Pennsy Diesels
1924 - 1968
A-6 to EF-36

by

Kenneth L. Douglas
and
Peter C. Weiglin

Pennsy Diesels
1924-1968
A-6 to EF-36
by Kenneth L. Douglas and
Peter C. Weiglin

Copyright 2002 by Hundman Publishing, Inc.
Hundman Publishing, Inc.
13110 Beverly Park Road
Mukilteo, Washington 98275

Library of Congress No. 2002106125

ISBN No. 0-945434-68-5

Printed in Hong Kong

Publisher
Robert L. Hundman

Graphics/Photo Reproduction
Sandy Mewhorter

Captions:

Page 1: This photo of PRR #6186 was taken at Sugar St. Tower in Lima, Ohio on August 19, 1948.

Page 2: PRR #5775 is seen at Summit Street in Dayton, Ohio on July 25, 1951.

Right: PRR #3495 is in Bradford, Ohio on November 10, 1952.

Page 8: K4 #3747 and EMD E7 #5883 are in South Amboy, New Jersey in April of 1956.

Dedication:
This book is gratefully dedicated to...

Fred Cheney, Jr.
David Sweetland
William D. Volkmer

... and to the dozens of other young engineers who played a role in keeping the Pennsylvania's diesels rolling in spite of physical and human obstacles.

Table of Contents

**A detailed listing of page references for sections in this book covering specific classes
of Pennsylvania Railroad diesel locomotives appears on Page 29.**

Preface and Acknowledgements

The Dieselization of the Pennsylvania Railroad is a story of machines, but more so a story of men, who at first resisted and then undertook nothing less than replacement of almost 4,400 familiar locomotives with a new technology.

The Pennsylvania Railroad was unique. Its uniqueness lay not only in the railroad's size, but was brought about by the PRR railroaders' collective attitude. It was the Standard Railroad of the World. Although the PRR's track mileage was not the largest in the United States, it carried the most traffic. During the l950s, in freight tonnage and passenger miles, the Pennsy exceeded its archrival New York Central (the next highest) by about 2s percent and 18 percent respectively.

In steam motive power, the Pennsylvania was the largest railroad to build its own locomotives in vast quantities, and its people were justifiably proud of their inhouse locomotive designs. The affiliated Norfolk and Western was the only other railroad that approached this level of in-house devotion.

When the PRR dieselized, the traffic level dictated a locomotive fleet correspondingly larger than other U. S. railroads of the period. The replacement diesel fleet was unique in its diversity. With hindsight, it is now apparent that a diesel roster including 68 different models (not differentiating A and B units) from five builders could not have been the most economical to operate. It should be recognized, however, that it would not have

been possible to purchase so large a diesel fleet in that time span from one or two builders.

The PRR was not first in line. Virtually every railroad in the country had realized the savings possible by dieselization and the order books of the builders were overflowing.

By the way, it is a form of shorthand to say, for example, that "The Pennsylvania Railroad dieselized," or that "Germany attacked Poland." To do so obscures the fact that it is people who do things, well or poorly, not the organizations. The PRR's approach to locomotive development and dieselization was determined by its people, and by their shared experience and inclinations, Much of their steam power philosophy was applied to diesel locomotives; not always appropri-

ately, but always consistently as experience accumulated. The evolution of a motive power philosophy over the forty-five years from 1923 to 1968 is part of this story.

About this book

This book is the story of a varied and numerous roster of diesel locomotives. In telling the story, it is fortunate that the PRR was so highly institutionalized. For the paper trail was considerable. There are numerous periodic lists that tabulated, referenced, assigned and classified the diesels, just as the steam locomotives had been extensively documented in previous years.

In addition to material which has been preserved privately, considerable PRR diesel locomotive documentation has been preserved in such archives as the Pennsylvania State Archives in Harrisburg, the Hagley Library and Museum in Wilmington, Delaware and the Railroad Museum of Pennsylvania near Strasburg, Pennsylvania. While it is a useful clue, for example, to hear an anecdote that a certain diesel model was expensive to maintain, an actual memo between PRR motive power executives stating that "we can obviously ill-afford to continue to operate these locomotives," makes it possible to present the facts with assurance.

Three types of tables appear throughout this book. All of them are there to provide detailed information without unduly bogging down the flow of text. These tables, and the roster that is included as an Appendix, are the distillation of many hours of painstaking research and cross-checking through the pertinent files. The first table type is the Order Summary, showing which locomotives in a class were part of which order. The second series of tables groups together similar locomotives in a series of Locomotive Characteristics tables showing equipment and ratings. The third category of tables covers unit assignments and special equipment, directly from PRR documents retrieved from various archives.

The details included in this book make it likely that despite considerable checking, errors are probable. The authors welcome the identification of any error so that corrections may be made.

Acknowledgements

The dedication to William D. Volkmer, Fred D. Cheney and David R. Sweetland recognizes their major contributions to this book. Ken Douglas first met them almost forty years ago when they were Junior Engineers for the Pennsylvania Railroad in the Maintenance of Equipment Department. As time passed, they provided considerable information about PRR motive power that would have otherwise gone into the trash. Among them they subsequently served Penn Central, Conrail, Tri-rail, Amtrak, Delaware and Hudson and the Iowa Interstate.

Richard O. Adams also contributed significantly to this book. Another friend for forty years, Dick provided photos, sought out PRR Form MP-229 copies and assisted in travel to the various archives at Hagley, Strasburg and the Pennsylvania State Archives.

A major effort by Dick Adams was a review of many publications to identify the resale of former PRR diesels after their disposal by Penn Central or Conrail. Significant help on the resale list was also provided by Kenneth M. Ardinger, Kermit Geary Jr., Allen M. Miller, Timothy J. Sposato, and Dick Will.

Photographs were also directly contributed by Bill Volkmer, Jack Consoli, Hugh Debberthine and Jerry Moyers. A number of the photos used were not supplied by the original photographer, but are part of one of the collections that were used. Among these photographers are the late Raymond J. Muller, the late H. N. Procter, J. David Engman, Richard Short, and Paul Dunn. These gentlemen were all dedicated railroad photographers and their contributions are hereby acknowledged. Uncredited photos are by Kenneth L. Douglas.

Dr. Louis A. Marre opened the resources of his large collection of diesel locomotive photographs for use in this book. The size of this collection masks the fact that Lou is an accomplished railroad photographer who chided us when we wanted to credit the "L. A. Marre Collection" for one photograph. "I took that shot myself" said he. Additionally, his advice as the author of numerous railroad books is also gratefully acknowledged.

James Mischke aided this effort with material he encountered in his project on Baltimore and Ohio diesel locomotives. Perhaps the most valuable item from Jim was an unpublished thesis by Mark Mapes detailing PRR's development of motive power in the years just prior to the decision to dieselize. The source material is available at the Hagley Library, but Mr. Mapes has applied scholarly organization and analysis of this material. This paper contributed considerably to Chapter One.

The following individuals (not already acknowledged) supplied valuable information and advice: Ben Anthony, P. A. Copeland, Don Dover, Lee Gregory, Tom Harley, Dave Ingles, john Kirkland, Carl Korn, Larry Russell, John Scala, Elbert Simon, Joe Strapac and Frank Tatnall.

The folks at Hundman Publishing, particularly Bob Hundman and Sandy Mewhorter, were more than helpful, and the authors appreciate an attitude that focused on the highest quality rather than the "easy way out."

Finally, a special acknowledgement must be given to Peter's wife, Jeanne. She "fueled" this project with her excellent cooking and good humor during the periods when the authors worked together on the book.

Kenneth L. Douglas
Long Beach, California

Peter C. Weiglin
San Mateo, California

Chapter 1

Muzzling The Ox

Before World War II, the Pennsylvania Railroad could never be accused of dragging its corporate feet in the area of system improvements and railroad technology development. Under Alexander Cassatt in the first years of the twentieth century, the railroad made a massive investment in system improvements, including the Hudson and East River tunnels, New York's Pennsylvania Station, its first electrification, creation of a four-track main line virtually all the way from Newark to Pittsburgh, dozens of new stations and bridges, Enola Yard, and numerous cutoffs and realignments. These improvements generated sufficient pride for the leaders of the company to style it The Standard Railroad of the World.

The emergence of the large shop complex at Altoona, Pennsylvania as a center of steam locomotive technology also dates to this period. The famous locomotive test facility, for example, was constructed in 1904 as a display for the St. Louis World's Fair, and then moved to Altoona after the Fair closed. The Pennsylvania, more than any other American railroad, designed its own steam and electric locomotives, and built many of its own as well. Baldwin and other locomotive builders may have constructed engines for the PRR, but by and large, supervision of the design work was done in Altoona. That competence was a considerable source of pride for the people involved. It was pride that permeated the culture of the place.

The Pennsylvania people saw four different and distinct service needs: passenger, freight, drag freight/pusher and switching, or shifting, as it was called on the Penn. The Altoona motive power philosophy was to develop specialized locomotive types for each of these different train services, rather than to design engines that were capable of performing a broader range of assignments. This was seen as an improvement on the old American Standard 4-4-0 wheel arrangement, which had been used for both passenger and freight service. The railroad's mechanical engineers at Altoona designed some of America's finest steam locomotives to meet each of those requirements.

SPECIALIZED LOCOMOTIVES

Thus the steam-powered heritage of the Pennsylvania called for different steam locomotive designs for passenger service (e.g., 4-4-2 Atlantics, 4-6-2 Pacifics), and freight service (e.g., 2-8-0 Consolidations, 2-8-2 Mikados). In general, the freight locomotives were designed to perform best hauling heavier trains at slower speeds, while the passenger locomotives performed best with their lighter trains at higher speeds, some in excess of 100 miles per hour. There was comparatively little use of a passenger engine for freight service, or vice versa; the railroad's operating people maintained a clear distinction between services.

Even though the Pennsylvania's people developed a variety of steam locomotive types suited to specific jobs, many aspects of their design and construction were standardized. Parts and subassemblies were designed to fit more than one locomotive type. For example, the K4s and L1s boilers were virtually identical. The I1s boilers were similar in many respects to the L1s, and the M1 boilers closely followed the I1s boilers. Many running gear parts were also interchangeable. More than most railroads, the Pennsylvania knew all about parts interchangeability long before the diesel locomotive manufacturers began to preach that particular virtue of their product.

But the Pennsylvania's people continued to think of passenger and freight services as separate entities sharing the same tracks, each with its own cars, each with its own crews, and each with its own locomotives. This concept had proven more than successful for them. For example, the K4s 4-6-2 Pacific was among the very best passenger locomotives ever designed and built; it shone on medium and long distance runs. The E6s 4-4-2 Atlantic was an outstanding performer with lighter trains at higher speeds, on

Class M1a 4-8-2 Mountain-type locomotives such as 6736 were the mainstays of the PRR locomotive fleet in the days before the diesels came. Number 6736 was a survivor; she is shown here with a westbound freight at Mount Union, Pennsylvania in May 1953. Mainline steam lasted until 1957.

Class I1s 2-10-0 locomotives were designed for pusher and slow drag service. If there was any attempt to achieve an aesthetic design, it failed miserably. PRR 3537 is still classified I1s in this photo at Altoona, several years before its conversion to class I1sa in January 1949.

more level track. For short-haul commuter trains the PRR people designed their own custom locomotive, the G-5s 4-6-0 Ten-Wheeler.

On the freight side, the H-class 2-8-0 Consolidations, L1s 2-8-2 Mikados and M1 4-8-2 Mountains hauled the goods. During World War II, under government orders, the Pennsylvania used J1 2-10-4 engines, built in Altoona to a Chesapeake and Ohio/Lima Locomotive Works design.

The third category of locomotive service was drag freight and helper service. This also was handled by a specialized design locomotive on the Pennsylvania: the I1s 2-10-0 Decapod, which provided brute strength at low speeds.

But the steam philosophy was changing, driven by longer trains on more demanding schedules. When dual service steam locomotive designs that could be used for both passenger and freight service (4-8-2 Mountain and 4-8-4 Northern types, for example) came off the builders' drawing boards in the 1920s and 1930s, they represented a return to the concept used in the 4-4-0s of the Nineteenth century. Some railroads embraced the reborn dual service locomotive concept. The PRR's archrival New York Central, for example, assigned its new 4-8-2 and 4-8-4 engines (which it haughtily called Mohawks and Niagaras respectively, rather than the more common Mountain and Northern) to both passenger and freight trains.

But while the Penn used at least 270 of its 300 M1 4-8-2 locomotives in freight service, the relatively few passenger M1s were carefully segregated. Dual service capability was a part of PRR design philosophy, but dual service operationally was not.

SHIFTERS

It was in the fourth type of locomotive service, shifting, that diesel locomotives made their first marks in American railroading. But there are two quite different categories of car movement called switching by the railroads: light-duty short-distance movement of one or a few cars, usually in an industrial setting; and heavy-duty low-speed persuasion of long freight-car strings in and between freight yards. We normally think of shifters as small engines, but particularly where a hump yard is involved, a switching locomotive can take on truly massive proportions.

The Pennsylvania developed steam shifters for both light and heavy work. The A5s 0-4-0 (tractive force 30,190 lbs.) and B6 0-6-0 (tractive force 36,140 lbs.) models handled the low end admirably. The newest examples of these classes were built in 1924 and 1926 respectively. For heavy switching, the newest units available were 90 Juniata-built C1 class 0-8-0 shifters (tractive force 78,110 lbs.) dating from 1925 and 1927. Before 1920, the railroad had also built a handful of experimental articulated brutes for *real-*

ly heavy shifting work. The articulateds didn't work out economically, and the relatively modern 0-8-0s proved to be unpopular. Many PRR operating people showed a preference for using 2-8-0 Consolidation engines reassigned from freight service (H10, tractive force 53,197 lbs.) rather than the 0-8-0s for some heavy shifting duties. Only 90 of the 150 projected C1's were built. Such duty by the Consolidations, one of the few cases of an engine designed for one service (i.e., freight) used in another service, was a precursor of the varied work later performed by diesel road-switchers.

During the 1920s, the Pennsylvania's locomotive designers had covered their shifting requirements, better on the low end than the high end. No new steam switcher development was undertaken. The 2-8-0 classes could be used in more places because of their lower axle loading than the 70,000 lb. per axle class C1. Also, the Consolidations were available in great numbers after having been bumped from mainline runs by larger freight engines. Another new heavy switcher design was not needed. The A5s and B6 carried the light-service load well. Steam engines could do, and were doing, the many jobs of the PRR.

THE KAUFMANN ACT

Given that serene situation, it probably comes as no surprise to learn that it was an external force, a law, that gave diesel switchers their first venue on American railroads. The arena was the group of small "riverside" freight switching yards maintained by each of the railroads serving New York City. The Pennsylvania had two such yards in New York City, at 37th Street on Manhattan's Hudson shore, and at West 4th Street on the Brooklyn waterfront. These isolated facilities each contained industry sidings and team tracks, and each was connected to the world by a float bridge. Freight cars arrived and departed on car floats, which were tracked barges shepherded across the rivers by railroad tugboats. In these riverside yards, switchers emptied and loaded the car floats, and moved cars about within the confines of the yard areas. Sharp curves dictated the use of small locomotives, usually 0-4-0 types.

The proximate cause for placing

PRR 6214 is a typical class B6as switcher on the Pennsy. Built in Altoona's Juniata Shop in 1913 as a superheated locomotive. Seen here in Altoona in July 1940 with the Futura lettering applied on PRR locomotives in the late 1940s.

diesel-electrics in the riverside yards was New York's Kaufmann Act of 1923, as amended. Earlier ordinances had required mainline electrification in New York City by June 30, 1908. Those earlier laws resulted in both the Grand Central Terminal and Pennsylvania Station electrification projects.

In February 1924, the New York Public Service Commission notified the Pennsylvania Railroad (along with the other railroads with riverside yards) that, under the Kaufmann Act, effective January 1, 1926, all railroad operations in the City of New York would require electric motive power to reduce smoke. Replacement of steam at Sunnyside yard on Long Island and two small float yards was required to bring the PRR into compliance. Sunnyside Yard was not a problem since third rail electrification was installed there; steam could be eliminated with additional electric locomotives and minor extension of the third rail.

That left the small isolated switching yards on the Hudson and in Brooklyn, which still used steam switchers. The costly nightmare of erecting overhead wires or installing dangerous third rails in these switching areas caused the Pennsylvania much concern. But the Motive Power Department was at that time looking into gas-electric motor cars with Westinghouse Electric. It dawned on someone that this was an electrically-driven vehicle, one that in effect carried an onboard capability to generate the electricity. Over the next several months after February 1924, a plan evolved for a similar method to

resolve the motive power problem at the two float yards.

First things first: would this be an acceptable solution to comply with the law? By June, the PRR's Chief of Motive Power requested a legal opinion from the railroad's Vice President and Chief Counsel, Judge C. B. Heiserman, to confirm that a gas-electric or oil-electric locomotive would comply with the Kaufmann Act's requirement for electrically operated locomotives. The answer in part was:

"I beg to advise that in my opinion an engine propelled in the manner described would not violate the New York Act, but such an engine can only be used after the Public Service Commission of New York has approved such a method of generating the electricity."

Not exactly a simple "Yes," but after all, as Chief Counsel of the Pennsylvania Railroad, Judge Heiserman was a Philadelphia lawyer. The Public Service Commission did subsequently approve the use of an electric locomotive that carried its own power generating station. With its legal flank protected, the PRR next arranged for the loan of a General Electric 37-ton gas electric locomotive to test at the two float yards.

The Central Railroad of New Jersey is credited with putting the first diesel-electric switcher into continuous service, in October 1925, at its riverside yard on the Harlem River in The Bronx. This was a 300-hp Alco-GE-Ingersoll Rand box-cab unit. The Baltimore & Ohio, Erie, Lehigh Valley, Long Island, and Delaware Lackawanna & Western

railroads placed similar units at their carfloat yards in New York between 1926 and 1928, to meet the requirements of the ordinance. The New York Central bought a fleet of three-power locomotives from General Electric, capable of operating from the third rail as electrics, operating from storage batteries, or from electricity produced by an onboard diesel engine.

Rather than purchasing internal combustion locomotives from an outside commercial manufacturer, the proud and independent Pennsylvania's 1924-1925 response for its riverside yards was to ask Altoona to construct three electric shifters with onboard power-generating capability. Altoona, no stranger to traction motors, married the running gear and box-cab design concepts of the PRR's B1 six-coupled electric shifters with the internal combustion engine. All of the necessary equipment had to be shoehorned into a carbody less than 24 feet long, above a four-wheel frame.

Since the last 0-4-0 steam shifters had been designated Class A5s, the new internal combustion locomotives became Class A6. Built and rebuilt between 1925 and 1928, two of the three locomotives were placed in service in the Pennsylvania's New York riverside yards. As noted elsewhere in this volume, the A6 units ended up with gasoline engines because of development problems with the diesel engine.

Switching is a low-speed task, involving less than 2000 miles per month per locomotive. In the riverside yards, the distances were much smaller and

PRR 4883 is seen here in Greenwich yard, Philadelphia, Pennsylvania on a most prestigious assignment--a Presidential Special. The day is December 2, 1961 and the Army-Navy football game is in progress. In attendance is President John F. Kennedy. The president had arrived for the game by air, but would return to the capital aboard this train. The first car in the train is an Army Signal Corps car ready to communicate with the world. Railroad personnel are inspecting the train continually. Considering what happened less than two years later, would the photographer have been allowed this close to the train for the 1964 game?

mileages even lower. The key measure of switcher usefulness is the hours of availability per month, which are reduced by the time it is in the shop being maintained. The steam switchers that had been working these isolated yards were not immune from the need for regular maintenance, and moving them back and forth to the shops by carfloat was a considerable pain. Replacement of steam locomotives in the riverside yards, while forced upon the railroads by law, showed that once the diesel shifters were in place, they had considerably greater availability than even the well-designed steam shifters from Altoona. The diesels didn't need to have their flues cleaned, their fires dumped, their ashes removed, etc.; they just ran.

Thus the Pennsylvania's first internal combustion locomotives were special-use shifters, operating on a relatively obscure part of the railroad. And that was that, until 1937, when one Model SW 600-hp switcher (starting tractive force 51,600 lbs.) was purchased from the Electro-Motive Corporation. As we note elsewhere, even the rationale for purchase of this locomotive had to do with external forces. Its assignment was shifting cars in the General Motors plant at Linden, New Jersey. GM, a large

shipper, owned the Electro-Motive Corporation, and was made happy by having one of its own products working on its premises. A second unit, a 1000-hp NW2 (starting tractive force 61,200 lbs.), came in 1941.

By the summer of 1947, only 35 more diesel shifters had joined the Pennsylvania's Brunswick Green ranks, 20 from the Baldwin Locomotive Works, three from Alco and 12 more (making a total of 13) from Electro-Motive. The total roster in 1947 showed, in addition to these 36 store-bought shifters and the three Altoona-built A6 veterans, 591 steam shifters: 46 0-4-0s, 455 0-6-0s, and the 90 unpopular 0-8-0s. Despite the fact that the Pennsylvania's smaller steam shifters (0-4-0 and 0-6-0) were excellent examples of their type, they were no less than 20 years old in 1947, and they were showing their age. The era of the steam switcher was clearly ending.

The new diesel-electric switchers demonstrated greater availability and economy than their steam counterparts, a condition which paralleled the experience of other railroads. It is significant that, while the Pennsylvania's Motive Power Department conducted extensive steam power experiments in the 1940s, none of this effort was expended on shifters. With their greater availability,

the diesel units from Baldwin and General Motors won that battle early on.

ELECTRIFICATION

Of course, another major improvement program, conducted in the 1930s, gave the Pennsylvania something that no other railroad had: an extensive mainline electrification network covering the busiest portion of its route, the area east of Harrisburg, Pennsylvania, including New York, Philadelphia and Washington.

Electric traction motors were not unknown in Altoona. The PRR's first electrification, the Hudson River (and East River) tunnels in New York City had been opened in 1910. A second electrification, in metropolitan Philadelphia, was opened in 1915.

The 1930 electrification project extended wires to Harrisburg and Washington. With the help of Philadelphia-based Baldwin Locomotive Works, Pittsburgh-based Westinghouse Electric and New York-based General Electric, the PRR motive power men had created a fleet of straight electric locomotives second to none, of which the crown jewel was the unsurpassed GG1.

Implementation of the large 1930s electrification project was supervised by Martin W. Clement, Vice President-Operations until his promotion to First Vice President in 1933. Mr. Clement had built a reputation for knowing the intimate details of what really going on in the railroad's operation. He became President of the PRR just after the electrification opened in 1935.

There were plans to extend the electrified territory westward from Harrisburg, but nothing ever came of them. On the non-electrified trackage west to Pittsburgh and beyond, the Penn continued to rely upon its faithful steamers for passenger, freight and helper service.

PASSENGER AND FREIGHT

In the late 1930s, although other railroads were experimenting with early diesels for passenger and freight service, the Pennsylvania took no part in these experiments. All of its road trains were either steam or electric powered. It should be noted here that the PRR was absent from the far-ranging list of railroads visited by EMD's FT demonstrators. Further, there was no discernible interest in trains like the Chicago Burlington & Quincy's Pioneer Zephyr or the Union Pacific's M-10000. The Pennsylvania's Blue Ribbon Fleet needed to have more muscle and more flexibility than those early diesels could provide.

There had been one proposal made by General Motors around 1937, for model EA diesels to power the *Broadway Limited* and the *Spirit of St. Louis*. But when data from tests in March 1936 showed that a two-unit 3600-hp EA set could not match the time schedules maintained by the railroad's trusty K4s's, the PRR smugly declined the opportunity. Let the Baltimore & Ohio become the first EA customer; they didn't have the K4s's and M1's that were operating on the Standard Railroad of the World. Let the Santa Fe, the Union Pacific and the Burlington buy passenger diesels; those roads have different needs and problems than the Pennsylvania. Those roads also didn't have the personnel and facilities of Altoona.

PHILOSOPHY, HISTORY AND FRIENDSHIPS

In summary then, before World War II, the diesel was of no interest to the Penn as road service motive power for three general reasons:

1. PRR steam engines were rated at or near the best in the industry in performing their intended tasks, and the body of steam locomotive knowledge and talent represented on the Pennsylvania payroll was unmatched in America. A bias of these people against engines "not designed here" is quite understandable. If better motive power was needed, the obvious answer was to build improved, Altoona-designed, steamers, not locomotives of an unproven technology designed elsewhere.

2. The Pennsylvania Railroad carried more coal than any other railroad; coal represented more than 25 per cent of the railroad's revenue tonnage. Pennsylvania people showed a natural bias toward using an on-line fuel, and salespeople were reluctant to offend such a large category of shippers. In the final analysis, this does not seem to have been a major problem. The coal industry came to understand that no one could haul coal better than the PRR, and that the diesel would allow lower freight rates.

3. Most significantly, the Pennsylvania Railroad and the Baldwin Locomotive Works were both Philadelphia-based companies, whose executives had longstanding relationships that bred frequent and friendly contact with each other. While Baldwin was indeed building diesels, most of its people had

grown up with steam locomotives, and remained committed to steam even after many railroad executives around the country had become convinced that the days of steam were numbered.

A 1935 speech by Baldwin Vice-President Robert S. Binkerd to the New York Railroad Club illustrates the point. The talk carried the title, *"Muzzle Not the Ox that Treadeth out the Corn."* The title was Biblical (Deuteronomy 25:4), and the speech was indeed a sermon; a fervent appeal not to abandon the improved versions of the faithful steamer which had served so well. Here are two quotes from Mr. Binkerd's remarks:

"The inherent nature of the Diesel locomotive and its accompanying electrical equipment in the present state of development debar it from high speed road service because of the physical characteristics of the power itself, its excessive capital cost, and its probable high maintenance cost . . . the field of profitable application of the Diesel locomotive is pretty generally indicated at work speeds not exceeding 10 miles per hour."

"There is no ground in recorded experience for the claim that Diesel locomotives can be maintained at a lower cost than steam. On the contrary, everything indicates that maintenance costs will be higher, but how

A classic steam locomotive photo: PRR K4s Pacific 3654 gets under way from Englewood station near Chicago with the eastbound Liberty Limited *on March 29, 1941.*

much higher no one can say with certainty."

The Binkerd speech was received by many of the New York attendees with some shock and shaking of heads, as it was clearly a more ringing endorsement of "steam power forever" than many of the railway men, particularly the younger railway men, were eager to make. But it was entirely consistent with the Pennsylvania's motive power philosophy. The Philadelphia environment, and the close cultural relations between PRR and Baldwin people, created a climate in which decisions were being made that assumed the continuing primacy of steam locomotives for services other than low-speed, unglamorous shifting work. That collective opinion was not changed easily.

THE VIEW FROM CHICAGO

Also in 1935, a PRR executive named James M. Symes began a leave from the railroad to serve a four-year term as Vice-President of Operation and Maintenance for the Association of American Railroads. He was thus more exposed to other railroads' practices than he would have been in the insular Quaker City. When Mr. Symes rejoined the Penn in 1939, he became General Manager (and later Vice-President) of the Western Region, with offices in Chicago. From that vantage point, he watched the progress of the railroads that had moved early to diesels, particularly the Burlington and the Santa Fe. He clearly was impressed, and he brought to the PRR a perspective on diesel locomotives that was certainly not common (and apparently not greatly appreciat-

---

On its way to helping America win the War, PRR J1 6474 pauses for a builder's photo in February 1943. The 2-10-4 was a Chesapeake and Ohio design without a Belpaire firebox. Juniata did use a PRR cab window design and front end touches, possibly to make the "furriner" look more at home.

ed) in Altoona or Philadelphia.

DUPLEXES AND TURBINES

Remember that until 1945, the collective judgment of the people responsible for the decisions on PRR motive power regarded the diesel-electric locomotive only as a helpful shifter. A possible use of passenger diesels in joint service on a new Chicago-Miami train, the *South Wind* (the Western Region; Mr. Symes' territory) with the Louisville & Nashville Railroad in 1940 was aborted. The PRR actually placed a passenger loco-

motive order with EMD for two E6 locomotives to be used on the *South Wind* on May 9, 1941 with delivery promised in October 1942. By the spring of 1942, the War Production Board had intervened in the process and informed the PRR that the diesels could not be built because of wartime production and material priorities. The PRR cancelled its order for the E6 units. The Louisville & Nashville did, however, receive E6 units of its own in 1942.

For line haul freight and passenger services, Altoona's main effort was on

making improvements to the faithful and familiar steamers. As far back as 1936, Vice-President-Operations John F. Deasy had ordered design work on new, more powerful steamers. In this, he was responding to direction from President Clement, who urged Deasy to review "both our steam passenger and freight engine designs for increasing the speed and tractive effort with less axle weight."

The first result of the design effort was the S1 duplex locomotive, built at the railroad's Juniata Shops. Completed

PRR 5502 is an immaculately turned out Class T1 4-4-4-4 at Chicago on July 11, 1948. The "exhibition finish" may relate to the Chicago Railroad Fair being held at that time.

in 1938 (with a startling $370,000 cost overrun), the engine was exhibited at the World's Fair in New York. The static Fair exhibit was apparently the S1's finest hour. Despite the S1's power, chronic maintenance problems plagued it whenever it was in motion. It logged only 200,000 miles in its ten-year life, and when all the S1 costs were added up, it was regarded as a $660,000 mistake. Worse was to come.

Such mistakes are not treated lightly in Corporate America. Chief of Motive Power Frederick W. Hankins was replaced by Harry W. Jones just in time to receive the first T1 locomotives for test in 1942. This was hoped to be the answer for passenger service.

For the PRR's passenger train fleet, there was a developing need for a heavier locomotive. Passenger train weights and lengths had increased beyond the capacity of a single K4s; doubleheading had become commonplace, and a second locomotive and engine crew greatly increased operating costs.

To meet the need for heavier passenger power, the Altoona designers created the T1, a 6000-hp duplex drive 4-4-4-4 locomotive to be capable of pulling a 16-car passenger train across Ohio and Indiana at speeds in excess of 100 miles per hour. Based on glowing reports from tests of the first two units conducted between 1942 and 1944, 50 T1s were built during 1945 and 1946. But after being placed in real-world service, the T1's showed alarmingly high operating and

maintenance costs, as well as some driver-slip problems. There were also so many problems with the T1's that Harry Jones's worries increased.

Freight power improvements took the form of the powerful Q1 and Q2 duplex steamers. The lone Q1 was built at Altoona in 1942, and the first of the revised Q2 model in 1944. Based on these initial tests, the railroad quickly ordered 25 more Q2's. The first of these registered almost 8000-hp, with a tractive force of 100,800 lbs. Those readings approached the maximum possible on the Altoona test bed.

Meanwhile, wartime traffic requirements forced the Pennsylvania to do something that did not come easily: build locomotives from another railroad's design. This was the J1, a 2-10-4 best known on the Chesapeake and Ohio. The PRR built a total of 125 J1's at Juniata from borrowed blueprints. The J1's were pronounced "disappointing" despite their relative efficiency. One wonders to what degree xenophobia influenced the analysis.

One more locomotive deserves mention here: the S2 6-8-6 steam turbine, No. 6200. The experimental PRR steam turbine-electric, developed with friendly Westinghouse Electric in 1944, became considerably more famous than its own merits would have indicated when it was selected by Lionel as a prototype for thousands of model train engines. The Lionel models gave their owners considerably more satisfaction than did the pro-

totype. The Pennsylvania's S2 died from inherent inefficiency and bleeding maintenance costs. Harry Jones' worries increased.

There were no freight diesels on the Pennsylvania during this period, hence there was no direct cost and performance comparison as was the case in passenger service. But during 1945 and 1946, the accountants raised red flags about the high operating costs of the Q2 freighters and turbine as well as the T1's.

By early 1946, it had become apparent that the T1 and Q2 duplex locomotives were not the answer, despite extensive corrective efforts and more than $14 million invested in them.

MR. CLEMENT'S ACTIONS

Whether the Pennsylvania should have purchased road diesels in 1941 instead of investing in improved steamers was a question made moot by World War II. During the war, only EMD was allowed to produce road units, while Alco and Baldwin were limited to switchers. There were enough orders from other railroads to clog the EMD pipeline.

By 1944, the somewhat competitive Baltimore & Ohio owned 24 freight diesels. However, it was the locomotive orders from one particular railroad that were the object of intense interest by Mr. Clement.

That was the New York Central Railroad, which ordered two four-unit (A-B-B-A) 5400-hp FT freight locomotives; they were delivered in June 1944.

Note that it wasn't all diesels in 1944; the Central also ordered its 25 Niagaras, while the Penn ordered 50 T1s.

But in 1944 Mr. Clement also arranged for that earlier order for the first two E7 diesels, accelerating the delivery schedule by calling it a resurrection of the original *South Wind* order. Interestingly, he gave the diesel procurement task to his Vice President of Real Estate and Purchases, largely bypassing the Operating Department and its Motive Power Department. Given his reputation for "knowing what was going on," we can speculate that Mr. Clement was hedging his motive power bet after receiving some disturbing early reports about the experimental steamers, and maybe a conversation or two about diesels west of Chicago.

More significantly, two black 4000-hp. (A-A) passenger E7 pairs, ordered in 1944, arrived on the New York Central in March 1945. The new E7's were tried on the *Twentieth Century Limited*, and both performance and publicity were favorable, even compared to the NYC's Niagaras, which outperformed the PRR's newest steam darlings. More diesels were being ordered by the Central. In mid-1945, the NYC also ordered a large number of new passenger cars for its postwar fleet. The PRR was a few months late in placing orders for competitive equipment, which would have frustrated any chief executive.

So, in 1945, Martin Clement saw his motive power department working mightily to improve the breed of steam locomotives, but the breed was proving to be resistant. He also saw his chief

competitor conducting a well-publicized campaign to "modernize" its passenger train fleet. Even if, as Harry Jones was saying, 75 Q2 steam engines could be had for the same price as 33 diesels, and one Q2 yielded far more horsepower and tractive effort than a four-unit FT set, the fact remained that the hated New York Central was successfully using diesels to improve its passenger market share. The fare-paying public was responding to the contrast between a "modern" dieselized *Century* and an "old-fashioned," steam-powered *Broadway*. It had become obvious, to Mr. Clement, at least, that for passenger service west of Harrisburg, the K4's would be replaced not by T1's, but by something else. The potential loss of cachet and customers to the Central was itself sufficient to cause Mr. Clement to override his Motive Power people.

Another memo went from Mr. Clement to Operations Vice-President Deasy, this one asking how many diesels would be required to power at least one train on the major passenger routes: not "whether," or "if", but "how many." While few in the management ranks supported Mr. Clement's position, no one overtly argued with the boss. The answer came back with apparent reluctance: "we need ten." Not enough; Mr. Clement authorized an order for 24 more E7's in November 1945. The hated New York Central would not win the competitive and publicity war if he could help it!

It was no accident that the Pennsylvania Railroad calendar for 1946, sent to friends and customers, prominently

featured the diesel locomotive.

THE NEW TEAM

Motive Power Chief Harry Jones had followed his instincts, his tradition, his training—and his predecessors—toward the conservative course. Better Altoona steam engines were the answer. Back in 1944, even as President Clement revived the original E7 order, Mr. Jones was telling the trade press that the PRR had "no diesels on order and no expansion contemplated." No freight diesels were on order.

Now it had all come crashing down. The E7 diesel locomotive had far outperformed all of the passenger steamers in terms of availability and operating costs. Mr. Jones died early in 1946, after shouldering the blame for the steam engine failures, many of which were beyond his control or understanding.

Contemporary documents show that the PRR's management, including new Chief of Motive Power Howell (Hal) Cover, was gradually becoming aware that the diesel's advantage was inherent, and not a result of bugs in the new steam locomotive models. Even when the new steamers worked perfectly (which was seldom), the diesels still showed greater availability, and much lower costs. Diesel-electrics would have a great cost advantage over all existing steam locomotives, duplexes as well as 2-10-4s, in freight and helper work as well as passenger and shifting services.

And one Regional Vice President in particular was urging that the diesel not be ignored. From Chicago, James Symes presented an analysis showing

This left side photograph of PRR 6184 taken at Altoona, clearly illustrates the conventional location of the rear engine cylinders on class Q2 locomotives. On the only class Q1 locomotive, these cylinders were behind the drivers and adjacent to the firebox.

PRR's lone S-1 6-4-4-6 "World's Fair" locomotive, in all its 1939 glory. It looked better than it ran. Chicago, August 19, 1945

that even if 75 Q2 steam engines could be had for the same price as 33 diesels, as the Motive Power Department had said, those 33 diesels could do the work of *more* than 75 Q2 steamers, and at a lower overall cost.

Within three months, Mr. Clement promoted the boat-rocking James

Symes to the post of Deputy Vice-President of Operations. Among his responsibilities: dieselization. In April 1947 Mr. Symes replaced the reluctant John

PRR 6200 is the Pennsy's experimental steam turbine locomotive, Class S2. The single member of Class S2 is seen here in Chicago, Illinois between passenger train assignments in July 1948.

PRR 5511 was not one of the two prototypes. It was one of fifty production model T1 locomotives to serve on the Pennsy.

Deasy as Vice-President of Operations. Another changing economic relation-ship also affected the course of locomotive development on the Pennsylvania.

The end of wartime price regulations meant that the price of coal doubled between 1945 and 1946. The alarming increase in fuel costs and other cost increases, along with a contraction in traffic revenues after the war, meant that the once-mighty Pennsylvania Railroad actually lost money in 1946.

The question at that point was no longer whether diesel-electrics would replace steam, but how quickly. The once-proud railroad, now fallen on hard times, would need to accelerate any programs that would save money, including locomotive replacement.

Clearly, EMD's order book was back-logged to the point where locomotives had to be bought from other suppliers if the plan for dieselization was to be implemented promptly. Enter Baldwin, Alco, Fairbanks-Morse and later Lima.

Martin Clement had made the decision to dieselize with all deliberate speed, based on economics and fear of losing competitive advantage. He found the people to do the job and he placed them where they could do it, notably James Symes (who himself became President of the PRR in 1954). The passenger, freight and helper locomotive replacement plan was in place by late 1946. The first orders to implement that plan were placed before year-end.

Shortly thereafter, in the March 1947 issue of *Trains* magazine (actually written about Christmas 1946, given magazine deadlines), the following appeared:

"Pennsylvania Railroad motive power policy has clearly changed in the past two or three years. Considering the road's long-time pre-eminence in steam locomotive engineering, it seems most likely that the shift was dictated by the changing economic relationship of coal and oil as fuels."

Of course, the whole story was not publicly known at that time. While fuel was not the only factor, in the end, the decision was clearly based on a larger economic picture than fuel costs alone.

This side view of PRR 8724 illustrates the lettering applied on the center cab transfer units. The BS-24m unit awaits an assignment at the engine terminal at Greenwich Yard in Philadelphia on June 8, 1958.

Chapter 2

The PRR Was *Unique...*

The Pennsylvania Railroad was well-known for the singular and parochial attitudes that governed its operating and motive power practices. Simply put, PRR people did not look to other railroads for inspiration. They had designed their own steam locomotives, passenger and freight cars, signal and communications systems, and operating/personnel practices. The railroad's position as the largest hauler of goods and people tended to reinforce feelings of superiority among managers of the "Standard Railroad of the World." We'll take a moment here to reflect on a few of the areas relevant to our story, in which the PRR did things differently.

SIZE OF THE DIESEL FLEET

Perhaps the most unique aspect of the PRR was the size of its operations. Quite simply, the Pennsy carried more freight and passengers than any other U. S. railroad. This in turn required the largest locomotive roster of its era. Full dieselization after World War II required the replacement of several thousand steam locomotives, many of which had seen several hard years of wartime service.

After an abortive start in the late 1920s (see Chapter 3), the PRR began the purchase of diesel switchers in 1937, but still had only 35 of these units by the end of the railroad's centennial year of 1946. At this time PRR's operations depended on more than 4350 steam engines and 282 electric units. With the delivery of the last GP9s in December 1959 the diesel locomotive roster of the Pennsylvania Railroad reached a total of 2465 units. In addition, the locomotive roster also included 277 electric units, most of which were used in the 11,000 Volt AC electrification system on the New York, Washington-Harrisburg lines. There were still four class DD-1 DC electrics in use out of Sunnyside Yard for maintenance at New York's Penn Station.

Aside from the retirement of a fire-damaged 44-tonner in 1961, the PRR diesel roster remained stable during 1960 and 1961. In 1962, the railroad started a program of purchasing second-generation diesel units and the retirement of its older diesels. In 1962 and 1963, 98 new Alco, EMD and GE second generation four-axle road-switchers were added to the fleet. In 1962 and 1963, 233 units were retired.

The pattern of purchasing second generation road-switchers for freight service and the retirement of older, less efficient units continued until the PRR and the NYC merged on February 1, 1968. At that time the PRR diesel roster numbered 2079 diesel units. A total of 579 units were delivered to the PRR from January 1, 1962 to February 1, 1968; and 964 units were retired. While this appears to be an unworkable balance of new vs. retired units, the units being retired ranged from 380 horsepower to 2500 horsepower, while the units being purchased ranged from 2250 horsepower to 3600 horsepower. The total retired horsepower was 1.41 million while the new units totaled 1.62 million horsepower.

During its diesel era, the PRR owned a total of 3044 units. The 2465 units were the largest number owned at any one time, however. The unit totals broke down as follows by builder:

Alco	494
Baldwin	643
Electro Motive	1539
Fairbanks-Morse	200
General Electric	145
Lima-Hamilton	22
PRR	1

CLASSIFICATION

Locomotive classification was an important reference system on the Pennsylvania Railroad, because it is the primary indicator to the operating personnel of a given locomotive's capabilities and suitability for a particular assignment. Classification was

STEAM/ELECTRIC LOCOMOTIVE CLASSIFICATION SYSTEM
Selected Railroads

Wheel Arr.	PRR	NYC	B&O	ERIE	C&O
0-4-0	A	--	C	--	--
0-6-0	B	B	D	B	C
0-8-0	C	U	L	C	C
2-6-0	F	F	K	F	E
2-8-0	H	G	E	H	G
2-10-0	I	--	Y	J	--
2-6-2	J	--	--	--	--
2-8-2	L	H	Q	U	K
2-10-2	N	--	S	R	B
2-8-4	--	A	--	S	K
2-10-4	J	--	--	--	T
4-4-0	D	--	--	D	A
4-4-2	E	I	A	E	A
4-6-0	G	F	B	G	F
4-6-2	K	K	P	K	F
4-6-4	P	J	V	--	L
4-8-2	M	L	T	--	J
4-8-4	R	S	--	--	J

Erie also had Class L-1 0-8 8-0, Class M 2-6-8-0, and Class P 2-8-8-8-2 (Triplex).

C&O Class C also included 0-10-0 and Shay type locomotives

B&O Class G, H, I, J and M were all 4-4-0's

vital during the steam locomotive era because there was very little standardization of steam locomotive designs from railroad to railroad, and even locomotives of the same wheel arrangement differed in their ability to handle a given train.

A common locomotive classification system was based on the Whyte system of locomotive identification by arrangement of leading truck wheels, drivers, and trailing truck wheels. For example, a four-wheel switcher had no leading truck, four drivers, and no trailing truck; it was called an 0-4-0 ("Oh-four-oh"). A Pacific-type locomotive had four leading wheels, six drivers and two trailing truck wheels; the Whyte system called it a 4-6-2. Many railroads adopted letter identification codes for the different Whyte wheel arrangements. They were not standardized. The PRR's steam locomotive letter code is shown in Table 1, along with that of a few other railroads.

The letter was followed by a number designating different groups of locomotives with the same wheel arrangement. Thus, PRR people could refer to K4, H9, I1, L1, or A5 locomotives, and understand each other. They knew, for example, that an H6 was not the same as an H9, although both shared the same wheel arrangement (2-8-0).

The steam classification system shown on page 23 shows how the designations were constructed. Note that the 0-8-0 switchers were classed in the C series and the 0-8-8-0 articulated locomotives, which had two sets of eight drivers, were classed as CC. Even the electric locomotives were fitted into the steam locomotive system. The famous GG-1 electric had a 4-6-6-4 wheel arrangement, and the system classified it as two ten-wheelers (4-6-0, Class G) back to back.

As might be expected, the first classification system used for PRR internal combustion locomotives was another extension of the steam/electric locomotive system that the railroad had used for years. But the Whyte-based classification system didn't work out well for diesel locomotives.

The gasoline powered 3905, built in 1928, had an 0-4-0 wheel arrangement and was classed A6, consistent with 0-4-0 steam locomotives on the PRR. When the first standard model diesel—the 3908, later 5911—was purchased from Electro-Motive in 1937, its wheel arrangement, two four-wheeled trucks, was described under the Whyte system as an 0-4-4-0. Under the Whyte-based PRR classification system, that called for an AA designation, and the EMC

unit was classed as AA5 when delivered.

The railroad struggled with this hyperextension of the steam/electric system for nine years after the purchase of the 3908. During this period the PRR purchased only switchers. The first EMC model NW2 was classed AA5a, the EMC model SW1 was classified AA5b, and the Baldwin VO-600 units were classified AA6 when they arrived in 1941-1942. When Baldwin delivered the VO-1000 units in 1943, another classification element was introduced. The new 1000 horsepower Baldwins were classified AA10B. Shortly after (September, 1943), EMC's model NW2 was reclassified to AA10E, to make its classification consistent with the Baldwin VO-1000 units.

So far, so good; the classification system was stretched, but only moderately. But the next new diesel model to arrive was the EMC model E7 in September, 1945, and it blew the classification system apart.

The E7 units were the first to operate in multiple, and the two back-to-back A units were considered to be one 4000 horsepower locomotive. This perception of multiple-unit locomotives was to pervade the classification system concept until the institution of the 1951 classification system. The E7 pairs were viewed as having a 0-6-6-6-6-0 wheel arrangement (back-to-back 0-6-6-0). To make matters worse, the E7 trucks contained both drivers and trailing wheels in each group. The existing or first classification scheme, based on the Whyte system, just could not adequately describe this diesel locomotive.

But they tried. The pair of E7 A-units in multiple was designated as class 4B, as if it were four 0-6-0 or B-class switchers coupled together. (Some switcher!). The E7 units were to carry the class 4B identification for less than a year, as the PRR looked for a new and better way to classify diesel locomotives.

The Whyte system, while adequate for steam locomotives, was finally acknowledged to be insufficiently descriptive of the differences in diesel-electric locomotives, which might vary widely by horsepower, type of body, builder and model, number of powered and unpowered wheels/axles, intended service, etc. An alternate system had been developed to identify powered and unpowered axles on electric and diesel locomotives. Within a truck, axles with traction motors are designated with letters (one axle = A, two axles = B, three axles = C), while unpowered axles are described with numbers. Thus, a locomotive riding on two trucks, each having two powered axles, is classified as B-B. Two trucks, each containing three powered axles, yields a C-C designation.

The two E7A units were a special case. Their six-wheel trucks were not C-C, because not all of the three axles in each truck were powered. "A1A" thus describes a three-axle truck with the center axle unpowered, and the E7s were described as A1A-A1A.

THE SECOND (1946) CLASSIFICATION SYSTEM

On many railroads, the in-house locomotive classification systems for diesels fell into disuse and the manufacturer's model designations were adopt-

The PRR's first Baldwin diesel and its third "store-bought" diesel switcher overall, 5907, is a Baldwin VO-660, classified AA5A originally, then (B-B) 6B in 1946, and finally BS-6 in 1947. The 5907 is seen here in Baltimore, Maryland in October 1949.

1946 Reclassification

Class (B-B)6E-Odd	had been class AA5	EMC Model SW
Class (B-B)6B	had been class AA5A	BLW VO-660
Class (B-B)6E	had been class AA5B	EMC Model SW1
Class (B-B)10B	had been class AA10B	BLW VO-1000
Class (B-B)10E	had been class AA10E	EMC Model NW2
Class (A1A-A1A)20E	had been class 4B	EMD Model E7

ed instead, because these models were highly standardized. Not surprisingly, when it became clear that the Whyte system would not be adequate, the Pennsylvania Railroad followed its normal independent instincts and developed its own, unique, diesel classification system. But, the diesel classification system did not evolve easily on the PRR. In fact, the road's first attempt at classification, in 1946, proved to be unsatisfactory. It was not until 1951, on the fourth try, that the classification system which is most associated with PRR diesels was instituted. This fourth scheme was to last for fourteen years until the classification system to be used on the Penn Central was instituted.

The second scheme, or 1946 classification system, dated from July 1, 1946. It divorced the diesel classes from the Whyte steam locomotive system. The wheel arrangement was shown, along with the unit horsepower. Only six classes were required. The reclassification is shown in the table on this page.

As shown, a B-B designation was given to a locomotive with two two-axle trucks, all wheels powered. The horsepower followed (in hundreds), followed by a suffix letter designating the builder. **A** was used for Alco, **B** for Baldwin, **E** for Electro-Motive (GMC), **F** for Fairbanks-Morse. The letters **G** for General Electric and **L** for Lima were added later as locomotives were purchased from those manufacturers.

The two E7 units on the roster had been reclassified from 4B to (A1A-A1A) on April 26, 1946 but reclassed again on July 1, 1946 to (A1A-A1A)20E on the individual unit data cards. However, the monthly report of totals of each locomotive class (PRR Form MP-11a) tabulated the two-unit E7 set as one, 2(A1A-A1A)20E locomotive. This was changed to one, 3(A1A-A1A)20E locomotive in the April 1, 1947 report in anticipation of the arrival that month of the B unit for the set, the 5900B.

Only one other new model, the Baldwin Centipede, arrived during the use of this system, and it proved to be the downfall of the 1946 theory of classification. The first set of Centipedes was delivered to the PRR in April 1947, and required the unwieldy classification of (2D+D2+2D+D2)60B.

Three other classes would have been applied had the 1946 system been retained. The FM three unit Erie-built would have been 3(A1A-A1A)20F, the EMD four unit F3 units would have been 4(B-B)15E and the Alco S-1 switchers would have been (B-B)6A. The awkwardness of the 1946 classification system was increasingly apparent, and in May 1947 a new locomotive classification system was introduced.

THE THIRD (1947) CLASSIFICATION SYSTEM

The third, or 1947, Classification system had many of the elements of the subsequent 1951 system. The engines which were used as single units were assigned a classification almost identical to the system applied to them in 1951. The first letter in the class was the builder, and the second indicated the service or function. After a dash a number representing the unit horsepower in hundreds was used. Thus for example, the former class (B-B)6B became a class BS-6 unit in the 1947 system: a Baldwin-built switcher of 660 horsepower.

For the road units the 1947 system used the number after the dash not for horsepower, but to indicate the number of units in the set for that class. This worked reasonably well except that it did assume that the E7 units would be used in three unit sets: the E7s were class EP-3. The 1947 system dictated class BP-1 for the Baldwin Centipedes which recognized that the unit pairs could not be operated separately. But with the purchase of the new models EMD E8A, EMD F7 and revised design of Baldwin 1500 horsepower freight units, a new difficulty became apparent. The E8s were classed "EP-3 (After 1-1-50)" and the E7s were then classified

"EP-3 (Before 1-1-50)." The EMD and Baldwin freighters were similarly classified.

Another problem was the fact that all cab unit sets did not operate in three or four unit sets indicated by the class shown in the classification documents. In some documents where the number of units in the set was significant, a two unit set of E7 units was identified as an EP-2. On the other hand, the term EF-3 most often meant the three unit helper sets of F3 or F7 units geared for 50 mph. But they couldn't be sure, and that kind of uncertainty defeated the purpose of a classification system.

THE FOURTH (1951) CLASSIFICATION SYSTEM

And so the Pennsylvania people went back to the drawing board to rethink the classification problem once more. These problems of multiple-unit confusion were eliminated in September 1951, when the locomotive classes were changed to the system we have shown in the table as both the 1951 Class and the Base Class. (The Base Class is used in this publication as the primary reference for diesel classes.) The new system met the test: no other new models required changing the class of former units, or necessitated complicated qualifying designations.

The 1951 system continued to use first letter for the builder and the second for the service or function. (A third letter was sometimes used, as with EFP-15.) The major change of the 1951 system was that all classes indicated the unit horsepower by numbers after the dash. There was also the option of subletters indicating certain equipment such as an **m** for multiple unit, an **s** for a steam generator. In addition, a **z** subletter was used on the class BF-16z road freighters for what was termed a major modification.

The modifying letter "**a**" was used to describe a new diesel model whose designation had been previously used. For example, the Baldwin VO-1000 switcher was the BS-10, and its successor model DS 4-4-1000 became the BS-10a. The letter "**a**" was also used to distinguish between the GE U25B (class GF-25) and the U25C (class GF-25a). A curious twist to this last convention was the EMD model SD-40 (classified EF-30a).

The PRR did not purchase any GP-40's, and class "EF-30" was not used. It was a case of a modifier having nothing to modify.

The 1951 classification system also had the flexibility to designate and distinguish the Baldwin freight cab units rebuilt in later years by Alco as ABF-18. In this case, the first letter indicated the rebuilder and the second letter the original builder. The number indicated the rebuilt horsepower. In several other cases a class capable of either freight or passenger service used both the **F** and the **P** to indicate both services. The dual service EMD FP7 and Alco PA-1 models used this convention as classes EFP-15 and AFP-20 respectively.

An interesting curiosity of the system was that in several cases the differences between builders' models was not deemed sufficient to add a modification letter. Class ES-12 included three similar EMD 1200 horsepower switcher models, SW7, SW9 and SW1200. Also, class AS-6 covered both the S-1 and S-3 Alco models and class AS-10 included both models S-2 and S-4.

The original Pennsy-built A6, No. 3907, was the only diesel not affected by the 1946, 1947, or 1951 classification system changes. It never became "PS-4," but retained its A6 designation until class A6b 3907 was retired in 1962.

The only expansion of the 1951 system came in 1955, recognizing the road switcher as a freight engine rather than a switcher. Prior to the arrival of the EMD GP9, road switchers were rarely used in through freight service and the letter "S" in their class was a recognition of their basic switcher function. But the GP9s were assigned to the main east-west freight service upon delivery; their classification as EFS-17m units (Electro-Motive/Freight/Switcher) recognized this assignment. Assignment of class APS-24ms to the Alco RSD-7 road switchers used in passenger helper service was a similar classification system extension.

The PRR also purchased the SD9, the six-axle equivalent of EMD's model GP9. Despite their capabilities, these units were true switchers on the PRR, rather than road-switchers. They were almost always used as hump pushers.

The SD9s on the PRR were classed as ES-17m. This was somewhat the reverse of the case of the PRR's GP7 and SD7 units, where the former were classed as ES-15m and ES-15ms and the latter were class ES-15a. The lack of MU coupling capability on the SD7 during the PRR period is indicated by the lack of the "m" sub letter in the classification. This was also the case of the PRR 8914, an Alco RS-3 without MU, which was classed AS-16.

The first second generation units began arriving in 1962; they were all road switchers. Despite this body configuration, the function letter on these locomotive classes were all **F**, recognizing that these were road units and not switchers.

During 1966 the final Pennsylvania Railroad classification system was adopted, in anticipation of the merger between the PRR and the NYC. This 1966 system, applied jointly by both railroads, was based on the 1951 PRR system with minor modifications. The most significant change was that diesel models which were used as road-switchers were now designated as such. All first generation road switcher models from 1000 horsepower to 2000 horsepower were given the function letters **RS**. Another change for road-switchers was in the use of subletters. A road-switcher with MU was not given an **m** subletter; rather, a road-switcher *without* MU was given the subletter **x**. This recognized that almost all road-switchers had MU control. Therefore, the Alco RS-1 unit numbered 5906 (class AS-10s) prior to renumbering and reclassing became road number 9916 and was reclassed ARS-10sx. This meant that the 9916 had a steam generator but was not equipped with MU. Another minor change with the 1966 classification system was the recognition that certain models were retired. Since no more Baldwin VO-660 or VO-1000 units remained in PRR service, the former BS-6a and BS-10a units became classes BS-6 and BS-10.

The 1966 classification system was continued throughout the Penn Central period; it ended with the formation of Conrail in 1976. Under Conrail's system, the locomotive planners abandoned the home-grown classification system in favor of the builders' locomotive models, catching up to what many railroads had done years before.

PRR 5886A at Detroit, Michigan on June 24, 1950. At the time, this unit was classed EP-3 (after 1-1-50), under the Third Classification system. The builder's paint is still intact -- Brunswick Green with gold stripes. The coupler doors are still in place, although in the open position.

KEN ARDINGER COLLECTION

PENNSYLVANIA RAILROAD
DIESEL LOCOMOTIVE CLASSES
1951 or Base Class
with cross-reference to pages in this book.

Base Class	Builder	Model	Page	Base Class	Builder	Model	Page
Passenger Units				Switchers and Road-switchers			
AP-20/AFP-20	ALCO	PA-1/PB-1	62	A6/A6b	PRR		44
BP-20	BLW	DR 6-4-2000	60	AS-6	ALCO	S-1 and S-3	169
BP-60a	BLW	DR 12-8-3000	55	AS-10/AS-10m	ALCO	S-2 and S-4	180
EP-20	EMD	E7A/E7B	51	AS-10a	ALCO	T-6	193
EP-22	EMD	E8	64	AS-10s/am/ams/as	ALCO	RS-1	117
				AS-15m	ALCO	RS-3	145
Freight and Helper Units				AS-16/16m/16ms	ALCO	RS-3	131
AF-15	ALCO	FA-1/FB-1	79	AS-16a/AS-16am	ALCO	RSD-5	141
AF-16	ALCO	FA-2/FB-2	89	AS-18m	ALCO	RS-11	153
AF-24	ALCO	RS-27	100	AS-18am	ALCO	RSD-12	156
AF-24a	ALCO	C-424	102	APS-24ms	ALCO	RSD-7	148
AF-25	ALCO	C-425	103	AS-24m	ALCO	RSD-15	150
AF-27	ALCO	C-628	106				
AF-30	ALCO	C-630	112	BS-6	BLW	VO-660	163
				BS-6a	BLW	DS 4-4-660	173
BF-15 and BF-15a	BLW	DR 4-4-1500	80	BS-7/BS-7m	BLW	DS 4-4-750	183
BF-16	BLH	RF-16	85	BS-7	BLH	S-8	183
BF-16z	BLH	DR 6 4-2000	61	BS-10	BLW	VO-1000	167
ABF-18	BLW/Alco	Rd-Frt(A&B)	95	BS-10a/BS-10am	BLW	DS 4-4-1000	175
BH-50	BLW	DR 12-8-3000	55	BS-10as	BLW	DRS 4-4-1000	120
				BS-12/BS-12m	BLH	S-12	188
EF-15	EMD	F3A/F3B	69	BS-12am/12ams /12as	BLW	RS-12	121
EF-15a	EMD	F7A/F7B	81				
EH-15	EMD	F3 & F7	76	BS-16m/BS-16ms	BLH	AS-616	136
EFP-15	EMD	FP7A & F7B	87	BS-24/BS-24m	BLH	RT-624	197
EFS-17M	EMD	GP9/GP9B	90				
EF-22	EMD	GP30	101	ES-6(5911)	EMC	SW	159
EF-25	EMD	GP35	104	ES-6	EMD	SW1	165
EF-25a	EMD	SD35	104	ES-10	EMD	NW2	161
EF-30a	EMD	SD40	108	ES-12/ES-12m	EMD	SW9/7/1200	185
EF-36	EMD	SD45	113	ES-15m/ES-15ms	EMD	GP7	126
				ES-15a	EMD	SD7	142
FF-16	F-M	CFA/CFB16-4	84	EFS-17m	EMD	GP9/GP9B	90
FF-20/FP-20 /FP-20a	F-M	ERIE-A and B	72	ES-17m	EMD	SD9	155
				FS-10	F-M	H10-44	178
GF-25	GE	U25B	98	FS-12/FS-12m	F-M	H12-44	192
GF-25a	GE	U25C	108	FS-16m	F-M	H16-44	136
GF-28a	GE	U28B	110	FS-20/FS-20m	F-M	H20-44	124
GF-30a	GE	U30C	110	FS-24m	F-M	H24-66	151
				GS-4/GS-4m	GE	44 Ton	170
				LS-25/LS-25m	Lima	2500 HP Tr	195

This table is a summary list of the PRR locomotive classes from the 1951 system, as used in this volume.

The Baldwin models in this table and in the text of the book are modified from the official builders "class" for brevity. These are correlated to the Baldwin "class" in a table on Page 204.

PAINT SCHEMES

Paint and lettering schemes used on Pennsylvania diesels had sufficient variations to warrant scholarly attention beyond the scope of this volume. Here are the basics.

The primary feature of the PRR's diesel locomotive paint schemes was their base color, which was such a dark shade of green that it was mistaken for black unless directly compared with black, or seen in bright sunlight immediately after application. The color, popularly known as "Brunswick Green," was supposedly the result of an early 1900s Altoona Paint Shop Supervisor saying that he was bored with that same dull PRR color (black), throwing a bucket of green in a 50 gallon drum of standard black. The color was first used on PRR steam and electric locomotives, so its use on diesels, from the first A6 switcher to the last EF-36 road-switchers, was entirely normal.

The formal name used by the PRR on its drawings and color control cards for this shade of green was "dark green locomotive paint, PRR shade Ref. 47-2626."

The only use of a color other than Brunswick Green for diesel locomotives began in 1952, when the Pennsy changed the base color on passenger units to Tuscan Red (Ref. 47-3258), matching its passenger cars. At the same time, the lettering color on passenger units was changed from gold leaf to buff (Ref. 47-3294), although there were ten class EP-22 units lettered in gold leaf on Tuscan Red.

Trucks and underbody equipment were painted "real" black below the bottom of the frame.

The "**PENNSYLVANIA**" lettering appeared at various times on various units in an ornate block style, and sometimes in a light Roman or a Futura style. In later years, the lettering was left off altogether, with the famous keystone being the only indication of ownership.

In the original cab unit paint scheme, the unit number appeared inside the keystone on the nose of A-units. In June 1953, painting drawings for A-units were revised to change to the standard PRR monogram, with no unit number.

Despite systemwide standard paint and lettering drawings, many variations in paint scheme details came about through evolution, adaptation of general designs to specific models, and the individuality in minor details exercised by paint shop foremen when engines were repainted. Thus at any given time, one might see units of the same series or type in different liveries.

PASSENGER CAB UNITS

While there were some variations, passenger diesels generally carried four different schemes, depending on the unit and the era. They were: (1) Five-stripe; (2) Baldwin five-stripe; (3) Single-stripe; and (4) Keystone-only.

PRR 4204, in Tuscan Red, displays one of the latter-day variations on the passenger unit paint scheme. The only graphics are road numbers on the rear of the side and the number boards, two keystones on each side and one on the nose. Vestiges of the five-stripe image can be seen on the lower air filter behind the cab door. When originally built, metal strips carried the top three stripes over the air filter. Harrisburg, Pennsylvania, June 11, 1967

As indicated above, the earliest paint scheme for passenger units was Brunswick Green with gold leaf striping and letters. The word **"PENNSYLVANIA"** and the road number were applied in 8" characters on the side. On carbody units, the "A" or "B" adjacent to the road number was a 5" character. Five stripes were applied somewhat more than halfway up the side of the carbody. The stripes were 1-3/8" wide with a 2" separation, and on A-units they converged into a downward "V" on the front of the locomotive.

On cab units, these stripes were even carried over carbody filters with strips of metal. This feature was removed from painting drawings in 1953, but the metal strips could be seen for some years afterward. Keystone emblems with locomotive road numbers were applied to the center of the noses of A-units, just as they had been placed on steam locomotive smokeboxes. Keystone emblems bearing the "PRR" initials were placed on the side below the stripes on A and B units. The same image for passenger diesels was used with both Brunswick Green and Tuscan Red base colors.

A major variation of the five-stripe image appeared on the Baldwin class BP-20. This was used with both the Brunswick Green and Tuscan Red base color. In this variation, the keystone was placed inside a 30-3/4" diameter circle, placed a few feet behind the cab door and centered at about the level of the second stripe from the top. The 1952 painting drawing for the BP-20

Baldwin 2020A is at Dearborn, Michigan in May 1961. This view shows the striping and PRR emblem unique to the Baldwin cab units when delivered.

A-units shows the five stripes applied from nose to rear.

However, builder's photos and other early shots show the five stripes applied only to the rear of the keystone in the circle, and not over the nose. In 1949, the BP-20 painting drawings were changed to add striping forward of the circle. This image remained on some of the BP-20 until retirement in 1964.

In 1956, painting drawings for all passenger cab classes were issued that replaced the five stripes with a less expensive single 8" wide stripe. The 8" lettering on the side was increased to 16" and the style was changed to a serif style different from the steam locomo-

tive style previously used. On A-units, a keystone emblem was centered on the stripe about a third of the distance from front to rear. The five-stripe image did not go quietly. Even though painting drawings for the one-stripe image were issued in 1956, the Juniata paint shop turned out passenger units in the five-stripe image for several years thereafter.

In 1964, painting drawings were once more issued to change passenger units to a keystone-only image consistent with other units. The single 8" stripe was retained, but the word **"PENNSYLVANIA"** on the unit side was replaced with two keystone emblems below the

Some switchers and road-switchers were renumbered for the Penn Central merger without having the keystone image applied. RS-3 5557, shown at Wilmington, Delaware on December 30, 1967, illustrates the new 16-inch numbers on her cab side. The 8-inch "PENNSYLVANIA" lettering remains unchanged. This rear-quarter view also affords a good look at the steam boiler stack behind the cab, and the trainphone apparatus, including the transmitting antenna "fence" along the right side of the hood, and the receiving antenna disc on the short hood. There's also a "firecracker" antenna for a radio on the near corner; by this time, trainphones were out of service, but the equipment had not been removed.

stripe. The road number was increased to a 16" high character, again consistent with the image used on other types of units. Until the 1966 renumbering, cab units still used an "A" as part of the road number and the booster units used a "B". The "A" or "B" character was 5" high.

In addition to the four images described above, several non-standard variations were applied. Most of these appeared during the last year or two of the PRR, with a varying number of keystones and the absence of even a single stripe.

FREIGHT CAB UNITS

The earliest freight cab units were painted the Brunswick Green base color with a single narrow buff stripe from nose to rear. On EMD cab units (and later other builders), a "teardrop" extended from the rear of the number board for 3 feet toward the rear.

A single buff side stripe was applied to all Alco, EMD and F-M freight units. A single stripe was also applied to Baldwin freight cab units as discussed below. On the EMD units, the stripe was 2" wide while on the other units the single stripe was 3" wide.

As with the passenger units, the side

and nose stripe curved downward to a "V" at the front. The stripe on the Alcos, F-M's and later on the Baldwins tapered in front to a 1/2" width at the lower end, at the bottom, of the "V". The original stripe on most EMD's was not tapered. Later repaintings on these had a taper.

The word **"PENNSYLVANIA"** was lettered in 8" high buff-colored letters on the side of the unit. Road numbers were also applied in 8" high characters on the side of the A-unit nose. On the rear of each A-unit and the front of each B-unit side, the road number was painted in 1-3/4" high characters. A keystone emblem was placed on the sides, centered from front to rear. On most diesel models, the keystone was placed above the side stripe. On the EMD F-units and the two Alco PAs (Class AFP-20) painted Brunswick Green, grillwork dictated placing the keystone below the side stripe.

The Baldwin freight cab units were Brunswick Green, bu carried the same design that appeared on the Baldwin class BP-20s: the five-stripe scheme with a circled keystone. On A-units, the keystone in a 30-3/4" diameter circle was placed behind the cab doors, centered on the five stripes. On the first order of class BF-15, the five stripes extended from the keystone circle to the rear of the A-units. The last of these units was delivered in March 1949. One month later, the painting drawing for these was revised to extend the stripes to the front end of the A-unit. On B-units, the five stripes extended full length. All of the Baldwin freight cabs were originally painted in this image.

In September 1952 a new painting drawing was issued for both classes BF-15 and BF-16. It changed the Baldwins to the same single stripe design used on all other freight cab units. The stripe was 3" wide. While many Baldwin cab units were eventually repainted in the single stripe image, many others carried the original five-stripe paint scheme until their retirement. This was particularly true of the last order of Baldwin freighters.

In 1964 painting drawings were issued with the keystone-only image. With this paint scheme, the single keystone replaced the word **"PENNSYLVANIA"** on the side. The road number was painted in 16" characters, replacing

The same locomotive is shown in two images. ES-12m 8527 on September 21, 1965, above, shows the original lettering plan with the 8-inch "PENNSYLVANIA" on the long hood and 5-inch numbers on the cab side. The number adjacent to the headlight is two inches high.
Below: The 8527 was photographed six days after the view above, showing off her new keystone image after a session with the painter. The keystones replace the lettering, and the cab number is a 16-inch high sans-serif style.

The "Keystone Only" image was applied to new PRR units at the builders starting in 1962. PRR 6018 is an SD35 built in 1965 and seen here in August 1967. The image consisted of a keystone emblem placed on each end and on the hood side behind the cab.

the 8" high numbers previously used. Many EMD freight cab units were painted in this image.

There were, of course, variations from all of these schemes in individual cases, as one would expect where multiple shop locations were involved. While it is possible that a few Alco, Baldwin or F-M freight cab units were painted in the last keystone-only image, these units were scheduled to be retired soon after the new image was defined, and were deemed to be not worth the paint and labor.

FIRST GENERATION ROAD-SWITCHERS AND SWITCHERS

The paint scheme used on the first generation road-switchers and switchers was a simple one. Brunswick Green was the base color. The word "**PENNSYLVANIA**" was lettered in 8" high characters, placed more or less in the center of the long hood. Placement depended on the location of doors and louvers. A 6" high road number was placed on the cab sides. Some, but not all, classes of switchers had the road number placed on the upper right side of the hood ends on most classes in 3" high characters.

On the SD7 and SD9s, a keystone was placed high on the outer end of the short hood side. On the GS-4 units, the word "**PENNSYLVANIA**" was located

on the side sill, as neither hood was long enough for the road name.

The keystone-only image, initially applied to first generation units about 1964, was similar to the scheme used on the second-generation road-switchers delivered in 1962. In this image, the "**PENNSYLVANIA**" lettering on the hoods was replaced with keystones on the long and short hood sides and on the ends. The road number on the cab sides was 16" high.

The main variation to the two basic images described above was the use of 16" high road numbers on the cab side with the 8" high "**PENNSYLVANIA**" still lettered on the cab side. This occurred when some units were renumbered in preparation for the Penn Central merger and only the cab number was changed. In this case, the unit was not repainted at the time of renumbering.

TRANSFER UNITS

Transfer units had equal length hoods on both ends. The paint scheme used on these units was a variation of the first generation road-switcher image except that the road name applied to the hood was only used on the right hand hood when viewed from the side. On the left-hand hood, a 10-3/4" high keystone was roughly centered on the length of the hood.

SECOND GENERATION ROAD-SWITCHERS

The keystone-only image was introduced when second generation road-switchers were delivered to the PRR in 1962. Six keystones were used. One keystone was located on each end, and one each on the sides of the long and short hoods.

The hood side keystone locations varied by locomotive manufacturer, because of louver and radiator location. On GEs and Alcos, the keystone was toward the rear of the long hood, high on the Alcos, low on the GEs. On EMD units, this keystone was located near the cab. As additional second-generation road-switcher models were acquired, the short hood side keystone was omitted on the classes AF-25, AF-27, GF-25a, GF-28a, GF-30a and AF-30. The omission was understandable; on these models, the short hood was very short indeed, and on some engines, the hand brake wheel was located where the keystone would have been. On EMD classes EF-25a, EF-30a and EF-36, the cab signal equipment box was placed on the walkway on the right side of the short hood and the keystone was omitted from this side, appearing on the left side only.

Diesels Visiting the PRR:
Demonstrators, Test Units, Leased Units

The PRR operated a variety of diesel locomotives that they did not own. These units were on the railroad for a many reasons, including tests by the PRR, tests by a builder, sales demonstrations by builders, and the use of leased units.

RAILROAD TEST UNITS

Before the PRR operated diesel locomotives the railroad ran several tests with units borrowed from builders to obtain operational data. This information became the basis for applying the new locomotive technology. A very early test of this type was run during July and August of 1924 when a borrowed 37-ton GE gasoline-electric was tested at the float piers in New York City. This is discussed in detail in Chapter 3 in the article on Class A6. With this test, the PRR was able to define the type of unit it required for the float yards.

In 1937, Electro-Motive Corporation loaned a 600 horsepower switcher to the PRR to confirm that this type of unit would do the work at the General Motors plant in Linden, New Jersey. This test is described in the article on the Class ES-6 (5911) in Chapter 9. In this case the PRR purchased the unit after the test confirmed that it could do the job.

Another PRR test occurred in late 1947 when an F-M model H20-44 was tested as a helper on the Allegheny grades west of Altoona. The PRR had also wanted to test a set of EMD F3 demonstrators with a low gear ratio for the same service, but this could not be arranged. The PRR ended up taking delivery of a new A-B-A set of low-geared units. Within a month of this test, an order was placed for additional units of this type.

BUILDER TEST UNITS

Both Baldwin and General Electric operated diesel locomotives on the PRR not so much as sales demonstration units but to test them for their own purpose. In the late 1920s, Baldwin produced two prototype diesels. The first was the 58501, placed in service in July 1925. The second was the 61000, completed in May 1928. Both of these 1000 horsepower units operated on the PRR. The 58501 was operated primarily to provide Baldwin information on the design. The most significant piece of information was that the engine was not suitable for railroad service. The 61000 did much better, spending five days on the PRR. It eventually operated for a total of 15,000 miles on at least five railroads and the open pit iron mine of Oliver Iron Mining Co. Although the

61000 test was more encouraging than the 58501, railroads were not in a position to purchase diesels in the early 1930s because of the economic conditions brought on by the depression.

On several occasions, General Electric, whose locomotive plant was located in Erie, Pennsylvania, used the PRR's line from Emporium to Erie, Pennsylvania for testing new units. The setup was advantageous. Since Erie was at the end of the Pennsy's line, diesels were not changed out because their trains originated there. Therefore, GE's test units could be sent over to the PRR engine terminal, set up and coupled up to a departing train. The line south of Erie was useful for testing since there were at least two grades, which tested pulling power. Two sets of units known to have been tested were the four unit set of GE U25B demonstrators, 2501-2504 and first of the GE U25C units, which were tested on the Pennsylvania line south of Erie, Pennsylvania.

DEMONSTRATORS

Demonstrators are units used by the builder to sell new locomotive models by demonstrating their performance in operation. Before-World War II, most of the internal combustion locomotives being sold were switchers, so almost all of the demonstrations were of this type

GE U25C at Emporium, Pennsylvania. Oro Dam Constructors units 8012, 8011, and 8010 were the first model U25Cs built. They had been run down from Erie on test, prior to their being shipped to the customer in October 1963.

of unit. Switcher demonstrations on the PRR included the following:
• EMC 463, 400 horsepower gas-electric-October 1930
• Porter 7184, 300 horsepower diesel-September 1930
• Westinghouse 23, 800 horsepower diesel-May 1932
• EMC 518, 900 horsepower diesel-April to July 1935
• Westinghouse 18, 1600 horsepower diesel-February 1936
• EMC 647, 900 horsepower diesel-April 1937
• BLW 307, 1000 horsepower diesel-January to February 1940
• BLW 333, 1000 horsepower diesel-March 1940

While none of these demonstrations resulted in immediate sales, the characteristics and performance data were tabulated by the PRR for future reference.

One significant demonstration occurred between March 3 and March 27, 1936. Electro Motive Corporation (EMC) demonstrators 511 and 512 were 1800 horsepower passenger box cab units. The PRR ran them on various passenger trains between Philadelphia and Chicago every day between March 3 and March 16 and on March 25 and 26. A total of 14,624 miles was operated. In the opinion of various Road Foremen of Engines, the diesels exhibited somewhat better acceleration than a non-stoker fired K-4s 4-6-2. It was also stated that the performance of a stoker-fired K4s was somewhat better than the

The first Electro Motive Corporation (EMC) road demonstrators, 511 and 512, visited the PRR in March 1936. Each box cab contained two 900-hp Winton engines; the two units totalled 3600 hp. The PRR did not buy, but the B&O did acquire a copy, its No. 50. The Santa Fe also purchased two similar units.

pair of diesels. The test provided an opportunity for railroad personnel to witness this new wonder. The visitors list included PRR officials from F. W. Hankins, Chief of Motive Power down to Assistant Road Foreman of Engines and Trainmasters in the territory between Philadelphia and Chicago

After the PRR had completed dieselization in 1958, no new units were purchased until 1962. Since diesel builders were no longer competing against steam locomotives, the sales job was more difficult. Demonstrators by the remaining three builders (Alco, EMD and GE) were offered to railroads

for testing. The following were among the second generation diesel models demonstrated on the PRR.
• Alco model RS-27-2400 horsepower B-B
• Alco Century 628-2750 horsepower C-C
• Alco Century 415-1500 horsepower B-B
• EMD model SD24-2400 horsepower C-C
• EMD model GP20-2000 horsepower B-B
• GE model U25B-2500 horsepower B-B

GM 1000 at North Philadelphia station, on its way from New York to Pittsburgh in 1956. After June 23, 30th Street Philadelphia replaced New York as the eastern terminal.

LEASED UNITS

During the diesel period, the PRR leased a number of units from other railroads. (and in one case directly from General Motors). Locomotive leasing was a practice that allowed railroads a cost-effective method of temporarily acquiring motive power without capital spending. This was particularly the case with the agreement that the Pennsy made with the Bangor and Aroostook. The long term agreement allowed the BAR to purchase diesels which it would use in the winter season and lease to the PRR in the other part of the year for iron ore service. This is discussed in detail in Chapter 5.

Some of these leases lasted for a few days and other lasted for several years. The longest continuous lease period involved the P&WV 40, a Baldwin model AS-616, 1600 horsepower C-C unit. The 40 lease lasted for nine years and is discussed in Chapter 7. The 40 was finally purchased by the PRR in July 1963. The Pennsy also purchased other leased units. Six D&H model RS-3 units were leased for almost four years.

Between February 26, 1956 and June 30, 1957, the PRR operated one of the Aerotrain equipment sets leased from General Motors. This was a train set that included a lightweight passenger locomotive and coaches. The train ran between New York and Pittsburgh until June 23, 1956 and Philadelphia to Pittsburgh thereafter. The locomotive was a 1200 horsepower, B-2 wheel arrangement diesel that was one of three units, which EMD had built. EMD identified this locomotive as an LWT12. The unit was numbered 1000 on the Pennsy and was referenced as class EP-12 in PRR assignment documents.

Although the train made almost $350,000 out of pocket profit, the operation did not result in an equipment purchase. Those who rode the Aerotrain equipment were not complimentary about the quality of the ride, saying that it was "like riding a bus." This was not surprising since the coaches were actually a modification of a GM bus design.

During the 1954-1957 period, as the PRR moved toward dieselization, leasing accelerated the process. The cost of leasing was offset by the savings of diesel operation vs. steam. The tables on this page list the diesels leased by the PRR as of November 1 1957 and October 1967.

At the end of 1957, several large orders of diesels were arriving, and the units listed in the table were returned to their owners, except for the BAR Geeps and the P&WV 40.

During 1966 the PRR again needed to lease diesels. By October 7, 1967, a total of 67 were on lease. The next month, the PRR added 21 EMD SDs from the Duluth, Missabe and Iron Range. Thirteen of these were model SD9 and eight were model SD18.

Units Leased by PRR - November 1957

Owner	No. of Units	Road Numbers	Model
Wash. Term.	2	46, 49	Alco RS-1
BAR	7	66, 67, 68, 71, 73, 74, 75	EMD GP7
BAR	5	76, 77, 78, 79, 80	EMD GP9
Union	2	608, 611	Alco RS-2
Montour	2	71, 72	EMD SW7
Montour	1	73	EMD SW9
PC&Y	1	1	F-M H10-44
Wabash	10	1154, 1154A, 1165, 1165A, 1166, 1166A,1168, 1168A, 1169, 1169A	EMD F7A
D&H	6	4041, 4042, 4044, 4046, 4047, 4048	Alco RS-3
DT&I	6	964, 965, 966, 970, 972, 973	EMD GP7
P&WV	1	40	BLH AS-616
Ill. Nor.	1	34	Alco S-4
C&O	15	5907, 5932, 5936, 5937, 5938, 5940, 5944, 5958, 5950, 5952, 5954, 5955, 5956, 5958, 5960	EMD GP9
Total Units	59		

Units Leased by PRR - October 1967

Owner.	No. of Units	Road Numbers	Model
Alco Prod.	3	900, 901, 902	Alco RS-27
DT&I	4	955, 957, 958, 969	EMD GP7
DT&I	2	990, 992	EMD GP9
Reading	8	500, 510, 519, 514, 520, 521, 523, 524	Alco RS-3
N&W	41	315, 316, 317, 320, 324, 327, 331, 337, 345, 346, 348, 352, 354, 355, 356, 357, 358, 360, 361, 362, 365, 368, 378, 388, 2573, 2575, 2576, 2577, 2850, 2851, 2852, 2853, 2854, 2855, 2856, 2857, 2858, 2859,2860, 2862, 2863	Alco RS-11
N&W	9	2865, 2866, 2867, 2868, 2869 2870, 2871, 2872, 2873	Alco RS-36
Total Units	67		

Cab Signals

The Pennsylvania installed signal display units in a number of steam, electric and diesel locomotive cabs. The displays closely approximated the aspects of trackside signals.

The PRR's trackside signal system, first introduced in 1915, was unique in that it did not rely on the color of the signal lights to transmit information. The lights were not red, yellow and green; rather, they were all yellow, and arranged so that they replicated the position of the semaphore blades they replaced. Three lights in a horizontal pattern gave a STOP indication; three lights in a vertical pattern indicated CLEAR, while three lights at a 45-degree angle indicated CAUTION.

In practice, the trackside position-light signals went beyond the semaphore. They could show four aspects on each signal head: horizontal, vertical, and both diagonals. A fifth aspect lighted all of the lights in the outer circle.

The clear advantage to the PRR was maintenance; there were no moving parts, and the aspect was still decipherable even if one bulb in the pattern was burned out.

Cab signals were installed in many road locomotives, particularly passenger engines, to give the engineer continuous information about track occupancy conditions ahead. A 100-cycle alternating current in the rails was interrupted in four coded sequences, providing four signal aspects in the cab. Each cab signal had five round bezels or windows, each with a fixed aspect. The indication varied with the situation.

The bezels showed:

Top: Clear; no train in next two blocks.

2nd and 3rd: Approach-medium; train in second block ahead.

4th: Approach; train in next block ahead.

Bottom: Stop or restricting; train ahead in this block.

Cab signals were most useful in bad weather when bad visibility limited the view of the trackside signals. The cab signal system preceded the diesels; by 1946, the circuits covered the electrified main lines, the Middle Division through Pennsylvania, and the main line to St. Louis.

Cab signal aspects changed instantaneously as conditions caused the wayside signals immediately ahead to change. An engineer could then reduce or increase speed immediately, rather than waiting until he saw the next wayside signal.

CAB SIGNAL TERRITORY

Cab signal territory on the PRR extended on the major main lines from New York City to Indianapolis via Pittsburgh and Columbus and from Zoo Tower (Philadelphia) to Washington. Curiously, cab signal equipment was not installed on the Pittsburgh-Chicago main line although the line was suitable for maximum speed operation.

Other significant cab signal equipped lines included several electrified freight lines in the triangle bounded by Trenton, New Jersey, Perryville, Maryland and Harrisburg, Pennsylvania. On non-electrified lines, the line between Columbus, Ohio and New Paris, Ohio via Bradford, Ohio was equipped for cab signals. New Paris is six miles east of Richmond, Indiana.

View from the ground looking into the cab of PRR 1422A. Visible through the cab window is the cab signal box to the left of the engineer. Also note the newly applied emblem that indicated radio installation. This dates the photo to the latter half of 1966 when radios were being installed in road units in anticipation of the end of trainphone.

Trainphone

Trainphone was the name given to the mobile electronic communication system used by the Pennsylvania Railroad from 1944 until it was superseded by conventional radio at the end of 1966. Unlike other railroads, the PRR did not choose a two-way space radio system; trainphone used a frequency-modulated signal which was transmitted by electromagnetic induction from an antenna loop on an engine or caboose to a lineside wire or the rails.

Union Switch and Signal Co. began developing the system before World War II, in conjunction with the PRR and other railroads. The prototype installation on PRR's Belvedere branch was authorized in September 1941. By June 1942, a locomotive and caboose had been equipped and wayside equipment placed in service. The developmental installation was completed in 1944 on the line between Trenton and Phillipsburg, New Jersey. At that time, ten locomotives, ten cabooses and one wayside station (Frenchtown, New Jersey) were equipped for a full trial. For this installation, the carrier was a 5.7-kilocycle AM signal. (The unit of frequency was later changed from "kilocycles" to "kilohertz.")

A 1944 *Railway Age* article on trainphone described it as neither radio nor telephone but incorporating certain features of both systems. The signal was carried between a wayside station (such as a tower or station) and a receiver antenna on a caboose or locomotive. At the time, trainphone was considered a great advantage because the signal radiated in space was of such low power that no FCC radio licenses were required.

By 1947, the installation had evolved from the initial installation on the Bel-Del line to two mainline divisions, between Harrisburg and Pittsburgh. From Harrisburg to Altoona, enough locomotives and cabooses were equipped for use on both passenger and freight trains. Between Altoona and Pittsburgh, communications were initially limited to passenger trains.

The single carrier frequency had been changed from 5.7 kilohertz AM to two FM frequencies, 88 and 144 kilo-

hertz. The two frequencies made possible a backup in the event one frequency was down. In 1947, the convention was to use the "L" (lower) frequency for train to wayside traffic and the "H" (higher) frequency for train end to end conversations. The carrier signals were active at all times making a party line situation. Since the range of signals was about five miles, this was not a difficulty. There was also a provision for an emergency signal. All stations receiving this signal were required to cease conversations so that the emergency message could be sent.

Although early technical articles referred to the trainphone signal as carried by rails, the 1947 *Railway Age* stressed the lineside wire as the carrying medium. This could be either the normal communication wire line or a dedicated wire strung adjacent to the tracks and insulated from the ground. This was especially required when the lineside wires were separated from the tracks by more than about 150 feet.

The trainphone equipment on diesel

locomotives and cabooses included separate transmitting and receiving antennas. The transmitter antenna loops were partially on the roof, and were quite visible, often described as "fences." The "fences" were lengths of pipe with loop wires inside and supporting brackets to provide the required standoff from the roof. The antenna also included an electrical connection to the front and rear trucks; the rail completed the loop. On most diesel locomotives, the receiving antenna was also on the roof, and was similar to the transmitting antenna except that while one end of the antenna was connected to the trainphone, the other end was open (not connected). On caboose receiving antennas, the receiving loop was contained in a disc-like case with the loop in a vertical plane. One of these antennas was required for each of the two frequencies, which is why there were two discs on caboose roofs. This type of receiving antenna was also used on locomotives where space was a problem.

Trainphone operation in a PRR cabin car. The trainphone box has two levers. The upper lever (S) switches between the high (H) and low (L) channels. The trainman has his hand on the "C" lever, which was used to send an emergency signal over the trainphone system. To send the emergency signals, the "C" lever was shifted from the "L" side to the "H" side (as the trainman has just done) and held in that position for about two seconds. He then returned the lever to the "H" position and repeated this move again. The two-tone emergency signal was heard on both channels. All other transmissions were to cease and the emergency call answered.

PRR 8111 illustrates the typical trainphone antenna installation on road-switchers. The "fence" on the roof is the transmitting antenna. The disc on the end of the long hood is the receiving antenna.

The PRR gradually expanded trainphone coverage to most of its non-electrified main lines in the late 1940s. Interference from high-voltage power circuits made trainphone unsatisfactory in the electrified zone. The system saved time by allowing enginemen and conductors to converse with each other, and with wayside stations.

In addition to trainphone equipment installed on locomotives, cabooses and way stations, there was also a "portable" trainphone set, known as the "Carryphone." The set was a 16" x 13" x 5" piece of equipment weighing almost 30 lbs. and carried with a shoulder strap. The antenna was a 30" diameter loop of wires, which was attached to the bottom of the equipment case and looped around the case and over the shoulder of the user. The Carryphone was portable in the same sense that a tuba is a portable musical instrument. Evidence suggests that carryphones were not widely used (if at all!) after an initial, strenuous, evaluation period.

Although the PRR used train phone most extensively, there were others. The Kansas City Southern was also a major user. Using a system from

Aircraft Accessories Corporation. (not US&S), the entire Kansas City to Port Arthur main line was so equipped. The DM&IR, B&LE and ACL also used trainphone-type systems. Other railroads, including the NYC, L&N, N&W, CB&Q, CNJ and SP, used trainphone-type systems in local areas . Many of these local systems provided only one way transmission, such as from a yard tower to a switcher. The visible indication that the system is one-way is the presence of only a receiving antenna on a locomotive. The receiving antenna is contained in the disc-like casing described above.

The PRR also used conventional radio during the trainphone era, but the radio installations were usually limited to a specific yard such as Buttonwood yard near Wilkes-Barre, Pennsylvania. This type of radio use restricted assignments to radio-equipped locomotives. Although the trainphone provided satisfactory communications for more than 20 years, by the mid-1960s conventional radio improvements had caught up with the PRR. Trainphone equipment predated transistors; some thirty-odd vacuum tubes were used in the locomotive and caboose sets. As time passed, this

presented a maintenance problem.

By the mid-1960s, much of the trainphone equipment was out of repair, and technology had advanced to the point where radio was the obvious choice for the future. The last new locomotive purchased with trainphone installed was 2415, the Alco C-424 delivered in September 1963. The end of trainphone was near; by the end of 1966 the PRR had completed installation of conventional radio on locomotives and cars and at wayside stations. A general order was issued on April 30, 1967 formally discontinuing trainphone.

The PRR installed trainphone equipment in way stations and lineside on virtually all non-electrified main lines. This included the following lines:
- Harrisburg to Chicago
- Pittsburgh to St. Louis
- Harrisburg to Buffalo
- Emporium to Erie
- Columbus to Chicago
- Xenia to Cincinnati
- Wilmington to Cape Charles
- Baltimore to Harrisburg

Many secondary main lines and branches were also trainphone-equipped.

The PRR builder's photo of the only class A6b unit. Note the canvas background and paper in the windows. This has been done to produce a photo with no background. Although the lettering looks a bit dull, it is in fact gold leaf instead of the later buff paint. This photo was taken in Altoona in 1930.

Chapter 3

The First Diesels

Motor Cars

The first recorded use of internal combustion engines on the Pennsylvania Railroad dates back to about 1909, when a self-propelled Fairbanks-Morse car was delivered to the PRR. A 50-hp F-M gasoline engine powered its car, which, with its Brill-built carbody, resembled a trolley car. The unit was robust enough to be delivered under its own power from the F-M plant in Three Rivers, Michigan to the PRR at Wilmington, Delaware. Its initial service was between Clayton and Smyrna, Delaware, a distance of slightly more than a mile.

Even before World War I, the Pennsylvania was looking for ways to reduce the cost of passenger and mail operations on lightly-traveled branches; something less expensive than a steam-powered train. While that search was to evolve into the use of diesel locomotives, the path was neither rapid nor straightforward.

One approach to lowering operating costs was a self-propelled motor car, which was cheaper to operate than a full steam-propelled train. Many railroads used motor cars, but as we

might expect, PRR motor car operations, like their passenger operations in general, were more extensive than most. In their time, PRR motor cars popped up anywhere from Trenton to Grand Rapids, but after World War II they gradually collected in New Jersey.

FIRST MOTOR CARS

Before 1920, the PRR had operated two motor cars. The first was the 1909 four-wheel F-M motor car mentioned above. Although this car was delivered on its own wheels from the factory in Michigan to Wilmington, the car was judged "not a success" and sold to a dealer in September 1913. It was operated for about five months on the Smyrna branch near Wilmington, and for less than two months on the Kensington branch in Philadelphia.

The second was a 70-foot McKeen gas-mechanical car numbered 4701, purchased in 1910. It was used on the Buffalo Division, but by 1912 a PRR motive power official stated that the car "was not a success." The car remained in service for several more years but by 1919, another official stated that the car "has been a failure on our road." At that point, an unsuccessful attempt was made to sell the car.

PRR 4701 was scrapped by the railroad in January 1920.

In addition to gas motor cars, PRR tested at least five battery-electric cars during the 1913 to 1918 period. While some of the tests resulted in mildly satisfactory results, none of the cars were purchased.

The first successful PRR motor cars had mechanical transmissions and drives, similar to those used in trucks. The idea of electric traction motors for self-propelled cars came to the PRR later.

In 1921, a Mack model AC gas-mechanical rail-car was purchased for operation by the Lewisburg, Milton and Watsontown Passenger Railway, a trolley-operated street railway that ran between Watsontown and Lewisburg, Pennsylvania.

In 1911, the trolley company leased the rights to run passenger operation on the PRR's Montandon Branch between Montandon to Mifflinburg via Lewisburg. Between 1911 and 1921, the trolley company purchased a succession of battery cars, none of which were successful. The Mack rail-car replaced the battery cars in 1921. It was lettered "LM&WPRy" and numbered 20.

PRR 4663 is seen shortly after completion in June 1929 on the Westinghouse test track in East Pittsburgh, Pennsylvania.

HAMLEY COLLECTION

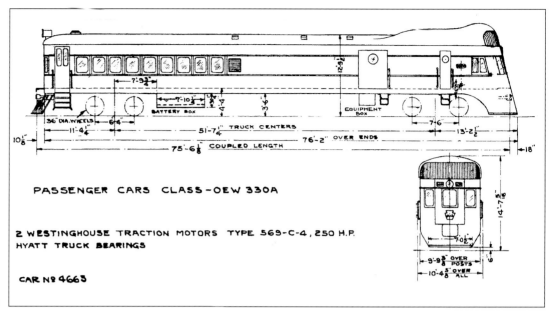

The diagram book drawing of PRR 4663 after being "dolled-up" in 1941. With the Zephyresque nose, the car became single ended for normal operation and required turning at each end of its run.

In 1928, the trolley company gave up its Montandon-Mifflinburg lease, at the same time it abandoned its other rail operations in favor of buses. The Mack rail-car was relettered for the PRR, numbered 4737, and operated on the Montandon branch for a short period. The car was sold in 1931 to the Artemus and Jellico in Kentucky. The car was acquired by the Buffalo Creek and Gauley in 1941 and numbered A. It operated on the BC&G until the abandonment of that operation. The most recent owner of this Mack motor car is the Strasburg Rail Road in East Strasburg, Pennsylvania.

MORE MOTOR CARS

Motor car procurement in the 1920s (after that initial Mack) began with 13 Brill gas-mechanical cars (including one trailer) purchased between 1924 and 1926. Of the Brill total, six were 68 horsepower Model 55 units, two were the 115 horsepower Model 65, and five were the 175 horsepower Model 75. One of the six Model 55s was assigned to the subsidiary West Jersey and Seashore. An additional Model 55 was purchased for the Long Island Rail Road.

We must note here that in those early days, an engine capable of generating 175 horsepower was much larger than an engine of the same power would be today. Higher horsepower ratings were to come, and engines would shrink; but that was in the future.

PRR motor cars operated either as single units or with a trailer. For most runs, light coaches were used as trailers, such as the MP-54 commuter cars.

The one Brill trailer purchased with the motor cars was designated a Model 75T. One of the powered Model 75 cars was purchased with a center entrance and was designated a model 75CE. These cars were smaller than the later gas-electrics and ranged in length from 43' 5" for the Model 55 to 60' for the model 75. They were variously equipped with Midwest, Sterling and Winton engines.

The Brill gas-mechanical motor cars did not have a long life on the PRR. The 4741 was converted to tower car 489500 in 1931, and the last remaining passenger unit was retired in 1935.

Between 1925 and 1930, the railroad's focus turned to electric motor power transmission instead of mechanical drives. This included the purchase of 37 gas-electrics. Two Westinghouse diesel-electric cars followed (described as "oil-electrics" at the time). Two early Budd motor cars came in 1933.

The gas-electric cars were primarily Brill cars ranging from the 250 horsepower Model 250 to the 415 horsepower Model 660. In addition, seven EMC and one Mack gas electric cars were also acquired. Six of the EMC cars were 275 horsepower, 75' 6" long with a seating capacity from 65 to 73 seats. The other EMC car was 400 horsepower with the same size and seating capacity as the earlier six. The single Mack car was a model AP with two engines totaling 240 horsepower, with a 75' 6" long carbody (built by Brill) and a seating capacity of 71.

More significant to this book were

the two Westinghouse "oil-electric" cars. PRR 4663 and 4664 were characterized by a *Railway Age* article (written by a Westinghouse engineer) as "the first cars of a coordinated design built for installation of a modern car-type Diesel-driven power plant, to be placed in service in the United States." These 1929 cars used a single Westinghouse engine, a six-cylinder, in-line machine with an 8-1/4" bore and 12" stroke. They were built at Westinghouse's South Philadelphia works to a design licensed from the Beardmore Company of Glasgow, Scotland. The carbodies were built by Pullman in Chicago, but the engines and electrical equipment were assembled at Westinghouse's East Pittsburgh Works. The 300-hp engine was representative of diesel engines available at the time for railway use. While the 300-hp. Westinghouse/Beardmore engine was more efficient than the earlier 175-hp. gasoline engines, it was a massive unit. The engine and generator extended for almost the total length of the motor car's 17' 6" engine compartment.

The Westinghouse/Beardmore engines were the first diesel power plants on the Pennsylvania. Many more were to follow. We must note here that the Westinghouse/Beardmore engine represented the size, weight and horsepower for a railroad diesel engine in 1929. This shows the impracticality of the Pennsy's premature effort (to be described later in this chapter) to shoehorn a smaller diesel engine into the A6 switcher four years earlier.

In 1932, the Pennsy purchased an advanced design pair of motor cars from the Budd Co. These cars used an early version of the Budd lightweight stainless steel carbody. They were mounted on Michelin-designed three-axle rubber-tired trucks. Each car was originally powered by a 125 horsepower Cummins diesel engine with mechanical drive. The cars were not successful in this form.

In 1936, the cars were rebuilt. The 4688 was converted to a trailer. The 4689 was re-engined with a 190 horsepower Lycoming gasoline engine. Both cars were rebuilt with two axle trucks and steel wheels. These mechanical-drive cars were still unsuccessful. In 1943, the cars were leased to the Washington and Old Dominion who purchased them in 1945. Unsuccessful on the W&OD as well as the PRR, the cars were finally and mercifully scrapped in 1949.

The electric traction system had been proven to be clearly superior. The diesel engines had also proven their worth in terms of reliability and safety as compared with gasoline. A fiery accident on July 31, 1940 tragically brought this issue into focus. Gas-Electric No. 4648 left Hudson Ohio for Akron at 5:49 PM, carrying passengers from mainline trains. The motor car's engineman over-ran the meet point with northbound freight FC-4. A head-on collision resulted, with the lead steam engine on the freight burying itself into almost half the length of the gas-electric. Forty-one people died as the car's gasoline tank exploded.

Between 1941 and 1953, the PRR gas-electric motor cars still in service were re-engined with diesels. The smaller cars received Cummins units while the larger cars had Hamilton engines installed.

Another notable development in PRR motor cars was the rebuilding of motor car 4663 in 1941. The 4663 was rebuilt as part of a program to improve the volume of freight traffic originating in Muskegon, Michigan. Later in August 1940, PRR people met with representatives of the larger industries in Muskegon. The railroad had wanted to terminate two passenger round trips to the city, but agreed to maintain the passenger service in return for materially improved freight business. By the end of the year, a significant gain in freight business had resulted. As a cooperative gesture, James M. Symes, who managed the PRR's Western Region, proposed that a motor car be "dolled up" for the Muskegon run.

In addition to the carbody modification, the PRR shop forces installed better seats, double pane windows (for the rigors of Michigan winters), and an oil-fired heating boiler to replace the original coal-burning unit. The car interior was generally brought up to the appearance standards of passenger cars that the PRR was improving at the time. Externally, 4663 received new sheet metal on its front end, obviously inspired by the Zephyr streamliners and ACF motor cars.

Although the engine was not replaced, it was given a heavy overhaul. One proposal not accepted was naming the car "City of Muskegon." The overhauled car was released from Altoona Shops in August 1941. Car 4663 was re-engined in 1947 and retired in 1954.

By the late 1950s, only 11 motor cars remained in passenger service. Four more had been converted to tower cars, equipped with rooftop platforms en-

PRR 4660 has just arrived in Phillipsburg, New Jersey after a run from Trenton as train number 2372. The date is July 6, 1959 and the train will be withdrawn the next year.

abling work on overhead wire in electrified territory. The cars' ability to move under their own power was helpful where the wires were not live.

Both of the Westinghouse cars had been retired by the late 1950s, and all of the others still in service had been dieselized. The remaining motor car runs were mostly in New Jersey. Motor cars were still used on the Camden-Trenton, Camden-Pemberton, Trenton-Phillipsburg and Trenton-Red Bank commuter runs. Outside this area motor cars were still used on the Baltimore-Parkston commuter run. This last run ended in 1959, the Trenton-Phillipsburg run in 1960 and the Pemberton and Red Bank runs in 1962. Finally, the last PRR motor car run was made from Camden to Trenton on Friday, June 21, 1963 using car 4666.

Classes A6 and A6b

The class A6 design was developed in 1924 and 1925 as the Pennsylvania Railroad's first diesel-electric locomotives. As noted in Chapter 1, the program for three 65-ton diesel switchers was initiated to eliminate steam at two small float yards in New York City, in compliance with the Kaufmann Act. The other railroads used 300-hp Alco-GE-Ingersoll Rand boxcab units for their New York harborside yard service. These locomotives had larger carbodies than the PRR's A6.

Considering the PRR's stated requirements for the 65-ton units, it is apparent that the railroad was overly ambitious in specifying the engine to be used. A 500 horsepower diesel small enough to fit into a 22 foot, 7 inch A6 carbody was beyond the technology of the time. Because of problems with the diesel engines designed for these units, and because of some urgency to meet the Kaufmann Act, gasoline engines were installed in all three units. The chronology worked out this way:

From July 10 to August 9, 1924, a borrowed GE 37-ton locomotive was tested at both W. 37th St. Yard, Manhattan and N. Fourth St. Yard in Brooklyn. The tests were successful. The gas-electric did the work of a class

A4 0-4-0 in Manhattan. The A4 had a tractive effort of 25,800 lbs. and was required to haul 8 cars weighing 415 tons at West 37th. At N. Fourth St., the work was being handled by a class A3a 0-4-0T, which had a tractive effort of 18,700 lbs.

In Brooklyn, the requirement was to haul four cars weighing 196 tons. The float bridge was restricted to 150,000 lbs., which accounts for the lighter loads. Although the 37-ton GE trial unit handled the work at both yards, it was observed in the report of the tests that operations in winter at W. 37th St. during periods of extreme high and low tide probably could not be handled satisfactorily by a similar unit. For this reason, a 50-ton unit was recommended in the test report.

By February 1925, letters had been sent to several prospective engine builders asking for details of their diesel engines. W. F. Kiesel, Jr., the PRR's Mechanical Engineer, had obtained a preliminary evaluation from Westinghouse Electric with their recommendations for switching the float yards. This evaluation recommended either a one-motor or two motor unit weighing between 100,000 and 125,000 lbs. and being powered with either one or two 250 HP engines.

The urgency to eliminate steam locomotives in New York City increased on April 14 when Governor Alfred E. Smith of New York vetoed the Thayer Bill, which would have deferred the date for electrification for three years. With eight and a half months before the Kaufmann Act deadline, PRR's motive power management acted. A meeting was convened on April 18, 1925 chaired by J. T. Willis, PRR Chief of Motive Power and attended by Messrs. Kiesel, Duer, Kleine and Henry of the railroad. William F. Kiesel, Jr. was Mechanical Engineer of the PRR; he had achieved significant accomplishments in the field of steam locomotive design. At the meeting, it was decided to proceed with the design and construction of three, 65-ton diesel-electric locomotives of 300-500 horsepower for the New York City float yards. These locomotives were designated class A6. The preference was for a horsepower of 500, which exceeded the horsepower of any single engine diesel-electric locomotive

at the time. The small carbody of the A6 proved to be an obstacle that the diesel engine manufacturers of the day could not overcome.

The order for the three diesel locomotives was placed with the Altoona Works on the same day as the meeting. In late May, letters soliciting bids were sent to several engine builders for proposals for a diesel engine in the 400-500 horsepower range. The group of builders included Worthington Pump and Machinery, Sun Shipbuilding and Drydock, Standard Motor Co., Ingersoll Rand, McIntosh and Seymour and American Krupp. Soon after, Willis stated that "We have experienced great difficulty in getting the manufacturers of Diesel engines to reduce their weights to a figure which it is necessary for us to comply with in the construction that we must use."

In early June 1925, officials of the Bessemer Gas Engine Company of Grove City, Pennsylvania met with Kiesel in order to exchange data on the engines that the PRR would require. By the end of October, Kiesel and the Bessemer people had agreed on the technical details and early in November an order was placed for three engines. At that time Kiesel believed that the engines would be delivered in time to complete the three locomotives by August 1, 1926.

At this point, the question arises about meeting the Kaufmann Act deadline of January 1, 1926. Surviving correspondence indicates that the New York Public Service Commission (NYPSC) was satisfied with reasonable progress. During December 1925, the PRR supplied the NYPSC with plans for compliance, including drawings of the locomotives being built. The PRR also stated that eight steam locomotives would continue operation after the deadline—six at Sunnyside and one each at the Manhattan and Brooklyn float yards. The NYPSC also issued an order that acknowledged acceptance of the use of diesel-electric locomotives at the float yards. This indicated acceptance of their use as electric powered locomotives. The PRR later received approval for delaying the completion of steam elimination until January 1, 1927. While Sunnyside electrification was completed by that time, the completion of the

44

A6 units did not even meet this deadline. Although the PRR was obviously motivated to complete the units and was respectful in informing the NYPSC of the lack of progress, questions about the legality of the Kaufmann Act seemed to deter the state from taking legal action.

The first engine from Bessemer was delivered a year and a half after the original projected delivery date. During that time, this engine (the second and third engines were never completed) was to reach testing three times at the engine company. Each time, engine failures during testing resulted in some degree of redesign. Two of these redesigns were characterized later by Bessemer as major redesigns. The first failure was in October 1926 when a timing gear became disengaged, damaging the cylinder heads and the valves which had been open at the time of failure. The camshaft and its supports were completely redesigned.

The second setback was in October 1927 when it was determined that the Duralumin (an aluminum alloy) connecting rods were not holding up. The resolution was to change the connect-ing rod material to forged steel. After about 12 hours of running with the new rod material in November 1927, another failure occurred, signaled by two small explosions in the crankcase during running. In the post-mortem, it was concluded that the clearances between the new connecting rods and the crankshaft were too tight. Severe connecting rod damage had occurred.

After the engine was rebuilt once again, the Bessemer company asserted that the generator being used to load the engine on test was somehow overloading the engine. Since the mechanical loading brake Bessemer had been using was damaged and could not be replaced for several months, Bessemer proposed shipping the engine to the PRR in Altoona for completion of the engine testing in actual locomotive operation. The Pennsy was still under pressure to complete the units, and agreed to take delivery of the first engine. The engine was invoiced by Bessemer on February 29, 1928 with payment to be made 90 days after successful operation of the diesel-electric locomotive in the Altoona yard.

The Pennsylvania Railroad's first diesel-electric locomotive, number 3905, was turned out of the Altoona Works on June 25, 1928, although the builder's plate states May 1928 and the builder's photographs were taken on May 22. Unit 3905 first operated in the Altoona yard on June 28. Within three weeks, it was obvious that the locomotive was not ready for New York City. In a letter of July 21, Kiesel informed the PRR Chief of Motive Power (now F. W. Hankins, since J. T. Willis had been promoted to Assistant Vice President-Operations) that the locomotive should not be sent to New York for service unless a protect engine is provided. The 3905 had operated for a total of 24 hours up to that time. It was apparent that considerable development would be required to make it satisfactory. Kiesel's letter also discussed the alternative of renting or purchasing of the Brill 500 horsepower gas unit (as used in the LIRR's first 402) or the installation of dual gas-electric motor car units in the second and third A6 frames.

Testing of the 3905 continued in the Altoona yard. Problems also continued. On September 29, 1928, the engine threw a connecting rod through the side

Railway Age's *June 18, 1927* issue contained an article describing the PRR's class A6 locomotives, equipped with the Bessemer diesel engine. This article was an abstract of a paper by F. K. Fildes, an Assistant Mechanical Engineer of the PRR. The side elevation below was included in the article.

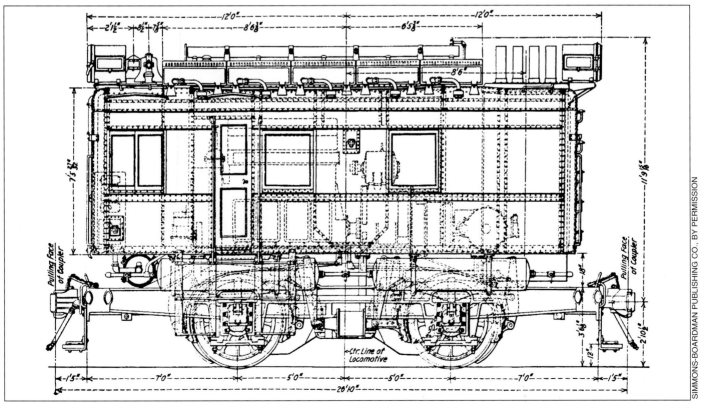

You are looking at the Pennsylvania Railroad's first internal combustion locomotive. Proudly bearing its Altoona builder's plate, No. 3905 and her crew pause during their labors at the railroad's Hudson (North) River float yard in New York, New York. Time is believed to be the late 1930s.

Below Left, Front of 3905, as-built. Below Right, Rear of 3905, as-built.

of the engine frame. This was repaired in late November and the 3905 was returned to service, but troubles with the engine persisted. Finally, on December 6, 1928, Kiesel wrote a letter to PRR motive power chief Hankins which ended the agony. After its most recent repairs, the unit had been in service for a total of 75 hours over a period of ten days. It had been taken out of service on December 1 on account of brush arcing. Kiesel stated: "However, we are continually working on the fuel injection system in order to balance the load on the cylinders. We are also having trouble retaining the oil in the exciter drive housing. Vibration is still excessive and this is causing trouble with the generator brushes which we believe is one of the causes for arcing mentioned above." The 3905 never ran again as a diesel-electric locomotive. The diesel had run about 100 total hours of service on the PRR. It had required major repairs twice during this period and had never developed more than 450 horsepower on test.

Above, gasoline-powered 3906 shoves an outside-braced wooden box car to its place in the float yard. Cars (and the engines, for that matter,) arrive and depart by car float. Did the neighbors appreciate the legislated lack of smoke?
Below, Rear quarter view of PRR 3907. The A6b unit sits unused in January 1962 at the engine terminal at 46th Street, Philadelphia. The pioneer locomotive had worked most of its life in nearby Norristown.

As early as July 1928, the Motive Power people were looking at using gasoline engine units, instead of the uncertain diesel, in the A6. At that time, discussions centered on single or dual 350 horsepower engine-generator units. These units were being installed in new PRR motor cars at the time. Consideration was also given to the use of a Cummins diesel. Intriguing as this was, a Cummins-powered A6 unit never came to pass. Even before Kiesel's letter of December 6, a request was made to the PRR Board of Directors in late November for more funds to purchase two 500-hp. dual sets (i.e. four 250-hp engine-generator packages) for the first two A6 frames. This proposal was made as the most expeditious method of replacing the steam engines at the New York City float yards.

By December 7, Kiesel had modified his proposal to use one 400 horsepower Winton Model 148 engine instead of two 250 horsepower units per locomotive. His reasons were that original cost and maintenance on one engine would be less than for two engines and that although the Winton engine was conservatively rated at 400 horsepower, it had produced up to 550 horsepower on the test stand. Kiesel also stated that based on personal observation, a 400 horsepower unit could handle the work at the float yards. In late December, the

Locomotive Characteristics			
Class	A6	A6b (As-built)	A6b (As Re-engined)
Builder	PRR Altoona	PRR Altoona	PRR Altoona
Model	None	None	None
Horsepower of engine	400	535	450
Horsepower for traction	320	375	
Wheel Arr,	B (0-4-0)	B (0-4-0)	B (0-4-0)
Total Weight, Lbs	130,000	130,000	130,000
Length over Couplers	26' 10"	26' 10"	26' 10"
Truck Wheelbase	10' 0"	10' 0"	10' 0"
Engine	Winton 148 Gasoline	Brill 860 Gasoline	Hamilton 68SA (Diesel)
Generator	Westinghouse 476	Westinghouse 476	Westinghouse 476
Traction Motors	2, Westinghouse 355	2, Westinghouse 355	2, Westinghouse 355
Gear Ratio	76:16	76:16	76:16
Maximum Speed	20 MPH	20 MPH	20 MPH
Starting Trac. Eff.	32,500 lbs.	32,500 lbs.	32,500 lbs.
Continuous Trac. Eff.	7,500 lbs.	8,500 lbs.	8,500 lbs.
Cont. Trac. Effort Speed	16.0 MPH	16.5 MPH	16.5 MPH

Winton engine order was placed. One engine would be used to replace the Bessemer diesel in the 3905 and the other would be used to complete the 3906.

Both of the A6 units were completed as gasoline-electric locomotives in May 1929. Although the 3905 carries a builder's date of May 1928, this represents its completion as a diesel-electric. The builder's date of the 3906 is May 1929, the date of its completion as a gasoline-electric. The 3905 was placed in service on June 10, 1929 at North 4th Street yard in Brooklyn. Although the 3906 was also completed in May, it was sent first to Philadelphia for an opera-

tional test which covered 125 hours of operation. It was placed in service at 37th Street Yard in Manhattan on July 9, 1929. In a June 28 letter requesting more funds to complete the third A6 unit, Hankins characterized the first few weeks of operation as entirely successful.

From the start, the project to build internal combustion locomotives for New York City included three units. The reason for having three locomotives was to have one for each of the float yards, plus a protect locomotive. Much of the material was on hand in Altoona for the third unit, including the cast

PRR 9316 at 37th Street Yard, Manhattan. By 1951, several class GS-4 units were available to relieve the A6's at the two float yards. In 1954, the last A6 was retired after 25 years in service. By January 1960 when this photo was taken, North 4th Street yard in Brooklyn had been shut down.

frame. A Hankins letter of July 9, 1929 requested additional funds to procure a gasoline engine for completion of the third A6 unit. This engine was a 535 horsepower, Brill model 860 engine.

The third unit was numbered 3907, classed A6b. (Class A6a had been assigned to a Cummins-powered diesel unit which was not built). As a result of testing on the 3906 in Philadelphia in June and July 1929, improvements were made in the design of the 3907. The most significant improvement was an upgraded cooling system to avoid over-heating of the engine and electrical systems, problems that had surfaced during the 3906 test. The 3907 was completed in May 1930 and arrangements were made to send it to Philadelphia for a test similar to that of the 3906.

The 3907 was placed in service on June 23, 1930 in Philadelphia; it was never sent to New York harbor, because the gas-electric was found to be an indispensable part of the Philadelphia terminal improvement project. This project included the building of the present 30th Street Station and the underground Suburban Station. After the completion of the project, it was further decided that the 3907 should be kept in Philadelphia as protection in case of electric power failures in Suburban Station, where steam locomotives were not allowed.

By late 1930, the three gasoline-powered units settled down to their assigned tasks. In November 1930 the availability of these units was 75%, 61% and 92% for the 3905, 3906 and 3907 respectively. The major reasons for the down time was identified as failure of generator armature bearings, replacement of fuel system parts (on the two A6 units) and delay in receipt of replacement parts. The replacement of the fuel system parts was considered necessary because the carburetors had been continually dripping gasoline. Furthermore, in June, a gasoline fire occurred on the 3906 which injured the fireman and scorched the front of the unit. It was determined that no significant damage had been done to the locomotive and it was possible to continue operation after minor repair to some ignition system wiring.

Another factor in down time for the gasoline units in New York was availability of maintenance personnel. Prior to their arrival in New York, it was decided that the logical maintenance shop for the A6 units was the Long Island Rail Road facility at Morris Park in Queens, New York City. The addition of the two PRR gasoline units to Long Island locomotives 401 and 402 and gas-electric rail car 4742, overtaxed the small internal combustion unit maintenance force at Morris Park. In October

1930, the General Manager of the Long Island identified shop overloading as a significant factor for the non-availability of the 3905 and 3906.

The two A6 units remained in New York City and the A6b stayed in the Philadelphia area through the 1930s and 1940s. By the late 1940's, the Pennsylvania Railroad was purchasing the diesel locomotives to replace steam. The replacement for the 0-4-0 class A5s steam engines was the General Electric 44-tonner (Class GS-4). Five GS-4s were assigned to the New York Division from the Pennsy's 1948 diesel locomotive order. Their initial assignments did not displace the gasoline locomotives, but they were satisfactory replacements. By 1951, two GS-4 units were assigned to the same Road Foreman of Engines as the two A6 units, and were soon riding the carfloats to assignments in the float yards. The 3905 was retired in April 1952 and the 3906 was retired in August 1954.

For the class A6b unit, replacement of the original Brill gasoline engine extended its life for almost 15 years. In 1947, a Hamilton model 68SA, six cylinder diesel engine was installed in the 3907. The unit continued in service (in the Norristown, Pennsylvania area most of the time) until the early 1960s when it was placed in storage at 44th St. engine terminal in Philadelphia and retired in late 1962.

Class A6a (Cummins-Engined Unit)

Units 3905 and 3906 were assigned Class A6, while locomotive 3907 became Class A6b. The question quite naturally arises, What about Class A6a? What was it?

The Pennsylvania Railroad's 1925 program to build three 65 ton, four-wheel diesel-electric units was being hampered by the inability of the Bessemer Gas Engine Company's engine to operate reliably after installation in the locomotive. Originally, the three locomotives were to be completed in August 1929, but because no locomotives had been produced by the middle of 1928, the PRR began considering alternatives.

The first mention of a Cummins-powered diesel locomotives appears in

incomplete correspondence on the subject in August, 1928. At that time, J. T. Wallis, Assistant V. P.—Operations and former Chief of Motive Power, was scheduled to visit the Cummins plant. W. F. Kiesel, Jr., PRR Mechanical Engineer, observed at the time that if a Cummins-engined unit was to be built, the A6 frames were not recommended because of the experience with the application of the Bessemer engine.

In a letter of November, 1928, F. W. Hankins, PRR Chief of Motive Power noted that $25,000 had been authorized to purchase a Cummins engine for installation in one of the A6 frames. Hankins stated that Cummins could not design a suitable diesel

engine which would fit on an A6 frame. A further $50,000 was requested for another frame, generator, traction motors and cooling system for completion of a diesel-electric unit using a Cummins engine.

A subsequent memo documented a meeting between the PRR and General Electric concerning the electrical equipment for the Cummins-powered diesel-electric unit. In that memo, the projected unit was identified as locomotive class A6a.

Later correspondence refers to the Cummins engine after delivery to Altoona. Further references indicate that the project became a casualty of Depression economics. The A6a was never built.

PRR 5824 presents this solid looking nose to the railroad world. As described in the text on the Centipedes, the carbody containing the engines, generators, control equipment and the cab, is mounted on a pair of cast frames at six points. The separation between the carbody and the frame is apparent in this view. Because of this construction, none of the buffing load was carried by the carbody.

Chapter 4

Passenger Locomotives

Some New York Central fans may disagree, but followers of the Pennsylvania Railroad will tell you (often at great length) that the Standard Railroad's passenger diesel locomotive fleet, like the steam locomotives that went before, powered the most intensive passenger train operations in America. One needed only to watch the parade of trains rounding Horsehoe Curve in the middle of any night to appreciate the magnitude of the operation. While most passenger operations east of Harrisburg were on electrified trackage, steam and diesel locomotives pulled the Penn's variety of trains west of the Pennsylvania capital city. As we will see, after shifting it was passenger service that most interested the Pennsylvania in the initial purchase of diesel-electric locomotives.

Class EP-20
EMD E7

The first two road diesel units on the Pennsylvania Railroad were two E7 A-units delivered in September 1945. Although these two units were ordered in September 1944, this was really the re-instatement of an order first placed in May 1941 for two E6 units intended for the PRR-L&N *South Wind*. The *South Wind* units were to be numbered 5900A and 5900B, but the total set was considered as being numbered 5900. The original order was never fulfilled, because wartime restrictions prohibited manufacture of new passenger diesel locomotives.

In 1944, the model then being offered was the E7, not the E6. The original information from EMD was that the PRR order had dropped from third to sixty-eighth in the builder's delivery sequence. However, in May of 1944, President Clement of the PRR stated that the President of General Motors had agreed to reinstate the PRR order

to its original delivery standing. The delivery date was to be in August 1945.

But the projected *South Wind* service for those locomotives was not to be. An exchange of letters between the PRR and the L&N shows that the plans for joint use were to be changed. The L&N stated that the PRR had not informed them of their *South Wind* motive power plans prior to March 1945. Since the PRR proposal would have required the L&N to rent the PRR diesels while they were on the L&N, agreement of the latter railroad was necessary for the operation.

The Louisville & Nashville had taken delivery of sixteen E6 passenger diesels in 1942; they were not strangers to the passenger diesel locomotive. Yet, with regard to the *South Wind* and the PRR, the L&N's position was that they had recently incurred considerable expense, including Tuscan red paint, to equip one of their modern steam passenger locomotives for service on the *South Wind* between Louisville and Montgomery. The payment of rental expenses to the PRR for their diesels would therefore be difficult to justify. The L&N letter closes with the statement that "Under the circumstances I hope that you will find it possible to use the diesel engine on some other assignment than the operation on the *South Wind* between Louisville and Montgomery."

When the two E7A units, bearing road numbers 5900A and 5901A, were delivered to the PRR, they were run light to Harrisburg for service. Their arrival at the Harrisburg roundhouse on an early fall day in 1945 is graphically described in an article in the January 1979 issue of *Trains*, entitled *A Reputation for Reliability* by W. A. Gardiner. Mr. Gardiner was working at Enola roundhouse when the first E7's arrived at Harrisburg. He was sent over to assist the EMD man assigned to the new units. PRR motive power management at Harrisburg was understandably steam oriented at the time and

paid very little attention to the diesel interlopers. Mr. Gardner was left to work out many of the details of early PRR road diesel operation for himself.

The *Trains* article also describes in interesting detail the tribulations of imposing diesel operation on a steam railroad. It was decided that the two units would run round trips to Altoona until a fueling station could be set up at Mansfield, Ohio. This "fueling station" was a tank car, a filter and a pump. With this in place, the units were used on one of the sections of the *Red Arrow* between Harrisburg and Detroit.

Mr. Gardiner relates a telling incident that highlighted the difference between steam and diesel road power. After the E7s had been in service for about six months, measurements showed that the legal wear limit on the wheels would be exceeded in another two months. Mr. Gardiner requested wheel turning to restore the required flange profile on the two units. The General Foreman at Harrisburg thought Gardiner was crazy. After all, it was perfectly obvious; anyone with experience would know that locomotive wheels lasted a year and a half before turning was required. After taking measurements and grumbling about "soft EMD wheels," the General Foreman agreed that the work was required.

The article points out that the facts were simple, and they gradually sank in at all executive levels. The E7s had run 69,000 miles in their first six months. The highest mileage on any one of the brand new T-1 steam locomotives delivered soon after the E7s was a mere 2,800. (Not twenty-eight *thousand*, twenty-eight *hundred*.) The General Foreman had been abruptly welcomed to the diesel age, and the PRR management was given a startling message about the difference between steam and diesel availability.

The 5900A and 5901A were to remain the only road diesels on the PRR for almost two years. In April 1947 a

PRR 5901A and 5900A at Harrisburg, Pennsylvania. The information provided by photographer Ray Muller on the envelope containing the negative for this photo is a tantalizing "first trip," but no date was noted. Considering the lack of trainphone, the pristine appearance of the units and the interest of the onlookers, this may be a view of the two units prior to their departure from Harrisburg on their first PRR trip in September 1945. The units glisten in their factory-applied five-stripe Brunswick Green paint. The early five-stripe scheme was labor intensive to apply. The stripes were carried across the windows; and a close look at the grillwork just behind the cab door shows five metal strips added just for the stripes.

B-unit was delivered to make an A-B-A set. The details of the orders and delivery of the PRR's E7's are shown in the table on Page 54.

Note the last two PRR E7 orders were for A-units only. This pattern was continued when orders for E8's were placed, as B-units were less versatile. The 46 E7A's, 14 E7B's and 74 EMD E8A's were to dominate the passenger diesel roster until the end of the PRR era. The sixty E7's were the largest group purchased by any single owner.

The first two A-units were given the classification of 4(B) as discussed in Chapter 2. Under the various classification schemes, the E7's were called "3(A1A-A1A)20E" and "EP-3." It was not until the 1951 system that this was re-solved when class EP-20 was applied.

EQUIPMENT

The equipment on EMD E7's was consistent with the F3, BL2, NW2 and SW1 models, which were produced at EMD at the same time. The engines and generators were arranged with the generators facing the front of the unit, and the air compressors and traction motor blowers were mechanically driven from the outboard ends of the engine/generator assembly. This meant that the forward compressor was connected to the generator end of the engine and the rear compressor was connected to the non-generator end. A single 3000 lb.-per-hour Vapor DRK-4530 steam generator to heat passenger cars was located in the rear of each of the A and the B-units.

The B-units had a set of hostler controls located in the right front corner. These controls were intended only for slow speed operation of the B-unit by itself in an engine terminal area. The length of the A-unit was 71' 1-1/4", which was almost ten feet shorter than the Baldwin class BP-20, but about five feet longer than the single engine Alco and F-M passenger units.

ASSIGNMENTS

During the entire PRR diesel era, the class EP-20's shared all diesel assignments in the passenger unit pool. Until 1963, they were almost always assigned to the system passenger unit mainte-

Passenger Locomotive Data Summary

Class	EP-20	EP-20	BP-60a	BH-50	BP-20	BP-20
Builder	EMD	EMD	BLW	BLW	BLW	BLW
Model	E7A	E7B	DR 8-4-3000	DR 8-4-3000	DR 6-4-2000	DR 6-4-2000
Type Unit	A	B	2(Cab-A)	2(Cab-A)	A	B
Horsepower	2000	2000	6000	5000	2000	2000
Wheel Arr,	A1A-A1A	A1A-A1A	2(2-D+D2)	2(2-D+D2)	A1A-A1A	A1A-A1A
Total Weight	319,600 lbs	306,100 lbs	1,187,420 lbs	1,187,420 lbs	387,100 lbs	374,500 lbs
Weight on Drivers	215,400 lbs	206,300 lbs	818,000 lbs	818,000 lbs	257,200 lbs	250,000 lbs
Length over Couplers	71' 1"	70' 0"	183' 0"	183' 0"	80' 0"	78' 2.5"
Truck Centers	43' 0"	43' 0"	n/a	n/a	46' 3.5"	46' 3.5"
Truck Wheelbase	14" 1"	14" 1"	n/a	n/a	15' 6"	15' 6"
Engine	2, EMD 12-567A	2, EMD 12-567A	4, BLW 8-600SC	4, BLW 8-600SC	2, BLW 6-606SC	2, BLW 6-606SC
Generator	2, EMD D4D	2, EMD D4D	4, W 471A	4, W 471A	2, W 471A	2, W 471A
Traction Motors	4, EMD D17B	4, EMD D17B	16, W 370F	16, W 370F	4, W 370DP	4, W 370DP
Gear Ratio	55:22	55:22	57:22	62:17	57:22	57:22
Maximum Speed	98 MPH	98 MPH	100 MPH	75 MPH	100 MPH	100 MPH
Starting Trac. Effort	53,800 lbs	51,575 lbs	204,500 lbs	204,500 lbs	64,300 lbs	62,500 lbs
Continuous Trac. Effort	18,750 lbs	18,750 lbs	105,600 lbs	147,200 lbs	26,400 lbs	26,400 lbs
CTE Speed	34.0 MPH	34.0 MPH	17.8 MPH	9.8 MPH	23.8 MPH	23.8 MPH
Steam Generator	1, DRK-4530	1, DRK-4530	2, DRK-4530	2, DRK-4530	DRK-4530	DRK-4530
Steam Gen, Capacity	3000 lb/hr	3000 lb/hr	6000 lb/hr	6000 lb/hr	3000 lb/hr	3000 lb/hr

R.J. MULLER PHOTO; DOUGLAS COLLECTION

nance facility at the Harrisburg enginehouse. Harrisburg was strategically located since it was there that all east-west passenger trains changed power from electric to diesel on the westbound trip and the reverse eastbound. Even units used on diesel passenger trains not operating through Harrisburg could be cycled there on east-west trains from locations such as Chicago or Pittsburgh.

An exception to Harrisburg maintenance was the assignment of four EP-20's to the New York and Long Branch for about a year in 1956 and 1957. For this period, they were assigned to Meadows engine terminal in Kearny, New Jersey for maintenance. Meadows was also the maintenance point for the BP-20 locomotives then on the NY&LB.

As the PRR cut back on passenger trains systemwide, the first locomotives removed from passenger service assignments were the non-EMD engines. The FP-20's were not used in passenger service after the early 1950s, the AFP-20s were not in passenger service after 1960, and the last BP-20s were retired in 1965. Starting in 1963, EP-20's were moved back to the NY&LB as the BP-20's were withdrawn.

With the re-assignment of EP-20s to the Long Branch, it was desired to maintain the units at the Harrisburg enginehouse and not Meadows as the

EP-20 5879A leads a pure three-unit set of E7s westbound just west of Gallitzin on July 15, 1958. The train has just shed its helpers and is accelerating toward Pittsburgh. The engines are now painted Tuscan red. Note that the metal grill strips are still in place to carry the 5-stripe motif, but that the stripes are no longer on the window glass. Also, large number boards and trainphone antenna have been added.

BP-20s had been. This would have required a deadhead move, but a clever MU arrangement was devised. Using a special MU cable it was possible to operate the E-units with the class E-44 straight electric locomotives used in freight service from the east to Harrisburg. The special MU cable only applied power up to Notch 1 on the diesels when power was applied on the lead electric motor. This meant that the engineer on the freight was paid for total weight on drivers (including the E-units), but not the extra pay for dead-

heading units. Not all of these units were deadheaded on freights, and as many as seven or eight EP-20 units were sometimes run light to and from Harrisburg for maintenance on weekends.

Use of EMD passenger units for freight service was not favored by many railroads. Ideally, freight service diesels had a lower gear ratio than passenger locomotives. Because of the 36-inch wheels used on E-units, it was not possible to use an axle gear large enough to obtain a higher freight gear ratio with-

Passenger Locomotive Data Summary

Class	BF-16z	BF-16z	AP-20	AP-20	AFP-20	AFP-20	EP-22
Builder	BLW	BLW	Alco	Alco	Alco	Alco	EMD
Model	DR 6-4-2000	DR 6-4-2000	PA-1	PB-1	PA-1	PB-1	E8A
Type Unit	A	B	A	B	A	B	A
Horsepower	1600	1600	2000	2000	2000	2000	2250
Wheel Arr,	A1A-A1A	A1A-A1A	A1A-A1A	A1A-A1A	A1A-A1A	A1A-A1A	A1A-A1A
Total Weight	387,100 lbs	374,500 lbs	312,200 lbs	300,000 lbs	312,200 lbs	306,900 lbs	335,000 lbs
Weight on Drivers	257,200 lbs	250,000 lbs	208,100 lbs	204,600 lbs	208,100 lbs	204,600 lbs	226,000 lbs
Length over Couplers	80' 0"	78' 2.5"	65' 8"	63' 6"	65' 8"	63' 6"	70' 3"
Truck Centers	46' 3.5"	46' 3.5"	34' 2"	34' 2"	34' 2"	34' 2"	43' 0"
Truck Wheelbase	15' 6"	15' 6"	15' 6"	15' 6"	15' 6"	15' 6"	14' 1"
Engine	2, BLW 6-606SC	2, BLW 6-606SC	1, Alco 16-244B	1, Alco 16-244B	1, Alco 16-244B	1, Alco 16-244B	2, EMD 12-567B
Generator	2, W 471A	2, W 471A	1, GE GT-566	1, GE GT-566	1, GE GT-566	1, GE GT-566	2, EMD D15B
Traction Motors	4, W 370DP	4, W 370DP	4, GE 752	4, GE 752	4, GE 752	4, GE 752	4, EMD D27B
Gear Ratio	63:15	63:15	60:23	60:23	64:19	64:19	55:22
Maximum Speed	65 MPH	65 MPH	100 MPH	100 MPH	80.5 MPH	80.5 MPH	98 MPH
Starting Trac. Effort	64,300 lbs	62,500 lbs	52,025 lbs	51,150 lbs	52,025 lbs	51,150 lbs	56,500 lbs
Continuous Trac. Effort	42,800 lbs	42,800 lbs	27,000 lbs	27,000 lbs	35,000 lbs	35,000 lbs	23,500 lbs
CTE Speed	11.3 MPH	11.3 MPH	23.0 MPH	23.0 MPH	17.5 MPH	17.5 MPH	30.0 MPH
Steam Generator	DRK-4530	DRK-4530	DRK-4530	DRK-4530	DRK-4530	DRK-4530	2, OK-4625
Steam Gen, Capacity	3000 lb/hr	3000 lb/hr	3000 lb/hr	3000 lb/hr	3000 lb/hr	3000 lb/hr	5000 lb/hr

out heavy modification. Only the Bangor and Aroostook was known to have done the alteration necessary to install the freight gear ratio on E's. They installed larger wheels and gears, which also required a change to the frame to lower the couplers by the amount that the axles had been raised.

The PRR did not make these extensive modifications. They did try E-units, with passenger gearing, in high-speed freight service on a regular basis. In early 1964, E7s were assigned to trains TT-1, TT-2, JET-1 and JET-2, top trains operating between New Jersey and Chicago. The test lasted for about two weeks. It was not a success for two reasons. First, the E7s did not have dynamic brakes, forcing the road to use helpers on both sides of the Allegheny grade. They pushed uphill and retarded on the downhill side. Second, the E-units would not backward transition automatically. On freight units, when train speed dropped the motor circuit was automatically reconnected from the higher speed parallel connection to the lower speed series motor connection, without returning to the engine idle position. On E-units, if the throttle was not returned to idle before the speed reduction, motor and/or generator damage followed. This damage quickly ended the assignment of E-units to freight service.

EP-20 retirement started in 1964, with unit 5847A; the 5876A followed in 1966. Just after this second retirement, the remaining E7s were renumbered 4200 to 4245 in anticipation of the Penn Central merger. By the time the merger took place, three additional A-units and two B-units had joined the retirement list.

Three E-units with train depart St. Louis Union Station in mid-day on March 27, 1964. The middle unit is an EP-22, with Roman lettering. The lead EP-20 has a later keystone-only paint scheme. (Note that the 5-stripe grill strips are still in place, but are not painted buff.)

E7 4201 (née 5901A) in 1967 at South Amboy, New Jersey. A train crewman is supervising the uncoupling. The GG1 electric that will haul this New York and Long Branch train into Penn Station is waiting just out of the photo at the right. This is one of the first PRR road units, delivered so long ago in 1945. It is preserved at the Pennsylvania State Railroad Museum, Strasburg.

R.J. MULLER PHOTO; DOUGLAS COLLECTION

By May 1, 1971, when the former PRR intercity passenger service was turned over to Amtrak by Penn Central, only twelve ex-PRR EP-20 class units had survived. None of them was a B-unit and none went to Amtrak. These remaining A-units were used mostly in New York and Long Branch service.

Only three EP-20s remained on the roster when Conrail took over on April 1, 1976. Two of these (4244 and 4224) were conveyed to New Jersey Transit in December 1976. All three of the surviving ex-PRR E7s were used as hangar queens on NJT. That is to say, they were picked over for parts to use on the E8's. The last remaining EP-20, #4233, was retired by Conrail in December 1979.

Fortunately, this was not the end of the former PRR EP-20's. One of the original two was donated to the Railroad Museum of Pennsylvania at Strasburg, Pennsylvania. The PC 4201, originally PRR 5901A, was retired in December 1973 before the end of the Penn Central. It was stored in the Harrisburg roundhouse until donated for preservation. This unit is the last EMD E7 locomotive still in existence.

Order Summary - EP20 Units

PRR ROAD NUMBERS	EMD ORDER NUMBER	NO. OF UNITS	TYPE UNITS	ORDER DATE	DELIVERY DATES
5900A-5901A	E671	2	A-units	Sep 44	Sep 45
5840A-5855A	E745	16	A-units	Nov 45	Aug 47-Sep 47
5840B-5854B (even)		8	B-units	Nov 45	Aug 47-Sep 47
5856A-5865A	E864	10	A-units	Jan 47	Feb 48
5856B-5864B (even)		5	B-units	Jan 47	Feb 48
5900B		1	B-unit	Jan 47	Apr 47
5866A-5879A	E1113	14	A-units	Jun 48	Mar 49-Apr 49
5880A-5883A		4	A-units	Nov 48	Apr 49

CLASS BP-60a BH-50 BALDWIN CENTIPEDE DR 12-8-1500/2

While the EMD E7 became a familiar sight on railroads all across the country, there was no diesel quite like the Centipede on American railroads. The running gear harkened to electric locomotive practice beginning near the turn of the century, and the use of two 1500 horsepower prime movers in each unit was not matched for a number of years on domestic railroads. They were mighty, if flawed machines.

The Pennsylvania Railroad ordered its first set of two Centipede units in January 1946; they were more formally known by Baldwin as Class DR 12-8-1500/2, denoting a Diesel Road unit with twelve axles, eight of them powered; and two 1500-hp. engines totalling a 3000-hp. power rating. As ordered by the PRR, the Centipedes were cab units in married pairs. While all of the Centipedes were cab units, they were not true "A-units" because the halves of the married pairs were not identical. Be-cause each of the units carried different equipment designed to serve the pair, they could not operate as single units. Each half was designated as either an A1 or an A2. For operating purposes, each *pair* was always considered and classed as one locomotive set.

A second order was placed for eleven sets in October 1946. The Centipede purchases were the third and fourth PRR orders for diesel passenger units, preceded only by two orders for EMD model E7's. The twelve Centipede sets were delivered more or less without a break from March 1947 to February 1948. When delivered, they were numbered 5823A1/5823A2 to 5834A1/5834A2. These actual unit numbers with the A1 or A2 only appeared in small letters on the sides at the rear. Both units displayed their four-digit number identification in the number boards and on the sides in the standard height numbers.

The first set delivered, 5823, was the only one classified in the 1946 system as (2D+D2+2D+D2)60B. This application of the 1946 system revealed the awkwardness of that system and in 1947 a new classification system was installed which identified the Centipedes as class BP-1. The final 11 sets of Centipedes were classified as BP-1 on delivery, and the 5823 was re-classified as BP-1 in May 1947. The in-flexibility of keeping like numbered pairs of units in rigid sets also proved impractical when work on one unit kept the other unit out of service. It was possible to marry any A1 unit to any A2 unit. Two units otherwise not utilized could be joined to make one Centipede set. In July 1949, units 5823A2 to 5834A2 were renumbered 5811 to 5823 to facilitate this practice.

EQUIPMENT

As previously noted, the construction of the Centipedes followed earlier electric locomotive practice, reflecting Baldwin's accumulated steam and electric knowledge. Each unit had two sets of cast driver frames, each of which had four driving axles. The driver frames were connected in the center with a heavy pin, called the Mallet Pin, which suggests the origin of the design.

On the outer end of each of the driver frames was a drawbar. On the front end of the PRR units, the drawbar was a coupler. On the rear, the drawbar was rigid and was connected to the rear of the other unit in the set. Also mounted under the outboard end of each driver frame was a two axle pilot truck, which provided guidance. This arrangement

The first Centipede, 5823A1 and A2, delivered as a married pair in 1947, is insufficiently honored in this black-and-white view. Imagine 184 feet of engine, Brunswick green and gold gleaming in the April sunlight, and the pride she instilled at that moment in the hearts of those involved in her creation. The disappointments were in the future; this was power!

The Friendship Train was part of a postwar effort to encourage donations of food for a Europe ravaged by war. When the train's second section visited Johnstown, Pennsylvania in mid-November 1947, picking up a car of foodstuffs in that city, the train was powered by BP-1 (later BP-60a) 5827. The locomotive had been delivered in October 1947; it was only about a month old at the time.

resulted in all of the tractive or buffing load being transmitted though the two driver frames, upon which rode the carbody. The carbody took none of the tractive load, but contained the engines, generators, control equipment and cab.

The design of the Centipedes thus differed substantially from the conventional road diesel configuration of a carbody frame mounted on two trucks. The Centipede carbodies were built on a bottom box frame with bridge trusses in the sides to form the main carbody structure. Each carbody was mounted on a pivot and two support pads on each driver frame. The pivot points were just inboard of the outboard drive axle. The two support pads were located at the inboard end of each driver frame.

A two-unit PRR Centipede set weighed 1,187,420 lbs and was 183 feet long. While that was impressive in terms of size and weight, an interesting comparison can be made with a three-unit set of EMD E7 units, which was also rated at 6000 horsepower for trac-

tion. The E7 A-B-A set was longer at 212 feet, 2-1/2 inches, but it was lighter at 945,300 lbs. The weight of the Centipede set was spread over 24 axles, vs. 18 on the E7 set, so the weight per axle on the Baldwin units was lower.

The equipment data table at the head of this chapter gives the characteristics of these units on a per-set (two-unit) basis.

SERVICE HISTORY

The first Centipede set (the 5823 pair) was placed in service at Harrisburg in April 1947. The initial trips were in freight service—one round trip on the Philadelphia Division and two on the Middle Division. The first passenger run was on Train 75, which carried 15 cars (1054 tons) as far as Pittsburgh and 16 cars on to Chicago. An optimistic memo noted that the train negotiated the East Slope grade (Altoona to Gallitzen) without a helper under adverse conditions—bad rail due to a heavy mist. The units returned from Chicago on Train 22 with 16 cars. The

next round trip was on the point of the premier Broadway Limited (Trains 28 and 29). Westbound Train 29 consisted of 16 cars and eastbound Train 28 had 15 cars.

As the big Baldwins were delivered, they all entered the Enola passenger pool. In this service, they were available for passenger trains west to Chicago and St. Louis, north to Buffalo and south to Baltimore. The assignment of all twelve of the sets to Enola continued until about the end of 1948, when three of the sets were assigned to Columbus.

By 1950, the Columbus-based Centipedes were in freight service, their passenger gearing and steam boilers notwithstanding. In December 1950, they were temporarily assigned back to passenger service for the holiday season, but they did not return to their freight assignments. Instead, they were returned to the Enola passenger pool in late March 1951. In 1951, the Centipedes were reclassified from BP-1 to BP-60a.

Available correspondence indicates dissatisfaction with the Centipedes in

56

A Centipede set in its later element, as a rear-end helper pushing caboose and train up the East Slope toward Gallitzin, Pennsylvania in October 1957. It is passing Slope tower in Altoona at about ten miles per hour. In later years, the maintenance priorities and reliability of these units had declined to the point that one engineer who had operated Centipedes in helper service recalled, "I never got to the top of the grade with all four engines still running."

passenger service. To try to cure the problem, one pair of units—5813 and 5834—was returned to Baldwin late in 1950 for modernization, to the improved 1951 Baldwin standards. They returned to service at Harrisburg in February 1951. A memo dated five years later states that the performance of the rebuilt units "has been no better than the remaining units which were not modernized." When this conclusion was reached, it was decided to replace the Centipedes in passenger service. In May 1951, 24 EMD model E8A units were ordered as part of the 1952 program. These units were intended in part to release the BP-60a units for conversion to BH-50 helper units.

CONVERSION

The helper conversions were performed at Juniata Shop between April 1952 and April 1953. As part of this conversion, each unit was de-rated to 2500 horsepower and the gear ratio was changed from 57:22 to 62:17. The re-gearing changed the continuous tractive effort for a two-unit set from 105,600 lbs at 17.8 mph, to 147,200 lbs at 9.8 mph. The converted units were used primarily as East Slope and West Slope helpers west of Altoona. Maintenance was performed by Juniata Shops.

The primary difficulty with Centipedes in helper service was that it was a role for which the units had not been designed. They had four-wheel pilot trucks, and now they were being used in pusher service. Hence, they tried very hard to derail when non-driving wheels were pushed laterally against rails on curves. Unhappily, they succeeded in so

derailing more often than the Operating Department preferred.

With the arrival of new Alco RSD-12's to Altoona in late 1957 and early 1958, the Centipedes were displaced from helper assignments and spent much of their time in storage. They would see occasional service on Altoona-Enola local freights and coal trains. A set was seen in this service as late as January 1962. Also, in late 1959 several units were sent to South Philadelphia for helper service on iron ore trains out of Greenwich yard up the Philadelphia Main Line grade to Bryn Mawr.

Finally, 14 of the class BH-50 units were retired in April 1962 and the remaining 10 were retired in September of the same year.

Six sets of Centipedes await their fate in the East Altoona deadline. It is September 1959, and their day is past. For the next three years, some of these units would occasionally be given a reprieve to meet a temporary need for local freight power on the Middle Division (between Altoona and Enola), or for helper service in the Philadelphia area.

W.D. VOLLKMER PHOTO

PRR 5829 is in Dayton, Ohio on May 16, 1948.
R.D. ACTON SR. PHOTO, DAVID OROZZI COLLECTION

The PRR's twenty-seven Baldwin 2000 horsepower passenger units were ordered in January 1947. At the same time, fifteen EMD and fifteen Alco passenger units were purchased. With a 2 to 1 ratio of A-units to B-units in all three orders, the intention to operate 6000-hp. A-B-A sets is apparent. These Baldwin passenger units would prove to be the only model DR 6-4-1000/2 units with the "Sharknose" carbody ordered by any railroad. In fact, they were the last passenger units built by Baldwin, with the intriguing exception of the single Xplorer unit built for the New York Central's ill-fated Train X in 1956.

Upon delivery, the units were classed BP-3 and numbered 5770A-5787A (A-units) and 5770B-5786B (even only, B-units). The units were re-classed BP-20 in the 1951 re-classification.

CONFIGURATION AND EQUIPMENT

The Baldwin passenger A-units were the longest 2000 horsepower, A1A-A1A wheel arrangement cab units to operate on the PRR. The A-units were 80' 0" long, and the B-units were 78' 2-1/2' in length. Baldwin needed this length to accommodate two engines. Baldwin used the 80-foot length for all its passenger A-units, again excepting the Xplorer unit. Other Baldwin passenger units included three NdeM units, three GM&O units, six double-cab CNJ units and the C&NW half-locomotive. These units had a carbody design known variously as Baby Face; or even "Gravel Gertie," after a comic strip character of the day. The C&NW unit had the same basic carbody as the GM&O.

The PRR's BP-3 units had a re-styled carbody, with a nose resembling the contemporary PRR class T-1 steam engines to some extent. This carbody and similar freight A-units came to be called Sharknoses. At an 80-foot length, the BP-3 was almost ten feet longer than the two-engined EMD E7A, and about 15 feet longer than the single-engined Alco PAs and F-M Erie-builts.

Another notable feature of the BP-20s was the installation of two WABCO Model 3-CD air compressors on each unit. This gave a total compressor capacity of 386 cubic feet per hour. This was more than twice the capacity of an EMD E7, 72% more than an E-8 and 25% more than the Alco passenger units.

SERVICE HISTORY

As with the other passenger units purchased by the PRR in the first rounds of orders, the BP-20's were used in the main east-west service early in their careers. As more EMD passenger units arrived, the BP-20's were assigned out of Columbus and used on the St. Louis mainline as well as on passenger runs from Cincinnati, Columbus and Louisville to Chicago. In the mid-1950's four A-units and four B-units were re-geared to 65 mph and de-rated to 1600 horsepower for freight service. These units were classed as BF-16z and are discussed below.

Except for two BP-20s (5782A and

Look closely: this is not a freight Sharknose. It was longer, heavier, more powerful, had six-wheel trucks, and it was unique to the Pennsylvania Railroad. The 2000-hp Baldwins started in mainline passenger service, and were gradually bumped to lesser and lesser passenger assignments. At the end of the electrified zone on the New York and Long Branch, we encounter 5772A and a single-stripe partner in September 1957, at South Amboy, New Jersey. Also present: K-4s Pacific No. 830, due to be retired within a few months.

5783A) assigned to Shire Oaks in the mid-50s for Pittsburgh commuter service, the BP-20's continued to work out of Columbus until mid-1957. At that time, the remaining Baldwin passenger units went to the New York and Long Branch to complete dieselization of that service.

The BP-20s spent the rest of their life on the New York and Long Branch, where they worked rather well. On the Long Branch, the passenger stops were spaced at close intervals. The Baldwins' rapid acceleration and rapid recharging of the brake system were of great value in maintaining their schedules.

By 1962 the class EP-20 EMD E7 units began replacing the BP-20s. During a March 1965 Sunday visit to the Bay Head Junction engine terminal at the end of the NY&LB, only three BP-20s were found. Within a few months all of the remaining Baldwins were withdrawn from service. The last BP-20s were retired in May 1965.

CLASS BF-16z

By the mid-1950s, the Pennsylvania Railroad had modified several passenger cab groups to make them suitable for freight service. The Alco passenger units were converted to dual service (passenger or freight), and the F-M Erie-built passenger units were converted to freight service.

During late 1952 and early 1953, eight of the Baldwin class BP-20's were converted to freight service and classed BF-16z. In the process, the Baldwins were de-rated to 1600 horsepower per unit and given 65-mph gearing. The steam boilers were retained. The units converted were 5784A to 5787A and 5780B to 5786B (even only).

The conversion resulted in freight units with two engines, an A1A-A1A wheel arrangement and a length that exceeded all freight units on the PRR except the Baldwin Centipedes. The continuous tractive effort was comparable to the Baldwin BF-15 and BF-15a classes at 42,800 lbs for both the A-units and B-units. The continuous

BP-20 B-unit No. 5772B in Louisville, Kentucky on December 22, 1955, is shown having recently received the single-stripe paint scheme with 16-inch Roman letters. Modelers may or may not appreciate the lack of a diaphragm.

tractive effort (CTE) speed on the BF-16z engines was 11.3 mph, which was slightly higher than the other Baldwin freight cab units. The CTE speed on the BF-15, BF-15a and BF-16 classes was 11.0 mph, 10.5 mph and 9.9 mph respectively. This meant when the units were mixed in MU (which they eventually were in the early 1960s), some care was required so that the rating of the BF-16z units in the set was not exceeded. The conversion of the BF-16z units did not change the air compressor. Each unit was still equipped with two Westinghouse Air

Brake Co. model 3-CD compressors, rated at 193 cubic feet per minute each. The BF-16z units therefore had twice the compressor capacity since the other Baldwin freight classes only had one compressor per unit.

The assignment of the class BF-16z units was the same as the other Baldwin freight classes, which is to say secondary fright service in most of the non-electrified territory.

All the class BF-16z units were retired on the same day in September 1962.

A de-rated and reclassified BF-16z, PRR 5784A, rumbles out of Altoona on October 12, 1958 with a westbound freight. Those are the Slope Tower home signals: our train is on Track 2, which is signaled for bi-directional operation.

CLASS AP-20/AFP-20 ALCO PA-1 AND PB-1

The PRR placed only one order for Alco passenger cab units. The Alco order was one of three placed in January 1947 for ten cab units and five booster units as discussed in the BP-20 section. At the time of these orders, only two passenger units - EMD E7A's - had been delivered to the railroad. Aside from some F-M Erie-builts ordered later in 1947 as passenger units, the only other passenger cab units ordered new by the PRR were 119 more EMD E units.

The purchase carried Alco sales orders 20123 (A-units) and 20124 (B-units). Ten were model PA-1 A's and five were model PB-1 B's. They were delivered between October and December 1947, numbered 5750A - 5759A (A-units) and 5750B - 5758B, even numbers only (B-units); and classed AP-3.

The big Alcos were equipped with 3000 lb. per hour steam generators, which was standard for the passenger cab units before the EMD E8's.

SERVICE HISTORY

In spite of being in the minority as passenger units were concerned, the Alcos worked on the PRR for almost fifteen years. They were delivered in late 1947, and were retired in September 1962. They were re-classed AP-20 in the 1951 classification system. Early in their careers they shared the main east-west service. As more EMDs were delivered and more passenger service was abandoned, they were bumped to lesser services. In late 1952 and early 1953, all fifteen were re-geared for a maximum of 80 mph and re-classed AFP-20. The gearing was changed from 60:23 to 64:19, which gave a continuous tractive effort of 35,000 lbs. at 17.5 mph. The classification indicates the purpose of the conversion—use in both passenger and freight service. After regearing, the Alcos were indeed used in both services, at first on the Northwest and Lake Regions.

By 1957, these assignments had been

modified. For instance, two units were based in Lewistown, Pennsylvania for use on a local to Altoona. Also, at least two units had been assigned to New York and Long Branch passenger service. All were stored early in 1958, but began to return to service by mid-year. In July 1958 the 5757A and 5758A were transferred to Camden, N. J. freshly repainted in Brunswick Green.

All of the passenger units delivered before 1952 were painted Brunswick green (with gold striping and letters) but they were re-painted Tuscan red starting in 1952. The class AFP-20 units except for 5757A and 5758A remained in Tuscan red until retirement.

For the Brunswick Green PA-1s, 1958 was the beginning of several years of service in the Camden-Philadelphia area. They were used both on Camden-Atlantic City passenger trains on the P-RSL and on local PRR freights. A standard freight run was the Pavonia (Camden) to Greenwich Yard (Philadelphia) transfer run, operating as PT-84 and PT-85.

In August 1960 four A-units and four B-units were transferred to Shire Oaks near Elrama, Pennsylvania for service

May, 1959: Alco 5756A leads a two-unit set in Baltimore's Pennsylvania Station, about to couple onto a train bound for Harrisburg. Some of the cars on these trains came up from Washington behind electric power; diesels took over for the 83-mile run over the old Northern Central Railway.

The PA-1s handled commuter trains on the New York and Long Branch. Here, in September 1957, a late afternoon outbound train heading for Bay Head Junction passes a CNJ caboose hop at the Raritan River interchange at South Amboy, New Jersey. Unit 5752A, in Tuscan red, shared Long Branch duties with BP-20s, K-4s, and locomotives of the Jersey Central, which jointly owned the New York and Long Branch with the PRR.

on coal trains from the coal producing areas south of Pittsburgh, to the Altoona area. As one observer said of this assignment, "It was like hooking a thoroughbred to a junk wagon."

By the end of 1960, two A-units and two B-units were set aside. The other four units continued on for several months. With only two A-units and two

B-units left in coal service, the AFP-20's ran in MU with Alco FA and FB units. By June 1961, nine of the class were set aside at East Altoona. The exceptions were the pair working out of Camden and the last four units that had been assigned to Shire Oaks stored at Pitcairn, near Pittsburgh. All except one of the nine units set aside at East Altoona had

the same problem—the crankshaft was scored. During July 1962 all of the units were scrapped at Hollidaysburg and used as trade-in for the class AF-24 Alco model RS-27 units. Curiously, the PA units were not officially retired from the PRR until September 1962.

One of the two AFP-20s to be given a Brunswick green single-stripe freight paint scheme. 5758A sports its new colors in Atlantic City, New Jersey on August 3, 1958, a few weeks after repainting. The unit was on lease that summer to the Pennsylvania-Reading Seashore Lines to help with the Summer passenger rush from Philadelphia. A more typical assignment was local freight transfer service.

CLASS EP-22
EMD E8

The PRR's purchase of 74 EMD model E8's continued the program started with the E7's. The PRR only ordered E8A units, which were classed EP-22. Actually, the first two groups were classed EP-3 (After 1-1-50) on delivery. Classing the E8 as EP-3 was rather strange since the PRR purchased no E8 B-units nor did the A-units have nose MU receptacles at the time. In any event, under the 1951 classification system the E8 units were classed EP-22, which was applied to the last two orders on delivery.

The delivery of the final order in November 1952 did not complete the dieselization of passenger trains on the PRR. Full dieselization was accomplished as a result of discontinuing passenger services. The last steam-powered PRR passenger train was a Camden-Pemberton local, dieselized during November 1957.

CONFIGURATION AND EQUIPMENT

The EMD model E8 was an improvement over the E7. The 567B engine replaced the 567A, the D15B main generator replaced the D4B and the D27B traction motor replaced the D17B. These equipment improvements allowed an increase in horsepower available for traction to 2250. As evidence of the upgraded electrical equipment, the continuous rating was raised to 23,500 lbs. from 18,750 and the speed for the continuous rating lowered from 34 mph to 30 with the 55:22 gear ratio used on the PRR's E-units.

The general arrangement of the engine, main generator, traction motor blowers and air compressors was revised from the E7 layout. On the E8's, the generator on the number 1 engine faced forward and the generator on the number 2 engine faced the rear. Also, the E8 electrical cabinets were relocated to the unit centerline, forward of the number 1 engine, which moved the front engine room bulkhead forward. The cab space on E8s was smaller than on E7s, but the actual operating area was not affected.

Another change from the E7 to E8 equipment was an engine-driven alternator which provided auxiliary AC power. The primary use of the alternating current was to power the cooling fans which had been mechanically driven from the engines on the E7's.

The E8 was offered with either one large steam generator or two smaller ones. The PRR ordered the second option; all EP-22 units were equipped with two Vapor 4625 steam generators for a total steam generator rated output of 5000 lbs. of steam per hour.

The EP-22's were assigned to virtually all of the PRR diesel non-commuter passenger trains at one time or another, as were the EP-20s. When first delivered, the units were primarily in the main east-west service. By the late 1950's, EMD passenger units covered all normal passenger locomotive assignments except the Long Branch service where the BP-20's reigned supreme. Train eliminations finally allowed the retirement of the BP-20s in 1965.

Aside from service on the PRR, EP-22 units were used on the interline *South Wind* service, the L&N having also retired its modern steam locomo-

The railroad brought out its finest newly-painted E8s for a Sunday fan trip on October 6, 1963. The 5838A and 5793A are ready to leave Tyrone, Pennsylvania for Philadelphia. It was the day the Los Angeles Dodgers won the fourth World Series game to sweep the New York Yankees, but baseball was far from the passengers' minds as the Trainmaster standing in the cab door confirmed everyone's readiness to depart. Railroad middle managers enjoyed at least part of their work.

Train 573 near Hyner's, Pennsylvania, is on its way to Buffalo, on April 22, 1967. EP-22 4281 leads an E7. By this time, head end traffic constituted the bulk of Passenger Department revenue, and even that was declining.

tive. In this operation, the PRR E-units operated as far south as Miami on the Atlantic Coast Line. The *South Wind* had run on the Florida East Coast before the withdrawal of through passenger trains in January 1963 because of the strike on that road. The strike ended in 1977 after FEC's passenger service had been abandoned. The strike was never settled.

At the startup of Amtrak on May 1, 1971, all of the ex-PRR EP-22 units were still in service. After the inauguration of Amtrak, 48 ex-PRR EP-22's were conveyed by Penn Central to the national passenger train operation. The remaining 26 former PRR class EP-22's were used on Boston, Chicago and Long Branch commuter services.

In December 1976, after the Conrail takeover of the Penn Central, seven former PRR E8's were sent to the Metropolitan Boston Transportation Authority and eleven were sent to New Jersey Transport (NJT), which had assumed operation of the New York and Long Branch. This left only two former PRR EP-22's in Conrail ownership, the 4249 and 4246. These two units were also used by NJT on the Long Branch but were retired in March and November 1980 by Conrail.

Curiously, the 4249 and 4246 were not the last former PRR E8's to be owned by Conrail. In late Summer, 1983, Conrail purchased units 498 and 499 from Amtrak. These units had originally been PRR 5809A and 5711A, and become CR 4020 and 4021. These road numbers were the fifth applied to these units. Amtrak removed the steam generators and installed diesel generator sets for train power and lighting.

Two other former PRR class EP-22's had extended lives. These are the ex-PRR 5706A and 5711A. The units were purchased from Amtrak in September 1985 by a private individual, and restored to their Tuscan Red five-stripe livery and original PRR road numbers. They operated for a time on the Blue Mountain and Reading Railroad, north of Reading, Pennsylvania. The latest information on these units at the time of publication is contained in Appendix C on Dispositions.

PRR ROAD NUMBERS	EMD ORDER NUMBER	NO. OF UNITS	ORDER DATE	DELIVERY DATES
Order Summary - EP22 Units				
5884A-5893A	6079	10	Nov 49	Mar 50-Apr 50
5808A-5810A, 5835A-5839A, 5894A-5899A, 5902A-5905A	6181	18	Aug 50	Jan 51-Apr 51
5765A-5769A 5788A-5799A 5801A-5807A	6354	24	May 51	Mar 52-Jul 52
5700A-5716A 5760A-5764A	2054	22	Nov 51	Sep 52-Nov 52

The Other
PASSENGER LOCOMOTIVES

The passenger cab unit classes described thus far in this chapter were not the only units to be used on the Pennsy's passenger trains. For example, the dual service EMD model FP7A and their companion F7B units (Class EFP-15) were occasionally used in passenger service. The PRR also operated three A-B-A sets of F-M Erie-built passenger units. These were classes FP-20 and FP-20a. These were converted to class FF-20 freight units by the end of 1953. See the description of the FP7 and Erie-builts in Chapter 5.

Road-switchers were also used on passenger trains, primarily but not exclusively in commuter service.

Above, An eastbound passenger train is operating between Cresson and Gallitzin, Pennsylvania on July 19, 1958. PRR FP7A 9860A heads an A-B-A set of class EFP-15 units.

Below, PRR 9479A leads a passenger train about 1948. This is a pure A-B-A set of FM Erie-Built units. The 9479A was delivered with a steam boiler and passenger gearing and classed FP-3 (later FP-20).

PRR 8553 was a class ES-15ms unit assigned for many years to the New York Division and New York Region. The EMD GP7 is seen here just after leaving South Amboy, New Jersey with a southbound commuter train on the New York and Long Branch. This view was taken on September 6, 1957. The NY&LB was jointly owned by the PRR and the CNJ and the locomotives and coaches from both roads were used. The 8553 was also used on another affiliated PRR operation, the Pennsylvania-Reading Seashore Lines, powering the Sunday Nellie Bly from Trenton to Atlantic City

PRR 8445 was a unique Alco RS-3. Because it was equipped with both a steam boiler and dynamic brakes, located in the short hood, this hood was raised above standard height to hold the equipment. At the time of this photo, the 8445 was assigned to the Northern Region and was often based at Emporium. At that location, it could protect the single E8A unit normally used on the Erie passenger train. Here 8445 leads the southbound Buffalo Day Express (Train #570) at Sunbury, Pennsylvania on June 6, 1966.

PRR 8473 heads the Delmarva passenger train prior to starting from Delmar, Delaware on July 23. 1960. The train consist includes two baggage cars, an RPO and a baggage-coach combination car. This run extended for 97.3 miles north to Wilmington, Delaware on the New York-Washington main line. At Dover, Delaware, about half-way through the run, the train length was more than doubled with additional head-end cars, containing outbound material from a catalog warehouse.

TOLEDO, OHIO, MAY 28, 1961. L.A. MARRE PHOTO

Chapter 5

The First Freighters

The first diesel locomotives to perform in Pennsylvania Railroad freight service on a regular basis began doing so in July 1947. These were diesel cab units, purchased from all four manufacturers. In 1947, the concept of road-switchers for through freight service (or even local freights) had not developed. The PRR bought cab units for freight service until the delivery of its last EMD F7 units in September 1952. Through freight service with road-switcher power did not begin on the PRR until the October 1955 delivery of the first EMD GP9s. The GP9s appear in this chapter because this model was the only first-generation road-switcher to be used primarily in PRR mainline through freight service.

Class EF-15
EMD F3

The 85 EMD model F3 freight cab units initiated diesel road freight service on the Pennsylvania Railroad. The F3 diesels with 62:15 gearing came to the PRR in seven groups. Six of these groups were ordered new from EMD and the last consisted of four B-units purchased secondhand from the Bangor and Aroostook. Delivery of the six groups ordered new by the PRR is shown in the accompanying table.

Four F-units joined the PRR roster secondhand. In 1952, the PRR purchsed four EMD model F3B units from the Bangor and Aroostook. BAR 600B to 603B became PRR 9530B, 9532B, 9534B and 9536B. The first two ex-BAR B-units had been built in October 1947 and the final two in May 1948, on EMD order E875.

CLASSIFICATION

Classification of PRR F3 and F7 units was somewhat complex prior to the 1951 classification system. The original F3s were all purchased with the 62:15 gearing (that is, 15 teeth on the driving motor pinion and 62 teeth on the driven axle gear), and a rated top speed of 65 mph. Classed EF-4, they were operated in A-B-B-A sets. When the helper F3 units arrived with their lower 65:12 gearing, they were classed EF-3 and run in A-B-A sets. After the F7 units with the 62:15 gearing were delivered, they became class "EF-4 (after 1-1-50)," which ignores the fact that the first of them arrived in March 1949. The F3

units in class EF-4 became "EF-4 (before 1-1-50)." The F7 units delivered with helper gearing were classed EF-3, just like the helper F3's. The 1951 classification system simplified things: the F3 units with 62:15 gearing became class EF-15, the F7 units with the 62:15 gearing became class EF-15a and both models with the 65:12 gearing were classed EH-15. Class EH-15 will be discussed later in a separate section.

EQUIPMENT

When EMD introduced the model F3 freight cab model in 1946, the General Motors subsidiary had a great advantage over the competition. Under War Production Board restrictions dur-

Order Summary - EF-15 Units

PRR ROAD NUMBERS	EMD ORDER NUMBER	NO. OF UNITS	ORDER DATE	DELIVERY DATES
9500A-9503A	E843	4	Nov 45	Jul 47
9500B-9503B		4		
9504A-9505A	E922	2	Jun 47	Sep 47
9504B-9505B		2		
9506A-9517A	E863	12	Jan 47	Apr 48-May 48
9506B-9517B		12		
9520A-9528A	E896	9	Jun 47	May 48-Jul 48
9540A-9541A		2	Feb 48	Jul 48-Sep 48
9520B-9527B		8	Jun 47	May 48-Jul 48
9540B		1	Feb 48	Jul 48
9529A-9539A	E921	11	Jul 47	Sep 48
9556A-9561A		6	Jul 47	Sep 48
9563A-9567A		5	Jul 47	Sep 48
9677A-9678A		2	Jun 48	Sep 48
9679A	E1138	1	Jun 48	Oct 48

A trio of F units, led by PRR F3 9509A, moves through East Liberty in Pittsburgh, Pennsylvania, on a frigid afternoon in December 1962. The lead A-unit wears a Chaplinesque moustache of snow while the photographers rejoice that their frigid wintry vigil has been rewarded. These locomotives were retired as trade-ins for second-generation Geeps in late 1962 and early 1963. They were hardly clunkers on the trade-in market. Still, EMD's policy at the time was not to resell trade-ins.

ing World War II, only EMD was allowed to build freight cab units, their model FT. Since Baldwin did not have a road unit in production, development of such a unit was severely restricted. Alco was given WPB authority for only a small number of road units. EMD delivered over a thousand model FTs and more than 100 model F2s prior to the introduction of the first F3s in late 1946. Both the FT and F2 were rated at 1350-hp for traction with the F2 using some F3 equipment.

Using the experience gained from a thousand freight units in the field, EMD made a number of improvements in the F3. Engine horsepower was increased to 1500 hp from 1350 for traction. The engine in the F3 also incorporated a number of mechanical improvements to increase serviceability and reliability. In addition, the engine governor was changed from an electro-pneumatic type to the electro-hydraulic type. Changes in the auxiliaries included electric drive of the traction motor blowers and cooling fans instead of mechanical drive auxiliaries used in FT diesels.

EMD's new model D12 generator went into the F3s, a substantial design change from the D8 generator in the FT's and F2's. Although the horsepower available for traction increased 11 percent, the traction generator continuous current rating was increased 19 percent. To achieve this, the physical size was increased with more iron and copper added. The armature diameter was increased from 36 inches on the older D8

to 42 inches on the D12 machine. The generator was so improved that it remained unchanged in the F7 model.

The units delivered by EMD on orders E921 and E1138 were "F5s." These looked like F7's except for the lack of an external dynamic brake fan. They were not equipped with all of the F7 electrical modifications. EMD officially classified these units as model F3.

SERVICE HISTORY

When the class EF-15 units were first delivered (classed EF-4 at the time), they were assigned to "arranged" freight service operating out of Enola. Arranged freight trains were the major east-west trains, which carried high-class freight, then mostly in box cars. As the EMD model F7s were delivered, the F3 were not so much supplanted as augmented to replace steam power. Most of the F3s with 65-mph gearing remained assigned to Enola until early 1956. The few exceptions were the 9524A/9524B/9525A set that was assigned to Columbus and Fort Wayne in 1951-52. Also, in what proved to be a prediction of the future, units 9500A-9503A and 9500B-9503B went to the Enola-Buffalo line about 1953. By 1956, these units were joined by 9504A and 9505A.

Delivery of large orders of GP9s in 1956 changed the EF-15 assignments. With the arrival of the GP9s, small groups of EF-15 units were added to the Northern Region to join the 10 already there. Other EF-15s were sent to the

Buckeye Region. A major change was made at the end of 1957: the entire fleet of EF-15 units was assigned to the Northern Region where they dominated the freight motive power assignments on the Enola-Buffalo mainline and its major branches.

Class EF-15 actually increased in numbers from 1959 to 1962 when eight of the earliest class EH-15 locomotives were rebuilt with 62:15 gearing. This conversion was part of Betterment Code 1298 to change all of the EH-15s to the 65-mph gearing. The eight units converted to class EF-15 did not have the heavier wiring required for the F7 rating. All of the former EH-15 units remained assigned to the Pittsburgh Region until retirement.

The Northern and Pittsburgh Region assignments prevailed until 1962 when large numbers the EF-15 units were traded in on the GP30 order. Class EF-15 was further reduced when more F3s were used as trade-ins for GP35s. By the end of 1963, all of the 36 class EF-15 units in the first three EMD orders, the four ex-Bangor and Aroostook B-units and 15 of the 45 units in the last three EF-15 orders had been retired. After 1963, the class EF-15 units (not including the re-geared EH-15 units) were assigned to secondary freight services with maintenance at Conway. Four of these units remained when they entered Penn Central service. Only the 1403 remained after the end of 1968. The 1403 was retired in April 1971.

Locomotive Characteristics

Class	EF-15	EF-15	EH-15	EH-15	EH-15	EH-15
Builder	EMD	EMD	EMD	EMD	EMD	EMD
Model	F3A	F3B	F3A	F3B	F7A	F7B
Type Unit	A	B	A	B	A	B
Horsepower	1500	1500	1500	1500	1500	1500
Wheel Arr,	B-B	B-B	B-B	B-B	B-B	B-B
Total Weight	238,000 lbs	227,000 lbs	238,000 lbs	234,800 lbs*	238,000 lbs	234,800 lbs
Weight on Drivers	238,000 lbs	227,000 lbs	238,000 lbs	234,800 lbs*	238,000 lbs	234,800 lbs
Length over Couplers	50' 8"	50' 1"	50' 8"	50' 1"	50' 8"	50' 1"
Truck Centers	30' 0"	30' 0"	30' 0"	30' 0"	30' 0"	30' 0"
Truck Wheelbase	9' 0"	9' 0"	9' 0"	9' 0"	9' 0"	9' 0"
Engine	EMD 16-567B	EMD 16-567B	EMD 16-567B	EMD 16-567B	EMD 16-567B	EMD 16-567B
Generator	EMD D12	EMD D12	EMD D12	EMD D12	EMD D12	EMD D12
Traction Motors	EMD D17	EMD D17	EMD D7E	EMD D7E	EMD D27E	EMD D27E
Gear Ratio	62:15	62:15	65:12	65:12	65:12	65:12
Maximum Speed	65 MPH	65 MPH	50 MPH	50 MPH	50 MPH	50 MPH
Starting Trac. Effort	59,500 lbs	56,750 lbs	59,500 lbs	58,700 lbs*	59,500 lbs	58,700 lbs
Continuous Trac. Effort	32,500 lbs	32,500 lbs	42,500 lbs	42,500 lbs	40,100 lbs	40,100 lbs
CTE Speed	14.25 MPH	14.25 MPH	11.0 MPH	11.0 MPH	11.0 MPH	11.0 MPH

*--Units 9515B, 9542B and 9544B only, weight 227,000 lbs. STE on these units is 56,750 lbs

W.D. VOLKMER PHOTO, DOUGLAS COLLECTION

Above, unit 1408 at Northumberland, Pennsylvania in October 1966. It was built in September 1948 as 9541A shortly before EMD had begun to produce F3's with F7 carbody features such as the the 9537A shown below. Both the 1408 and the GP9 coupled behind have been repainted in the Keystone-only image used at the end of the PRR era.

Below, three F3s pull an outbound ore train from Greenwich Yard in Philadelphia, assisted by pushers out of sight at the end of the train. Note the grillwork on the roof behind the cab for the dynamic brake; F7s had a visible fan.
Photo taken in October 1962.

The Fairbanks-Morse 2000 horse-power, A1A-A1A wheel arrangement diesel locomotive design was the prestige model in the F-M line of locomotives when introduced in 1945. The Pennsylvania Railroad owned the largest fleet of this model with 48 units out of a total of 111 sold by F-M. The PRR ordered both A-units and B-units as tabulated.

FAIRBANKS MORSE AND DIESEL LOCOMOTIVES

The engine used in the Erie-built units was the 10-cylinder Fairbanks-Morse model 38D8-1/8 opposed piston engine, a land adaptation of the engine built by F-M in great numbers to power U. S. Navy submarines during World War II. See pages 70-71 for a discussion of this engine. The production facilities for Navy engine building were in fact F-M's reason for entry into the diesel locomotive business. The engine building capabilities were there at Beloit, and locomotives were logical postwar products. But F-M did not yet have locomotive erection shop facilities sufficient for its plans. The solution was to sub-contract construction of the initial F-M road units to General Electric in Erie, Pennsylvania.

An F-M model designation such as P20-64 was never assigned to these units. The term "Erie-built" was applied informally and in due time was used in an F-M trouble-shooting manual issued by the builder. The Erie-builts were unusual in that they carried builders' numbers from both F-M and GE.

EQUIPMENT

F-M used Westinghouse electrical equipment for most of its locomotives, up until Westinghouse abandoned the diesel locomotive electrical equipment business. The Erie-built units were the

---

The Erie-Builts, PRR class FF-20, were perhaps the best example of the lengths to which a railroad would go to dieselize in a hurry. Consider the inefficiency of a freight engine with only two-thirds of its weight on the drivers. But they could be had more quickly than other models, and they did indeed run. It seems that even an inefficient diesel design was preferable to steamers. Below, the FF-20s appear in the configuration intended by the Motive Power Department: as a 6000-hp. A-B-A set. We are west of Gallitzin Pennsylvania in July, 1958.

(Note: the authors have resisted the temptation to use a computer photo retouching program to "remove" the telephone pole.)

Locomotive Characteristics

Class	FF-20	FF-20	FP-20	FP-20	FP-20a	FP-20a
Builder	F-M	F-M	F-M	F-M	F-M	F-M
Model	Erie-A	Erie-B	Erie-A	Erie-B	Erie-A	Erie-B
Type Unit	A	B	A	B	A	B
Horsepower	2000	2000	2000	2000	2000	2000
Wheel Arr,	A1A-A1A	A1A-A1A	A1A-A1A	A1A-A1A	A1A-A1A	A1A-A1A
Total Weight	355,170 lbs	354,100 lbs	331,400 lbs	332,800 lbs	341,180 lbs	334,880 lbs
Weight on Drivers	245,720 lbs	245,140 lbs	232,100 lbs	230,800 lbs	236,200 lbs	232,600 lbs
Length over Couplers	64' 10"	64' 10"	64' 10"	64' 10"	64' 10"	64' 10"
Truck Centers	36' 5"	36' 5"	36' 5"	36' 5"	36' 5"	36' 5"
Truck Wheelbase	15' 6"	15' 6"	15' 6"	15' 6"	15' 6"	15' 6"
Engine	FM 10-38D8-1/8	FM 10-38D8-1/8	1, FM 10-38D8-1/8	1, FM 10-38D8-1/8	1, FM 10-38D8-1/8	1, FM 10-38D8-1/8
Generator	GE GT-567	GE GT-567	1, GE GT-567	1, GE GT-567	1, GE GT-567	1, GE GT-567
Traction Motors	4,GE 746	4,GE 746	4, GE 746	4, GE 746	4, GE 746	4, GE 746
Gear Ratio	70:17	70:17	64:23	64:23	64:23	64:23
Maximum Speed	69 MPH	69 MPH	100 MPH	100 MPH	100 MPH	100 MPH
Starting Trac. Effort	61,430 lbs	61,285 lbs	57,700 lbs	58,025 lbs	59,050 lbs	58,150 lbs
Continuous Trac. Effort	41,000 lbs	41,000 lbs	27,500 lbs	27,500 lbs	27,500 lbs	27,500 lbs
CTE Speed	15.5 MPH	15.5 MPH	22.0 MPH	22.0 MPH	22.0 MPH	22.0 MPH
Steam Generator			1, DRK-4530	1, DRK-4530	1, DRK-4530	1, DRK-4530
Steam Gen, Capacity			3000 lb/hr	3000 lb/hr	3000 lb/hr	3000 lb/hr

FF-20 9481A leads another A unit with a coal train, westbound at Gray Tower, Tyrone, Pennsylvania in October 1957.

exception among early F-Ms; they contained GE electrical equipment. Since General Electric manufactured the units, this is not surprising. The main traction generator was the GE GT567 and the traction motors were the GE746 model. The 746 motor was larger than the 752 used in Alco and GE road locomotives and had greater electrical capacity. The PRR joined other roads by specifying the 746 motor and 42" diameter wheels on their Erie-built units instead of the 40" diameter wheels used with GE752 traction motors and on EMD freight road units. The Erie-builts used General Electric's amplidyne control system in which an amplidyne gen-

erator produced the traction generator excitation current and was capable of close control of the generator. In fact, the locomotive control system used in the Erie-builts was very similar to the Alco passenger units.

Most of the PRR Erie-builts were ordered as freight units with 65-mph gearing. These were originally classed FF-3 (or FF-2 for the 9480A-9491A group). One A-B-A set, 9478A/9478B/9479A, was delivered with a 3000 lb. per hour steam boiler and 100-mph gearing. These were classed FP-3. Three more A-B-A sets (9472A-9477A, 9472B, 9474B and 9476B) were delivered with the 3000 lb. per hour boiler but with the 65-mph gear-

ing. These were classed FF-3s. In April 1949, the FF-3s group was re-equipped at Juniata Shop with 100-mph gearing and reclassed as FP-3. In the 1951 re-classification the FF-2 and FF-3 units were reclassified FF-20, the as-built FP-3 units reclassified FP-20 and the converted FP-3 units reclassified as FP-20a.

Special equipment on the A-units included cab signals and trainphone. The first two orders of FF-20s were built with dynamic brakes. The third order (9480A-9491A) had no dynamic brakes.

The less glamorous aspect of diesels was the B-unit; the "bridesmaid." Because they were seldom photographed in detail, we present this picture here, along with others to come. Note that B-units had a designated front end, the letter "F" at the right edge tells us this, even though the large shutter location on an Erie-built is a more visible indication. Note also, at the front, what looks like a cab window hatch in the side, shuttered with a steel plate. It was a window, through which a hostler could observe conditions while using a rudimentary set of controls to move the B-unit by itself for short distances in an engine terminal. PRR 9466B is at Richmond, Indiana in June 1961.

SERVICE HISTORY

When delivered, the first two orders of Erie-builts were assigned to operate out of Enola. For the freight units at Enola, most of the assignments were east-west through freights. For units in passenger service, the destinations were the same, although operations to Baltimore and Buffalo were possibilities. The third order of Erie-builts (9480A-9491A) was delivered for service on the Pittsburgh Division except for the last two units. These last two initially went to the Eastern Division but were transferred to the Lake Division after a short period.

By February 1952, six A-B-A sets of Class FF-20 units were assigned to the Enola pool. This was the first PRR order of Erie-builts and they had been assigned to the Enola pool since delivery. In this pool, the units were assigned to through freights to Chicago, St. Louis, Detroit, Cincinnati, Cleveland, Buffalo and Hagerstown. The one-way mileage from Enola (Harrisburg) ranged from 858 to East St. Louis to 31 for the run to York on trains YE-1 and YE-2. At this time the FP-20 and FP-20a units were still in passenger service. On the Pittsburgh Division 9480A-9489A were used as two-unit sets in the Pitcairn-Derry helper pool. The pair of Lake Division units, 9490A-9491A, was assigned to Canton for service to Cambridge on CDC-1 and CDC-2. By the end of 1952, the Lake units had been moved to the Pittsburgh Division.

By May 1952, the assignment of the first two orders was changed from Enola to Columbus, although the boiler equipped units remained at Harrisburg until they were converted to freight service, which was completed in 1953. The third order of FF-20s remained assigned to the Pittsburgh Division as before. These assignments were to remain in force for the remainder of the service of this class. Despite operational assignment to the Pittsburgh and Lake Divisions (later the Pittsburgh and Lake Regions), Class FF-20 maintenance remained at Columbus. Although assigned to Columbus and Pittsburgh operationally, Erie-builts were assigned to secondary freights on most of the non-electrified PRR system.

In 1959, PRR began to rewire the units to replace main traction busses, which had been laid on the carbody floor. Although the busses were insulated, their location on the floor made them the target of lubricant leaks, and oil impregnation led to loss of insulation. The rewiring relocated the conductors in areas out of harm's way for better reliability. The second modification was the installation of nose MU receptacles on the A-units in the class during the last two years or so of service. This made it possible to run FF-20 A-units in the middle of sets and added to the utility of the units. This was particularly important in winter since the FF-20 A-units had a reputation for poor cab heating; engineers preferred to ride in a different model unit on the head end.

While Class FF-20 continued well into 1962, this was to be the last full year of operation. The first Class FF-20 units were retired in September 1962 and the last in December 1963.

The engine on the Erie-builts was the 10-cylinder F-M model 38D8-1/8 opposed piston diesel. As used in diesel locomotives, this engine was rated at 2000 horsepower for traction. The opposed piston design was unique to F-M in North American diesel locomotives and had been developed for U.S. Navy submarine propulsion.

The opposed piston engine has two pistons per cylinder. One piston in each cylinder is connected to a crankshaft at the top of the engine and the other to the crankshaft at the bottom of the engine. The engine is a two stroke cycle design and during the compression stroke, the two pistons in each cylinder approach each other compressing the air between them. At the moment in the cycle when fuel combustion is required, the fuel is sprayed into the cylinder between the pistons. Fuel ignition occurs because the charged air in the cylinders has been heated by compression to a temperature higher than the ignition temperature of the fuel.

While this process is the basis of fuel ignition in all diesel engines, the opposed piston engine is unique in that compression is achieved by two pistons approaching each other instead of one piston compressing the air in a cylinder closed at one end by a cylinder head. The opposed piston engine does not have cylinder heads. The upper and lower crankshafts of the engine are connected with suitable gearing for power output.

The two pistons in each cylinder are not actually synchronized to reach their individual top dead centers simultaneously. The lower piston leads the top piston by twelve degrees in timing for the ten cylinder engine.

The twelve-degree lead of the low-

Order Summary - FF20 Units				
PRR ROAD NUMBERS	F-M ORDER NUMBER	NO. OF UNITS	ORDER DATE	DELIVERY DATES
9456A-9471A	LD-29	16	Apr 47	Nov 47-Apr 48
9456B-9470B (even)	LD-29	8	Apr 47	Nov 47-Dec 47
9472A-9477A	LD-35	6	Jul 47	Jun 48-Jul 48
9472B-9476B (even)	LD-35	3	Jul 47	Jun 48-Jul 48
9478A-9479A	LD-35	2	Jul 47	Sep 48
9478B	LD-35	1	Jul 47	Sep 48
9480A-9491A	LD-45	12	Feb 48	Sep 48-Dec 48

Fairbanks-Morse Opposed Piston Locomotive Diesel Engine

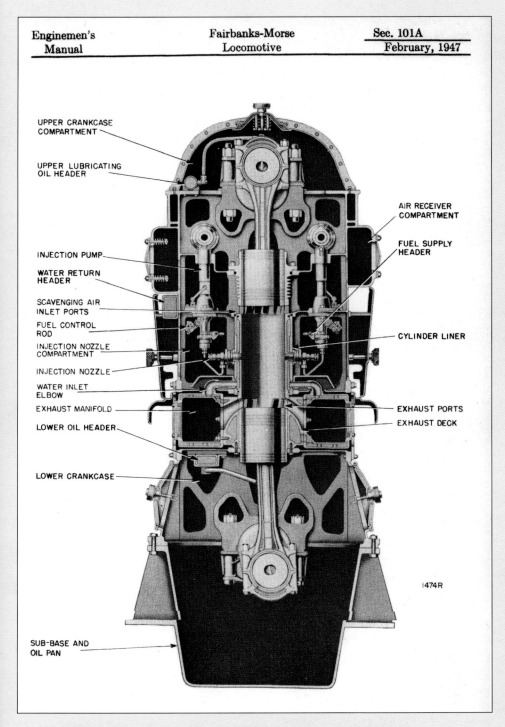

UPPER CRANKCASE COMPARTMENT

UPPER LUBRICATING OIL HEADER

INJECTION PUMP

WATER RETURN HEADER

SCAVENGING AIR INLET PORTS

FUEL CONTROL ROD

INJECTION NOZZLE COMPARTMENT

INJECTION NOZZLE

WATER INLET ELBOW

EXHAUST MANIFOLD

LOWER OIL HEADER

LOWER CRANKCASE

SUB-BASE AND OIL PAN

AIR RECEIVER COMPARTMENT

FUEL SUPPLY HEADER

CYLINDER LINER

EXHAUST PORTS

EXHAUST DECK

1474R

Transverse Cross Section of Engine

er piston over the upper provides a port-opening sequence that contributes to engine operating economy. This sequence starts during the last segment of the power stroke when the lower piston uncovers the exhaust port. Because of the lead, this precedes the upper piston uncovering the intake port. This means that the burned gasses start exhausting by the remaining pressure resulting from the fuel combustion. As the pistons continue to move, the upper piston uncovers the intake port and the blower forces air into the cylinder. This scavenges out the remaining exhaust gasses and forces clean air into the cylinder for the next power stroke.

On the 10-cylinder version of the engine, the result of the 12-degree lead is that 72-percent of the power is generated from the lower crankshaft. Very little of the power generated in the upper piston is used for traction since the auxiliaries are driven from the upper crankshaft.

The model 38D8-1/8 F-M engine had a bore of 8-1/8" and each piston stroked 10". Because of the unique design, the opposed piston engine was greater in height than competing engines, which is why the F-M hoods and carbodies were typically higher than hoods on other makes of diesel locomotives.

CLASS EH-15
EMD F3 AND F7

The Pennsylvania was one of the few American railroads to order cab units specificlly for helper duty. This requirement developed in late 1947 after the PRR had dieselized several major Enola-Chicago and Enola-St. Louis premium freights with three A-B-B-A sets of EMD model F3s. Examples were the westbound LCL-1 that required two steam helpers to assist the diesel road set in only one place: the westbound grade at Altoona. For eastbound CG-8, no helpers were needed on thegrade near Altoona. With steam operation, these trains needed five helpers on four grades on the eastbound trip and six helpers on four grades, westbound.

Even with this magnitude of improvement, the PRR operating department wanted diesel helpers on diesel freights. Soon after the delivery of the first F3 units, the PRR negotiated with EMD to borrow an F3 A-B-A demonstrator set with a 65:12 gear ratio, lower than the conventional 62:15 ratio. Lower speed, more push. The test units would be run on the East Slope grade (Altoona west to Cresson). The PRR and EMD discussed several plans to regear an EMD demonstrator and one or two existing PRR F3 units. The PRR was not willing to regear existing units since the

advantages of dieselization of the hot-shots were so great.

They finally worked out the delivery of an A-B-A set from existing PRR orders, whose delivery was moved up by shuffling the EMD production schedule. Units 9518A/9518B/9519A were delivered in January 1948, equipped with the 65:12 gear ratio for the desired trial. They were built on EMD order E1021 and classed EF-3 under the 1947 classification system.

The success of the first set of low-speed helpers was evident when an order for seven more A-B-A sets with the 65:12 gear ratio was placed in February 1948, within a month after the delivery of the trial units. Delivery of additional EH-15 units followed as shown in

the table below, until a total of 60 were on the property. Of this total, 39 units were model F3 and 21 were model F7. They were arranged in 20 A-B-A helper sets.

The F3s delivered after October 1948 were a transition model, equipped with a number of F7 features, such as low-profile roof fans, as EMD moved to the later model. EMD sold these as F3s. Some confusion has grown around an internal EMD designation of these transitional units as "F5." We follow the convention that, officially, there never was an "F5."

The PRR's orders for EMD freight cab units are confusing since several of the orders were changed between original order placement and unit delivery.

In service as head-end helpers, 9547A and B-unit lead a two-unit Erie-built set westbound to move a train of empty hoppers back to the coal mines. They are passing Slope Tower just west of Altoona on the East Slope grade. Horseshoe Curve lies ahead. At this time, in October 1957, the nose multiple-unit connections had not yet been installed.

Order Summary - EH-15 Units

PRR ROAD NUMBERS	NO. OF UNITS	EMD ORDER NUMBER	MODEL	DELIVERY DATE	ORDER DATES
9518A-9519A	2	E1021	F3A	Jun 47	Jan 48
9518B	1		F3B	Jun 47	Jan 48
9542A-9555A	14	E1004	F3A	Feb 48	Oct 48-Jan 49
9542B-9554B (even)	16		F3B	Feb 48	Oct 48-Jan 49
9680A-9683A	4	E1108	F3A	Jun 47	Jan-Feb 49
9519B, 9528A	2		F3B	Jun 47	Jan-Feb 49
9684A-9689A	6	E1080	F3A	Jun 48	Feb 49
9541B-9545B (odd)	3		F3B	Feb 48	Feb 49
9690A-9699A	10		F7A	Jun 48	Apr 49
9547B-9555B (odd)	5		F7B	Feb 48	Apr 49
9652A-9655A	4	3038	F7A	Nov 49	Feb 50
9652B, 9654B	2		F7B	Nov 49	Feb 50

As a result, some orders were split between models F3 and F7 and between 62:15 and 65:12 gear ratios. All of the units tabulated in the EH-15 order summary are equipped with the 50 mph, 65:12 gear ratio.

The class EH-15 (as they were reclassed from EF-3 in 1951) units were pretty straight F3 and F7 units aside from the gear ratio and some F7 features on the late F3s. The A-units equipped with trainphone, dynamic brakes plus whistle and acknowledger. The B-units all had dynamic brakes. A distinguishing feature of the EH-15 A-units was the 2-inch wide horizontal yellow stripe painted on the cab doors designating a 50 mph unit.

The original plan for the first eighteen three-unit sets was for helper duty on the East and West Slope grades (east or west of Cresson, the Allegheny summit). This plan was not carried out exactly. A report written in late 1949 identified the actual uses of the helper units. The report stated that on October 13, 1949, only six sets were in the intended service (with another set in the shop for monthly inspection; the "boiler wash"), while the other units had been assigned to various other jobs. Two three unit sets had been broken up into three two-unit sets for local freights in the Pitcairn-Blairsville-Youngwood area. Two sets were in mine run service—one on the Cresson Branches and the other on the Altoona-Osceola Mills turn. Of the other sets, three were in a Canton-Columbus pool and five sets were being used to dieselize BEC-1 and BEC-2 between Buffalo and Crestline and PB-1 and PC-2 between Pitcairn and Buffalo.

Within two years after the report on the helper F-units, more diesel units had arrived and the helper F-units (now Class EH-15) had almost all been returned to their originally intended helper assignments. The assignments for February 15, 1952 are detailed in the table. Within another year, the conversion of the Baldwin Centipedes to class BH-50 helpers was almost complete. This pushed a lot of the EH-15s from their original duty as helpers, but they remained assigned to the Pittsburgh Division, where there was plenty of drag service to perform. About the time of the reorganization of the operating divisions into nine operating regions in late 1955, the two three-unit sets assigned to Columbus were reassigned to the Pittsburgh Region. After this move, all of the Class EH-15 units remained assigned to the Pittsburgh Region until retirement or conversion to either Class EF-15 or EF-15a. In the late 1950s, all of the class was assigned to Pitcairn for maintenance.

CONVERSIONS

By May 1959, delivery of Class AS-18am units for helper service reduced the need for the EH-15s, and the PRR decided to convert them to the more conventional 62:15 gear ratio. Part of the reason for conversion was to eliminate the troublesome 65:12 gear ratio in F-units. Because the 12-tooth

PRR 9519A is seen soon after rebuild from a head-on collision with a Centipede set. The 9519A was rebuilt to an F7 rating. The basic "chicken wire" F3 carbody was retained, but close examination shows cab doors with the rounded corners used on F7 production and an F9 style headlight enclosure. Such parts would have been the current ones available from EMD. The photo is dated August 24, 1956.

J. J. CONSOLI COLLECTION

pinion was cut directly on the armature shaft of the traction motor, a gear problem in a 65:12 unit meant the total loss of the traction motor instead of the replacement of the motor pinion only. In the words of the PRR letter which instituted this betterment (Betterment Code 1298), the conversion was to be performed "to provide greater flexibility in regular freight service." A little cost reduction didn't hurt either.

When Betterment Code 1298 was issued, one EH-15 unit had already been converted from Class EH-15 to Class EF-15a. It was one of the first EH-15s

delivered—9519A. On December 3, 1955, this unit had been leading a diesel set with a caboose on the Cresson secondary track, having left Cresson as Extra 9519 North in mine run service. At 7:35 AM, on single track at Bradley Jct., Extra 9519 North collided head-on with a 20 car train headed by Centipedes 5811 and 5819. Three railroaders were killed and seven injured. The 9519A was derailed but remained upright at an angle of approximately 120 degrees from its original direction. ICC Report 3671 on this wreck, dated February 17, 1956, stated that the front

Assignment of Pennsylvania Railroad Class EH-15 units as of February 15, 1952

UNIT SETS	DIVISION	ASSIGNMENT
9682A 9528B 9683A	Middle	Tyrone-Osceola Coal Trains
9544A 9544B 9545A	Pittsburgh	Altoona-Pgh, 43rd St (PC-5/PC-2) and side trip Pgh, 43rd St-Kiski Jct. (KC-1/KC-2)
9680A 9519B 9681A	Pittsburgh	Altoona-Pgh, 43rd St (PC-5/PC-2) and side trip Pgh, 43rd St-Kiski Jct. (KC-1/KC-2)
9684A 9541B 9685A	Pittsburgh	East Slope Helper
9686A 9543B 9687A	Pittsburgh	East Slope Helper
9694A 9551B 9695A	Pittsburgh	East Slope Helper
9696A 9553B 9697A	Pittsburgh	East Slope Helper
9698A 9555B 9699A	Pittsburgh	East Slope Helper
9518A 9518B 9519A	Pittsburgh	West Slope Helper
9542A 9548B 9543A	Pittsburgh	West Slope Helper
9546A 9546B 9547A	Pittsburgh	West Slope Helper
9548A 9542B 9549A	Pittsburgh	West Slope Helper
9550A 9550B 9551A	Pittsburgh	West Slope Helper
9552A 9552B 9553A	Pittsburgh	West Slope Helper
9554A 9554B 9555A	Pittsburgh	West Slope Helper
9688A 9545B 9689A	Pittsburgh	West Slope Helper
9690A 9547B 9691A	Pittsburgh	West Slope Helper
9692A 9549B 9693A	Pittsburgh	East and West Slope Helper Protect
9652A 9652B 9653A	Columbus	Indianapolis-Bicknell Coal Trains
9654A 9654B 9655A	Columbus	Columbus Yard (Grandview-Grogan)

This listing indicates that as late as 1952, these units were still assigned in rigid three unit sets.

Diesel Operation of Trains
BEC-1 and BEC-2

A report on helpers dated October 20, 1949 provides a specific example of diversion of helper units away from their intended service, in this case to trains BEC-1 and BEC-2. The locomotives had been reassigned because it was believed that greater savings would be achieved.

BEC-1 and BEC-2 were freight trains operating between Buffalo New York and Crestline Ohio via Corry, Erie, Wheatland, Youngstown, Alliance and Canton. Prior to dieselization, each BEC-1 was handled by three different class I-1s (2-10-0) locomotives with power being changed at Erie and Canton. This westbound train also required single helpers from Orrville to Smithville (5.5 miles) and Millbrook to Ross (32.8 miles). From Brockton to Summerdale (20.7 miles), two helpers were required. Each eastbound BEC-2 also used three different class I1s loco-

motives, changed at the same locations as BEC-1; but it needed no more than a single helper at any point. The westbound trip was scheduled for 28.5 hours with setouts and pickups at Erie, Youngstown and Canton. The eastbound trip was scheduled for 33.4 hours with intermediate work at Canton, Sharon and Erie.

In October, 1949, BEC-1 and BEC-2 were converted to diesel power with three A-B-A sets of EMD model F3 units with the 65:12 gearing purchased for helper service. In addition to operating the two trains without any helpers, BEC-1 and BEC-2 were able to handle cars formerly moved by BEC-3 and BEC-4 between Erie and Canton.

BEC-1 and BEC-2 were consistently late using steam power. The diesels reduced the running times by as much as eight hours. The early arrival also made it possible to use the diesels to

perform extra work before the return trip. For example, one of the sets was frequently used to assist train BNY-16 from Buffalo to Machias New York, returning in time to cover its westbound assignment on BEC-1 to Crestline. The railroad was able to consider shortening the BEC-1/BEC-2 schedule, and eliminating trains BEC-3 and BEC-4.

The BEC-1/BEC-2 runs gave the Operating Department an example of savings possible with dieselization. It had been calculated that in helper service, the diesels would provide a 29.8% return on investment. Use of the units on BEC-1 and BEC-2 resulted in a calculated return of 35.5%. What could not be calculated was the impact on the service improvement through earlier delivery of cars to connections and consignees and lowered per diem charges through earlier turnover of cars to connections.

end and control compartment of the 9519A was demolished. This damage required considerable reconstruction of the unit and the PRR converted it to the F7 rating as part of the rebuild. The 9519A came out of Juniata shop in mid-1956 as a Class EF-15a.

Originally, the 1959 conversion program would have reclassified the model F3 units as EF-15 and the F7s as EF-15a. A few days after the original betterment memo defined just such a change, another memo revised the arrangement. The PRR found only eight of the F3 units (9518A, 9542A to 9545A, 9518B, 9542B and 9544B) that had not already been equipped with the heavier traction power cabling and traction motor blowers required for the F7 rating. The units with the heavier equipment had actually been the transitional design (the so-called "F5") and could be converted to the F7 rating by replacing the D17 traction motors with the newer EMD model D27.

The first locomotive converted under Betterment Code 1298 was 9547A, which was turned out of Pitcairn shop on May 16, 1959 as Class EF-15a, even though it was a model F3A. The conver-

sion program continued for the next three years at Juniata, Pitcairn and Columbus shops until the last unit, 9553B, left Columbus on July 1, 1962. Only three EH-15s retained the 65:12 gear ratio until their retirement in December 1963: 9541B, 9549B and 9681A.

After conversion, all of the ex-EH-15 units returned to the Pittsburgh Region except for the 9519A. The 9519A had been converted as part of the wreck

rebuild and not under the betterment code. It had been assigned to the Northern Region after its rebuild.

Only nine of the former EH-15 F-units were on the PRR roster on February 1, 1968 when they were included in the Penn Central's locomotive roster. Only the former 9686A (by then 1423) lasted more than a year under the PC banner, being retired in March 1970.

PRR 9690A was built (April 1949) as an F7 model by EMD, with 1500-hp. Since it was purchased as a helper, it was reclassified as EH-15 from its original EF-3. This unit confounds those railfans who insist that F3s had small number boards, F7s had large number boards. Fact is, EMD did not follow its automotive parent in making all changes at once with a model change, which leads to visual anomalies. It is shown here eastbound at Pitcairn Yard in February 1964, after its conversion to class EF-15a.

CLASS AF-15
ALCO FA-1

The sixteen class AF-15 units on the PRR consisted of eight 1500-hp Alco model FA-1 A-units and eight model FB-1 B-units. The first order was placed in July 1947 for four A-units and four B-units. They were delivered in July and August 1948. The four A-units were on Alco sales order 20241 and the four B-units on order 20242. The A-units were numbered 9600A to 9603A and the B-units numbered 9600B to 9603B.

The second order was for an additional eight units, placed on November 1949 and delivered in March and April 1950. The four A-units were on Alco sales order 20472 and the four B-units were on Alco sales order 20473. The A-units were numbered 9604A to 9607A and the B-units numbered 9604B to

9607B. The second order was among the last of this model that Alco built; they were rated at 1600-hp, not 1500-hp. Special equipment included trainphone, cab signals and whistle/acknowledger for passenger service.

SERVICE HISTORY

All of the class AF-15 units were assigned to Crestline for maintenance upon delivery. They stayed there through 1952. An early 1952 list of assignments shows all of the units assigned to the Crestline-Canton-Conway-Pitcairn pool which covered three eastbound and four westbound symbol freights in the area. They were set up in two A-B-A sets, two A-B-B sets and one A-B-B-A set. In early 1953, maintenance was moved to Enola.

By the middle of 1957, the AF-15s were almost all assigned to secondary freight service. With the arrival of large orders of GP9s in 1958, the AF-15 units were assigned to Shire Oaks and

Juniata maintenance. Later, the Juniata maintenance assignment was changed to East Altoona but the service was the same—coal service from Shire Oaks (below Pittsburgh on the Monongahela River) to the Altoona area.

The Pittsburgh Region and later Central Region assignments lasted until the units were gradually set aside and retired. In June 1961, seven of the sixteen units were set aside, one with a defective main generator but the remainder with scored crankshafts.

In 1963 and 1964, two of the A-units were sent east. During these years, 9606A and 9607A were assigned to the Bel-Del line from Trenton to Phillipsburg. They shared duties with Alco road-switchers—mostly RS-11s. During this period, five symbol freights operated in each direction on the Bel-Del line.

The 9600A-9603A and 9600B-9603B were retired in December 1963 and the remaining units in 1964 and 1965.

Above: Buttonwood engine terminal, south of Wilkes-Barre, Pennsylvania is the locale; Alco FA-1 No. 9605A (second group, 1600-hp) is found being serviced while awaiting an assignment in November 1964. The coupled unit to the right is 9616A, an AF-16. Unit 9605A had six months to go until retirement.

Locomotive Characteristics

Class	AF-15	AF-15	BF-15	BF-15	BF-15a	BF-15a
Builder	Alco	Alco	BLW	BLW	BLW	BLW
Model	FA-1	FB-1	DR 4-4-1500	DR 4-4-1500	DR 4-4-1500	DR 4-4-1500
Type Unit	A	B	A	B	A	B
Horsepower	1500	1500	1500	1500	1500	1500
Wheel Arr,	B-B	B-B	B-B	B-B	B-B	B-B
Total Weight	244,600 lbs	235,200 lbs	266,000 lbs	257,000 lbs	257,000 lbs	250,400 lbs
Weight on Drivers	244,600 lbs	235,200 lbs	266,000 lbs	257,000 lbs	257,000 lbs	250,400 lbs
Length over Couplers	51' 6"	50' 2"	54' 5"	52' 7"	54' 8"	53' 2"
Truck Centers	27' 2"	27' 2"	28' 2"	28' 2"	28' 2"	28' 2"
Truck Wheelbase	9' 4"	9' 4"	9' 2"	9' 2"	9' 2"	9' 2"
Engine	Alco 12-244B	Alco 12-244B	BLW 8-608SC	BLW 8-608SC	BLW 8-608SC	BLW 8-608SC
Generator	GE GT-564	GE GT-564	W 471A	W 471A	W 471A	W 471A
Traction Motors	GE 752	GE 752	W 370G	W 370G	W 370GL	W 370GL
Gear Ratio	74:18	74:18	63:15	63:15	63:15	63:15
Maximum Speed	65 MPH	65 MPH	65 MPH	65 MPH	65 MPH	65 MPH
Starting Trac. Effort	61,150 lbs	58,800 lbs	66,500 lbs	64,250 lbs	64,450 lab	62,600 lbs
Continuous Trac. Effort	42,500 lbs	42,500 lbs	43,000 lbs	43,000 lbs	42,800 lbs	42,800 lbs
CTE Speed	11.0 MPH	11.0 MPH	11.0 MPH	11.0 MPH	10.5 MPH	10.5 MPH

CLASS BF-15 AND BF-15A BALDWIN DR 4-4-1500

Baldwin freight cab units were second only in number to EMD on the PRR, and easily outnumbered Baldwin freight cab units on other American railroads. There were two classes of Baldwin 1500 horsepower cab units on the Pennsy. Originally classed "BF-4 (before 1-1-50) "and" BF-4 (after 1-1-50)," under the 1951 classification system, this was simplified to BF-15 and BF-15a, as shown in the accompanying table.

The carbody on PRR's 1500-hp Baldwin freight units evolved from the so-called "Baby Face" design Baldwin built for the Central of New Jersey, Missouri Pacific and New York Central. This design was similar to the 1500-hp A1A-A1A model and the Centipedes. The PRR Class BF-15s were built with the newer sharknose carbody styling done by the design firm of Hadley, Ryder and Pederson (*not* Raymond Loewy, who is often mistakenly credited). Baldwin had introduced the sharknose design on the PRR's 2000 horsepower class BP-20s.

Unlike the earlier models of Baldwin 1500 horsepower freight units, the BF-15's used a fabricated underframe. The only other Baldwin 1500 horsepower freight units with the sharknose styling (other than the BF-15a) were the A-B-B-A demonstrators which were built at the same time as the PRR's BF-15 units. The Baldwin demonstrator set was sold to the EJ&E, which subsequently sold it to the B&O.

The PRR's class BF-15a freighters were built after the BF-15 units and used the same carbody as the later Baldwin model RF-16 diesels. The BF-15a and BF-16 A-units were three inches longer than the BF-15 A-units and almost 10,000 pounds lighter. The B-units compared similarly.

SERVICE HISTORY

The class BF-15 units were originally put in service at such diverse locations as Crestline, Altoona, Enola and Columbus, and all class BF-15as were initially assigned to Renovo. While assignments were shifted periodically, these original assignments illustrate the BF-15 and BF-15a areas of operation.

Above, class BF-15a # 9707A is at Canton, Ohio, in June 1964, less than a year before retirement. The carbody is different from the class BF-15. A welded underframe on the BF-15a results in a visible side sill.

Unit 9607A leads 9606A on the Bel-Del line (Belvidere-Delaware River), at Milford, New Jersey, bound from Phillipsburg to Trenton during their short (1963-1964) tenure in that part of the country.

Class BF-15 unit 9574A rumbles westbound solo with a local freight train through Edgewood, Pennsylvania, near Pittsburgh in April 1962. The photo documents an unusual condition; Baldwin cab units did not often run as single locomotives.

Secondary freight service was the usual assignment.

Retirement of class BF-15 units began at the end of 1963 and was completed in August 1964. The class BF-15as lasted about a year more being retired between February and May 1965. One exception is unit 9583B which was re-engined by Alco in 1959 and reclassed ABF-18. See this class for the history of this unit.

Class Summary - BF-15 Units

PRR ROAD NUMBERS	NO. OF UNITS	UNIT TYPE	ORIGINAL CLASS	1951 CLASS	ORDER DATE	DELIVERY DATES
9568A-9573A	6	A-unit	BF-4 (before 1-1-50)	BF-15	Jul 47	Feb 49-Mar 49
9568B-9573B	6	B-unit	BF-4 (before 1-1-50)	BF-15	Jul 47	Feb 49-Mar 49
9574A-9593A	20	A-unit	BF-4 (before 1-1-50)	BF-15	Nov 48	Mar 49-Jul 49
9574B-9593B	20	B-unit	BF-4 (before 1-1-50)	BF-15	Nov 48	Mar 49-Jul 49
9700A-9707A	8	A-unit	BF-4 (after 1-1-50)	BF-15a	Nov 49	Apr 50-Jun 50
9700B-9707B	8	B-unit	BF-4 (after 1-1-50)	BF-15a	Nov 49	Apr 50-Jun 50

CLASS EF-15A
EMD F7

EMD F7 units with the 62:15 gear ratio continued the replacment of steam power in mainline east-west freight service. They came to the PRR in six orders, as shown in the table. Originally, they were classified as "EF3 (after 1-1-50)." They were reclassified as EF-15a in 1951.

Deliveries of F7s from EMD to U. S. railroads commenced in February 1949 after a pause of only about two weeks after F3 production ended. The PRR had received some of the last F3 units early in February and got their first F7's the next month. Performance was the most important improvement for the F7 over the F3. Even when the F3s were introduced, Alco and Baldwin offered a 1500 horsepower freight cab unit with

better performance than the EMDs. For the 65 mph gearing used by the PRR, both Alcos and Baldwins provided about 42,000 lbs continuous tractive effort at about 11 mph, while an F3 produced only 32,500 at 14 mph. The advantage of the non-EMD builders was the use of GE and Westinghouse electrical equipment, which had higher electrical capacity than the EMD-designed equipment. The diesel models introduced by EMD in 1949 closed the competitive gap almost completely. The new F7 models had a continuous tractive effort of 40,000 lbs. at 11 mph for the 65-mph gearing.

EQUIPMENT

The PRR's F7s were equipped with the 567B engine and D12 main traction generator, which were the same machines used on the F3. The big improvement was the new D27 traction motor used on the F7's. The new motor was designed with a higher electrical rating

than the D17 used on the F3s. Other improvements required to achieve the better ratings were heavier main traction wiring and higher capacity traction motor blowers. These changes improved the performance to the extent that EMD claimed that an F7 could haul 25 percent more tonnage on a one-percent grade than an F3. Automatic transition was standard on all F7 units in both forward and reverse transition, i.e., making transition in both increasing and decreasing speed conditions. Another major change was a 23 percent increase in dynamic brake capacity.

SERVICE HISTORY

When first delivered, about two-thirds of the PRR's class F7s joined the F3s at Enola for major east-west freight service. The others were assigned to Renovo, Canton, Cleveland, Fort Wayne and Cincinnati. Units 9656A to 9661A were equipped at an early date with the New York Central type intermittent inductive train stop equipment, enabling them to operate into Erie, Pennsylvania from Girard Junction to the west over NYC trackage rights. By 1951, the 9666A had also been equipped with the same equipment. Units equipped with the ITS equipment were called "hook" units on the PRR because of the shape of the electrical inductive pickup gear attached to the engineer's side of the front truck.

Until 1957 the assignments were largely unchanged although the non-Enola assignments were shuffled from time to time. As with the class EF-15 units, the arrival of large numbers of EMD model GP9s caused major relocations. By early 1958, more than half the EF-15a's were assigned to the Buckeye Region and a little less than a quarter to Enola. The rest went to the Northern Region except for the seven "hook" units assigned for maintenance to Canton, Ohio for service over the NYC into Erie.

THE FORMER EH-15 UNITS

Note that an additional group of F7s were delivered with the 65:12 gear ratio, to be used in helper service. They were not classified EF-15a, but EH-15, and have been discussed under that class. As noted in that section, all but one of the Class EH-15 units built as F7s were re-geared to 62:15 and reclassed EF-15a between 1959 and 1962.

Twenty-nine more EH-15s with 65:12 gearing were also upgraded to F7 stan-

The PRR main line descends the East Slope grade from Gallitzin to Altoona; we are at Alto Tower, where the H&P (Hollidaysburg and Petersburg) Branch is seen joining the main at the left. Smoke from protesting brake shoes accompanies a downhill freight train led by EF-15a 9815A. The second of four units is a GP9B. Photo was taken from the 17th Street overpass, Altoona in July 1965.

dards, Class EF-15a. These newer F3 units had heavier wiring and other equipment which made it possible to achieve F7 rating with just the change in gearing and installation of D27 traction motors. These former EH-15s remained assigned to the Pittsburgh Region for the remainder of the PRR period.

By 1964, all Class EF-15as were assigned to Conway for maintenance. About a quarter of the class was retired between 1963 and the renumbering in 1966. The 1966 renumbering assigned

the A-units in the class to the 1440-1538 and 1900-1906 road number blocks. The 1900 group was the "hook" units. The B-units were renumbered from 3508 to 3563. None of the number series was ever completely filled because many were retired before renumbering.

While assigned to Conway, the class EF-15as were used in secondary and local freight service over most of the PRR. This type of assignment continued for the final years prior to retirement of the class. At the end of PRR service, only 56 Class EF-15a units were turned

Locomotive Characteristics

Class	EF-15a	EF-15a	FF-16	FF-16	BF-16	BF-16	EFP-15	EFP-15
Builder	EMD	EMD	F-M	F-M	BLH	BLH	EMD	EMD
Model	F7A	F7B	CFA16-4	CFB16-4	RF-16	RF-16	FP7A	F7B
Type Unit	A	B	A	B	A	B	A	B
Horsepower	1500	1500	1600	1600	1600	1600	1500	1500
Wheel Arr,	B-B	B-B	B-B	B-B	B-B	B-B	B-B	B-B
Total Weight	234,000 lbs	230,600 lbs	258,000 lbs	254,000 lbs	257,800 lbs	250,400 lbs	260,000 lbs	247,000 lbs
Weight on Drivers	234,000 lbs	230,600 lbs	258,000 lbs	254,000 lbs	257,800 lbs	250,400 lbs	260,000 lbs	247,000 lbs
Length over Couplers	50' 8"	50' 0"	56' 6"	56' 6"	54' 8"	53' 2"	54' 8"	50' 0"
Truck Centers	30' 0"	30' 0"	43' 4"	43' 4"	28' 2"	28' 2"	34' 0"	30' 0"
Truck Wheelbase	9' 0"	9" 0"	9' 4"	9' 4"	9' 10"	9' 10"	9' 0"	9' 0"
Engine	EMD 16-567B	EMD 16-567B	FM 8-38D8	FM 8-38D8	BLW 8-608A	BLW 8-608A	EMD 16-567B	EMD 16-567B
Generator	EMD D12	EMD D12	W 497B	W 497B	W 471B	W 471B	EMD D12	EMD D12
Traction Motors	EMD D27B	EMD D27	W 370G	W 370G	W 370DZ	W 370DZ	EMD D27B	EMD D27B
Gear Ratio	62:15	62:15	63:15	63:15	63:15	63:15	60:17	60:17
Maximum Speed	65 MPH	65 MPH	66.4 MPH	66.4 MPH	70 MPH	70 MPH	77 MPH	77 MPH
Starting Trac. Effort	58,500 lbs	57,650 lbs	64,500 lbs	63,500 lbs	64,450 lab	62,600 lbs	65,000 lbs	61,750 lbs
Continuous Trac. Effort	40,000 lbs	40,000 lbs	42,800 lbs	42,800 lbs	48,600 lbs	48,600 lbs	34,000 lbs	34,000 lbs
CTE Speed	11.0 MPH	11.0 MPH	11.7 MPH	11.7 MPH	9.9 MPH	9.9 MPH	13.2 MPH	13.2 MPH
Steam Generator							OK-4625	OK-4625
Steam Gen, Capacity							2500 lb/hr	2500 lb/hr

over to Penn Central. These were almost all retired during the first four years of the PC: 34 in 1968, 19 in 1969, seven in 1970 and three in 1971. The last B-unit (3548) was retired in 1975, but A-units 1482 and 1501 were turned over to Conrail on April 1, 1976. The 1482 was to be renumbered to CR 1651, but was not. It was relettered Conrail but retained the 1482 road number. On the other hand, 1501 was assigned the Conrail road number of 1652 and for a time was renumbered 1652, but retained its Penn Central lettering. The 1482 was retired with that road number in April 1977. Conrail 1652 was retired in March 1978, the last ex-PRR class EF-15a to operate.

Order Summary - Class EF- 15a

PRR ROAD NUMBERS	EMD ORDER NUMBER	NO. OF UNITS	ORDER DATE	DELIVERY DATES
9667A-9676A	E1144	10	Oct 48	Mar 49-Jul 49
9667B-9676B		10		
9640A-9647A	E1221	8	Nov 49	Feb 50-Mar 50
9664A-9665A		2		
9640B-9647B		8		
9648A-9651A	3025	4	Nov 49	Feb 50-Mar 50
9662A-9663A		2		
9666A		1		
9648B, 9650B		2		
9656A-9661A	3037	6	Nov 49	Mar 50
9656B-9660B (even)		3		
9764A-9831A	3051	68	Aug 50	Jan 51-Jun 51
9764B-9818B (even)		28		
9872A-9879A	3144	8	Nov 51	Sep 52
9872B-9878B (even)		4		

PRR 1905 and 1906 are between runs at Renovo, Pennsylvania in November 1966. In the 1966 renumbering plan, the 1900 series F7A units were equipped with the New York Central intermittent train stop apparatus. The pickup for the ITS can be seen on the first axle of the front truck. It has been renumbered recently; the paint is fresher in that spot.

9773A represents a straightforward F7A unit, at Richmond, Indiana in January 1961. Note the large number board, more typical of EMD's F7. The nose M-U receptacles had not yet been installed; that modification started to be made a bit later.

CLASS FF-16
FM CFA16-4 AND CFB16-4 C-LINER

The "Consolidation" line of Fairbanks-Morse cab diesel locomotive was the successor to the Erie-built. These were built at F-M's Beloit, Wisconsin plant. The product line consisted of a cleverly designed group of models which used carbody modules in various combinations to provide for freight and passenger designs, A-units and B-units, B-B and B-A1A wheel arrangements and 1600, 2000 and 2400 horsepower. The Pennsylvania Railroad purchased sixteen model CFA16-4 A-units and eight CFB16-4 B-units. These were 1600 horsepower, B-B freight units. They were ordered on builder's order LD-88 in November 1949 and delivered between September and November 1950. The A-units were numbered 9448A-9455A and 9492A-9499A. The B-units were numbered 9448B-9454B and 9492B-9498B, even only. Originally classed as FF-3a, they were reclassed FF-16 in 1951.

SERVICE HISTORY

When delivered, the Class FF-3a units were divided between the Pittsburgh, Panhandle, Eastern and Lake Divisions. By the end of 1951, the Panhandle and Eastern Division units were moved to join the other units of the class on the Pittsburgh and Lake Divisions. In February 1952, five three-

Two FF-16s, with 9455A leading, provide power for a northbound freight in electrified territory at Crum Lynne, Pennsylvania in February 1958. A fine powder snowstorm had crippled the GG-1 electrics that usually powered these runs, by clogging the air intakes. Crum Lynne is a suburban stop north of Chester on the line from Philadelphia to Wilmington, Delaware.

unit C-Liner sets (by now reclassed FF-16) were assigned to the West Brownsville to Altoona pool. In this assignment, the C-Liners powered coal trains from the gathering yards at West Brownsville and Shire Oaks to Altoona. The five sets included 9448A-9455A, 9492A, 9293A and their corresponding B-units. Of the remaining Class FF-16 units, two A-B-A sets were assigned to a Columbus-Zanesville-Dennison-Mingo Jct.-Pitcairn pool and one A-B-A set was assigned to the Columbus-Canton-Cleveland pool.

The FF-16 assignments stayed relatively stable until retirement, although the specific assignment of the 1952

pools did not continue. The 9448-9455 and 9492-9493 groups were on the Pittsburgh Division or Region, the 9494-9497 group were on the Panhandle Division or Buckeye Region and 9498-9499 were on the Lake Division or Region. During these remaining years, secondary freight service was the assignment. Maintenance for most of that period was performed at Columbus, but for the last year or so, at Conway.

During 1964, more and more of the class were set aside for heavy repairs until at the end of the year, only 9451A, 9496A and 9497A were in service. All Class FF-16 units were retired on April 1, 1965.

9451A and companion at the Shire Oaks engine terminal, Elrama, Pennsylvania in April 1958. Elrama was a yard on the Monongahela River that served as a collecting point for coal from the area's mines.

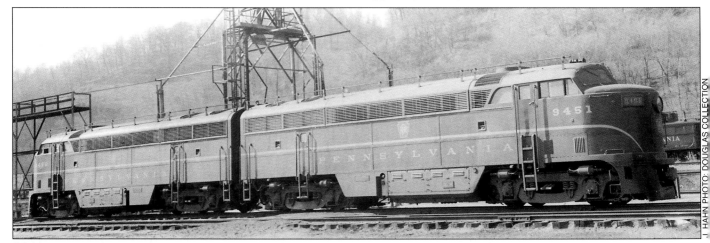

CLASS BF-16
BALDWIN RF-16

The PRR purchased a total of 102 Baldwin model RF-16 road freighters in two orders totalling 72 A-units and 30 B-units. The Pennsy owned the largest RF-16 fleet, far exceeding the 32 units owned by the B&O and 26 on the NYC. The 1600 horsepower units on the PRR became Class BF-16 under the 1951 classification system. When delivered, they shared Class BF-4 (after 1-1-50)

Left, BF-16 9599A and a B-unit are serving as a head-end helper hauling a morning ore train out of the Whiskey Island yard on Lake Erie. The train is eastbound, coming off the Cuyahoga River bridge on the New York Central line in Cleveland Ohio. The Pennsylvania had trackage rights over the NYC route to reach the PRR line in East Cleveland. The heavy ore traffic was primarily to mills in Weirton and Steubenville. The photo was taken in September 1964. The 9599A was retired in July 1966.

Below, we are at Gallitzin, the Allegheny summit, just east of the three tunnels at the summit. The train headed by 2009A has just emerged from the center tunnel bore, and is headed eastbound to Altoona. The configuration today, July 15, 1962, has two B-units coupled to 2009A.

with the units that later became class BF-15a. This illustrates one of the problems of the pre-1951 system. Purchases of the 1600 horsepower Baldwin freighters are tabulated on the order summary on the next page.

The BF-16 units were very similar to the Class BF-15a units. The major change was the improved model 608A engine. Of course, the horsepower available for traction was higher at 1600 and the continuous tractive effort was increased over the BF-15a with 48,600 lbs compared to 42,800 lbs on the older model. The CTE speed was slightly

Order Summary - Class BF-16

PRR ROAD NUMBERS	NO. OF UNITS	TYPE UNITS	ORDER DATE	DELIVERY DATES
9708A-9745A 9594A-9599A	44	A-unit	Aug 50	Dec 50-May 51
9708B-9714B (even) 9728B-9744B (even) 9594B-9598B (even)	16	B-unit	Aug 50	Dec 50-May 51
2000A-2027A	28	A-unit	May 51	Jun 51-Apr 52
2000B-2026B (even)	14	B-unit	May 51	Jun 51-Apr 52

lower on the newer units, 9.9 mph vs. 10.5. These characteristics were 20 percent better than the EMD F7 units, but only 92 percent of the continuous rating of an Alco FA-2.

Units 9734A to 9739A and 2024A to 2027A were equipped with the Intermittent Train Stop "hook" equipment for operation over the NYC trackage rights from Girard to Erie, Pennsylvania. Seven class EF-15a EMD F7As were also so equipped.

The BF-16s were also used in secondary service on the dieselized mainlines, the same use as classes BF-15 and BF-15a

The class BF-16 units were retired in two groups, one in July 1966 and the other in January 1967. The exceptions were the two BF-16 units that were re-engined by Alco and reclassed as ABF-18. See this class for information on these units.

A side/rear view of a BF-16 B-unit, 9596B, at the engine terminal in Canton, Ohio, taken in June 1964. PRR practice was to place B-unit numbers in small lettering only, on the sides near the front stirrup step, and on the ends.

With a racetrack special passenger extra, FP7 9835A, F7 9834B and FP7 9834A are parked near the track at Bowie, Maryland, awaiting the cash-depleted equine enthusiasts. The date is March 24, 1955. Although this is a black-and-white photo, we know that this three-year old trio is painted Tuscan red, not Brunswick green. Lettering and five-striping is buff, not gold leaf. Note the closed coupler door in the pilot; a touch of elegance removed after 1955 because of high maintenance costs.

CLASS EFP-15
EMD FP7A/F7B

The class EFP-15 diesels formed the PRR's largest group of dual service freight-passenger cab units. The 42 A-units were EMD model FP7A. Additionally, the class included 12 F7Bs that matched the 42 A-units. These were ordered in May 1951 and delivered between April and August of 1952. The A-units were numbered 9832A to 9871A and the B-units were numbered 9832B to 9858B (even only).

In June 1950, the PRR had issued a report identifying the number and type of diesel's estimated to complete dieselization, which was about half completed at the time. This report projected the need for 32 freight units equipped with steam generators in addition to 93 more dedicated passenger cab units.

The PRR actually purchased only 48 passenger cab units (all EMD model E8A) and the 54 Class EFP-15's. The greater number of dual service cab units gave the railroad more flexibility in locomotive assignments. The EFP-15 units were useful because there were many passenger assignments that didn't need an E8A with the 98-mph gearing that the PRR used. The class EFP-15's, geared for a maximum of 77 mph, were satisfactory for secondary passenger services. These assignments included mail and express trains, passenger extras, and end of the year holiday extra trains. This was in addition to their

9870A leads an eastbound freight emerging from Tunnel No. 5, just west of Gould Siding, near Mingo Junction, Ohio. By January 1965, when this photo was taken, the FP7s had received M-U and dynamic brake nose connectors.

standard assignment to freight service.

EQUIPMENT

The special equipment that the EFP-15 shared with most of the other Pennsy F-units were cab signals, trainphone and dynamic brakes. The first two features were on the A-units only. Late in the PRR period, radio replaced the trainphone. In the early 1960s, almost all of the A-units received nose MU receptacles. By May 1967, 4350 (former 9850A) was the only unit in the class to lack this feature.

The difference between FP7A units and F7A units was an additional four feet of length behind the front truck. The space was taken up with additional boiler water capacity. On the PRR, the boiler water capacity was 1180 gallons on the Class EFP-15 A-units and 1400 gallons on the B-units. By comparison, the F7A passenger service units on the Santa Fe had a water capacity of only 600 gallons.

The reason why the F7B units (which were essentially the same length as the A-units) had a higher boiler water storage capacity than either FP7A or F7A units was because there was a large space available in the area taken up by an operating cab on A-units. On F7B units without steam generators, this space was taken up by a sizable piece of concrete ballast.

The PRR EFP-15 A-units weighed 260,000 lbs vs. 234,000 lbs for a class EF-15a, F7A unit. This gave the dual service units 7,500 lbs more starting tractive effort. However, the higher gear ratio resulted in a lower continuous tractive effort of 34,000 vs. the 40,000 lbs for the F7A. The class EFP-15s had speed control, unlike most EF-15a units.

Some of the EFP-15 units carried a Tuscan red passenger paint scheme, including three coats of synthetic Tuscan red enamel, reference 47-3258. Five 1-3/8" wide stripes were applied

FP7 9854A is painted Brunswick green, and has no skirts or coupler door. She rests at Richmond, Indiana, in January 1960. The FP7's extra length made room for a cylindrical boiler water tank under the front porthole.

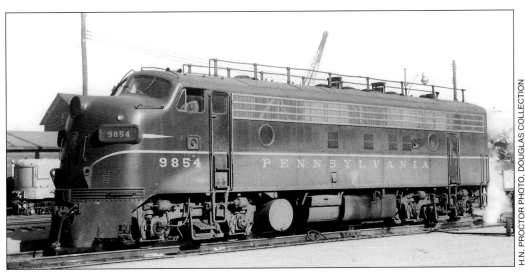

over the base color (described on the drawings as buff color, reference 47-2616). Exactly which units received the Tuscan scheme at EMD or in PRR shops is shrouded in some mystery, because units shown as red on the paint drawings were sighted as green shortly after delivery. EMD apparently applied red to four A-units (9832A-9835A) and two B-units (9832B and 9834B).

Similar sightings of Brunswick green units in the 9836A-9839A group indicate that PRR painting drawings for the red class EFP-15 units are in error since they state that the drawings applied to units 9832A to 9839A and 9832B to 9838B (even only). Therefore, there were two A-B-A sets of red EFP-15 units, not four. Some of these units remained in the red scheme through the 1950s.

SERVICE HISTORY

The class EFP-15 units were assigned primarily west of Pittsburgh for almost the entire PRR period. Initial assignments were to the Panhandle, Cincinnati and Ft. Wayne Divisions. For a few months 9836A, 9836B and 9837A were assigned to the Northern Division. About the end of 1952, 9832A to 9839A and 9832B to 9838B (even only) were transferred to Enola, where they were available for main east-west passenger service. About the time that the PRR reorganized operations from divisional groupings into nine regions in 1955, all the class EFP units except these at Enola were assigned to Columbus in the Buckeye Region. After about three years, the Enola units were also transferred to Columbus where maintenance was assigned to Columbus Diesel Shop. By the mid-1960s, maintenance was transferred to Conway. The final reassignment of the PRR period was applied to the A-units only when maintenance responsibility was moved to Harrisburg roundhouse.

For most of their lives, the class worked on the western end the PRR. Their work could be called regional freight assignments. This would apply to freight operations other than local freights but not the main east-west work. The class was still observed on passenger trains until the end of the PRR period. In 1967 for instance, the 4357 (former 9847A) was seen heading a pair of A-units on a New Jersey race train. Also, early in the Penn Central period, the class was assigned to mail trains in four and five unit sets.

In the general renumbering in preparation for the Penn Central merger, the units were not reclassified but all units were renumbered. Units 9832A to 9871A became 4332 to 4371 in order. The B-units, 9832B to 9858B (even only) became 4150 to 4163, again in order.

The class suffered no retirements until almost the end of their PRR service. In October 1967, six B-units were dropped. Between 1968 and 1976, under Penn Central ownership, 17 A-units and six more B-units were retired. Seventeen A-units and two B-units were on the roster at the beginning of Conrail ownership. Conrail retired the remaining class EFP-15 units before the end of 1978.

This FB-2 B-unit photo is for the modelers. Note the small numbers, the lift rings, the absence of a diaphragm. This is the front end of the unit. 9612B on March 17, 1962, at Conway Pennsylvania engine terminal.

PRR's six-year old AF-16 9616A and a B-unit are passing Alto tower at Altoona, Pennsylvania. This train was on Horseshoe Curve not too many minutes ago; it's eastbound to Enola on October 12, 1957. Alto tower was the last operational tower in the Altoona area; it lasted into the 1990s.

CLASS AF-16
ALCO FA-2/FB-2

The PRR purchased more than twice the number of Alco 1600 horsepower freight cab and booster diesels than their 1500 horsepower predecessors. The class AF-16s were purchased in two orders for a total of 24 A-units and 12 A-units. The first group was ordered in August 1950 and delivered in May 1951. In this first group, the 12 B-units were ordered on Alco sales order 20583 and the six B-units were ordered on Alco sales order 20584. They were numbered 9608A-9619A and 9608B-9618B (even only). The second group was ordered in May 1951 and delivered in November and December 1951. The 12 A-units were ordered on Alco sales order 20712 and the 6 B-units were ordered on Alco

sales order 20713. They were numbered 9620A-9631A and 9620B-9630B (even only).

The Alco model FA-2/FB-2 were basically the same as the predecessor FA-1/FB-1 but had somewhat improved horsepower and continuous tractive effort ratings. The horsepower was raised from 1500 to 1600. The generator was the GE GT-581, the successor to the GE GT 564. The traction motors were the GE 752 used on almost all Alco road units. Some rearrangement of equipment was part of the change from the 1500 horsepower units. This was most evident in the relocation of the radiators, fans and batteries.

The AF-16 units used the same 74:18 gearing as did the AF-15's for a maximum speed of 65 mph. The improved electrical system was evidenced with the continuous tractive effort raised by 23 percent to 52,500 lbs. The continuous tractive effort speed was lowered to 9.5

mph from 11 mph.

Special equipment included train-phone and cab signals. Units 9620A to 9621A also had speed control.

On delivery, they were assigned to several Ohio locations. Three A-B-A sets were assigned to the Lake Division with one each of the sets being assigned to the Cleveland-Conway-Mingo pool, the Columbus-Canton-Cleveland pool and the Ashtabula-Conway-Canton pool. Seven A-B-A sets were assigned to the Eastern Division's Canton-Toledo pool for use on symbol freights ST-1 and ST-2. The last two A-B-A sets were assigned to the Crestline-Canton-Conway pool which also included the class AF-15 units. This was also an Eastern Division assignment. This initial assignment period only lasted for about a year and a half when the units were scattered more widely. At this time, the AF-16s were assigned to the Lake, Eastern, Susquehanna, Maryland, Phila-

PRR 9622A leads an EF-15a unit with a westbound freight at the west end of Pitcairn yard. This location is not in the municipality of Pitcairn, but in the neighboring jurisdiction of Wall, Pennsylvania. This photo was taken on October 7, 1962.

delphia and Middle Divisions. Coincident with regionalization in 1955, all of the class was assigned to Enola. Again, this assignment only lasted for a couple of years.

The assignment after the arrival of the large numbers of GP9s starting in 1958 were the same as the AF-15s— Shire Oaks to Altoona area coal trains. This lasted until late 1960 when the Alco freight cab units were assigned general system secondary freight service.

After this last move, if problems occurred, the AF-16s were set aside for heavy repairs, which were never made. For the next several years, more of the units were set aside, but 9614A seemed to lead a charmed life. After mid-1965, it was the only class AF-16 in service. Although 9614A was stored for brief peri-

ods, it remained in service until mid-1966.

Retirement of the first order of 18 AF-16 units took place in July 1966, and the second 18 were retired in January 1967. Several of the AF-16's had been set aside for as long as six years with such varied problems as fire damage, damaged engine A-frames and the typical malady—scored crankshafts.

CLASS EFS-17m
EMD GP9

There were more GP9s on the PRR diesel roster—310 of them— than any other model. From the end of 1957 until

the Penn Central merger, at least one out of ten PRR diesels was a GP9. At the end of 1959, it was 12.5 per cent. The GP9 percentage rose to 14.8 percent just before the Penn Central merger because unit retirements exceeded locomotive purchases. Additionally, there were enough GP9s to power many secondary freights and locals in addition to the mainline through freights.

The PRR's fleet of GP9s included 40 cabless B-units out of the 310-unit total. Only the PRR and Union Pacific purchased the GP9B. The Santa Fe had GP7 B-units. As long as a railroad utilized the road-switchers in multi-unit sets, the B-units allowed a saving in cab control equipment maintenance. The downside was that a B-unit was inflexible because a set had to be led by a cab

A westbound freight just east of Gallitzin in June 1963 is pulled by a three-unit GP9 set, 7003 in the lead. 7003, delivered as part of the first order late in 1955, has two 36-inch cooling fans at the top front of the hood. The GP9s were sufficient in number on the Pennsylvania to discourage photography for a time: "Isn't there any other kind of engine on this $@&%@ railroad?"

Locomotive Characteristics

Class	AF-16	AF-16	EFS-17m	EFS-17m	ABF-18	ABF-18
Builder	Alco	Alco	EMD	EMD	BLH	BLW
Model	FA-2	FB-2	GP9	GP9B	RF-16	DR 4-4-1500
Type Unit	A	B	A	B	A	B
Horsepower	1600	1600	1750	1750	1800	1800
Wheel Arr,	B-B	B-B	B-B	B-B	B-B	B-B
Total Weight	246,400 lbs	245,200 lbs	249,000 lbs	248,000	249,000 lbs	246,000 lbs
Weight on Drivers	246,400 lbs	245,200 lbs	249,000 lbs	248,000	249,000 lbs	246,000 lbs
Length over Couplers	53' 6"	52' 8"	56' 2"	56' 2"	54' 8"	52' 7"
Truck Centers	29' 2"	29' 2"	31' 0"	31" 0"	28' 2"	28' 2"
Truck Wheelbase	9' 4"	9' 4"	9' 0"	9' 0"	9' 10"	9' 10"
Engine	Alco 12-244D	Alco 12-244D	EMD 16-567C	EMD 16-567C	Alco 12-251	Alco 12-251
Generator	GE GT-581	GE GT-581	EMD D12B	EMD D12B	GE GT-581	GE GT-581
Traction Motors	GE 752	GE 752	EMD D37 (*)	EMD D37 (*)	W 370DZ	W 370G
Gear Ratio	74:18	74:18	62:15	62:15	63:15	63:12
Maximum Speed	65	65	65 MPH	65 MPH	65 MPH	65 MPH
Starting Trac. Effort	61,600 lbs	61,300 lbs	62,250 lbs	62,000 lbs	62,250 lbs	61.500 lbs
Continuous Trac. Effort	52,500 lbs	52,500 lbs	¥	¥	48,600 lbs	48,600 lbs
CTE Speed	9.5 MPH	9.5 MPH	¥	¥	11.2 MPH	11.2 MPH

(*) Units 7230-7269 and 7230B-7239B originally had EMD D47B traction motors.
(¥) When the model GP9 was introduced, EMD stated that improvements in traction motors made short time ratings unnecessary.

unit. At engine terminals, a unit shuffle could be required to assure a cab unit was on the front end for outbound moves. This negative side of B-unit operation was less of a factor to the PRR when the B-units could be utilized in through freight service, but it became a problem to the successor Penn Central and Conrail when the units had been bumped down to local service.

The Pennsylvania acquired its GP9s in five orders with deliveries spread over five years. The 1750 horsepower, B-B wheel arrangement road-switchers were classed as EFS-17m. These orders are summarized on this page.

Order 5556 was a curiosity since delivery of these fifty units was deferred for about two years. The contract for order 5570 was signed seven months after order 5556, but the units on 5570 were delivered very shortly after order placement. There were two apparent reasons for this situation. First, order 5570 was part of a large 175 unit group that the PRR leased from an EMD subsidiary named El-Mo Leasing Corp. Order 5556 was financed by the PRR itself. Secondly, the economic downturn in 1958 (which was made more acute by a steel strike in that year) resulted in the units in order 5570 being surplus when delivered. Fortunately for the PRR, there was a need on the friendly Norfolk and Western. For almost all of 1958, 30 of the order 5570 GP9s were leased to the N&W. Eighteen of these stayed on well into 1959. It is apparent that the order 5556 units and order 5570

units were not needed for the traffic on the PRR in 1958 and 1959.

EQUIPMENT

The GP9 was to become the biggest seller of the ten new models introduced by EMD at the end of 1954. The V-16 version of the model 567 engine was upgraded to 1750 horsepower for traction. Improved traction generators and motors provided higher ratings. Of the ten new EMD models, the PRR purchased only the GP9, SD9 and SW1200.

The EFS-17m units on the Pennsy were all equipped with one 16-cylinder EMD model 567C engine which provided 1750 horsepower for traction. In common with all model 567 engines, the bore was 8-1/2 inches and the stroke was 10 inches. The main traction gener-

ator was an EMD model D12D. Two models of traction motors were applied to the units as delivered. The first three orders (units 7000 to 7144) were delivered with EMD model D37B traction motors while the remainder of the GP9 units were delivered with EMD model D47B. All were equipped with the 62:15 gear ratio. The cab unit weight was 249,000 lbs, which gave a tractive effort of 62,250 lbs. The booster units weighed 248,000 lbs, which gave a tractive effort of 62,000 lbs. This was both the starting and continuous tractive effort since theoretically the EMD units introduced in 1954 had a zero mph continuous rating.

All of the EMD GP9s were equipped with multiple unit control, air brakes with the pressure maintaining feature and dynamic brakes. All of the cab units

Order Summary - Class EFS-17m

PRR ROAD NUMBERS	EMD ORDER NUMBER	NO. OF UNITS	ORDER DATE	DELIVERY DATES	NOTES
7000-7049	5408	50	May 55	Oct 55-Dec 55	
7050-7104	5461	55	Mar 56	Oct 56-Nov 56	
7105-7144	5541	40	Nov 56	May 57-Jun 57	
7145-7229	5570	85	Nov 57	Nov 57-Dec 57	See note below
7175B-7204B		30	Nov 57	Nov 57-Dec 57	B-units
7230-7269	5556	40	Apr 57	Oct 59-Dec 59	
7230B-7239B		10	Apr 57	Oct 59-Dec 59	B-units

Note: The contract date of order 5570 was November 1, 1957. Delivery of the first unit was November 21, 1957. The builder s date of the 7145 to 7182 group was October, 1957 which indicates that EMD built much of this order before the contract date.

In January 1958, within a month after delivery, these two units posed for the railroad photographer Above, one of 85 GP9 "cab units." Note the single 48-inch fan at the top left, instead of the two 36-inch fans inherited from the GP7 design. Note too, in the photo of GP9 B-unit number 7185B the minimal differences in the hood configuration. A metal plate with a porthole filled in the gap where a cab would have been between the two hoods. The PRR had 40 of these, the only fleet of GP9 B-units other than the Union Pacific.

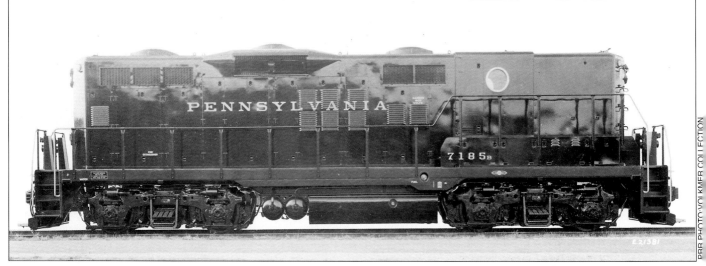

had cab signals. Only units 7000 to 7144 were equipped with trainphone. All units up to 7229A and 7204B were equipped with 24RL brakes while units 7230-7269 and 7230B-7239B were equipped with schedule 26L brakes.

SERVICE HISTORY

The entire EFS-17m class was assigned to Enola maintenance for use in the system freight pool when they were delivered. Their major assignment was to main east-west arranged schedule freight trains. Until late 1962, very few other classes of diesel locomotive were used on these trains west of Enola. The first break in this pattern came in 1964, when some of the Enola GP9s (all cabs) were designated for service on the Northern Region. It should be noted that as the GP9s arrived, most

of the class EF-15 units (EMD model F3) had been assigned to through freights on the Northern Region. Since many of the EF-15 units had been used for EMD trade-ins starting in 1962, the move of the EFS-17m units to the Northern Region is understandable.

In late 1962, the PRR began purchasing second generation units from Alco, GE and EMD. A total of 505 new units were acquired between 1962 and 1968. These units bumped the EFS-17m units from first class freight assignments. Assignment away from Enola for the GP9 cab units started in 1965. By July 1965, 56 were assigned to Conway. In June 1966, 93 were assigned to Conway and 26 to East Altoona.

The 1966 pre-Penn Central renumbering did not change the road numbers of the GP9 cab units on the Pennsy. The

class was changed from EFS-17m to ERS-17. The B-units were renumbered from 7175B-7204B and 7230B-7239B to 3800-3839. The B-units were reclassed as EF-17. This was recognition that these units could not be used as roadswitchers in the strictest sense.

All 310 GP9 units acquired by the PRR did not survive to the Penn Central merger. Three were retired because of wreck damage. Both 7071 and 7129 were damaged beyond economical repair in the Harmarville, Pennsylvania wreck in the early 1960s and were retired in September 1964. The 7225 was involved in the rear-end accident near Mansfield, Ohio in March 1964 and was also retired in September 1964. After the Penn Central merger, the 7095 was in a wreck at Herndon, Pennsylvania and was retired in January 1973. All of the GP9 B-units made it through the PRR and Penn Central years without any retirements and were taken over in the Conrail merger.

Under Conrail, the ex-PRR GP9 fleet has had a varied history. First, Conrail's primary assignment of the GP9 B-units was as hump pushers in MU with cab units. All of the B-units were retired between 1979 and 1981. The ex-PRR GP9 cab units have met a variety of fates on Conrail. First, most of them have been retired, starting in 1979. Those not scrapped or rebuilt were sold or returned to the lessor. As a result, former PRR GP9s have seen further service on C&NW, Atlantic Northwestern, New Jersey Transit, SEPTA and Pocono Northeast. Some units got a heavy in-kind rebuild at Altoona Shops. During these rebuilds, the units were completely rewired and the dynamic brakes removed. Last, another group of the ex-PRR GP9 cab units were given

Above, three of the thirty GP9 units leased to the Norfolk & Western in 1958 appear at Christianburg, Virginia on June 14, 1958. PRR 7224, 7221 and 7210 were leading a westbound non-coal freight train. At the right, N&W GP9 731 awaits a helper assignment.

capital rebuilds. The first 15 Conrail GP9 units to receive this type of rebuild got the complete "Paducah" rebuild by the Illinois Central Gulf at their Paducah, Kentucky backshop. Ten of the 15 units were originally PRR units. In the process, the short hood was chopped and the short end was made the front end. After this rebuild program, a number of additional ex-PRR units were rebuilt by Morrison-Knudson at Boise, the Rock Island at Silvis and more by the ICG at Paducah. This was not as extensive a rebuild as the first Paducah group; the short hood was not lowered. Finally, two ex-PRR GP9 cab units have been placed on display. The first was the 7024, which replaced the K4s steam locomotive at Horseshoe Curve. The second was the 7006 at the Pennsylvania State Railroad Museum at East Strasburg, Pennsylvania.

Above, GP9 7172 (and two sisters) in March 1965, with an eastbound freight approaching Enola yard. 7172 is equipped with one 48-inch fan at the end of the long hood. GP9s numbered below 7145 had two 36-inch fans. This is also an example of the keystone-only lettering scheme, first seen on new units delivered in late 1962.

Right, This GP9B started life as 7195B, and received 3820 in the pre-Penn Central renumbering wave. She is shown coupled to an SD45 at Renovo, Pennsylvania within a month of the Penn Central effective date.

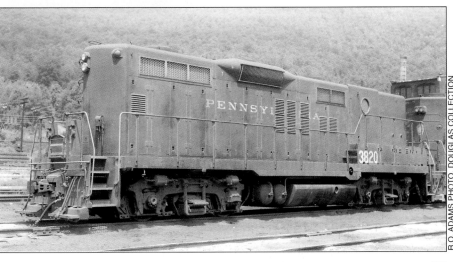

BANGOR AND AROOSTOOK GP7 AND GP9 LEASED UNITS

The lease of GP-7 and GP-9 units to the Pennsylvania Railroad by the Bangor and Aroostook Railroad was an agreement which provided both railroads diesel locomotives during the season of the year when the need was the greatest. From 1951 to end of the PRR's existence, the BAR leased the PRR from eight to fifteen units from mid-May to mid-November of every year. From 1951 to 1953, the agreement provided for ten GP7 units being leased to the PRR. A new agreement in 1954 expanded the agreement to fifteen units every year. This 1954 agreement allowed the BAR to purchase the last five units required for complete diesel operation. These last five units were EMD GP9s and until 1963, these five were leased to the PRR every year. The exception to the lease of fifteen units every year was 1958, when only eight units came south because of reduced traffic requirements on the PRR.

The 1951 agreement provided for the lease of ten GP7s from the BAR to the PRR between May and November. In 1951, BAR units 560-569 were leased. These were from the first order of GP7s (units 560-571) built for the BAR in October and November of 1950. For the

next two years of the agreement, four additional GP7 units were added to the group from which the ten units were drawn. These were road numbers 572-575, built in August, 1952.

Before the 1954 season, the BAR GP7s were renumbered from 560-575 to 60-75. The five GP9s delivered in June, 1954 were numbered 76-80. Until 1965 (the last year for which road numbers of the leased units are known) the five GP9s went to the PRR every year except for 1963, when only two GP9s were in the leased group.

The only year when less than the ten or fifteen units were leased to the PRR was 1958. Traffic that year on the PRR was affected both by recession and by a steel strike. Since the BAR units were all assigned to Erie for handling iron ore traffic, the PRR predicted lower traffic and requested that the lease agreement be modified to cover only eight units instead of fifteen for the year 1958 only. In return, the PRR agreed to extend the 1954 agreement one year to cover the year 1967.

Until 1960, the leased BAR units were all used at Erie at the ore docks. By 1960, this ore traffic had subsided at Erie and the next year the leased BAR

units were assigned to Cleveland and Ashtabula where they were assigned to the ore dock traffic. Later, in the 1960s, the BAR units were assigned further west, in Fort Wayne and Sandusky. The latter assignment ended with the 1964 season when the PRR's Sandusky line was sold to the N&W.

The agreements provided for the Bangor sending the units to the PRR between May 5th and May 15th of each year and for the PRR to return the units between November 5th and November 15th of each year. This was not an absolute requirement and the November return was seldom observed. During the PRR period, the return of the units was quite often delayed until December or January. In 1964-65, BAR 76 was not even returned at all and wintered on the PRR.

The lease agreement to send the BAR units south lasted after the end of the PRR and was extended though the Penn Central era. It was terminated by Conrail. In later years as trucks took over more and more of the Maine potato traffic, the BAR's traffic peak was less pronounced, but the income from the lease kept coming in.

BAR 79 on a radial track in August 1967 at the roundhouse in Fort Wayne, Indiana. PRR GP-9 unit 7205 occupies the adjacent track. Bell and horn placement are the most obvious differences. The BAR unit is short hood forward, while the long hood is the front on the Pennsy unit.

CLASS ABF-18 BALDWIN CAB UNITS, ALCO REPOWERING

The Class ABF-18 cab units were the Pennsylvania Railroad's major attempt to extend the life of diesel locomotives. Three Baldwin wreck-damaged freight units, two As and a B, were taken in hand by Alco for the work. They had been out of service since a collision at Thomson, Pennsylvania in December 1958. In December 1959, Alco replaced the engine, main generator, auxiliary generator, exciter generator and control system with equipment then being installed in its 1800 horsepower, four-axle road-switchers. The installation of sealed beam headlights was an added touch.

The three units were numbered immediately after the class AF-16 Alco freight cab units. Unit 2001A became the 9632A, 9583B became the 9632B and the former 9726A became the 9633A.

After rebuilding, the units were a combination of Baldwin carbody and running gear, Alco engine, GE generators and controls and Westinghouse traction motors. The engine was the Alco V-12 model 251, the generator was the GE GT-581 and the traction motors were Westinghouse model 370 (370-DZ in the A-units and 370-G in the B-unit). The rated tractive effort of the units was similar to a 1600-hp Baldwin freight cab unit. The continuous tractive effort was identical to a class BF-16 but at a somewhat higher speed, 11.2 miles per hour vs. 9.9 miles per hour.

The three units were first tried out on the helper grade out of Williamsport on the Elmira branch. After that, they were in the same secondary freight service pool as the Alco freight cab units. Since the control system was now the same as contemporary Alco road units, the AFB-18s were capable of multiple unit operation with the same models as were the Alcos. They could not operate in multiple unit with Baldwins since they no longer had a Baldwin control system with its air throttle. The ABF-18s did, however, MU with Alcos. This provided those with partial knowledge about compatibility a start to see an apparent Baldwin freight unit in MU with an Alco.

The class ABF-18 units lasted in service for a relatively brief period. The B-unit was retired in May 1965 and the A-units in July 1966. The project to re-engine Baldwin freight units with Alco engines was a trial to determine the feasibility of life extension for these units. From a technical standpoint, the rebuilding was a success, but from a cost standpoint it was not. Aside from the three ABF-18 units, no more Baldwin freight cab units were rebuilt. The trio worked out their lives as oddities.

The PRR 9632A MUed with 9632B at Cresson, Pennsylvania on December 19, 1960. The second unit is identified with class ABF-18 B-unit because the carbody has the features of a class BF-15 unit from which it was rebuilt. The differences between ABF-18 A-unit (rebuilt from class BF-16) and the ABF-18 B-unit (rebuilt from Class BF-15) are apparent.

PRR 9633A and 9632A at Erie, Pennsylvania in October, 1962. The most significant modification to the Baldwin carbody is the use of an Alco fan and radiator, visible in this photograph.

RENOVO, PENNSYLVANIA, NOVEMBER 24, 1966.

Chapter 6

The Second Generation

In A 1962 *Trains* magazine article, editor David P. Morgan defined second generation diesel locomotive models as "those diesels which can economically supplant the diesels which replaced steam." In 1962, after a five year pause in locomotive purchases, the Pennsylvania Railroad began buying new diesels to replace its earliest locomotives, which were becoming less economical to operate as they aged. PRR purchases that year totaled 92 units, from GE, EMD and Alco. General Motors, presumably guided by its automotive instincts, was leading

the way toward a "unit trade-in" concept, which on some railroads extended to the remanufacturing and re-use in new engines of some components from the old ones.

The Pennsylvania never involved itself in extensive remanufacturing. You just did not see traded-in Blomberg trucks under a new Alco or GE unit, or Type B trucks under a new EMD hood unit. The PRR policy was for "all-new" equipment, even though the financial picture was not bright.

More than mere replacement was involved in these purchases; there was

also the opportunity to upgrade. Units of higher horsepower had become available, and improvements in design and components had been made. The second generation also saw the road-switcher carbody becoming universal, replacing the earlier "covered wagon" cab unit design.

True to its relatively narrow concept of service assignments, the Pennsylvania considered its second-generation locomotives (like its GP9s) to be road freight units, not "switchers," in spite of their carbodies and they were classified accordingly.

A U-boat trio, led by PRR 2506, caught in March 1965 at Slope Tower in Altoona, Pennsylvania with a westbound freight. The second and third units, 2535 and 2534, are brand new and do not have the characteristic trainphone antenna that ran the length of so many PRR diesel roofs. The increasingly unreliable trainphone system was soon to be replaced by radios. Newer units came without the trainphone.

Locomotive Characteristics

Class	GF-25	AF-24	EF-22	AF-24a	AF-25	EF-25
Builder	GE	Alco	EMD	Alco	Alco	EMD
Model	U25B	RS-27	GP30	C-424	C-425	GP35
Horsepower	2500	2400	2250	2400	2500	2500
Wheel Arr.	B-B	B-B	B-B	B-B	B-B	B-B
Total Weight	270,090 lbs	260,990 lbs	263,170 lbs	260,000 lbs	268,850 lbs	261,860 lbs
Length over Couplers	60' 2"	57' 3"	56' 2"	58' 10"	59' 4"	56 2
Truck Centers	36' 2"	31' 0"	32' 0"	32' 6"	32' 6"	32 0
Truck Wheelbase	9' 4"	9' 4"	9' 0"	9' 0"	9' 4"	9 0
Engine	GE 16-FDL16	Alco 16-251B	EMD 16-567D3	Alco 16-251	Alco 16-251C	EMD-16-567D3A
Generator	GE GT-598C1	GE GT-564	EMD D22	GE GT-564	GE GT-598D2	EMD D32
Traction Motors	GE 752	GE 752	EMD D57	GE 752	GE 752	EMD D67B1
Gear Ratio	74:18	74:18	62:15	74:18	74:18	62:15
Maximum Speed	70 MPH	70 MPH	71 MPH	70 MPH	70 MPH	71 MPH
Starting Trac. Effort	67,522 lbs	65,248 lbs	65,792 lbs	65,000 lbs	67,212 lbs	65,465 lbs
Continuous Trac. Effort	53,000 lbs	50,800 lbs	50,000 lbs	53,000 lbs	57,200 lbs	51,700 lbs
CTE Speed	14.7 MPH	14.0 MPH	12.0 MPH	14.0 MPH	13.8 MPH	12.0 MPH

CLASS GF-25
GE U25B

Order Summary - Class GF-25				
PRR ROAD NUMBERS	GE SHOP REQUISITION NO.	NO. OF UNITS	ORDER DATE	DELIVERY DATES
2500-2506	320-95203	7	Feb 62	Aug 62
2507-2528	320-95207	22	Aug 62	Sep 62-Oct 62
2529-2533	320-59765	5	Jan 64	Sep 64
2534-2548	320-63177	15	Nov 64	Feb 65-Mar 65
2649-2658	320-65187	10	Aug 65	Nov 65-Dec 65

The diesel locomotive model that best seemed to exemplify the second generation designs was the General Electric U25B. In marketing the U25B, GE offered a design with a higher horsepower (2500 hp) on four axles than Alco or EMD, and including features designed to reduce maintenance.

The U25B diesel was the result of a long development program, started by GE soon after the 1953 dissolution of its joint agreement with Alco for marketing diesel-electric locomotives. An important early event in the new program was the start of work with Cooper-Bessemer on development of a suitable new engine for a road freight diesel. To outside observers, the first visible result of the development program was an A-B-B-A demonstrator/test set of cab units produced in 1954. These were equipped with V-8 engines in each of two units, and V-12 engines in each of the other two units. More demonstrators followed. In 1959, two 2500 horsepower road switcher units were produced with V-16 engines and many of the design

features of the U25B; these were numbered 751 and 752. In 1960, demonstrators 753-756 hit the road with the first 2500 horsepower GE production engines. These were followed the next year by demonstrators 2501-2504. The last two sets of demonstrators were eventually sold to railroads—the 753-756 to the Frisco and the 2501-2504 to the Union Pacific. The GE 2501 was the first U25B built with the now familiar low short hood or chop-nosed arrangement.

The results of the U25B's higher horsepower were touted in a GE advertisement of the period, stating that the Frisco had replaced 17 of its older diesel units with eight U25Bs, and that the U25Bs were averaging between 18,000 and 20,000 miles per month. (That statement by GE as to the extent of mileage improvement on the Frisco

has been characterized as "pure fiction" by an eminent SL-SF diesel expert and author.)

Other GE advertisements during the same period contended that reduced maintenance was achieved by design features new to diesel locomotives. The major new feature was an air cleaning system designed to deliver very clean air for engine combustion and equipment cooling.

In February 1962, GE's 2501-2504 demonstrator set made several trips on the PRR—notably on the premier trailer-train hotshots, TT-1 and TT-2. During the same month the railroad placed an order for seven GE model U25B units. These units, numbered 2500-2506, were purchased with money received in compensation from the federal government because of construction of the Kinzua Dam in northwestern Pennsylvania. The

The first seven GF-25 units were equipped with dual controls and were therefore capable of running long hood forward. Above, PRR 2501 is doing so as it leads a morning westbound freight at the Brickyard Crossing just west of Altoona, Pennsylvania on May 14, 1965.

Below, 2630 suns itself (to use a caption cliché) at Renovo, Pennsylvania in July, 1967. Both the PRR and NYC had numbered their U25B units in the 2500-series. This was resolved in the 1966 renumbering by placing the PRR units in the 2600-series. The last ten PRR U25B units were delivered as 2649-2658. The 2630 seen here in July, 1967 had been the 2530.

waters impounded by the dam covered the PRR's line used by trains from Conway yard near Pittsburgh to Buffalo. Government compensation to the PRR for locomotive power was based on the added power required for running the Conway-Buffalo trains on other PRR lines.

Four more orders for U25B diesels followed in the next three years. The units were classed GF-25 in recognition that despite their road switcher carbodies, these were mainline freight units. The units were numbered 2500 and upward, except for the last order.

The last PRR U25B order was numbered in the 2600 series starting with 2649. This was an early clue to the impending PRR-NYC merger locomotive numbering system. Since the NYC model U25B units were already numbered from 2500-2560, one group would require renumbering. When the U25B units in PRR's August 1965 order were delivered in the 2649 to 2658 number block, it was a good sign that the older class GF-25 units would become 2600-2648, as indeed they did. The PRR class GF-25 orders are detailed in the accompanying table.

EQUIPMENT

All units were equipped with cab signals, dynamic brakes and schedule 26-L air brakes (which included the pressure maintaining feature). Units 2500-2528 were originally equipped with trainphone, but this equipment was removed in 1966 when radio was applied to the engines in that class. The Kinzua Dam-related GF-25 units, 2500-2506, were also equipped with dual control; they had two control stands in the cab, allowing the engineer to run the unit in either direction with controls on the right hand side when facing forward. Units in the 2500-2506 group were occasionally observed leading a set of units running with the long high hood forward, contrary to normal practice.

SERVICE HISTORY

Units 2500-2506 did operate Buffalo-Conway freights immediately after delivery for a few months, but moved to the system pool thereafter. Later PRR U25B units were assigned to the system pool on delivery and were maintained at Enola. New U25B's were to be found on the prestige trains like TT-1 and TT-2 and similar first rank east-west trains.

As time passed, the units could be observed on any freight whose units came from the system pool. Therefore, the class GF-25 units served their time on the PRR on through freights over most of the non-electrified main lines.

As mentioned above, the pre-Penn Central renumbering changed the road numbers of PRR 2500-2548 to 2600-2648. The GF-25 classification was unchanged and in fact was also applied to the NYC U25B units.

All of the ex-PRR class GF-25 units were active throughout the Penn Central period with two exceptions. The 2603 was retired in January 1973 after sustaining heavy wreck damage. Late in the PC period, the 2653 was heavily damaged in a wreck at Archbold, Ohio in February 1976. It was the first ex-PRR GF-25 unit to be retired by Conrail—in June 1976. Between 1978 and 1983 the ex-PRR U25B's were retired in small groups. Conrail retirements of PRR U25Bs proceeded as follows during that period: one in 1978, one in 1979, eight in 1980, five in 1981, three in 1982 and five in 1983. All of the remaining units in the group were retired in 1984, the last on November 7.

Fifteen Alco model RS-27's were ordered by the Pennsylvania Railroad in September 1962 on Alco sales order 21170, and delivered in October 1962. The fifteen model PA-1 and PB-1 class AFP-20 units were traded in on the AF-27s.

The RS-27 locomotives were four-axle, high horsepower improved designs. It must be noted that the 2400-hp. Alco RS-27, having been introduced before the other builders' new models, was not completely competitive in design with the GE U25B and the EMD GP30. The air system was not the fully contained "cleaner air" system used by GE and EMD. These features were introduced by Alco in its Century series in 1963.

The PRR's Alco model RS-27's were class AF-24 and were numbered 2400-2414.

SERVICE HISTORY

The AF-24 units were delivered to Enola and were initially used on the main east-west high-class freights such as TT-1 and TT-2. With the arrival of more EMD GP-30's, EMD GP-35's and GE U25B's, the class AF-24 units were bumped down to the general freight unit pool operating out of Enola. In this pool the AF-24 units could be found on

Two-year old AF-24 2409 is MUed with two EMD B-units to pull an ore jenny train past a storage yard east of Altoona. Date is October 9, 1964. That's not a recently renumbered unit; the crews just cleaned off a spot on the filthy cab side so they could read the number.

Alco RS-27 2400 is in Chicago; it's March 27, 1966. But it's still wearing the paint scheme which it was delivered in four years earlier. This was one of the first groups of PRR diesels to have the "keystone only" identification rather than the name of the railroad.

almost any PRR mainline and many secondary lines. The AF-24 units were used for more than sixteen years on the PRR, the Penn Central, and finally by Conrail. Conrail retired most of the units in 1978, but the 2401 lasted until 1979 and the 2407 (renumbered 5099) wasn't retired until March 1980.

During their service on the PRR, the Class AF-24 units averaged a total of 470,000 miles and two of the class operated more than a half million miles. The average mileage for the class for 64 months of PRR service was 7427 miles per month. This was greater than the 6124 average miles per month that the first seven class GE U25B units turned during their 66 months of PRR service. As a comparison, a unit in first class east-west service could be expected to average more than 10,000 miles per month.

A group of PRR diesels hauls an eastbound freight past Fairhope Tower just east of Canton, Ohio. GP30 2245 leads; second unit is 2273, a GP35 (Class EF25). It's June 7, 1964.

CLASS EF-22
EMD GP30

Delivery of the first EMD model GP30 in April 1962 to the Reading Railroad brought the three-way competitive picture of the second-generation diesel locomotive market into sharp focus. By then, GE had been shipping their 2500-hp U25B units for almost nine months and Alco's four-axle, 2400-hp model RS-27 had been working on several roads since late 1959.

Even with the delivery of the first production GP30, Electro-Motive was not only late in getting to the market, but it was behind in the "horsepower race," with only 2250.

The new EMD entry still used the model 567 engine. To achieve higher horsepower, the old war-horse required turbocharging, which was also used on both the GE and Alco second generation units. The EMD 567 engine had always been equipped with Roots blower because the two-stroke cycle requires an external device to purge the exhaust gasses at the end of the power stroke.

The PRR placed only one order for EMD GP30s, purchasing 52 of them in November 1962. First-generation units were traded in. (Remember, the PRR had also ordered 15 Alco RS-27 units in

September 1962 and 27 GE U25B units in February and August 1962.) The GP30 units were delivered on EMD sales order 7643 between February and May of 1963. They were numbered 2200 to 2251 and classed EF-22.

Special equipment included dynamic brakes, cab signals and trainphone.

SERVICE HISTORY

The EF-22 units were assigned all their PRR lives to the Enola system freight pool. Their life on the PRR was only a little more than five years. Early in the period they were found primarily on the main east-west freights. Within a few years, they were moved down to more general service by newer units. This general service extended to most of the railroad.

In 1966, only two of the class were renumbered. Units 2250 and 2251 were renumbered 2198 and 2199. This made it possible to number all of the GP35 units from the PRR and the NYC in the 2250 to 2399 block of road numbers. The NYC's ten GP30 units were numbered from 2188 to 2197. The GP30's remained in class EF-22.

The entire PRR GP30 fleet remained intact throughout the Penn Central period and became Conrail units on April 1, 1976, without renumbering. Conrail subsequently retired all GP30s.

2223 heads an eastbound Trailer Train in August 1964, crossing the Brickyard Crossing west of Altoona.

In June 1963, about a month after delivery from LaGrange, PRR EF-22 No. 2240 poses at 59th St. engine terminal, Chicago.

W.D. VOLKMER PHOTO

CLASS AF-24a
ALCO C-424

The PRR owned only one Century 424 unit, classed AF-24a. The unit was a true C-424, but it was a special case since much of the mechanical and electrical equipment was re-used from Alco model RS-27 demonstrator 640-1. The 2415 was ordered in April 1963 on Alco sales order 21189 and delivered in September 1963.

EQUIPMENT

The four axle, 2400 horsepower Century 424 was one of the original Century series of locomotive models that Alco introduced in early 1963, as the company sought to match the 1962 design improvements made by GE and EMD. On the Century 424, the engine, main traction generator, control system and traction motors were virtually the same as the RS-27. The big change was the redesigned carbody, which accommodated the improved air handling system, designed to draw in air through inertial filters prior to being used for engine combustion and cooling of equipment. The air for these purposes was pressurized at intake and completely ducted from intake to exhaust to maintain air cleanliness.

One of the more interesting aspects of the Alco air system design was the use of a duct in the center sill to direct clean air to the traction motors for cooling. Air for traction motor cooling was drawn into the system through an intake in the roof right behind the cab, through the air blower, down into the space between the two heavy I-beams that formed the frame center sill and finally carried to the traction motors using the frame as an air duct. The Alco main floor frame differed from the GE frame in that the Alco center sill was the main strength member. On a four axle GE U-boat, several parallel I-beams made up the main frame longitudinal members.

SERVICE HISTORY

On the PRR, the 2415 was the only example of the Century 424. It was in the same general freight service as the Class AF-24, model RS-27's and the Class AF-25, Century 425.

In common with the AF-24 and AF-25 units, the 2415 worked its way from its start as a PRR locomotive through the entire Penn Central era and finally ended its service as a Conrail unit. On Conrail it was renumbered 2474 and was retired in November 1978.

This was not the end for the former PRR 2415. After its Conrail retirement, the unit was sold to the GE Hornell operation. The unit was given a heavy rebuild and became Green Bay and Western 319.

The Pennsylvania's lone Century 424, No. 2415. The emblem under the road number on the cab side indicates that the radio equipment replacing the train phone has been installed. The trainphone antenna is gone. On this unit when built, the limited clearance caused by the high hoods meant that the antenna was not a "fence," but only a wire, as close to the hood as possible. Renovo, Pennsylvania in February 1967.

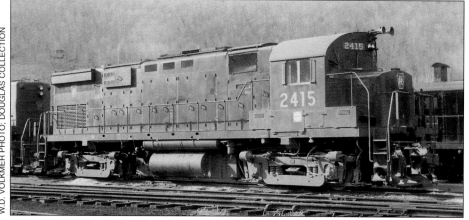

W.D. VOLKMER PHOTO; DOUGLAS COLLECTION

CLASS AF-25
ALCO C-425

In 1964 and 1965, the Pennsylvania Railroad continued to purchase Alco four axle road units. Two orders were placed: 21 units in November 1964 (Alco sales order 21214) and 10 units in August 1965 (Alco sales order 21247). The units on the first order became road numbers 2416-2436 and the second order units became road numbers 2437-2446. These were the model Century 425 and were class AF-25 on the PRR.

Alco C-425 2417 was at Northumberland, Pennsylvania in September 1965. Note absence of the trainphone antenna; these units were delivered without trainphone.

W.D. VOLKMER PHOTO; DOUGLAS COLLECTION

EQUIPMENT

The four axle, 2500 horsepower Century 425 was perceived as a unit with a somewhat more robust main traction generator than the Century 424. Whereas the Century 424 used a main generator which was originally used in the early 1950s on 1500 and 1600-hp. four axle Alco units, the Century 425 used a new generator which was basically the same as the generator used on GE model U25B and U25C.

The main generator used on the Century 425 was the GE model GT-598D2 unit. The GE model U25B and U25C used the GE GT-598C1 and GT-598C4 generators respectively. The difference between the GT-598C (both variations 1 and 4) and the GT-598D2 accommodated the 50 RPM speed difference on the Alco and GE engines at

full horsepower. The GT-598 permitted the four-step transition instead of the problem plagued multi-step controllers used on Alco RS-27 and Century 424.

All of the units in the class were equipped with cab signals, radio (after late 1966) and dynamic brakes.

SERVICE HISTORY

The class was all assigned to Enola for maintenance after delivery. Their assignments were the system freight pool. When they were new, they were often seen on piggyback trains (typical of new four-axle units) but later ordinary boxcar freights and coal service assignments were common. In March 1966, the class was assigned to Conway for maintenance.

The 1966 renumbering and reclassification did not change the Century 425s. They entered Penn Central service in 1968 and were relettered to the PC image in due time. In Penn Central service they were joined by the ten former New Haven Century 425s (2450-2459), which also did not need to be renumbered by PC. All of the class AF-25's continued for the entire Penn Central period and entered Conrail service in April 1976. They initially retained their original numbers. In 1979, all were renumbered to the 5060-5088 series.

Starting in September 1977 with the retirement of 2424, the ranks of the class started to thin. The remaining units were retired by October 1981.

AF-25 No. 2443 on January 20, 1968, eleven days before Penn Central. We are shivering at West Brownsville. Pennsylvania, where loaded hoppers were received from the Monongahela Railway.

CLASS EF-25
EMD GP35

Order Summary - Class EF-25 Units				
PRR ROAD NUMBERS	EMD ORDER NUMBER	NO. OF UNITS	ORDER DATE	DELIVERY DATES
2252-2296	7713	45	Jan 64	May 64-Jun 64
2297-2298	7753	2	May 64	Nov 64
2299-2310	7765	12	May 64	Nov 64
2311-2370	7793	60	Nov 64	Jan 65-Apr 65

In 1964, the Pennsylvania Railroad ordered its last four axle units. In the remaining three-plus years of PRR's existence, only six-axle units were ordered. Thus, for example, the PRR had no GP40's, however popular that model may have been elsewhere.

The PRR placed orders for a total of 119 GP35s in January, May and November 1964. All were classed EF-25. The GP35 represented EMD's makeover of the model GP30. Two obvious changes were made. The first was an increase in horsepower to 2500 to meet Alco and GE competition. The second was the simplification of the carbody using the squared off and angular cab which has been used by EMD in several forms to the present.

Special equipment included cab signals and dynamic brakes. There was no trainphone; by 1964, radio was in the immediate future for the PRR. Installation of radios began late in 1966.

The class EF-25 units followed the EF-22 units in the Enola system freight pool, and were used throughout the system. This assignment was not changed during the PRR period.

The 1966 renumbering affected relatively few of the GP35 units. Units 2309 and 2310 were renumbered 2250 and 2251. Units 2369 and 2370 were renumbered to 2309 and 2310. This move accomplished two things. First, the combined PRR and NYC GP35 fleet was placed in the 2250 to 2399 number block. Additionally, the units in the PRR January, May and November 1964 orders remained in the same number blocks.

All of the PRR GP35's were passed on to Penn Central on February 1, 1968. The same cannot be said of the Penn Central to Conrail transfer. Units 2253, 2318 and 2352 were retired by PC due to wreck damage. Starting in 1981, Conrail retired all of the ex-PRR GP35's. The 2363 was de-turboed in November 1984 and rated at 2000 horsepower for traction.

CLASS EF-25a
EMD SD35

The 40 Class EF-25a EMD model SD35 units were part of the PRR's first group of six-axle road-switchers assigned to through freight service. Until the arrival of the new six-axle units in early 1965, almost all of the PRR's six-axle motive power had been used as heavy switchers, hump pushers or helper units. The forty Class EF-25a units were ordered in November 1965 on EMD order 7795. They arrived between February and May 1965, numbered 6000-6039. This was the first use of the 6000 road number series for PRR diesels. When the PRR re-numbered diesels in 1966 in preparation for the Penn Central merger, all six-axle units were re-numbered into the 6000s.

The SD35 was EMD's companion unit to the four-axle GP35, and was the first six-axle road-switcher to incorporate EMD's second-generation features. (The GP30 had been EMD's first second-generation road-switcher, but it had no companion six-axle model.)

EMD increased the horsepower of its second generation units by turbocharg-

An EMD GP35, No. 2309, pairs with Alco Century 425 No. 2420 to bring joy to children of all ages. They are hauling a circus train; wagons, animals, performers, and popcorn. Location is Northumberland, Pennsylvania, in October 1965. The diesels are less than a year old.

The EMD units pictured on this page are General Motors' response to the higher horsepower of the GE and Alco second generation models. In the GM line, they replaced the GP30 (PRR class EF-22) and the six-axle SD24, which the Penn never purchased. At Left, GP35 (EF-25) No. 2257 leads a three-unit set on a westbound freight train at Wilmerding, Pennsylvania, in May 1967. The large building in the background is the Westinghouse Air Brake plant.
Below, shiny new SD35 (class EF-25a) 6016 as she was delivered in March 1965 at Riverdale, Illinois.

ing the model 567 engine. The SD35 also had the enclosed and ducted air system that improved the cleanliness of cooling air for the engine and electrical equipment.

Because the Class EF-25a units arrived in early 1965, they served the PRR for not quite three years. Assigned to

Conway for maintenance, they were used system-wide in mainline freight. In addition to through freight service, the SD35s could be found in coal train service in the Altoona area and in iron ore service in Cleveland. These assignments were unchanged during the entire PRR period of service.

The 1966 renumbering resulted in neither a change in road number nor reclassification for the Class EF-25a units. The class served through the Penn Central without retirement and well into the Conrail period, again without renumbering. Conrail retired the entire class during 1983 and 1984.

PRR 6300 and 6301, Class AF-27, had been on the property less than a month when this photo was taken in April 1965. They displaced the Class AS-18am units from helper duty on the East Slope from Altoona to Gallitzin. The ten Century 628's replaced the 25 RSD-12's. This pair is running light, on its way back to Altoona for another push. They are stopped at the Slope Tower home signal, awaiting clearance to proceed.

CLASS AF-27
ALCO C-628

In November 1964, the Pennsylvania Railroad placed orders for 156 new locomotives. This order included six axle units in the 2500-2750 horsepower range from all three active builders—Alco, GE and EMD. Alco's meager share of the six axle unit orders was ten Century 628 locomotives, which Alco had first offered a year before.

In early 1963 Alco had announced the Century line of diesel locomotives. The original Alco Century line consisted of the Century 420, the Century 424 and the Century 624. The 624 was a six-axle, 2400 horsepower unit for which Alco re-

ceived no immediate orders. Late in 1963, Alco announced the 2750 horse-power Century 628, to replace the Century 624. The PRR order for Century 628's (Alco sales order 21215) was the seventh order for the model. Previously, single orders had been placed by the Monon, Louisville and Nashville, Delaware and Hudson, Alco (for four demonstrators), and two orders by the Atlantic Coast Line. The PRR's Century 628's were delivered in March 1965, numbered 6300-6309 and classed AF-27. A further five were ordered in August 1965 (Alco sales order 21248) and delivered in the last two months of 1965. The last five AF-27 units were numbered 6310-6314.

EQUIPMENT

The class AF-27 on the PRR had the model's standard equipment; the Alco

16 cylinder model 251-C engine, the GE GT-586 main traction generator and six GE 752 traction motors. Revision "C" of Alco's 251 engine represented an increase of 350 horsepower to 2750 traction horsepower, achieved by three basic changes in the engine. The first was a 50-rpm increase in maximum full power crankshaft speed from 1000 to 1050 rpm. The second was an increase in the injection pump bore from 15 to 16 millimeters. The third was a change in the fuel injection nozzle hole size from .325 to .350 millimeters. These changes increased the horsepower by increasing the amount of fuel fed to the engine at full power.

The GT-586 generator had first been used on the six-axle, 1800-hp model RSD-12. It was also used in the six-axle, 2400-hp model RSD-7 and RSD-15 Alco road-switchers. That a main generator

Locomotive Characteristics

Class	EF-25a	AF-27	GF-25a	EF-30a	GF-28a	GF-30a	AF-30	EF-36
Builder	EMD	Alco	GE	EMD	GE	GE	Alco	EMD
Model	SD35	C-628	U25C	SD40	U28C	U30C	C-630	SD45
Horsepower	2500	2750	2500	3000	2800	3000	3000	3600
Wheel Arr,	C-C	C-C	C-C	C-C	C-C	C-C	C-C	C-C
Total Weight	388,550 lbs	389,200 lbs	385,500 lbs	391,000 lbs	395,500 lbs	395,500 lbs	391,500 lbs	389,000 lbs
Length over Couplers	68' 8"	69' 6"	64' 6"	65' 8"	67' 3"	67' 3"	69' 6"	65' 8"
Truckbase	35' 0"	46' 5"	42' 0"	40' 0"	40' 11"	40' 11"	46 5"	40' 0"
Truck Wheelbase	13' 7"	12' 6"	13' 0"	13' 7"	13' 7"	13' 7"	12' 6"	13' 7"
Engine	EMD 16-567D3A	Alco 16-251C	GE 16-FDL16	EMD 16-645E3	GE 16-FDL16	GE 16-FDL16	Alco 16-251E	EMD 20-645E
Generator	EMD D32	GE GT-586	GE GT-598C4	EMD AR10	GE GTA-9	GE GTA-9	GE GTA-981	EMD AR10
Traction Motors	EMD D67B1	GE 752	GE 752	EMD D77	GE 752	GE 752	GE 752	EMD D77
Gear Ratio	62:15	74:18	74:18	62:15	74:18	74:18	74:18	62:15
Maximum Speed	71 MPH	70 MPH	70 MPH	71 MPH	70 MPH	70 MPH	70 MPH	71 MPH
Starting Trac. Effort	97,135 lbs	97,300 lbs	96,375 lbs	97,750 lbs	98,875 lbs	98,875 lbs	97,895 lbs	97,250 lbs
Continuous Trac. Effort	75,000 lbs	85,800 lbs	85,000 lbs	82,000 lbs	85,800 lbs	85,800 lbs	90,600 lbs	82,100 lbs
CTE Speed	9.4 MPH	9.5 MPH	8.3 MPH	11.1 MPH	9.5 MPH	9.5 MPH	9.9 MPH	11.1 MPH

Unit 6313 retains its Pennsylvania livery, but less than five months after the merger, the second unit has already been painted in the Penn-Central (absence of) colors. The four units are in Rochester, Pennsylvania in June 1968, westbound with pigs.

designed originally for an 1800 horse-power locomotive could be used with a 2750-hp. unit was a tribute to the generous capacity of the original design.

SERVICE HISTORY

The first assignment of the original ten class AF-27's was as East Slope helpers west out of Altoona. The East Slope helpers were used on freights from Altoona (usually coupled on at Rose tower in East Altoona) to Gallitzin at the top of the grade above Horseshoe Curve.

The standard helper set was two AF-27 units, together exerting a tractive effort of 171,600 lbs at the 9.5-mph continuous tractive effort speed. This was actually slightly more than the 165,000

lbs. at 9.5-mph rating of the three-unit AS-18am sets that each pair of AF-27 units replaced. While three AS-18am units had a higher tractive effort at a lower speed (238,500 lbs. continuous at 6 mph,) the continuous rating of the road units being helped was somewhat above 10 mph. The mismatch in CTE speeds between road units and the old AS-18am units could slow down the road sets to speeds below their safe continuous rating speed and motor amperages. That condition pushed the short time ratings and shortened the motor life on the road units. The AF-27s represented a better match.

In this service only about 2000 miles per month were accumulated. After about a year, the AF-27s were trans-

ferred to Conway maintenance and used primarily in iron ore and coal traffic, mostly in an area bounded by Cleveland, Mingo Junction (near Steubenville, Ohio), and Altoona. Although the AF-27's wandered out of this area with regularity, this was the main assignment.

All the class AF-27's went on to both the Penn Central in February 1968 and Conrail in April 1976. The units were not renumbered by Penn Central but became 6738 to 6752 on Conrail. On Conrail the Century 628's were still used in the Cleveland to Mingo Junction iron ore service. The first unit was retired in November 1977 and the last in December 1980. A few were repainted in Conrail blue.

PRR units 6517, 6509 and 6510 form a matched trio of GF-25a units power a Trailer Train hotshot through Wilmerding, Pennsylvania on May 22, 1965. Leading unit 6517 and trailing unit 6510 were from the second group of PRR U25Cs, while the second unit was from the first group.

Unit 6504 at Northumberland, October 6, 1965. This was one of the first group of GF25a locomotives delivered, six months previously. In this two-order cycle, the PRR bought 15 six-axle Alco C628's, 20 GE U25C's, and 105 EMD SD35's and SD40's.

CLASS GF-25a
GE U25C

The General Electric model U25C diesel locomotive was the six axle design that evolved from the four axle U25B. The first U25C units were shipped to the Oro Dam Constructors in California in September 1963. Oro Dam 8013 stopped off at the Chicago Railroad Fair in October sharing the GE locomotive display with Rock Island 213 (a U25B) and UP 31 (a U50).

The six axle GE fell right into the Pennsylvania's 1964-65 motive power plans. A little more than a year after the shipment of the first U25C, the PRR placed a 150 unit order with GE, Alco and EMD. Sixty of these were six axle units, also divided between the three builders. The PRR placed two orders for U25C's, each for ten units. The first order (6500-6509) was placed in November 1964; delivery was made in April 1965. The second order (6510-6519) was placed in August 1965, with delivery in November and December 1965. The Pennsy classed them GF-25a.

EQUIPMENT

The layout of equipment for the U25C was virtually identical to the U25B. The length of the U25C was 64' 6" compared to the U25B length of 60' 2",

because of the longer trucks. Inside the long hood of a U25B, the equipment was quite close to the rear bulkhead of the cab. On a U25C, there was sufficient room for installation of a steam boiler, but no U25C was ever so-equipped. In most U25C's, this space was used for a crew toilet. In the U25B, the toilet was located in the short hood. Locating of the toilet behind the cab in the U25C made it possible to equip the six-axle units with a shorter nose. The arrangement of the equipment behind the air compressor was virtually identical on both the U25C and U25B. This equipment (from front to rear) included the air compressor, main and auxiliary generators, engine, radiators and cooling fans.

SERVICE HISTORY

Like most of the U25B's, the U25C's on the PRR were assigned to the system pool at Enola for operation and maintenance. This meant that they were to be seen on most of the PRR mainlines in freight service. Although six axle units are associated with heavy services (coal and iron ore trains on the PRR), these units were seen in trailer trains in addition to drag service. The units also were used on the helper services west of Altoona.

The renumbering of PRR units in preparation for the Penn Central merger did not affect the GE U25C's. They remained numbered 6500-6519 and classed GF-25a.

Neither the Pennsylvania Railroad nor the Penn Central retired any Class GF-25a units. The GE U25C's entered Conrail service intact and without renumbering. In 1979 the twenty units were renumbered from 6500-6519 to 6800-6819 to make room for new GE units. Conrail retired 6813 and 6817 in December 1980. All of the remainder of the class GF-25a units were retired by Conrail in April 1983.

CLASS EF-30a
EMD SD40

In June 1965, EMD introduced a completely new line of diesel locomotives, incorporating significant mechanical and electrical changes. However, from the nine new models EMD offered, the PRR's September 1965 order only included the model SD40 six axle, 3000 horsepower road switcher.

The SD40 was the first EMD six-axle diesel locomotive whose maximum continuous tractive effort (CTE) speed was almost the same as its companion four-axle model. In the 1965 models, the SD40 had a rated CTE of 82,000 lbs at 11.1 mph while the four-axle GP40 had a rated CTE of 51,200 lbs at 11.3 mph. In the predecessor SD35, the CTE was 75000 lbs at 9.4 mph. The four-axle GP35 had a CTE of 51,700 lbs at 12 mph.

Since this mismatch also was characteristic of Alco and GE four and six-axle units, operation of mixed four and six-axle units within the CTE rating of the six-axle units could exceed the rating of the four-axle unit. Therefore, in considering the 1965 purchase, it was possible for the PRR to make a valid comparison between two SD40 units with a total of 164,000 lbs tractive effort at the CTE rated speed, and three GP40s with a total of 155,000 lbs tractive effort at the same speed. The PRR never ordered GP40s.

A total of 65 EMD model SD40's were ordered by the PRR in September 1965 on Order No. 7862, delivered in February and March 1966, numbered 6040 to 6104 and classed EF-30a.

Above, SD40 6074 heads a decidedly non-hotshot freight west of Columbus, Ohio on a hot summer day in August 1966. These units were at home on any kind of service, a blessing to the motive power assignment clerks released from the traditional shackles of the Pennsylvania's "dedicated unit for a given service" approach to locomotives.

THE EMD IMPROVEMENTS

Seldom had the ElectroMotive Division made such significant changes as those made in the new models introduced in June 1965.

The venerable Model 567 engine was at last replaced after being manufactured for 27 years. The direct current main traction power system was replaced by a more competitive alternating current (AC-DC) system, described on Page 111.

The new engine was designated Model 645. The external dimensions of the power assemblies (the cylinder liner, cylinder head and piston) were unchanged from the 567, but there were major improvements, including a cylinder bore increase from 8-1/2" to 9-1/16", resulting in a displacement *in each cylinder* of 645 cubic inches. (For comparison, the three-liter engine in a current passenger automobile displaces about 183 cubic inches in the *entire engine*.)

The new engine also had a heavier frame, a higher capacity turbo-charger and increased cooling capacity because of a higher capacity water pump and larger water manifolds. These changes increased the horsepower of the 16-cylinder version of the engine from 2500 to 3000. Unchanged were the 10" stroke, the cylinder spacing, the crankshaft and the compression ratios of both the turbocharged and blower-aspirated versions of the engines.

EMD's D32 DC generator in the 2500-hp units had reached the limits of space available in the road-switcher body. The new AR10 alternator in the 3000-hp units not only fit into the required space but also was rated at 4000 amperes compared to the 2600 ampere rating of the D32 DC machine.

The traction motors were also improved and increased in rating. EMD had worked with DuPont on motor insulation and the result was an improved insulating sheet material, which DuPont named Kapton, with ten times the dielectric strength of mica insulation. Kapton's greater insulating capability allowed for thinner layers of insulation, which in turn made it possible to build the new D77 traction motor with 18 percent more copper windings in the same space as that used in the previous D67 motor design. This increased the electrical capacity of the traction motor.

SERVICE HISTORY

The SD40 units served the Pennsylvania Railroad just short of two years. They were assigned to Enola for maintenance and service in the system pool. This meant that their operating assignments were system wide, primarily in mainline freight service.

The Class EF-30a's were neither renumbered nor reclassed in the 1966 renumbering plan, which preceded the Penn Central merger. They worked through the Penn Central period in the same general service as during their brief PRR ownership. All but one of the former PRR SD40 units made it to Conrail ownership. The exception was the 6072, which was severely damaged in the Leetonia, Ohio wreck of June 1975. This unit was not conveyed to Conrail. After the Conrail merger, the group was renumbered from 6040-6104 to 6293-6357 less the 6325, which would have been the number slot of the PRR/PC 6072.

Below, the profile of power is displayed by EF-30a 6060 at Pitcairn engine terminal, Wall, Pennsylvania on a Sunday four days before Thanksgiving, 1966.

A quick comparison of the two types of truck underneath the GE U28C (GF28a) and U30C (GF30a) locomotives. Above, the Adirondack; below, the General Steel Industries design.

CLASS GF-28a and GF-30a
GE U28C and U30C

In its 1966 and 1967 locomotive purchase programs, the PRR bought only high horsepower, six-axle units from Alco, EMD and GE. Twenty GE model U28C's were ordered as part of the 1966 program. The units ordered from GE in April 1966 had the lowest horsepower

of the three builders. When the 1966 order was placed, the highest horsepower that GE had available in a single engine unit was 2800. Alco offered the 3000-hp Century 630 diesels, while EMD had the 3600-hp SD45 units.

The fifteen GE model U28C units were delivered to the Pennsy in September and October 1966, with AC-DC drive. They were numbered 6520 to 6534 and were classed GF-28a. The last five units on the GE U28C order were actually model U30C's, delivered in January and February 1967. They were numbered 6535 to 6539 and were classed GF-30a.

The PRR units weighed 395,500 lbs, resulting in a 98,875-lb starting tractive effort. The class GF-28a and GF-30a's were the heaviest PRR six-axle diesel locomotives. They outweighed the PRR SD-45s by 6500 lbs and the SD-40s by 4500 lbs.

OTHER IMPROVEMENTS

The U28C had a number of detail differences from the U25C, resulting from equipment relocation and arrangement changes. Perhaps the most obvious change was the three axle truck design used on the U28C. The U25C had used a drop equalizer truck which utilized a three point support system between each truck and the locomotive frame. The new truck consisted of the three wheel and axle sets with journals mounted in a cast steel frame. A bolster was mounted on the top of the frame. A GE brochure dated June 1966 uses the term "Floating Bolster" to describe the truck design. The brochure describes this feature as the cast steel bolster which floats on four sandwiches of curved rubber and steel permanently bonded together. These bolster mounts, along with two lateral snubbers, allow controlled lateral motion and excellent high-speed riding qualities. Long life is assured because there are no wearing parts, and the transmission of vibration and road shocks to the cab is greatly reduced.

Two foundries supplied the trucks: Adirondack Steel Casting Co., and General Steel Industries, Inc. Although structurally the same, trucks from the two foundries each had their own distinctive appearance. The PRR Class GF-28a (and GF-30a) units used trucks

Only five U30C locomotives were built for the PRR; here is unit 6538 (Adirondack truck) eight months into the Penn Central era, at Gallitzin, Pennsylvania.

The AC – DC Transmission

As the mid-1960s approached, American diesel locomotive builders were marketing the advantages of higher unit horsepower. By 1964, GE (which started the horsepower race in 1961) was still shipping the 2500 horsepower U25C and U25B. Alco had responded with the 2750-hp Century 628, while EMD was selling the 2500-hp SD35 and GP35.In December 1964, Alco accepted an order from the Atlantic Coast Line for three Century 630 units, rated at 3000 horsepower for traction. These units were the first to be equipped with an AC-DC transmission system, using GE electrical equipment. In an AC-DC system, the diesel engine drives an alternating current (AC) generator (or alternator), after which silicon rectifiers convert the power to direct current (DC) to drive the traction motors. The system's heart is the control circuitry to smooth out the DC for use in the traction motors. AC-DC systems became both necessary and advantageous because DC traction generator designs for 2800 horsepower had reached the size limit that could be installed in a diesel locomotive. Also, an AC alternator does not require a commutator for picking up the current from its rotor, eliminating a high maintenance item. The AC-DC traction power system for locomotives was made possible by the development of solid state silicon rectifiers. These rugged and dependable devices had been introduced into locomotive service in the early 1960s and

succeeded the less rugged mercury arc rectifiers used previously in electric locomotives. In the 3000-hp EMD models introduced in 1965, two banks of 30 silicon rectifier diodes each were mounted on the front face of the alternator (i.e. the end opposite the engine). Because those 60 rectifiers supplied a surplus capacity, a diode failure did not cause the locomotive to shut down. EMD recommended periodic inspection and replacement of any defective diodes to keep the required minimum number of diodes in service at any one time.Alco delivered the first Century 630, a six-axle, 3000-hp unit with AC-DC drive, to the Atlantic Coast Line in July 1965. During the previous month, EMD had announced its new line with AC-DC drive, including the 3000-hp model GP40 and SD40 units, and the 3600-hp model SD45.In September, General Electric announced their new 2800-hp U28B and U28C road-switchers, with a straight DC drive. At the time, a trade journal article related GE's justification for staying with DC: "GE points out that the GT-598 direct-currant generator was originally designed for growth beyond 3000-hp output and is conservatively rated at 2800-hp for 1966, that it has established an enviable reputation for trouble-free operation and will remain basically unchanged." Additionally, GE also said that they did not foresee that the space limitations of a higher horsepower DC generator would become a

factor until the unit horsepower reached the range of 3000 to 3500 horsepower in GE locomotives. Someone in GE management must have realized that continuing with straight DC would put GE at a competitive disadvantage. Having helped Alco with their designs, GE was not unaware of the AC-DC system and its benefits. So, when the PRR ordered its first 20 U28C units in April 1966, GE was putting the finishing touches on two prototype 2800-hp, four-axle road-switchers with AC-DC drive. These two units had a builder's date of May 1966; they were followed the next month by two similar units. The four prototypes were then sent out for extensive testing in the real railroad world.

This development was timed particularly well for the PRR. Their 15 model U28C units were the first ones to be delivered with AC-DC drive. What the Penn received were the first U28s with the new GTA-9 main traction generator and the rest of the AC/DC drive equipment. So much for the evolution of the DC drive to 3000 plus horsepower. The last five units of the 20-unit order were delivered as 3000-hp model U30C's. Eventually, the PRR operated 65 model SD40's, 125 model SD45's, 15 GE model U28C units, 5 GE model U30C's, and 15 Alco Century 630's. These 225 AC-DC drive units were all acquired in the last two years of PRR operation.

from both suppliers. In later years the interchangeability of the trucks from the two foundries was demonstrated on a PRR locomotive with one truck from each supplier.

The PRR class GF-28a's were almost the last model U28C's built and the class GF-30a units were almost the first model U30C's built. In between, there were units on other railroads which were transitional in that they were originally designated U28C but identified in later GE documents as model U30C. On the PRR, units of both models had very similar appearance. The PRR purchased no more model U30C's. The 1967 order

to GE included model U33C units but these locomotives were delivered after Penn Central took over operations and these were never part of the Pennsy locomotive roster.

Special equipment on the PRR Class GF-28a and GF-30a units included extended range dynamic brakes and cab signals.

SERVICE HISTORY

The Class GF-28a and GF-30a locomotives were assigned to Enola for maintenance and were used in the system freight pool. Although the uses of these six-axle units included east-west

though freights, their primary use was in the heavy coal and iron ore service which made up a significant percentage of PRR's freight tonnage.

Since the U28C and U30C's were delivered in late 1966 and early 1967, they were numbered at the builder in a number series consistent with the Penn Central system. After 11 to 14 months of PRR service, all of the units in the two classes passed on to Penn Central. Further, on April 1, 1976, all of the units were passed on to Conrail without renumbering. In January 1979, Conrail renumbered them when the acquisition of new SD-40-2 units pushed into the number series above 6520. The U28C's were renumbered 6820 to 6834 and the U30C's were renumbered 6835 to 6839. All units in the two classes were retired by Conrail in November 1984 after eighteen years of service.

Fifteen six axle 3000-hp locomotives comprised Alco's share of the PRR's three April 1966 orders totaling 100 high horsepower six-axle units. The Alco units were ordered on sales order 21273, delivered between October and December 1966, numbered 6315-6329 and classed AF-30.

An orange N-8 caboose trails GF-28a unit 6527 and SD40 6046; the caboose hop is at Pitcairn Yard, 15 miles west of Pittsburgh. The U28C, riding on Adirondack trucks, is less than two months old in this October 1966 photo. The Pennsylvania Railroad, by the way, had about sixteen months to live. The lettering style of the numbers on unit 6527 does not match the PRR standard; GE apparently applied the wrong style lettering, but the PRR inspectors accepted it.

CLASS AF-30
ALCO C-630

The Alco Century 630 locomotive was the first domestic diesel model that utilized an alternating current-direct current transmission instead of a straight direct current transmission. It was a significant development, and it should be noted that Alco was there

first. The Alco Century 630 utilized a 144-silicon diode cell rectifier.

Special equipment included cab signals, extended range dynamic brakes and radio.

SERVICE HISTORY

The Century 630s were assigned to Conway on delivery and were not relocated during the PRR period.

The Class AF-30 units only worked on the PRR for little more than a year before Penn Central. They operated in the system freight pool and were seen

throughout the system.

Because they arrived after the pre-Penn Central renumbering, the C-630s had no reason to be renumbered or reclassed. The class operated intact throughout the Penn Central era and right into Conrail service.

The entire class was renumbered by Conrail. Road numbers 6315 to 6329 became Conrail 6765 to 6779. All were retired between May 1979 and March 1981, In later PC and Conrail service, the class was primarily used in ore service from Cleveland to Mingo Jct.

It's Sunday, October 30, 1966. C-630 No. 6316 is stopped momentarily going through Pitcairn (Pennsylvania) Yard on her very first westbound trip after delivery at Enola from Alco (with the correct style numbers).

C-630 6328 and another unit with a train including auto racks and piggyback cars eastbound at Cavittsville, Pennsylvania, just east of Pitcairn Yard. Photo dates to May 1967, before auto racks were enclosed with rock guard grills.

CLASS EF-36
EMD SD45

The 1966 and 1967 locomotive orders of the Pennsylvania Railroad consisted entirely of six-axle road switchers in the 2800-3600 horsepower range. More than half of them were EMD model SD45. All of the GE 3300-hp model U33C and Alco 3600 horsepower Century 636 units ordered by the PRR were delivered after February 1, 1968 to Penn Central. All but five of the EMD 3600 horsepower model SD45 units arrived on January 31, 1968 or earlier. It is obvious that in its last few years the PRR was committed to high horsepower, six-axle road switchers for freight service.

Both the SD40 and SD45 were built on frames of the same length. The SD45 appeared larger since the hoods extended over a greater length of the frame. In addition, to achieve greater radiator cooling area, the SD45 radiators were set on an angle from the vertical that allowed more radiator height within the same vertical dimension used in the SD40. The outward flare of the radiators on the long hood of the SD45s contributed to the more bulky look of the units.

EMD had announced the SD45 in June 1965 in its new line of locomotives using the new 645 engine. The SD45 engine was a V-20, an extrapolation of the V-16, which had previously been

A northbound freight near Renovo, Pennsylvania is headed by SD45 unit No. 6113 in April 1967. An SD40 and a GP9 B-unit are second and third in the set.

Order Summary - Class EF-36 Units

PRR ROAD NUMBERS	EMD ORDER NUMBER	NO. OF UNITS	ORDER DATE	DELIVERY DATES	NOTES
6105-6169	7928	65	Apr 1966	Oct 66-Jan 67	
6170-6194, 6196-6199 6210-6234	7993	54	Oct 1967	Dec, 67-Feb 68	
6200, 6202, 6204, 6206, 6208	7090	5	Oct 1967	Jan 68	Radio control master units
6205	7091	1	Oct 1967	Jan 68-Mar 68	Radio control slave units

Units, 6195 (order 7993), 6203, 6207 and 6209 (order 7091) were delivered after January 1, 1968 and were never PRR-owned units.

EMD's largest engine. The PRR did not include the new SD45 in its orders placed in August 1965, ordering 65 SD40's at that time. This was to be the only PRR order for SD40s.

Details of the two groups of SD45's ordered by the PRR are shown in the accompanying Order Summary Table.

The five class EF-36 units delivered on February 1, 1968 or later were 6195, 6201, 6203, 6207 and 6209. These were never owned by the Pennsylvania Railroad and are therefore not included in the roster in this publication. Delivery of the 6207, the last unit on the October 1967 order, was made to Penn Central on March 3, 1968.

The PRR class EF-36's were equipped with a V-20 model 645E engine, along with a model AR10 alternator as the main traction generator. Six model D77 traction motors with a 62:15 gear ratio provided a 82,100-lb. continuous tractive effort rating at 11.1 mph. The units weighed 389,000 lbs, resulting in a 97,250 lb. starting tractive effort. Curiously, the class EF-30, SD40 units weighed 2000 pounds more than the SD45 units, and therefore produced 500 lb. more starting tractive effort. But starting tractive effort doesn't tell the whole story. What the PRR got for the added cost of the SD45 and the additional 600 horsepower was more tractive effort in the higher speed ranges. For instance, at 45 mph, the tractive effort of the SD40 was 22,000 lbs while the tractive effort of the SD45 at the same speed was 26,500 lbs.

At the time the second group of PRR EF-36's was being ordered, the railroad was investigating the use of radio-controlled helper units. On the October 1967 order, five of the units (6200, 6202, 6204, 6206 and 6208) were equipped as radio transmitters. Five other units (6201, 6203, 6205, 6207 and 6209) had radio receivers. The intention was to use these on iron ore trains. Although the PRR's first monster (35,805 ton) ore train from Cleveland to Mingo Jct. ran on September 21, 1967, most of these trains ran after the merger of PRR into PC. While successful on an experimental and well-supervised basis, these huge trains were not a long-term success because of the difficulty of maintaining a pool of specially trained enginemen to handle them.

Photographed two months after the Penn Central merger (February 1968), the 6202 was one of the last units delivered to the PRR. This SD45 was set up as a radio control master unit.

PRR 6192 on a coal train at Bayview Yard in Baltimore, Maryland. Photographed in November 1968, ten months after the Penn Central merger, none of the units has been relettered.

Class EF-36 units served the PRR for an even shorter period than the EF-30a's. The first SD45s were delivered in September 1966 and served the PRR for a little more than a year. For the last order of 65 units, the first were operated by the PRR for a month and a half. The class EF-36s were assigned to Enola and were in a common system pool with the class EF-30a's. They were therefore also used primarily in mainline freight service.

The class EF-36 units were neither renumbered or reclassed in the 1966 renumbering plan that preceded the Penn Central merger. The ex-PRR units served the Penn Central without retirement. They served in the same general type of service as during the PRR period. All of the group was conveyed to Conrail on April 1, 1976. They were not renumbered.

The 6105-6169 group of SD45's retired during 1979 to 1986. Seven of the 6170-6234 group were retired in January 1981 and remainder were returned to the lessor in January 1983.

After being returned to the lessor, almost all the units in the last group were sold to the Chicago and Northwestern. The C&NW did not release all of these (numbered in their 6500 series) for service. After C&NW service, most of the ex-PRR units were sold to locomotive rebuilders such as VMV Industries and National Railway Equipment. This group became a significant source of "hulks" used as the basis for rebuilding.

Morrison-Knudson did most of this rebuilding. The common rebuild replaced the 20-cylinder engine with a 16-cylinder EMD model 645 engine and upgraded the locomotive to SD40-2 standards. This configuration was identified as an "SD40M-2." Many former PRR SD-45 units were thus reborn for further service on CSX and SP (now UP).

PRR 6120 at Renovo, Pennsylvania on November 4, 1966. This SD45 is only a month old.

Chapter 7

Early Road Switchers

Until the middle of 1950, freight dieselization on the PRR meant cab units. The only locomotives on the railroad of the type that came to be known as road-switchers were the 1000-hp Alcos and Baldwins and the 2000-hp F-M units. Even at that, the PRR's June 1950 dieselization study listed them as "switchers."

Up to that time, this was not an unusual practice. Most major railroads were using cab units for freight service. While Alco, Baldwin and F-M offered road-switchers, EMD had only produced the first GP7 in November 1949 after producing the flawed BL2 (for "Branch Line") a few years before.

The Pennsy had a great need for the function filled by the road-switcher as a single unit, namely a combination road unit and switcher. The railroad was to find that when combined in multiple, road switchers could perform the same freight service function as cab units. By the end of PRR's dieselization, their 310 GP9s confirmed this.

With the application of a boiler in the short hood, a road-switcher could be used in passenger service, again, both as a road unit and as a switcher.

For local freights and moderately heavy switching on the PRR through 1950, the primary steam locomotives used were the H9s and H10s (plus a very few H6s) 2-8-0 engines. More than 500 were in use at that time, and diesel road-switchers replaced many of them.

LIGHT ROAD-SWITCHERS

The PRR's light road switchers were the 1000 and 1200 HP units. At the time of the June 1950 dieselization study, the PRR owned three of these and the study projected a requirement for 26 more. The PRR subsequently purchased 26 more RS-'s plus eight Baldwin model RS-12's, in three classes. Further, there were some 87 additional 1200 HP end cab switchers purchased from four builders for use as light road-switchers. The total number of PRR's light road-switchers came to 41, which was matched only by the Alaska Railroad and the GM&O in the U. S.

> ## CLASSES
> ## AS-10s, AS-10am,
> ## AS-10as and
> ## AS-10ams
> ## *Alco RS-1*

There were four Alco RS-1 classes, each with its own mix of special equipment, reflecting assignment to different services. Some of them had steam generators, some were MU equipped and some had both. The model RS-1 units were ordered from Alco with the special equipment indicated in the table on page 119.

Class AS-10s

The first single class AS-10s (road number 5906), had a total weight of 249,700 lbs with a starting tractive effort of 62,425 lbs. The 5906 was purchased as power for the Parkton commuter local out of Baltimore. It was equipped with a Vapor model 4225 boiler rated at 2250 lbs. per hour of steam generation, and was not MU-equipped.

The 5906 was purchased to replace steam power on the Parkton Local, a 29-mile commuter operation on the Northern Central line north of Baltimore. The AS-10s diesel with passenger cars worked this assignment, along with a motor car, until 1952 when the arrival of Baldwin RS-12 No. 8776 bumped the 5906 back to protection power for the Parkton service, and switching at Baltimore's Pennsylvania Station. The last Parkton Local ran on June 27, 1959. The 5906 continued in the Baltimore area until 1963, when it was assigned to Canton, Oho. In Canton, the unit was used in general switching, with little use of the steam boiler. In 1965, 5906 was assigned to the Northern Division with maintenance at Ebenezer engine terminal near Buffalo.

The 5906 was renumbered 9916 in 1966 in preparation for the Penn Central merger, and re-classed ARS-10sx. In May 1967 it was assigned to 46th Street engine terminal in Phila-

There was only one AS-10s, the 5906. Here this unit is working in Philadelphia, Pennsylvania in October, 1966. The rear quarter view shows the stack for the boiler, which is still in place, but rarely, if ever used in Philadelphia.

R.J. MULLER PHOTOS; DOUGLAS COLLECTION

delphia and stayed there past the Penn Central merger. Shortly before the merger, unit 9916 was assigned on paper to Conway in the Central Region for maintenance, but it stayed on loan to Philadelphia. It was still in there in 1969. The unit was retired by Penn Central in February 1970.

Class AS-10am

The 22 RS-1 units in class AS-10am weighed 242,400 lbs with a starting tractive effort of 60,600 lbs. They were purchased for branchline freight service in several locations. The PRR viewed their use to be as 2000-hp two-unit locomotives, and had them equipped for back-to-back MU operation. The MU connections were installed at the rear ends of the units only.

SERVICE HISTORY

Class AS-10am units were sent to three areas when delivered. Eight units were assigned to the New York Division with two units at South Amboy and six at Trenton. Six units were assigned to the Northern Division at Olean, NY. The last eight units were assigned to the Eastern Division at Canton, Ohio; but two of them (5629 and 5630) were assigned to Buffalo and Olean in the mid-1950s. These assignments were relatively unchanged through the remaining PRR period.

On the New York Division, the two South Amboy units were intended for service between Brown yard, just outside of town and the coal dumper, which was adjacent to the engine terminal. The six Trenton units were used to dieselize the Bel-Del line from Trenton to Phillipsburg, New Jersey. For this service, trainphone was installed on the locomotives. The AS-10am units continued on the Bel-Del until the trains got too heavy for the paired RS-1 units.

After being bumped from the main

AS-10am was the most numerous of the RS-1 subclasses. 5622 is at Phillipsburg, Pennsylvania in July 1965. Phillipsburg was the north end of the Bel-Del line, originally dieselized by this class locomotive. All of the units in the class were built with rear-end MU only. Later, the PRR added front-end MU on six units in the class.

Bel-Del freights, the RS-1 units found plenty of employment in the Bristol-Morrisville-Trenton-Phillipsburg area. They worked New York Division switcher and local freight jobs for the remainder of the PRR period.

The Canton-assigned units also had trainphone. The units were assigned to local freights. These operated out of Salem and Dover, Ohio in addition to Canton. By the early 1960s, three of the class were sent to Toledo for transfer runs.

The six Northern Division AS-10am units were originally divided between two assignments. Two units were assigned to the Olean and Rochester freights, OR-15 and OR-16. The other four units were used as helpers between Emporium and Keating Summit on the Enola-Buffalo mainline. The later assignment lasted for only a few years because the helper service required more push than two RS-1's could provide. By 1955, all eight of the class on the Northern Division were assigned to Olean, where operation of the Rochester Branch and other shorter branches required them. As discussed below, the

addition of the AS-10ams made it possible to run RS-1 sets of more than two units. In the late 1950s, front end MU was applied to the six Olean-based class AS-10am units (5625, 5626, 5628, 5629, 5637 and 5638). After this modification, these six and the two class AS-10ams made the Northern Region RS-1's more flexible.

Operation of the Rochester Branch from Olean ended about 1962 when it was abandoned south of the Lehigh Valley crossing 14.5 miles south of Rochester. Thereafter, PRR service to Rochester was run via trackage rights over the LV out of Buffalo.

In the mid-1960s the long-time assignments of the AS-10am's was altered. By May 1967, the units were assigned to Buffalo (9), Meadows (6), Morrisville (4) and Philadelphia (2). The 5628 had been retired in 1965 because of wreck damage. In the 1966 numbering plan, the class was renumbered from 5619-5640 to 9919-9940 except there was no 5628 to renumber. The units were reclassed ARS-10. When the PRR merged into Penn Central on February 1, 1968 all were assigned to Conway for maintenance. For three units, 9922, 9925 and 9935, this did not take effect because they remained at Morrisville. Also, 9923 went to 46th St., Philadelphia on loan. All but four of the class were retired by Penn Central. The remaining four were retired by Conrail, two in October 1976 and the last two in early 1977.

PRR ROAD NUMBERS	ALCO SALES ORDER	NO. OF UNITS	PRR CLASS	ORDER DATE	DELIVERY DATES	SPECIAL EQUIPMENT
5906	20329	1	AS-10s	Oct 47	Dec 48	SG
5619-5640	20485	22	AS-10am	Nov 49	Jun 50-Aug 50	MU
8857-8858	20592	2	AS-10as	Aug 50	Mar 51-Apr 51	SG
8485-8486	20782	2	AS-10ams	Nov 51	May 52	SG, MU

Order Summary - Alco Model RS-1 Units

Class AS-10as

The class AS-10as had a total weight of 244,000 lbs. with a starting tractive effort of 61,000 lbs. The 8857 and 8858 were purchased for passenger car switching and transfer service between Newark, Jersey City and Meadows yard on the New York Division. They were not equipped for MU operation but were equipped with steam generators. The Vapor OK-4616 was rated at 1600 lbs. per hour. This was a smaller unit than the OK-4225 used on the class AS-10s.

The 8857 and 8858 were assigned to North Jersey for the passenger drill service until 1955 when they were re-assigned to Morrisville to join the AS-10am's assigned there. Even though they were not equipped with MU, they could be used in the same local freights and switcher assignments as AS-10am diesels if a single unit was sufficient for the job. Since they did have boilers, one of these units could be assigned to the Trenton-Camden passenger local on the New Jersey side of the Delaware River through Bordentown.

In the 1966 renumbering, the two units became 9917 and 9918 and were re-classed ARS-10sx. Both units were retired by Penn Central—the 9917 in June 1975 and the 9918 in October 1975.

Equipment and Assignment Table
Classes AS-10s, AS-10am, AS-10as and AS-10ams (Alco RS-1)

Orig. Road No.	Orig. Class	1966 Road No.	1966 Class	May 1959 Assignment	T P	S G	C S	M U
5619	AS-10am	9919	ARS-10	South Amboy			Y	Y
5620	AS-10am	9920	ARS-10	South Amboy			Y	Y
5621	AS-10am	9921	ARS-10	Morrisville	Y			Y
5622	AS-10am	9922	ARS-10	Morrisville	Y			Y
5623	AS-10am	9923	ARS-10	Morrisville	Y			Y
5624	AS-10am	9924	ARS-10	Morrisville	Y			Y
5625	AS-10am	9925	ARS-10	Olean				Y
5626	AS-10am	9926	ARS-10	Olean				Y
5627	AS-10am	9927	ARS-10	Olean				Y
5628	AS-10am			Olean				Y
5629	AS-10am	9929	ARS-10	Olean	Y			Y
5630	AS-10am	9930	ARS-10	Olean	Y			Y
5631	AS-10am	9931	ARS-10	Canton	Y			Y
5632	AS-10am	9932	ARS-10	Canton	Y			Y
5633	AS-10am	9933	ARS-10	Canton	Y			Y
5634	AS-10ms	9934	ARS-10	Canton	Y			Y
5635	AS-10ms	9935	ARS-10	Canton	Y			Y
5636	AS-10ms	9936	ARS-10	Canton	Y			Y
5637	AS-10ms	9937	ARS-10	Olean				Y
5638	AS-10ms	9938	ARS-10	Olean				Y
5639	AS-10ms	9939	ARS-10	Morrisville	Y		Y	Y
5640	AS-10ms	9940	ARS-10	Morrisville	Y		Y	Y
5906	AS-10s	9916	ARS-10sx	Baltimore		Y	Y	
8485	AS-10ams	9914	ARS-10s	Olean		Y		Y
8486	AS-10ams	9915	ARS-10s	Olean		Y		Y
8857	AS-10as	9917	ARS-10sx	Morrisville		Y	Y	
8858	AS-10as	9918	ARS-10sx	Morrisville		Y	Y	

TP = Train Phone; SG = Steam Generator; CS = Cab Signal; MU - Multiple-unit connections
Special Equipment as of January, 1960

LOCOMOTIVE CHARACTERISTICS

Class	AS-10s	AS-10am	AS-10as	AS-10ams	BS-10as	BS-12as	BS-12ams	BS-12am
Builder	Alco	Alco	Alco	Alco	BLW	BLH	BLH	BLH
Model	RS-1	RS-1	RS-1	RS-1	DRS-4-4-1000	RS-12	RS-12	RS-12
Horsepower	1000	1000	1000	1000	1000	1200	1200	1200
Wheel Arr,	B-B	B-B	B-B	B-B	B-B	B-B	B-B	B-B
Total Weight	249,700 lbs	242,400 lbs	244,000 lbs	246,000 lbs	240,600 lbs	243,000 lbs	243,200 lbs	233,200 lbs
Length over Couplers	55' 0"	55' 0"	55' 0"	55' 0"	58' 0"	58' 0"	58' 0"	58' 0"
Truck Centers	31' 0"	31' 0"	31' 0"	31' 0"	32' 3"	32' 3"	32' 3"	32' 3"
Truck Wheelbase	9' 4"	9' 4"	9' 4"	9' 4"	9' 10"	9' 10"	9' 10"	9' 10"
Engine	Alco 6-539SC	Alco 6-539SC	Alco 6-539SC	Alco 6-539SC	BLW 6-606SC	BLH 6-606A	BLH 6-606A	BLH 6-606A
Generator	GE GT-553	GE GT-553	GE GT-553	GE GT-553	W 480	W 480	W 480	W 480
Traction Motors	GE 731	GE 731	GE 731	GE 731	W 362D	W 372DF	W 372DF	W 372DF
Gear Ratio	75:16	75:16	75:16	75:16	68:14	68:14	68:14	68:14
Maximum Speed	60 MPH	60 MPH	60 MPH	60 MPH	60 MPH	60 MPH	60 MPH	60 MPH
Starting Trac. Effort	62,425 lbs	60,600 lbs	61,000 lbs	61,500 lbs	60,150 lbs	60,750 lbs	60,750 lbs	58,300 lbs
Continuous Trac. Effort	34,000 lbs	34,000 lbs	34,000 lbs	34,000 lbs	32,400 lbs	32,400 lbs	32,400 lbs	32,400 lbs
CTE Speed	8.0 MPH	8.0 MPH	8.0 MPH	8.0 MPH	9.5 MPH	11.4 MPH	11.4 MPH	11.4 MPH
Steam Generator	OK-4225		OK-4616	OK-4616	OK-4516	OK-4616	(*)	
Steam Gen, Capacity	2250		1600	1600	1600	1600	(*)	

(*) PRR 8776 was equipped with an OK4616 steam generator rated at 1600 lb/hr. PRR 8110 was equipped with an OK4625 steam generator rated at 2500 lb/hr

Class AS-10ams

The class AS-10ams units weighed 246,000 lbs, which resulted in a starting tractive effort of 61,500 lbs. The units were equipped with a Vapor OK 4616 steam generator rated at 1600 lbs. per hour. The units were equipped for MU operation and had MU connections on both ends. The trucks were equipped with roller bearings.

The two units in this class were originally assigned to Erie, but within a few months they were reassigned to Olean to join the six AS-10am units. The arrival of the AS-10ams with MU at both ends made it possible to plug together four unit RS-1 sets for the Rochester Branch local. As noted above, when six of the AS-10am units had front end MU applied, the 8485 and 8486 were no longer the only units needed to make up RS-1 sets of more than two units.

When the access to Rochester was changed from Olean to Buffalo, several of the AS-10am and AS-10ams units were transferred to Buffalo. In 1967, a typical Friday evening-Saturday assignment for the pair of class AS-10ams units was observed. First, the two AS-10ams units left Ebenezer Yard near Buffalo late Friday evening with a transfer run to Fort Erie, Ontario on the Canadian National. They returned to Ebenezer a few hours later. Next, the same two AS-10ams units made a round trip to Olean with a local freight run. This occupied most of Saturday.

In the 1966 renumbering, the 8485

The engineer on PRR 9918 is pouring on the sand as the unit digs in to move a cut of cars past the passenger station in Trenton, New Jersey in June, 1968. The unit spent most of its PRR time assigned to the Trenton area. Originally numbered 8858, it was purchased to shift passenger cars around Newark. The passenger shifting assignment only lasted a few years.

and 8486 were renumbered 9914 and 9915 and reclassed ARS-10s. In early 1967, the 9915 was transferred to 46th Street Philadelphia. The 9914 stayed in Buffalo. These were the final PRR assignments of the class. The 9914 was retired by Penn Central in March 1972. The 9915 served through the Penn Central period but was retired by Conrail in March 1977.

CLASS BS-10as
Baldwin
DRS 4-4-1000

An intriguing aspect of the PRR diesel locomotive roster is the number of rare model types, of which the Centipedes and the large center cab transfer switchers are examples. The Baldwin model DRS 4-4-1000 road switcher was another rare type. Only two other railroads (the Tennessee Central and the Canadian Pacific) purchased that model, and the PRR owned six of the total of 22 built. Of course, 1000-hp. road switchers were not unique, because Alco had built more than 400 of the competitive model RS-1.

Although Baldwin did not have much success selling 1000 horsepower road switchers, the model had been offered since the late World War II period when the post-war locomotive line had been proposed. The earliest incarnation was proposed with an 8-cylinder VO engine and indeed such a unit was built for the Soviet Union, albeit with a full cab carbody.

The PRR purchased its BLW DRS 4-4-1000's in two groups. The first order was placed in February 1948 for two units, which were delivered in February 1949 and numbered 9276 and 9277. The second order was placed in November 1949 and delivered in February 1950. The later order was for four units that were numbered 5591 to 5594. None were MU-equipped but they did have steam boilers. They were all classified BS-10s when delivered but were reclas-

These two RS-1's had steam generators, and the front end MU connections visible in the photo. Nos. 8485 and 8486 were found at Olean, New York on August 27, 1966.

sified as BS-10as in the 1951 classification scheme.

The units had the same major equipment as the class BS-10a Baldwin DS 4-4-1000. The trucks, however, were the same 9' 10" wheelbase General Steel Castings truck used on Baldwin road units. The only special equipment was the Vapor model 4516 steam generator rated at 1600 lbs. per hour.

SERVICE HISTORY

When these were delivered, all were assigned to Chicago, where they were capable of coach yard work, light local freight assignments or even the Valparaiso commuter train. For most of the 1950's, they were assigned to Chicago, Fort Wayne, Toledo, Cleveland, Canton and Pittsburgh.

In Camden, 9276 and 9277 shared duties with Class BS-12as 8975 on Camden-Pemberton commuters and local freights.

In the early 1960s, the six units were dispersed as follows:

5591: Lake Region–Canton
5592: Northwest Region--59th St., Chicago
5593: Lake Region–Cleveland
5594: Northwest Region--59th St., Chicago
9276: Philadelphia Region, Camden
9277: Philadelphia Region, Camden

These assignments were stable throughout the early half of the 1960s, except that the 5591 was moved to the Chesapeake Region. In the spring of 1965, all of the BS-10as units not already there were moved to the Philadelphia Region, where they remained until retirement.

In the 1966 renumbering, they were renumbered 8050 to 8055, but they were not renumbered in order. 5591 to 5594 became 8051 to 8054, 9276 became 8050 and 9277 became 8055. They were reclassed BS-10sx. 9277 and 5594 were retired in February 1967 and May 1966 respectively without renumbering. The remainder of the class passed to Penn Central on February 1, 1969.

All of the remaining four Class BS-10sx units lasted throughout the Penn Central period. All were renumbered in October 1972 to make room in the numbering system for new GP-38's. Units 8050 to 8053 became 8300 to 8303. All of the class was retired three days

PRR 8050 has been renumbered from 9276 for almost a year. In this rear quarter view, the boiler stack shows prominently. Camden, New Jersey, November 11, 1967.*

DRS4-4-1000 5594 was one of the second group of this model purchased by the Pennsylvania, shown at Frankford Jct., in November 1965. The number style on the cab is borrowed from the GG-1 electrics; what was that about local option in the paint shops?

before Conrail acquired the Penn Central--on March 29, 1976.

CLASSES BS-12as, BS-12ams, and BS-12am
Baldwin RS-12

The purchases of the Baldwin model RS-12 1200-hp road switchers continued the PRR's use of 1000 and 1200 horsepower road-switchers for switching and light local freight assignments. The PRR's RS-12's were assigned to three classes and were ordered in four groups, as shown in the Order Summary Table.

The RS-12 road-switchers had the same major equipment as the class

BS-12 switcher, but with the 9' 10" wheelbase General Steel Castings truck design used on Baldwin road units.

Class BS-12as

The first Baldwin model RS-12 road-switcher purchased by the PRR was classified BS-12as and numbered 8975. It was equipped with a steam generator and trainphone, but no MU or cab signals. The steam generator was the Vapor OK-4616 model, rated at 1600 lbs. per hour.

It was originally assigned to Cleveland where it could be used on light local freights, heavy switching, and trains 353 and 354, the Cleveland-Alliance commuter trains. In late 1957, the 8975 was reassigned to Camden, NJ. There were still several passenger commuter trains operating out of Camden at the time, using both motor cars and lo-

Order Summary - Baldwin RS-12 Units

PRR ROAD NUMBERS	BLH SALES ORDER	NO. OF UNITS	CLASS	ORDER DATE	DELIVERY DATES
8975	50525	1	BS-12as	Aug 50	Apr 51
8776	51531	1	BS-12ams	Nov 51	Sep 52
8105-8109	300320	5	BS-12am	Jun 53	Feb 54
8110	300317	1	BS-12ams	Jun 53	Feb 54

The many faces of RS-12: 8975 is at Pemberton, New Jersey on a March, 1966 weekend, awaiting a Monday run. Pemberton commuter service lasted into the Penn Central era.

comotive hauled equipment. The light road-switchers were also used on commuter runs when the motor cars could not respond to the call. The 8975 remained in the Camden-Philadelphia area for the remainder of its PRR service.

The 8975 received number 8084 in the 1966 pre-Penn Central renumbering program. It was also reclassed BRS-12sx. The 8084 remained in the Philadelphia area through the Penn Central era. The unit was renumbered again in October 1972 to 8306, to make room for new GP-38's. Retirement came in December 1974.

Class BS-12ams

The two BS-12ams units were delivered two years apart; the 8776 in 1952 and the 8110 in the last Baldwin delivery in February 1954. Both were equipped with a steam generator, cab signals, trainphone and MU-control. The 8776 carried a Vapor OK-4616 steam generator rated at 1600 lbs. per hour, while the 8110 was equipped with the

larger Vapor OK-4624 unit rated at 2500 lbs. per hour.

The 8776 was assigned to the Baltimore area and the 8110 to the Philadelphia area for the entire PRR period. PRR 8776 was used on the commuter locals, sharing this assignment with PRR 5906. From 1957 until the last Parkton local trips on June 27, 1959, one of the trainsets wes 8776 and two or three cars and the other motor car.

The two units had the same type of renumbering record as the 8975. The 8110 became 8085 and the 8776 became 8086 in 1966. Both were reclassed BRS-12s at the same time. The 8776/8086 did not make it to the Penn Central as it was retired in October 1967. The 8085 lasted three years longer and worked through the Penn Central merger until retirement in December 1970.

Equipment and Assignment Table
Classes BS-12am, BS-12ams and BS-12as
(Baldwin RS-12)

Orig. Road No.	Orig. Class	1966 Road No.	1966 Class	Original Assignment	May 1959 Assignment	TP	SG	CS	MU	RA
8105	BS-12am	8090	BRS-12	Oil City	Ebenezer				Y	
8106	BS-12am	8091	BRS-12	Oil City	Ebenezer				Y	
8107	BS-12am	8087	BRS-12	Oil City	Ebenezer				Y	
8108	BS-12am	8088	BRS-12	Oil City	Ebenezer				Y	
8109	BS-12am	8089	BRS-12	Oil City	Ebenezer				Y	
8110	BS-12ams	8085	BRS-12s	Philadelphia	Phila.-46th St.		Y	Y	Y	Y
8776	BS-12ams	8086	BRS-12s	Baltimore	Baltimore	Y	Y	Y	Y	
8975	BS-12as	8084	BRS-12sx	Cleveland	Camden	Y	Y			

TP = Train Phone; SG = Steam Generator; CS = Cab Signal; MU = Multiple-unit; RA = Radio
Special Equipment as of January, 1960

8087 awaits assignment at Conway engine terminal on February 18, 1968, the first month of Penn Central operation. It was originally PRR 8107. Note the high short hood used on later RS-12's which provided more clearance for steam generators (although there was no steam generator on this unit).

Class BS-12am

The four BS-12am units were delivered to the Northern Region in February 1954. Their only special equipment was MU control installed on both ends, so they were not limited to two-unit combinations. In the Northern Region, they were used on local freights in both the Buffalo and Olean areas.

Reassignments in Spring 1965 moved the class BS-12ams to heavy switching and local freight service based at Pitcairn, just east of Pittsburgh. The assignment lasted until the end of the PRR era and well into the Penn Central period. The Pitcairn assignment meant they could be found in many locations to the east and south of Pittsburgh, working out of such diverse locations as Pitcairn itself, Wilkinsburg Yard, Kiski Junction, and Thompson yard on the west side of the Monongahela River.

In the 1966 renumbering, units 8105 and 8106 became 8090 and 8091, while 8107 to 8109 became 8087 to 8089. They were reclassed to BRS-12. In the Penn Central period, 8087, 8090 and 8091 were retired in June 1969. The 8088 and 8089 were transferred to the Philadelphia-Wilmington area in 1970. The 8089 was retired in November 1971. The 8088 was renumbered to 8307 in October 1972 to make its road number available for new GP-38's and was retired in November 1973.

8110 is at Wilmington, Delaware in July 1965. When the PRR attempted to abandon the DelMarVa passenger train earlier, citing an annual loss of $180,000, the state Public Utilities Commission urged one last effort. The PRR mounted a publicity campaign which included a train naming contest. The resulting "Blue Diamond Express" was given a six months trial beginning on July 1, 1965 with an improved schedule. It was not successful, but this photo is evidence of the trial.

HEAVY ROAD-SWITCHERS

Classes FS-20, FS-20m
F-M H20-44

The Fairbanks-Morse model H20-44 was unique during the dieselization of America's railroads. This F-M was a 2000 horsepower, end cab road-switcher. Twenty-five years later, Montreal Locomotive offered a unit with the same configuration, but it only sold 17 (M420TR). F-M sold 96 model H20-44 units between 1947 and 1954.

In addition to the largest fleet of H10-44s, the PRR owned the largest number of H20-44s with a total of 38. They purchased them on two orders. Builder's order LD-65 for 12 units was placed in June 1948 by PRR and was delivered from December 1948 to February 1949. Eight of the units on this order were non-MU and four were MU-equipped. All twelve were classified as FS-20 when delivered.

The second PRR order for H20-44s was builder's order LD-105, placed in August 1950 for 26 units, which were delivered in May and June 1951. Order LD-105 was the largest order that F-M received for the model. The units on order LD-105 were all MU-equipped. Under the revised PRR classification system which began to be applied in September 1951, the MU-equipped units on both orders were reclassified as FS-20m.

The model H20-44 followed the pattern of the other F-M hood units with their carbody variations. Most H20-44s, including all of the PRR units, used the first carbody which was similar to the H15-44 and first H16-44s. The Loewy touches were the same—the sculptured headlight base and the sheet metal curves on the cab and battery box sides. Only the last seven H20-44's built had the simplified carbody that was similar to the second H16-44. All model H20-44's received the early F-M road-switcher truck.

SERVICE HISTORY

The class FS-20 and FS-20m's were widely distributed over most of the PRR west of Altoona. Locations included Conemaugh, Pitcairn, Mingo Jct., Canton, Cleveland, Toledo, Cincinnati, Lancaster, Ohio, Louisville and Chicago. Although they were moved from time to time, the wide range of maintenance points on the Equipment and Assignment Tabulation is typical of the assignments up until about 1965 when all FS-20 and FS-20m's were moved to Columbus to concentrate maintenance of F-M units.

Almost all of the assignments for the class were for heavy switching, hump pushing and mine runs. The class FS-20 and FS-20m units assigned at Conemaugh (Johnstown) and Mingo Junction certainly filled these heavy switching jobs.

Another assignment in the early 1960s was true road-switcher service. Three of the Canton-maintained FS-20m's were used on the Marietta branch to Marietta, Ohio. Almost all of the traffic handled on the Marietta branch originated at a coal mine at Dexter City, Ohio. Most of the coal from the branch was interchanged with the B&O at Cambridge, Ohio, where the three FS-20m's were based.

The Chicago-based FS-20's had typical assignments for the non-MU units, including hump pushing and transfer runs. No other location on the PRR required as much freight car transfer work between railroads as did the Chicago area.

The 1966 renumbering scheme reclassed the FS-20 as FRS-20x and the class FS-20m units as FRS-20. Units 9300-9311 were to be renumbered 7700-7711 and 8917-8942 were to be renumbered 7717-7742. However, none of the H20-44 engines ever saw service on the Penn Central. Half of the 38 units were retired in 1966 before they were renumbered, and the rest, renumbered as shown in the Assignment Table, were retired by the end of September 1967. The last units retired were 7705, 7734 and 7741.

Road-switchers 9305 and 8936 in MU, one from each of the H20-44 orders, haul a freight on Front Street in Cincinnati, Ohio, in what was then a warehouse district. September 18, 1965.

L.A. MARRE PHOTO

Equipment and Assignment Table
Classes FS-20 and FS-20m
(Fairbanks-Morse H20-44)

Orig. Road No.	1966 Road No.	May, 1959 Assignment	M U	T P	C S
8917	7717	Lancaster OH	Y	Y	Y
8918		Lancaster OH	Y	Y	Y
8919		Conemaugh	Y	Y	Y
8920	7720	Conway	Y	Y	Y
8921	7721	Conway	Y	Y	Y
8922		Conway	Y	Y	Y
8923	7723	Lancaster OH	Y	Y	Y
8924		Conway	Y	Y	Y
8925		Conway	Y	Y	Y
8926		Conway	Y	Y	Y
8927		Conway	Y	Y	Y
8928		Mingo Jct.	Y	Y	Y
8929	7729	Conemaugh	Y	Y	Y
8930	7730	Conemaugh	Y	Y	Y
8931	7731	Conemaugh	Y	Y	Y
8932		Conemaugh	Y	Y	
8933		Conemaugh	Y	Y	
8934	7734	Mahoningtown	Y	Y	
8935		Toledo	Y	Y	
8936		Mingo Jct.	Y	Y	Y
8937		Mingo Jct.	Y		
8938		Canton	Y		
8939	7739	Canton	Y		
8940	7740	Canton	Y		
8941	7741	Toledo	Y		
8942		Mahoningtown	Y		
9300	7700	Chicago-59th St			
9301		Cincinnati			
9302		Lancaster, OH			Y
9303		Chicago-59th St			
9304		Louisville			
9305	7705	Conemaugh	Y		Y
9306		Conemaugh	Y		Y
9307		Conemaugh			Y
9308		Conemaugh			Y
9309		Conemaugh			Y
9310		Canton	Y		
9311	7711	Canton	Y		

MU = Multiple Units
TP = Train Phone
CS = Cab Signal

Freshly-painted PRR 8941 at Canton, Ohio, February 20, 1964. The paint drawing for the keystone-only image had not yet been issued, so the local motive power foreman located the side keystone as shown here. When the drawing was issued, it showed the keystone centered on the long hood. The authors believe the foreman got it right.

Above: PRR 8940 at Alliance, Ohio on November 9, 1963. This F-M road switcher would be retired in just over three years.

Below: PRR 9301, one of the eight non-MU H20-44s, at Richmond, Indiana, July 1961.

W.D. VOLKMER PHOTO; DOUGLAS COLLECTION

Classes ES-15m and ES-15ms *EMD GP7*

Order Summary - Class ES-15m Units

PRR ROAD NUMBERS	NO. OF UNITS	EMD SALES ORDER	ORDER DATE	DELIVERY DATES
8797-8806	10	5060	May 51	Jan 52
8500-8501	2	5169	Nov 51	Aug 52
8503-8507	5	5194	Nov 51	Aug 52
8508-8512	5	5195	Nov 51	Aug 52
8502	1	5196	Nov 51	Aug 52
8545-8546	2	5290	Jun 53	Aug 53
8583-8587	5	5291	Jun 53	Aug 53-Sep 53
8554-8582	29	5292	Jun 53	Aug 53-Sep 53
8547-8550	4	5293	Jun 53	Sep 53
8551-8552	2	5294	Jun 53	Sep 53
8553	1	5295	Jun 53	Sep 53

The EMD model GP7's on the Pennsylvania Railroad performed in standard road-switcher assignments. These were not the first road switchers on the PRR, because more than 60 Baldwin, Alco and FM road-switchers had been delivered to the railroad prior to the arrival of the first GP7s in January 1952. Only three groups of GP7 were ordered by the PRR. The second and third had a great variety of special equipment and were built under a total of ten EMD order numbers. The adjacent table defines the orders.

The Equipment and Assignment Table on Page 130 defines the special equipment installed on each unit. All were equipped with MU control.

All of the ten ES-15ms units had Vapor OK-4625 2500-lb. per hour steam generators. They had a fuel capacity of 800 gallons and a boiler water capacity of 800 gallons, achieved by mounting two separate tanks under the center of the road-switcher. These two tanks took up the same space as the single 1600 gallon fuel tank mounted on the Class

ES-15m, which was not steam-generator equipped.

Other special equipment was customized for the intended service areas. For instance, cab signals were not used in the Chicago or Williamsport areas. Because units 8583-8587 were intended and purchased for Chicago service and units 8551-8552 for Williamsport, they were delivered without cab signals. Units 8583-8587 were also built without trainphone equipment even though trainphone was used in the Chicago area. Units 8551-8552 destined for Williamsport were the only GP7's with

dual control. The 8553 was purchased for Trenton where it might operate in both trainphone and cab signal territory; hence it was equipped with both devices.

SERVICE HISTORY

Assignments for May 1959 are detailed on Page 130. Although these assignments changed from time to time, the tabulated locations are representative. Prior to the large-scale reassignment in the spring of 1965, the Class ES-15m units were mostly assigned within what was known after 1964 as

Freshly painted 8574 displays the keystone-only image in July 1966, at Northumberland, Pennsylvania. The keystone is not centered on the hood. Same foreman as PRR 8941, previous page, different location. The new paint job also included a bright yellow pilot plow, whose freshness will not last long.

GP7 5853 leads two more Geeps on a caboose hop at Kiski (Kiskiminetas) Junction in September 1966. Kiski Junction is located upstream on the Allegheny River near Freeport, Pennsylvania.

the Central Region. After the 1965 reassignment, most of the class was assigned to the Western Region.

The assignment of the ten boiler-equipped Class ES-15ms units was virtually unchanged from delivery until about 1963. Units 8500 and 8501 were assigned to Buffalo. 8551 and 8552 were assigned to Williamsport, where they were available for use on passenger

trains 595 and 596 from Williamsport to Canandaigua, New York, until these trains were withdrawn in 1956. 8553 was assigned to Trenton and Morrisville for use on Trenton-Camden trains and Sunday *Nellie Bly* from Trenton to Atlantic City. The P-RSL handled the train on days other than Saturday. The *Nellie Bly* was diesel powered from Trenton to Atlantic City, with the last part of the

run over the Pennsylvania-Reading-Seashore Lines. Units 8583-8587 were all assigned to Northwest Region, Chicago and Logansport. Chicago area units assigned to the Chicago-Valparaiso, Indiana commuter runs, collectively nicknamed "the Dummy."

In the 1966 renumbering, the Class ES-15m units were renumbered into the 5840-5899 block and reclassed ERS-15.

PRR GP7 5954 leads the South Wind *(with diesels at last) at Clagg Tower, Louisville, Kentucky. Second unit is ACL E7 No. 525. The date is May 5, 1967, significant as the PRR's last Kentucky Derby Day.*

PRR 9302 H-20-44 is in Brookville, Ohio on July 24, 1951.
R.D. ACTON SR. PHOTO, DAVID OROZZI COLLECTION

The renumbering is shown in the assignment table.

The ES-15ms units were renumbered into the 5950-5959 block and were reclassed ERS-15s as detailed in the Assignment Table.

All 66 of the Class ERS-15 and ERS-15s units carried on through the Penn Central period although four of the ERS-15s units were given capital rebuilds and were renumbered.

After Conrail commenced operating in April 1976, the ex-PRR GP7 fleet remained intact for a short period. Aside from the five units given heavy rebuilds during 1976 to 1979, all of the former PRR class ES-15m and ES-15ms units were retired during the 1979-1985 period. Unit 5856 was included in the first ten GP7 units sent to the ICG shop at Paducah for a heavy rebuild—coming out as 5727 in 1976, and being renumbered 5407 in 1978. Four others were

Equipment and Assignment Table Classes ES-15m and ES-1ms (EMD GP7)

Orig. Road No.	1966 Road No.	May 1959 Assignment	SG	TP	CS	DC	SC	DB	PMF
8500	5950	Ebenezer	Y	Y					
8501	5951	Ebenezer	Y	Y					
8502	5852	Ebenezer							
8503	5853	Osceola		Y	Y		Y	Y	Y
8504	5884	Morrisville		Y	Y		Y	Y	Y
8505	5885	Osceola		Y	Y		Y	Y	Y
8506	5886	Osceola		Y	Y		Y	Y	Y
8507	5887	Meadows		Y	Y		Y	Y	Y
8508	5888	Cincinnati		Y	Y			Y(*)	Y
8509	5889	Logansport			Y				
8510	5890	Logansport			Y				
8511	5891	East Altoona			Y				
8512	5892	Bellefonte			Y				
8545	5845	Lewistown		Y	Y				
8546	5846	East Altoona		Y	Y				
8547	5847	Northumberland							
8548	5848	Northumberland							
8549	5849	Northumberland							
8550	5850	Northumberland							
8551	5952	Williamsport	Y	Y		Y			
8552	5953	Williamsport	Y	Y		Y			
8553	5954	Morrisville	Y	Y	Y				
8554	5854	Conway		Y	Y			Y	Y
8555	5855	Conway		Y	Y			Y	Y
8556	5856	Pitcairn		Y	Y			Y	Y
8557	5857	Cincinnati		Y	Y			Y	Y
8558	5858	Conway		Y	Y			Y	Y
8559	5859	Conway		Y	Y			Y	Y
8560	5860	Pitcairn		Y	Y			Y	Y
8561	5861	Pitcairn		Y	Y			Y	Y
8562	5862	Cincinnati		Y	Y			Y	Y
8563	5863	Conway		Y	Y			Y	Y

SG = Steam generator; TP = Train Phone; CS = Cab Signal; DC = Dual Control;
SC = speed control, DB = dynamic brakes, PMF = pressure maintaining feature

Locomotive Characteristics

Class	FS-20	FS-20m	ES-15m	ES-15ms
Builder	F-M	F-M	EMD	EMD
Model	H20-44	H20-44	GP7	GP7
Horsepower	2000	2000	1500	1500
Wheel Arrangement	B-B	B-B	B-B	B-B
Total Weight	254,000 lbs	254,000 lbs	245,600 lbs (#)	249,000 lbs (+)
Length over Couplers	51' 0"	51' 0"	56' 2"	56' 2"
Truck Centers	27' 0"	27' 0"	31' 0"	31' 0"
Truck Wheelbase	9' 6"	9' 6"	9' 0"	9' 0"
Engine	FM 10-38D8-1/8	FM 10-38D8-1/8	EMD 16-567B	EMD 16-567B
Generator	W 474A	W 474A	EMD D12B	EMD D12B
Traction Motors	W 370D	W 370D	EMD D27B	EMD D27B
Gear Ratio	63:15	63:15	62:15	62:15
Maximum Speed	65 MPH	65 MPH	65 MPH	65 MPH
Starting Trac. Effort	63,500 lbs	63,500 lbs	61,400 lbs (#)	62,250 lbs (+)
Continuous Trac. Effort	42,800 lbs	42,800 lbs	40,000 lbs	40,000 lbs
CTE Speed	14.7 MPH	14.7 MPH	11.0 MPH	11.0 MPH
Steam Generator				OK-4616
Steam Gen, Capacity, Lb./Hr.				1600

Notes

(#) - Units 8564 and 8567 had weight of 250,400 lbs and a STE of 62,600 lbs.

(+) - Units 8551 to 8553 had weight of 252,000 lbs and a STE of 63,000 lbs.

(*) - This data applies also to the non-MU class AS-16 unit, 8914.

($) - Units 8435 to 8438 had weight of 252,000 lbs and a STE of 63,000 lbs.

(^) - Units 8903, 8905, 8910 to 8913, 8915 and 8516 had weight of 250,200 lbs, and a STE of 62,550 lbs.

Orig. Road No.	1966 Road No.	May 1959 Assignment	S G	T P	C S	D C	S C	D B	P M F
8564	5864	Conway		Y	Y			Y	Y
8565	5865	Pitcairn-Wst Al		Y	Y			Y	Y
8566	5866	Conway		Y	Y			Y	Y
8567	5867	Pitcairn		Y	Y			Y	Y
8568	5868	Conway		Y	Y			Y	Y
8569	5869	Pitcairn		Y	Y			Y	Y
8570	5870	Pitcairn		Y	Y			Y	Y
8571	5871	Conway		Y	Y			Y	Y
8572	5872	Pitcairn		Y	Y			Y	Y
8573	5873	Pitcairn		Y	Y			Y	Y
8574	5874	Pitcairn		Y	Y			Y	Y
8575	5875	Pitcairn		Y	Y			Y	Y
8576	5876	Pitcairn		Y	Y			Y	Y
8577	5877	Conway		Y	Y			Y	Y
8578	5878	Pitcairn		Y	Y			Y	Y
8579	5879	Ebenezer		Y	Y			Y	Y
8580	5880	Pitcairn		Y	Y			Y	Y
8581	5881	Lewistown		Y	Y			Y	Y
8582	5882	Cincinnati		Y	Y			Y	Y
8583	5955	Logansport	Y						
8584	5956	Logansport	Y						
8585	5957	Logansport	Y						
8586	5958	Chicago-16th St	Y						
8587	5959	Logansport	Y				-	---	---
8797	5897	Morrisville		Y	Y				
8798	5898	Meadows		Y	Y				
8799	5899	Morrisville		Y	Y				
8800	5840	Logansport		Y	Y				
8801	5841	Logansport		Y	Y				
8802	5842	Pitcairn		Y	Y				
8803	5843	Pitcairn		Y	Y				
8804	5844	Pittsburgh-28th		Y	Y				
8805	5895	Pitcairn		Y	Y				
8806	5896	Conway		Y	Y				

(*) = By PRR: All units had MU control. Units 8547, 8797, 8798 were also equipped with two-way radio.

Locomotive Characteristics

Class	AS-16m (*)	AS-16ms	FS-16m
Builder	Alco	Alco	F-M
Model	RS-3	RS-3	H16-44
Horsepower	1600	1600	1600
Wheel Arr	B-B	B-B	B-B
Total Weight	248,600 lbs ($)	259,600 lbs (^)	256,000 lbs
Length over Couplers	56' 0"	56' 0"	54' 0"
Truck Centers	30' 0"	30' 0"	30' 0"
Truck Wheelbase	9' 4"	9' 4"	9' 4"
Engine	Alco 12-244D	Alco 12-244D	FM 8-38D8-1/8
Generator	GE GT-581	GE GT-581	W 472
Traction Motors	GE 752	GE 752	W 370DEZ
Gear Ratio	74:18	74:18	63:15
Maximum Speed	65 MPH	65 MPH	70 MPH
Starting Trac. Effort	62,150 lbs ($)	64,900 lbs (^)	64,000 lbs
Continuous Trac. Effort	52,500 lbs	52,500 lbs	48,600 lbs
CTE Speed	9.5 MPH	9.5 MPH	9.9 MPH
Steam Generator		OK-46256	
Steam Gen, Capacity, Lb./Hr.		2500	

($) - On 8435-8438, weight was 252,000 lbs and starting tractive effort was 63,000 lbs.
(^) On 8910-8913, 8915, 8916, weight was 250,200 lbs and starting tractive effort was 62,550 lbs.

involved in the second wave of rebuilding, which wasn't nearly as complete. Units 5874 and 5879 were rebuilt by Paducah as 5428 and 5429 while 5860 and 5861 were rebuilt by the Rock Island at Silvis and were renumbered 5430 and 5431.

CLASSES AS-16, AS-16m, AS-16ms *Alco RS-3*

The PRR's August 1950 locomotive order started their purchases of Alco 1600 horsepower road-switchers. Eventually, 121 RS-3's operated on the PRR, outnumbering all road-switcher models until the EMD GP9s arrived. (And remember that the PRR considered the GP9's freight units, not road switchers.) The RS-3's were ordered from Alco in five groups: 15 in August 1950, 50 in May 1951, 33 in November 1951, 11 in June 1953 and 16 in September 1953. Another six RS-3's were purchased second-hand from the D&H in January 1958 and were classed AS-15m. These units are discussed in a separate section.

Before September 1952, units without steam generators were all classed AS-16 and units with steam generators were classed AS-16s. The 1951 system assigned AS-16m to all of the former AS-16 units except the 8914, which retained Class AS-16 since it did not have MU control. The AS-16s units became Class AS-16ms.

Mechanically and electrically, the RS-3 was the same as the model FA-2 and FB-2 Alco road-freight cab units, with the 12-cylinder model 244 engine, a GE model GT-581 main traction generator and GE 752 traction motors. A major improvement on the RS-3 over the predecessor RS-2 was the use of a geared drive for the auxiliary and exciter generator instead of a belt drive. All the RS-3 units on the PRR were equipped with 74:18 gearing which resulted in a continuous tractive effort of 52500 lbs. at 9.5 mph. This gearing provided a maximum speed of 65 mph, the standard PRR freight gearing.

The PRR RS-3's were equipped with a great variety of special or extra equipment. Extra equipment ranged from none on the 8914 (which was not even equipped with MU control), to the units purchased for the Pittsburgh and Chicago commuter service, which more than made up for the barren 8914. Those commuter units carried steam generators, MU control, trainphone, cab signals, dual control and speed control, all features appropriate for units in commuter passenger service. The dual control was particularly useful since train reversal became a matter of running the diesel around the train instead of turning it.

The 8903 was the only RS-3 to have both a steam generator and hump control, allowing it to be used for both hump pushing and passenger train protection service. Another "singleton" was the 8445, equipped with both a steam boiler and dynamic brakes. This combination required a higher short hood to allow installing the dynamic brake in the expanded space above the steam boiler. The steam generator installed in all class AS-16ms units was the Vapor model OK-4625, which produced 2500 lbs. per hour of steam.

The class AS-16m units were assigned to various types of freight service and the special equipment consisted of various mixes of trainphone, cab signal, dynamic brakes and pressure maintaining feature on the air brake system. Neither cab signal or trainphone applications were required in all assignments since the required lineside equipment was not installed on all lines of the PRR. It should be noted that the final group of AS-16m units delivered in

Equipment and Assignment Table
Classes AS-16, AS-16m and AS-16ms
(Alco RS-3)

Orig. Road No.	Class	1966 Road No.	May 1959 Assignment	SG	TP	CS	DC	HC	DB	PMF	SC	RA
8435	AS-16m	5415	Olean		Y				Y	Y		
8436	AS-16m	5416	Olean		Y				Y	Y		
8437	AS-16m	5437	Olean		Y				Y	Y		
8438	AS-16m	5438	Olean		Y				Y	Y		
8439	AS-16m	5439	Indianapolis		Y							
8440	AS-16m	5440	Indianapolis		Y							
8441	AS-16m	5441	Indianapolis		Y							
8442	AS-16m	5442	Indianapolis		Y							
8443	AS-16ms	5567	Baltimore	Y		Y						
8444	AS-16ms	5568	Baltimore	Y		Y						
8445	AS-16ms	5569	Olean	Y	Y				Y	Y		
8452	AS-16m	5452	Terre Haute		Y							
8453	AS-16m	5453	Terre Haute		Y							
8454	AS-16m	5454	Indianapolis		Y							
8455	AS-16m	5455	Erie		Y							
8456	AS-16m	5456	Toledo									
8457	AS-16m	5457	Ebenezer									Y
8458	AS-16m	5458	Toledo									
8459	AS-16m	5459	Erie									
8460	AS-16m	5460	Ebenezer									Y
8461	AS-16m	5461	Erie									
8462	AS-16m	5462	Indianapolis									
8463	AS-16m	5463	Crestline									
8464	AS-16m	5464	Indianapolis									
8465	AS-16m	5465	Erie		Y							
8466	AS-16m	5466	Ebenezer		Y							Y
8467	AS-16m	5467	Erie		Y							
8468	AS-16m	5468	Erie		Y							
8469	AS-16m	5469	Indianapolis		Y							
8470	AS-16m	5470	Erie		Y							
8471	AS-16ms	5571	Pittsburgh-28th St.	Y	Y	Y	Y				Y	
8472	AS-16ms	5572	Pittsburgh-28th St.	Y	Y	Y	Y				Y	
8473	AS-16ms	5573	Wilmington	Y		Y						
8474	AS-16ms	5574	Wilmington	Y		Y						
8475	AS-16ms	5575	Shire Oaks	Y		Y						
8476	AS-16ms	5576	Wilmington	Y		Y						
8577	AS-16ms	5577	Wilmington	Y		Y						
8478	AS-16ms	5578	Wilmington	Y		Y						
8479	AS-16ms	5579	Harrisburg (Nor. Reg.)		Y		Y					
8480	AS-16ms	5580	Toledo	Y	Y							
8481	AS-16ms	5581	Erie	Y	Y							
8482	AS-16ms	5582	Erie	Y	Y							
8483	AS-16ms	5583	Erie	Y	Y							
8484	AS-16ms	5584	Erie	Y	Y							
8590	AS-16m	5450	Wilmington		Y	Y			Y	Y		
8591	AS-16m	5451	Wilmington		Y	Y			Y	Y		
8592	AS-16m	5411	Ebenezer		Y	Y			Y	Y		
8593	AS-16m	5443	Ebenezer		Y	Y			Y	Y		
8594	AS-16m	5444	Pitcairn		Y	Y			Y	Y		
8595	AS-16m	5445	Wilmington		Y	Y			Y	Y		
8596	AS-16m	5446	Mahoningtown		Y	Y			Y	Y		
8597	AS-16m	5447	Chicago-16th St		Y	Y			Y	Y		Y
8598	AS-16m	5448	Chicago-16th St		Y	Y			Y	Y		Y
8599	AS-16m	5449	Ebenezer		Y	Y			Y	Y		
8600	AS-16m	5400	Erie		Y	Y			Y	Y		
8601	AS-16m	5401	Erie		Y	Y			Y	Y		
8602	AS-16m	5402	Harrisburg		Y	Y			Y	Y		
8603	AS-16m	5403	Harrisburg		Y	Y			Y	Y		
8604	AS-16m	5404	Shire Oaks		Y	Y			Y	Y		
8605	AS-16m	5405	Shire Oaks		Y	Y			Y	Y		

Equipment and Assignment Table
Classes AS-16, AS-16m and AS-16ms
(Alco RS-3)

Orig. Road No.	Class	1966 Road No.	May 1959 Assignment	SG	TP	CS	DC	HC	DB	PMF	SC	RA
8817	AS-16m	5417	Crestline		Y	Y						
8818	AS-16m	5418	Shire Oaks		Y	Y						Y
8819	AS-16m	5419	Shire Oaks		Y	Y						
8820	AS-16m	5420	Shire Oaks		Y	Y						
8821	AS-16m	5421	Shire Oaks		Y	Y						
8822	AS-16m	5422	Shire Oaks		Y	Y						
8823	AS-16m	5423	Shire Oaks		Y	Y						
8824	AS-16m	5424	Shire Oaks		Y	Y						
8825	AS-16m	5425	Shire Oaks		Y	Y						
8826	AS-16m	5426	Shire Oaks		Y	Y						
8827	AS-16m	5427	Shire Oaks		Y	Y						
8828	AS-16m	5428	Shire Oaks		Y	Y						
8829	AS-16m		Shire Oaks		Y	Y						
8830	AS-16m	5430	Shire Oaks		Y	Y						
8831	AS-16m	5431	Toledo		Y	Y						
8832	AS-16m	5432	Toledo		Y	Y						
8833	AS-16m	5433	Toledo		Y	Y						
8834	AS-16m	5434	Mingo Jct.		Y	Y		Y				
8835	AS-16m	5435	Renovo		Y	Y						
8836	AS-16m		Crestline		Y	Y						
8837	AS-16ms	5537	Pittsburgh-28th St.	Y	Y	Y	Y				Y	
8838	AS-16ms	5538	Pittsburgh-28th St.	Y	Y	Y	Y				Y	
8839	AS-16ms	5539	Pittsburgh-28th St.	Y	Y	Y	Y				Y	
8840	AS-16ms	5540	Pittsburgh-28th St.	Y	Y	Y	Y				Y	
8841	AS-16ms	5541	Pittsburgh-28th St.	Y	Y	Y	Y				Y	
8842	AS-16ms	5542	Pittsburgh-28th St.	Y	Y	Y	Y				Y	
8843	AS-16ms	5543	Chicago 16th St.	Y	Y	Y	Y				Y	
8844	AS-16ms	5544	Chicago 16th St.	Y	Y	Y	Y				Y	
8845	AS-16ms	5545	Pittsburgh-28th St.	Y	Y	Y	Y				Y	
8846	AS-16ms	5546	Pittsburgh-28th St.	Y	Y	Y	Y				Y	
8847	AS-16ms	5547	Pittsburgh-28th St.	Y	Y	Y	Y				Y	
8848	AS-16ms	5548	Pittsburgh-28th St.	Y	Y	Y	Y				Y	
8849	AS-16ms	5549	Pittsburgh-28th St.	Y	Y	Y	Y				Y	
8850	AS-16ms	5550	Pittsburgh-28th St.	Y	Y	Y	Y				Y	
8851	AS-16ms	5551	Pittsburgh-28th St.	Y	Y	Y	Y				Y	
8852	AS-16ms	5552	Pittsburgh-28th St.	Y	Y	Y	Y				Y	
8853	AS-16ms	5553	Pittsburgh-28th St.	Y	Y	Y	Y				Y	
8854	AS-16ms	5554	Pittsburgh-28th St.	Y	Y	Y	Y				Y	
8855	AS-16ms	5555	Pittsburgh-28th St.	Y	Y	Y	Y				Y	
8856	AS-16ms	5556	Pittsburgh-28th St.	Y	Y	Y	Y				Y	
8902	AS-16m	5412	Indianapolis		Y							
8903	AS-16ms	5557	Mingo Jct.	Y	Y	Y		Y				
8904	AS-16m	5414	Mingo Jct.		Y	Y		Y				
8905	AS-16ms	5558	Crestline	Y	Y	Y						
8906	AS-16m	5406	Mingo Jct.		Y			Y				
8907	AS-16m	5407	Pitcairn					Y				
8908	AS-16m	5408	Pitcairn					Y				
8909	AS-16m	5409	Pitcairn					Y				
8910	AS-16ms	5560	Cleveland	Y	Y							
8911	AS-16ms	5561	Pitcairn	Y	Y	Y						
8912	AS-16ms	5562	Pitcairn	Y	Y	Y						
8913	AS-16ms	5563	Cleveland	Y	Y							
8914	AS-16	5499	Sandusky									
8915	AS-16ms	5565	Mingo Jct.	Y	Y	Y						
8916	AS-16ms	5566	Morrisville	Y	Y	Y						

Notes to Table
SG = Steam generator; TP = Train Phone;
CS = Cab Signals; DC = Dual control;
HC = Hump control; DB = Dynamic brake;
PMF = Pressure maintenance feature;
SC = Speed control; RA = Two-way radio
Special equipment as of January 1960

late 1955 and early 1956 had the full set of freight-type equipment. The last group of RS-3's was equipped with static traction generator excitation, subsequently used on the Alco RS-11.

SERVICE HISTORY

The Equipment and Assignment Table illustrates that the PRR RS-3's were assigned in all regions of the system in 1959. Of all the various assignments, perhaps the most common for the non-boiler units was local freight runs. For instance, a 1964 visit to the Emporium and Ridgeway area in Pennsylvania found four RS-3's in each location. The units at Ridgeway were used on local freights to Falls Creek, Johnsonburg and St. Marys. The Emporium set (which included the 8445) was used in helper service from Emporium to Keating summit on the line to Buffalo. The 8445 gave passenger protect for both the Erie and Buffalo passenger trains. This was particularly important for the Erie train since it usually ran with one E-unit on a nightly Erie-Emporium-Erie turn.

Most of the class AS-16ms units were used in Pittsburgh commuter service. The heaviest of these services ran eastward on the mainline to Derry, Pennsylvania with some trains terminating at Trafford. Other Pittsburgh commuter services ran on the main lines toward St. Louis and Chicago, on both sides of the Allegheny River northeast of Pittsburgh, and on the line south along the Monongahela River.

During the 1950's the AS-16ms units assigned to Chicago were used on the Valparaiso commuter "Dummy" locals. Other passenger assignments included the Delmarva line south of Wilmington, Delaware and in various protect passenger assignments. One of the protection services was at Emporium, Pennsylvania noted above.

The RS-3 units were renumbered in 1966 into the 5400 and 5500 series, as shown on the Assignment Table.

The first Alco RS-3 to be retired was the 8911 in July 1966. After this date, units were retired every year until only 23 ex-PRR units remained to be passed on to Conrail from Penn Central. This included 8 units that Penn Central had re-engined with EMD model 12-567 engines and generators from E-units.

The much-renumbered high-short hood RS-3 unit, unique on the PRR, in January 1967 at Renovo, Pennsylvania. She's still numbered 8445, but not for long. Later, the Alco served Penn Central, the Lehigh Valley and Conrail. On LV and CR, new road numbers were used.

These were re-rated to 1200 horsepower with the smaller engines. After the start of Conrail on April 1, 1976, ten of the former PRR model RS-3's were conveyed to Amtrak for service on work trains. Both the Conrail and Amtrak units have since been retired. Some of these were sold to shortlines for further use.

Three other former PRR model RS-3's came to Conrail through a different set of circumstances. Because the PRR and PC had a substantial ownership in the Lehigh Valley Railroad, several motive power transactions occurred during the diesel era. One of these was a 1971 exchange of three older Lehigh Valley RS-2's sent to Penn Central for trade-in units, while the LV received three ex-PRR, RS-3 units that were in newer and in better condition for further service. The units that went to the LV were PC 5461, which became LV (II)210, PC 5569, which became LV (II) 211, and PC 5401, which became LV (II)212. PC 5569 was the unique high short hood RS-3 with both dynamic brake and steam boiler. The three passed to Conrail from the Lehigh Valley on April 1, 1976 and were again renumbered, to 5586, 5587 and 5588 respectively. Conrail retired units 5586 and 5588 in October 1976.

High short hood 5587 survived in its original Alco form until January 1979, when it was rebuilt with an EMD 12-567

Below, PRR 8599 was in the last group of RS-3 switchers purchased by the PRR. The 16 units in the group were all class AS-16m and illustrate the last carbody configuration of this model. Instead of louvers on the side of the hood, the late RS-3s used two sets of air filters oriented vertically in two groups. The 8599 is seen at New Castle, Pennsylvania in June, 1962.

Above, one is reminded of the introduction to radio's "Gunsmoke," describing the Marshal as "The first man they call for; the last man they want to see." The wreck train is operating between Renovo and Lock Haven Pennsylvania in February 1965, with RS-3 8436 providing the power.

engine and the matching generator from a retired E-unit. This was a continuation of the program started by PC as mentioned above. In this form (still with the high short hood), PRR 8445 /PRR 5569/PC 5569/LV211(II)/CR 5587 continued in service with the number 9920 until it was retired by Conrail in April 1985.

A commuter train headed for Pittsburgh on April 20, 1962 stops at Edgewood, Pennsylvania. RS-3 8846 is running short-hood forward thanks to the dual controls that enabled bi-directional operation. The Pittsburgh area commuter service would be abandoned in November 1964; the straight, unmodified P-70 coaches never would receive air-conditioning.

CLASS FS-16m
F-M H16-44

Fairbanks-Morse model H16-44 road-switchers totaled about five percent of the 1500/1600 horsepower, B-B road-switchers on U. S. railroads. The ten class H16-44 units on the Pennsylvania Railroad were almost exactly that percentage of the total of H16-44, EMD GP7 and Alco RS-3 diesels on the railroad. The class FS-16m locomotives were ordered on one of the PRR's first purchases of road-switchers in the 1500/1600 horsepower range. But no other orders for F-M H16-44 units followed, although 55 more GP7s and more than a hundred RS-3's arrived over the next four years. As for the H16-44 units, they were ordered as part of builders order LD-129 in May 1951 and were delivered in April and May 1952. The ten units were numbered 8807 to 8816 and classed FS-16m.

The model H16-44 was built in three carbody variations. The PRR FS-16m's were the first type, with C-liner trucks and without the decorative striping around the side cab windows. A modification made in later years on the PRR was to add four louvres on the battery box side to reduce the possibility of gas explosions from the hydrogen generated by the batteries.

Special equipment on the class FS-16m's included trainphone and cab signals.

SERVICE HISTORY

The class FS-16m units were initially assigned to Conemaugh (Johnstown), Pennsylvania for maintenance and stayed there throughout the 1950's. Assignment to Conemaugh meant a variety of road-switcher duties, almost all of which were associated with coal service operating out of Cresson, Pennsylvania. Also working out of Cresson were six to eight FS-20m units which could and did operate in MU with the FS-16m diesels. At Cresson, heavy switching of coal hoppers in the yard and mine runs on the numerous Cresson branches were the assignments for the class. A typical run on one of the Cresson branches would use two or three F-M units to handle the work.

As the 1950s ended, maintenance was transferred to East Altoona for the entire class. A year or so later, six of the class were transferred to Conway for maintenance. By the spring of 1962, several of the class FS-16m's were being used at Conway as heavy switchers and as local freight engines. By the end of 1964, all but the 8807 (which was still assigned to East Altoona) were assigned to Conway for maintenance.

In 1965, all of the class was transferred to Columbus to concentrate F-M maintenance; all of the H20-44 and H24-66 units were similarly assigned. In this assignment there was more heavy switching and local freight service, both in Columbus and working from satellite locations such as Dennison, Ohio. The class FS-16m units ended their PRR service at Columbus.

In the 1966 renumbering, the FS-16m's units became class FRS-16 and were to be renumbered from 8807-8816 to 5150-5159. Not all were renumbered, however, since 8807, 8808, 8810, 8812, 8814 and 8816 were retired in January 1967 with their original road numbers. The remaining four saw service in the 5150 series, but for three, their remaining service time was brief. All but 5158 were retired late in 1967. The 5158 worked for two more years in Penn Central service. It was moved to Chicago shortly after the PC merger. Before it moved, it received a full Penn Central road switcher lettering job with both Penn Central and the PC noodle emblem on the long hood and non-standard numbers on the cab side.

Penn Central 5158 was retired in February 1970.

CLASS BS-16m, BS-16ms
BLH AS-616

Most of the Pennsylvania Railroad's 1500-1750 horsepower six-axle road switchers were utilized as heavy switchers. The ten class BS-16m and two class BS-16ms six-axle Baldwin road switchers were no exception. This group includes the P&WV 40, which spent almost its entire life on the PRR before being purchased in July 1963. The units were acquired in three groups as shown in the summary table.

The Baldwin-Lima-Hamilton model AS-616 was one of three road switcher designs introduced by the builder in

PRR 8808 and 8815 switch cars at busy Conway (Pennsylvania) Yard on May 5, 1962. Note that this set was not in hump service when this photo was taken; this is just a bit of 3200-hp. flat switching.

1950. The three shared a common car-body, engine and generator arrangement but differed in trucks and number of traction motors. Model AS-16 was the four-axle, four traction motor design (B-B); Model AS-416 was the six-axle, four traction motor design (A1A-A1A); and AS-616 was the six-axle, six traction (C-C) motor design. The PRR purchased none of the B-B or A1A-A1A models, and only nine of the C-C units new from Baldwin. While the Pennsy had little use for the A1A units (which were intended for light axle loading applications), it is odd that none of the four axle AS-16 units were purchased since the Penn purchased so many EMD, Alco and F-M units of this type.

The Pennsylvania-Reading Seashore Lines, which was jointly owned by the PRR and Reading, purchased 16 model AS-16 units and the Reading itself owned the largest fleet—43.

The boiler on the class BS-16ms units was the Vapor Corporation OK-4625 2500 lbs. per hour steam generator.

Other special equipment varied over the years on the class. Hump control was originally installed on 8966, 8972-8974 and 8111-8112. During their years at Conway, all units of the class had hump control installed, but by 1963 it had been removed from all of the units. On units 8966-8969, 8972-8974 and 8111-8112, both hump cab signals and yard trainphone were installed during the

The opposed piston design throbs under the hood of 8813 in Zanesville, Ohio, in 1966. Note the keystone in the middle of the long hood.

years assigned to Conway. PRR 8969-8972 and 8111-8112 had road cab signals and trainphone during all but the last few years of PRR service.

When the PRR purchased the first nine Baldwin AS-616 units, the plan was to assign them as follows:

8966: Scully, for turns to Burgettstown
8967-68: Shire Oaks
8969-74: Mingo Junction, Weirton, Wheeling and Benwood

When the units were delivered, the plan was carried out, except the 8966 went to Mingo Junction and the 8972 went to Scully. But within a few months, the Scully unit went to Mingo Junction and the two Shire Oaks units

were transferred to Canton.

These assignments all involved heavy switching and hump service in conjunction with iron ore and coal traffic. At Mingo Junction both were handled. The coal came from the Cadiz branch in Ohio's Harrison County and from the Powhatan branch, which fed into the Mingo Junction yard from the south. The iron ore came primarily from the Cleveland docks and required distribution to the Wheeling Steel and Weirton Steel mills in the Weirton and Steubenville areas.

Although the two Class BS-16ms units had steam boilers, their primary assignment was the same heavy duty as the other AS-616 units. The photo on page 245 of the book *Pennsy Power II* illustrates 8971 on a high school football special, indicating the type of passenger service to which the two BS-16ms units were assigned.

Early assignments of the other BS-16m units were similar. The 8111 and 8112 received the Scully assignment on delivery. P&WV 40 was assigned to Columbus yard for a very short time when first leased in February 1952, but was soon dispatched to Terre Haute for assignment to the Brazil mine run.

During the 1950s, the BS-16m and BS-16ms units remained in the general area of Mingo Junction, Pitcairn and Conway as heavy switchers. After 1956, more and more of the class were assigned to Conway, until mid-1957 when all of the PRR AS-616 units were assigned to that location as hump pushers and other heavy switching assign-

Portrait of a classic C-C road switcher, in Zanesville Ohio in January 1963. In the early stages of dieselization (1946-51), Baldwin was the clear leader in C-C road switchers. The photographer was Paul Dunn of Zanesville Ohio, in front of whose camera lens an incredible variety of PRR power appeared in his home town. The 8971, shown here, is one of the two steam generator-equipped Baldwin AS-616s.

PRR AS-616 No. 8111 MU'd with transfer unit 8729 at North Philadelphia station, in August 1964. 8111 and 8112 (not shown) were the last two new AS-616s purchased by the Penn. In fact, they were part of the PRR's last order for Baldwin engines of any kind. Note the later drop equalizer truck, instead of the Commonwealth rigid bolster type.

ments. In May 1958, these units were joined by the P&WV 40 from Terre Haute.

About the start of 1960, the Conway assignment ended when the eight SD9 units from Altoona and four SD9s from Columbus were transferred to Conway. In return, 8966-8969, 8972-8974 and P&WV 40 were transferred to Altoona and 8111, 8112, 8970 and 8971 were transferred to Columbus. In October 1962, the units assigned to Columbus were sent to Philadelphia. Units 8111 and 8112 were assigned to 46th St. enginehouse and 8970 and 8971 were

assigned to Camden. The Altoona units were still used in heavy switching. The Philadelphia units were also used in both switching and transfer service. The BS-16m units in the Philadelphia area were often MUed with the BS-24m units on the Greenwich yard to Camden transfer runs.

In mid-1965, four of the Altoona units moved to Cleveland: 8966-8968 and 8114. The latter unit was the former P&WV 40, which was renumbered PRR 8114 after its purchase by the Pennsy in July 1963. By mid-1966 three more units had joined them: 8973, 8974 and 8112.

In Cleveland, there was much heavy switching at Whiskey Island where the iron ore was transferred from the lake boats to hopper cars.

In the 1966 renumbering, the class was to have been renumbered from 8966-8974, 8111-8112 and 8114 to 6966-6977. However, 8968, 8969, 8970, 8971 and 8972 were retired in July 1966 without being renumbered. The class BS-16m units became class BRS-16 and the two BS-16ms units would have become class BRS-16s. These remaining were all renumbered after July 1966.

In 1967, units 6966, 6973 and 6974

Penn Central 6966 at Edge Moor yard near Wilmington after replacement of original trucks.
September 19, 1971

Order Summary - Class BS-16m Units

PRR ROAD NOS.	BLH SALES ORDER	NO. OF UNITS	PRR CLASS	ORDER DATE	DELIVERY DATES
8966-8969, 8972-8974	50518-C	7	BS-16m	Aug 50	May 51-Jun 51
8970-8971	50518-C	2	BS-16ms	Aug 50	Jun 51
P&WV 40/ PRR 8114	50529-A	1	BS-16m	Nov 50 (*)	May 51 (*)
8111-8112	300318	2	BS-16m	Jun 53	Feb 54

(*) Date of order by P&WV. Leased to PRR effective on Feb. 1, 1952. PRR renewed this lease several times by the PRR until the unit was purchased by PRR effective July 1, 1963.

Below: Fans of Baldwin diesel locomotives have been known to shed tears at this sight. When an elderly locomotive is judged to require more investment in its continuance than is justified by the economic result of estimated useful life, the locomotive is moved to the "dead line" and stored. This photo of what had been No. 8111 was taken in the Altoona dead line on November 11, 1967. The unit has been renumbered to 6975 in anticipation of Penn Central. Since it was unlikely that 8111/6975 would ever move under its own power again, the numbering was sloppily done with an aerosol can, which required the least labor.

returned to their original assignment— Mingo Junction. Here they were on the other end of the Cleveland to Mingo iron ore trip where they continued in old duties, heavy switching and hump pushing.

Equipment and Assignment Table
Classes BS-16m and BS-16ms
(Baldwin AS-616)

Orig. Road No.	1966 Road No.	May 1959 Assignment	TP	YP	CS	SG	HC	HS
8111	6975	Conway	Y	Y	Y		Y	Y
8112	6976	Conway	Y	Y	Y		Y	Y
8114	6977	Conway-P&WV 40					Y	Y
8966	6966	Conway		Y			Y	Y
8967	6967	Conway		Y			Y	Y
8968		Conway		Y			Y	Y
8969		Conway	Y	Y	Y		Y	Y
8970		Conway	Y			Y	Y	
8971		Conway	Y			Y	Y	
8972		Conway		Y			Y	Y
8973	6973	Conway		Y			Y	Y
8974	6974	Conway		Y			Y	Y

TP = Train Phone; YP = Yard Trainphone; CS = (Road) Cab signal;
SG = Steam Generator; HC = Hump control; HS = Hump cab signals

In September 1967, former P&WV 6977 was retired. Otherwise, several of the other BRS-16 units were in the dead line at East Altoona. Four of the class were retired soon after the PC merger with 6975 and 6976 going in June 1969. The remaining four (6966, 6967, 6973 and 6974) were assigned to the Baltimore-Wilmington area. After the transfer east, 6966 received an interesting modification by Penn Central. It was re-trucked with a set of Baldwin three-axle drop-equalizer trucks and continued in service. The 6966 also received partial Penn Central lettering and the 6974 received the full PC lettering. The final retirement dates were: 6966, February 1972; 6967, August 1970; 6973, August 1970; and 6974, March 1972.

PITTSBURGH AND WEST VIRGINIA 40

Pittsburgh and West Virginia engine 40 led a diesel locomotive schizoid life. P&WV 40 was a Baldwin model AS-616 (1600 horsepower, C-C wheel arrangement) which spent only the first two and two-thirds years of its life on its home railroad. For the next ten years, the unit was leased to the PRR, but it worked in P&WV livery and lettering. It was finally purchased by the PRR in 1963 after several lease extensions. Numbered 8114 and then 8977 on the PRR roster, the Baldwin worked four more years before being retired.

The P&WV 40 was delivered to its owner in May, 1951 at Rook shop in Green Tree borough near Pittsburgh. From the start it was an orphan among a P&WV roster of Fairbanks-Morse road-switchers. Starting on February 1, 1954, the unit was leased by the Pennsylvania Railroad for $55 per day for a period of three years. The initial intention was to assign the unit to Columbus yard in conjunction with Cincinnati Chevrolet plant traffic. However, the P&WV 40 was sent to Terre Haute for mine run work within a month. The PRR considered the six-axle unit to be particularly useful in this assignment. In May, 1958 the Baldwin was transferred to Conway yard north of Pittsburgh for hump service. This reassignment brought the P&WV 40 together with the PRR's similar class BS-16m's serving at Conway. In September 1960 the P&WV 40 was transferred to Altoona for heavy yard service.

As early as 1956, the PRR considered an outright purchase of the P&WV 40. This was but the first of several evaluations of acquisition either by purchase or trade. In 1959, the P&WV proposed that the PRR trade one of its FM model H20-44 road-switchers to the P&WV in exchange for the P&WV 40. This proposal received serious consideration by the PRR. Within a month a P&WV mechanical department man inspected the PRR 9305 at Johnstown and a favorable report resulted. The PRR 9305 was a FM model H20-44 very similar to the 23 P&WV H20-44 units although it only had MU connections on the rear end. In addition the depreciated value of the P&WV 40 and the PRR 9305 were within a few thousand dollars. This was an important

P&WV No. 40 at Hollidaysburg, Pennsylvania in May 1960. This is a rear-quarter view; the great majority of Baldwin road-switchers were run long hood forward.

consideration for the equipment trust holders. For whatever reason, the trade was not made and by the end of 1959, the PRR proposed continuing the lease.

In 1963, after further lease extensions, the PRR and the P&WV came to an agreement for the PRR to purchase the unit. The PRR's initial offer was to pay the $1650 scrap price for the Baldwin. The P&WV countered stating that the depreciated book valve was $78,689. Finally, the PRR agreed to a purchase price of $35,000 since this was what the P&WV still owed to the equipment trust for the unit. The P&WV 40 was purchased by the PRR on July 1, 1963.

In approving the $35,000 purchase of the P&WV 40, Mr. A. J. Greenough, president of the Pennsylvania Railroad was critical of the situation which resulted in payment of $186,450 in lease payments ($55 per day for the whole period) over the ten years of the lease. Mr. Greenough noted that this was more than the P&WV had paid for the Baldwin.

The PRR numbered the former P&WV 40 as its road number 8114. The road number followed the 1954 group of Baldwin switchers and road-switchers. Detailed instructions were issued for painting which included the painting diagram for classes AS-16m and AS-16ms units (PRR drawing B462763, Revision A) and the various drawings for letters, numbers and Keystones. This paint scheme was the one which originated for the new units purchased in 1962 where the PENNSYLVANIA lettering on the long hood was replaced by a Keystone emblem and the cab side numbers were 16" instead of 5". These instructions were not carried out exactly. The PRR 8114 rolled out of the paint shop on September 13, 1963 with the Keystone emblems but with the 5" numbers on the cabside. The Baldwin finally received the 16" cab numbers when it was renumbered 6977.

PRR 8114 was transferred to Cleveland in early 1965, where it worked thereafter. The 8114 was renumbered 8977 and reclassed BRS-16 as part of the 1966 renumbering plan. PRR 8977 was retired in September, 1967.

CLASS AS-16a (later AS-16am) *Alco RSD-5*

The six Alco model RSD-5 units on the PRR got the jobs that most of the railroad's first generation six-axle units were assigned, namely the dirty work. These gritty tasks included heavy yard work (particularly hump pushing), heavy local freights and helper service. Both double engine and single engine, six axle units were ordered by the Pennsy in the 1950's, and they all got this type of assignment.

The PRR ordered its six Alco model RSD-5 road switchers in November 1951 on Alco sales order 20785. The first two were delivered in October 1952 and the last four in March 1953. The gap in delivery was caused by a labor strike at Alco. These units were numbered 8446 to 8451 and classed AS-16a.

All six diesels were equipped with hump control. Units 8449 to 8451 were equipped with cab signals. None of the six were built with multiple unit control, but in 1965, all six PRR model RSD-5 units were MU-equipped by the PRR, and were reclassed AS-16am.

Addition of multiple-unit control equipment involved connection of certain control wires and pneumatic hoses to cables and hoses that run the length of the unit, terminating at MU cable and hose connectors front and rear. This allows a group of locomotives all to be controlled from any one of them. The

PRR improved flexibility by later applying MU equipment to some engines that, for economy reasons, it had purchased without MU.

When delivered, the six AS-16a units were assigned to the Maryland Division for heavy yard duty in Baltimore, Maryland and Wilmington. By 1955, the 8446 was assigned to Enola and Harrisburg, typically used for both yard switching and to Enola-Harrisburg transfer runs. These assignments remained in effect throughout the 1960s. During this time, one or two of the AS-16a units were assigned to York, Pennsylvania.

In late 1960, the 8446 was moved from the Harrisburg area to Terre Haute, Indiana, used in a heavy coal run from the Green River mine, east of Terre Haute. By the end of 1964, another change was made. Units 8446 to 8448 were moved to East Altoona on the Pittsburgh Region. The other three units in the class remained on the Chesapeake Region.

The pre-Penn Central renumbering changed the road numbers from 8446-8451 to 6800-6805. The units were reclassed to ARS-16a. By May 1967, all six units were assigned to Wilmington (6800 and 6801) and Baltimore (6802 to 6805), but by September 1967, all of the class were assigned to Conway maintenance. All of the class ARS-16a units were on the roster on February 1, 1968, the first day of Penn Central operation.

Four of the six RSD-5 units were retired in the post-PRR years. The 6800 in April 1977 by Conrail, 6801 in December 1977 by Penn Central, 6802 in October 1978 by Conrail and 6805 in

Harrisburg, Pennsylvania is the site at which RSD-5 No. 8446 was captured, switching the stockyard on September 9, 1959.

Locomotive Characteristics

Class	BS-16m	BS-16ms	AS-16a(*)	ES-15a	AS-15m
Builder	BLH	BLH	Alco	EMD	Alco
Model	AS-616	AS-616	RSD-5	SD7	RS-3
Horsepower	1600	1600	1600	1500	1500
Wheel Arr,	C-C	C-C	C-C	C-C	B-B
Total Weight	331,000 lbs	339,600 lbs	360,000 lbs	360,000 lbs	245,400 lbs
Length over Couplers	58' 0"	58' 0"	56' 0"	60' 9"	56' 0"
Truck Centers	32' 3"	32' 3"	34' 9"	35' 0"	30' 0"
Truck Wheelbase	13' 0"	13' 0"	12' 6"	13' 7"	9' 4"
Engine	BLH 8-608A	BLH 8-608A	Alco 12-244D	EMD 16-567BC	Alco 12-244B
Generator	W 471	W 471	GE GT-566	EMD D12	GE GT-564
Traction Motors	W 370DZ	W 370DZ	GE 752	EMD D27E	GE 752
Gear Ratio	63:15	63:15	74:18	65:12	74:18
Maximum Speed	60 MPH	60 MPH	60 MPH	55 MPH	65 MPH
Starting Trac. Effort	82,750 lbs	84,900 lbs	90,000 lbs	90,000 lbs	61,350 lbs
Continuous Trac. Effort	72,900 lbs	72,900 lbs	78,750 lbs	87,700 lbs	52,500 lbs
CTE Speed	6.5 MPH	6.5 MPH	5.0 MPH	4.6 MPH	9.0 MPH
Steam Generator		OK-4625			
Steam Gen. Capacaity		2500			

(*) Reclassed as AS-16m in 1965

October 1976 by Conrail. In the first part of 1972, units 6803 and 6804 switched road numbers. The former 6804, now 6803, was retired in May 1972.

The second 6804 had a more interesting history. In the first part of 1975, this unit was converted to a hump slug to work with an EMD-re-engined Alco RSD-15. This coversion included removal of the engine, generator and cab. The hump set was originally numbered 6849 and was passed on to Conrail. Conrail renumbered the set 6899 before retiring it in January 1980.

CLASS ES-15a
EMD SD7

The PRR's two EMD model SD7's were very special units, ordered for a very special service. They were purchased for what the Association of American Railroads characterized as the steepest known grade on a line-haul railroad in this country. This was the fearsome Madison Hill, the 1.5-mile, 5.89 percent average grade between Madison and North Madison, Indiana. We should note that in railroading circles, any grade greater than 2 per cent (a rise or drop of two feet in 100 feet) is considered to be severe. 5.89 per cent is cause for alarm, special equipment, special procedures, and great care.

The PRR ordered two 1500 horse-power, C-C wheel arrangement road-switchers in June 1953 (EMD order 5300); they were delivered five months later. They were classed ES-15a by the PRR and numbered 8588 and 8589. In November 1953, the new diesels replaced a small group of Class H-6 2-8-0 steam locomotives specially equipped for the Madison Hill, augmented by class H-10s 2-8-0s.

The Class ES-15a units alternated between service on the Madison line and switching duty at Hawthorne Yard, the main PRR yard in Indianapolis. Each unit spent half a month on each assignment, which allowed the units to receive their monthly inspections in Indianapolis during their Hawthorne periods.

The 16-cylinder EMD model 567BC diesel engine installed in PRR's SD7 units was a transition model between the 567B and 567C. This model incorporated some C model features on the "B" engine. The Model D12 main traction generator was standard. The 65:12 gear ratio was achieved by a modification to

the EMD model D27 traction motor. This modified motor was designated D27E. In model D27E traction motors, the 12-tooth motor pinion was quite small; the motor pinion teeth were cut directly into the motor shaft. This was similar to the gear configuration in the EH-15 units.

The PRR SD7's weighed 360,000 lbs. each. It has become part of railfan folk-lore that these two units were unusually heavy, having been specially ballasted for Madison Hill service. While this weight was at the maximum of the normal EMD weight range (300,000 to 360,000 lbs) for SD7 units, several other railroads purchased SD7 units weighing from 360,000 to 370,000 lbs for heavy service. The low gear ratio installed for hill-climbing did, however, yield a continuous tractive effort of 87,700 lbs at 4.6 miles per hour and a maximum speed of 55 mph.

SPECIAL EQUIPMENT

EMD optional equipment included dynamic brakes, the pressure maintain-

PRR 6801 demonstrates its latter-day capability to operate in multiple unit, here with RSD-12 6873. Location is Morrisville Yard, on November 25, 1967.

PRR 8589 switches the grocery warehouse track at the top of the Madison grade, North Madison, Indiana. The date is July 3, 1964.

ing feature and a special wheel-slip control feature with an automatic sanding device. An item of optional equipment not related to operation on Madison hill was hump control, for use during the half of each month when the unit operated in hump pushing service at Hawthorne Yard. Because the PRR operated the SD7s singly, they were not equipped for multiple unit operation.

An unusual feature on the class ES-15a units was rail washing equipment, that sprayed water ahead of the lead truck to assure that the rails were clean. This helped to maximize traction by removing leaves and other foreign material from the railheads. The rail washer was designed by the PRR mechanical department, and consisted of a water tank in the short hood, pressurized from the locomotive's air system, and the pipes and control valves necessary to spray the water onto the railhead.

It should be noted that the critical direction of movement on the Hill was downhill, not uphill. The danger of a

downgrade runaway far exceeded the inconvenience of an upgrade stall on the Hill. The heavy grade from North Madison south to Madison was so exceptional that special operating rules were necessary. They took a page and a half in the PRR employee timetables governing the territory. For example, Western Region timetable Number 1 effective October 25, 1964, stated:

"Enginemen and Conductors required special qualification for the Madison Hill, and were required to work the Hill at least once a year to avoid re-qualification."

Only an ES-15a unit could be used on the Hill; and the dynamic brakes, pressure maintaining feature and rail washers all had to be operational if the a train was operated on the Hill. The locomotive was required to be on the south (downgrade) end of the train.

Trains could not exceed 15 cars, or 350 tons, or 51 tons per effective brake exclusive of the engine. Movement of light engines was prohibited because the braking safety margin was question-

able without the additional braking capacity of coupled cars.

Prior to operating down the hill, the engineman had to inspect the fuel and lube oil to verify an adequate supply. Because of the heavy grade, the lube oil had to be two inches above the minimum mark on the dipstick to be adequate in a tilted condition.

A thorough brake test was required on the train before proceeding down the grade.

The following rules are quoted verbatim concerning actual train handling:

"After passing derail and while on the grade:

(a) The dynamic brake must be manipulated to obtain the maximum dynamic braking effect, without allowing the load-meter to go above 700 amperes. The train speed will be controlled by supplementing the dynamic brake with the train brakes.

(b) While descending grade, the train air brakes and dynamic brake must be manipulated to avoid speed in excess of eight (8) miles per hour

The other half of the SD7 assignment; 6950 (ex-8588) is drilling Hawthorne Yard, Indianapolis, Indiana in April 1968, less than three months into the Penn Central era.

Right: Hawthorne Yard in Indianapolis was home to more than an SD7; here is ex-D&H Alco RS-3 4044 in April 1965, working Hawthorne. The paint job is no longer new.

Below: RS-3 No. 4047 had been on PRR property for two years in D&H livery. When the Penn bought them, they were repainted; this photo captures No. 4047 in April 1958, about three months after acquisition. There appear to be minor deviations from the lettering drawing in the cab numbers and hood letters (is the letter "S" in "PENNSYLVANIA" upside down?)

at any point on the grade and a minimum running time of twelve (12) minutes from the derail to Bridge 44.14 must be observed.

(c) If a condition arises making the use of hand brakes necessary, the engineman will give the prescribed signal for brakes to be applied from the train. Trainmen, when practicable, will apply hand brakes. Hand brakes and conductor's valve are to be applied in accordance with Paragraph 19 and 19A of the Brake and Train Air Signal Instructions No. 99-D-1.

(d) If the diesel engine stops, dynamic brake becomes inoperative, or an electrical failure develops while on the Hill, the movement must be STOPPED and all hand brakes applied. The train must not be started until the Diesel engine is operating properly, the brake system charged, and proper main reservoir pressure established, unless otherwise authorized by the Superintendent Transportation."

The dual Madison Hill/Hawthorne yard assignment lasted for about 25 years through PRR, Penn Central and into the Conrail era. In the late 1970s on Conrail, the ES-15a units were first assigned to Stanley yard in Toledo and then to Allentown yard on the former Lehigh Valley line.

The two units were renumbered to 6950 and 6951 in the 1966 renumbering scheme and reclassed ERS-15ax. Penn Central renumbered them in 1970 to 6998 and 6999 to make room in the numbering system for new SD38s. Multiple unit control was also applied by Penn Central and were reclassed ERS-15a. Conrail retired 6999 in February 1984 and the 6998 in April 1985. Conrail 6999 was sold for further service on the Glasgow Railway in Kentucky.

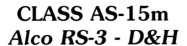

CLASS AS-15m
Alco RS-3 - D&H

In 1955 the PRR was filling its motive power needs with leased motive power, both steam and diesel. As part of this program, by early 1956 six Alco RS-3's were leased from the Delaware and Hudson Railroad. The units were D&H 4041, 4042, 4044, 4046, 4047 and 4048.

Unlike most of the leased units of the period, the ex-D&H units were not returned to their original owners. Instead, the PRR purchased the units in January, 1958. The D&H road numbers were retained by the Pennsy and the units were classified AS-15m.

The D&H units had the same basic equipment described for PRR Alco RS-3's. The PRR class for the RS-3s purchased from the D&H, (AS-15m) indicates that the horsepower available for traction on the units was 1500. This reveals a practice unique to the D&H.

When the D&H purchased their first model RS-3's after previously buying 27 RS-2's (including two for the subsidiary Napierville Junction Ry.), the road made the decision to operate the units at 1500 horsepower.

After their purchase in 1958, the six units were given local assignments in Fort Wayne, including Fort Wayne-Chicago local freights and switching at Indianapolis. They could not MU with other RS-3's because they were equipped with 6-SL brakes. They were all retired in May and July 1965.

Chapter 8

Later Road Switchers

By the mid-1950s, Alco, EMD and F-M had all made product improvements in their locomotives in order to maintain their market positions. By this time, Baldwin was losing its grip on the locomotive business. The Eddystone plant would ship its last diesel-electric locomotive in 1956. Having received its last Baldwin diesel early in 1954, the PRR finished its dieselization with the products of the other main builders.

The most obvious improvement in diesel locomotives was the increase in horsepower per unit. Although this was an important feature, there was more to it than that.

Alco replaced its Model 244 with the Model 251 engine. This was an improvement which was vital to meeting customer complaints about the Model 244. The rating of the Model 251 12-cylinder engine was raised to 1800 horsepower.

EMD's improvements included upgrades to both the engine and the electrical equipment. The Model 567 engine's horsepower was increased to 1750 horsepower in the 16-cylinder version. Electrical equipment changes included an insulation material so improved that short term ratings were not required (in theory).

In 1953, F-M began to produce their Train Master road-switcher, Model H24-66. This 2400 horsepower, six-axle unit was described by Fairbanks-Morse as the "the most useful locomotive

ever built," and it was to be F-M's masterpiece. But even the Train Master did not prolong F-M's production of locomotives much beyond the completion of dieselization.

All of these developments were taken into consideration by the PRR in their remaining purchases of road-switchers. These models have been characterized here as later road-switchers.

We note that EMD's GP9 unit indeed had a road-switcher carbody, and was produced contemporaneously with the road-switchers described in this chapter. However, because the PRR saw the GP9 as a freight unit, not a road-switcher, it has been included in Chapter 5.

Train No. 17 is just departing from Altoona, Pennsylvania on October 12, 1957, after disgorging the photographer. EP-22 No. 5712A is getting assistance from APS-24ms No. 8609 as the assault on the East Slope grade commences. About a year earlier, this would have been an Aerotrain, testifying to the fact that not all progress is improvement.

PRR RSD-7 8608 and RSD-15 8614 make an unusual visit to Pittsburgh, having run in from Altoona on Train No. 13 on February 12, 1966. They normally ran only from Altoona to Gallitzen as East Slope helpers, but continued on this day because of a road engine failure.

Class APS-24ms
Alco RSD-7

The five units of class APS-24ms were purchased as East Slope passenger helpers out of Altoona. This seemingly contradictory term refers to the East Slope of the Alleghenies and actually applies to trains moving westbound from Altoona to Gallitzin.

The class APS-24ms units were ordered in September 1955, and delivered in December 1955 and January 1956. Alco designated these 2400 horsepower, C-C wheel arrangement road-switchers as model RSD-7. The PRR class was APS-24ms and the road numbers 8606-8610. On delivery, the units were placed in the service for which they were intended—almost exclusively as passenger helpers. Even when the East Slope Passenger Helper pool was merged with the freight helper pool about 1960, the APS-24ms units remained assigned to Altoona.

The primary piece of special equipment on the APS-24ms units was a Vapor OK-4740 steam generator rated at 4500 lbs. of steam per hour. This was the largest steam generator installed in a PRR diesel. Other special equipment included trainphone, cab signals, and dynamic brakes. Both the APS-24ms units and the AS-24m units discussed in the next section were arranged to operate short hood forward. They were the only PRR road-switchers to be so operated.

SERVICE HISTORY

As indicated, the class was assigned to Altoona for almost the entire PRR period. In helper service, one or two of the units would be coupled ahead of the

Coming off the reversing track at AR Tower, Gallitzin Pennsylvania, PRR 8610 and 8607 are on their way back to Altoona after helping a passenger train up the East Slope grade. The date is July 18, 1958.

July 1965: PRR unit 8613 leads a trio of Alco road-switchers past Alto Tower in Altoona. They are returning from a helper assignment. Note the trainphone "fence" transmission antenna, and the disc-shaped receiving antenna on top of the short hood. Alco notched the hood corners to provide better access for sand filler hatches, and angled surfaces for number boards.

passenger units in the Altoona station, and would help the train to Gallitzen at the top of the Allegheny grade. At Gallitzen, the train would stop and the helpers would cut off and proceed around the loop track to AR tower, reversing direction in the process. At AR tower, a favorable signal would allow the helper set onto one of the eastbound main tracks for the return trip to Altoona. Aside from the location where the helpers were attached, this process was also used for freight helpers.

Although the assignment to Altoona is indicated on assignment sheets for the PRR period, one exception was noted. The 8606 was sighted at Bay Head Jct. in March of 1958, indicating at least a trial on the New York and Long Branch.

The assignments for the APS-24ms remained essentially the same during their entire PRR period—heavy work around Altoona, mainly helper service. One non-helper assignment during the 1965-66 period was their use on LA-1 and LA-2, the Altoona to Lewistown local freights. Late in the PRR diesel era, the units wandered to some extent.

Use on the Keating Summit grade north from Emporium, Pennsylvania is one example. In the mid-1960s, maintenance was transferred from East Altoona to Conway.

The impending Penn Central merger resulted in the units being renumbered from 8606-8610 to 6806-6810 in order. The class was changed from APS-24ms to ARS-24s. All of the units were on the Penn Central roster at merger time, but didn't last long. Except for 6809, all of the class was retired in December 1970. The 6809 was lettered for Penn Central, but was retired in November 1973.

Locomotive Characteristics

Class	APS-24ms	AS-24m	FS-24m	AS-18m	ES-17m	AS-18am
Builder	Alco	Alco	F-M	Alco	EMD	Alco
Model	RSD-7	RSD-15	H24-66	RS-11	SD9	RSD-12
Horsepower	2400	2400	2400	1800	1750	1800
Wheel Arr,	C-C	C-C	C-C	B-B	C-C	C-C
Total Weight	366,000 lbs	348,000 lbs	376,000 lbs	249,000 lbs	356,000 lbs	347,000 lbs
Length over Couplers	65' 1"	66' 7"	66' 0"	57' 0"	60' 9"	58' 2"
Truck Centers	43' 6"	43' 6"	41' 6"	31' 0"	35' 0"	35' 5"
Truck Wheelbase	12' 6"	12' 6"	13' 0"	9' 4"	13' 7"	12' 6"
Engine	Alco 16-244G	Alco 16-251B	FM 12-38D8-1/8	Alco 12-251B	EMD 16-567C	Alco 12-251B
Generator	GE GT-586	GE GT-586	GE GT-567	GE GT-581	EMD D12B	GE GT-586
Traction Motors	GE 752	GE 752	GE 752	GE 752	EMD D47	GE 752
Gear Ratio	65:18	74:18	74:18	74:18	62:15	74:18
Maximum Speed	75 MPH	65 MPH	66 MPH	65 MPH	65 MPH	65 MPH
Starting Trac. Effort	91,500 lbs	87,000 lbs	94,000 lbs	62,250 lbs	89,000 lbs	86,750 lbs
Continuous Trac. Effort	69,800 lbs	79,500 lbs	79,500 lbs	53,000 lbs	---	79,500 lbs
CTE Speed	9.0 MPH	8.5 MPH	8.6 MPH	10.0 MPH	---	6.0 MPH
Steam Generator	OK-4740					
Steam Gen, Capacity	4500					

W.D. VOLKMER PHOTO; DOUGLAS COLLECTION

Class AS-24m
Alco RSD-15

The Alco RSD-15 road-switchers were Alco's most advanced first generation diesel. The PRR ordered six examples of these units on Alco sales order 21025 in February 1956, at the same time they ordered nine F-M Train Masters. The Alco units were delivered between June and August 1956, numbered 8611 to 8616 and classed AS-24m. Special equipment included trainphone, cab signals and the brake pressure maintaining feature.

SERVICE HISTORY

The AS-24m's were delivered to the Pennsy at Wilkes-Barre via the D&H from Schenectady. All were assigned to Enola after delivery. The six units stayed at Enola until 1959 when the 8611 and 8613 were transferred to Morrisville. At Morrisville, they were assigned heavy work serving the Fairless Works of U. S. Steel. Hauling ore from the docks on the Delaware River into the mill was enough work on level ground, but on this run there were heavy grades approaching the overpass line crossing the PRR mainline.

In 1960, the Enola units were sent to the Northern Region, being assigned at various times to Williamsport, Renovo and Olean. Assignments here included

the helpers out of Emporium and Williamsport. In 1963, the Northern Region units were sent to Altoona and were followed in 1965 by the two units which had been at Morrisville. At Altoona, their main assignments were helper service on both the East and West Slopes and coal trains from Cresson. Even while they were based at Altoona, some of the units were sent to Renovo on occasion.

The 1966 PRR renumbering and reclassing resulted in the class AS-24m's being renumbered 6811 to 6816 and being reclassed ARS-24. During the PC period, 8611 was retired in July 1972. Otherwise, the 6815 was converted to a slug mother, re-engined with a 12 cylinder 567 engine and renumbered 6849. It was married to an ex-PRR RSD-5 con-

Above: The 6816 and 6815 head a freight train that has stopped near Renovo, Pennsylvania on July 6, 1967. They used to be 8616 and 8615 before repainting in the keystone-only image. The RSD-15s ran short hood forward

verted to a slug for hump pusher service at Dewitt yard, near Syracuse, New York. Otherwise, 6812, 6813, 6814 and 6816 entered Conrail service in April 1976. These last four Alcos were retired in June 1978 (6812 and 6813) and October 1978 (6814 and 6816). The converted 6849 was renumbered 6899 and was retired in January 1980.

As noted, the APS-24ms and AS-24m were the only two first-generation road switcher models that were normally operated short hood forward on the PRR.

RSD-15 8611 in MU with RS-11 8635 with a cut of hoppers in Morrisville, Pennsylvania. February 15, 1959

Class FS-24m
F-M H24-66

Fairbanks-Morse Train Master diesels did not play the significant role on the Pennsylvania Railroad that they did in their highly visible commuter train assignments on the Lackawanna, Jersey Central and Southern Pacific, or on the Virginian where the model formed more than a third of the diesel roster. On the PRR the nine F-M model H24-66's were tucked away in a roster of more than two thousand units. Moreover, they were not concentrated in one location until late in their PRR service lives.

All Pennsy first generation six-axle road switchers were assigned the same type of duty—heavy pusher, heavy mine gathering, transfer and yard service. The PRR's Train Masters were no exception. The nine F-M 2400 horsepower, C-C road switchers were ordered by the PRR on builder's order LD-200 in February 1956, and delivered in August and September 1956. They were assigned road numbers 8699-8707 and classified FS-24m.

EQUIPMENT

In the discussions of the PRR's F-M models H12-44, H16-44 and H20-44 it has been observed that the carbodies and equipment evolved during the production of these models. F-M concur-

rently offered the Train Master in two carbody types: high end platforms and low end platforms. Two railroads disliked the high end platform design because of a potentially unsafe mismatch of platform heights when these Train Masters were MUed with units of other builders. The Lackawanna, for example, operated the high end platform version, but restricted the H24-66 units to MU operation only with other H24-66s.

Southern and most Wabash TM units used the second carbody variation, which had steps along the side to make the transition from the height of the cab floor and high walkways down to the lower side walkway and end platforms. The end platforms thus matched the height of other units.

PRR Train Master 6701 is doing some heavy switching in Columbus, Ohio in March 1967. Late in the PRR diesel era, all FS-24m engines were concentrated in Ohio's capital, where there was plenty of heavy switching and transfer work to be done.

Blue smoke drifts skyward as the train's brake shoes protest a downhill ride west of Altoona. Train Master 8703 was here displaying its power by singlehandedly working a heavy coal train on October 12, 1957.

151

Another variation was the use of GE electrical equipment after the withdrawal of Westinghouse from the locomotive electrical equipment business.

On the PRR, the FS-24m's were built with the more conventional high platforms and GE electrical equipment. The high platforms were not a problem since the Train Masters usually operated as single units. Although some class FS-24m units were assigned to Conemaugh with other F-M road-switchers, they could not MU since the FS-16m and FS-20m units were equipped with air throttles and the FS-24m units had electric throttles.

Special equipment included train-phone, cab signals, and dynamic brakes.

SERVICE HISTORY

When delivered to the PRR, the first four class FS-24m units were assigned to the Buckeye Region at Columbus. The last five were assigned to the Pittsburgh Region. The Columbus units remained there until retired. The Pittsburgh Region units were originally assigned to Pitcairn maintenance, but within a year and a half units 8703-8706 were transferred to Conemaugh for maintenance. In the Pittsburgh area, they were used largely as helpers. At Conemaugh the FS-24m's were used as West Slope helpers and on coal trains into Altoona. In the Pittsburgh district, helpers were required on many trains eastbound from the north side of the Allegheny River to Wilkinsburg via the Brilliant Branch and from Pitcairn to Derry.

For several years in the late '50s, the 8707 was commonly stationed at UY tower at the north end of the Brilliant branch waiting for freights to help. The Brilliant branch was a short (1.8 miles) but a vital link for operations in the Pittsburgh area. It ran from UY tower on the Conemaugh line to CM tower on the mainline on the east side of Pittsburgh. What made the Brilliant branch a vital link was that freights routed to the main line east could run on the Conemaugh line from the north side of Pittsburgh to UY tower, run across the Brilliant branch and then connect with the main line at CM tower. This avoided running freight trains through the passenger station in downtown Pittsburgh.

The West Slope refers to the west slope of the Alleghenies; the grade requiring helpers from Johnstown (Conemaugh) to Gallitzin. In addition to serving as West Slope helpers, one class FS-24m could take a respectable coal train from Cresson into Altoona.

About 1963, the Pittsburgh Region-assigned class FS-24m units were transferred to Columbus where all units in the class performed heavy transfer and switching work.

In 1966, the Train Masters were reclassed and renumbered in preparation for the Penn Central merger. Units 8700-8708 were renumbered 6700-6707. Unit 8699 was renumbered 6708. The units were reclassed FRS-24. By this time, 8702 and 8704 had been taken out of service (never to return) because of serious mechanical problems. They were sent to the dead line in East Altoona. Since the two units were still under their equipment trust, they were renumbered while in the dead line. The new road numbers on the cab sides were applied with a spray can.

After renumbering, the FS-24 engines, except for 6700, were shipped to Altoona for storage if repairs wererequired. The 6700 worked on and was sent to Chicago about the time of the Penn Central merger in February 1968. It was renumbered 6799 in November 1969 to make way for new GE model U23C's. All of the Train Masters were retired at the end of 1970.

PRR Fairbanks-Morse Train Master 8707 giving a big push to an eastbound train at Springdale, Pennsylvania in 1961. The train is definitely going away from the photographer despite the headlight being lit.

Class AS-18m
Alco RS-11

The RS-11 road switcher improved Alco's competitive position in two ways. First, the 251 engine was a significant improvement over the Alco 244 engine; second, the 1800 horsepower rating had a 50-hp edge over the EMD competition.

The Pennsylvania used the competitive Alco RS-11 and EMD GP-9 differently, although they were purchased at the same time in 1956 and 1957. The EMDs were used primarily as through freight power while the Alcos were given assignments typical for road switcher —local freights, mine run and heavy switcher assignments. Classed as AS-18m, the 38 RS-11's were purchased in three orders, as shown in the order summary table on the next page.

The PRR was a relatively early buyer of the RS-11, purchasing the first lot of nine from Alco's third production order of the model. The last PRR RS-11s were built in 1957, although Alco continued to produce the model until 1964.

The major improvement on the Alco RS-11 over the RS-3 was the engine. Although the bore and stroke of the 251 engine was the same as the Model 244 (9" bore, 12-1/2 stroke), the 251's design was so different that the only part common to the two was the wrist pin con-

Equipment and Assignment Table
Class AS-18m
(Alco RS-11)

Orig. Road No.	1966 Road No.	May 1959 Assignment	TP	PM	RA	Orig. Road No.	1966 Road No.	May 1959 Assignment	TP	PM	RA
8617	7617	Enola-Cum. Val.	Y	Y		8636	7636	Renovo		Y	
8618	7618	Enola-Cum. Val.	Y	Y		8637	7637	Renovo		Y	
8619	7619	Enola-Cum. Val.	Y	Y		8638	7638	Renovo		Y	
8620	7620	Renovo	Y	Y		8639	7639	Renovo		Y	
8621	7621	Enola-Cum. Val.	Y	Y		8640	7640	Northumberland		Y	Y
8622	7622	Elmira	Y	Y		8641	7641	Northumberland		Y	Y
8623	7623	Elmira	Y	Y		8642	7642	Renovo		Y	
8624	7624	Elmira	Y	Y		8643	7643	Northumberland		Y	Y
8625	7625	Morrisville	Y	Y		8644	7644	Renovo		Y	
8626	7626	Enola-Sys. Pool	Y	Y		8645	7645	Renovo		Y	
8627	7627	Enola-Sys. Pool	Y	Y		8646	7646	Renovo		Y	
8628	7628	Cleveland	Y	Y		8647	7647	Renovo		Y	
8629	7629	Cleveland	Y	Y		8648	7648	Northumberland		Y	Y
8630	7630	Morrisville	Y	Y		8649	7649	Enola-General		Y	
8631	7631	Enola-Sys. Pool	Y	Y		8650	7650	Enola-General		Y	
8632	7632	Enola-Sys. Pool	Y	Y		8651	7651	Enola-General		Y	
8633	7633	Morrisville	Y	Y		8652	7652	Enola-General		Y	
8634	7634	Morrisville	Y	Y		8653	7653	Chicago-16th St.		Y	
8635	7635	Morrisville	Y	Y		8654	7654	Chicago-16th St.		Y	

TP = Train Phone; PM = Pressure maintaining feature; RA = Two-way radio.
All units had cab signal and dynamic brake. Special Equipment as of January, 1960.

necting the piston to the connecting rod. The reason for the new engine as stated in *The Diesel Builders, Volume Two* by John Kirkland was that "by the time of the redesign, . . . the shortcomings of the Model 244 engine had become all too evident. Mr. Kirkland points out further that Alco had been fulfilling warranty obligations because of the 244 engine. This had strained relations with their customers so that a new engine design was vital.

All class AS-18m units had multiple unit control, cab signals, and dynamic brakes. Additionally, 8617-8635 (the units on the first two orders) were equipped with trainphone.

PRR 8627 leading a three-unit set of RS-11s on a westbound coal train at Tyrone, PA in June 1963. This was the common PRR practice of running long hood forward.

SERVICE HISTORY

Between the delivery of the last order of RS-11's to the PRR and early 1960, the 38 class AS-18m units were primarily assigned to the Philadelphia Region (12) and the Northern Region (17). The other units in the class were divided between the New York Region, the Lake Region, and the Northwest Region.

The 17 assigned to the Northern Region before 1960 were placed in Renovo (10), Northumberland (4) and Elmira (3). The Elmira units worked on the Sodus Point branch, where the major traffic was coal moving north to the docks on Lake Ontario for transshipment to Canada. The Renovo units powered Northern Region locals in northern Pennsylvania. The Northumberland units shared local freight jobs with four GP7s.

Early in 1960, the unit distribution was changed to seven in the New York Region, 20 in the Northern Region and 11 in the Pittsburgh Region. On the Pittsburgh Region, at least six AS-18m units were assigned to Osceola Mills, Pennsylvania, just north of Altoona. The Osceola work was strictly a coal mine run and gathering assignment.

Three of the units were used in Osceola Mills mine run service. The other three units hauled the gathered loads south to Tyrone. During this period, a crew was called at Osceola Mills at about 8 AM and was assigned a set of three class AS-18m units. First, 25 loads were moved to the top of the mountain on the line to Tyrone. Securing the brakes on the first 25 loads, the crew returned to Osceola for another 25 loads of coal and struggled to the top of the mountain with this train. Then the two cuts were combined into one 50-car train and run under heavy braking down grade into Tyrone for forwarding to Altoona.

Another Pittsburgh Region assignment in the early 1960s was 8617 to Lewistown. This was a three shift, six-day job working between Lewistown and Huntingdon. On the first shift, the job worked local between Huntingdon and Mount Union. Most of the first shift work was at the Mapleton Sand Co. in Mapleton, Pennsylvania. On the second shift, the 8617 worked the Mountt Union yard, moving loaded cars over the scales for weighing and blocking cars for both eastbound and westbound pickups. On the third trick, the 8617 switched the Huntingdon yard, which included working several industries.

Early in 1964, the PRR leased six Alco RS-11's, 8640-8644 and 8648, to the Lehigh Valley Railroad. The PRR rebuilt the units to 2000 horsepower at Juniata Shop and repainted the units for Lehigh Valley. The units were relettered but not renumbered. The six units eased the LV's locomotive shortage and remained on the roster until it was merged into Conrail on April 1, 1976.

In 1966 the PRR RS-11 units were renumbered from 8617-8654 to 7617-7654 and reclassed ARS-18. The six PRR RS-11 units leased to the Lehigh Valley were included in the renumbering but were reclassed ARS-20.

In May 1967, 23 class AS-18m units were assigned to Morrisville maintenance, while the remainder of the class worked out of Conway and Columbus. The Morrisville units worked local freights in the area from Philadelphia to Newark-Jersey City. In the Trenton area, one of the major jobs was switching the U.S. Steel Morrisville mill. The class AS-18m units were also regulars on the Bel-Del line from Trenton up the east side of the Delaware River to Philipsburg, Pennsylvania, where the traffic was turned over to the Lehigh Valley Railroad. A significant part of the business on this line was hauling iron ore from the Delaware River docks near Philadelphia to Bethlehem Steel in Bethlehem.

Assignments of the units continued much the same as described in the previous paragraph until the merger of the PRR into the Penn Central. None of the ARS-18s was retired by the PRR and only the 7622 was retired by Penn Central (in April 1971). Conrail eventually retired all of the units, starting in January and February 1977. The last of the ex-PRR RS-11 units were retired in March 1981, including the last of the 2000 horsepower rebuilds that came to Conrail via the Lehigh Valley.

Order Summary - Class AS-18m Units

PRR ROAD NUMBERS	ALCO SALES ORDER	NO. OF UNITS	ORDER DATE	DELIVERY DATES
8617-8625	21024	9	Mar 56	Aug 56
8626-8635	21054	10	Nov 56	Feb 57-May 57
8636-8654	21074	19	Sep 57	Nov 57-Dec 57

Alco's replacement for the RS-3 was the RS-11. Here is PRR AS-18M 7629 late in the PRR era at Camden, New Jersey, October, 1967. The unit had been renumbered from 8629 in preparation for the Penn Central merger. The 7629 was originally equipped with train-phone, but by this date, this equipment had been removed.

Class ES-17m
EMD SD9

The PRR's 25 EMD SD9 units were used almost exclusively as hump pushers and heavy yard switchers. They were purchased on EMD order 5567 in November 1957, one of the orders placed to complete dieselization. The 1750-hp, C-C wheel arrangements were delivered between November 1957 and January 1958, numbered 7600-7624 and classed ES-17m.

EMD introduced the SD9 in late 1953, at the same time as the GP9; they used similar equipment. The engine was the 16-cylinder EMD model 567C, the main generator was the D12B and six D47 traction motors were applied.

Special equipment on the class included cab signals (although the units were almost never used in road service), hump control, and dynamic brakes.

SERVICE HISTORY

The class ES-17m units were assigned to large freight classification hump yards for their entire lives on the PRR. In April 1959, eight units (7600-7607) were assigned to East Altoona; six (7608-7613) were assigned to Enola, and eleven (7614-7624) to Columbus. The East Altoona and Enola units had two-way radios; the Columbus units did not. By January 1962, six were still at Enola but twelve were in the Pittsburgh Region at Conway and Pitcairn, with seven at Columbus.

As hump pushers, the SD9s were used in two-unit sets and as single

Above, The PRR's SD9 road switchers almost never got out on the road. This view of PRR 7611 is not really an exception. The class ES-17m unit is on a transfer run from Harrisburg. Near the west end of Enola Yard about 1963.

Below, Another two-unit set at Conway yard on July 24 1966. The two units are 6917 and 7600. The 1966 renumbering had only started the previous month. The change had been made on 6917 only twelve days previously but the 7600 would wait until September 6, 1966 for renumbering. In many cases, it was necessary to confirm that a first unit had been renumbered before a second unit could be changed, to avoid a conflict. Since there was no original 6900 series, the SD9s could be renumbered with impunity.

units. At Conway yard north of Pittsburgh, the class ES-17m units pushed the hump in pairs.

The 1966 renumbering changed the road numbers to 6900-6924 and the class was changed to ERS-17a. By May 1967 the distribution was twelve at Conway, six at Enola, three at Columbus, three at Cleveland and one at Chicago.

The group of SD9s remained intact throughout the Penn Central period, although they were displaced as the primary hump pushers by the arrival of 35 SD38 units in 1970. The SD9s remained though the Conrail period until all were retired and returned to the lessor in January 1983.

A two-unit SD9 set; PRR 7606 and 7614 is shown at Conway Yard on March 17, 1962, an appropriate day for green locomotives. Cabooses were not normal on hump pushers, unless the caboose was being picked up and added to a soon-to-depart freight train.

155

Class AS-18am
Alco RSD-12

The class AS-18am units spent most of their PRR lives helping freight trains on the east slope grade from Altoona to Gallitzin. The 25 1800 horsepower, six-axle road switchers were ordered from Alco on their Sales Order 21083 in November 1957, and were delivered between December 1957 and April 1958. They were numbered 6855-6879 and classed AS-18am. By the time the RSD-12's were delivered, the PRR had been completely dieselized, but their arrival allowed the PRR to store the high-maintenance Baldwin Centipedes.

Class AS-18am's were equipped with a GE model 586 main traction generator, the standard model on RSD-12 Alcos and all other Alco six-axle road switchers up to the Century 628. It was capable of providing the amperage required for the six traction motors. All of the PRR RSD-12 units were equipped with cab signals, hump control, and dynamic brakes.

For a little more than two years, all but one of the class AS-18am locomotives, were used in the Altoona East Slope freight helper pool. The 24 units thus assigned were set up in eight three-unit sets, making it possible to have seven three unit sets in service with one set available for shopping.

The 25th AS-18m was assigned to Terre Haute, Indiana for the Green Valley coal turn until 1960, when it was reassigned to Altoona to rejoin the rest of the class. After the 8679 joined the rest of the class in Altoona, four units could be shopped at once, making assignments more flexible.

Starting at Rose tower on the east end of the Altoona shop complex, the helpers were coupled onto freights for the push either to Gallitzin or to Cresson. At Gallitzin there was sufficient distance between the eastbound and westbound tracks for a reverse loop. This allowed the helpers to return to Altoona without changing ends.

In March 1965, the monopoly of the class AS-18am units on the East Slope helper assignment was broken with the delivery of ten Alco Century 628's, which were also assigned to East Slope helper duty. These new larger Alcos were used in two-unit sets, with a total of 5500 horsepower and a total continuous tractive effort of 171,600 lbs. at 9.5 miles per hour. This compared to 5400 horsepower and about 165,000 lbs. of tractive effort at 9.5 miles per hour for the RSD-12s. Although the class AS-18am units were rated at a higher continuous tractive effort at six miles

an hour, this speed was considerably lower than the continuous rating speed of the road units. The PRR determined that the traction motors of head end units were failing because of excessive heat generated by operation of the trains at speeds below the head end engines' safe continuous ratings.

With the arrival of the six-axle Centuries, the RSD-12s were given only occasional helper turns, and other assignments. By the middle of 1966, six units had been reassigned to Morrisville and a year later six others were assigned to Columbus. In mid-1967 the remaining East Altoona units were reassigned to Conway for maintenance.

In the late PRR years, as many as six of the Altoona/Conway maintained AS-18am units were based at Renovo for operation. They pushed the hump, worked locals such as coal trains, and were occasionally used as helpers from Emporium to Keating Summit. The Morrisville units were used in yard service and in local freights, which sent them from Camden on the south to Philipsburg on the north. One particularly demanding assignment at Morrisville was the haulage of cuts of ore dumped at the Morrisville ore dock into the yard for marshalling into ore trains for movement west.

The 1966 pre-Penn Central renumbering saw the 25 Alcos reclassed

The RSD-12s were bought to push freight trains up hills, particularly the East Slope. Here, 8667, 8672 and 8669 unite to do that job, pushing a westbound freight into Gallitzin tunnel on June 23, 1963.

Above, an early inkling of the reassignment of RSD-12s away from helper service came with discovery of 8666 at the head end of a train, MU'd with an RS-3, hauling gondolas. It was March 13, 1965, and we are at Slope Tower, Altoona.

ARS-18a and renumbered from 8655-8679 to 6855-6879. All units saw service through the entire Penn Central era, but they were scattered throughout the system. Many went to former New York Central locations for maintenance. A November 1970 list shows two units at DeWitt, near Syracuse, four at Selkirk, near Albany, two at Buffalo, four at Baltimore, one at Wilmington, two at Meadows (near Newark, New Jersey) and the remaining ten at Morrisville. At these locations, the units performed heavy yard work and ran on local freights. The entire class was included in the Conrail merger in the same service seen on Penn Central. All were retired by the end of 1978.

Below, No. 6876 (ex-8676) and 6879 (ex-8679) combine to move a northbound Alpha Jet at Lambertville on New Jersey's Bel-Del line in 1968.

157

CRESSON, PENNSYLVANIA, APRIL 4, 1965.

Chapter 9

Shifters

Class ES-6 (5911) *EMD SW*

Prior to 1937, the only internal combustion locomotives on the property were the Altoona-built gasoline-fueled class A6 and A6b. After constructing the A6s, the PRR had run trials on numerous internal combustion switchers from Westinghouse, EMC, Porter and Baldwin, but they bought none of them.

But in 1937, the Pennsylvania purchased its first standard model or "off-the-shelf" diesel-electric locomotive. In that year, General Motors built an automobile assembly plant on the PRR in Linden, New Jersey. It was estimated that the plant would receive 70 freight cars a day by rail. The general manager of the GM plant insisted that an internal combustion locomotive must be used for switching inside the plant, because of smoke hazards with steam switchers.

To meet this demand, the PRR tried out one of its Class A6 gasoline locomotives, along with a borrowed Long Island Rail Road 600-horsepower Ingersoll-Rand diesel locomotive. The A6 unit produced excessive fumes inside the plant and the I-R diesel made too much smoke. Also, the I-R exhaust stack was considered to be too tall for some of the overhead piping above the tracks inside the plant.

After these unsuccessful trials, (and likely not unmindful of GM's desires,) the PRR consulted with Electro-Motive Corporation (EMC) for a solution. The General Motors subsidiary predicably recommended one of its 600 horsepower switchers with a redesigned exhaust stack to satisfy the Linden plant management. EMC further offered to provide a trial unit of this type. The PRR expected to purchase the unit, although there was no commitment made to EMC.

EMC supplied a 600 horsepower model SW switcher for the trial. Both the EMC serial number and the road number were 680. The builder's photo below illustrates that this switcher was painted a very dark hue and had no lettering whatsoever. The road number 680 was carried in the headlight number boards only.

EMC 680 arrived at Waverly enginehouse dead in tow from Wilmington at 4:15 AM on Thursday, June 24, 1937. It had been fully serviced with fuel and sand prior to arrival, so it was able to go into service immediately. In an hour's time, the new unit was cranked up and left Waverly with 17 cars for Stiles Avenue yard at Linden. It worked until midnight that day switching the Stiles Avenue yard, the GM plant and the Gordon Gin Company. The 680 also made two runs between Linden and Waverly transferring cars.

During the next week, the 680 was given a thorough workout at both Stiles Avenue and Waverly. On Tuesday, the 29th, the 680 was assigned to one of the Waverly to Greenville yard runner jobs usually handled by a class H9s 2-8-0. For this run, 680 tied onto 51 loaded cars and set out for Greenville with a 3138-ton train. The run took 34 minutes compared to 15 minutes for a 2-8-0 with the same tonnage. On the ascending .44% grade going onto the Newark Bay Bridge, the train's speed dropped to 4.32 mph, but never stalled. A similar performance was turned in the next day on a Waverly to Harsimus Cove runner with a 2757-ton train of 45 loads and one empty.

This is the original builder's photo of EMD 680. The only place that number appeared was in the number board integral to the headlight (not readable in this photo.) The locomotive looked like this during its first tests on the PRR; only after it was purchased did the railroad's painters have at it.

EMD PHOTO, MARRE COLLECTION

PRR 3908 at Linden, New Jersey, circa 1938. After purchase from Electro-Motive, the unit was painted at Meadows Shop near Kearny, New Jersey. The Futura lettering style was then considered "Modern."

After two weeks of this type of trial, it was concluded that the unit was more than ample to take care of the switching service at the General Motors plant and at other local yards. However, the speed in runner service was too slow. It was also concluded that the performance of the 600-hp diesel on transfer runs from Waverly to Linden was not satisfactory. With 2242 ton trains between these two points, the diesel required 36 minutes vs. 23 minutes for transfers powered with a class B6sb 0-6-0. However, since there was enough switching at Linden to require two or three-shift service, the diesel would be effectively utilized there.

The good news was in the costs. The estimated cost to operate the 680 was $2.91 per hour in two-trick shifting. This compared to $4.43 per hour for a class B6sb 0-6-0 and $5.47 per hour for a class H9s 2-8-0. In a memo dated July 14, 1937, which outlined these results, purchase of the unit for $70,000 was recommended to M. W. Clement, President of the Pennsylvania Railroad. Due to Clayton Act requirements, the PRR was required to put the purchase out for bid. Electro-Motive was the only bidder and the purchase was made early in August 1937.

The locomotive was painted at Meadows Shop to save deadheading the unit to Wilmington. Meadows had some men characterized as old passenger car painters who did work on steam locomotives. Their handiwork can be seen in the photos taken by the PRR at Meadows. The lettering was described as the "Modern" type. Since the railroad performed the lettering, EMC gave them a $50 credit for this work.

The PRR classified the SW diesel as class AA5 and numbered it 3908, which was in the same number series as the three gasoline locomotives 3905-3907.

The original SC switcher went through a few changes in its lifetime. Even by August, 1964, the unit had been re-engined (and re-hooded). The replacement 567 engine had to be mounted higher on the frame, hence the "blister" on the hood. Note too the outboard handrails in addition to the normal SW1 hood-side railings. Seen here at Renovo, Pennsylvania, the stack is covered, indicating that the unit was temporarily out of service. The pioneer PRR unit was not quite done yet; it was to be renumbered 8511 and not retired until after the Penn Central merger.

EQUIPMENT

A Winton model 201A engine powered the unit. This was an eight-cylinder in-line engine with a bore of 8" and a stroke of 10". The main generator was a General Electric 5GT-534E1. The four traction motors were GE model 287-E51 machines geared at 68:16 for a maximum speed of 35 mph. With its original weight of 200,000 lbs, the starting tractive effort was 50,000 lbs and the continuous tractive effort was 20,000 lbs at nine mph. In 1946, the diagram book page for the 5911 was revised to specify a weight of 206,500 lbs. and a starting tractive effort of 51,640 lbs.

During its first four years of service, the 3908 was the PRR's only diesel locomotive. Monthly reports detailing the unit's operating costs, availability and general suitability were prepared and sent to Philadelphia to allow the Chief of Motive Power and other powers to scrutinize the newcomer's operation.

In 1941, a 1000 horsepower model NW2 switcher was purchased and assigned to the New York Zone. The purpose of purchasing this unit (road number 3909) was to compare its capabilities with the 3908. In early 1942 the two EMD switchers were renumbered from 3908 and 3909 to 5911 and 5912 to be in the same series as the two planned (but later canceled) E6A units which the PRR would have numbered 5900A and 5901A. By 1943 the larger 5912 had succeeded to the assignment at Linden and the 5911 was assigned to nearby Harsimus Cove yard.

The 5911 was reclassed several times as the PRR searched for a suitable diesel classification system. In the 1946 classification system, the unit was reclassed from AA5 to (B-B)6E-(Odd). In the 1947 system, the 5911 became class ES-6. This was changed to ES-6(5911) in the 1951 classification system to differentiate it from the standard EMD SW1. Of course, the unit was an odd one on the Pennsy. It was the road's only Winton-engined unit and the only EMC/EMD unit with GE electrical equipment.

SERVICE HISTORY

The 5911 stayed in the New York Zone until the late 1940s. A couple of years in Philadelphia were followed by an assignment at Northumberland. This assignment stayed constant until about 1962 when the unit was reassigned to Renovo. In the mid-1960s the 5911 was assigned to Enola.

In November 1956, the 5911 was re-engined with a 6-cylinder EMD model 567A engine, the same engine used in EMD model SW1 switchers. The GE electrical equipment was not replaced. Because the 567 engine, more overhead room in the hood than the Winton 201A engine required, a sheet metal hump was installed on the hood to provide the required space. The 5911 looked like no other ES-6 unit. The specified weight and tractive effort did not change.

In the 1966 renumbering the 5911 was renumbered 8511 and reclassed ES-6. After the mid-1960s the unit was in storage most of the time and was retired about a month after the Penn Central merger on April 9, 1968.

| Class ES-10 |
| EMD NW2 |

The Pennsylvania Railroad purchased only 32 EMD model NW2's between 1941 and 1948. For most railroads, 32 switcher's would have been a respectable representation of a switcher model. On the PRR however, the 32 EMD 1000-horsepower switchers were in fourth place numerically compared to the 145 Baldwin, 55 F-M and 42 Alco 1000-horsepower switchers purchased during the same period. This situation developed even though the first EMC model NW2 was the second production model diesel purchased by the PRR. The NW2s were purchased in five orders, described in the Order Summary.

The NW2s were equipped with a V-12 model 567-A engine, except for the 3909/5912, which had the pre-war model 567 engine. The main generator was an EMD model D4D and the four traction motors were EMD model D17B. Again, the pre-war 3909 had four EMC model D7D traction motors when originally delivered instead of the D17B motors. The gear ratio was 62:15, which allowed a maximum speed of 65 mph for the D17B traction motors and a 60-mph maximum speed for the D7D traction motors.

Locomotive Characteristics

Class	ES-6(5911) [*]	ES-6(5911) [+]	ES-10	BS-6	ES-6	BS-10
Builder	EMC	EMC	EMD	BLW	EMD	BLW
Model	SW	SW	NW2	VO-660	SW1	VO-1000
Horsepower	600	600	1000	660	600	1000
Wheel Arr,	B-B	B-B	B-B	B-B	B-B	B-B
Total Weight	206,650 lbs	206,560 lbs	248,400 lbs	197,600 lbs	194,000 lbs	240,000 lbs
Length over Couplers	43' 8"	43 8	44' 5"	45 10	44' 5"	48' 10"
Truck Centers	22' 0"	22 0	22' 0"	22 6	22' 0"	25' 6"
Truck Wheelbase	8' 0"	8 0	8' 0"	8 0	8' 0"	8' 0"
Engine	Win. 8-201A	EMD 6-567A	EMD 12-567A	BLW 6-VO	EMD 6-567A	BLW 8-VO
Generator	GE 5GT-534E1	GE 5GT-534E1	EMD D4D	W 486K4	EMD D4D	W 480
Traction Motors	GE 287E	GE 287E	EMD D17B[#]	W 362D or 362E	EMD D17B	W 362D
Gear Ratio	68:16	68:16	62:15	76:16 or 68:14	62:15	68:14
Maximum Speed	35 MPH	40 MPH	65 MPH	60 MPH	65 MPH	60 MPH
Starting Trac. Effort	51,640 lbs	51,640 lbs	62,100 lbs	49,400 lbs	48,500 lbs	60,000 lbs
Continuous Trac. Effort	20,000 lbs	20,000 lbs	30,000 lbs	29,200 lbs	23,500 lbs	34,000 lbs
CTE Speed	9.0 MPH	9.0 MPH	10.0 MPH	6.5 MPH	7.5 MPH	8.3 MPH

[*]--As built
[+]--As re-engined

[#]--PRR 3909/5912 had EMD D7D traction motors

Order Summary - Class ES-10 Units

PRR ROAD NUMBERS	EMD ORDER NUMBER	NO. OF UNITS	ORDER DATE	DELIVERY DATES
3909 (*)	E416	1	Mar 41	Oct 41
5921-5922	E680	2	Jan 45	Apr 46, Nov 45
5923-5925	E849	3	Dec 46	Oct 47
9155-9176	E897	22	Oct 47	Feb 48-Nov 48
9247-9250	E1024	4	Feb 48	Dec 48

(*) Renumbered 5912 in 1942.

SERVICE HISTORY

The first PRR NW2, 5912, was in a class by itself for five years, although the class name changed from the initial class AA6, to AA10E in 1943 and (B-B)10E in 1946 before finally being reclassed to ES-10 in 1947. All that time and for several years thereafter, 5912 was assigned to the Philadelphia area. Specifically, the April 1943 assignment of 5912 was a Norristown job.

When the full complement of ES-10 units was on hand in 1949, the largest concentration was in the Pittsburgh area, with six locomotives assigned to the Conemaugh Division and nine to the Pittsburgh Division. Other assignments included seven to the Chicago Terminal Division, six to the Eastern Division, three to the Maryland Division and the 5912 to the Philadelphia Terminal Division.

During the 1950s, the Class ES-10's were spread over all of the PRR, excepting only the Indianapolis, Louisville, and St. Louis areas. By 1959, the Northwest Region had the largest concentration; eleven in Chicago, one in Fort Wayne, two in Logansport and two in Grand Rapids. Five were still in Pittsburgh but all of the others were scattered to places like Elmira, Sandusky, Columbus and Meadows, all of which had one or two of the units. The Meadows assignment was an exception to the almost solid assignment of Alco switchers to the New York Region. As you might expect, the lone ES-10's assignment included switching the Linden, New Jersey GM assembly plant, just as 5911 had done back in 1937.

The 1959 assignment pattern continued through the mid-1960s. In the 1966 pre-Penn Central renumbering, the ES-10's were assigned road numbers between 8647 and 8678. By the end of the

PRR period, the class had been shuffled somewhat in assignment. Only one was left in Chicago but nine were in Fort Wayne and three were in Logansport (Northwest Region). Five were in Indianapolis and seven were in York, PA. The original NW2, 5912, was in Elmira, New York, where it had been since the middle 1950s, along with one other NW2. Pitcairn and Altoona each had one ES-10, and two were assigned to Harrisburg.

None of the ES-10s were retired by either the PRR or Penn Central. During the Penn Central period, 17 of the 32 ex-PRR class ES-10's was given a capital rebuild and renumbered in the 9100 series. During this rebuild the horsepower was raised to 1200 and all were given multiple unit control and axle roller bearings. All the 32 units survived to become Conrail units, and were retired between 1981 and 1985

All of the ex-PRR un-rebuilt model NW2's were numbered 9248 to 9262 on Conrail. They were retired between 1981 and 1986.

Several of the former PRR class ES-10's continued to operate. Former PRR 9165 was operated by Central Soya in Indianapolis. Former PRR 9170 was owned by the Brandywine Valley Railroad in Coatesville, Pennsylvania, and numbered 8203. The Pocono Northeast 87 was one of the ES-10 units rebuilt by Penn Central. It was originally PRR 9167.

Builder's photograph of PRR 5925, taken July 22, 1948. This is an early "plain vanilla" NW2, which spent a good deal of its lifetime in Cleveland.

PENNSYLVANIA
5925

Class BS-6
Baldwin "VO-660"

Pennsylvania #5907 was a Baldwin 660 horsepower switcher with a model VO engine. It was the first of more than 600 Baldwin-built diesel locomotives on the Pennsy, the largest fleet of Baldwin units on any American railroad. Although the 12 diesels of class BS-6 were a small part of the eventual PRR diesel fleet, in 1945 they formed almost half of the railroads diesel fleet.

The 660 horsepower Baldwin switcher's were delivered in four orders. Baldwin sales order 41505-N for one unit (the 5907) was entered in March 1942 and delivered the same month. Baldwin sales order 41518-N for two units (5908 and 5909) was also entered in March 1942 but was not delivered until October 1942. Baldwin sales order 41518-R for six units (5932-5937) was also entered in March 1942 and was delivered between September and October 1942. The final order for class BS-6's was Baldwin sales order 45504-D

for three units (5941-5943). It was placed in February 1945 and delivered in October and November 1945. The PRR class BS-6's had no official Baldwin model, but have unofficially become known as "VO-660" based on the use of the model VO engine and the

660 horsepower available for traction.

The VO-660's were originally classed AA-5a. During the brief period the 1946-47 classification scheme was in effect, the units were classed (B-B)6a. Finally, during the 1947 and subsequent schemes, they were classed BS-6.

ORIG. ROAD NO.	1966 ROAD NO.	MAY 1959 ASSIGNMENT	ORIG. ROAD NO.	1966 ROAD NO.	MAY 1959 ASSIGNMENT
5912	8677	Elmira	9167	8667	Chicago 59th St.
5921	8651	Grand Rapids	9168	8668	Pittsburgh 28th St.
5922	8652	Grand Rapids	9169	8669	Pittsburgh 28th St.
5923	8653	Meadows	9170	8670	Logansport (NW Reg.)
5924	8654	Sandusky	9171	8671	Chicago 59th St.
5925	8678	Cleveland	9172	8672	East Altoona
9155	8655	Cleveland	9173	8673	Pittsburgh 28th St.
9156	8656	Logansport (NW Reg.)	9174	8674	Chicago 59th St.
9157	8657	Pittsburgh 28th St.	9175	8675	Chicago 59th St.
9158	8658	Chicago 16th St.	9176	8676	Chicago 59th St.
9159	8659	Chicago 16th St.	9247	8647	Chicago 59th St.
9160	8660	Chicago 16th St.	9248	8648	Logansport (Bl Reg.)
9161	8661	Cleveland	9249	8649	Chicago 59th St.
9162	8662	Columbus St. Clair	9250	8650	Fort Wayne
9163	8663	Columbus St. Clair			
9164	8664	Pittsburgh 28th St.			
9165	8665	Chicago 16th St.			
9166	8666	Chicago 59th St.			

Assignment Table
Class ES-10
(EMD NW2)

PRR 9169 is shown at York, Pennsylvania, in October 1966. The paint scheme is the transitional design, with the original 8-inch lettering on the hood, but with the 16-inch numbers on the cab.

Here is PRR 5936, working in Philadelphia in March 1963. This unit was delivered in Fall 1942, shortly before Baldwin suspended production of Baldwin 660-hp. switchers by order of the War Production Board. Note the curved sheet metal fillets around the cab, and the single exhaust stack.

EQUIPMENT

The Baldwin 660 horsepower switcher equipped with the VO engine was larger than the 600 or 660 horsepower models offered by other builders. The VO-660s had a length over coupler faces of 45' 10". This was more than a foot longer than the Alco model S-1 at 44' 5-3/4" and the EMD model SW1 at 44' 5". The engine in the Baldwin 660 horsepower switchers was the straight six-cylinder Baldwin VO engine with a 12-3/4" bore and 15-1/2" stoke. The engine weighed 26,500 lbs all by itself. Although it had a larger bore and stroke than the equivalent Alco switcher engine, the non-turbocharged model 539 engine, which weighed 33,700 lbs. The six-cylinder model 567 engine from EMD, on the other hand, scaled out at only 15,000 lbs.

The electrical equipment installed on the units built in 1945 differed from that on the 1942 units. The War Production Board controlled production of diesel locomotives built during World War II and had directed that only 1000 horsepower diesel switchers would be produced by any builder. This limitation was relaxed as the war proceeded, permitting Baldwin to resume building 660 horsepower switchers in late 1944. At this time Baldwin decided that the same electrical equipment used on the 1000 horsepower switchers would be used on the 660 horsepower switchers. The PRR class BS-6 units included units equipped with both types of electrical equipment.

The 1942 #5907-5909 and 5932-5937 were equipped with a Westinghouse model 485K4 generator (except for 5907, which had a 485H4 machine,) and four Westinghouse model 362B traction motors geared to the axles with a 76:16 gear ratio. This gave the units a continuous tractive effort of 25,000 lbs at 7 miles per hour.

PRR 5941-5943 were built in 1949, equipped with a Westinghouse model 480C generator and four Westinghouse model 362D traction motors geared to the axles with a 68:14 gear ratio. The continuous tractive effort of these units was 29,200 lbs. at 6.5 miles per hour. As early as 1948, PRR classification data lists all class BS-6's with the later continuous tractive effort characteristic. By 1952, the PRR classification data states that the traction motors in the BS-6 units were both models 362D and 362E, but no 362C.

SERVICE HISTORY

April 1943 assignment data states that the nine VO-660 units then in class AA5a were assigned to Philadelphia (7 units) Linden, NJ (1 unit) and Chicago (1 unit). By 1947, one unit was still on the New York Division, five at the Philadelphia Terminal, and six on the Maryland Division. The New York Division's unit 5932 went to the Conemaugh Division in 1947 and the Lake Division in 1949 before going to Philadelphia by May 1950. By the 1953-54 period, two of the Maryland Division units and one from Philadelphia were assigned to the Susquehanna Division. These assignments stayed pretty constant until late 1961, when all but the 5934 at Northumberland and 5937, 5942 and 5943 assigned to Wilmington, were assigned to Philadelphia. By October 1962, all class BS-6's were assigned to the Philadelphia area where they ended their days. The 12 class BS-6 units were retired in the 1964-65 period; none were sold for further service.

PRR 5941, found in Philadelphia in August 1964, was built in October 1945. It represents VO-660 postwar production. The carbody design is simplified; the sheet metal fillets are gone. The exhaust manifold was redesigned to route the gases to two pairs of stacks.

Class ES-6
EMD SW1

Order Summary - Class ES-6 Units

PRR ROAD NUMBERS	EMD ORDER NUMBER	NO. OF UNITS	ORDER DATE	DELIVERY DATES
5910	E512	1	Jan 42	Aug 42
5944-5946	E679	3	Feb 45	Jun 46
5947-5951	E694	5	Dec 45	Jun 46-Jul 46
5952-5953	E850	2	Dec 46	Oct 47
5987-5999	E934	13	Jun 47	Mar 48-Apr 48
9137-9154	E898	18	Oct 47	Apr 48-Oct 48
9104, 9200-9203, 9205-9209	E1049	10	Feb 48	Apr 49
9396-9428	6081	33	Nov 49	Jul 50-Nov 50

The PRR's first SW1 was only the sixth production model diesel it owned, and it was one of only a handful of diesels on the railroad until after World War II. Their eighty-five 600 horsepower EMD SW1 switchers were assigned to almost every part of the system at one time or another. The SW1 units were originally classed AA5b, reclassed (B-B) 6E in 1946 and finally ES-6 in 1947.

EQUIPMENT

Major equipment used on Class ES-6 was as indicated on the Characteristics table. The exception was the first of the class, 5910, which had a model 567 engine and four model D-7A1 traction motors.

Alco, Baldwin and EMD all offered 600 or 660 horsepower switchers during the 1940s. EMD was the only one with the 600 horsepower rating. The SW1 also typically weighed less than the competition. The SW1s on the PRR weighed 194,000 lbs as compared to 199,000 lbs. for most of the Alco model S-1 units and 196,000 lbs. for the Baldwin DS 4-4-660. The lower weight also meant lower starting tractive effort and lighter work for the EMDs as compared to these Alcos and Baldwins.

SERVICE HISTORY

While ES-6's were used in most PRR locations at one time or another, there were three points where they were concentrated. First, the 5987-5999 started their life in the Pittsburgh area, and all but three of the units were still there through the first year of Conrail operation. The 9138-9154 and 9206-9209 plus the 9428 were first assigned to Chicago, and remained until 1968. The third concentration of EMD SW1's was the Harrisburg-Enola area. The 9396-9414 were delivered to that area and stayed there throughout the PRR period.

The SW1's were assigned to a variety of duties appropriate for light switchers, including passenger terminal switching, hump yard trimmer duty, and miscellaneous switching assignments. A February 1952 system switcher assignment sheet gives a look at typical Class ES-6 assignments. Fourteen 600-hp. switchers were assigned to the passenger station yard in Pittsburgh. In Harrisburg, some of the seven Class ES-6 units assigned there also served the passenger station.

Eight ES-6 units were assigned to Enola Yard, and were used as trimmers in the hump yards. The 19 Class ES-6's assigned to the Philadelphia Division in 1952 included one at Lancaster, one at Hagerstown and one at Chambersburg. Another Class ES-6 was assigned to Chambersburg for use on local freight between Chambersburg and Kingston (CV-56 and CV-57). This unit was also used on a local freight between Chambersburg and Waynesboro, CV-58 and CV-59.

The Chicago Division had 16 Class ES-6's in 1952. Two were assigned to Damon Avenue, one at 16th St., one at the Campbell Soup plant, three at 55th St. yard, three at 12th Street, three at Colehour yard on the Indiana border and two at 59th St. yard. One ES-6 was assigned to Logansport yard.

The ES-6 class units survived the PRR relatively intact. In 1966, the pre-Penn Central renumbering placed them in the 8500 number series. Only three ES-6 units were retired before renumbering, but no more were retired from the class before the PC merger. Between 1968 to 1976, the Penn Central retired five more former PRR Class ES-6's, and passed the remaining units on to Conrail or to Amtrak. Eight of the former PRR Class ES-6 units were conveyed to Amtrak on April 1, 1976. The Conrail units were all retired between 1977 and 1984.

Passenger train switching was a large part of the work done by ES-6 locomotives on the PRR. This photo of Unit 9410 was taken in August 1958, shortly after SW1's replaced the electric B-1 switchers at Harrisburg.

Equipment and Assignment Table
Class ES-6 (EMD SW1)

ORIG. ROAD NO.	1966 ROAD NO.	MAY 1959 ASSIGNMENT	ORIG. ROAD NO.	1966 ROAD NO.	MAY 1959 ASSIGNMENT	ORIG. ROAD NO.	1966 ROAD NO.	MAY 1959 ASSIGNMENT
5910	8510	Cincinnati	9141	8541	Indianapolis	9402	8562	Chambersburg
5944	8544	Columbus St. Clair	9142	8542	Indianapolis	9403	8563	Enola (Non-system)
5945	8545	Pittsburgh 28th St.	9143	8543	Grand Rapids	9404	8564	Enola (Non-system)
5946	8546	Pittsburgh 28th St.	9144		Chicago 16th St.	9405	8565	Enola (Non-system)
5947	8547	Elmira	9145	8575	Chicago 16th St.	9406	8566	Enola (Non-system)
5948	8548	Northumberland	9146	8576	Logansport (NW Reg.)	9407	8567	Enola (Non-system)
5949	8549	Indianapolis	9147		Chicago 16th St.	9408	8568	Harrisburg (Non-system)
5950	8550	Louisville	9148	8578	Columbus St. Clair	9409	8569	Enola (Non-system)
5951	8551	Pittsburgh 28th St.	9149	8579	Indianapolis	9410	8570	Harrisburg (Non-system)
5952	8552	Pittsburgh 28th St.	9150	8530	Grand Rapids	9411	8571	Harrisburg (Non-system)
5953	8553	Pitcairn	9151	8531	Pitcairn	9412	8512	Enola (Non-system)
5987	8587	Pittsburgh 28th St.	9152	8532	Logansport (NW Reg.)	9413	8513	Enola (Non-system)
5988	8588	Pittsburgh 28th St.	9153	8533	Columbus St. Clair	9414	8514	Enola (Non-system)
5989	8589	Pittsburgh 28th St.	9154	8554	Pittsburgh 28th St.	9415	8515	Mahoningtown
5990	8590	Pittsburgh 28th St.	9200	8580	Pittsburgh 28th St.	9416	8516	Cleveland
5991	8591	Pittsburgh 28th St.	9201	8501	Pittsburgh 28th St.	9417	8517	Cleveland
5992	8592	Pittsburgh 28th St.	9202	8502	Pittsburgh 28th St.	9418	8518	Cleveland
5993	8593	Pittsburgh 28th St.	9203	8503	Pittsburgh 28th St.	9419	8519	Mahoningtown
5994	8594	Pittsburgh 28th St.	9205	8505	Pittsburgh 28th St.	9420	8520	Pittsburgh 28th St.
5995	8595	Pittsburgh 28th St.	9206	8506	Chicago 16th St.	9421		Cleveland
5996	8596	Pittsburgh 28th St.	9207	8507	Chicago 16th St.	9422	8522	Pittsburgh 28th St.
5997	8597	Pittsburgh 28th St.	9208	8508	Logansport (NW Reg.)	9423	8523	Pittsburgh 28th St.
5998	8598	Pittsburgh 28th St.	9209	8509	Terre Haute	9424	8524	Columbus St. Clair
5999	8599	Pittsburgh 28th St.	9396	8556	Enola (Non-system)	9425	8525	Pittsburgh 28th St.
9104	8504	Pittsburgh 28th St.	9397	8557	Harrisburg (Non-system)	9426	8526	Cleveland
9137	8537	Pittsburgh 28th St.	9398	8558	Enola (Non-system)	9427	8527	Mahoningtown
9138	8538	Columbus St. Clair	9399	8559	Enola (Non-system)	9428	8528	Logansport (Bl Reg.)
9139	8539	Chicago 16th St.	9400	8560	Enola (Non-system)			
9140	8540	Chicago 16th St.	9401	8561	Enola (Non-system)			

SW1's have proven to be desirable units for new shortlines, and a number of former PRR Class ES-6s saw further use in this type of operation. Former PRR 9150 and 9200 served Amtrak (as 254, later 741 and 258, later 745) before going to the Berlin Mills Ry. in New England. PRR 9425 served PC and Conrail as 8525, going to the West Shore with the former PC and Conrail road number. PRR 9404 ended up operating at the A. E. Staley Co. in Morrisville, Pennsylvania after being retired by Conrail as 8564 in January 1982. In this case, the SW1 was transferred to Staley in settlement of a claim. Finally, former PRR 9423 was operating on the New Hope and Ivyland in its original PRR livery and lettering in late 1989. This is not a complete list but it can be seen that ex-PRR class ES-6 units still survive.

Freshly painted in the Keystone-only image, PRR 9137 sparkles in the sun at Northumberland PA. The month is April 1966. There's some question as to whether the keystone on the front sandbox was an extra creative detail added by the Motive Power foreman. Looks good, though ("If the drawing didn't have it, it should have.")

W.D. VOLKMER PHOTO, DOUGLAS COLECLTION

Here we see PRR 8594 switching the east end of the Wilkensburg, Pennsylvania yard several months after the Penn-Central merger.

Class BS-10
Baldwin "VO-1000"

Only eight Baldwin 1000 horsepower switchers with VO engines appeared on the PRR roster. They were acquired in two groups. The 1943 group consisted of six units, ordered on Baldwin sales orders 42530-R and 43502-E, placed in March 1942 and delivered in September and October 1943. They carried PRR numbers 5913-5918. The PRR's two-unit 1945 group was ordered on Baldwin sales order number 44511-H in February 1945 and delivered in October 1945. The Pennsy numbered these units 5919 and 5920. As with the 660 horsepower VO-engined Baldwin switchers, the 1000

horsepower switchers had no official Baldwin "model" designation, but are commonly called VO-1000 units. On the PRR, the VO-1000 units were originally classed AA-10b, they were reclassed (B-B)10B in 1946 and BS-10 in 1947.

EQUIPMENT

The Baldwin VO-1000's were also longer than the competitive EMD NW2's and Alco S-2's. The Baldwins were 48' 10" inside coupler knuckles, vs. the Alcos' 45" 5-3/4" and the EMDs' 44' 5" in length. The solid frame casting was the base for the straight eight cylinder VO engine with its 12-3/4" bore and 15-1/2" stroke. This frame casting on both VO models also incorporated the steps on the four corners of the locomotive. This was continued until January 1948 on 1000 horsepower Baldwin switchers through the 608NA engined units, and

on the 660 horsepower switchers. By deleting the steps from the frame, the depth of the foundry mould, and therefore the casting cost, was reduced considerably. The cost of attaching the separately fabricated steps was less than the more expensive casting with the integral steps. Note that the 1000 horsepower Baldwin switchers with the turbo-charged six-cylinder engine came after the changeover to fabricated steps.

SERVICE HISTORY

The 1943 group was part of a group of twelve Baldwin switchers assigned to New York and Philadelphia. Estimates at the time concluded that these twelve diesels allowed the release of 22 steam locomotives for other work. The 1945 group was part of a 10-unit order of both Baldwin and EMD switchers,

Locomotive Characteristics

Class	AS-6	AS-6 (#)	AS-6	GS-4, GS-4m	BS-6a	BS-10a, BS-10am
Builder	Alco	Alco	Alco	GE	BLW	BLW
Model	S-1	S-1	S-3	44-Ton	DS 4-4-660	DS 4-4-1000
Horsepower	660	660	660	380 or 400	660	1000
Wheel Arr,	B-B	B-B	B-B	B-B	B-B	B-B
Total Weight	199,900 lbs	202,400 lbs	199,900 lbs	88,550 lbs	196,000 lbs	228,500 lbs
Length over Couplers	44' 6"	44' 6"	44' 6"	33' 5"	46' 0"	46' 0"
Truck Centers	22' 0"	22' 0"	22' 0"	18' 9"	22' 8"	22' 8"
Truck Wheelbase	8' 0"	8' 0"	8' 0"	6' 10"	8' 0"	8' 0"
Engine	Alco 6-539	Alco 6-539	Alco 6-539	2, Cat. D-17000	BLW 6-606NA	BLW 6-606SC
Generator	GE 552	GE 552	GE 552	2, GE GT-555	W 480	W 480
Traction Motors	GE 731	GE 731	GE 731	4, GE 733	W 362D	W 362D
Gear Ratio	75:16	75:16	75:16	26:15/51:23	68:14	68:14
Maximum Speed	60 MPH	60 MPH	60 MPH	30 MPH	60 MPH	60 MPH
Starting Trac. Effort	49,975 lbs	50,600 lbs	49,975 lbs	22,137 lbs	49,000 lbs	57,125 lbs
Continuous Trac. Effort	29,200 lbs	29,200 lbs	29,200 lbs	13,000 lbs	34,000 lbs	34,000 lbs
CTE Speed	6.3 MPH	6.3 MPH	6.3 MPH	7.2 MPH	5.3 MPH	9.0 MPH

(#) This column refers to AS-6 units 5934, 9100-9103 and 9237-9244, which were heavier than the remaining AS-6s.

Here's another in the passing parade of Baldwin switchers, VO-1000 No. 5917 in Philadelphia in August 1963. The unit was built in 1943; note the cab sheet metal fillets and single stack characteristic of the prewar units. The War Production Board ordered Baldwin to concentrate on 1000-hp. switchers for the duration, which ended the company's production of 660-hp. units until after the war.

replacing 14 steam locomotives in the Baltimore district.

The first six class AA10b units, as they were then classed, were assigned to the New York Division (5913-5916) and the Chicago Terminal Division (5917 and 5918) in June 1944. By early 1948, this had been changed to an even split of four each on the New York and Maryland Divisions. These assignments were unchanged into the mid-1950s.

During the late 1950s, the BS-10s were shuffled somewhat with assignments of one or two units on the Susquehanna and Atlantic Divisions and more units moved to the Philadelphia area. At the end of the decade three units were maintained at Camden, New Jersey, one at Harrisburg, one at Meadows (Kearny, New Jersey), two at Wilmington, Delaware and one at Northumberland, Pennsylvania. In 1962, all of the class was assigned to the Philadelphia area where they worked out their days until all were retired in 1964 and 1965.

Northbound at Crum Lynne, Pennsylvania with a local freight, the 5920 shows the details of its rear end. The corner steps were cast integrally with the underframe.

Class AS-6
Alco S1, S3

Order Summary - Class AS-6 Units

PRR ROAD NUMBERS	ALCO SALES ORDER	NO. OF UNITS	ALCO MODEL	ORDER DATE	DELIVERY DATES
5954-5956	20096	3	S-1	Nov 46	May 47-Jun 47
9100-9103	20214	4	S-1	Oct 47	Feb 49-Mar 49
9237-9246	20297	10	S-1	Feb 48	Mar 49-May 49
5661-5670	20487	10	S-1	Nov 49	May 50-Jun 50
8873-8885	20580	13	S-3	Aug 50	Nov 50-Mar 51

The PRR lumped its Alco model S-1 and S-3 switchers into one class, AS-6. The first three of these Alco 660 horsepower, B-B wheel arrangement, end cab switchers, numbers 5954-5956, were purchased by the PRR in 1946 and delivered in 1947. They escaped being classed as (B-B)6A because the units were delivered the very month that a new classification system went into effect, designating them as class AS-6. The table above shows the acquisitions.

EQUIPMENT

The major difference between Alco models S-1 and S-3 was the truck. Until early 1950, Alco 660 and 1000 horsepower switchers (Alco models S-1 and S-2 respectively) were equipped with the distinctive Alco Blunt truck. Beginning in 1950, Alco changed over to the General Steel Castings trucks used by EMD, Baldwin, F-M and Lima on their switchers. Model designations S-3 (600-hp) and S-4 (1000-hp) were assigned to the GSC-equipped switchers.

The PRR segregated its class AS-6 units into two groups, but weight, and not the Alco model was the basis for

this distinction. Units 5954, 9100-9103 and 9237-9244 were ballasted to 202,400 lbs. total weight which resulted in starting tractive effort of 50,600 lbs. The rest of the class weighed 199,900 lbs and had a starting tractive effort of 49,975 lbs.

SERVICE HISTORY

Until the early 1950s, the S-1s were assigned almost exclusively to the New York Division, with only the 9237 and 9238 assigned to Buffalo. In February 1952, twenty-nine 660 horsepower diesel switchers were assigned to the New York Division of which twenty-five were Alco model S-1. The other four were Baldwin Class BS-6a. The Class AS-6 assignments included seven units at Harsimus Cove yard, one at Greenville yard, five at Meadows yard and shop, eight at Waverly yard, one at Harrison, one at New Brunswick, one at Bristol, and four at Trenton yard. The

remaining two worked BL-22/BL-23, a local freight from Trenton to Stockton and on various locals out of Phillipsburg yard. Waverly, Meadows, Harsimus Cove and Greenville were the large PRR yards in the Newark-Jersey City area. The Class AS-6 units working these yards were maintained at Meadows Shops. Meadows also maintained the Harrison and New Brunswick units. The other switchers were maintained at Trenton until the new shop was built at Morrisville yard in the mid-1950s.

The S-3s were all initially assigned to Mingo Junction (9 units) and Dennison (2 units) on the Panhandle Division, except for 8873 assigned to New Castle on the Lake Division and 8874 assigned to Canton on the Eastern Division.

These assignments were relatively stable well into the mid-1960s except for one or two S-1s being assigned to

---

Alco S-1 9450 is caught between switching moves in Philadelphia about 1967 after it had been renumbered from 9100. By this year, Alco switchers were replacing Baldwins in the Philadelphia area. The Alcos had the "outboard" handrails as standard equipment, rather than rails attached to the hood.

R.J. MULLER PHOTO, DOUGLAS COLLECTION

ORIG. ROAD NO.	MODEL	1966 ROAD NO.	MAY 1959 ASSIGNMENT
5661	S-1	9461	Meadows
5662	S-1	9462	Meadows
5663	S-1	9463	Morrisville
5664	S-1	--	Meadows
5665	S-1	9465	Morrisville
5666	S-1	9466	Meadows
5667	S-1	9467	Indianapolis
5668	S-1	9468	Morrisville
5669	S-1	9469	Morrisville
5670	S-1	9470	Meadows
5954	S-1	9454	Meadows
5955	S-1	9455	Meadows
5956	S-1	9456	Meadows
8873	S-3	9473	Enola (Non-system)
8874	S-3	9474	Columbus St. Clair
8875	S-3	9475	Enola (Non-system)
8876	S-3	9476	Mingo Jct. (BI Reg.)
8877	S-3	9477	Mingo Jct. (Pgh. Reg.)
8878	S-3	9478	Mingo Jct. (Pgh. Reg.)
8879	S-3	9479	Mingo Jct. (Pgh. Reg.)
8880	S-3	9480	Mingo Jct. (Pgh. Reg.)
8881	S-3	9481	Williamsport
8882	S-3	9482	Elmira
8883	S-3	9483	Mingo Jct. (BI Reg.)
8884	S-3	9484	Mingo Jct. (BI Reg.)
8885	S-3	9485	Mingo Jct. (Pgh. Reg.)
9100	S-1	9450	Meadows
9101	S-1	9451	Meadows
9102	S-1	9452	Enola (Non-system)
9103	S-1	9453	Meadows
9237	S-1	9437	Mingo Jct. (Pgh. Reg.)
9238	S-1	9438	Williamsport
9239	S-1	9439	Meadows
9240	S-1	9440	Meadows
9241	S-1	9441	Meadows
9242	S-1	9442	Meadows
9243	S-1	9443	East Altoona
9244	S-1	9444	Indianapolis
9245	S-1	9445	Meadows
9246	S-1	9446	Meadows

**Assignment Table
Class AS-6
(Alco S-1 and S-3)**

The S-3 version of the AS-6 class had AAR switcher trucks rather than the Blunt design. Unit 8878 sits in the Canton Ohio engine terminal on a Sunday morning in November 1963, accompanied by a variety of other motive power, including a Baldwin Sharknose freighter.

9461-9470 number blocks, and the S-3 units were given the 9473-9485 block. Only 5664 was not renumbered; it had been retired in May 1966; number 9464 was unused.

All of the remaining Class AS-6's were retired by Penn Central. The 9455, 9456, 9461, 9470, 9473, and 9476 lasted until the last day of PC operation, being retired as of 12:01 AM March 31, 1976, just as Conrail took over on April 1.

Class GS-4 and GS-4m GE 44-ton

The GE 44-ton switcher was created as a common carrier locomotive to take advantage of a 1937 labor agreement that allowed operation without a fire-man of locomotives with less than 90,000 lbs. on the drivers.

The 46 General Electric 44-tonners owned by the PRR between 1950 and 1962 formed the largest group of this type owned by any one railroad. The PRR normally assigned only an engineer to single-unit Class GS-4 operation. The units were numbered in one block, 9312 to 9357, which was somewhat unusual on the PRR.

On one hand the GS-4s' ability to operate around tight curves and on light trackage was a distinct advantage. Unfortunately, their low tractive effort more than offset this advantage in most assignments. Since the units were a desirable commodity on the second-hand locomotive market of the early 1960s, all but one were sold by the time of the Penn-Central merger. Even the

The GE 44-ton switcher was the only diesel locomotive model that even remotely deserved to be called "cute." To the engineers who were frustrated by its lack of pulling power, it was anything but cute. Unit 9318 is at Zanesville Ohio in November 1951.

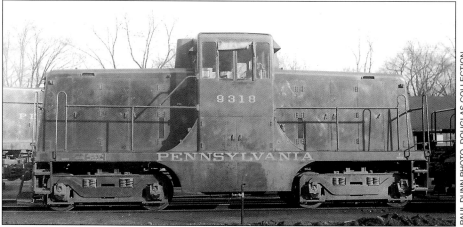

locations such as Philadelphia, Altoona, Indianapolis; and S-3s at Columbus, Williamsport and Elmira. The New York Division became an even stronger Alco 660 hp switcher center during the last years of the PRR, as most of the S-3's were reassigned to that area. By 1966, the only Class AS-6 units not in the New York area were the nine S-1 and S-3 units assigned to Philadelphia and the 9238 (as 9438 after 1966), which remained assigned to Williamsport until the end of PRR operations.

The AS-6 switchers were renumbered into the 9400 series in 1966, but the class remained the same. The S-1's were assigned the 9437-9446, 9450-9456 and

A pair of GS-4m units utilizing the "m" feature passing the Altoona passenger station with a shop train. The units are headed for Juniata Shops from South Altoona. The presence of the old train shed dates the photo to mid-1957 at the latest.

tan Island at 37th Street, replacing an A-6. This trackage was connected to the rest of the PRR by carfloat. The Juniata Shop assignments were just that, shop switchers, although the MU sets made local runs to the 12th Street shop and South Altoona shop. Another assignment was the lease to the Wabash of 9313 and 9318, for service on a Wabash branch where they had replaced the 2-6-0s that were the last steamers operating on that road.

MU OPERATION

None of the GS-4 units was equipped for multiple unit operation when built by GE. Between 1955 and 1957, the PRR tried to improve the utilization of the 44-tonners and equipped 11 of them with MU control. On most of the GS-4m locomotives (as they became), the MU connection was on the rear only. This meant that the GS-4m's with MU could only be plugged up in two-unit sets. However, at least one of the GS-4m units assigned to the Juniata shops had MU receptacles on both ends, and three-unit sets were run. In the Juniata assignment, the two and three unit GS-4m sets were used on the shop train that ran between Altoona area shops.

EQUIPMENT

The units utilized two Caterpillar D17000 V-8 engines, each rated at 190 HP. This was later increased to 200 HP for units produced starting in 1949. Each engine drove a 250 volt DC generator which supplied traction current to the pair of traction motors on the truck under the respective engines. Each traction motor was in turn connected to its axle with a double reduction gear set. The twin power plants were controlled simultaneously by the locomotive throttle. The main traction electrical circuits were separate. This meant that it was not possible to power the traction motors on one end from the main generator on the other end.

SERVICE HISTORY

The class data table indicates the location assignments for maintenance in May 1959. Two areas were centers of GS-4 operation: the Philadelphia-Camden area and Altoona. The Philadelphia 44-tonners operated out of Frankford Junction and Reed Street on the Delaware River waterfront, in as-

signments that required switching on tight curves. Another waterfront assignment was the GS-4 that worked the small yard on the west side of Manhat-

one survivor was not retained for service on the PRR or PC but was leased out.

ORIG. ROAD NO.	MAY 1959 ASSIGNMENT	M-U EQUIP	ORIG. ROAD NO.	MAY 1959 ASSIGNMENT	M-U EQUIP
9312	Juniata Shops		9335	Juniata Shops	Y
9313	Leased-Wabash		9336	Juniata Shops	Y
9314	Meadows		9337	Camden-PRSL	
9315	Lancaster, OH	Y	9338	Juniata Shops	
9316	Meadows		9339	Juniata Shops	Y
9317	Columbus-St. Cl		9340	Philadelphia-46	
9318	Leased-Wabash		9341	Philadelphia-46	
9319	Mingo Jct		9342	Philadelphia-46	
9320	Wilmington		9343	Philadelphia-46	
9321	Meadows		9344	Enola	
9322	Columbus-St. Cl	Y	9345	Philadelphia-46	
9323	Juniata Shops		9346	Philadelphia-46	
9324	Juniata Shops		9347	Philadelphia-46	
9325	Philadelphia-46		9348	Philadelphia-46	
9326	Camden-PRSL		9349	Philadelphia-46	
9327	Camden-PRSL		9350	Mahoningtown	
9328	Camden-PRSL		9351	Louisville	Y
9329	Juniata Shops	Y	9352	Oil City	
9330	Louisville	Y	9353	Philadelphia-46	
9331	Juniata Shops		9354	Renovo	
9332	Juniata Shops	Y	9355	Meadows	
9333	Enola		9356	Enola	
9334	Juniata Shops	Y	9357	Erie	

Equipment and Assignment Table
Class GS-4
(GE 44-ton Switcher)

Order Summary - Class GS-4 Units

PRR ROAD NUMBERS	GE ORDER NUMBER	NO. OF UNITS	ORDER DATE	DELIVERY DATES
9325-9328	P-24455	4	Oct 47	Nov 47
9328-9349	P-24455	22	Oct 47	Sep 48-Dec 48
9312-9321	P-67382	10	Oct 48	Mar 49-Apr 49
9322-9324	P-84351	3	Oct 48	Apr 49-May 49
9350-9356	P-84351	7	Oct 48	May 49
9357	P-113566	1	Nov 49	Feb 50

GS-4m units were also assigned to Louisville (site of a large GE factory complex). As indicated on the class data table, the 9330 and 9351 were assigned in Louisville in February 1959. These two units were later joined by GS-4m 9315.

Despite the application of MU, even three 44-tonners still could not muster the tractive effort of a common 120 ton, 1000 horsepower switcher. In Philadelphia it was found that 600-hp switchers could be used on the tight curve switching assignments. In the early 1960s, more and more Alco class AS-6 units were seen at Reed Street engine terminal on the waterfront in place of the GS-4's. Outside Philadelphia during this period many of the GS-4's were put in storage in ones and twos.

Finally, the PRR concluded that a reasonable price could be realized by selling the units. Between 1963 and 1966 almost all of them were sold. Locomotive dealers like Striegel in Baltimore, Preston W. Duffy near Columbus and Birmingham Rail and Loco in Alabama purchased most of them.

The 9353 was a survivor, however. It was leased out in 1959 when the Union Transportation Co. in New Egypt, New Jersey sent back the PRR class B-6sb 0-6-0 it had been leasing and dieselized with the PRR GS-4. The 9353 was left out of the 1966 pre-Penn Central renumbering plan. When it was belatedly realized that the 9353 was to be around awhile, it became the 9999. In due time it was relettered Penn Central and lasted into the Conrail era. The Union Transportation Co. finally ceased operations just before the end of the Penn Central. The 9999 was returned to Camden engine terminal where it was finally retired by Conrail in November 1977--never being relettered for Conrail.

PRR 9348 switching cars on Delaware Avenue in Philadelphia in February 1965. By this time, the GS-4 units assigned to Philadelphia were among the last GE 44-ton locomotives still operating on the Pennsylvania. The sharp curvature of the industrial tracks on Delaware Avenue was the reason for their survival.

The 1966 re-numbering plan did not originally include any 44-tonner renumbering. However, it was necessary to retain the 9353 on the roster for leasing to the Union Transportation Co. in New Jersey. So, the unit was renumbered to the highest number slot available--9999. PRR 9999 is seen here switching near Fort Dix, New Jersey at Union Transportation in October, 1967.

Class BS-6a
Baldwin DS 4-4-660

By a wide margin, the Pennsylvania Railroad owned the largest (371 units) fleet of Baldwin diesel switchers in the U. S. The PRR was also the largest owner of Baldwin diesel locomotives, with 643 units. Although the class BS-6a fleet of 99 units was not the largest class of Baldwin diesel switchers on the Pennsy, they constituted almost three-quarters of Baldwin's production of their DS 4-4-660 switchers.

The class was purchased in four orders. The last order was for 50 units. These Baldwins were designated class BS-6a by the railroad, which distinguished them from their class BS-6 660 horsepower VO engine switchers. The order summary details the four PRR orders for the Baldwin DS 4-4-660 units.

The DS 4-4-660 switchers were the 660 horsepower, B-B wheel arrangement switcher design in Baldwin's post-World War II diesel locomotive line. The engine was a BLW model 606NA prime mover with a 12-3/4" bore and a 15-1/2" stroke. This engine was naturally aspirated, which was Baldwin's terminology for non-turbocharged. This meant that the engine air was drawn in by the suction from the cylinder combustion chamber during the intake stroke of the four-stroke engine. With no turbocharger, an observer of a hardworking PRR class BS-6a unit could readily observe the exhaust of each cylinder. At night, this was visibly dramatized by successive fiery traces from the three exhaust stacks as the 1-2-4-6-5-3 cylinder ignition sequence repeated over and over.

The 99 class BS-6a units on the PRR were the fourth largest group of a single diesel switcher model on a U. S. rail-

PRR 9221 is shown in March 1965 with a cut of tank cars on Westmoreland Street in Philadelphia. This was one of the many industrial tracks (albeit with curves not as sharp as on Delaware Avenue) that required the assignment of so many switchers to the Philadelphia area.

Northumberland was a favorite place to photograph freshly-painted diesels. Here is a well-turned out 9113 in March 1965. Unfortunately, the mechanical condition of the unit didn't match the exterior, and the unit became one of the BS-6a's to be retired (in May 1966) before the pre-Penn Central renumbering sweep.

road. Until retirements reduced this number in the 1960s, the class was scattered over most of the PRR's system with the exception of the Southwest Region.

Despite this scattering of assignments, about half of the BS6a's were assigned to Philadelphia, making up the largest group of Baldwin switchers in the Philadelphia area. Aside from the 44-ton GE units in Philadelphia and Camden, all of the diesel switching assignments in the 50s and early 60s were Baldwins--classes BS-6, BS-6a, BS-10, BS-10a and BS-10am.

Fifty 660 horsepower Baldwin switchers (this included four 660 VO units) were needed at Philadelphia because the PRR switched a large number of industries there. Anyone riding the PRR's passenger service though the city in the 1950s could observe countless small industries with sidings on the PRR main line. In a 1952 tabulation of the locations from which switchers operated, the largest number of such

Order Summary - Class BS-6a Units

PRR ROAD NUMBERS	NO. OF UNITS	ORDER DATE	DELIVERY DATES
5957-5966	10	Jun 47	Mar 48-Apr 48
9110-9121	12	Oct 47	Jul 48-Aug 48
9210-9236	27	Feb 48	Nov 48-Feb 49
9000-9049	50	Nov 48	Mar 49-May 49

Equipment and Assignment Table
Class BS-6a
(Baldwin DS 4-4-660)

ORIG. ROAD NO.	1966 ROAD NO.	MAY 1959 ASSIGNMENT	RADIO	ORIG. ROAD NO.	1966 ROAD NO.	MAY 1959 ASSIGNMENT	RADIO	ORIG. ROAD NO.	1966 ROAD NO.	MAY 1959 ASSIGNMENT	RADIO
5957		Baltimore	Y	9024	7867	Mahoningtown	--	9118	7818	Philadelphia 46th St	--
5958	7858	Wilmington	Y	9025	7845	Mahoningtown	--	9119		Wilmington	Y
5959		Baltimore	Y	9026		Cleveland	--	9120	7820	Philadelphia 46th St.	--
5960	7860	Wilmington	Y	9027	7827	Mahoningtown	--	9121	7821	Philadelphia 46th St.	--
5961	7861	Baltimore	Y	9028		Mingo Jct. (Pgh. Reg.)	--	9210	7870	Philadelphia 46th St.	--
5962	7862	Baltimore	Y	9029	7809	Mingo Jct. (BI Reg.)	--	9211	7871	Philadelphia 46th St.	--
5963		Baltimore	Y	9030	7880	Mingo Jct. (BI Reg.)	--	9212	7872	Philadelphia 46th St.	--
5964	7864	Baltimore	Y	9031	7881	Mingo Jct. (Pgh. Reg.)	--	9213	7873	Philadelphia 46th St.	--
5965		Meadows	Y	9032	7882	East Altoona	--	9214		Philadelphia 46th St.	--
5966	7866	Meadows	Y	9033		Philadelphia 46th St.	--	9215	7875	Philadelphia 46th St.	--
9000		Camden	--	9034		Philadelphia 46th St.	Y	9216	7876	Philadelphia 46th St.	--
9001	7801	Philadelphia 46th St.	--	9035		Camden	--	9217		Philadelphia 46th St.	--
9002	7802	Philadelphia 46th St.	--	9036	7847	Philadelphia 46th St.	Y	9218		Philadelphia 46th St.	--
9003	7803	Camden	--	9037	7837	Philadelphia 46th St.	Y	9219		Philadelphia 46th St.	--
9004	7804	Philadelphia 46th St.	--	9038	7838	Philadelphia 46th St.	Y	9220	7800	Philadelphia 46th St.	--
9005	7805	Mingo Jct. (Pgh. Reg.)	--	9039	7839	Philadelphia 46th St.	Y	9221	7865	Philadelphia 46th St.	--
9006		Mingo Jct. (Pgh. Reg.)	--	9040	7840	Philadelphia 46th St.	Y	9222	7822	Philadelphia 46th St.	--
9007	7807	Cleveland	--	9041	7841	Philadelphia 46th St.	Y	9223	7823	Baltimore	Y
9008	7808	Canton	--	9042		Philadelphia 46th St.	--	9224		Philadelphia 46th St.	--
9009		Lancaster, OH	--	9043	7843	Philadelphia 46th St.	--	9225	7825	Philadelphia 46th St.	--
9010		Mingo Jct. (BI Reg.)	--	9044	7844	Canton	--	9226	7826	Camden	--
9011		Philadelphia 46th St.	Y	9045		Canton	--	9227		Lancaster, OH	--
9012		Philadelphia 46th St.	Y	9046	7846	Canton	--	9228	7828	Baltimore	--
9013	7853	Philadelphia 46th St.	Y	9047		Mingo Jct. (Pgh. Reg.)	--	9229	7829	Wilmington	--
9014	7854	Philadelphia 46th St.	Y	9048	7848	Philadelphia 46th St.	--	9230	7830	Wilmington	--
9015	7855	Philadelphia 46th St.	Y	9049	7849	Philadelphia 46th St.	--	9231	7831	Fort Wayne	--
9016	7856	Philadelphia 46th St.	Y	9110	7810	Baltimore	Y	9232	7832	Fort Wayne	--
9017		Philadelphia 46th St.	Y	9111	7811	Philadelphia 46th St.	--	9233	7833	Enola	--
9018		Philadelphia 46th St.	--	9112	7812	Philadelphia 46th St.	--	9234	7834	Meadows	--
9019	7819	Mingo Jct. (Pgh. Reg.)	--	9113		Northumberland	--	9235	7835	Meadows	--
9020	7850	Lancaster, OH	--	9114	7814	Baltimore	Y	9236	7836	Philadelphia 46th St.	--
9021	7851	Mingo Jct. (Pgh. Reg.)	--	9115	7815	Philadelphia 46th St.	--				
9022	7852	Mahoningtown	--	9116	7816	Philadelphia 46th St.	--				
9023	7842	Mahoningtown	--	9117		Wilmington	Y				

PRR 9233 was equipped with cab signals.
Special equipment as of January, 1960

operation bases were listed for the Philadelphia Terminal Division. The number of 660 horsepower Baldwin units ranged from six locations with one unit to Frankford Junction with eleven.

Most of the first two orders of the class were sent to the Maryland and Delmarva Divisions. As of 1949, these two divisions had 21 Class BS-6a units. Shortly thereafter, there was a reassignment of the class and the number on the Maryland and Delmarva Divisions was reduced to 16, with most moving to Philadelphia. In February 1952 on the Delmarva Division, two of the class were assigned to Norfolk and one to Cape Charles. Most of the Baldwin 660 horsepower switchers (12 units) on the Maryland Division were assigned to Baltimore proper.

Outside of the Philadelphia,

The Sunday calm at the Wilkinsburg, Pennsylvania yard is momentarily broken by the sweet-sounding Baldwin engine; the photographer was drawn by the sound. It is May, 1967, and the unit (which started life as 9029) has just been renumbered.

174

Wilmington and Baltimore areas, the BS-6a's were less concentrated. In 1959, regions other than the Philadelphia and Chesapeake Regions were all assigned BS-6a units except the Southwest Region.

Assignments were:

New York Region   4
Pittsburgh Region   11
Lake Region   11
Buckeye Region   6
Northwest Region   2

A more comprehensive assignment table appears on the prevous page.

Retirements of class BS-6a units started in May 1964 when PRR 9000 was retired. The unit had been leased to the Pennsylvania-Reading Seashore Lines and had been enveloped in fire when the freight house at Salem, New Jersey burned in June, 1963. The 9000 was a complete loss. Retirements continued until 55 remained at the end of the PRR.

In the 1966 renumbering, the BS-6a's were all renumbered into the 7800 series and reclassed as BS-6. In 1969, there were two further renumberings of the class, to clear road numbers for new GP-38's. The first renumbering in May 1969 affected unretired units in the 7800 to 7821 group, which were renumbered into open slots up to 7879. In November 1969, all of the remaining BS-6's were numbered into the 8350-8378 series. The class served almost throughout the entire Penn Central period, with the last three of the class being retired in August 1975. The numbers of those last three survivors were 8350, 8369 and 8374, originally PRR 9226, 9024 and 9003.

The Penn had 137 of these Baldwin DS 4-4-1000's. PRR 7955, typical of the non-MU group, is working at Trainer, Pennsylvania on January 25, 1969. The unit had been renumbered from 5555 well in advance of the PC merger. It had a cast underframe as did most of the class BS-10a units. The sheet metal below the walkway was just that; sheet metal, not a structural member.

Class BS-10a and Class BS-10am BLW DS 4-4-1000

The largest single-model switcher group on the Pennsylvania was the 137 DS 4-4-1000 Baldwin engines. Only the New York Central's 152 EMD model NW2s made up a larger group of first-generation switchers of the same model.

The PRR's DS 4-4-1000s included 125 non-MU and 12 MU-equipped units. The table shows the five orders under which they were purchased.

EQUIPMENT

The Baldwin DS 4-4-1000 was the 1000-horsepower companion of the DS 4-4-660 in the 1946 Baldwin diesel locomotive line. The model was initially introduced with the eight cylinder, non-turbocharged 608 NA engine. The frames were castings with integrally cast steps, of the type used on the Baldwin VO-1000 switchers.

Starting in late January 1948, Baldwin began delivering of a 1000 horsepower switcher with a six-cylinder turbocharged engine, the model 606SC. The 660-hp. switchers used the same engine, but without the turbocharger. The underframe on the DS 4-4-1000, along with the 660-hp units, was a re-designed and less expensive casting without the integrally cast steps. The first exception to cast underframes was PRR 5550, which was the production prototype for the welded fabricated underframe that became standard for later Baldwin switchers.

Delivery of the first PRR Class BS-10a switchers started about a month and a half after Baldwin began shipping 606SC-equipped switchers. All of the class PRR BS-10a and BS-10am units were equipped with this engine. The engine had the same 12-3/4" bore, 15-1/2" stroke as the non-turbocharged model 606NA engine used on the Class BS-6a's. The Westinghouse electrical equipment

Order Summary Class BS-10a Units			
PRR ROAD NUMBERS	NO. OF UNITS	ORDER DATE	DELIVERY DATES
5967- 5977, 9177-9179	14	Jun 47	Mar 48-Apr 48
5978-5979, 9180-9183	6	Jun 47	Apr 48-May 48
9122-9136	15	Oct 47	Jun 48-Jul 48
9251-9275	25	Feb 48	Dec 48-Feb 4
9050-9079	30	Nov 48	Mar 49-Apr 49
5551-5590	40	Nov 49	Jan 50-Apr 50
5550	1	Nov 49	Mar 50
9429-9434	6	Nov 49	May 50

was also the same, namely the 480F main traction generator and the four 362D traction motors.

The 68:14 gear ratio was used on both Class BS-6a and BS-10a units. Both classes produced the same continuous tractive effort: 34,000 lbs. The difference was that on the 1000 horsepower unit this effort was produced at 9.0 mph, while on the 660 horsepower unit, the 34,000 lbs of pull was exerted at only 5.3 mph. The starting tractive effort for the BS-10a was 57,125 lbs. This was also higher than the 660 horsepower, because the 228,500 lb. weight of the 1000 horsepower units was some 15 tons greater than for the 660 horsepower units.

Equipment and Assignment Table
Classes BS-10a and BS-10am
(Baldwin DS 4-4-1000)

ORIG. ROAD NO.	1966 ROAD NO.	MAY 1959 ASSIGNMENT	MU	CS	RA
5550	7950	Wilmington	--	Y	Y
5551	7951	Phila. 46th St.	--	--	--
5552	7952	Phila. 46th St.	--	--	--
5553	7953	Phila. 46th St.	--	--	--
5554	7954	Phila. 46th St.	--	Y	--
5555	7955	Phila. 46th St.	--	--	--
5556	7956	Phila. 46th St.	--	--	--
5557	7957	East Altoona	--	--	--
5558		Enola	--	Y	Y
5559	7959	Harrisburg	--	Y	Y
5560	7960	Phila. 46th St.	--	Y	Y
5561	7961	Phila. 46th St.	--	Y	--
5562	7962	Phila. 46th St.	--	Y	Y
5563	7963	Phila. 46th St.	--	Y	Y
5564	7964	Phila. 46th St.	--	Y	Y
5565	7965	Phila. 46th St.	--	Y	Y
5566	7966	Phila. 46th St.	--	--	Y
5567	7967	Phila. 46th St.	--	--	Y
5568	7968	Phila. 46th St.	--	--	Y
5569	7969	Phila. 46th St.	--	--	Y
5570	7970	Phila. 46th St.	--	--	Y
5571	7971	Phila. 46th St.	--	--	Y
5572	7972	Phila. 46th St.	--	--	--
5573	7973	Phila. 46th St.	--	--	--
5574	7974	Phila. 46th St.	--	--	--
5575	7975	Phila. 46th St.	--	--	--
5576	7976	Phila. 46th St.	--	--	--
5577	7977	Phila. 46th St.	--	--	--
5578	7978	York	--	--	Y
5579		York	--	--	Y
5580	7980	York	--	--	Y
5581	7981	Harrisburg	--	--	Y
5582		Ivy City (D. C.)	--	--	Y
5583	7983	Ivy City (D. C.)	--	--	Y
5584		Baltimore	--	--	Y
5585	7985	Canton	--	--	--
5586	7986	Conway	--	--	--
5587	7987	Conway	--	--	Y
5588	7988	Conway	--	--	Y
5589	7989	Canton	--	--	--
5590	7990	Conway	--	--	Y
5967		Wilmington	--	Y	Y
5968	7938	Wilmington	--	Y	Y
5969	7939	Wilmington	--	Y	Y
5970	7940	Baltimore	--	Y	--
5971	7941	Baltimore	--	--	Y
5972	7942	Baltimore	--	--	Y
5973	7943	Camden	--	--	--
5974	7944	Baltimore	--	--	Y
5975	7945	Baltimore	--	--	Y
5976	7946	Renovo	--	--	--
5977	7947	Ivy City (D. C.)	--	--	Y
5978	8038	Baltimore	Y	--	Y
5979	8039	Baltimore	Y	--	Y
9050		Cleveland	--	--	--
9051	8001	Mahoningtown	--	--	--
9052	8002	Mahoningtown	--	--	--
9053	8003	Cleveland	--	--	--
9054	8004	Meadows	--	--	--
9055	8005	Cleveland	--	--	--
9056	8006	Cleveland	--	--	--
9057	8007	Mahoningtown	--	--	--
9058	8008	Mahoningtown	--	--	--
9059	8009	Mahoningtown	--	--	--
9060	8010	Canton	--	--	--
9061	8011	Cleveland	--	--	--
9062	8012	Canton	--	--	--
9063	8013	Conway	--	--	Y
9064	8014	Conway	--	--	Y
9065	8015	Meadows	--	--	--
9066	8016	Meadows	--	--	--
9067		Mingo Junction	--	--	--
9068	8018	Canton	--	--	--
9069	8019	Chicago 16th St.	--	--	--
9070	8020	Canton	--	--	--
9071		Cleveland	--	--	--
9072		Conway	--	--	Y
9073	8023	Conway	--	--	Y
9074		Ebenezer	--	--	--
9075	8025	Conway	--	--	Y
9076	8026	Fort Wayne	--	--	--
9077	8027	Mahoningtown	--	--	--
9078	8028	Mahoningtown	--	--	--
9079	8029	Cleveland	--	--	--
9122	7922	Phila. 46th St	.--	--	Y
9123	7923	Phila. 46th St	.--	--	Y
9124		Phila. 46th St.	--	--	Y
9125	7925	Phila. 46th St.	--	--	Y
9126		Baltimore	--	--	Y
9127		Baltimore	--	--	Y
9128	7928	Phila. 46th St.	--	--	Y
9129	7929	York	--	--	Y
9130	7930	Phila. 46th St.	--	--	--
9131	7931	Phila. 46th St.	--	--	--
9132	7932	Wilmington	--	--	Y
9133	7933	Wilmington	--	--	Y
9134		Wilmington	--	--	Y
9135	7935	Phila. 46th St.	--	--	--
9136	7936	Camden	--	--	--
9177		Ivy City (D. C.)	--	--	Y
9178		Wilmington	--	--	Y
9179	7999	Meadows	--	--	--
9180	8040	Baltimore	Y	--	Y
9181	8041	Baltimore	Y	--	Y
9182	8042	Baltimore	Y	--	Y
9183	8043	Baltimore	Y	--	Y
9251	7991	Camden	--	--	--
9252		Camden	--	--	--
9253	7993	Ebenezer	--	--	--
9254	7994	Ebenezer	--	--	--
9255	7995	Toledo	--	--	--
9256	7996	Toledo	--	--	--
9257	7997	East Altoona	--	--	--
9258	8035	Fort Wayne	Y	--	--
9259	8036	Fort Wayne	Y	--	--
9260	8037	Fort Wayne	Y	--	--
9261	8044	Fort Wayne	Y	--	--
9262	7984	Phila. 46th St.	--	--	--
9263	7924	Conway	--	--	Y
9264	7914	Mingo Junction	--	--	--
9265		Mahoningtown	--	--	--
9266	7916	Conway	--	--	Y
9267	7917	Meadows	--	--	--
9268	7918	Meadows	--	--	--
9269	7919	Meadows	--	--	--
9270	7920	Meadows	--	--	--
9271	7921	Meadows	--	--	--
9272	8017	Meadows	--	--	--
9273	7948	Phila. 46th St.	--	--	Y
9274	8024	Phila. 46th St.	--	--	Y
9275	7949	Phila. 46th St.	--	--	Y
9429	8045	East Altoona			
9430	8046	East Altoona			
9431	8031	East Altoona			
9432	8032	Lewistown			
9433	8033	Phila. 46th St.			
9434	8034	Phila. 46th St.			

Hump control on units 5978, 5979
and 5980-5983.
MU - Multiple Unit
CS - Cab Signals
RA - Radio

Special equipment as of January, 1960

SPECIAL EQUIPMENT

Not much special equipment was applied to the BS-10 units. About 18 or so units assigned to the New York-Washington corridor were equipped with cab signals. In addition, somewhat fewer than half of the units were equipped with the Bell Mobil Phone, a yard radio. The BS-10am units in Baltimore (5978-5979 and 9180-9183) were equipped with hump control after about 1960. Units 5973-5979, 9180-9183 and 9429-9434 were MU-equipped by the builder. The PRR installed MU on units 9258-9261 in 1952.

SERVICE HISTORY

Assignments of the BS-10a class were more widespread than the BS-6a units, although more than half of the units were concentrated in the Philadelphia and Chesapeake Regions. The May 1959 distribution shown in the table on the next page is typical of the location of the class from their initial delivery until some redistribution in early 1965.

Heavy switchers in the Philadelphia area often were found on local freight trains, because they were handy. Above, near suburban Crum Lynne, in February 1959, PRR 5550 leads such a freight.

REGION	NO. OF UNITS
New York	10
Philadelphia	45
Chesapeake	30
Northern	4
Pittsburgh	19
Lake	22
Buckeye	1
Northwestern	5
Southwestern	0

In early 1965, some 20 of the BS-10a units were moved from the East Coast to the Pittsburgh-Canton-Cleveland area. Additionally, two from Columbus and one from Chicago were moved to Conway, and the four were moved from Fort Wayne to Cleveland. From 1965 to the end of PRR ownership, distribution of the class was approximately 25 in Philadelphia and also in the Baltimore-Wilmington areas and some 60 units in the Pittsburgh-Cleveland area.

In the 1966 reclassing and renumbering, the BS-10a units were all numbered between 7914 and 8030. They were reclassed to BS-10. The MU equipped units in class BS-10am were renumbered from 8031 to 8046 and reclassed BS-10m.

Retirements of the class BS-10a units started with five in 1965, 16 in 1966, 18 in 1967 and one in 1968. Three of the class BS-10am units were retired in 1967.

Class BS-10 and BS-10m units survived on the Penn Central roster until almost the last day of PC operation. The next to last Penn Central retirement instruction letter included the remaining class BS-10's (9 units) and the last class BS-10m. The retirement letter ordered them to be retired effective March 29, 1976; they were dropped from the accounts as of 12.01 AM on March 30, 1976. Penn Central thus had no class BS-10's on its last day of operation.

9433 and 9434 are in MU at Greenwich Yard in South Philadelphia in March 1966. These units have the Baldwin fabricated underframe. The structure below the walkway is the side sill, a structural member of the frame.

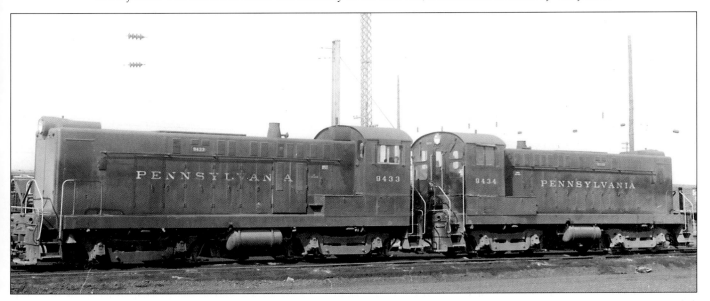

Class FS-10
F-M H10-44

The H-10-44 1000 horsepower switcher was the model that established Fairbanks-Morse in the diesel locomotive business. The PRR's fleet of 55 of these switchers, assigned Class FS-10, was the largest of any railroad. They totaled more than a quarter of the 197 H10-44 units built. The three PRR orders were also the three largest orders for the model.

EQUIPMENT

All the Class FS-10 units were equipped with the six-cylinder F-M model 38D8 1/8 opposed piston diesel engine. Westinghouse electrical equipment was used on the first two PRR orders. This equipment included a model 481B main traction generator and four model 362D traction motors on each switcher. Starting in 1949 (after building a prototype in March 1948), F-M started equipping switchers with electrical equipment of their own design, although Westinghouse electrical equipment was also offered. On the final PRR order, F-M used model DGZ-J main traction generators and F-M model DRZ-H traction motors.

The F-M model H10-44 utilized pneumatic engine speed control. With the F-M pneumatic control, the engine governor was actuated by a small air cylinder. The throttle was mechanically connected to an air valve, which increased air pressure to the governor air cylinder

Equipment and Assignment Table
Classes FS-10
(F-M H10-44)

ORIG ROAD NO.	1966 ROAD NO.	MAY 1959 ASSIGNMENT	CAB SIG.	ORIG ROAD NO.	1966 ROAD NO.	MAY 1959 ASSIGNMENT	CAB SIG.
5980	8211	Cincinnati	--	9186	8220	Chicago 59th St.	--
5981	8212	Cincinnati	--	9187		Columbus St. Clair	Y
5982	8213	Cincinnati	--	9188	8222	Fort Wayne	--
5983	8214	Cincinnati	--	9189	8223	Cincinnati	--
5984	8215	Cincinnati	--	9190	8224	Fort Wayne	--
5985	8216	Cincinnati	--	9191	8225	Cincinnati	--
5986	8217	Cincinnati	--	9192	8226	Fort Wayne	--
9080	8244	Chicago 59th St.	--	9193	8227	Rose Lake	--
9081	8245	Columbus St. Clair	Y	9194	8228	Rose Lake	--
9082		Columbus St. Clair	Y	9195	8229	Louisville	--
9083	8247	Columbus St. Clair	--	9196	8230	Cincinnati	--
9084	8248	Cincinnati	--	9197	8231	Indianapolis	--
9085	8249	Columbus St. Clair	Y	9198	8232	Rose Lake	--
9086	8250	Chicago 59th St.	--	9199		Chicago 59th St.	--
9087		Columbus St. Clair	--	9288	8233	Cincinnati	--
9088		Columbus St. Clair	--	9289	8234	Cincinnati	--
9089	8252	Fort Wayne	--	9290	8235	Cincinnati	--
9090		Columbus St. Clair	Y	9291	8236	Cincinnati	--
9091	8254	Chicago 59th St.	--	9292	8237	Indianapolis	Y
9092	8255	Louisville	--	9293	8238	Rose Lake	--
9093	8256	Louisville	--	9294	8239	Cincinnati	--
9094	8257	Columbus St. Clair	--	9295	8240	Chicago 59th St.	--
9095	8258	Cincinnati	--	9296	8241	Chicago 59th St.	--
9096	8259	Fort Wayne	--	9297		Chicago 59th St.	--
9097	8260	Columbus St. Clair	--	9298	8242	Chicago 59th St.	--
9098	8261	Columbus St. Clair	--	9299	8243	Chicago 59th St.	--
9099		Columbus St. Clair	--				
9184	8218	Rose Lake	--				
9185	8219	Rose Lake	--				

Units 9085, 9087 and 9088 had radio.
Special equipment as of January, 1960

in order to increase engine speed.

A unique control stand featured operation of the reverser and throttle with one handle, which could be advanced through either of two horizontal slots on the stand. The two slots were connected on their right ends with a vertical slot, which was the engine idle position. If the handle was moved in the vertical slot to the lower horizontal slot, the traction motor electrical circuits were connected for locomotive forward motion. If the handle was raised in the vertical slot and into the upper horizontal slot, the motor circuits were connected for reverse operation. Advancing the handle to the left increased the speed in the chosen direction.

The crew disembarks from a northbound local freight pulled by F-M H10-44 9098. We are at Orrville, Ohio in November 1963. The H10 carbody was the original Loewy design, including overhanging cab roof, sheet metal fillets at the cab, and the "sculpted" three-facet nose. Pretty fancy for a switcher!

SERVICE HISTORY

Class FS-10 units were assigned to the PRR west of Columbus almost without exception. Until the early 1960s, the PRR assigned FS-10's to Cincinnati, Columbus, Rose Lake (East St. Louis), Louisville, Chicago, Indianapolis, Ft. Wayne and Toledo in varying numbers.

The Rose Lake assignment was the first one for eight of the new FS-10's. Five were sufficient to handle yard operations there. The three other FS-10s were used on local freights between Rose Lake and Terre Haute and accomplished the following:

- Eliminated seven trains, replacing them with four locals.
- Eliminated an engine terminal at Greenville, reducing force by two laborers.
- Reduced the assigned laborers at Effingham by three.
- Produced an actual savings of $395,663 per year.
- Permitted operation of two tricks in Terre Haute yard with diesel units between the arrival of Train SL-2 and the departure of Train SL-1, a saving not included in the $395,663 per year.

The memo detailing the changes proclaimed them to be a splendid accomplishment. It is safe to assume that the five men whose jobs were eliminated did not share this enthusiasm.

In 1965, the units which had been assigned to the Southwest Region (Indianapolis, Louisville and Rose Lake) were moved to the Toledo-Detroit area. This left the remainder of the FS-10s in

FS-10 #5980 heads a transfer run to the Norfolk & Western's Clare Yard east of Cincinnati, Ohio in October 1965. With seven railroads entering Cincinnati, transfer runs went in all directions. The Queen City area was the home of many PRR FS-10's, e.g., 17 units in 1959. The louvers on the battery box (ahead of the cab) were cut in by the PRR after problems with accumulation of gases from the batteries.

Order Summary - Class FS-10 Units

PRR ROAD NUMBERS	F-M ORDER NUMBER	NO. OF UNITS	ORDER DATE	DELIVERY DATES
5980-5986, 9184-9199	LD-50	23	Oct 47	Jun 48-Sep 48
9288-9299	LD-53	12	Feb 48	Mar 49-Apr 49
9080-9099	LD-71	20	Nov 48	Jul 49-Nov 49.

Cincinnati, Columbus and Chicago in addition to Detroit and Toledo. This was the assignment pattern until the end of the PRR.

The first FS-10's were retired in February 1966. Retirements continued until only 29 remained by February 1968, when the units entered Penn Central service. In 1966, the class had been re-

numbered into the 8211 to 8291 number block for the integration of the PRR and NYC locomotive rosters. As retirements continued during the PC period, the remaining class FS-10's were concentrated in Chicago. The last three former PRR class FS-10's were retired in August 1970.

Blasting through Columbus, Ohio in March, 1967, PRR 8260 wears her new number (previously 9097). The renumbering was a minimum effort, replacing only the road numbers on the cab side and in the numberboards. The "PENNSYLVANIA" lettering on the hood was not replaced with a keystone emblem.

The Pennsy classed both Alco models S-2 and S-4 as AS-10. The only difference between the two models was the truck. Until early 1950, both Alco 660 and 1000 horsepower switchers were equipped with the distinctive Alco Blunt truck (Models S-1 and S-2). After the change, Alco equipped these switchers with the General Steel Castings trucks also used by EMD, Baldwin, F-M and Lima on their switchers.

The PRR placed seven orders for Alco model S-2 and S-4 switchers, as noted in the Order Summary. An eighth order for Alco 1000 horsepower switchers was placed in late 1957 but these were for the model T-6, which was classified as AS-10a, the subject of a separate section. All the S-2 and S-4 units were classed as AS-10 except for road numbers 8490 to 8499, which were the MU equipped class AS-10m. The MU-equipped units were part of the November 1951 diesel purchase by the PRR which also included MU-equipped 1200 horsepower switchers from EMD, Baldwin and F-M.

PRR 9204 had received the Keystone-only image by the time it was photographed in Northumberland, Pennsylania in 1966. Otherwise, it is a typical Alco model S-2 like 41 others on the PRR roster.

Model S-2

The assignments of the model S-2's can be divided into three time periods. The first lasted from unit delivery to about 1953 or 1954. During this time, about 19 or 20 were assigned to the New York Division, a few less to Buffalo and two to Wellesville, Ohio.

From the end of the first period until about 1963, the Wellsville units and about seven others were assigned in ones and twos to locations such as Canton, Pitcairn, Harrisburg, Indianapolis and Williamsport. The New York Division fleet remained at about 20 during this second period.

Finally, after 1963, all but the four Buffalo-based units were concentrated in the New York Division and the Philadelphia area. By 1967, there were 28 assigned to the New York Division, six in Philadelphia, and the old faithful two in Buffalo plus two in Renovo.

PRR 8901, seen here at Harsimus Cove on the west bank of the Hudson River, was one of two PRR Alco switchers equipped with trainphone and assigned to the Bel-Del branch on delivery. These units were on this assignment for only a few months when they were sent to Eastern Ohio, where they spent most of the their PRR lives. Instead, it was first sent to eastern Ohio. The 8901 made it to New Jersey shortly before this photo was taken in November 1966.

Model S-4

As described in John Kirkland's *The Diesel Builders: American Locomotive Co. and Montreal Locomotive Works*, the Association of American Railroads (AAR) had adopted the General Steel Casting switcher truck as an AAR Recommended Practice in 1949. In order for Alco (and MLW) to sell their switchers as conforming to AAR standards, use of the Blunt truck on the S-1 and S-2 models could not be continued. Alco changed the truck, and switcher models S-1 and S-2 became models S-3 and S-4. The PRR took delivery of both models beginning in 1950.

Order Summary - Class AS-10 Units

PRR ROAD NUMBERS	ALCO SALES ORDER	NO. OF UNITS	ALCO MODEL	ORDER DATE	DELIVERY DATES
5926-5931,9204	20184	7	S-2	Jun 47	Jul 48-Aug 48
9105-9109	20298	5	S-2	Oct 47	Feb 49
9278-9287	20298	10	S-2	Feb 48	Feb 49-Mar 49
5641-5660	20482	20	S-2	Nov 49	Mar 50-Apr 50
8886-8901	20581	16	S-4	Aug 50	Nov 50-Jun 51
8487-8499	20851	13	S-4	Nov 51	May 52-Jun 52
8430-8434	20898	5	S-4	Jun 53	Jan 54-Feb 54

The class AS-10 S-4 non-MU units were concentrated between Toledo and Buffalo. Until the mid-1960s, between three and six of the units were assigned to Toledo, Canton, Youngstown, and Buffalo. The 8430-8434 group in particular was assigned to Toledo from delivery in 1954 until the mid-1960s. Unit

Equipment and Assignment Table
Class AS-10 and AS-10m
(Alco S-2 and S-4)

ORIG. ROAD NO.	MODEL	1966 ROAD NO.	MAY 1959 ASSIGNMENT	CAB SIG.	MULT. UNIT	RADIO	ORIG. ROAD NO.	MODEL	1966 ROAD NO.	MAY 1959 ASSIGNMENT	CAB SIG.	MULT. UNIT	RADIO
5641	S-2	9841	Meadows	--	--	--	8495	S-4	9775	Morrisville	--	Y	Y
5642	S-2	9842	Meadows	--	--	Y	8496	S-4	9776	Morrisville	--	Y	Y
5643	S-2		South Amboy	--	--	--	8497	S-4	9777	Morrisville	--	Y	Y
5644	S-2	9824	Meadows	Y	--	--	8498	S-4	9768	Morrisville	--	Y	--
5645	S-2	9825	Meadows	Y	--	--	8499	S-4	9769	Morrisville	--	Y	--
5646	S-2	9816	Enola (Non-system)	--	--	--	8886	S-4	9803	Mahoningtown	--	--	--
5647	S-2		Meadows	Y	--	--	8887	S-4	9817	Mahoningtown	--	--	--
5648	S-2	9818	Morrisville	Y	--	--	8888	S-4	9788	Indianapolis	--	--	--
5649	S-2	9819	South Amboy	Y	--	--	8889	S-4	9789	Toledo	--	--	--
5650	S-2	9810	Meadows	Y	--	--	8890	S-4	9790	Canton	--	--	--
5651	S-2	9811	Meadows	--	--	Y	8891	S-4	9791	Canton	--	--	--
5652	S-2	9812	South Amboy	--	--	--	8892	S-4	9792	Toledo	--	--	--
5653	S-2	9813	Meadows	--	--	--	8893	S-4	9793	Mahoningtown	--	--	--
5654	S-2	9814	Conway	--	--	Y	8894	S-4	9794	Canton	--	--	--
5655	S-2	9785	Conway	--	--	Y	8895	S-4	9795	Conway	--	--	Y
5656	S-2	9836	Meadows	--	--	Y	8896	S-4	9796	Conway	--	--	Y
5657	S-2	9837	Meadows	--	--	--	8897	S-4	9797	Canton	--	--	--
5658	S-2	9838	Meadows	--	--	--	8898	S-4	9798	Conway	--	--	Y
5659	S-2	9839	Conway	--	--	Y	8899	S-4	9799	Conway	--	--	Y
5660	S-2	9802	Conway	--	--	Y	8900	S-4	9800	Mahoningtown	--	--	--
5926	S-2	9826	Ebenezer	--	--	Y	8901	S-4	9801	Mahoningtown	--	--	--
5927	S-2	9827	Ebenezer	--	--	Y	9105	S-2	9805	Meadows	--	--	--
5928	S-2	9828	Ebenezer	--	--	Y	9106	S-2	9806	Indianapolis	--	--	--
5929	S-2	9829	Ebenezer	--	--	Y	9107	S-2	9807	Meadows	--	--	--
5930	S-2	9820	Ebenezer	--	--	Y	9108	S-2	9808	Meadows	--	--	--
5931	S-2	9821	Ebenezer	--	--	Y	9109	S-2	9809	Meadows	--	--	--
8430	S-4	9830	Toledo	--	--	--	9204	S-2	9804	Ebenezer	--	--	Y
8431	S-4	9831	Toledo	--	--	--	9278	S-2	9778	Ebenezer	--	--	Y
8432	S-4	9832	Toledo	--	--	--	9279	S-2	9779	Ebenezer	--	--	Y
8433	S-4	9833	Toledo	--	--	--	9280	S-2	9780	Indianapolis	--	--	--
8434	S-4	9834	Toledo	--	--	--	9281	S-2	9781	Canton	--	--	--
8487	S-4	9815	Ebenezer	--	--	Y	9282	S-2	9782	Canton	--	--	--
8488	S-4	9822	Ebenezer	--	--	Y	9283	S-2	9783	Northumberland	--	--	Y
8489	S-4	9823	Erie	--	--	--	9284	S-2	9784	Ebenezer	--	--	Y
8490	S-4	9770	Morrisville	--	Y	Y	9285	S-2		Indianapolis	--	--	--
8491	S-4	9771	Morrisville	--	Y	Y	9286	S-2	9786	Ebenezer	--	--	Y
8492	S-4	9772	Morrisville	--	Y	Y	9287	S-2	9787	Ebenezer	--	--	Y
8493	S-4	9773	Morrisville	--	Y	Y							
8494	S-4	9774	Morrisville	--	Y	Y							

Units 8900 and 8901 equipped with trainphone.
Special equipment as ot January, 1960.

Equipment and Assignment Table
Classes BS-7 and BS-7m
(BLW DS 4-4-750 and BLH S-8)

ORIG. ROAD NO.	MODEL	CLASS	1966 ROAD NO.	MAY 1959 ASSIGNMENT	CAB SIG.	MULT. UNIT	RADIO
5595	DS 4-4-750	BS-7m	7911	East Altoona	--	Y	--
5596	DS 4-4-750	BS-7	7886	Enola	Y	--	--
5597	DS 4-4-750	BS-7m	7912	East Altoona	--	Y	--
5598	DS 4-4-750	BS-7	7888	Philadelphia 46th St.	Y	--	--
5599	DS 4-4-750	BS-7	7889	Meadows	--	--	--
5600	DS 4-4-750	BS-7m	7913	Meadows	--	--	--
5601	DS 4-4-750	BS-7		Williamsport	--	--	--
5602	DS 4-4-750	BS-7	7902	Philadelphia 46th St.	--	--	--
5603	DS 4-4-750	BS-7	7903	Enola (Non-system)	--	--	Y
5604	DS 4-4-750	BS-7	7904	Enola (Non-system)	--	--	Y
5605	DS 4-4-750	BS-7		Philadelphia 46th St.	--	--	--
5606	DS 4-4-750	BS-7	7906	Enola (Non-system)	Y	--	--
5607	DS 4-4-750	BS-7		York	--	--	Y
5608	DS 4-4-750	BS-7	7908	York	--	--	Y
5609	DS 4-4-750	BS-7		Baltimore	--	--	Y
5610	DS 4-4-750	BS-7	7910	York	--	--	Y
5611	DS 4-4-750	BS-7	7891	York	--	--	Y
5612	DS 4-4-750	BS-7	7892	Baltimore	--	--	--
5613	DS 4-4-750	BS-7	7893	Baltimore	--	--	--
5614	DS 4-4-750	BS-7	7900	Ivy City (D. C.)	--	--	Y
5615	DS 4-4-750	BS-7	7901	Ivy City (D. C.)	--	--	Y
5616	DS 4-4-750	BS-7	7890	Baltimore	--	--	Y
5617	DS 4-4-750	BS-7	7887	Ivy City (D. C.)	--	--	Y
5618	DS 4-4-750	BS-7		Baltimore	--	--	Y
8994	S-8	BS-7		Mingo Junction	--	--	--
8995	S-8	BS-7		Chicago 16th St.	--	--	--
8996	S-8	BS-7	7896	Canton	--	--	--
8997	S-8	BS-7		Canton	--	--	--
8998	S-8	BS-7	7898	Lancaster, OH	--	--	--
8999	S-8	BS-7		Lancaster, OH	--	--	--

Special equipment as of January 1960

8430 departed first, going to the New York Division in 1962.

Between two and four non-MU S-4's were assigned to Conway from delivery in 1952 until 1961. In addition, a single S-4 was assigned to Indianapolis from 1958 to 1961, and a single S-4 to Williamsport in 1963. In the mid-1960s, most of the non-MU S-4's were sent to the New York Division (12 units) plus

eight to Philadelphia, with single units to Williamsport and Renovo.

The Class AS-10m (MU equipped) units had stable assignments on the New York Division upon delivery; they stayed there until the mid-1960s when they were reassigned to the Northern Region. On the New York Division, the AS-10m units were divided between Meadows and Morrisville assignments,

with six usually at Morrisville and four at Meadows. At Meadows the units were used in MU on transfer drags.

A notable and demanding AS-10m assignment was the use of three in multiple on the Waverly to Weehawken transfer to the New York Central. Tortuously threading their way past junctions, multi-track crossings and lift bridges, with frequent and unpredictable waits, this job usually required sixteen hours.

At Morrisville, the AS-10m's were used in two-unit MU sets between the steel mill and the Morrisville yard. This job also was a rugged one, with the curves in the steel mill and the grades over the mainline overhead bridge and in the yard itself. On one occasion, a long time observer did note a three-unit set at Morrisville. Fortunately he was in a position to photograph the event and the results are shown on this page. In the mid-1960s, all ten of the AS-10m's were moved to the Northern Region where six were assigned to Buffalo and four to Erie.

In the 1966 renumbering, class AS-10 non-MU units were renumbered into the 9778-9842 series, although 5643, 5647 and 9285 were retired in May 1965 before being made part of the renumbering. The units remained classified as AS-10 on the PC. See the adjacent table for unit by unit renumbering. The AS-10m units retained the AS-10m classification and were renumbered from 8498-8499 and 8491-9497 to 9768-9777.

Most of the class AS-10 and AS-10m units were retired during Penn Central ownership. Class AS-10m units 9770 and 9777 plus eighteen class AS-10 units survived to Conrail ownership but this was short-lived. All were retired by March 1978.

PRR 8496 leads 8493 and 8495 with a train of loaded ore-jennies at Morrisville yard in 1959.

R.D. ADAMS PHOTO

Class BS-7 and BS-7m
BLW DS 4-4-750 and BLH S-8

In November 1958, Thorndale, Pennsylvania was home for PRR 5606, a Baldwin DS4-4-750 without MU equipment. This was the "standard" configuration for this class of switchers.

The Pennsylvania Railroad's November 1949 purchase of Baldwin 750-hp switchers showed the railroad's continued preference for Eddystone's nominal 100-ton switcher. Switchers of this weight were also offered by Alco (the 660-hp model S-1) and by EMD (the 600-hp model SW1). During this period, Fairbanks-Morse cataloged only one pure switcher, the 1000 horsepower model H10-44, which weighed about 120 tons. Before the 1949 order, the PRR had acquired 101 Baldwin, 17 Alco and 40 EMD switchers rated at 600 and 660 hp—the nominal 100-ton category.

Before 1948, Baldwin's nominal "100-ton" switcher matched its competition with the 660 horsepower model DS 4-4-660. Except for the PRR, which had purchased almost all of Baldwin's production of the model, it had not sold well. In 1948, Baldwin replaced the 660 horsepower unit with the 750 horsepower DS 4-4-750. Compared to the DS 4-4-660, the DS 4-4-750 provided the same continuous tractive effort (34,000 lbs.) at a slightly greater speed—6.2 mph vs. 5.3 mph. The increase in horsepower was accomplished primarily by increasing the compression ratio of the model 606NA engine from 13.45:1 to 14.88:1, raising the full rated gross horsepower of the non-supercharged engine from 750 to 825.

In November 1949, the Pennsylvania ordered 24 Baldwin 750-hp switchers. The units were produced on Baldwin sales order 49511 in May and June 1950. They were numbered 5595 to 5618 and classed BS-7. Three of these units were later modified with multiple unit controls and re-classed BS-7m.

The PRR's August 1950 locomotive orders included the last nominal 100-ton switchers purchased by the road. Six 800-hp, model S-8 Baldwin switchers were ordered at the same time as thirteen model S-3 Alco switchers. The S-8 was part of the 1950 overhaul of the Baldwin locomotive line, which included the increase of switcher horsepower from 1000 to 1200 and from 750 to 800. The PRR's model S-8 units, numbered 8994 to 8999, were the first S-8's produced by Baldwin. Delivery was in March and April 1951 on Baldwin sales order 50525; class was BS-7 instead of BS-8.

The 750 horsepower units were equipped with a Baldwin 6-cylinder model 606NA engine that had a 12-3/4" bore and a 15-1/2" stroke. The engine drove a Westinghouse 480-F main generator.

The 800 horsepower units used a new engine, which Baldwin designated as simply the model 606. This 6-cylinder, non-supercharged engine also had a 12-3/4" bore and a 15-1/2" stroke and 14.88:1 combustion ratio, but the full rated gross horsepower had been increased from 825 to 875. The improvements needed to accomplish this increased the engine weight from 28,600 lbs to 31,500 lbs. The electrical equipment was unchanged between the 750 and 800 horsepower units.

SERVICE HISTORY

The 750 horsepower units were all assigned east of Buffalo and Altoona, mostly in the Philadelphia and Chesapeake Regions. These assignments were similar to the Class BS-6a units except that the 750 horsepower BS-7's were even more concentrated on the eastern end of the system. In a tabulation of switcher assignments in early 1952 however, none of the Class BS-7 units were assigned to the Philadelphia area itself. Instead, the assignments included one at Waverly yard in north Jersey, one at Harrisburg, seven at Enola yard, one at Cumbo yard, one at Hagerstown, one at Buttonwood (south of Wilkes-Barre, Pennsylvania), one at Northumberland, four at Washington, DC and five at York. All of these locations indicate work assignments in light local freight and yard service.

Locomotive Characteristics

Class	FS-10	AS-10	AS-10, AS-10m	BS-7, BS-7m
Builder	F-M	Alco	Alco	BLW
Model	H10-44	S-2	S-4	DS 4-4-750 (*)
Horsepower	1000	1000	1000	750
Wheel Arr,	B-B	B-B	B-B	B-B
Total Weight	242,000 lbs	234,100 lbs	234,100 lbs	197,600 lbs
Length over Couplers	48' 10"	45' 6"	45' 6"	46' 0"
Truck Centers	25' 6"	22' 6"	22' 6"	22' 8"
Truck Wheelbase	8' 0"	8' 0"	8' 0"	8' 0"
Engine	FM 6-38D8-1/8	Alco 6-539SC	Alco 6-539SC	BLW 6-606NA (*)
Generator	W 481B (+)	GE GT-553	GE GT-553	W 480
Traction Motors	W 362D (+)	GE 731	GE 731	W 362D
Gear Ratio	68:14	75:16	75:16	68:14
Maximum Speed	60 MPH	60 MPH	60 MPH	60 MPH
Starting Trac. Effort	60,500 lbs	58,525 lbs	58,525 lbs	49,400 lbs
Continuous Trac. Effort	34,000 lbs	34,000 lbs	34,000 lbs	34,000 lbs
Cont. Trac. Effort Speed	8.9 MPH	8.0 MPH	8.0 MPH	6.2 MPH

(+) FS-10 units 9080 and 9085-9099 had F-M model DGZJ main generator and DRZH traction motors.

(*) BS-7 units 8994-8999 were BLH Model S-8 using model 6-606 engine

Baldwins 5595 and 5600 at Cresson, Pennsylvania in April 1965. MU equipment had been applied to 5600 only two years previously to provide a relief unit for the two-unit MU set used from Altoona over the Western Maryland into Cumberland MD. The three BS-7ms went to other assignments after the WM rebuilt its line.

The 800 horsepower BS-7 units received initial assignments in eastern Ohio. The early 1952 list of switcher assignments tabulate one at Salem, two at Canton yard, one at Mansfield, one at Cambridge, Ohio and one at Lancaster. The sixth unit in this group was assigned to locals ZB-11 and ZB-12 between Lancaster and Circleville, Ohio on the Panhandle Division.

These assignments remained remarkably stable over the years with regard to assigned area if not specific location. By 1963, the 750-hp units were distributed as follows:

New York Region: 1 unit
Philadelphia Region: 7 units
Chesapeake Region: 12 units
Northern Region: 1 unit
Pittsburgh Region: 3 units

The 800-hp units were distributed as follows:

Pittsburgh Region: 3 units
Buckeye Region: 2 units
Northwest Region: 1 unit

A major assignment shuffle in Spring 1965 moved all of the 750 horsepower units from other areas into the Philadelphia and Chesapeake Regions. At that time, the 22 remaining units (two were retired in 1965) were all assigned to Baltimore, Wilmington and the 46th St. enginehouse in Philadelphia.

The surviving 800- horsepower units were all assigned to Conway except the 8995, which remained at 59th St. in Chicago for maintenance until retired.

The PRR converted three BS-7 750

horsepower units to multiple unit operation. The first two units (5595 and 5597) were converted in late 1952, a conversion made to dieselize the PRR operation from Altoona down the Bedford Secondary Track to Cumberland, Maryland. Although the actual Bedford Secondary Track of the PRR was rated for heavier units than 100 tons, the PRR reached Cumberland over trackage rights on the Western Maryland Railway. The WM section extending from the Pennsylvania-Maryland state line into Cumberland was restricted to locomotives with working weights less than 100 tons. The restriction was a bridge over the B&O in the Cumberland Narrows at GC Junction. The only PRR steam locomotives which had been allowed on this line were the 0-6-0 classes. The application of MU on the two BS-7 diesels allowed one-crew diesel operation over the weight restricted section with units totaling 1500 horsepower.

There was still one problem, however. When a BS-7m was out of service for maintenance, it was necessary to use two diesels, with two engine crews. In those cases any pair of class ES-6, BS-6, BS-7 or AS-6 units could be used with the cost penalty of an extra engine crew. In July, 1963, a third BS-7 (the 5600) was converted to class BS-7m with MU equipment, to avoid the cost of the second crew. Ironically, within a short time after the conversion, the WM upgraded the line from State Line south so that heavier power could be used. All three of the class BS-7m's were transferred to Philadelphia in 1965 and the MU feature was rarely, if ever, used.

In the 1966 renumbering, the BS-7 class was allocated the 7886 to 7910 number block, but the renumbering was not done in order of old road number. The 800 horsepower units would have occupied the 7894 to 7899 block in numerical order, but only the 8996 and 8998 stayed in service long enough to be renumbered. BS-7m's 5595, 5597 and 5600 were renumbered 7911 to 7913.

Prior to the Penn Central merger, nine BS-7's were retired, including three of the 800 horsepower units. The remaining BS-7's were retired by Penn Central; the last two in September 1972. Eight BS-7's were renumbered in November 1969 into the 8381 to 8388 number block to make way for new GP38 units. The 8388 was the only BS-7m so renumbered, and it was retired in August 1970. The last two BS-7's retired were 8381 (originally 5596) and 8381 (originally 5615).

PRR 8998, seen here at Zanesville Ohio in January 1958, is one of the six model S-8 units which the railroad mysteriously included in the BS-7 class rather than creating a new, more accurate "BS-8" class.

Class ES-12 and ES-12m
EMD SW7, SW9, SW1200

The Pennsylvania Railroad purchased some of all three EMD 1200 horsepower models--SW7, SW9 and SW1200, placing all three in classes ES-12 and ES-12m. Non-MU class ES-12 originally totaled 78 units of all three models. The MU Class ES-12m originally totaled 41 SW7's and SW9's. These totals changed in 1956 and 1957 when six of the non-MU model SW7's were equipped with multiple unit connections. The totals were altered to 72 class ES-12 and 47 class ES-12m.

The table defines the MU and non-MU locomotives as originally built. The ten model SW7's originally built as MU on EMD order number 4031 were equipped for back-to-back operation, with MU connections on the rear only. They were never modified. The rear ends of these ten units had MU type end handrails with walkways installed, while the front ends had the non-MU type end handrails.

The six model SW7 units (8868, 8871, 8872, 9386, 9387 and 9388) equipped by the PRR with MU control in 1956 and 1957 were equipped with MU connections on *both* ends, with the end railings on both ends modified to the MU configuration. The model SW9 ES-12m had MU connections on both ends with the MU type end handrails.

SERVICE HISTORY

The 38 non-MU equipped SW7's were all originally assigned west of Pittsburgh. The five non-MU equipped SW9's were based in the Pittsburgh area (8859 and 8860) and Wilmington, Delaware (8542-8544). The SW1200 diesels (all of which were non-MU equipped) had widespread assignments; they were located in seven of the nine PRR regions--all but the Chesapeake and Southwest regions.

The assignment table details the assignment of each unit in May 1959. Prior to the major reassignment of units in Spring 1965, location of the ES-12 switchers was relatively stable. Some reassignment took place, but most of

PRR 9074 is seen here at the Pitcairn yard engine terminal at Pitcairn, Pennsylvania on November 20, 1966. This non-MU SW7 switcher was renumbered in September, 1966 from 9374. The PRR's ES-12 models had all the usual distinctions between the three models in the class. The SW7's had the louvres above the "PENNSYLVANIA" on the hood. The model SW9 did not have these louvres. The SW1200 was the same as the SW9 except for five louvres instead of six on the battery box aft of the cab.

This is one of only five non-MU SW9's on the PRR. This photo illustrates the difference between SW9s and SW7s: the SW9s have no louvers above the lettering. It's is shown at Perryville, Maryland in the Keystone only image. The photo was taken in late 1966 or early 1967.

the class at least stayed in the same region over that period. The 1965 reassignment was intended primarily to locate units of the same builder in the same area. This was the reason for sending SW1200 units to Rose Lake, Illinois, for instance. The FS-10 units formerly assigned to the Southwest Region were centralized in Chicago.

The original ES-12m assignments of the class were also relatively stable between delivery and the 1965 reassignment. The SW7's in the class assigned to Terre Haute operated on the Peoria branch. The New York region MU-equipped assignments included heavy transfer work in North Jersey, heavy work at South Amboy on the coal dumpers, and the steel mill work in the Trenton area after the Fairless Works of

US Steel opened in the early 1950s. The MU-equipped units in Erie worked at the ore docks. As ore traffic dwindled between 1952 and 1959, the number of ES-12m units at Erie was reduced.

After the 1965 reassignment, more MU-equipped switchers were sent to Chicago, for both local freights and steel mill work. Units assigned to East Altoona and Enola were also used in local freights. The Enola units, for instance, were used at Northumberland and on the Bald Eagle local. Some of the class ES-12m model SW7 units remained in Terre Haute after 1965 on the Peoria branch.

The 1966 renumbering placed the ES-12's in the block from 9009-9080, and the ES-12m in the block from 9081-9141, as shown in the table on Page 187.

PRR 9372 and 9363 are at Terre Haute, Indiana in April 1965. These SW7s had M-U connectors only on the cab ends, and worked the long branch out of Terre Haute (via Farrington) to Peoria, Illinois.

None of the PRR class ES-12 or ES-12m units was retired by Penn Central. After the Conrail merger, the SW7 and SW9's retained their PC road numbers. Conrail renumbered the ex-PRR SW1200's from 9009-9034 and 9050-9058 to 9328-9363. Most of the SW7 and SW9 units were retired by Conrail starting in 1981. Retirements of SW1200's began in 1983.

Order Summary - Class ES-12 Units

PRR ROAD NUMBERS	EMD ORDER NUMBER	NO. AND TYPE OF UNITS	EMD MODEL	ORDER DATE	DELIVERY DATES
9358-9363, 9369-9370 9371-9372	4061	10, MU	SW7	Nov 49	Jun 50 Jun 50 Jul 50
9364-9368	6022	5, Non-MU	SW7	Nov 49	Apr 50-May 50
9373-9395	6079	23, Non-MU	SW7	Nov 49	Mar 50-May 50
8861-8868, 8871-8872	6230	10, Non-MU	SW7	Aug 50	Jan 51
8859-8860	6180	2, Non-MU	SW9	Aug 50	Mar 51
8869-8870	6231	2, MU	SW9	Aug 50	Mar 51
8513-8522, 8529-8536	4170	18, MU	SW9	Nov 51	Dec 52-Mar 53 Mar 53
8523-8528 8537-8541	4194	11, MU	SW9	Nov 51	Dec 52
8542-8543	4195	3, Non-MU	SW9	Nov 51	Mar 53
7900-7934	4414	35, Non-MU	SW1200	Nov 57	Oct 57-Apr 58

Locomotive Characteristics

Class	BS-12, BS-12m	FS-12	FS-12m	ES-12, ES-12m	ES-12, ES-12m	ES-12	AS10a
Builder	BLH	F-M	F-M	EMD	EMD	EMD	Alco
Model	S-12	H12-44	H12-44	SW7	SW9	SW1200	T-6
Horsepower	1200	1200	1200	1200	1200	1200	1000
Wheel Arr,	B-B	B-B	B-B	B-B	B-B	B-B	B-B
Total Weight	228,000 lbs (*)	246,800 lbs	249,000 lbs	246,600 lbs	246,600 lbs	246,600 lbs	243,000 lbs
Length over Couplers	46' 0"	48' 10"	48' 10"	44' 5"	44' 5"	44' 5"	45' 6"
Truck Centers	22' 8"	25' 6"	25' 6"	22' 0"	22' 0"	22' 0"	22' 0"
Truck Wheelbase	8' 0"	8' 0"	8' 0"	8' 0"	8' 0"	8' 0"	8' 0"
Engine	BLH 6-606A	FM 6-38D8-1/8	FM 6-38D8-1/8	EMD 12-567A	EMD 12-567B	EMD 12-567C	Alco 6-251
Generator	W 480	FM DGZJ	FM DGZJ	EMD D15A	EMD D15A	EMD D15A	GE GT-584
Traction Motors	W 362 DF	FM DRZH	FM DRZH	EMD D27A	EMD D27B	EMD D47B	GE 752
Gear Ratio	68:14	68:14	68:14	62:15	62:15	62:15	74:18
Maximum Speed	60 MPH	60 MPH	60 MPH	65 MPH	65 MPH	65 MPH	60 MPH
Starting Trac. Effort	57,000 lbs	61,700 lbs	62,250 lbs	61,650 lbs	61,650 lbs	61,650 lbs	60,750 lbs
Continuous Trac. Effort	34,000 lbs	34,000 lbs	34,000 lbs	36,000 lbs	36,000 lbs		53,000 lbs
CTE Speed	10.8 MPH	11.3 MPH	11.3 MPH	10.0 MPH	10.0 MPH		5.0 MPH

(*) Class BS-12m units weighed 240,000 lbs. with a starting tractive effort of 60,000 lbs

Equipment and Assignment Table
Classes ES-12 and ES-12m
(EMD SW7, SW9, and SW1200)

ORIG ROAD NO.	1966 ROAD NO.	BLDR S MODEL	CLASS	MAY 1959 ASSIGNMENT	C S	R A
7900	9050	SW1200	ES-12	Pittsburgh-28th		
7901	9051	SW1200	ES-12	Pittsburgh-28th		
7902	9052	SW1200	ES-12	Pittsburgh-28th		
7903	9053	SW1200	ES-12	Pittsburgh-28th		
7904	9054	SW1200	ES-12	Pittsburgh-28th		
7905	9055	SW1200	ES-12	Pittsburgh-28th		
7906	9056	SW1200	ES-12	Elmira		
7907	9057	SW1200	ES-12	Elmira		
7908	9058	SW1200	ES-12	Cleveland		
7909	9009	SW1200	ES-12	Cleveland		
7910	9010	SW1200	ES-12	Columbus-St. Cl		
7911	9011	SW1200	ES-12	Columbus-St. Cl		
7912	9012	SW1200	ES-12	Columbus-St. Cl		
7913	9013	SW1200	ES-12	Columbus-St. Cl		
7914	9014	SW1200	ES-12	Columbus-St. Cl		
7915	9015	SW1200	ES-12	Enola		
7916	9016	SW1200	ES-12	Enola		
7917	9017	SW1200	ES-12	Enola		
7918	9018	SW1200	ES-12	Enola		
7919	9019	SW1200	ES-12	East Altoona		
7920	9020	SW1200	ES-12	East Altoona		
7921	9021	SW1200	ES-12	East Altoona		
7922	9022	SW1200	ES-12	East Altoona		
7923	9023	SW1200	ES-12	East Altoona		
7924	9024	SW1200	ES-12	East Altoona		
7925	9025	SW1200	ES-12	Lewistown		
7926	9026	SW1200	ES-12	Crestline		
7927	9027	SW1200	ES-12	Crestline		
7928	9028	SW1200	ES-12	Chicago-59th St		
7929	9029	SW1200	ES-12	Chicago-59th St		
7930	9030	SW1200	ES-12	Chicago-59th St		Y
7931	9031	SW1200	ES-12	Chicago-59th St		Y
7932	9032	SW1200	ES-12	Chicago-59th St		Y
7933	9033	SW1200	ES-12	Chicago-59th St		Y
7934	9034	SW1200	ES-12	Chicago-59th St		Y
8513	9113	SW9	ES-12m	Logansport		
8514	9114	SW9	ES-12m	Logansport		
8515	9115	SW9	ES-12m	Erie		
8516	9116	SW9	ES-12m	Logansport		
8517	9117	SW9	ES-12m	Logansport		
8518	9118	SW9	ES-12m	Erie		
8519	9119	SW9	ES-12m	Erie		
8520	9120	SW9	ES-12m	Erie		
8521	9121	SW9	ES-12m	Logansport		
8522	9122	SW9	ES-12m	Pittsburgh-28th		
8523	9123	SW9	ES-12m	Meadows	Y	
8524	9124	SW9	ES-12m	Meadows	Y	
8525	9125	SW9	ES-12m	Morrisville	Y	
8526	9126	SW9	ES-12m	Enola	Y	
8527	9127	SW9	ES-12m	Meadows	Y	
8528	9128	SW9	ES-12m	Enola	Y	
8529	9129	SW9	ES-12m	South Amboy		
8530	9130	SW9	ES-12m	South Amboy		
8531	9131	SW9	ES-12m	Meadows		
8532	9132	SW9	ES-12m	Morrisville		
8533	9133	SW9	ES-12m	Morrisville		
8534	9134	SW9	ES-12m	Meadows		
8535	9135	SW9	ES-12m	Meadows		
8536	9136	SW9	ES-12m	Morrisville		
8537	9137	SW9	ES-12m	Morrisville	Y	
8538	9138	SW9	ES-12m	Morrisville	Y	
8539	9139	SW9	ES-12m	Meadows	Y	
8540	9140	SW9	ES-12m	Meadows	Y	
8541	9141	SW9	ES-12m	Meadows	Y	Y
8542	9042	SW9	ES-12	Wilmington	Y	Y
8543	9043	SW9	ES-12	Wilmington	Y	Y
8544	9044	SW9	ES-12	Wilmington	Y	Y
8859	9059	SW9	ES-12	Pittsburgh-28th	Y	
8860	9060	SW9	ES-12	Pittsburgh-28th	Y	
8861	9061	SW7	ES-12	Mingo Junction		
8862	9062	SW7	ES-12	Mingo Junction		
8863	9063	SW7	ES-12	Mingo Junction		
8864	9064	SW7	ES-12	Mingo Junction		
8865	9065	SW7	ES-12	Mingo Junction		
8866	9066	SW7	ES-12	Mingo Junction		
8867	9067	SW7	ES-12	Mingo Junction		
8868	9094	SW7	ES-12m(*)	Logansport		
8869	9095	SW9	ES-12m	Terre Haute		
8870	9096	SW9	ES-12m	Terre Haute		
8871	9097	SW7	ES-12m(*)	Logansport		
8872	9098	SW7	ES-12m(*)	Lewistown		
9358	9084	SW7	ES-12m	Terre Haute		
9359	9085	SW7	ES-12m	Terre Haute		
9360	9086	SW7	ES-12m	Logansport		
9361	9087	SW7	ES-12m	Logansport		
9362	9088	SW7	ES-12m	Terre Haute		
9363	9089	SW7	ES-12m	Indianapolis		
9364	9038	SW7	ES-12	Grand Rapids		
9365	9035	SW7	ES-12	Pittsburgh-28th		
9366	9036	SW7	ES-12	Sandusky		
9367	9037	SW7	ES-12	Indianapolis		
9368	9068	SW7	ES-12	Sandusky		
9369	9090	SW7	ES-12m	Terre Haute		
9370	9091	SW7	ES-12m	Terre Haute		
9371	9092	SW7	ES-12m	Terre Haute		
9372	9093	SW7	ES-12m	Terre Haute		
9373	9073	SW7	ES-12	Sandusky		
9374	9074	SW7	ES-12	Mahoningtown		
9375	9075	SW7	ES-12	Sandusky		
9376	9076	SW7	ES-12	Sandusky		
9377	9077	SW7	ES-12	Mingo Junction		
9378	9078	SW7	ES-12	Mingo Junction		
9379	9079	SW7	ES-12	Grand Rapids		
9380	9080	SW7	ES-12	Pittsburgh-28th		
9381	9041	SW7	ES-12	Grand Rapids		
9382	9039	SW7	ES-12	Grand Rapids		
9383	9040	SW7	ES-12	Grand Rapids		
9384	9046	SW7	ES-12	Sandusky		
9385	9045	SW7	ES-12	Mahoningtown		
9386	9081	SW7	ES-12m(*)	Chicago-59th St		
9387	9082	SW7	ES-12m(*)	Lewistown		
9388	9083	SW7	ES-12m(*)	Chicago-59th St		
9389	9069	SW7	ES-12	Sandusky		
9390	9070	SW7	ES-12	East Altoona		
9391	9071	SW7	ES-12	Chicago-59th St		
9392	9072	SW7	ES-12	Crestline		
9393	9073	SW7	ES-12	Chicago-59th St		
9394	9048	SW7	ES-12	East Altoona		
9395	9049	SW7	ES-12	Chicago-59th St		

Unit 8514 had Hump Control

(*) MU applied by PRR, not builder

CS is cab signal

RA is yard radio

Specail equipment as of January 1960

187

Seen from yet another overpass in Altoona, EMD SW1200 No. 7922 is switching cars at South Interlocking in June 1963.

Class BS-12 and BS-12m
Baldwin S-12

The Pennsylvania Railroad's acquisition of the Baldwin 1200 horsepower switchers was the final phase of their purchase of Baldwin end cab switchers. The Pennsy's Baldwin switcher orders totaled 373, almost 44% of the total of the PRR's 851 diesel switchers. The 373 Baldwin switchers greatly outnumbered the 236 EMD end cab switchers. The EMD total included 35 model SW1200 switchers purchased after Baldwin left the diesel locomotive business.

The PRR classed its 87 Baldwin S-12 switchers BS-12 and BS-12m, the latter class being equipped with multiple unit control. The units were acquired under four orders as detailed in the table on Page 183.

The BS-12m units were part of the PRR's November 1951 order that included a total of 84 MU-equipped switchers from Alco, EMD and F-M in addition to Baldwin. Almost all of these units were used as light road-switchers. The class BS-12m group fit this description by

working primarily on the Delmarva line and its branches.

For the first 18 months of model S-12 production, which started in September 1950, these units were built with both cast and fabricated underframes at the buyer's option. The first order of PRR BS-12's were the last Baldwin switchers delivered to the railroad with cast underframes. All other PRR Class BS-12 units were built with a frame fabricated by welding steel shapes and plate. After March 1952 all S-12's were built with a fabricated underframe.

SERVICE HISTORY

When the 18 non-MU units ordered in August 1950 were delivered in early 1951 they were divided between the Lake and Pittsburgh divisions. On the Lake Division, three went to yards in Cleveland, three to Akron and Barberton, one to the yard in Niles and one to the yard in Wheatland, Pennsylvania. On the Pittsburgh Division, all ten went to the coal country south of Shire Oaks yard in Elrama, Pennsylvania on what had been the Monongahela Division before 1951.

PRR 8990 is shown at Pitcairn Yard in May 1965. The unit is from the railroad's first order for 18 Baldwin-Lima-Hamilton model S-12 units, which were built with cast underframes. The remainder of the Penn's S-12s had fabricated underframes.

The 20 non-MU units ordered in July 1951 were assigned somewhat more widely than the first 18. In the east, four were divided between Philadelphia (three units) and Hagerstown, Maryland. In the west, six went to Toledo. Otherwise, five went to the Pittsburgh Division, being divided between Cresson and Youngwood. Of the remaining five, three went to the Conemaugh Division at Blairsville and two went to Panhandle Division at Pittsburgh and Mingo Jct.

The 12 non-MU diesels delivered in August and September 1952 all went to the Chesapeake Division at Wilmington, Delaware. The last five Class BS-12's were delivered to the PRR in February 1954 at Pitcairn yard, east of Pittsburgh.

Generally, these assignments remained in force until the last two years of PRR operation. The units assigned to the Pittsburgh Division and Region gravitated to Pitcairn maintenance by the mid-1950s. Also in the mid-1950s, the two Panhandle Division units were assigned to Lancaster, Ohio. In 1957, 8785-8787 (originally assigned to Blairsville, Pennsylvania on the Conemaugh Division) were reassigned from the Pittsburgh Region to Philadelphia.

Except for the units assigned to Philadelphia and Wilmington, class BS-12 units were involved with switching at locations handling the PRR's bread and butter commodities, coal and iron ore. The units assigned to Shire Oaks and Pitcairn worked the yards in the coal region south of Pittsburgh. The BS-12's were the switching units at West Brownsville, Youngwood and Shire Oaks, where the coal trains were made up and then fed to the PRR's coal customers in the east and on the Great Lakes.

The Class BS-12's assigned to Toledo and Cleveland were more involved with iron ore. The ore docks at Cleveland on Whiskey Island marshaled the ore hoppers loaded off the ore boats into trains, which ran south to the steel mills in the Weirton, West Virginia-Steubenville, Ohio area.

The BS-12 units assigned to Wilmington, Delaware and Philadelphia did general switching. At Philadelphia, work could also include iron ore handling at the huge ore handling dock adjacent to Greenwich yard in South Philadelphia. The single BS-12 unit (8777) assigned to Hagerstown, Maryland, stayed in that location from delivery until 1965 when it was transferred to Pitcairn. At Hagerstown, 8777 worked the Hagerstown to Winchester, Virginia job on the Cumberland Valley Branch. In 1952, before this section of line was downgraded to the Winchester Secondary Track, freights to and from Winchester were CV-93, CV-94, CV-95 and CV-96.

The 32 MU-equipped Class BS-12m's were all assigned to Wilmington or Baltimore on delivery. Twenty-one of these were assigned to what until 1955 was the Delmarva Division, extending from Wilmington to Cape Charles, Virginia, with many branches. Within a very

Order Summary - Class BS-12 Units

PRR ROAD NUMBERS	BLH SALES ORDER	NO. OF UNITS	PRR CLASS	ORDER DATE	DELIVERY DATES
8976-8993	50512	18	BS-12	Aug 50	Jan 51-Mar 51
8777-8796	50545	20	BS-12	May 51	Dec 51-Feb 52
8753-8764	51530	12	BS-12	Nov 51	Aug 52-Sep 52
8732-8752	51530	21	BS-12m	Nov 51	Sep 52-Oct 52
8765-8775	51530	11	BS-12m	Nov 51	Oct 52-Dec 52
8100-8104	300316	5	BS-12	Jun 53	Feb 54

In 1967, recently renumbered from 8794, S-12 No. 8114 idles at Philadelphia's 46th Street engine terminal. The side sill on this fabricated underframe is actually a structural member. On the eighteen cast-underframe S-12 units the corresponding under-walkway part was sheet metal.

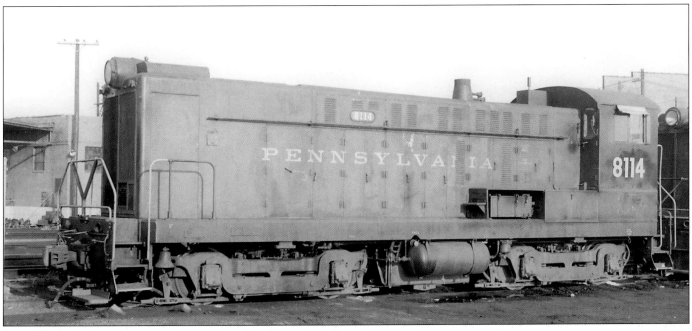

J. D. ENGMAN PHOTO, DOUGLAS COLLECTION

PRR 8751 leads a three-unit set of MU'd BS-12ms at Delmar, Delaware in July 1960. These units were equipped with both trainphone and roller bearing trucks, and were in fact used as road-switchers.

short time after delivery, four were sent to other locations, with 8732 and 8733 going to Buffalo on the Northern Division, 8734 going to Northumberland on the Susquehanna Division and 8735 going to the Middle Division. These assignments also remained stable, except that in the middle 1950s, 8767 and 8768 were transferred from Wilmington to Philadelphia.

The operation of the BS-12m's on the Delmarva line and its branches was an efficient light road-switcher assignment. With the many branches from the main Wilmington-Cape Charles line, the PRR operated trains south from Wilmington,

and dropped off both cars and a single unit at the branch junction point. The single unit that was dropped off was then able to deliver and pick up on the branch. On the Wilmington-bound trip, the trains were re-assembled, as both the cars and the single unit were picked up at the branch junction.

The Delmarva BS-12m's had extra equipment for the road-switcher function. The units were purchased with roller bearing trucks, while the BS-12 units used friction bearings. Most of the Delmarva BS-12m's also had trainphone, making communication with the units possible when they were on the road.

In the 1966 renumbering, Class BS-12's was placed in the 8113-8167 number block, although six units had been retired before renumbering. Class BS-12m's was renumbered into the 8168-8199 block. Some reassignments were made in the late PRR period. The six BS-12's at Toledo were reassigned to Canton in 1965 and the Cleveland area BS-12 was transferred to Philadelphia. The three Buffalo Class BS-12m's were reassigned in 1965, one to Pitcairn and two to Baltimore.

As indicated in the Equipment and Assignment Table, BS-12's were retired before being renumbered. Units 8986,

This BS-12 and caboose are based at Burlington, New Jersey. It worked a local freight from Bordentown southward, on the east shore of the Delaware River. On this Sunday in May, 1966, PRR 8794 is parked and awaiting the next week's work.

Equipment and Assignment Table
Class BS-12 and BS-12M
(BLH S-12)

ORIG. ROAD NO.	1966 ROAD NO.	CLASS	MAY 1959 ASSIGNMENT	RADIO	ORIG. ROAD NO.	1966 ROAD NO.	CLASS	MAY 1959 ASSIGNMENT	RADIO
8100	8135	BS-12	Pitcairn	--	8770	8170	BS-12m	Baltimore	Y
8101	8136	BS-12	Pitcairn	--	8771	8171	BS-12m	Baltimore	Y
8102	8165	BS-12	Pitcairn	--	8772	8172	BS-12m	Baltimore	Y
8103	8167	BS-12	Pitcairn	--	8773	8173	BS-12m	Wilmington	--
8104	8134	BS-12	Pitcairn	--	8774	8174	BS-12m	Baltimore	Y
8732	8182	BS-12m	Ebenezer	--	8775	8175	BS-12m	Baltimore	Y
8733	8183	BS-12m	Ebenezer	Y	8777	8137	BS-12	Hagerstown	--
8734	8184	BS-12m	Northumberland	--	8778	8138	BS-12	Pitcairn	--
8735	8185	BS-12m	Lewistown	--	8779	8139	BS-12	Pitcairn	--
8736	8186	BS-12m	Wilmington	--	8780	8140	BS-12	Pitcairn	--
8737	8187	BS-12m	Wilmington	Y	8781	8141	BS-12	Pitcairn	--
8738	8188	BS-12m	Wilmington	Y	8782		BS-12	Pitcairn	--
8739	8189	BS-12m	Wilmington	Y	8783	8143	BS-12	Lancaster, OH	--
8740	8190	BS-12m	Wilmington	--	8784	8144	BS-12	Lancaster, OH	--
8741	8191	BS-12m	Wilmington	--	8785	8145	BS-12	Phila. 46th St.	--
8742	8192	BS-12m	Wilmington	--	8786	8146	BS-12	Phila. 46th St.	--
8743	8193	BS-12m	Wilmington	--	8787	8147	BS-12	Phila. 46th St.	--
8744	8194	BS-12m	Wilmington	--	8788		BS-12	Toledo	--
8745	8195	BS-12m	Wilmington	--	8789	8149	BS-12	Toledo	--
8746	8196	BS-12m	Wilmington	--	8790	8150	BS-12	Toledo	--
8747	8197	BS-12m	Wilmington	--	8791	8151	BS-12	Toledo	--
8748	8198	BS-12m	Wilmington	--	8792	8152	BS-12	Toledo	--
8749	8199	BS-12m	Wilmington	--	8793	8113	BS-12	Toledo	--
8750	8180	BS-12m	Wilmington	--	8794	8114	BS-12	Camden	--
8751	8181	BS-12m	Wilmington	--	8795		BS-12	Phila. 46th St.	--
8752	8178	BS-12m	Wilmington	--	8796	8116	BS-12	Phila. 46th St.	--
8753	8153	BS-12	Wilmington	Y	8976	8166	BS-12	Mahoningtown	--
8754	8154	BS-12	Wilmington	Y	8977	8117	BS-12	Cleveland	--
8755	8155	BS-12	Wilmington	Y	8978	8118	BS-12	Cleveland	--
8756	8156	BS-12	Wilmington	Y	8979	8119	BS-12	Cleveland	--
8757	8157	BS-12	Wilmington	Y	8980	8120	BS-12	Cleveland	--
8758	8158	BS-12	Wilmington	Y	8981	8121	BS-12	Cleveland	--
8759	8159	BS-12	Wilmington	Y	8982	8122	BS-12	Canton	--
8760	8160	BS-12	Wilmington	Y	8983	8123	BS-12	Cleveland	--
8761	8161	BS-12	Wilmington	Y	8984	8124	BS-12	Pitcairn	--
8762	8162	BS-12	Wilmington	Y	8985	8125	BS-12	Shire Oaks	--
8763	8163	BS-12	Wilmington	Y	8986		BS-12	Shire Oaks	--
8764	8164	BS-12	Wilmington	Y	8987		BS-12	Shire Oaks	--
8765	8179	BS-12m	Baltimore	Y	8988	8128	BS-12	Pitcairn	--
8766	8176	BS-12m	Wilmington	--	8989	8129	BS-12	Shire Oaks	--
8767	8177	BS-12m	Camden	--	8990	8130	BS-12	Pitcairn	--
8768	8168	BS-12m	Camden	--	8991	8131	BS-12	Shire Oaks	--
8769	8169	BS-12m	Baltimore	Y	8992	8132	BS-12	Shire Oaks	--
					8993		BS-12	Shire Oaks	--

All units in class BS-12m were equipped with MU control. Units 8736 — 8752 and 8773 were equipped with Trainphone. Units 8769 — 8775 and 8794 — 8796 were equipped with Cab Signals.

Special equipment as of Janaury 1960

8987 and 8993 were retired in 1966. Units 8795, 8782 and 8788 were retired in 1967. Twelve more BS-12's were retired before the end of the PRR: 8118 in 1966; and 8119, 8121, 8124, 8137, 8141, 8143, 8150, 8155, and 8159 in 1967. In Class BS-12m, 8172, 8174, 8178, 8181, 8185, 8188, 8191, 8194 and 8196 were retired in October 1967. The remainder of the two classes worked on the Penn Central and were renumbered again into the 8317-8344 block in October 1972 to make room for new GP-38 road numbers. All the remainder of the class were retired by Penn Central except the 8334. This unit (originally 8765, class BS-12m, then 8179) was on the Conrail roster until October 1976. It was assigned road number 8334 on Conrail but was never repainted or relettered.

Classes FS-12 and FS-12m
F-M H12-44

The PRR's Fairbanks-Morse model H12-44 units were purchased in two groups. The earliest were the MU-equipped Class FS-12m units, which were actually used as light road-switchers. The second group were non-MU diesels which were used as conventional switchers. The thirteen FS-12m's were purchased on builders order LD-135 in November 1951 and delivered in November 1952. They were numbered 8711 to 8723. The three Class FS-12's were entered as builders order LD-156 in June 1953 and delivered in February 1954. They were numbered 8708-8710.

The November 1951 orders by the PRR were noteworthy because 1000-1200 horsepower multiple unit switchers were purchased from all four of the major diesel locomotive builders of the period—EMD, Alco, F-M and Baldwin. PRR bought 196 units in that month and 90 of those units were MU-equipped switchers: 35 EMD, 10 Alco, 13 F-M and 32 Baldwin. These units could be used in a variety of assignments but the ability to work local freights using two or more units in multiple made them very versatile diesels.

The F-M model H12-44 diesel was produced in four distinguishable carbody variations. The PRR's Class FS-12m used the second carbody and the FS-12 had the third carbody. The first carbody had been the same as the H10-44, with the Loewy design. The second carbody style eliminated most of the three Loewy features found on the first carbody. The third carbody shuffled the louver/filter arrangement, but most importantly added louvers to the battery box to improve ventilation in that compartment. Ventilation of the battery box was vital to reduction of gas explosions in that confined space.

The F-M model H12-44 used the same model 38D8 1/8 engine as the model H10-44, but it was rated at 1200 horsepower for traction. The most important engine change was the increase in maximum RPM from 800 to 850. The traction generator on the PRR units was the F-M model DGZ-J and the four traction motors were the F-M model DRZ-H. This combination was also used in the H10-44 after 1948 and was also the most common arrangement for the model H12-44. The Westinghouse equipment, used in most of the model H10-44 units, was still available, but it was used in only about a sixth of the total number of H12-44's produced.

On the PRR, the FS-12m units spent most of their life assigned in the Oil City, Pennsylvania-Olean, New York area. As discussed above, the units were used as light road-switchers and switchers on secondary lines. In 1965 the FS-12m's which remained were moved to Chicago, where they joined the FS-10 and FS-12 switchers and spent their remaining service time on the PRR and PC as pure switchers.

The FS-12's were assigned to Chicago for their entire life. Operating out of the 59th Street engine terminal, they worked the jobs which PRR Chicago switchers worked, which meant yard jobs and transfer jobs which could be handled by one unit.

Assignment Table Classes FS-12, FS-12m (F-M H12-44)

ORIG 1966 ROAD ROAD NO. NO.		CLASS	MAY 1959 ASSIGNMENT
8708	8340	FS-12	Chicago 59th St.
8709	8341	FS-12	Chicago 59th St.
8710	8342	FS-12	Chicago 59th St.
8711	8327	FS-12m	Olean
8712	8328	FS-12m	Olean
8713	8329	FS-12m	Olean
8714	8330	FS-12m	Olean
8715	8331	FS-12m	Olean
8716	8332	FS-12m	Olean
8717	8333	FS-12m	Olean
8718	8334	FS-12m	Olean
8719	8335	FS-12m	Olean
8720	8336	FS-12m	Olean
8721	8337	FS-12m	Olean
8722	8338	FS-12m	Olean
8723	8339	FS-12m	Olean

All of the class FS-12m and FS-12 units remained on the PRR roster through 1966 and were renumbered into the 8300 series in preparation for the merger of the PRR and NYC rosters. The Class FS-12m's were renumbered in order from 8711-8723 to 8327-8339. The Class FS-12 units were renumbered in order from 8708-8710 to 8340-8342. With the retirement of eight in October 1967, only five of the class FS-12m units joined the NYC class FS-12 units in Penn Central service. None of the ex-PRR units were relettered for PC, as four of the FS-12m units were retired in 1968, and the last FS-12m plus all of the FS-12 units remained in the dead line at East Altoona until they were retired in June 1969. Only the 8330 and 8337 remained active.

Not many units retired by either the PRR or the PC were sold for service after retirement. The GE 44-tonners and the two FM model H12-44 units were exceptions. Class FS-12m units 8330 and 8337 were retired from PC in June 1968 and sold to U. S. Steel Corp. for service at the Fairless Works near Morrisville, Pennsylvania. At this location they joined eight other model H12-44 units at the steel mill. At the Fairless works, the ex-PRR units were numbered 23 and 24. They were renumbered in reverse order: 23 was ex-PRR 8721/8337 and 24 was ex-PRR 8714/8330. Both of these units were retired by Fairless in the late 1980s.

Units 8714 and 8716, H12-44, idling at their long-time home, Oil City, Pennsylvania, in January 1964. From here, the duo served on branch lines in the area.

Class AS-10a
Alco T-6

The six Alco model T-6 1000-horse-power switchers were among the last diesel switchers ordered by the Pennsylvania Railroad. Only the 30 EMD model SW1200s came later. The Alco T-6 units were ordered in August 1957 on Alco sales order 21080 and were delivered in March 1958. The PRR numbered them 8424-8429 and classed them AS-10a.

The Alco model T-6 was an end cab, B-B wheel arrangement switching and transfer unit. It was equipped with a 6-cylinder, in-line model 251 engine with a bore of 9" and a stroke of 10-1/2". The main traction generator was the GE GT-584, which was also used in the 900 horsepower model S-6 switcher and in export models with a horsepower rating in the 900 HP range. The four traction motors were GE model 752, geared to 74:18. This yielded a continuous tractive effort of 53,000 lbs at 5 mph. This was considerably more than the continuous rating of 34,000 lbs at 8 mph rating of Alco's S-2 and S-4 switchers. The T-6's better rating resulted from a more robust electrical system. The major element was the 752 traction motor, which was the same motor used in virtually all of Alco's road units after 1946.

The right side of PRR 9847 at Bristol, Pennsylvania. During the last few years of PRR operation, the switching of the large Rohm and Haas plant in Bristol was usually performed by one of the AS-10a units. The unit had been renumbered from 8427 in preparation for the PC merger.

SERVICE HISTORY

The assignments of the class AS-10a units were very stable. All of the T-6's were assigned to Enola when delivered, and remained there until the units were moved to Morrisville in the mid-1960s. At Enola, the units worked the Philadelphia Region/Division assignments, ranging from Enola to Camp Hill. At Morrisville, the units worked the Morrisville yard and assignments such as the Bristol Pennsylvania jobs. The Bristol switchers spent some of their time working the large Rohm and Haas chemical plant at this location.

In 1966, the six units were renumbered from 8424-8429 to 9844-9849. The AS-10a class designation was un-changed. The units remained intact throughout Penn Central ownership, were taken over by Conrail on April 1 1976 and were not renumbered. All of the group were retired by Conrail in November 1978 except the 9846 which was retired in January 1980. The 9844 and 9846 even received a Conrail blue paint scheme.

Retirement did not mean scrapping for the units, however. At least three of the units saw service after Conrail. CR 9844 and 9826 became Maryland and Delaware 17 and 19. The M&D also bought CR 9848, and leased it the North Country. These are only the initial re-sales. These units subsequently moved on to other operations.

The left side of PRR 8426 at the Morrisville yard engine terminal in Morrisville, Pennsylvania. In the background is a GG-1 electric and the inactive coal tower. Note also the "firecracker" radio antenna on the cab roof.

Control stand of PRR 8961 (Class BS-24M). The engineer's hand is on the handle of the throttle.

Chapter 10

Transfer Units

Heavy center-cab transfer units were an interesting early approach to developing a high-horsepower diesel unit for heavy, slow-speed freight runs. "Transfer" in this instance refers to moving strings of cars from one railroad's yard to another railroad's yard in the same city.

The center-cab transfer locomotive was developed before the day of high-horsepower diesel locomotives, when the largest single-unit diesel engine was 1500-hp. The center-cab was an early "brute force" method of building a 2400-hp. locomotive: marry two 1200-hp. switcher hoods with one cab spliced between them, and place the resulting combination on two six-wheel trucks.

The Elgin, Joliet and Eastern, whose purpose in life was transfer work around Chicago, had 27 Baldwin center-cabs on its roster. Center-cabs were also used for heavy non-transfer drags on the DSS&A, MN&S, Trona, and Santa Fe.

The Pennsylvania Railroad operated more two-engine, center-cab, transfer-switcher diesel locomotives than any U. S. railroad. The PRR owned a total of 45, almost evenly divided between Baldwin and Lima-Hamilton. The units were used on transfer runs, and in such other heavy slow-speed services as mine runs, hump pushing, helper service and general heavy switching. By the end of the PRR in 1968, the center-cab era had passed. All of the transfer units were permanently out of service if not actually retired.

Classes LS-25 and LS-25m
Lima 2500-hp

The 22 Lima units on the PRR were the only ones of this type built by Lima. They were ordered in two lots. The first 12 were all non-MU and were classed LS-25. They were ordered in November 1949 and delivered between May and July 1950. The second order included eight units with MU and two

without. The second group was ordered at the same time as the Baldwin center cabs in August 1950 and was delivered between May and September 1951. The last unit of the second group, road number 5683, was the last locomotive that Lima built.

The Lima transfer units (Lima never assigned model designations to their diesel units) were originally offered as 2400 horsepower units, which is logical since their switchers were rated at 800 and 1200-hp for traction at the time. However, the PRR ordered 2500-hp units, and that is what they got. The transfer units were essentially two 1250-hp switchers in one carbody. Controlled from one cab, each of the two engines powered its own traction generator and powered the three-axle truck located under its end of the unit.

EQUIPMENT

The class LS-25 and LS-25m's were equipped with two Hamilton model T-89-SA engines. The engines were turbo-charged straight eight cylinder machines with a maximum RPM of 950. Each engine drove a Westinghouse model 499-B traction generator. The six traction motors were the common Westinghouse model 370-DZ, geared at the common 63:15 gear ratio. With this gear ratio, the units had a theoretical maximum speed of 70 mph and a continuous tractive effort of 64,000 lbs. at 11.5 mph.

They had a variety of equipment. Dynamic brakes, pressure maintaining feature and multiple unit are covered on the Class Equipment and Assignment Table. The yardphone installed on LS-25 5671-5675 was a one-way communication set used by base stations (such as hump towers).

SERVICE HISTORY

The first nine Limas were all class LS-25 and were delivered to Columbus, which was to remain a center of LS-25 operation for the entire life of the class. When the two final LS-25 units were delivered a year after the first

group, these two plus another were assigned to Chicago for a few years. By the middle 1950s, the assignments of the class became remarkably stable. Units 5671, 5672, 5673, 5675, 5677, 5678, 5680, 5681 and 5683 were assigned to Columbus, St. Clair roundhouse for maintenance. The 5674 was assigned to Chicago's 59th St. engine terminal, the 5676 and 5679 were assigned to Indianapolis and the 5682 went to Fort Wayne. Heavy switching and hump pushing was the most common class LS-25 assignment. The class worked until the early 1960s when they were set aside as they came due for heavy repairs. All but the last two units delivered were retired in 1965. The last

Equipment and Assignment Table Class LS-25 and LS-25m (Lima Transfer)

ROAD NO.	CLASS	MAY 1959 ASSIGNMENT
5671	LS-25	Columbus St. Clair
5672	LS-25	Columbus St. Clair
5673	LS-25	Columbus St. Clair
5674	LS-25	Chicago 59th St.
5675	LS-25	Columbus St. Clair
5676	LS-25	Indianapolis
5677	LS-25	Columbus St. Clair
5678	LS-25	Columbus St. Clair
5679	LS-25	Indianapolis
5680	LS-25	Columbus St. Clair
5681	LS-25	Columbus St. Clair
5682	LS-25	Fort Wayne
5683	LS-25	Columbus St. Clair
8943	LS-25m	Mingo Jct. (Pgh. Reg.)
8944	LS-25m	Mingo Jct. (Pgh. Reg.)
8945	LS-25m	Mingo Jct. (Pgh. Reg.)
8946	LS-25m	Mingo Jct. (Pgh. Reg.)
8947	LS-25m	Mingo Jct. (Pgh. Reg.)
8948	LS-25m	Mingo Jct. (BI Reg.)
8949	LS-25m	Mingo Jct. (BI Reg.)
8950	LS-25m	Mingo Jct. (Pgh. Reg.)
8951	LS-25m	Mingo Jct. (Pgh. Reg.)

All units had dual control.
Units 8948 and 8949 had dynamic brake and pressure maintaining feature.
Class LS-25m was equipped with MU control and trainphone.
Units 5671-5675 had yard trainphone.
All units except 5673 and 5874 had cab signals.
Special equipment as of January 1960

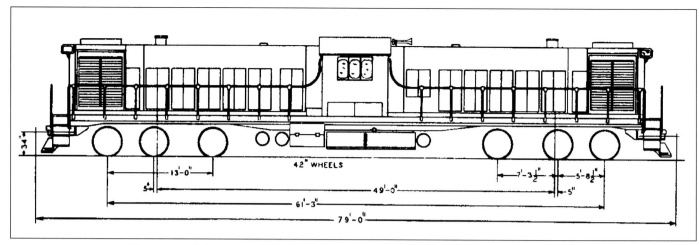

Dimensional drawing of the LS-25 as it appeared in the Lima operating manual.

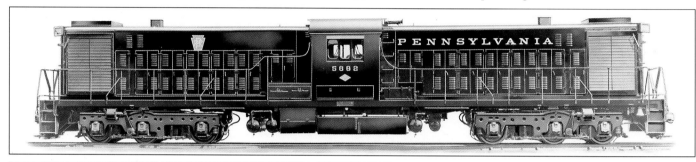

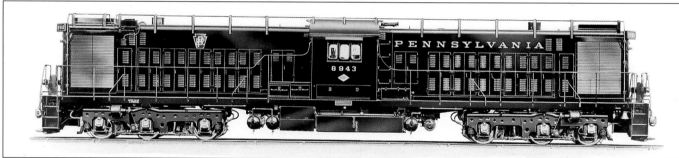

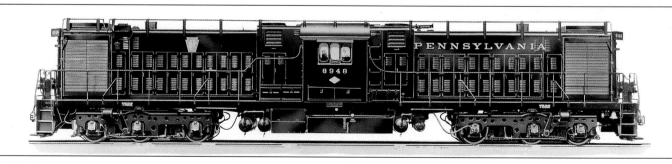

The three faces (or sides) of Lima Transfer units. At top, 5682 represents the non-MU LS-25 with no trainphone and no-frills end platform railings. The center image is 8943, Class LS-25m, with trainphone, M-U connections and end walkways. At bottom, Class LS-25m unit 8948, fitted with dynamic brakes in addition to the equipment on 8943. The engineers probably did not appreciate being flanked by loud dynamic brake equipment close by, on each side of the cab.

two delivered, the 5682 and 5683, were retired with the class LS-25m units in July 1966.

The class LS-25m units were all assigned for maintenance to that center of gritty railroading—Mingo Jct., Ohio. The yard at Mingo handled both iron ore and coal, the two commodities that contributed the heaviest tonnages to the

Pennsylvania Railroad's totals. The iron ore came primarily from the ore boats unloaded at the Whiskey Island ore docks in Cleveland. The coal came from the southeast Ohio coalfields. Primary destination for these bulk products was the complex of steel mills in the Steubenville, Ohio- Weirton, W. Virginia area, primarily the Weirton Steel and

Wheeling Steel companies. Many tons of coal went to the Great Lakes for shipment on lake boats—the opposite of the flow of iron ore traffic. The LS-25m units performed both mine runs to the south and west of Mingo Jct., transfer work to Weirton and the heavy switching and hump pushing in Mingo yard.

Someone left the sand filler hatch open as this transfer unit performs heavy switching at Columbus, Ohio in July 1956. PRR 5683 was the last locomotive built by the Lima Locomotive Works (known as Baldwin-Lima-Hamilton by that time).

Locomotive Characteristics

	LS-25, LS-25m	BS-24, BS-24m
Class	LS-25, LS-25m	BS-24, BS-24m
Builder	Lima	BLH
Model	2500HP Transfer	RT-624
Horsepower	2500	2400
Wheel Arr	C-C	C-C
Total Weight	362,000 lbs.	359,000 lbs
Length over Couplers	79 0	74 0
Truck Centers	49 0	41 0
Truck Wheelbase	13 0	13 0
Engine	2,Hamilton T-89-SA	2, BLH 6-606SC
Generator	2, W 449B	2, W 480
Traction Motors	6, W 370DZ	6, W 370DZ
Gear Ratio	63:15	63:15
Maximum Speed	70MPH	60 MPH
Starting Trac. Effort	90,500 lbs.	89,750 lbs.
Continuous Trac. Effort	64,000 lbs.	72.900 lbs.
CTE Speed	11.5 MPH	9.9 MPH

Before 1956, all of the class LS-25m units were assigned to the Panhandle Division, which included all of the mine areas whose output was gathered into Mingo. With the reorganization of the PRR into a regional arrangement in 1956, the Cadiz Jct. to Cadiz line was made part of the Buckeye Region while the remaining lines out of Mingo were assigned to the Pittsburgh Region. This didn't change the maintenance location of the two dynamic brake-equipped LS-25m units (8948 and 8949) which worked the Cadiz line, but it did mean that the two units were designated as Buckeye Region units.

The work described above for the class LS-25m units continued for the entire service life of the class. This continued until the mid-1960's when the units were set aside as problems occurred. Before that time, such problems would have been corrected. In December 1964 only

three of the nine were set aside for heavy repairs but by the following August, all were set aside. During the spring of 1965, 8945, 8946 and 8950 were still seen active at Mingo Jct. Being set aside meant a trip to the East Altoona dead line, which is where the class spent its last days on PRR rails. All the units of class LS-25m were retired in July 1966.

Classes BS-25 and LS-25m
Baldwin RT-624

The class BS-24 and BS-24m units on the PRR were Baldwin's model RT-624 transfer-switcher, introduced in 1950. The August 1950 orders placed by the PRR included double-engined, center cab units from both Lima and Baldwin to add to the Limas of this type already on the property. Both of these August 1950 orders were for MU locomotives (except for two each of the Baldwins and Limas). The previously purchased Limas had been non-MU. It is somewhat ironic that the PRR had ordered the type first from Lima, because Baldwin had first delivered the center-cab design in 1946 with a 2000-hp model. Six other railroads (but not the Pennsylvania) purchased a total of 46 2000-hp Baldwin center cab units. The PRR did buy all but one of the 24 model RT-624 2400-hp. units produced. The Minneapolis, Northfield and Southern purchased the only "non-PRR" RT-624.

The two class BS-24's ordered in August 1950 (8952 and 8953) were delivered in July 1951. Also ordered in August 1950 were 12, class BS-24m units (8954-8965), delivered between August 1951 and November 1951. These 14 units were equipped with the same rigid bolster truck used by Baldwin on their domestic six-motor transfer units and road-switchers since 1946.

The next order was placed in November 1951 for eight class BS-24m units (8724-8731). These were delivered between September 1952 and December 1952, and were equipped with a new drop equalizer, three-motor truck that Baldwin had first installed under model AS-616 demonstrator 1600 in late summer 1952. The new truck provided better tracking and improved crew com-

Before 1956, all of the class LS-25m

LS-25 8949 at Mingo Junction, Ohio in May 1955. This unit and 8948 were equipped with dynamic brakes.

R.J. MULLER PHOTO, DOUGLAS COLLECTION

Equipment and Assignment Table
Class BS-24
(Baldwin RT-624)

ROAD NO.	ORIGINAL ASSIGNMENT	MAY 1959 ASSIGNMENT	MU	TP	DB	CS	DC	RA	PM
8113	Philadelphia	Phila-46th St	Y						
8724	Philadelphia	Phila-46th St	Y			Y		Y	
8725	Elmira	Phila-46th St	Y			Y		Y	
8726	Elmira	Phila-46th St	Y			Y		Y	
8727	Philadelphia	Phila-46th St	Y			Y		Y	
8728	Philadelphia	Phila-46th St	Y			Y		Y	
8729	Philadelphia	Phila-46th St	Y			Y		Y	
8730	Philadelphia	Phila-46th St	Y			Y		Y	
8731	Philadelphia	Phila-46th St	Y			Y		Y	
8952	Conway	Conway					Y		
8953	Cleveland	Phila-46th St					Y	Y	
8954	Mingo Jct.	Mingo Jct	Y	Y		Y	Y		
8955	Mingo Jct.	Mingo Jct	Y	Y		Y	Y		
8956	Mingo Jct.	Mingo Jct	Y	Y		Y	Y		
8957	Mingo Jct.	Mingo Jct	Y	Y		Y	Y		
8958	Conemaugh	Conemaugh	Y	Y	Y	Y	Y		Y
8959	Shire Oaks	Pitcairn	Y	Y	Y	Y	Y		Y
8960	Shire Oaks	Pitcairn	Y	Y	Y	Y	Y		Y
8961	Conemaugh	Phila-46th St	Y	Y	Y	Y	Y	Y	Y
8962	Conemaugh	Conemaugh	Y	Y	Y	Y	Y		Y
8963	Conemaugh	Conemaugh	Y	Y	Y	Y	Y		Y
8964	Conemaugh	Phila-46th St	Y	Y	Y	Y	Y	Y	Y
8965	Conemaugh	Conemaugh	Y	Y	Y	Y	Y		Y

MU = Multiple-Unit; TP = Trainphone; DB = Dynamic Brake; CS = Cab Signals; DC = Dual Controls; RA = Radio; PM = Pressure Maintaining Feature

Unit 8113 was renumbered 8966, then 08966 after being removed from service.
Special equipment as of January 1960

fort. The final class BS-24m unit was ordered in June 1953 and put in service on February 1954 (8113), one of a group of diesels which were the last of 600 Baldwins bought by the PRR.

EQUIPMENT

The BS-24 and BS-24m units were equipped with two Baldwin 606SC engines, each driving a Westinghouse 480 main traction generator. Six Westinghouse 370-DZ traction motors provided the driving power. Aside from the basic equipment, the PRR RT-624 units were equipped with a great variety of special equipment. This is tabulated in the Special Equipment and Assignment Table. Note that the 8724-8731 group was equipped with radios and not trainphone. This was because the group was assigned to the Philadelphia area and spent a lot of time under the 11,000 volt AC electric overhead, which was incompatible with trainphone operation. Almost all of the units had cab signals installed, an indication that road operation was an important part of the plan for the units.

SERVICE HISTORY

As with the big Limas, the Class BS-24 and BS-24m units were used for the very purposes projected for the type. Heavy switching, hump pushing, transfer service, heavy mine runs and pusher service was the service for which the units were intended and that's how the Pennsy used them. Like the Limas, the unit assignments were remarkably stable over the years, as tabulated in the adjacent box. The 1959 assignments were the assignment of most of the units from delivery until retirement.

The 8113 and 8724-8731 almost never left the Philadelphia area. Iron ore moves were the primary work. Assignments involving iron ore included heavy switching at Greenwich yard in south Philadelphia, along with pusher service from Greenwich yard to Bryn Mawr and Paoli on the line to Harrisburg. This traffic was primarily the iron ore unloaded at PRR's ore dock just east of Greenwich Yard. In later years the BS-24m units were occasionally used on ore trains to Bethlehem via Trenton and the Bel-Del line. Other Philadelphia assignments included freights on the Schuylkill branch. The units were often assigned to S-1 and S-2 to Phoenixville, Pennsylvania and transfer runs to Camden, New Jersey. In this service they were sometimes operated in MU with one of the late class BS-16m (Baldwin model AS-616) units 8111 or 8112, which were also equipped with the drop equalizer, three motor truck.

The Mingo Junction assignments were the same as described for the Lima transfer units; switching of coal and iron ore, iron ore transfer to Weirton and mine runs. The Johnstown (Conemaugh) assignment was on coal trains running from South Fork to Altoona. The units were run in pairs and ran light on their return. Units 8961 and 8964, originally assigned to Conemaugh, were moved to Philadelphia at the end of 1957. The two units assigned to Pitcairn (8959 and

February, 1966, and snow is blanketing North Philadelphia. BS-24m No. 8730 and a second (understandably) unidentified BS-24m have been assigned to assist a GG-1 electric with a passenger train. GG-1 electrics were known to have problems in snowy weather, and the RT-24s provided insurance.

8960) were almost exclusively used as hump pushers at this yard just east of Pittsburgh.

The two non-MU BS-24 units were also moved once. The 8952 was originally assigned to Conway but was moved to Mingo Jct. in late 1959. The 8953 was originally assigned to Cleveland and was moved to Philadelphia late in 1956.

Starting in 1964, units 8954-8965 were gradually set aside or stored as heavy repairs were required. All were retired in July 1966. The 8113 and 8724-8724 group worked a little later in the Philadelphia area.

The original plan was to retire all of these units without renumbering. Since their equipment trusts precluded retirement until after 1967, it was necessary to renumber the units in 1966. The 8113 was renumbered to 8966 in September 1966 at 46th Street enginehouse, where it was permanently out of service. The 8724-8731 group was renumbered to 08724-08731 in May 1967, even though these units were also permanently out of service. This group was renumbered in the East Altoona dead line using spray cans to apply a rough zero on the cab side. A month later, the ex-8113 was renumbered 08966 at 46th Street Philadelphia. On this unit, the first renumbering had been performed crudely with a paintbrush while the zero was applied with a spray can. The East Altoona units were retired in October 1967, and the 08966 was retired in June 1969 by Penn Central.

In better weather (October 1962), units 8959 and 8960 are moving into position to push the eastbound Pitcairn hump yard at Wall, Pennsylvania: 4800 horsepower on the hump was presumed to be adequate for the job.

In June 1958, we're looking at RT-24 No. 8724 with a cut of ore jennies at the west end of Greenwich Yard in Philadelphia.

The Tale of Two Trucks

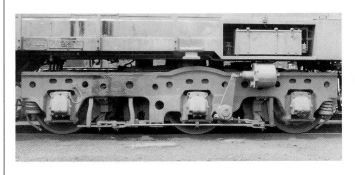

The first RS-24 units and the LS-25s, for that matter, were equipped with the same Commonwealth cast six-wheel trucks as used on the first Baldwin AS-616s, as shown in the photo on the left. The offset center axle provided room for the third traction motor, allowing all three axles to be powered.

The drop equalizer truck shown in the photo on the right was introduced in 1952 to provide improved riding quality, which was easier on trackwork and crew spines alike.

Pennsylvania Railroad Operational Organization

The organization charted below applied during most of the PRR diesel era. During 1955, the term "District" instead of "Division" was used. In the transition, the 1955 "regions" did not follow exactly the boundaries of the 1951 "divisions." For instance, the eastern boundary of the Panhandle Division was in Pittsburgh. The eastern boundary of the Buckeye Region was west of Mingo Junction. The chart shows the division or region names, and their headquarters cities

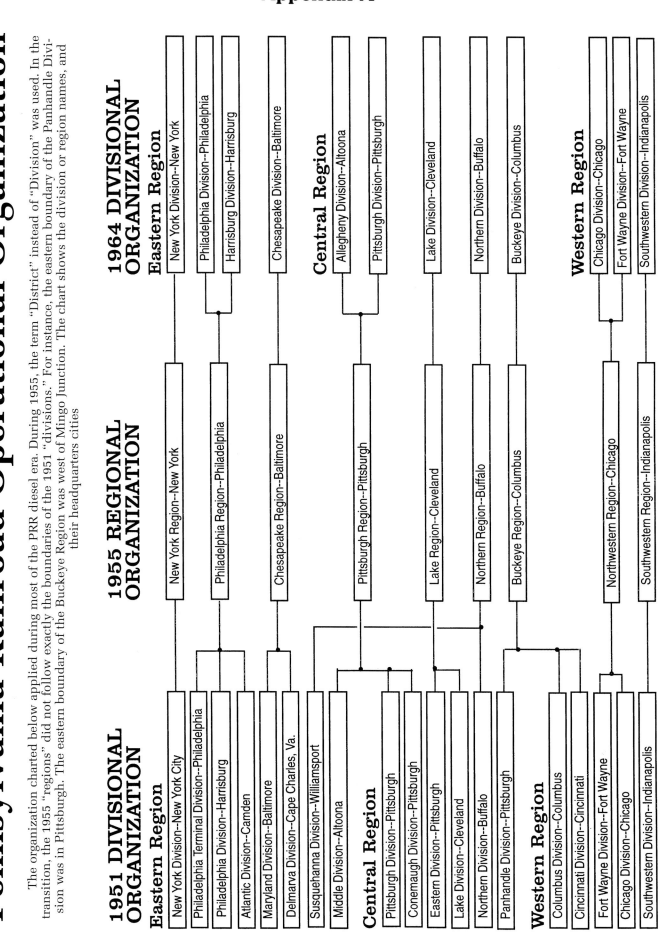

1964 DIVISIONAL ORGANIZATION

Eastern Region

- New York Division--New York
- Philadelphia Division--Philadelphia
- Harrisburg Division--Harrisburg
- Chesapeake Division--Baltimore

Central Region

- Allegheny Division--Altoona
- Pittsburgh Division--Pittsburgh
- Lake Division--Cleveland
- Northern Division--Buffalo
- Buckeye Division--Columbus

Western Region

- Chicago Division--Chicago
- Fort Wayne Division--Fort Wayne
- Southwestern Division--Indianapolis

1955 REGIONAL ORGANIZATION

- New York Region--New York
- Philadelphia Region--Philadelphia
- Chesapeake Region--Baltimore
- Pittsburgh Region--Pittsburgh
- Lake Region--Cleveland
- Northern Region--Buffalo
- Buckeye Region--Columbus
- Northwestern Region--Chicago
- Southwestern Region--Indianapolis

1951 DIVISIONAL ORGANIZATION

Eastern Region

- New York Division--New York City
- Philadelphia Terminal Division--Philadelphia
- Philadelphia Division--Harrisburg
- Atlantic Division--Camden
- Maryland Division--Baltimore
- Delmarva Division--Cape Charles, Va.
- Susquehanna Division--Williamsport
- Middle Division--Altoona

Central Region

- Pittsburgh Division--Pittsburgh
- Conemaugh Division--Pittsburgh
- Eastern Division--Pittsburgh
- Lake Division--Cleveland
- Northern Division--Buffalo
- Panhandle Division--Pittsburgh

Western Region

- Columbus Division--Columbus
- Cincinnati Division--Cincinnati
- Fort Wayne Division--Fort Wayne
- Chicago Division--Chicago
- Southwestern Division--Indianapolis

PRR 5780A is posed by itself in the "Circle" area of the Altoona Works, in the Juniata section of Altoona, Pennsylvania. The date is July 28, 1949 and the unit is not quite a year old.

The location is Bay Head Junction, New Jersey at the south end of the New York and Long Branch Railroad. The NY&LB was a jointly owned operation between the PRR and CNJ, both of whom supplied cars and locomotives. In this September, 1964 scene, the transition from the Baldwin DR 6-4-2000 units to EMD E7 is only about eight months from completion. The last of the BP-20's were retired in May, 1965. The 5771A has a blanked off headlight mounting which had been filled with a Mars light. The 5858A would be renumbered 4218 but would be retired in May, 1967.

Pennsylvania Railroad Locations

The PRR locations referenced in the test of this book are tabulated below. Locations which are well known are not included, such as New York City, Philadelphia, Chicago and St. Louis. Even locations such as Altoona, Wheeling, Youngstown, Trenton and Steubenville should be located without difficulty.

The direction shown is not purely geographical, but is given in the general direction of railroad operation.

LOCATION	STATE	PRR DIVISION	NEAREST CITY OR LOCATION	DISTANCE AND DIRECTION	NOTES
Alliance	Ohio	Eastern	Pittsburgh	82 mi. west	
Ashtabula	Ohio	Lake	Pittsburgh	125 mi. north	Iron ore docks, transfer from lake boats
Bay Head Junction	New Jersey	NY & LB	South Amboy	36 mi. south	At south end of New York and Long Branch
Benwood	West Virginia	Panhandle	Wheeling	2.5 mi. south	
Bellwood	Pennsylvania	Middle	Altoona	7 mi. east	
Blairsville	Pennsylvania	Conemaugh	Pittsburgh	66 mi. east	
Bordentown	New Jersey	New York	Trenton	6 mi. south	On east side of Delaware River
Bowie	Maryland	Maryland	Baltimore	25 mi. south	PRR service to the racetrack here.
Bradley Junction	Pennsylvania	Pittsburgh	Cresson	11 mi. north	Cresson is 15 miles east of Altoona
Bristol	Pennsylvania	New York	New York	69 mi. south	
Brockton	New York	Northern	Buffalo	51 mi. south	
Bryn Mawr	Pennsylvania	Phila. Terminal	Philadelphia	10 mi. west	
Burgettstown	Pennsylvania	Panhandle	Pittsburgh	28 mi. west	
Buttonwood	Pennsylvania	Susquehanna	Wilkes-Barre	3 mi. south	
Cadillac	Michigan	Fort Wayne	Fort Wayne	239 mi. north	
Cambridge	Ohio	Lake	Newcomerstown	27 mi. south	Newcomerstown is 82 miles east of Columbus
Canandaigua	New York	Susquehanna	Elmira	68 mi. north	
Canton	Ohio	Eastern	Pittsburgh	101 mi. west	
Cavittsville	Pennsylvania	Pittsburgh	Pittsburgh	18 mi. east	Just east of Pitcairn yard
Chambersburg	Pennsylvania	Philadelphia	Harrisburg	52 mi. south	
Chester	Pennsylvania	Maryland	Philadelphia	13 mi. south	
Circleville	Ohio	Panhandle	Trinway	80 mi. west	Trinway is 55 mi. east of Columbus
CM Tower	Pennsylvania	Pittsburgh	In Pittsburgh	6 mi east	Distance is from Pittsburgh station
Coatesville	Pennsylvania	Philadelphia	Philadelphia	38 mi. west	
Conemaugh	Pennsylvania	Pittsburgh	Johnstown	2 mi. east	
Conway	Pennsylvania	Eastern	Pittsburgh	22 mi. west	Large classification yard
Corry	Pennsylvania	Northern	Erie	37 mi. south	
Cresson	Pennsylvania	Pittsburgh	Altoona	15 mi. east	
Crestline	Ohio	Fort Wayne	Fort Wayne	131 mi. east	
Crum Lynne	Pennsylvania	Maryland	Philadelphia	11 mi. south	
Cumbo Yard	West Virginia	Philadelphia	Harrisburg	90 mi. south	Yard at Martinsburg, W. Va. on Cumb. Valley branch
Dennison	Ohio	Panhandle	Columbus	100 mi. east	
Derry	Pennsylvania	Pittsburgh	Pittsburgh	46 mi. east	
Dexter City	Ohio	Lake	Newcomerstown	57 mi. south	Newcomerstown is 82 miles east of Columbus
Dover	Ohio	Lake	Newcomerstown	19 mi. north	Newcomerstown is 82 miles east of Columbus
East Liberty	Pennsylvania	Pittsburgh	In Pittsburgh	5 mi east	Distance is from Pittsburgh station
Ebenezer	New York	Northern	Buffalo	7 mi. south	Main PRR base in Buffalo area
Edgewood	Pennsylvania	Pittsburgh	Pittsburgh	7 mi. east	
Elrama	Pennsylvania	Pittsburgh	Pittsburgh	23 mi. south	Town nearest Shire Oaks yard on Mon. river.
Emporium	Pennsylvania	Northern	Buffalo	121 mi. south	Junction of Erie line with Buffalo line
Enola	Pennsylvania	Philadelphia	Harrisburg	4 mi. west	Location of large freight yard and diesel shop
Falls Creek	Pennsylvania	Northern	Red Bank	63 mi. east	Red Bank is 64 mi. north of Pittsburgh
Frankford Jct.	Pennsylvania	Phila. Terminal	Phila. 30th St.	8 mi. north	In northern part of city
Frazer	Pennsylvania	Philadelphia	Philadelphia	24 mi. west	
Freeport	Pennsylvania	Conemaugh	Pittsburgh	28 mi. east	Very near Kiski Jct.
Frenchtown	New Jersey	New York	Trenton	32 mi. north	
Gallitzin	Pennsylvania	Pittsburgh	Altoona	12 mi. west	
Girard	Pennsylvania	Northern	Erie	17 mi. west	On PRR, Erie to Girard was via trackage rights on NYC
Greenville Yard	New Jersey	New York	Lane Tower	5.4 mi. east	Lane tower is 3.5 miles south of Newark
Greenwich Yard	Pennsylvania	Phila. Terminal	Phila. 30th St.	6.5 mi. south	In southern part of city
Hagerstown	Maryland	Philadelphia	Harrisburg	74 mi. south	
Harrison	New Jersey	New York	New York	9.5 mi. south	
Harsimus Cove Yd	New Jersey	New York	Waverly Yard	8 mi. east	On Passaic and Harsimus branch
Hollidaysburg	Pennsylvania	Middle	Altoona	7.5 mi. south	Site of major PRR car building and repair shop
Horseshoe Curve	Pennsylvania	Pittsburgh	Altoona	4 mi. west	The world famous Horseshoe Curve
Huntingdon	Pennsylvania	Middle	Harrisburg	98 mi. west	
Hyner	Pennsylvania	Susquehanna	Lock Haven	21 mi. north	
Johnsonburg	Pennsylvania	Northern	Erie	110 mi. south	
Juniata Shops	Pennsylvania	Middle	Altoona	2 mi. east	Main PRR locomotive shop
Keating Summit	Pennsylvania	Northern	Buffalo	108 mi. south	
Kingston	Pennsylvania	Philadelphia	Harrisburg	12 mi. south	Location is New Kingston, Penna.
Kiski Junction	Pennsylvania	Conemaugh	Pittsburgh	30 mi. west	On Conemaugh line. Actually Kiskiminetas Jct.

LOCATION	STATE	PRR DIVISION	NEAREST CITY OR LOCATION	DISTANCE AND DIRECTION	NOTES
Lambertville	New Jersey	New York	Trenton	16 mi. north	
Lancaster	Ohio	Panhandle	Trinway	60 mi. south	Trinway is 55 mi. east of Columbus
Leaman Place	Pennsylvania	Philadelphia	Lancaster	11 mi. east	Junction with Strasburg Rail Road
Leetonia	Ohio	Eastern	Pittsburgh	63 mi. west	
Lewistown	Pennsylvania	Middle	Harrisburg	61 mi. west	
Linden	New Jersey	New York	Newark	9 mi. south	
Lock Haven	Pennsylvania	Susquehanna	Williamsport	25 mi. north	
Logansport	Indiana	Chicago	Chicago	117 mi. south	
Machias	New York	Northern	Buffalo	44.5 mi. south	
Madison	Indiana	Southwestern	Indianapolis	85.5 mi. south	
Mahoningtown	Pennsylvania	Lake	Pittsburgh	48 mi. north	New Castle Jct.on employee timetables
Mapleton	Pennsylvania	Middle	Harrisburg	90 mi. west	
Marrietta	Ohio	Lake	Newcomerstown	84 mi. south	Newcomerstown is 82 miles east of Columbus
Meadows	New Jersey	New York	New York	8 mi. west	
Milford	New Jersey	New York	Trenton	35 mi. north	
Millbrook	Ohio	Eastern	Canton	38 mi. west	
Mingo Jct.	Ohio	Panhandle	Pittsburgh	46 mi. west	Large yard services steel mills
Morrisville	Pennsylvania	New York	Trenton	2 mi. south	Site of major PRR freight yard
Mount Union	Pennsylvania	Middle	Harrisburg	86 mi. west	
New Brunswick	New Jersey	New York	New York	33 mi. south	
Niles	Ohio	Lake	Cleveland	35 mi. south	
Norristown	Pennsylvania	Phila. Terminal	Philadelphia	17.5 mi. north	
North Madison	Indiana	Southwestern	Indianapolis	83 mi. south	
North Philadelphia	Pennsylvania	New York	Phila. 30th St.	5 mi. north	In City of Philadelphia
Northumberland	Pennsylvania	Susquehanna	Harrisburg	102 mi. north	
Oceola Mills	Pennsylvania	Middle	Tyrone	19 mi. north	Tyrone is 14 miles east of Altoona
Oil City	Pennsylvania	Northern	Buffalo	117 mi. south	
Olean	New York	Northern	Buffalo	70 mi. south	
Orrville	Ohio	Eastern	Canton	22 mi. west	
Parkton	Maryland	Maryland	Baltimore	29 mi. north	
Pemberton	New Jersey	Atlantic	Camden	25 miles east	
Phila. 46th St.	Pennsylvania	Phila. Terminal	Phila. 30th St.	2 mi. west	Engine terminal just west of Zoo Tower
Phillipsburg	New Jersey	New York	Trenton	51 mi. north	
Pitcairn	Pennsylvania	Pittsburgh	Pittsburgh	15 mi. east	Site of major PRR freight yard
Renovo	Pennsylvania	Northern	Harrisburg	111 mi. north	
Richmond	Indiana	Columbus	Indianapolis	68 mi. east	
Ridgeway	Pennsylvania	Northern	Erie	118 mi. south	
Rochester	Pennsylvania	Eastern	Pittsburgh	26 mi. west	
Rose Lake	Illinois	Southwestern	St. Louis	12 mi. west	Main PRR yard in St. Louis area
Ross	Ohio	Eastern	Canton	71 mi. west	
Salem	Ohio	Eastern	Pittsburgh	70 mi. west	
Scully Yard	Pennsylvania	Panhandle	Pittsburgh	7 mi. west	On its own branch
Sharon	Pennsylvania	Lake	Erie	77 mi. south	
Shire Oaks yard	Pennsylvania	Pittsburgh	Pittsburgh	24 mi. south	Coal gathering yard, south on Mon. river line
Smithville	Ohio	Eastern	Canton	27.5 mi. west	
Snedikerville	Pennsylvania	Susquehanna	Elmira	16 mi. south	Called Snediker by PRR. Also Sned interlocking.
South Amboy	New Jersey	New York	Newark	20 mi. south	On New York and Long Branch
St. Mary s	Pennsylvania	Northern	Erie	123 mi. south	
Steubenville	Ohio	Pittsburgh	Pittsburgh	43 mi. west	Wheeling Steel Co. mills
Stockton	New Jersey	New York	Trenton	19.5 mi. north	On Bel-Del branch
Summerdale	New York	Northern	Buffalo	71 mi. south	
Summerdale	Pennsylvania	Philadelphia	Enola	2 mi. west	At west end of Enola yard
Sunbury	Pennsylvania	Susquehanna	Harrisburg	54 mi. north	
Thompson	Pennsylvania	Pittsburgh	Pittsburgh	10 mi. south	On Mon. River line.
Thorndale	Pennsylvania	Philadelphia	Philadelphia	35 mi. west	
Trafford	Pennsylvania	Pittsburgh	Pittsburgh	17 mi. west	Just east of Pitcairn yard
Tyrone	Pennsylvania	Middle	Altoona	14 mi. east	
UY Tower	Pennsylvania	Conemaugh	Pittsburgh	7 mi. east	
Valparaiso	Indiana	Chicago	Chicago	42 mi. west	
Wall	Pennsylvania	Pittsburgh	Pittsburgh	15 mi. east	South side of Pitcairn yard
Waverly Yard	New Jersey	New York	Newark	2 mi. south	
Waynesboro	Pennsylvania	Philadelphia	Harrisburg	70 mi. south	On branch, junction just north of Chambersburg
Wellsville	Ohio	Eastern	Steubenville	17 mi. north	
West Brownville	Pennsylvania	Pittsburgh	Pittsburgh	52 mi. south	On Mon. River line Junc. with Monogahela Ry
Wheatland	Pennsylvania	Lake	Erie	79 mi. south	
Whiskey Island	Ohio	Lake	Cleveland	In city	PRR s large iron ore unloading docks
Weirton	West Virginia	Pittsburgh	Pittsburgh	41 mi. west	Weirton Steel Co. mills
Wilkinsburg	Pennsylvania	Pittsburgh	Pittsburgh	7 mi. east	
Wilmerding	Pennsylvania	Pittsburgh	Pittsburgh	13 mi. east	
Winchester	Virginia	Philadelphia	Harrisburg	116 mi. south	
Youngwood	Pennsylvania	Pittsburgh	Greensburg	7 mi. south	Greensburg is 31 miles east of Pittsburgh
Zanesville	Ohio	Panhandle	Trinway	16.5 mi. south	Trinway is 55 mi. east of Columbus

Pennsylvania Railroad
Detailed Roster of Diesel Locomotives

The locomotive roster on the following pages includes all 3044 diesel units and three gasoline switchers owned by the PRR. One of the gasoline units (3907) was re-engined with a diesel engine and is included in the 3044 total. Three of the diesel locomotives are listed twice. These are the three Baldwin freight units, two A-units and a B-unit that were rebuilt by Alco and renumbered.

PRR 8077 at Milliken Rick Company in Pitcairn, Pennsylvania on May 11, 1968.

Baldwin Models/Class			
PRR Class	**Baldwin Class (*)**	**Baldwin Model Used In This Book**	**Notes**
BP-20 & BF-16z	DR-6-4-1000/2 SC	DR 6-4-2000	Sharknose Passenger
BP-60a & BH-50	DR-12-8-1500 SC	DR-12-8-3000	Centipede
BF-15 & BF-15a	DR-4-4-1500/1 SC	DR 4-4-1500	Sharknose Freight
BF-16	DR-4-4-1600/1 SC (608A) RF-16	RF-16	Sharknose Freight
BS-6	0-4-4-0 660/1 DE	VO-600	
BS-6a	DS-4-4-660/1 NA	DS-4-4-660	
BS-7	DS-4-4-750/ NA	DS-4-4-750	
BS-7	DS-4-4-800/1 NA (606) S-8	S-8	
BS-10	0-4-4-0 1000/1 DE	VO-1000	
BS-10a & BS-10am	DS4-4-1000/1 SC	DS-4-4-1000	
BS-10as	DS-4-4-1200/1 SC (606A) S-12	S-12	
BS-12am & BS-12ams and BS-12as	DRS-4-4-1200/1 SC (606A) RS-12	RS-12	
BS-16m & BS-16ms	DRS-6-6-1200/2 SC (606A) RT-24	RT-24	
(*) As tabulated on the Builders list in The Diesel Builder, Volume 3 by John F. Kirkland			

Pennsylvania Railroad Diesel Locomotive Roster

RF-16 (road numbers 2000A–2013A)

ORIG ROAD NUM.	PRR BASE CLASS	PRR REBLT CLASS	1966 ROAD NUM.	PRR CLASS (1966)	BLDR	BLDR MODEL	BLDR SERIAL NUM.	BLDR DATE	RETIRE DATE	NOTE
2000A	BF-16				BLH	RF-16	75197	Jun 51	Jul 66	
2000B	BF-16				BLH	RF-16	75215	Jun 51	Jul 66	
2001A	BF-16	ABF-18			BLH	RF-16	75198	Jun 51	Jul 66	(12)
2001B	BF-16				BLH	RF-16	75199	Jun 51	Jul 66	
2002A	BF-16				BLH	RF-16	75216	Jun 51	Jul 66	
2002B	BF-16				BLH	RF-16	75200	Jun 51	Jul 66	
2003A	BF-16				BLH	RF-16	75201	Jul 51	Jul 66	
2003B	BF-16				BLH	RF-16	75217	Jul 51	Jul 66	
2004A	BF-16				BLH	RF-16	75202	Jul 51	Jul 66	
2004B	BF-16				BLH	RF-16	75203	Aug 51	Jul 66	
2005A	BF-16				BLH	RF-16	75218	Aug 51	Jul 66	
2005B	BF-16				BLH	RF-16	75204	Aug 51	Jul 66	
2006A	BF-16				BLH	RF-16	75205	Oct 51	Jul 66	
2006B	BF-16				BLH	RF-16	75219	Oct 51	Jul 66	
2007A	BF-16				BLH	RF-16	75206	Oct 51	Jul 66	
2008A	BF-16				BLH	RF-16	75207	Feb 52	Jan 67	
2008B	BF-16				BLH	RF-16	75220	Feb 52	Jan 67	
2009A	BF-16				BLH	RF-16	75208	Feb 52	Jan 67	
2010B	BF-16				BLH	RF-16	75209	Feb 52	Jan 67	
2012A	BF-16				BLH	RF-16	75221	Feb 52	Jan 67	
2013A	BF-16				BLH	RF-16	75210	Feb 52	Jan 67	

RF-16 (road numbers 2014A–2027A) and GP30

ORIG ROAD NUM.	PRR BASE CLASS	PRR REBLT CLASS	1966 ROAD NUM.	PRR CLASS (1966)	BLDR	BLDR MODEL	BLDR SERIAL NUM.	BLDR DATE	RETIRE DATE	NOTE
2014A	BF-16				BLH	RF-16	75211	Feb 52	Jan 67	
2014B	BF-16				BLH	RF-16	75222	Feb 52	Jan 67	
2015A	BF-16				BLH	RF-16	75212	Feb 52	Jan 67	
2016B	BF-16				BLH	RF-16	75223	Mar 52	Jan 67	
2017A	BF-16				BLH	RF-16	75214	Mar 52	Jan 67	
2018A	BF-16				BLH	RF-16	75358	Mar 52	Jan 67	
2018B	BF-16				BLH	RF-16	75400	Mar 52	Jan 67	
2019A	BF-16				BLH	RF-16	75359	Mar 52	Jan 67	
2020A	BF-16				BLH	RF-16	75378	Mar 52	Jan 67	
2020B	BF-16				BLH	RF-16	75409	Mar 52	Jan 67	
2021A	BF-16				BLH	RF-16	75379	Mar 52	Jan 67	
2022A	BF-16				BLH	RF-16	75380	Mar 52	Jan 67	
2022B	BF-16				BLH	RF-16	75410	Mar 52	Jan 67	
2023A	BF-16				BLH	RF-16	75381	Mar 52	Jan 67	
2024A	BF-16				BLH	RF-16	75411	Apr 52	Jan 67	
2024B	BF-16				BLH	RF-16	75382	Apr 52	Jan 67	
2025A	BF-16				BLH	RF-16	75383	Apr 52	Jan 67	
2026A	BF-16				BLH	RF-16	75384	Apr 52	Jan 67	
2026B	BF-16				BLH	RF-16	75412	Apr 52	Jan 67	
2027A	BF-16				BLH	RF-16	75385	Apr 52	Jan 67	
2200	EF-22		2200	EF-22	EMD	GP30	28108	Feb 63	to PC	
2201	EF-22		2201	EF-22	EMD	GP30	28109	Feb 63	to PC	
2202	EF-22		2202	EF-22	EMD	GP30	28110	Feb 63	to PC	
2203	EF-22		2203	EF-22	EMD	GP30	28111	Feb 63	to PC	
2204	EF-22		2204	EF-22	EMD	GP30	28112	Mar 63	to PC	
2205	EF-22		2205	EF-22	EMD	GP30	28113	Mar 63	to PC	
2206	EF-22		2206	EF-22	EMD	GP30	28114	Mar 63	to PC	
2207	EF-22		2207	EF-22	EMD	GP30	28115	Mar 63	to PC	
2208	EF-22		2208	EF-22	EMD	GP30	28116	Mar 63	to PC	
2209	EF-22		2209	EF-22	EMD	GP30	28117	Mar 63	to PC	
2210	EF-22		2210	EF-22	EMD	GP30	28118	Mar 63	to PC	
2211	EF-22		2211	EF-22	EMD	GP30	28119	Mar 63	to PC	
2212	EF-22		2212	EF-22	EMD	GP30	28120	Mar 63	to PC	
2213	EF-22		2213	EF-22	EMD	GP30	28121	Mar 63	to PC	
2214	EF-22		2214	EF-22	EMD	GP30	28122	Mar 63	to PC	
2215	EF-22		2215	EF-22	EMD	GP30	28123	Mar 63	to PC	
2216	EF-22		2216	EF-22	EMD	GP30	28124	Mar 63	to PC	
2217	EF-22		2217	EF-22	EMD	GP30	28125	Mar 63	to PC	
2218	EF-22		2218	EF-22	EMD	GP30	28126	Mar 63	to PC	
2219	EF-22		2219	EF-22	EMD	GP30	28127	Mar 63	to PC	
2220	EF-22		2220	EF-22	EMD	GP30	28128	Mar 63	to PC	
2221	EF-22		2221	EF-22	EMD	GP30	28129	Apr 63	to PC	
2222	EF-22		2222	EF-22	EMD	GP30	28130	Apr 63	to PC	
2223	EF-22		2223	EF-22	EMD	GP30	28131	Apr 63	to PC	
2224	EF-22		2224	EF-22	EMD	GP30	28132	Apr 63	to PC	
2225	EF-22		2225	EF-22	EMD	GP30	28133	Apr 63	to PC	
2226	EF-22		2226	EF-22	EMD	GP30	28134	Apr 63	to PC	
2227	EF-22		2227	EF-22	EMD	GP30	28135	Apr 63	to PC	
2228	EF-22		2228	EF-22	EMD	GP30	28136	Apr 63	to PC	
2229	EF-22		2229	EF-22	EMD	GP30	28137	Apr 63	to PC	
2230	EF-22		2230	EF-22	EMD	GP30	28138	Apr 63	to PC	
2231	EF-22		2231	EF-22	EMD	GP30	28139	Apr 63	to PC	

DOUGLAS COLLECTION

PRR 2012A was delivered to the railroad on February 26, 1952 and put into service at Enola. On March 13,1952, the 2012A is seen on an A-B-A set, photographed from the Enola shop roof.

Pennsylvania Railroad Diesel Locomotive Roster

ORIG ROAD NUM.	PRR BASE CLASS	PRR REBLT CLASS	1966 ROAD NUM.	PRR CLASS (1966)	BLDR	BLDR MODEL	BLDR SERIAL NUM.	BLDR DATE	RETIRE DATE	NOTE
2232	EF-22		2232	EF-22	EMD	GP30	28140	Apr 63	to PC	
2233	EF-22		2233	EF-22	EMD	GP30	28141	Apr 63	to PC	
2234	EF-22		2234	EF-22	EMD	GP30	28142	Apr 63	to PC	
2235	EF-22		2245	EF-22	EMD	GP30	28143	Apr 63	to PC	
2236	EF-22		2236	EF-22	EMD	GP30	28144	May 63	to PC	
2237	EF-22		2237	EF-22	EMD	GP30	28145	May 63	to PC	
2238	EF-22		2238	EF-22	EMD	GP30	28146	May 63	to PC	
2239	EF-22		2239	EF-22	EMD	GP30	28147	May 63	to PC	
2240	EF-22		2240	EF-22	EMD	GP30	28148	May 63	to PC	
2241	EF-22		2241	EF-22	EMD	GP30	28149	May 63	to PC	
2242	EF-22		2242	EF-22	EMD	GP30	28150	May 63	to PC	
2243	EF-22		2243	EF-22	EMD	GP30	28151	May 63	to PC	
2244	EF-22		2244	EF-22	EMD	GP30	28152	May 63	to PC	
2245	EF-22		2245	EF-22	EMD	GP30	28153	May 63	to PC	
2246	EF-22		2246	EF-22	EMD	GP30	28154	May 63	to PC	
2247	EF-22		2247	EF-22	EMD	GP30	28155	May 63	to PC	
2248	EF-22		2248	EF-22	EMD	GP30	28156	May 63	to PC	
2249	EF-22		2249	EF-22	EMD	GP30	28157	May 63	to PC	
2250	EF-22		2198	EF-22	EMD	GP30	28158	May 63	to PC	
2251	EF-22		2199	EF-22	EMD	GP30	28159	May 63	to PC	
2252	EF-25		2252	EF-25	EMD	GP35	29001	May 64	to PC	
2253	EF-25		2253	EF-25	EMD	GP35	29002	May 64	to PC	
2254	EF-25		2254	EF-25	EMD	GP35	29003	May 64	to PC	
2255	EF-25		2255	EF-25	EMD	GP35	29004	May 64	to PC	
2256	EF-25		2256	EF-25	EMD	GP35	29005	May 64	to PC	
2257	EF-25		2257	EF-25	EMD	GP35	29006	May 64	to PC	
2258	EF-25		2258	EF-25	EMD	GP35	29007	May 64	to PC	
2259	EF-25		2259	EF-25	EMD	GP35	29008	May 64	to PC	
2260	EF-25		2260	EF-25	EMD	GP35	29009	May 64	to PC	
2261	EF-25		2261	EF-25	EMD	GP35	29010	May 64	to PC	
2262	EF-25		2262	EF-25	EMD	GP35	29011	May 64	to PC	
2263	EF-25		2263	EF-25	EMD	GP35	29012	May 64	to PC	
2264	EF-25		2264	EF-25	EMD	GP35	29013	May 64	to PC	
2265	EF-25		2265	EF-25	EMD	GP35	29014	May 64	to PC	
2266	EF-25		2266	EF-25	EMD	GP35	29015	May 64	to PC	
2267	EF-25		2267	EF-25	EMD	GP35	29016	May 64	to PC	
2268	EF-25		2268	EF-25	EMD	GP35	29017	May 64	to PC	
2269	EF-25		2269	EF-25	EMD	GP35	29018	May 64	to PC	
2270	EF-25		2270	EF-25	EMD	GP35	29019	May 64	to PC	
2271	EF-25		2271	EF-25	EMD	GP35	29020	May 64	to PC	
2272	EF-25		2272	EF-25	EMD	GP35	29021	May 64	to PC	
2273	EF-25		2273	EF-25	EMD	GP35	29022	May 64	to PC	
2274	EF-25		2274	EF-25	EMD	GP35	29023	May 64	to PC	
2275	EF-25		2275	EF-25	EMD	GP35	29024	Jun 64	to PC	
2276	EF-25		2276	EF-25	EMD	GP35	29447	Jun 64	to PC	
2277	EF-25		2277	EF-25	EMD	GP35	29448	Jun 64	to PC	
2278	EF-25		2278	EF-25	EMD	GP35	29449	Jun 64	to PC	
2279	EF-25		2279	EF-25	EMD	GP35	29450	Jun 64	to PC	
2280	EF-25		2280	EF-25	EMD	GP35	29451	Jun 64	to PC	
2281	EF-25		2281	EF-25	EMD	GP35	29452	Jun 64	to PC	
2282	EF-25		2282	EF-25	EMD	GP35	29453	Jun 64	to PC	
2283	EF-25		2283	EF-25	EMD	GP35	29454	Jun 64	to PC	
2284	EF-25		2284	EF-25	EMD	GP35	29455	Jun 64	to PC	
2285	EF-25		2285	EF-25	EMD	GP35	29456	Jun 64	to PC	
2286	EF-25		2286	EF-25	EMD	GP35	29457	Jun 64	to PC	
2287	EF-25		2287	EF-25	EMD	GP35	29458	Jun 64	to PC	
2288	EF-25		2288	EF-25	EMD	GP35	29459	Jun 64	to PC	
2289	EF-25		2289	EF-25	EMD	GP35	29460	Jun 64	to PC	
2290	EF-25		2290	EF-25	EMD	GP35	29461	Jun 64	to PC	
2291	EF-25		2291	EF-25	EMD	GP35	29462	Jun 64	to PC	
2292	EF-25		2292	EF-25	EMD	GP35	29463	Jun 64	to PC	
2293	EF-25		2293	EF-25	EMD	GP35	29464	Jun 64	to PC	
2294	EF-25		2294	EF-25	EMD	GP35	29465	Jun 64	to PC	
2295	EF-25		2295	EF-25	EMD	GP35	29466	Jun 64	to PC	
2296	EF-25		2296	EF-25	EMD	GP35	29467	Jun 64	to PC	
2297	EF-25		2297	EF-25	EMD	GP35	29605	Nov 64	to PC	
2298	EF-25		2298	EF-25	EMD	GP35	29606	Nov 64	to PC	
2299	EF-25		2299	EF-25	EMD	GP35	29607	Nov 64	to PC	
2300	EF-25		2300	EF-25	EMD	GP35	29608	Nov 64	to PC	
2301	EF-25		2301	EF-25	EMD	GP35	29609	Nov 64	to PC	
2302	EF-25		2302	EF-25	EMD	GP35	29610	Nov 64	to PC	
2303	EF-25		2303	EF-25	EMD	GP35	29611	Nov 64	to PC	
2304	EF-25		2304	EF-25	EMD	GP35	29612	Nov 64	to PC	
2305	EF-25		2305	EF-25	EMD	GP35	29613	Nov 64	to PC	
2306	EF-25		2306	EF-25	EMD	GP35	29614	Nov 64	to PC	
2307	EF-25		2307	EF-25	EMD	GP35	29615	Nov 64	to PC	
2308	EF-25		2308	EF-25	EMD	GP35	29616	Nov 64	to PC	
2309	EF-25		2250	EF-25	EMD	GP35	29617	Nov 64	to PC	
2310	EF-25		2251	EF-25	EMD	GP35	29618	Nov 64	to PC	
2311	EF-25		2311	EF-25	EMD	GP35	30328	Jan 65	to PC	
2312	EF-25		2312	EF-25	EMD	GP35	30329	Jan 65	to PC	
2313	EF-25		2313	EF-25	EMD	GP35	30330	Jan 65	to PC	
2314	EF-25		2314	EF-25	EMD	GP35	30331	Jan 65	to PC	
2315	EF-25		2315	EF-25	EMD	GP35	30332	Jan 65	to PC	
2316	EF-25		2316	EF-25	EMD	GP35	30333	Jan 65	to PC	

Led by PRR 2322, this westbound Trailer Train has just passed the unique Federal Street tower on the north side of Pittsburgh on February 20, 1965. The train has gone through the Pittsburgh station and crossed the upper deck of the Fort Wayne Bridge.

Pennsylvania Railroad Diesel Locomotive Roster

ORIG ROAD NUM.	PRR BASE CLASS	PRR REBLT CLASS	1966 ROAD NUM.	PRR CLASS (1966)	BLDR	BLDR MODEL	BLDR SERIAL NUM.	BLDR DATE	RETIRE DATE	NOTE
2317	EF-25		2317	EF-25	EMD	GP35	30334	Jan 65	to PC	
2318	EF-25		2318	EF-25	EMD	GP35	30335	Jan 65	to PC	
2319	EF-25		2319	EF-25	EMD	GP35	30336	Jan 65	to PC	
2320	EF-25		2320	EF-25	EMD	GP35	30337	Jan 65	to PC	
2321	EF-25		2321	EF-25	EMD	GP35	30338	Jan 65	to PC	
2322	EF-25		2322	EF-25	EMD	GP35	30339	Jan 65	to PC	
2323	EF-25		2323	EF-25	EMD	GP35	30340	Jan 65	to PC	
2324	EF-25		2324	EF-25	EMD	GP35	30341	Jan 65	to PC	
2325	EF-25		2325	EF-25	EMD	GP35	30342	Jan 65	to PC	
2326	EF-25		2326	EF-25	EMD	GP35	30343	Jan 65	to PC	
2327	EF-25		2327	EF-25	EMD	GP35	30344	Jan 65	to PC	
2328	EF-25		2328	EF-25	EMD	GP35	30345	Jan 65	to PC	
2329	EF-25		2329	EF-25	EMD	GP35	30346	Jan 65	to PC	
2330	EF-25		2330	EF-25	EMD	GP35	30347	Jan 65	to PC	
2331	EF-25		2331	EF-25	EMD	GP35	30348	Feb 65	to PC	
2332	EF-25		2332	EF-25	EMD	GP35	30349	Feb 65	to PC	
2333	EF-25		2333	EF-25	EMD	GP35	30350	Feb 65	to PC	
2334	EF-25		2334	EF-25	EMD	GP35	30351	Feb 65	to PC	
2335	EF-25		2335	EF-25	EMD	GP35	30352	Feb 65	to PC	
2336	EF-25		2336	EF-25	EMD	GP35	30353	Feb 65	to PC	
2337	EF-25		2337	EF-25	EMD	GP35	30354	Feb 65	to PC	
2338	EF-25		2338	EF-25	EMD	GP35	30355	Feb 65	to PC	
2339	EF-25		2339	EF-25	EMD	GP35	30356	Feb 65	to PC	
2340	EF-25		2340	EF-25	EMD	GP35	30357	Feb 65	to PC	
2341	EF-25		2341	EF-25	EMD	GP35	30358	Feb 65	to PC	
2342	EF-25		2342	EF-25	EMD	GP35	30359	Feb 65	to PC	
2343	EF-25		2343	EF-25	EMD	GP35	30360	Feb 65	to PC	
2344	EF-25		2344	EF-25	EMD	GP35	30361	Feb 65	to PC	
2345	EF-25		2345	EF-25	EMD	GP35	30362	Feb 65	to PC	
2346	EF-25		2346	EF-25	EMD	GP35	30363	Feb 65	to PC	
2347	EF-25		2347	EF-25	EMD	GP35	30364	Feb 65	to PC	
2348	EF-25		2348	EF-25	EMD	GP35	30365	Feb 65	to PC	
2349	EF-25		2349	EF-25	EMD	GP35	30366	Feb 65	to PC	
2350	EF-25		2350	EF-25	EMD	GP35	30367	Feb 65	to PC	
2351	EF-25		2351	EF-25	EMD	GP35	30368	Mar 65	to PC	
2352	EF-25		2352	EF-25	EMD	GP35	30369	Mar 65	to PC	
2353	EF-25		2353	EF-25	EMD	GP35	30370	Mar 65	to PC	
2354	EF-25		2354	EF-25	EMD	GP35	30371	Mar 65	to PC	
2355	EF-25		2355	EF-25	EMD	GP35	30372	Mar 65	to PC	
2356	EF-25		2356	EF-25	EMD	GP35	30373	Mar 65	to PC	
2357	EF-25		5657	EF-25	EMD	GP35	30374	Mar 65	to PC	
2358	EF-25		5658	EF-25	EMD	GP35	30375	Mar 65	to PC	
2359	EF-25		5659	EF-25	EMD	GP35	30376	Mar 65	to PC	
2360	EF-25		5660	EF-25	EMD	GP35	30377	Mar 65	to PC	
2361	EF-25		2361	EF-25	EMD	GP35	30378	Mar 65	to PC	
2362	EF-25		2362	EF-25	EMD	GP35	30379	Mar 65	to PC	
2363	EF-25		2363	EF-25	EMD	GP35	30380	Mar 65	to PC	
2364	EF-25		2364	EF-25	EMD	GP35	30381	Mar 65	to PC	
2365	EF-25		2365	EF-25	EMD	GP35	30382	Mar 65	to PC	
2366	EF-25		2366	EF-25	EMD	GP35	30383	Apr 65	to PC	
2367	EF-25		2367	EF-25	EMD	GP35	30384	Apr 65	to PC	
2368	EF-25		2368	EF-25	EMD	GP35	30385	Apr 65	to PC	
2369	EF-25		2309	EF-25	EMD	GP35	30386	Apr 65	to PC	
2370	EF-25		2310	EF-25	EMD	GP35	30387	Apr 65	to PC	
2400	AF-24		2400	AF-24	Alco	RS-27	83607	Sep 62	to PC	
2401	AF-24		2401	AF-24	Alco	RS-27	83608	Sep 62	to PC	
2402	AF-24		2402	AF-24	Alco	RS-27	83609	Sep 62	to PC	
2403	AF-24		2403	AF-24	Alco	RS-27	83610	Oct 62	to PC	
2404	AF-24		2404	AF-24	Alco	RS-27	83611	Oct 62	to PC	
2405	AF-24		2405	AF-24	Alco	RS-27	83612	Oct 62	to PC	
2406	AF-24		2406	AF-24	Alco	RS-27	83613	Oct 62	to PC	
2407	AF-24		2407	AF-24	Alco	RS-27	83614	Oct 62	to PC	
2408	AF-24		2408	AF-24	Alco	RS-27	84373	Oct 62	to PC	
2409	AF-24		2409	AF-24	Alco	RS-27	84374	Oct 62	to PC	
2410	AF-24		2410	AF-24	Alco	RS-27	84375	Oct 62	to PC	
2411	AF-24		2411	AF-24	Alco	RS-27	84376	Oct 62	to PC	
2412	AF-24		2412	AF-24	Alco	RS-27	84377	Oct 62	to PC	
2413	AF-24		2413	AF-24	Alco	RS-27	84378	Oct 62	to PC	
2414	AF-24		2414	AF-24	Alco	RS-27	84379	Oct 62	to PC	
2415	AF-24a		2415	AF-24	Alco	C-424	84558	Sep 63	to PC	
2416	AF-25		2416	AF-25	Alco	C-425	3394-01	Oct 64	to PC	
2417	AF-25		2417	AF-25	Alco	C-425	3394-02	Oct 64	to PC	
2418	AF-25		2418	AF-25	Alco	C-425	3394-03	Oct 64	to PC	
2419	AF-25		2419	AF-25	Alco	C-425	3394-04	Nov 64	to PC	
2420	AF-25		2420	AF-25	Alco	C-425	3394-05	Nov 64	to PC	
2421	AF-25		2421	AF-25	Alco	C-425	3394-06	Nov 64	to PC	
2422	AF-25		2422	AF-25	Alco	C-425	3403-01	Feb 65	to PC	
2423	AF-25		2423	AF-25	Alco	C-425	3403-02	Feb 65	to PC	
2424	AF-25		2424	AF-25	Alco	C-425	3403-03	Feb 65	to PC	
2425	AF-25		2425	AF-25	Alco	C-425	3403-04	Feb 65	to PC	
2426	AF-25		2426	AF-25	Alco	C-425	3403-05	Feb 65	to PC	

Rear quarter view of PRR 2420 at Kiski Junction engine terminal near Freeport, Pennsylvania on December 18, 1967.

ORIG ROAD NUM.	PRR BASE CLASS	PRR REBLT CLASS	1966 ROAD NUM.	PRR CLASS (1966)	BLDR	BLDR MODEL	BLDR SERIAL NUM.	BLDR DATE	RETIRE DATE	NOTE
2427	AF-25		2427	AF-25	Alco	C-425	3403-06	Feb 65	to PC	
2428	AF-25		2428	AF-25	Alco	C-425	3403-07	Feb 65	to PC	
2429	AF-25		2429	AF-25	Alco	C-425	3403-08	Mar 65	to PC	
2430	AF-25		2430	AF-25	Alco	C-425	3403-09	Mar 65	to PC	
2431	AF-25		2431	AF-25	Alco	C-425	3403-10	Mar 65	to PC	
2432	AF-25		2432	AF-25	Alco	C-425	3403-11	Mar 65	to PC	
2433	AF-25		2433	AF-25	Alco	C-425	3403-12	Mar 65	to PC	
2434	AF-25		2434	AF-25	Alco	C-425	3403-13	Mar 65	to PC	
2435	AF-25		2435	AF-25	Alco	C-425	3403-14	Mar 65	to PC	
2436	AF-25		2436	AF-25	Alco	C-425	3403-15	Mar 65	to PC	
2437	AF-25		2437	AF-25	Alco	C-425	3433-01	Dec 65	to PC	
2438	AF-25		2438	AF-25	Alco	C-425	3433-02	Dec 65	to PC	
2439	AF-25		2439	AF-25	Alco	C-425	3433-03	Dec 65	to PC	
2440	AF-25		2440	AF-25	Alco	C-425	3433-04	Dec 65	to PC	
2441	AF-25		2441	AF-25	Alco	C-425	3433-05	Dec 65	to PC	
2442	AF-25		2442	AF-25	Alco	C-425	3433-06	Dec 65	to PC	
2443	AF-25		2443	AF-25	Alco	C-425	3433-07	Dec 65	to PC	
2444	AF-25		2444	AF-25	Alco	C-425	3433-08	Dec 65	to PC	
2445	AF-25		2445	AF-25	Alco	C-425	3433-09	Dec 65	to PC	
2446	AF-25		2446	AF-25	Alco	C-425	3433-10	Dec 65	to PC	
2500	GF-25		2600	GF-25	GE	U25B	34528	Aug 62	to PC	
2501	GF-25		2601	GF-25	GE	U25B	34529	Aug 62	to PC	
2502	GF-25		2602	GF-25	GE	U25B	34530	Aug 62	to PC	
2503	GF-25		2603	GF-25	GE	U25B	34531	Aug 62	to PC	
2504	GF-25		2604	GF-25	GE	U25B	34532	Aug 62	to PC	
2505	GF-25		2605	GF-25	GE	U25B	34533	Aug 62	to PC	
2506	GF-25		2606	GF-25	GE	U25B	34534	Aug 62	to PC	
2507	GF-25		2607	GF-25	GE	U25B	34539	Sep 62	to PC	
2508	GF-25		2608	GF-25	GE	U25B	34540	Sep 62	to PC	
2509	GF-25		2609	GF-25	GE	U25B	34541	Sep 62	to PC	
2510	GF-25		2610	GF-25	GE	U25B	34542	Sep 62	to PC	
2511	GF-25		2611	GF-25	GE	U25B	34543	Sep 62	to PC	
2512	GF-25		2612	GF-25	GE	U25B	34544	Sep 62	to PC	
2513	GF-25		2613	GF-25	GE	U25B	34545	Oct 62	to PC	
2514	GF-25		2614	GF-25	GE	U25B	34546	Oct 62	to PC	
2515	GF-25		2615	GF-25	GE	U25B	34547	Oct 62	to PC	
2516	GF-25		2616	GF-25	GE	U25B	34548	Oct 62	to PC	
2517	GF-25		2617	GF-25	GE	U25B	34549	Oct 62	to PC	
2518	GF-25		2618	GF-25	GE	U25B	34550	Oct 62	to PC	
2519	GF-25		2619	GF-25	GE	U25B	34551	Oct 62	to PC	
2520	GF-25		2620	GF-25	GE	U25B	34552	Oct 62	to PC	
2521	GF-25		2621	GF-25	GE	U25B	34553	Oct 62	to PC	
2522	GF-25		2622	GF-25	GE	U25B	34554	Oct 62	to PC	
2523	GF-25		2623	GF-25	GE	U25B	34555	Oct 62	to PC	
2524	GF-25		2624	GF-25	GE	U25B	34556	Oct 62	to PC	
2525	GF-25		2625	GF-25	GE	U25B	34557	Oct 62	to PC	
2526	GF-25		2626	GF-25	GE	U25B	34558	Oct 62	to PC	
2527	GF-25		2627	GF-25	GE	U25B	34559	Oct 62	to PC	
2528	GF-25		2628	GF-25	GE	U25B	34560	Oct 62	to PC	
2529	GF-25		2629	GF-25	GE	U25B	35124	Sep 64	to PC	
2530	GF-25		2630	GF-25	GE	U25B	35125	Sep 64	to PC	
2531	GF-25		2631	GF-25	GE	U25B	35126	Sep 64	to PC	
2532	GF-25		2632	GF-25	GE	U25B	35127	Sep 64	to PC	
2533	GF-25		2633	GF-25	GE	U25B	35128	Sep 64	to PC	
2534	GF-25		2634	GF-25	GE	U25B	35530	Feb 65	to PC	
2535	GF-25		2635	GF-25	GE	U25B	35531	Feb 65	to PC	
2536	GF-25		2636	GF-25	GE	U25B	35532	Feb 65	to PC	
2537	GF-25		2637	GF-25	GE	U25B	35533	Feb 65	to PC	
2538	GF-25		2638	GF-25	GE	U25B	35534	Feb 65	to PC	
2539	GF-25		2639	GF-25	GE	U25B	35535	Feb 65	to PC	
2540	GF-25		2640	GF-25	GE	U25B	35536	Feb 65	to PC	
2541	GF-25		2641	GF-25	GE	U25B	35537	Feb 65	to PC	
2542	GF-25		2642	GF-25	GE	U25B	35538	Feb 65	to PC	
2543	GF-25		2643	GF-25	GE	U25B	35539	Feb 65	to PC	
2544	GF-25		2644	GF-25	GE	U25B	35540	Feb 65	to PC	
2545	GF-25		2645	GF-25	GE	U25B	35541	Feb 65	to PC	
2546	GF-25		2646	GF-25	GE	U25B	35542	Feb 65	to PC	
2547	GF-25		2647	GF-25	GE	U25B	35543	Mar 65	to PC	
2548	GF-25		2648	GF-25	GE	U25B	35544	Mar 65	to PC	
2649	GF-25		2649	GF-25	GE	U25B	35773	Nov 65	to PC	
2650	GF-25		2650	GF-25	GE	U25B	35774	Nov 65	to PC	
2651	GF-25		2651	GF-25	GE	U25B	35775	Nov 65	to PC	
2652	GF-25		2652	GF-25	GE	U25B	35776	Nov 65	to PC	
2653	GF-25		2653	GF-25	GE	U25B	35777	Nov 65	to PC	
2654	GF-25		2654	GF-25	GE	U25B	35778	Dec 65	to PC	
2655	GF-25		2655	GF-25	GE	U25B	35779	Dec 65	to PC	
2656	GF-25		2656	GF-25	GE	U25B	35780	Dec 65	to PC	
2657	GF-25		2657	GF-25	GE	U25B	35781	Dec 65	to PC	
2658	GF-25		2658	GF-25	GE	U25B	35782	Dec 65	to PC	
3905	A6			A6	PRR	A6	4192	May 28	Ca. 52	(2)
3906	A6			A6	PRR	A6	4206	May 29	Ca. 54	(3)
3907	A6b	A6b		A6b	PRR	A6b	4226	Jun 30	Ca. 62	(4)

PRR 2658 is less than a month old in December, 1965 as it leads a southbound freight at Case interlocking at Sunbury, Pennsylvania. It was delivered in the 2600 series into which all of the PRR U25B diesels would be renumbered as part 1966 plan for the Penn-Central merger.

Pennsylvania Railroad Diesel Locomotive Roster

Pennsylvania Railroad Diesel Locomotive Roster

ORIG ROAD NUM.	PRR BASE CLASS	PRR REBLT CLASS	1966 ROAD NUM.	PRR CLASS (1966)	BLDR	BLDR MODEL	BLDR SERIAL NUM.	BLDR DATE	RETIRE DATE	NOTE
4041	AS-15m				Alco	RS-3	78340	Oct 50	Jul 65	(5)
4042	AS-15m				Alco	RS-3	78341	Oct 50	May 65	(5)
4044	AS-15m				Alco	RS-3	78343	Oct 50	Jul 65	(5)
4046	AS-15m				Alco	RS-3	78353	Oct 50	Jul 65	(5)
4047	AS-15m				Alco	RS-3	78354	Oct 50	May 65	(5)
4048	AS-15m				Alco	RS-3	78355	Oct 50	Jul 65	(5)
5550	BS-10a		7950	BS-10	BLW	DS 4-4-1000	74759	Mar 50	to PC	
5551	BS-10a		7951	BS-10	BLW	DS 4-4-1000	74638	Feb 50	Sep 67	
5552	BS-10a		7952	BS-10	BLW	DS 4-4-1000	74639	Feb 50	to PC	
5553	BS-10a		7953	BS-10	BLW	DS 4-4-1000	74641	Feb 50	to PC	
5554	BS-10a		7954	BS-10	BLW	DS 4-4-1000	74642	Feb 50	to PC	
5555	BS-10a		7955	BS-10	BLW	DS 4-4-1000	74643	Feb 50	to PC	
5556	BS-10a		7956	BS-10	BLW	DS 4-4-1000	74644	Feb 50	to PC	
5557	BS-10a		7957	BS-10	BLW	DS 4-4-1000	74645	Feb 50	to PC	
5558	BS-10a				BLW	DS 4-4-1000	74651	Feb 50	May 66	
5559	BS-10a		7959	BS-10	BLW	DS 4-4-1000	74652	Feb 50	to PC	
5560	BS-10a		7960	BS-10	BLW	DS 4-4-1000	74653	Feb 50	to PC	
5561	BS-10a		7961	BS-10	BLW	DS 4-4-1000	74654	Feb 50	to PC	
5562	BS-10a		7962	BS-10	BLW	DS 4-4-1000	74655	Feb 50	Jun 67	
5563	BS-10a		7963	BS-10	BLW	DS 4-4-1000	74656	Feb 50	to PC	
5564	BS-10a		7964	BS-10	BLW	DS 4-4-1000	74657	Feb 50	to PC	
5565	BS-10a		7965	BS-10	BLW	DS 4-4-1000	74658	Feb 50	to PC	
5566	BS-10a		7966	BS-10	BLW	DS 4-4-1000	74198	Jan 50	to PC	
5567	BS-10a		7967	BS-10	BLW	DS 4-4-1000	74199	Jan 50	to PC	
5568	BS-10a		7968	BS-10	BLW	DS 4-4-1000	74200	Jan 50	to PC	
5569	BS-10a		7969	BS-10	BLW	DS 4-4-1000	74201	Jan 50	to PC	
5570	BS-10a		7970	BS-10	BLW	DS 4-4-1000	74202	Jan 50	to PC	
5571	BS-10a		7971	BS-10	BLW	DS 4-4-1000	74621	Jan 50	to PC	
5572	BS-10a		7972	BS-10	BLW	DS 4-4-1000	74622	Jan 50	Feb 67	
5573	BS-10a		7973	BS-10	BLW	DS 4-4-1000	74623	Jan 50	to PC	
5574	BS-10a		7974	BS-10	BLW	DS 4-4-1000	74624	Jan 50	to PC	
5575	BS-10a		7975	BS-10	BLW	DS 4-4-1000	74625	Jan 50	to PC	
5576	BS-10a		7976	BS-10	BLW	DS 4-4-1000	74626	Jan 50	to PC	
5577	BS-10a		7977	BS-10	BLW	DS 4-4-1000	74636	Jan 50	Sep 67	
5578	BS-10a		7978	BS-10	BLW	DS 4-4-1000	74659	Jan 50	to PC	
5579	BS-10a				BLW	DS 4-4-1000	74660	Apr 50	Dec 66	
5580	BS-10a		7980	BS-10	BLW	DS 4-4-1000	74661	Apr 50	to PC	
5581	BS-10a		7981	BS-10	BLW	DS 4-4-1000	74662	Apr 50	to PC	
5582	BS-10a				BLW	DS 4-4-1000	74663	Apr 50	May 66	
5583	BS-10a		7983	BS-10	BLW	DS 4-4-1000	74664	Apr 50	Sep 67	
5584	BS-10a				BLW	DS 4-4-1000	74665	Apr 50	Feb 65	
5585	BS-10a		7985	BS-10	BLW	DS 4-4-1000	74197	Feb 50	to PC	
5586	BS-10a		7986	BS-10	BLW	DS 4-4-1000	74666	Feb 50	to PC	
5587	BS-10a		7987	BS-10	BLW	DS 4-4-1000	74704	Feb 50	to PC	
5588	BS-10a		7988	BS-10	BLW	DS 4-4-1000	74705	Feb 50	to PC	
5589	BS-10a		7989	BS-10	BLW	DS 4-4-1000	74706	Feb 50	to PC	
5590	BS-10a		7990	BS-10	BLW	DS 4-4-1000	74707	Feb 50	to PC	
5591	BS-10as		8051	BRS-10sx	BLW	DRS 4-4-1000	74744	Mar 50	Feb 67	
5592	BS-10as		8052	BRS-10sx	BLW	DRS 4-4-1000	74745	Mar 50	to PC	
5593	BS-10as		8053	BRS-10sx	BLW	DRS 4-4-1000	74746	Mar 50	to PC	
5594	BS-10as				BLW	DRS 4-4-1000	74747	Mar 50	Dec 66	
5595	BS-7	BS-7m	7911	BS-7m	BLW	DS 4-4-750	74720	May 50	to PC	(6)
5596	BS-7		7886	BS-7	BLW	DS 4-4-750	74721	May 50	to PC	
5597	BS-7	BS-7m	7912	BS-7m	BLW	DS 4-4-750	74722	May 50	to PC	(6)
5598	BS-7		7888	BS-7	BLW	DS 4-4-750	74723	May 50	Dec 66	
5599	BS-7		7889	BS-7	BLW	DS 4-4-750	74724	Jun 50	to PC	
5600	BS-7	BS-7m	7913	BS-7m	BLW	DS 4-4-750	74725	Jun 50	to PC	(6)
5601	BS-7				BLW	DS 4-4-750	74726	Jun 50	Jul 65	
5602	BS-7		7902	BS-7	BLW	DS 4-4-750	74727	Jun 50	to PC	
5603	BS-7		7903	BS-7	BLW	DS 4-4-750	74728	Jun 50	Jun 67	
5604	BS-7		7904	BS-7	BLW	DS 4-4-750	74729	Jun 50	to PC	
5605	BS-7				BLW	DS 4-4-750	74730	Jun 50	Jul 66	
5606	BS-7		7906	BS-7	BLW	DS 4-4-750	74731	Jun 50	to PC	
5607	BS-7				BLW	DS 4-4-750	74732	Jun 50	Feb 66	
5608	BS-7		7908	BS-7	BLW	DS 4-4-750	74733	Jun 50	Feb 67	
5609	BS-7				BLW	DS 4-4-750	74734	Jun 50	to PC	
5610	BS-7		7910	BS-7	BLW	DS 4-4-750	74735	Jun 50	to PC	
5611	BS-7		7891	BS-7	BLW	DS 4-4-750	74736	Jun 50	to PC	
5612	BS-7		7892	BS-7	BLW	DS 4-4-750	74737	Jun 50	to PC	
5613	BS-7		7893	BS-7	BLW	DS 4-4-750	74738	Jun 50	to PC	
5614	BS-7		7900	BS-7	BLW	DS 4-4-750	74739	Jun 50	to PC	
5615	BS-7		7901	BS-7	BLW	DS 4-4-750	74740	Jun 50	to PC	
5616	BS-7		7890	BS-7	BLW	DS 4-4-750	74741	Jun 50	to PC	

Rear quarter view of PRR 3907. The A6b unit sits unused in January 1962 at the engine terminal at 46th Street, Philadelphia. The pioneer locomotive had worked most of its life in nearby Norristown.

Pennsylvania Railroad Diesel Locomotive Roster

ORIG ROAD NUM.	PRR BASE CLASS	PRR REBLT CLASS	1966 ROAD NUM.	PRR CLASS (1966)	BLDR	BLDR MODEL	BLDR SERIAL NUM.	BLDR DATE	RETIRE DATE	NOTE
5617	BS-7		7887	BS-7	BLW	DS 4-4-750	74742	Jun 50	to PC	
5618	BS-7			BS-7	BLW	DS 4-4-750	74743	Jun 50	Sep 65	
5619	AS-10am		9919	ARS-10	Alco	RS-1	78106	Jun 50	to PC	
5620	AS-10am		9920	ARS-10	Alco	RS-1	78107	Jun 50	to PC	
5621	AS-10am		9921	ARS-10	Alco	RS-1	78110	Jul 50	to PC	
5622	AS-10am		9922	ARS-10	Alco	RS-1	78111	Jul 50	to PC	
5623	AS-10am		9923	ARS-10	Alco	RS-1	78112	Jul 50	to PC	
5624	AS-10am		9924	ARS-10	Alco	RS-1	78113	Jul 50	to PC	
5625	AS-10am		9925	ARS-10	Alco	RS-1	78100	Jun 50	to PC	
5626	AS-10am		9926	ARS-10	Alco	RS-1	78101	Jun 50	to PC	
5627	AS-10am		9927	ARS-10	Alco	RS-1	78102	Jun 50	May 65	
5628	AS-10am			ARS-10	Alco	RS-1	78103	Jun 50	to PC	
5629	AS-10am		9929	ARS-10	Alco	RS-1	78114	Aug 50	to PC	
5630	AS-10am		9930	ARS-10	Alco	RS-1	78116	Aug 50	to PC	
5631	AS-10am		9931	ARS-10	Alco	RS-1	78117	Aug 50	to PC	
5632	AS-10am		9932	ARS-10	Alco	RS-1	78159	Aug 50	to PC	
5633	AS-10am		9933	ARS-10	Alco	RS-1	78160	Aug 50	to PC	
5634	AS-10am		9934	ARS-10	Alco	RS-1	78161	Aug 50	to PC	
5635	AS-10am		9935	ARS-10	Alco	RS-1	78162	Aug 50	to PC	
5636	AS-10am		9936	ARS-10	Alco	RS-1	78163	Aug 50	to PC	
5637	AS-10am		9937	ARS-10	Alco	RS-1	78104	Jun 50	to PC	
5638	AS-10am		9938	ARS-10	Alco	RS-1	78105	Jun 50	to PC	
5639	AS-10am		9939	ARS-10	Alco	RS-1	78108	Jul 50	to PC	
5640	AS-10am		9940	ARS-10	Alco	RS-1	78109	Jul 50	to PC	
5641	AS-10		9841	AS-10	Alco	S-2	77061	Mar 50	to PC	
5642	AS-10		9842	AS-10	Alco	S-2	77062	Mar 50	to PC	
5643	AS-10			AS-10	Alco	S-2	77063	Mar 50	May 65	
5644	AS-10		9824	AS-10	Alco	S-2	77489	Apr 50	to PC	
5645	AS-10		9825	AS-10	Alco	S-2	77490	Mar 50	to PC	
5646	AS-10		9816	AS-10	Alco	S-2	77064	Mar 50	to PC	
5647	AS-10			AS-10	Alco	S-2	77491	Apr 50	May 65	
5648	AS-10		9818	AS-10	Alco	S-2	77492	Apr 50	to PC	
5649	AS-10		9819	AS-10	Alco	S-2	77493	Apr 50	to PC	
5650	AS-10		9810	AS-10	Alco	S-2	77494	Apr 50	to PC	
5651	AS-10		9811	AS-10	Alco	S-2	77065	Mar 50	to PC	
5652	AS-10		9812	AS-10	Alco	S-2	77066	Mar 50	to PC	
5653	AS-10		9813	AS-10	Alco	S-2	77067	Mar 50	to PC	
5654	AS-10		9814	AS-10	Alco	S-2	77068	Mar 50	to PC	
5655	AS-10		9785	AS-10	Alco	S-2	77444	Mar 50	to PC	
5656	AS-10		9836	AS-10	Alco	S-2	77447	Mar 50	to PC	
5657	AS-10		9837	AS-10	Alco	S-2	77448	Mar 50	to PC	
5658	AS-10		9838	AS-10	Alco	S-2	77449	Mar 50	to PC	
5659	AS-10		9839	AS-10	Alco	S-2	77445	Mar 50	to PC	
5660	AS-10		9802	AS-10	Alco	S-2	77446	Mar 50	to PC	
5661	AS-6		9461	AS-6	Alco	S-1	77982	May 50	to PC	
5662	AS-6		9462	AS-6	Alco	S-1	77983	May 50	to PC	
5663	AS-6		9463	AS-6	Alco	S-1	77992	May 50	May 66	
5664	AS-6			AS-6	Alco	S-1	77993	May 50	to PC	
5665	AS-6		9465	AS-6	Alco	S-1	77994	Jun 50	to PC	
5666	AS-6		9466	AS-6	Alco	S-1	77995	Jun 50	to PC	
5667	AS-6		9467	AS-6	Alco	S-1	77996	Jun 50	to PC	
5668	AS-6		9468	AS-6	Alco	S-1	77997	Jun 50	to PC	
5669	AS-6		9469	AS-6	Alco	S-1	77984	Jun 50	to PC	
5670	AS-6		9470	AS-6	Alco	S-1	77985	May 50	to PC	
5671	LS-25				L-H	2500T	9402	May 50	May 65	
5672	LS-25				L-H	2500T	9403	May 50	Feb 65	
5673	LS-25				L-H	2500T	9404	May 50	Feb 65	
5674	LS-25				L-H	2500T	9405	May 50	Mar 65	
5675	LS-25				L-H	2500T	9406	Jun 50	May 65	
5676	LS-25				L-H	2500T	9407	Jun 50	May 65	
5677	LS-25				L-H	2500T	9408	Jun 50	Feb 65	
5678	LS-25				L-H	2500T	9409	Jun 50	Mar 65	
5679	LS-25				L-H	2500T	9410	Jun 50	Feb 65	
5680	LS-25				L-H	2500T	9411	Jul 50	Apr 65	
5681	LS-25				L-H	2500T	9412	Jul 50	Mar 65	
5682	LS-25				L-H	2500T	9537	Aug 51	Jul 66	
5683	LS-25				L-H	2500T	9538	Sep 51	Jul 66	
5700A	EP-22		4300	EP-22	EMD	E8A	16769	Sep 52	to PC	
5701A	EP-22		4271	EP-22	EMD	E8A	16770	Sep 52	to PC	
5702A	EP-22		4272	EP-22	EMD	E8A	16771	Sep 52	to PC	
5703A	EP-22		4273	EP-22	EMD	E8A	16772	Sep 52	to PC	
5704A	EP-22		4274	EP-22	EMD	E8A	16773	Sep 52	to PC	
5705A	EP-22		4275	EP-22	EMD	E8A	16774	Sep 52	to PC	
5706A	EP-22		4276	EP-22	EMD	E8A	16775	Oct 52	to PC	
5707A	EP-22		4277	EP-22	EMD	E8A	16776	Oct 52	to PC	
5708A	EP-22		4278	EP-22	EMD	E8A	16777	Oct 52	to PC	
5709A	EP-22		4279	EP-22	EMD	E8A	16778	Oct 52	to PC	
5710A	EP-22		4280	EP-22	EMD	E8A	16779	Oct 52	to PC	
5711A	EP-22		4311	EP-22	EMD	E8A	16780	Oct 52	to PC	

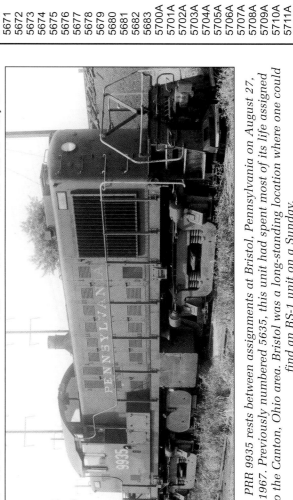

PRR 9935 rests between assignments at Bristol, Pennsylvania on August 27, 1967. Previously numbered 5635, this unit had spent most of its life assigned to the Canton, Ohio area. Bristol was a long-standing location where one could find an RS-1 unit on a Sunday.

Pennsylvania Railroad Diesel Locomotive Roster

PRR 5794A accelerates past Homewood station in Pittsburgh with Train #16. The train has left Pittsburgh station about ten minutes before on its trip east to New York's Penn Station. The date is March 31, 1963.

ORIG ROAD NUM.	PRR BASE CLASS	PRR REBLT CLASS	1966 ROAD NUM.	PRR CLASS (1966)	BLDR	BLDR MODEL	BLDR SERIAL NUM.	BLDR DATE	RETIRE DATE	NOTE
5712A	EP-22			EP-22	EMD	E8A	16781	Oct 52	to PC	
5713A	EP-22			EP-22	EMD	E8A	16782	Oct 52	to PC	
5714A	EP-22			EP-22	EMD	E8A	16783	Nov 52	to PC	
5715A	EP-22			EP-22	EMD	E8A	16784	Nov 52	to PC	
5716A	EP-22			EP-22	EMD	E8A	16785	Nov 52	to PC	
5750A	AP-20	AFP-20			Alco	PA-1	74697	Oct 47	Sep 62	(7)
5750B	AP-20	AFP-20			Alco	PB-1	75343	Oct 47	Sep 62	(7)
5751A	AP-20	AFP-20			Alco	PA-1	74698	Oct 47	Sep 62	(7)
5752A	AP-20	AFP-20			Alco	PA-1	74699	Oct 47	Sep 62	(7)
5752B	AP-20	AFP-20			Alco	PB-1	75344	Oct 47	Sep 62	(7)
5753A	AP-20	AFP-20			Alco	PA-1	74700	Oct 47	Sep 62	(7)
5754A	AP-20	AFP-20			Alco	PA-1	74701	Nov 47	Sep 62	(7)
5754B	AP-20	AFP-20			Alco	PB-1	75345	Nov 47	Sep 62	(7)
5755A	AP-20	AFP-20			Alco	PA-1	75323	Nov 47	Sep 62	(7)
5756A	AP-20	AFP-20			Alco	PA-1	75324	Nov 47	Sep 62	(7)
5756B	AP-20	AFP-20			Alco	PB-1	75346	Nov 47	Sep 62	(7)
5757A	AP-20	AFP-20			Alco	PA-1	75325	Nov 47	Sep 62	(7)
5758A	AP-20	AFP-20			Alco	PA-1	75326	Dec 47	Sep 62	(7)
5758B	AP-20	AFP-20			Alco	PB-1	75347	Dec 47	Sep 62	(7)
5759A	AP-20	AFP-20			Alco	PA-1	75327	Dec 47	Sep 62	(7)
5760A	EP-22		4260	EP-22	EMD	E8A	16786	Nov 52	to PC	
5761A	EP-22		4261	EP-22	EMD	E8A	16787	Nov 52	to PC	
5762A	EP-22		4262	EP-22	EMD	E8A	16788	Nov 52	to PC	
5763A	EP-22		4263	EP-22	EMD	E8A	16789	Nov 52	to PC	
5764A	EP-22		4264	EP-22	EMD	E8A	16790	Nov 52	to PC	
5765A	EP-22		4265	EP-22	EMD	E8A	15648	Mar 52	to PC	
5766A	EP-22		4266	EP-22	EMD	E8A	15649	Mar 52	to PC	
5767A	EP-22		4267	EP-22	EMD	E8A	15650	Apr 52	to PC	
5768A	EP-22		4268	EP-22	EMD	E8A	15651	Apr 52	to PC	
5769A	EP-22		4269	EP-22	EMD	E8A	15652	May 52	to PC	
5770A	BP-20				BLW	DR 6-4-2000	73505	Jun 48	Jun 64	
5770B	BP-20				BLW	DR 6-4-2000	73523	Jun 48	Mar 62	
5771A	BP-20				BLW	DR 6-4-2000	73506	Jun 48	May 65	
5772A	BP-20				BLW	DR 6-4-2000	73507	Aug 48	Jun 64	
5772B	BP-20				BLW	DR 6-4-2000	73524	Aug 48	Dec 63	
5773A	BP-20				BLW	DR 6-4-2000	73508	Aug 48	May 65	
5774A	BP-20				BLW	DR 6-4-2000	73509	Sep 48	Aug 64	
5774B	BP-20				BLW	DR 6-4-2000	73525	Sep 48	Dec 63	
5775A	BP-20				BLW	DR 6-4-2000	73510	Sep 48	Mar 64	
5776A	BP-20				BLW	DR 6-4-2000	73511	Sep 48	Jun 64	
5776B	BP-20				BLW	DR 6-4-2000	73526	Sep 48	Dec 63	
5777A	BP-20				BLW	DR 6-4-2000	73512	Sep 48	May 65	(8)
5778A	BP-20				BLW	DR 6-4-2000	73513	Oct 48	Mar 64	
5778B	BP-20				BLW	DR 6-4-2000	73527	Oct 48	Dec 63	
5779A	BP-20				BLW	DR 6-4-2000	73514	Oct 48	May 65	
5780A	BP-20				BLW	DR 6-4-2000	73515	Oct 48	Nov 64	
5780B	BP-20	BF-16z			BLW	DR 6-4-2000	73528	Oct 48	Sep 62	(8)
5781A	BP-20				BLW	DR 6-4-2000	73516	Oct 48	Jun 64	
5782A	BP-20				BLW	DR 6-4-2000	73517	Oct 48	Mar 65	
5782B	BP-20	BF-16z			BLW	DR 6-4-2000	73529	Nov 48	Sep 62	(8)
5783A	BP-20				BLW	DR 6-4-2000	73518	Nov 48	Nov 64	
5784A	BP-20	BF-16z			BLW	DR 6-4-2000	73519	Nov 48	Sep 62	(8)
5784B	BP-20	BF-16z			BLW	DR 6-4-2000	73530	Nov 48	Sep 62	(8)
5785A	BP-20	BF-16z			BLW	DR 6-4-2000	73520	Nov 48	Sep 62	(8)
5786A	BP-20	BF-16z			BLW	DR 6-4-2000	73521	Dec 48	Sep 62	(8)
5786B	BP-20	BF-16z			BLW	DR 6-4-2000	73531	Dec 48	Sep 62	(8)
5787A	BP-20	BF-16z			BLW	DR 6-4-2000	73522	Dec 48	Sep 62	(8)
5788A	EP-22		4248	EP-22	EMD	E8A	15653	May 52	to PC	
5789A	EP-22		4249	EP-22	EMD	E8A	15654	May 52	to PC	
5790A	EP-22		4250	EP-22	EMD	E8A	15655	May 52	to PC	
5791A	EP-22		4251	EP-22	EMD	E8A	15656	May 52	to PC	
5792A	EP-22		4252	EP-22	EMD	E8A	15657	May 52	to PC	
5793A	EP-22		4253	EP-22	EMD	E8A	15658	Jun 52	to PC	
5794A	EP-22		4254	EP-22	EMD	E8A	15659	Jun 52	to PC	
5795A	EP-22		4255	EP-22	EMD	E8A	15660	Jun 52	to PC	
5796A	EP-22		4256	EP-22	EMD	E8A	15661	Jun 52	to PC	
5797A	EP-22		4257	EP-22	EMD	E8A	15662	Jun 52	to PC	
5798A	EP-22		4258	EP-22	EMD	E8A	15663	Jun 52	to PC	
5799A	EP-22		4259	EP-22	EMD	E8A	15664	Jun 52	to PC	
5801A	EP-22		4301	EP-22	EMD	E8A	15665	Jul 52	to PC	
5802A	EP-22		4282	EP-22	EMD	E8A	15666	Jul 52	to PC	
5803A	EP-22		4283	EP-22	EMD	E8A	15667	Jul 52	to PC	
5804A	EP-22		4281	EP-22	EMD	E8A	15668	Jul 52	to PC	
5805A	EP-22		4270	EP-22	EMD	E8A	15669	Jul 52	to PC	
5806A	EP-22		4306	EP-22	EMD	E8A	15670	Jul 52	to PC	
5807A	EP-22		4307	EP-22	EMD	E8A	15671	Jul 52	to PC	
5808A	EP-22		4308	EP-22	EMD	E8A	13101	Jan 51	to PC	
5809A	EP-22		4309	EP-22	EMD	E8A	13102	Jan 51	to PC	
5810A	EP-22		4310	EP-22	EMD	E8A	13103	Jan 51	to PC	
5811	BP-60a			BH-50	BLW	DR 12-8-3000	73131A2	Mar 47	Apr 62	(9)

Pennsylvania Railroad Diesel Locomotive Roster

ORIG ROAD NUM.	PRR BASE CLASS	PRR REBLT CLASS	1966 ROAD NUM.	PRR CLASS (1966)	BLDR	BLDR MODEL	BLDR SERIAL NUM.	BLDR DATE	RETIRE DATE	NOTE
5812	BP-60a	BH-50			BLW	DR 12-8-3000	73377A2	Apr 47	Apr 62	(9)
5813	BP-60a	BH-50			BLW	DR 12-8-3000	73378A2	May 47	Sep 62	(9)
5814	BP-60a	BH-50			BLW	DR 12-8-3000	73379A2	Sep 47	Apr 62	(9)
5815	BP-60a	BH-50			BLW	DR 12-8-3000	73380A2	Oct 47	Sep 62	(9)
5816	BP-60a	BH-50			BLW	DR 12-8-3000	73381A2	Nov 47	Sep 62	(9)
5817	BP-60a	BH-50			BLW	DR 12-8-3000	73382A2	Dec 47	Sep 62	(9)
5818	BP-60a	BH-50			BLW	DR 12-8-3000	73383A2	Jan 48	Apr 62	(9)
5819	BP-60a	BH-50			BLW	DR 12-8-3000	73384A2	Jan 48	Apr 62	(9)
5820	BP-60a	BH-50			BLW	DR 12-8-3000	73385A2	Feb 48	Sep 62	(9)
5821	BP-60a	BH-50			BLW	DR 12-8-3000	73386A2	Feb 48	Apr 62	(9)
5822	BP-60a	BH-50			BLW	DR 12-8-3000	73387A2	Feb 48	Sep 62	(9)
5823	BP-60a	BH-50			BLW	DR 12-8-3000	73131A1	Mar 47	Apr 62	(9)
5824	BP-60a	BH-50			BLW	DR 12-8-3000	73377A1	Apr 47	Apr 62	(9)
5825	BP-60a	BH-50			BLW	DR 12-8-3000	73378A1	May 47	Apr 62	(9)
5826	BP-60a	BH-50			BLW	DR 12-8-3000	73379A1	Sep 48	Sep 62	(9)
5827	BP-60a	BH-50			BLW	DR 12-8-3000	73380A1	Oct 48	Sep 62	(9)
5828	BP-60a	BH-50			BLW	DR 12-8-3000	73381A1	Nov 48	Apr 62	(9)
5829	BP-60a	BH-50			BLW	DR 12-8-3000	73382A1	Dec 48	Apr 62	(9)
5830	BP-60a	BH-50			BLW	DR 12-8-3000	73383A1	Jan 48	Sep 62	(9)
5831	BP-60a	BH-50			BLW	DR 12-8-3000	73384A1	Jan 48	Sep 62	(9)
5832	BP-60a	BH-50			BLW	DR 12-8-3000	73385A1	Feb 48	Apr 62	(9)
5833	BP-60a	BH-50			BLW	DR 12-8-3000	73386A1	Feb 48	Apr 62	(9)
5834	BP-60a	BH-50			BLW	DR 12-8-3000	73387A1	Feb 48	Apr 62	(9)
5835A	EP-22		4317	EP-22	EMD	E8A	13104	Jan 51	to PC	
5836A	EP-22		4246	EP-22	EMD	E8A	13105	Feb 51	to PC	
5837A	EP-22		4247	EP-22	EMD	E8A	13106	Feb 51	to PC	
5838A	EP-22		4318	EP-22	EMD	E8A	13107	Feb 51	to PC	
5839A	EP-22		4319	EP-22	EMD	E8A	13108	Feb 51	to PC	
5840A	EP-20		4240	EP-20	EMD	E7A	3976	Aug 47	to PC	
5840B	EP-20		4115	EP-20	EMD	E7B	3992	Aug 47	to PC	
5841A	EP-20		4241	EP-20	EMD	E7A	3977	Aug 47	to PC	
5842A	EP-20		4242	EP-20	EMD	E7A	3978	Aug 47	to PC	
5842B	EP-20		4116	EP-20	EMD	E7B	3993	Aug 47	to PC	
5843A	EP-20		4243	EP-20	EMD	E7A	3979	Aug 47	to PC	
5844A	EP-20		4244	EP-20	EMD	E7A	3980	Aug 47	to PC	
5844B	EP-20		4117	EP-20	EMD	E7B	3994	Aug 47	to PC	
5845A	EP-20		4245	EP-20	EMD	E7A	3981	Aug 47	to PC	
5846A	EP-20		4206	EP-20	EMD	E7A	3982	Aug 47	to PC	
5846B	EP-20		4118	EP-20	EMD	E7B	3995	Aug 47	to PC	
5847A	EP-20				EMD	E7A	3983	Aug 47	Jun 64	
5848A	EP-20		4208	EP-20	EMD	E7A	3984	Aug 47	to PC	
5848B	EP-20		4119	EP-20	EMD	E7B	3996	Aug 47	to PC	
5849A	EP-20		4209	EP-20	EMD	E7A	3985	Aug 47	to PC	
5850A	EP-20		4210	EP-20	EMD	E7A	3986	Aug 47	to PC	
5850B	EP-20		4120	EP-20	EMD	E7B	3997	Aug 47	to PC	
5851A	EP-20		4211	EP-20	EMD	E7A	3987	Aug 47	to PC	
5852A	EP-20		4212	EP-20	EMD	E7A	3988	Sep 47	to PC	
5852B	EP-20		4121	EP-20	EMD	E7B	3998	Sep 47	Sep 67	
5853A	EP-20		4213	EP-20	EMD	E7A	3989	Sep 47	to PC	

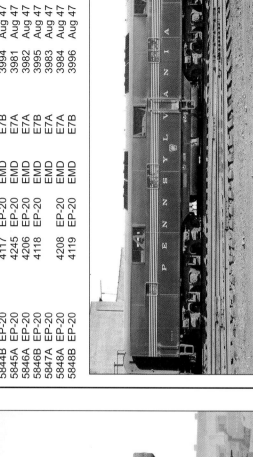

Full side view of E7B unit 5842B. The unit was only about four months old, but the reason why the painted stripes on the windows did not last long is apparent—the paint did not adhere to the glass.

PRR 5824 presents this solid looking nose to the railroad world. As described in the text on the Centipedes, the carbody containing the engines, generators, control equipment and the cab, is mounted on a pair of cast frames at six points. The separation between the carbody and the frame is apparent in this view. Because of this construction, none of the buffing load was carried by the carbody.

Left table

ORIG ROAD NUM.	PRR BASE CLASS	PRR REBLT CLASS	1966 ROAD NUM.	PRR CLASS (1966)	BLDR	BLDR MODEL	BLDR SERIAL NUM.	BLDR DATE	RETIRE DATE	NOTE
5854A	EP-20		4214	EP-20	EMD	E7A	3990	Sep 47	to PC	
5854B	EP-20		4122	EP-20	EMD	E7B	3999	Sep 47	to PC	
5855A	EP-20		4215	EP-20	EMD	E7A	3991	Sep 47	Sep 67	
5856A	EP-20		4216	EP-20	EMD	E7A	5073	Feb 48	to PC	
5856B	EP-20		4123	EP-20	EMD	E7B	5083	Feb 48	to PC	
5857A	EP-20		4217	EP-20	EMD	E7A	5074	Feb 48	to PC	
5858A	EP-20		4218	EP-20	EMD	E7A	5075	Feb 48	Mar 67	
5858B	EP-20		4124	EP-20	EMD	E7B	5084	Feb 48	to PC	
5859A	EP-20		4219	EP-20	EMD	E7A	5076	Feb 48	to PC	
5860A	EP-20		4220	EP-20	EMD	E7A	5077	Feb 48	to PC	
5860B	EP-20		4125	EP-20	EMD	E7B	5085	Feb 48	to PC	
5861A	EP-20		4221	EP-20	EMD	E7A	5078	Feb 48	to PC	
5862A	EP-20		4222	EP-20	EMD	E7A	5079	Feb 48	Sep 67	
5862B	EP-20		4126	EP-20	EMD	E7B	5086	Feb 48	to PC	
5863A	EP-20		4223	EP-20	EMD	E7A	5080	Feb 48	to PC	
5864A	EP-20		4224	EP-20	EMD	E7A	5081	Feb 48	to PC	
5864B	EP-20		4127	EP-20	EMD	E7B	5087	Feb 48	Mar 67	
5865A	EP-20		4225	EP-20	EMD	E7A	5082	Feb 48	to PC	
5866A	EP-20		4226	EP-20	EMD	E7A	7836	Mar 49	to PC	
5867A	EP-20		4227	EP-20	EMD	E7A	7837	Mar 49	to PC	
5868A	EP-20		4228	EP-20	EMD	E7A	7838	Apr 49	to PC	
5869A	EP-20		4229	EP-20	EMD	E7A	7839	Apr 49	to PC	
5870A	EP-20		4230	EP-20	EMD	E7A	7840	Apr 49	to PC	
5871A	EP-20		4231	EP-20	EMD	E7A	7841	Apr 49	to PC	
5872A	EP-20		4232	EP-20	EMD	E7A	7842	Apr 49	to PC	
5873A	EP-20		4233	EP-20	EMD	E7A	7843	Apr 49	to PC	
5874A	EP-20		4234	EP-20	EMD	E7A	7844	Apr 49	to PC	
5875A	EP-20		4235	EP-20	EMD	E7A	7845	Apr 49	to PC	
5876A	EP-20				EMD	E7A	7846	Apr 49	Mar 66	
5877A	EP-20		4237	EP-20	EMD	E7A	7847	Apr 49	to PC	
5878A	EP-20		4238	EP-20	EMD	E7A	7848	Apr 49	to PC	
5879A	EP-20		4239	EP-20	EMD	E7A	7849	Apr 49	to PC	
5880A	EP-22		4204	EP-22	EMD	E8A	8619	Apr 49	to PC	
5881A	EP-22		4205	EP-22	EMD	E8A	8620	Apr 49	to PC	
5882A	EP-22		4203	EP-22	EMD	E8A	8621	Apr 49	to PC	
5883A	EP-22		4284	EP-22	EMD	E8A	8622	Apr 49	to PC	
5884A	EP-22		4285	EP-22	EMD	E8A	10421	Mar 50	to PC	
5885A	EP-22		4286	EP-22	EMD	E8A	10422	Mar 50	to PC	
5886A	EP-22		4287	EP-22	EMD	E8A	10423	Apr 50	to PC	
5887A	EP-22		4288	EP-22	EMD	E8A	10424	Apr 50	to PC	
5888A	EP-22		4289	EP-22	EMD	E8A	10425	Apr 50	to PC	
5889A	EP-22		4290	EP-22	EMD	E8A	10426	Apr 50	to PC	
5890A	EP-22		4291	EP-22	EMD	E8A	10427	Apr 50	to PC	
5891A	EP-22		4292	EP-22	EMD	E8A	10428	Apr 50	to PC	
5892A	EP-22		4293	EP-22	EMD	E8A	10429	Apr 50	to PC	
5893A	EP-22		4294	EP-22	EMD	E8A	10430	Apr 50	to PC	
5894A	EP-22		4295	EP-22	EMD	E8A	13109	Mar 51	to PC	
5895A	EP-22		4296	EP-22	EMD	E8A	13110	Mar 51	to PC	
5896A	EP-22		4297	EP-22	EMD	E8A	13111	Mar 51	to PC	
5897A	EP-22		4298	EP-22	EMD	E8A	13112	Mar 51	to PC	
5898A	EP-22		4299	EP-22	EMD	E8A	13113	Mar 51	to PC	
5899A	EP-22			EP-22	EMD	E8A	13114	Mar 51	to PC	

Right table

ORIG ROAD NUM.	PRR BASE CLASS	PRR REBLT CLASS	1966 ROAD NUM.	PRR CLASS (1966)	BLDR	BLDR MODEL	BLDR SERIAL NUM.	BLDR DATE	RETIRE DATE	NOTE
5900A	EP-20		4200	EP-20	EMD	E7A	3356	Sep 45	to PC	
5900B	EP-20		4114	EP-20	EMD	E7B	5088	Apr 47	to PC	
5901A	EP-20		4201	EP-20	EMD	E7A	3357	Sep 45	to PC	
5902A	EP-22		4302	EP-22	EMD	E8A	13115	Mar 51	to PC	
5903A	EP-22		4303	EP-22	EMD	E8A	13116	Mar 51	to PC	
5904A	EP-22		4304	EP-22	EMD	E8A	13117	Apr 51	to PC	
5905A	EP-22		4305	EP-22	EMD	E8A	13118	Apr 51	to PC	
5906	AS-10s		9916	ARS-10sx	Alco	RS-1	76214	Dec 48	to PC	
5907	BS-6				BLW	VO-660	64247	Mar 42	Jun 64	
5908	BS-6				BLW	VO-660	64393	Aug 42	Jun 64	
5909	BS-6				BLW	VO-660	64395	Aug 42	Jun 64	
5910	ES-6		8510	ES-6	EMC	SW1	1852	Aug 42	to PC	(10)
5911	ES-6(5911)		8511	ES-6	EMC	SW	680	Jun 37	to PC	(11)
5912	ES-10		8677	ES-10	EMC	NW2	1426	Oct 41	Jun 64	
5913	BS-10				BLW	VO-1000	69662	Sep 43	Jun 64	
5914	BS-10				BLW	VO-1000	69663	Sep 43	Jul 65	
5915	BS-10				BLW	VO-1000	69664	Sep 43	Jun 64	
5916	BS-10				BLW	VO-1000	69665	Sep 43	Jun 64	
5917	BS-10				BLW	VO-1000	69666	Sep 43	Jun 64	
5918	BS-10				BLW	VO-1000	69784	Oct 43	Jul 65	
5919	BS-10				BLW	VO-1000	71552	Oct 45	Apr 65	
5920	BS-10				BLW	VO-1000	71553	Oct 45	Jun 64	
5921	ES-10		8651	ES-10	EMD	NW2	3417	Apr 46	to PC	
5922	ES-10		8652	ES-10	EMD	NW2	3418	Nov 45	to PC	
5923	ES-10		8653	ES-10	EMD	NW2	4954	Oct 47	to PC	

PRR 5900A-5900B-5901A at Harrisburg on June 16, 1947. The B-unit had been built two months previously and brought the original E7 set to the 3-unit standard set by the second order of these EMD units. The photo shows the train-phone antenna added to the A-units by PRR.

Pennsylvania Railroad Diesel Locomotive Roster

Pennsylvania Railroad Diesel Locomotive Roster

ORIG ROAD NUM.	PRR BASE CLASS	PRR REBLT CLASS	1966 ROAD NUM.	PRR CLASS (1966)	BLDR	BLDR MODEL	BLDR SERIAL NUM.	BLDR DATE	RETIRE DATE	NOTE
5924	ES-10		8654	ES-10	EMD	NW2	4955	Oct 47	to PC	
5925	ES-10		8678	ES-10	EMD	NW2	4956	Oct 47	to PC	
5926	AS-10		9826	AS-10	Alco	S-2	75916	Jul 48	to PC	
5927	AS-10		9827	AS-10	Alco	S-2	75917	Aug 48	to PC	
5928	AS-10		9828	AS-10	Alco	S-2	75918	Aug 48	to PC	
5929	AS-10		9829	AS-10	Alco	S-2	75920	Aug 48	to PC	
5930	AS-10		9820	AS-10	Alco	S-2	75921	Aug 48	to PC	
5931	AS-10		9821	AS-10	Alco	S-2	75922	Aug 48	to PC	
5932	BS-6				BLW	VO-660	64401	Sep 42	Jul 65	
5933	BS-6				BLW	VO-660	64402	Sep 42	Jul 65	
5934	BS-6				BLW	VO-660	64403	Sep 42	Jul 65	
5935	BS-6				BLW	VO-660	64404	Oct 42	Jun 64	
5936	BS-6				BLW	VO-660	64405	Oct 42	Aug 64	
5937	BS-6				BLW	VO-660	64406	Oct 42	Jul 65	
5941	BS-6				BLW	VO-660	72821	Oct 45	Jul 65	
5942	BS-6				BLW	VO-660	72822	Oct 45	Jun 64	
5943	BS-6				BLW	VO-660	72827	Nov 45	Jun 64	
5944	ES-6		8544	ES-6	EMD	SW1	3414	Jun 46	to PC	
5945	ES-6		8545	ES-6	EMD	SW1	3415	Jun 46	to PC	
5946	ES-6		8546	ES-6	EMD	SW1	3416	Jun 46	to PC	
5947	ES-6		8547	ES-6	EMD	SW1	3580	Jun 46	to PC	
5948	ES-6		8548	ES-6	EMD	SW1	3581	Jun 46	to PC	
5949	ES-6		8549	ES-6	EMD	SW1	3582	Jul 46	to PC	
5950	ES-6		8550	ES-6	EMD	SW1	3583	Jul 46	to PC	
5951	ES-6		8551	ES-6	EMD	SW1	3584	Jul 46	to PC	
5952	ES-6		8552	ES-6	EMD	SW1	4957	Sep 47	to PC	
5953	ES-6		8553	ES-6	EMD	SW1	4958	Sep 47	to PC	
5954	AS-6		9454	AS-6	Alco	S-1	75231	May 47	to PC	
5955	AS-6		9455	AS-6	Alco	S-1	75232	Jun 47	to PC	
5956	AS-6		9456	AS-6	Alco	S-1	75233	Jun 47	to PC	
5957	BS-6a				BLW	DS 4-4-660	73618	Mar 48	Mar 67	
5958	BS-6a		7858	BS-6	BLW	DS 4-4-660	73619	Mar 48	Sep 67	
5959	BS-6a				BLW	DS 4-4-660	73620	Mar 48	May 65	
5960	BS-6a		7860	BS-6	BLW	DS 4-4-660	73621	Mar 48	to PC	
5961	BS-6a		7861	BS-6	BLW	DS 4-4-660	73622	Mar 48	to PC	
5962	BS-6a		7862	BS-6	BLW	DS 4-4-660	73623	Mar 48	to PC	
5963	BS-6a				BLW	DS 4-4-660	73624	Mar 48	Feb 66	
5964	BS-6a		7864	BS-6	BLW	DS 4-4-660	73625	Apr 48	to PC	
5965	BS-6a				BLW	DS 4-4-660	73626	Apr 48	May 65	
5966	BS-6a		7866	BS-6	BLW	DS 4-4-660	73627	Apr 48	Jul 66	
5967	BS-10a				BLW	DS 4-4-1000	73585	Mar 48	to PC	
5968	BS-10a		7938	BS-10	BLW	DS 4-4-1000	73586	Mar 48	to PC	
5969	BS-10a		7939	BS-10	BLW	DS 4-4-1000	73587	Mar 48	to PC	
5970	BS-10a		7940	BS-10	BLW	DS 4-4-1000	73588	Mar 48	to PC	
5971	BS-10a		7941	BS-10	BLW	DS 4-4-1000	73589	Mar 48	to PC	
5972	BS-10a		7942	BS-10	BLW	DS 4-4-1000	73590	Mar 48	to PC	
5973	BS-10a		7943	BS-10	BLW	DS 4-4-1000	73591	Mar 48	to PC	
5974	BS-10a		7944	BS-10	BLW	DS 4-4-1000	73592	Mar 48	Mar 67	
5975	BS-10a		7945	BS-10	BLW	DS 4-4-1000	73593	Apr 48	to PC	
5976	BS-10a		7946	BS-10	BLW	DS 4-4-1000	73594	Apr 48	to PC	
5977	BS-10a		7947	BS-10	BLW	DS 4-4-1000	73595	Apr 48	to PC	
5978	BS-10am		8038	BS-10m	BLW	DS 4-4-1000	73603	May 48	to PC	
5979	BS-10am		8039	BS-10m	BLW	DS 4-4-1000	73604	May 48	to PC	
5980	FS-10		8211	FS-10	FM	H10-44	10L61	Jun 48	to PC	
5981	FS-10		8212	FS-10	FM	H10-44	10L62	Jun 48	to PC	
5982	FS-10		8213	FS-10	FM	H10-44	10L63	Jun 48	Jun 67	
5983	FS-10		8214	FS-10	FM	H10-44	10L66	Jun 48	Sep 67	
5984	FS-10		8215	FS-10	FM	H10-44	10L67	Jun 48	to PC	
5985	FS-10		8216	FS-10	FM	H10-44	10L68	Jun 48	to PC	
5986	FS-10		8217	FS-10	FM	H10-44	10L69	Jun 48	to PC	
5987	ES-6		8587	ES-6	EMD	SW1	5664	Mar 48	to PC	
5988	ES-6		8588	ES-6	EMD	SW1	5665	Mar 48	to PC	
5989	ES-6		8589	ES-6	EMD	SW1	5666	Mar 48	to PC	
5990	ES-6		8590	ES-6	EMD	SW1	5667	Mar 48	to PC	
5991	ES-6		8591	ES-6	EMD	SW1	5668	Apr 48	to PC	
5992	ES-6		8592	ES-6	EMD	SW1	5669	Apr 48	to PC	
5993	ES-6		8593	ES-6	EMD	SW1	5670	Apr 48	to PC	
5994	ES-6		8594	ES-6	EMD	SW1	5671	Apr 48	to PC	
5995	ES-6		8595	ES-6	EMD	SW1	5673	Apr 48	to PC	
5996	ES-6		8596	ES-6	EMD	SW1	5674	Apr 48	to PC	
5997	ES-6		8597	ES-6	EMD	SW1	5675	Apr 48	to PC	
5998	ES-6		8598	ES-6	EMD	SW1	5676	Apr 48	to PC	
5999	ES-6		8599	ES-6	EMD	SW1		Apr 48	to PC	
6000	EF-25a		6000	EF-25a	EMD	SD35	30388	Feb 65	to PC	
6001	EF-25a		6001	EF-25a	EMD	SD35	30389	Feb 65	to PC	
6002	EF-25a		6002	EF-25a	EMD	SD35	30390	Feb 65	to PC	
6003	EF-25a		6003	EF-25a	EMD	SD35	30391	Feb 65	to PC	
6004	EF-25a		6004	EF-25a	EMD	SD35	30392	Mar 65	to PC	
6005	EF-25a		6005	EF-25a	EMD	SD35	30393	Mar 65	to PC	
6006	EF-25a		6006	EF-25a	EMD	SD35	30394	Mar 65	to PC	
6007	EF-25a		6007	EF-25a	EMD	SD35	30395	Mar 65	to PC	

DOUGLAS COLLECTION

PRR 5921 at Cadillac, Michigan on July 15, 1964. The 5921 was one of the first units delivered to the PRR after World War II and it was assigned to the western end of the PRR for most of its life.

PRR's first EMD SD35 unit, the 6000 is seen here at Chicago on August 15, 1967. This is the unit that started a practice on the PRR, PC and Conrail of number-ing six-axle diesels in the 6000 series.

ORIG ROAD NUM.	PRR BASE CLASS	PRR REBLT CLASS	1966 ROAD NUM.	PRR CLASS (1966)	BLDR	BLDR MODEL	BLDR SERIAL NUM.	BLDR DATE	RETIRE DATE	NOTE
6008	EF-25a		6008	EF-25a	EMD	SD35	30396	Mar 65	to PC	
6009	EF-25a		6009	EF-25a	EMD	SD35	30397	Mar 65	to PC	
6010	EF-25a		6010	EF-25a	EMD	SD35	30398	Mar 65	to PC	
6011	EF-25a		6011	EF-25a	EMD	SD35	30399	Mar 65	to PC	
6012	EF-25a		6012	EF-25a	EMD	SD35	30400	Mar 65	to PC	
6013	EF-25a		6013	EF-25a	EMD	SD35	30401	Mar 65	to PC	
6014	EF-25a		6014	EF-25a	EMD	SD35	30402	Mar 65	to PC	
6015	EF-25a		6015	EF-25a	EMD	SD35	30403	Mar 65	to PC	
6016	EF-25a		6016	EF-25a	EMD	SD35	30404	Mar 65	to PC	
6017	EF-25a		6017	EF-25a	EMD	SD35	30405	Mar 65	to PC	
6018	EF-25a		6018	EF-25a	EMD	SD35	30406	Mar 65	to PC	
6019	EF-25a		6019	EF-25a	EMD	SD35	30407	Mar 65	to PC	
6020	EF-25a		6020	EF-25a	EMD	SD35	30408	Apr 65	to PC	
6021	EF-25a		6021	EF-25a	EMD	SD35	30409	Apr 65	to PC	
6022	EF-25a		6022	EF-25a	EMD	SD35	30410	Apr 65	to PC	
6023	EF-25a		6023	EF-25a	EMD	SD35	30411	Apr 65	to PC	
6024	EF-25a		6024	EF-25a	EMD	SD35	30412	Apr 65	to PC	
6025	EF-25a		6025	EF-25a	EMD	SD35	30413	Apr 65	to PC	
6026	EF-25a		6026	EF-25a	EMD	SD35	30414	Apr 65	to PC	
6027	EF-25a		6027	EF-25a	EMD	SD35	30415	Apr 65	to PC	
6028	EF-25a		6028	EF-25a	EMD	SD35	30416	Apr 65	to PC	
6029	EF-25a		6029	EF-25a	EMD	SD35	30417	Apr 65	to PC	
6030	EF-25a		6030	EF-25a	EMD	SD35	30418	Apr 65	to PC	
6031	EF-25a		6031	EF-25a	EMD	SD35	30419	Apr 65	to PC	
6032	EF-25a		6032	EF-25a	EMD	SD35	30420	Apr 65	to PC	
6033	EF-25a		6033	EF-25a	EMD	SD35	30421	Apr 65	to PC	
6034	EF-25a		6034	EF-25a	EMD	SD35	30422	Apr 65	to PC	
6035	EF-25a		6035	EF-25a	EMD	SD35	30423	May 65	to PC	
6036	EF-25a		6036	EF-25a	EMD	SD35	30424	May 65	to PC	
6037	EF-25a		6037	EF-25a	EMD	SD35	30425	May 65	to PC	
6038	EF-25a		6038	EF-25a	EMD	SD35	30426	May 65	to PC	
6039	EF-25a		6039	EF-25a	EMD	SD35	30427	May 65	to PC	
6040	EF-30a		6040	EF-30a	EMD	SD40	31285	Feb 66	to PC	
6041	EF-30a		6041	EF-30a	EMD	SD40	31286	Feb 66	to PC	
6042	EF-30a		6042	EF-30a	EMD	SD40	31287	Feb 66	to PC	
6043	EF-30a		6043	EF-30a	EMD	SD40	31288	Feb 66	to PC	
6044	EF-30a		6044	EF-30a	EMD	SD40	31289	Feb 66	to PC	
6045	EF-30a		6045	EF-30a	EMD	SD40	31290	Feb 66	to PC	
6046	EF-30a		6046	EF-30a	EMD	SD40	31291	Feb 66	to PC	
6047	EF-30a		6047	EF-30a	EMD	SD40	31292	Feb 66	to PC	
6048	EF-30a		6048	EF-30a	EMD	SD40	31293	Feb 66	to PC	
6049	EF-30a		6049	EF-30a	EMD	SD40	31294	Feb 66	to PC	
6050	EF-30a		6050	EF-30a	EMD	SD40	31295	Feb 66	to PC	
6051	EF-30a		6051	EF-30a	EMD	SD40	31296	Feb 66	to PC	
6052	EF-30a		6052	EF-30a	EMD	SD40	31297	Feb 66	to PC	
6053	EF-30a		6053	EF-30a	EMD	SD40	31298	Feb 66	to PC	
6054	EF-30a		6054	EF-30a	EMD	SD40	31299	Feb 66	to PC	
6055	EF-30a		6055	EF-30a	EMD	SD40	31300	Feb 66	to PC	
6056	EF-30a		6056	EF-30a	EMD	SD40	31301	Feb 66	to PC	
6057	EF-30a		6057	EF-30a	EMD	SD40	31302	Feb 66	to PC	
6058	EF-30a		6058	EF-30a	EMD	SD40	31303	Feb 66	to PC	
6059	EF-30a		6059	EF-30a	EMD	SD40	31304	Feb 66	to PC	
6060	EF-30a		6060	EF-30a	EMD	SD40	31305	Feb 66	to PC	
6061	EF-30a		6061	EF-30a	EMD	SD40	31306	Feb 66	to PC	
6062	EF-30a		6062	EF-30a	EMD	SD40	31307	Feb 66	to PC	
6063	EF-30a		6063	EF-30a	EMD	SD40	31308	Feb 66	to PC	
6064	EF-30a		6064	EF-30a	EMD	SD40	31309	Feb 66	to PC	
6065	EF-30a		6065	EF-30a	EMD	SD40	31310	Feb 66	to PC	
6066	EF-30a		6066	EF-30a	EMD	SD40	31311	Feb 66	to PC	
6067	EF-30a		6067	EF-30a	EMD	SD40	31312	Feb 66	to PC	
6068	EF-30a		6068	EF-30a	EMD	SD40	31313	Feb 66	to PC	
6069	EF-30a		6069	EF-30a	EMD	SD40	31314	Feb 66	to PC	
6070	EF-30a		6070	EF-30a	EMD	SD40	31315	Feb 66	to PC	
6071	EF-30a		6071	EF-30a	EMD	SD40	31316	Feb 66	to PC	
6072	EF-30a		6072	EF-30a	EMD	SD40	31317	Feb 66	to PC	
6073	EF-30a		6073	EF-30a	EMD	SD40	31318	Feb 66	to PC	
6074	EF-30a		6074	EF-30a	EMD	SD40	31319	Feb 66	to PC	
6075	EF-30a		6075	EF-30a	EMD	SD40	31320	Feb 66	to PC	
6076	EF-30a		6076	EF-30a	EMD	SD40	31321	Feb 66	to PC	
6077	EF-30a		6077	EF-30a	EMD	SD40	31322	Feb 66	to PC	
6078	EF-30a		6078	EF-30a	EMD	SD40	31323	Feb 66	to PC	
6079	EF-30a		6079	EF-30a	EMD	SD40	31324	Mar 66	to PC	
6080	EF-30a		6080	EF-30a	EMD	SD40	31325	Mar 66	to PC	
6081	EF-30a		6081	EF-30a	EMD	SD40	31326	Mar 66	to PC	
6082	EF-30a		6082	EF-30a	EMD	SD40	31327	Mar 66	to PC	
6083	EF-30a		6083	EF-30a	EMD	SD40	31328	Mar 66	to PC	
6084	EF-30a		6084	EF-30a	EMD	SD40	31329	Mar 66	to PC	
6085	EF-30a		6085	EF-30a	EMD	SD40	31330	Mar 66	to PC	
6086	EF-30a		6086	EF-30a	EMD	SD40	31331	Mar 66	to PC	
6087	EF-30a		6087	EF-30a	EMD	SD40	31332	Mar 66	to PC	
6088	EF-30a		6088	EF-30a	EMD	SD40	31333	Mar 66	to PC	
6089	EF-30a		6089	EF-30a	EMD	SD40	31334	Mar 66	to PC	
6090	EF-30a		6090	EF-30a	EMD	SD40	31335	Mar 66	to PC	
6091	EF-30a		6091	EF-30a	EMD	SD40	31336	Mar 66	to PC	

Pennsylvania Railroad Diesel Locomotive Roster

Pennsylvania Railroad Diesel Locomotive Roster

ORIG ROAD NUM.	PRR BASE CLASS	PRR REBLT CLASS	1966 ROAD NUM.	PRR CLASS (1966)	BLDR	BLDR MODEL	BLDR SERIAL NUM.	BLDR DATE	RETIRE DATE	NOTE
6092	EF-30a		6092	EF-30a	EMD	SD40	31337	Mar 66	to PC	
6093	EF-30a		6093	EF-30a	EMD	SD40	31338	Mar 66	to PC	
6094	EF-30a		6094	EF-30a	EMD	SD40	31339	Mar 66	to PC	
6095	EF-30a		6095	EF-30a	EMD	SD40	31340	Mar 66	to PC	
6096	EF-30a		6096	EF-30a	EMD	SD40	31341	Mar 66	to PC	
6097	EF-30a		6097	EF-30a	EMD	SD40	31342	Mar 66	to PC	
6098	EF-30a		6098	EF-30a	EMD	SD40	31343	Mar 66	to PC	
6099	EF-30a		6099	EF-30a	EMD	SD40	31344	Mar 66	to PC	
6100	EF-30a		6100	EF-30a	EMD	SD40	31345	Mar 66	to PC	
6101	EF-30a		6101	EF-30a	EMD	SD40	31346	Mar 66	to PC	
6102	EF-30a		6102	EF-30a	EMD	SD40	31347	Mar 66	to PC	
6103	EF-30a		6103	EF-30a	EMD	SD40	31348	Mar 66	to PC	
6104	EF-30a		6104	EF-30a	EMD	SD40	31349	Mar 66	to PC	
6105	EF-36		6105	EF-36	EMD	SD45	32315	Oct 66	to PC	
6106	EF-36		6106	EF-36	EMD	SD45	32316	Oct 66	to PC	
6107	EF-36		6107	EF-36	EMD	SD45	32317	Oct 66	to PC	
6108	EF-36		6108	EF-36	EMD	SD45	32318	Oct 66	to PC	
6109	EF-36		6109	EF-36	EMD	SD45	32319	Oct 66	to PC	
6110	EF-36		6110	EF-36	EMD	SD45	32320	Oct 66	to PC	
6111	EF-36		6111	EF-36	EMD	SD45	32321	Oct 66	to PC	
6112	EF-36		6112	EF-36	EMD	SD45	32322	Oct 66	to PC	
6113	EF-36		6113	EF-36	EMD	SD45	32323	Oct 66	to PC	
6114	EF-36		6114	EF-36	EMD	SD45	32324	Oct 66	to PC	
6115	EF-36		6115	EF-36	EMD	SD45	32325	Oct 66	to PC	
6116	EF-36		6116	EF-36	EMD	SD45	32326	Oct 66	to PC	
6117	EF-36		6117	EF-36	EMD	SD45	32327	Oct 66	to PC	
6118	EF-36		6118	EF-36	EMD	SD45	32328	Oct 66	to PC	
6119	EF-36		6119	EF-36	EMD	SD45	32329	Oct 66	to PC	
6120	EF-36		6120	EF-36	EMD	SD45	32330	Oct 66	to PC	
6121	EF-36		6121	EF-36	EMD	SD45	32331	Oct 66	to PC	
6122	EF-36		6122	EF-36	EMD	SD45	32332	Oct 66	to PC	
6123	EF-36		6123	EF-36	EMD	SD45	32333	Oct 66	to PC	
6124	EF-36		6124	EF-36	EMD	SD45	32334	Nov 66	to PC	
6125	EF-36		6125	EF-36	EMD	SD45	32335	Nov 66	to PC	
6126	EF-36		6126	EF-36	EMD	SD45	32336	Nov 66	to PC	
6127	EF-36		6127	EF-36	EMD	SD45	32337	Nov 66	to PC	
6128	EF-36		6128	EF-36	EMD	SD45	32338	Nov 66	to PC	
6129	EF-36		6129	EF-36	EMD	SD45	32339	Nov 66	to PC	
6130	EF-36		6130	EF-36	EMD	SD45	32340	Nov 66	to PC	
6131	EF-36		6131	EF-36	EMD	SD45	32341	Nov 66	to PC	
6132	EF-36		6132	EF-36	EMD	SD45	32342	Nov 66	to PC	
6133	EF-36		6133	EF-36	EMD	SD45	32343	Nov 66	to PC	
6134	EF-36		6134	EF-36	EMD	SD45	32344	Nov 66	to PC	
6135	EF-36		6135	EF-36	EMD	SD45	32345	Nov 66	to PC	
6136	EF-36		6136	EF-36	EMD	SD45	32346	Nov 66	to PC	
6137	EF-36		6137	EF-36	EMD	SD45	32347	Nov 66	to PC	
6138	EF-36		6138	EF-36	EMD	SD45	32348	Nov 66	to PC	
6139	EF-36		6139	EF-36	EMD	SD45	32349	Dec 66	to PC	
6140	EF-36		6140	EF-36	EMD	SD45	32365	Dec 66	to PC	
6141	EF-36		6141	EF-36	EMD	SD45	32366	Jan 67	to PC	
6142	EF-36		6142	EF-36	EMD	SD45	32367	Jan 67	to PC	
6143	EF-36		6143	EF-36	EMD	SD45	32368	Jan 67	to PC	
6144	EF-36		6144	EF-36	EMD	SD45	32369	Jan 67	to PC	
6145	EF-36		6145	EF-36	EMD	SD45	32370	Jan 67	to PC	
6146	EF-36		6146	EF-36	EMD	SD45	32371	Jan 67	to PC	
6147	EF-36		6147	EF-36	EMD	SD45	32372	Jan 67	to PC	
6148	EF-36		6148	EF-36	EMD	SD45	32373	Jan 67	to PC	
6149	EF-36		6149	EF-36	EMD	SD45	32374	Jan 67	to PC	
6150	EF-36		6150	EF-36	EMD	SD45	32375	Jan 67	to PC	
6151	EF-36		6151	EF-36	EMD	SD45	32376	Jan 67	to PC	
6152	EF-36		6152	EF-36	EMD	SD45	32377	Jan 67	to PC	
6153	EF-36		6153	EF-36	EMD	SD45	32378	Jan 67	to PC	
6154	EF-36		6154	EF-36	EMD	SD45	32379	Jan 67	to PC	
6155	EF-36		6155	EF-36	EMD	SD45	32380	Jan 67	to PC	
6156	EF-36		6156	EF-36	EMD	SD45	32381	Jan 67	to PC	
6157	EF-36		6157	EF-36	EMD	SD45	32382	Jan 67	to PC	
6158	EF-36		6158	EF-36	EMD	SD45	32383	Jan 67	to PC	
6159	EF-36		6159	EF-36	EMD	SD45	32384	Jan 67	to PC	
6160	EF-36		6160	EF-36	EMD	SD45	32385	Jan 67	to PC	
6161	EF-36		6161	EF-36	EMD	SD45	32386	Jan 67	to PC	
6162	EF-36		6162	EF-36	EMD	SD45	32387	Jan 67	to PC	
6163	EF-36		6163	EF-36	EMD	SD45	32388	Jan 67	to PC	
6164	EF-36		6164	EF-36	EMD	SD45	32389	Jan 67	to PC	
6165	EF-36		6165	EF-36	EMD	SD45	32390	Jan 67	to PC	
6166	EF-36		6166	EF-36	EMD	SD45	32391	Jan 67	to PC	
6167	EF-36		6167	EF-36	EMD	SD45	32392	Jan 67	to PC	
6168	EF-36		6168	EF-36	EMD	SD45	32393	Jan 67	to PC	
6169	EF-36		6169	EF-36	EMD	SD45	32394	Jan 67	to PC	
6170	EF-36		6170	EF-36	EMD	SD45	33804	Dec 67	to PC	
6171	EF-36		6171	EF-36	EMD	SD45	33805	Dec 67	to PC	
6172	EF-36		6172	EF-36	EMD	SD45	33806	Dec 67	to PC	
6173	EF-36		6173	EF-36	EMD	SD45	33807	Dec 67	to PC	

PRR 6104 was the highest numbered SD40 on the PRR. It is seen here at Columbus, Ohio on March 11, 1967. The square decal on the side of the cab indicates that a radio had been installed on the unit.

ORIG ROAD NUM.	PRR BASE CLASS	PRR REBLT CLASS	1966 ROAD NUM.	PRR CLASS (1966)	BLDR	BLDR MODEL	BLDR SERIAL NUM.	BLDR DATE	RETIRE DATE	NOTE
6174	EF-36		6174	EF-36	EMD	SD45	33808	Dec 67	to PC	
6175	EF-36		6175	EF-36	EMD	SD45	33809	Dec 67	to PC	
6176	EF-36		6176	EF-36	EMD	SD45	33810	Dec 67	to PC	
6177	EF-36		6177	EF-36	EMD	SD45	33811	Dec 67	to PC	
6178	EF-36		6178	EF-36	EMD	SD45	33812	Dec 67	to PC	
6179	EF-36		6179	EF-36	EMD	SD45	33813	Dec 67	to PC	
6180	EF-36		6180	EF-36	EMD	SD45	33814	Dec 67	to PC	
6181	EF-36		6181	EF-36	EMD	SD45	33815	Dec 67	to PC	
6182	EF-36		6182	EF-36	EMD	SD45	33816	Dec 67	to PC	
6183	EF-36		6183	EF-36	EMD	SD45	33817	Dec 67	to PC	
6184	EF-36		6184	EF-36	EMD	SD45	33818	Dec 67	to PC	
6185	EF-36		6185	EF-36	EMD	SD45	33819	Dec 67	to PC	
6186	EF-36		6186	EF-36	EMD	SD45	33820	Dec 67	to PC	
6187	EF-36		6187	EF-36	EMD	SD45	33821	Dec 67	to PC	
6188	EF-36		6188	EF-36	EMD	SD45	33822	Dec 67	to PC	
6189	EF-36		6189	EF-36	EMD	SD45	33823	Jan 68	to PC	
6190	EF-36		6190	EF-36	EMD	SD45	33824	Jan 68	to PC	
6191	EF-36		6191	EF-36	EMD	SD45	33825	Jan 68	to PC	
6192	EF-36		6192	EF-36	EMD	SD45	33826	Jan 68	to PC	
6193	EF-36		6193	EF-36	EMD	SD45	33827	Jan 68	to PC	
6194	EF-36		6194	EF-36	EMD	SD45	33828	Jan 68	to PC	
6195	EF-36		6195	EF-36	EMD	SD45	33829	Jan 68	to PC	
6196	EF-36		6196	EF-36	EMD	SD45	33830	Jan 68	to PC	
6197	EF-36		6197	EF-36	EMD	SD45	33831	Jan 68	to PC	
6198	EF-36		6198	EF-36	EMD	SD45	33832	Jan 68	to PC	
6199	EF-36		6199	EF-36	EMD	SD45	33833	Jan 68	to PC	
6200	EF-36		6200	EF-36	EMD	SD45	33859	Jan 68	to PC	
6201	EF-36		6201	EF-36	EMD	SD45	33864	Jan 68	to PC	
6202	EF-36		6202	EF-36	EMD	SD45	33860	Jan 68	to PC	
6203	EF-36		6203	EF-36	EMD	SD45	33865	Jan 68	to PC	
6204	EF-36		6204	EF-36	EMD	SD45	33861	Jan 68	to PC	
6205	EF-36		6205	EF-36	EMD	SD45	33866	Jan 68	to PC	
6206	EF-36		6206	EF-36	EMD	SD45	33862	Jan 68	to PC	
6207	EF-36		6207	EF-36	EMD	SD45	33867	Jan 68	to PC	
6208	EF-36		6208	EF-36	EMD	SD45	33863	Jan 68	to PC	
6209	EF-36		6209	EF-36	EMD	SD45	33868	Jan 68	to PC	
6210	EF-36		6210	EF-36	EMD	SD45	33834	Jan 68	to PC	
6211	EF-36		6211	EF-36	EMD	SD45	33835	Jan 68	to PC	
6212	EF-36		6212	EF-36	EMD	SD45	33836	Jan 68	to PC	
6213	EF-36		6213	EF-36	EMD	SD45	33837	Jan 68	to PC	
6214	EF-36		6214	EF-36	EMD	SD45	33838	Jan 68	to PC	
6215	EF-36		6215	EF-36	EMD	SD45	33839	Jan 68	to PC	
6216	EF-36		6216	EF-36	EMD	SD45	33840	Jan 68	to PC	
6217	EF-36		6217	EF-36	EMD	SD45	33841	Jan 68	to PC	
6218	EF-36		6218	EF-36	EMD	SD45	33842	Jan 68	to PC	
6219	EF-36		6219	EF-36	EMD	SD45	33843	Jan 68	to PC	
6220	EF-36		6220	EF-36	EMD	SD45	33844	Jan 68	to PC	
6221	EF-36		6221	EF-36	EMD	SD45	33845	Jan 68	to PC	
6222	EF-36		6222	EF-36	EMD	SD45	33846	Jan 68	to PC	
6223	EF-36		6223	EF-36	EMD	SD45	33847	Jan 68	to PC	
6224	EF-36		6224	EF-36	EMD	SD45	33848	Jan 68	to PC	
6225	EF-36		6225	EF-36	EMD	SD45	33849	Jan 68	to PC	

ORIG ROAD NUM.	PRR BASE CLASS	PRR REBLT CLASS	1966 ROAD NUM.	PRR CLASS (1966)	BLDR	BLDR MODEL	BLDR SERIAL NUM.	BLDR DATE	RETIRE DATE	NOTE
6226	EF-36		6226	EF-36	EMD	SD45	33850	Jan 68	to PC	
6227	EF-36		6227	EF-36	EMD	SD45	33851	Jan 68	to PC	
6228	EF-36		6228	EF-36	EMD	SD45	33852	Jan 68	to PC	
6229	EF-36		6229	EF-36	EMD	SD45	33853	Jan 68	to PC	
6230	EF-36		6230	EF-36	EMD	SD45	33854	Jan 68	to PC	
6231	EF-36		6231	EF-36	EMD	SD45	33855	Jan 68	to PC	
6232	EF-36		6232	EF-36	EMD	SD45	33856	Jan 68	to PC	
6233	EF-36		6233	EF-36	EMD	SD45	33857	Jan 68	to PC	
6234	EF-36		6234	EF-36	EMD	SD45	33858	Jan 68	to PC	
6300	AF-27		6300	AF-27	Alco	C-628	3404-1	Mar 65	to PC	
6301	AF-27		6301	AF-27	Alco	C-628	3404-2	Mar 65	to PC	
6302	AF-27		6302	AF-27	Alco	C-628	3404-3	Mar 65	to PC	
6303	AF-27		6303	AF-27	Alco	C-628	3404-4	Mar 65	to PC	
6304	AF-27		6304	AF-27	Alco	C-628	3404-5	Mar 65	to PC	
6305	AF-27		6305	AF-27	Alco	C-628	3404-6	Mar 65	to PC	
6306	AF-27		6306	AF-27	Alco	C-628	3404-7	Mar 65	to PC	
6307	AF-27		6307	AF-27	Alco	C-628	3404-8	Mar 65	to PC	
6308	AF-27		6308	AF-27	Alco	C-628	3404-9	Mar 65	to PC	
6309	AF-27		6309	AF-27	Alco	C-628	3404-10	Mar 65	to PC	
6310	AF-27		6310	AF-27	Alco	C-628	3434-1	Nov 65	to PC	
6311	AF-27		6311	AF-27	Alco	C-628	3434-2	Nov 65	to PC	
6312	AF-27		6312	AF-27	Alco	C-628	3434-3	Nov 65	to PC	
6313	AF-27		6313	AF-27	Alco	C-628	3434-4	Nov 65	to PC	
6314	AF-27		6314	AF-27	Alco	C-628	3434-5	Dec 65	to PC	
6315	AF-30		6315	AF-30	Alco	C-630	3466-1	Oct 66	to PC	
6316	AF-30		6316	AF-30	Alco	C-630	3466-2	Oct 66	to PC	
6317	AF-30		6317	AF-30	Alco	C-630	3466-3	Oct 66	to PC	
6318	AF-30		6318	AF-30	Alco	C-630	3466-4	Oct 66	to PC	
6319	AF-30		6319	AF-30	Alco	C-630	3466-5	Oct 66	to PC	

View of the front truck of PRR 6316 at Pitcairn yard, October 30, 1966

Pennsylvania Railroad Diesel Locomotive Roster

218

Pennsylvania Railroad Diesel Locomotive Roster

ORIG ROAD NUM.	PRR BASE CLASS	PRR REBLT CLASS	1966 ROAD NUM.	PRR CLASS (1966)	BLDR	BLDR MODEL	BLDR SERIAL NUM.	BLDR DATE	RETIRE DATE	NOTE
6320	AF-30		6320	AF-30	Alco	C-630	3466-6	Oct 66	to PC	
6321	AF-30		6321	AF-30	Alco	C-630	3466-7	Nov 66	to PC	
6322	AF-30		6322	AF-30	Alco	C-630	3466-8	Nov 66	to PC	
6323	AF-30		6323	AF-30	Alco	C-630	3466-9	Nov 66	to PC	
6324	AF-30		6324	AF-30	Alco	C-630	3466-10	Nov 66	to PC	
6325	AF-30		6325	AF-30	Alco	C-630	3466-11	Dec 66	to PC	
6326	AF-30		6326	AF-30	Alco	C-630	3466-12	Dec 66	to PC	
6327	AF-30		6327	AF-30	Alco	C-630	3466-13	Dec 66	to PC	
6328	AF-30		6328	AF-30	Alco	C-630	3466-14	Dec 66	to PC	
6329	AF-30		6329	AF-30	Alco	C-630	3466-15	Dec 66	to PC	
6500	GF-25a		6500	GF-25a	GE	U25C	35057	Apr 65	to PC	
6501	GF-25a		6501	GF-25a	GE	U25C	35058	Apr 65	to PC	
6502	GF-25a		6502	GF-25a	GE	U25C	35059	Apr 65	to PC	
6503	GF-25a		6503	GF-25a	GE	U25C	35056	Apr 65	to PC	
6504	GF-25a		6504	GF-25a	GE	U25C	35050	Apr 65	to PC	
6505	GF-25a		6505	GF-25a	GE	U25C	35051	Apr 65	to PC	
6506	GF-25a		6506	GF-25a	GE	U25C	35052	Apr 65	to PC	
6507	GF-25a		6507	GF-25a	GE	U25C	35053	Apr 65	to PC	
6508	GF-25a		6508	GF-25a	GE	U25C	35054	Apr 65	to PC	
6509	GF-25a		6509	GF-25a	GE	U25C	35055	Apr 65	to PC	
6510	GF-25a		6510	GF-25a	GE	U25C	35619	Nov 65	to PC	
6511	GF-25a		6511	GF-25a	GE	U25C	35620	Nov 65	to PC	
6512	GF-25a		6512	GF-25a	GE	U25C	35621	Dec 65	to PC	
6513	GF-25a		6513	GF-25a	GE	U25C	35622	Dec 65	to PC	
6514	GF-25a		6514	GF-25a	GE	U25C	35623	Dec 65	to PC	
6515	GF-25a		6515	GF-25a	GE	U25C	35624	Dec 65	to PC	
6516	GF-25a		6516	GF-25a	GE	U25C	35625	Dec 65	to PC	
6517	GF-25a		6517	GF-25a	GE	U25C	35626	Dec 65	to PC	
6518	GF-25a		6518	GF-25a	GE	U25C	35627	Dec 65	to PC	

ORIG ROAD NUM.	PRR BASE CLASS	PRR REBLT CLASS	1966 ROAD NUM.	PRR CLASS (1966)	BLDR	BLDR MODEL	BLDR SERIAL NUM.	BLDR DATE	RETIRE DATE	NOTE
6519	GF-25a		6519	GF-25a	GE	U25C	35628	Dec 65	to PC	
6520	GF-28a		6520	GF-28a	GE	U28C	36019	Sep 66	to PC	
6521	GF-28a		6521	GF-28a	GE	U28C	36020	Sep 66	to PC	
6522	GF-28a		6522	GF-28a	GE	U28C	36021	Sep 66	to PC	
6523	GF-28a		6523	GF-28a	GE	U28C	36022	Sep 66	to PC	
6524	GF-28a		6524	GF-28a	GE	U28C	36023	Sep 66	to PC	
6525	GF-28a		6525	GF-28a	GE	U28C	36024	Sep 66	to PC	
6526	GF-28a		6526	GF-28a	GE	U28C	36026	Sep 66	to PC	
6527	GF-28a		6527	GF-28a	GE	U28C	36027	Sep 66	to PC	
6528	GF-28a		6528	GF-28a	GE	U28C	36025	Sep 66	to PC	
6529	GF-28a		6529	GF-28a	GE	U28C	36028	Sep 66	to PC	
6530	GF-28a		6530	GF-28a	GE	U28C	36029	Sep 66	to PC	
6531	GF-28a		6531	GF-28a	GE	U28C	36030	Oct 66	to PC	
6532	GF-28a		6532	GF-28a	GE	U28C	36031	Oct 66	to PC	
6533	GF-28a		6533	GF-28a	GE	U28C	36032	Oct 66	to PC	
6534	GF-28a		6534	GF-28a	GE	U28C	36033	Oct 66	to PC	
6535	GF-30a		6535	GF-30a	GE	U30C	36096	Jan 67	to PC	
6536	GF-30a		6536	GF-30a	GE	U30C	36097	Jan 67	to PC	
6537	GF-30a		6537	GF-30a	GE	U30C	36098	Jan 67	to PC	
6538	GF-30a		6538	GF-30a	GE	U30C	36099	Jan 67	to PC	
6539	GF-30a		6539	GF-30a	GE	U30C	36100	Feb 67	to PC	
7000	EFS-17m		7000	ERS-17	EMD	GP9	20704	Oct 55	to PC	
7001	EFS-17m		7001	ERS-17	EMD	GP9	20705	Oct 55	to PC	
7002	EFS-17m		7002	ERS-17	EMD	GP9	20706	Oct 55	to PC	
7003	EFS-17m		7003	ERS-17	EMD	GP9	20707	Oct 55	to PC	
7004	EFS-17m		7004	ERS-17	EMD	GP9	20708	Oct 55	to PC	
7005	EFS-17m		7005	ERS-17	EMD	GP9	20709	Oct 55	to PC	
7006	EFS-17m		7006	ERS-17	EMD	GP9	20710	Oct 55	to PC	
7007	EFS-17m		7007	ERS-17	EMD	GP9	20711	Oct 55	to PC	
7008	EFS-17m		7008	ERS-17	EMD	GP9	20712	Oct 55	to PC	
7009	EFS-17m		7009	ERS-17	EMD	GP9	20713	Oct 55	to PC	
7010	EFS-17m		7010	ERS-17	EMD	GP9	20714	Oct 55	to PC	
7011	EFS-17m		7011	ERS-17	EMD	GP9	20715	Oct 55	to PC	
7012	EFS-17m		7012	ERS-17	EMD	GP9	20716	Oct 55	to PC	
7013	EFS-17m		7013	ERS-17	EMD	GP9	20717	Oct 55	to PC	
7014	EFS-17m		7014	ERS-17	EMD	GP9	20718	Oct 55	to PC	
7015	EFS-17m		7015	ERS-17	EMD	GP9	20719	Oct 55	to PC	
7016	EFS-17m		7016	ERS-17	EMD	GP9	20720	Oct 55	to PC	
7017	EFS-17m		7017	ERS-17	EMD	GP9	20721	Oct 55	to PC	
7018	EFS-17m		7018	ERS-17	EMD	GP9	20722	Nov 55	to PC	
7019	EFS-17m		7019	ERS-17	EMD	GP9	20723	Oct 55	to PC	
7020	EFS-17m		7020	ERS-17	EMD	GP9	20724	Nov 55	to PC	
7021	EFS-17m		7021	ERS-17	EMD	GP9	20725	Nov 55	to PC	
7022	EFS-17m		7022	ERS-17	EMD	GP9	20726	Nov 55	to PC	
7023	EFS-17m		7023	ERS-17	EMD	GP9	20727	Nov 55	to PC	
7024	EFS-17m		7074	ERS-17	EMD	GP9	20728	Nov 55	to PC	
7025	EFS-17m		7025	ERS-17	EMD	GP9	20729	Nov 55	to PC	
7026	EFS-17m		7026	ERS-17	EMD	GP9	20730	Nov 55	to PC	
7027	EFS-17m		7027	ERS-17	EMD	GP9	20731	Nov 55	to PC	
7028	EFS-17m		7028	ERS-17	EMD	GP9	20732	Nov 55	to PC	
7029	EFS-17m		7029	ERS-17	EMD	GP9	20733	Nov 55	to PC	
7030	EFS-17m		7030	ERS-17	EMD	GP9	20734	Nov 55	to PC	

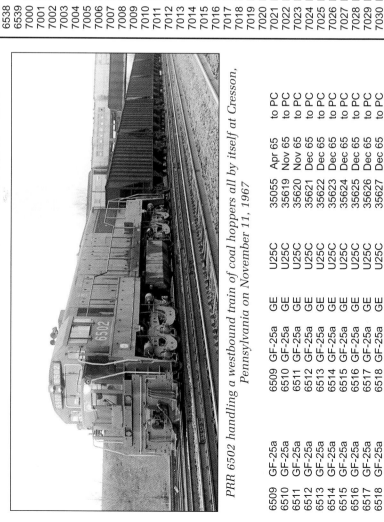

PRR 6502 handling a westbound train of coal hoppers all by itself at Cresson, Pennsylvania on November 11, 1967

ORIG ROAD NUM.	PRR BASE CLASS	PRR REBLT CLASS	1966 ROAD NUM.	PRR CLASS (1966)	BLDR	BLDR MODEL	BLDR SERIAL NUM.	BLDR DATE	RETIRE DATE	NOTE
7031	EFS-17m		7031	ERS-17	EMD	GP9	20735	Nov 55		to PC
7032	EFS-17m		7032	ERS-17	EMD	GP9	20736	Nov 55		to PC
7033	EFS-17m		7033	ERS-17	EMD	GP9	20737	Nov 55		to PC
7034	EFS-17m		7034	ERS-17	EMD	GP9	20738	Nov 55		to PC
7035	EFS-17m		7035	ERS-17	EMD	GP9	20739	Dec 55		to PC
7036	EFS-17m		7036	ERS-17	EMD	GP9	20740	Nov 55		to PC
7037	EFS-17m		7037	ERS-17	EMD	GP9	20741	Nov 55		to PC
7038	EFS-17m		7038	ERS-17	EMD	GP9	20742	Nov 55		to PC
7039	EFS-17m		7039	ERS-17	EMD	GP9	20743	Nov 55		to PC
7040	EFS-17m		7040	ERS-17	EMD	GP9	20744	Dec 55		to PC
7041	EFS-17m		7041	ERS-17	EMD	GP9	20745	Nov 55		to PC
7042	EFS-17m		7042	ERS-17	EMD	GP9	20746	Dec 55		to PC
7043	EFS-17m		7043	ERS-17	EMD	GP9	20747	Dec 55		to PC
7044	EFS-17m		7044	ERS-17	EMD	GP9	20748	Dec 55		to PC
7045	EFS-17m		7045	ERS-17	EMD	GP9	20749	Nov 55		to PC
7046	EFS-17m		7046	ERS-17	EMD	GP9	20750	Dec 55		to PC
7047	EFS-17m		7047	ERS-17	EMD	GP9	20751	Dec 55		to PC
7048	EFS-17m		7048	ERS-17	EMD	GP9	20752	Dec 55		to PC
7049	EFS-17m		7049	ERS-17	EMD	GP9	20753	Dec 55		to PC
7050	EFS-17m		7050	ERS-17	EMD	GP9	21855	Oct 56		to PC
7051	EFS-17m		7051	ERS-17	EMD	GP9	21856	Oct 56		to PC
7052	EFS-17m		7052	ERS-17	EMD	GP9	21857	Oct 56		to PC
7053	EFS-17m		7053	ERS-17	EMD	GP9	21858	Oct 56		to PC
7054	EFS-17m		7054	ERS-17	EMD	GP9	21859	Oct 56		to PC
7055	EFS-17m		7055	ERS-17	EMD	GP9	21860	Oct 56		to PC
7056	EFS-17m		7056	ERS-17	EMD	GP9	21861	Oct 56		to PC
7057	EFS-17m		7057	ERS-17	EMD	GP9	21862	Oct 56		to PC
7058	EFS-17m		7058	ERS-17	EMD	GP9	21863	Oct 56		to PC
7059	EFS-17m		7059	ERS-17	EMD	GP9	21864	Oct 56		to PC
7060	EFS-17m		7060	ERS-17	EMD	GP9	21865	Oct 56		to PC
7061	EFS-17m		7061	ERS-17	EMD	GP9	21866	Oct 56		to PC
7062	EFS-17m		7062	ERS-17	EMD	GP9	21867	Oct 56		to PC
7063	EFS-17m		7063	ERS-17	EMD	GP9	21868	Oct 56		to PC
7064	EFS-17m		7064	ERS-17	EMD	GP9	21869	Oct 56		to PC
7065	EFS-17m		7065	ERS-17	EMD	GP9	21870	Oct 56		to PC
7066	EFS-17m		7066	ERS-17	EMD	GP9	21871	Oct 56		to PC
7067	EFS-17m		7067	ERS-17	EMD	GP9	21872	Oct 56		to PC
7068	EFS-17m		7068	ERS-17	EMD	GP9	21873	Oct 56		to PC
7069	EFS-17m		7069	ERS-17	EMD	GP9	21874	Oct 56		to PC
7070	EFS-17m		7070	ERS-17	EMD	GP9	21875	Oct 56		to PC
7071	EFS-17m				EMD	GP9	21876	Oct 56	Sep 64	
7072	EFS-17m		7072	ERS-17	EMD	GP9	21877	Oct 56		to PC
7073	EFS-17m		7073	ERS-17	EMD	GP9	21878	Oct 56		to PC
7074	EFS-17m		7074	ERS-17	EMD	GP9	21879	Nov 56		to PC
7075	EFS-17m		7075	ERS-17	EMD	GP9	21880	Nov 56		to PC
7076	EFS-17m		7076	ERS-17	EMD	GP9	21881	Nov 56		to PC
7077	EFS-17m		7077	ERS-17	EMD	GP9	21882	Nov 56		to PC
7078	EFS-17m		7078	ERS-17	EMD	GP9	21883	Nov 56		to PC
7079	EFS-17m		7079	ERS-17	EMD	GP9	21884	Nov 56		to PC
7080	EFS-17m		7080	ERS-17	EMD	GP9	21885	Nov 56		to PC
7081	EFS-17m		7081	ERS-17	EMD	GP9	21886	Nov 56		to PC
7082	EFS-17m		7082	ERS-17	EMD	GP9	21887	Nov 56		to PC

ORIG ROAD NUM.	PRR BASE CLASS	PRR REBLT CLASS	1966 ROAD NUM.	PRR CLASS (1966)	BLDR	BLDR MODEL	BLDR SERIAL NUM.	BLDR DATE	RETIRE DATE	NOTE
7083	EFS-17m		7083	ERS-17	EMD	GP9	21888	Nov 56		to PC
7084	EFS-17m		7084	ERS-17	EMD	GP9	21889	Nov 56		to PC
7085	EFS-17m		7085	ERS-17	EMD	GP9	21890	Nov 56		to PC
7086	EFS-17m		7086	ERS-17	EMD	GP9	21891	Nov 56		to PC
7087	EFS-17m		7087	ERS-17	EMD	GP9	21892	Nov 56		to PC
7088	EFS-17m		7088	ERS-17	EMD	GP9	21893	Nov 56		to PC
7089	EFS-17m		7089	ERS-17	EMD	GP9	21894	Nov 56		to PC
7090	EFS-17m		7090	ERS-17	EMD	GP9	21895	Nov 56		to PC
7091	EFS-17m		7091	ERS-17	EMD	GP9	21896	Nov 56		to PC
7092	EFS-17m		7092	ERS-17	EMD	GP9	21897	Nov 56		to PC
7093	EFS-17m		7093	ERS-17	EMD	GP9	21898	Nov 56		to PC
7094	EFS-17m		7094	ERS-17	EMD	GP9	21899	Nov 56		to PC
7095	EFS-17m		7095	ERS-17	EMD	GP9	21900	Nov 56		to PC
7096	EFS-17m		7096	ERS-17	EMD	GP9	21901	Nov 56		to PC
7097	EFS-17m		7097	ERS-17	EMD	GP9	21902	Nov 56		to PC
7098	EFS-17m		9098	ERS-17	EMD	GP9	21903	Nov 56		to PC
7099	EFS-17m		7099	ERS-17	EMD	GP9	21904	Nov 56		to PC
7100	EFS-17m		7100	ERS-17	EMD	GP9	22596	Nov 56		to PC
7101	EFS-17m		7101	ERS-17	EMD	GP9	22597	Nov 56		to PC

PRR 7098 is actually the last unit of three in a pushing helper set on a westbound train. This train has crossed over from number 2 track to number 3 track just west of Slope tower in Altoona. The westbound is clearing for an eastbound move whose headlight can be seen through the haze of brakeshoe smoke from the coal train on the left. That's why they have four tracks here. The date is June 22, 1963.

Pennsylvania Railroad Diesel Locomotive Roster

Pennsylvania Railroad Diesel Locomotive Roster

At Williamsport, Pennsylvania on October 18, 1965, PRR 7166 has recently had the road number on its cab redone with the 16-inch numbers in lieu of the previous 8-inch size.

ORIG ROAD NUM.	PRR BASE CLASS	PRR REBLT CLASS	1966 ROAD NUM.	PRR CLASS (1966)	BLDR	BLDR MODEL	BLDR SERIAL NUM.	BLDR DATE	RETIRE DATE	NOTE
7102	EFS-17m		7102	ERS-17	EMD	GP9	22598	Nov 56	to PC	
7103	EFS-17m		7103	ERS-17	EMD	GP9	22599	Nov 56	to PC	
7104	EFS-17m		7104	ERS-17	EMD	GP9	22600	Nov 56	to PC	
7105	EFS-17m		7105	ERS-17	EMD	GP9	23305	May 57	to PC	
7106	EFS-17m		7106	ERS-17	EMD	GP9	23306	May 57	to PC	
7107	EFS-17m		7107	ERS-17	EMD	GP9	23307	May 57	to PC	
7108	EFS-17m		7108	ERS-17	EMD	GP9	23308	May 57	to PC	
7109	EFS-17m		7109	ERS-17	EMD	GP9	23309	May 57	to PC	
7110	EFS-17m		7110	ERS-17	EMD	GP9	23310	May 57	to PC	
7111	EFS-17m		7111	ERS-17	EMD	GP9	23311	May 57	to PC	
7112	EFS-17m		7112	ERS-17	EMD	GP9	23312	May 57	to PC	
7113	EFS-17m		7113	ERS-17	EMD	GP9	23313	May 57	to PC	
7114	EFS-17m		7114	ERS-17	EMD	GP9	23314	May 57	to PC	
7115	EFS-17m		7115	ERS-17	EMD	GP9	23315	Jun 57	to PC	
7116	EFS-17m		7116	ERS-17	EMD	GP9	23316	Jun 57	to PC	
7117	EFS-17m		7117	ERS-17	EMD	GP9	23317	Jun 57	to PC	
7118	EFS-17m		7118	ERS-17	EMD	GP9	23318	Jun 57	to PC	
7119	EFS-17m		7119	ERS-17	EMD	GP9	23319	Jun 57	to PC	
7120	EFS-17m		7120	ERS-17	EMD	GP9	23320	Jun 57	to PC	
7121	EFS-17m		7121	ERS-17	EMD	GP9	23321	Jun 57	to PC	
7122	EFS-17m		7122	ERS-17	EMD	GP9	23322	Jun 57	to PC	
7123	EFS-17m		7123	ERS-17	EMD	GP9	23323	Jun 57	to PC	
7124	EFS-17m		7124	ERS-17	EMD	GP9	23324	Jun 57	to PC	
7125	EFS-17m		7125	ERS-17	EMD	GP9	23325	Jun 57	to PC	
7126	EFS-17m		7126	ERS-17	EMD	GP9	23326	Jun 57	to PC	
7127	EFS-17m		7127	ERS-17	EMD	GP9	23327	Jun 57	to PC	
7128	EFS-17m		7128	ERS-17	EMD	GP9	23328	Jun 57	to PC	
7129	EFS-17m				EMD	GP9	23329	Jun 57	Sep 64	
7130	EFS-17m		7130	ERS-17	EMD	GP9	23330	Jun 57	to PC	
7131	EFS-17m		7131	ERS-17	EMD	GP9	23331	Jun 57	to PC	
7132	EFS-17m		7132	ERS-17	EMD	GP9	23332	Jun 57	to PC	
7133	EFS-17m		7133	ERS-17	EMD	GP9	23333	Jun 57	to PC	
7134	EFS-17m		7134	ERS-17	EMD	GP9	23334	Jun 57	to PC	
7135	EFS-17m		7135	ERS-17	EMD	GP9	23335	Jun 57	to PC	
7136	EFS-17m		7136	ERS-17	EMD	GP9	23336	Jun 57	to PC	
7137	EFS-17m		7137	ERS-17	EMD	GP9	23337	Jun 57	to PC	
7138	EFS-17m		7138	ERS-17	EMD	GP9	23338	Jun 57	to PC	
7139	EFS-17m		7139	ERS-17	EMD	GP9	23339	Jun 57	to PC	
7140	EFS-17m		7140	ERS-17	EMD	GP9	23340	Jun 57	to PC	
7141	EFS-17m		7141	ERS-17	EMD	GP9	23341	Jun 57	to PC	
7142	EFS-17m		7142	ERS-17	EMD	GP9	23342	Jun 57	to PC	
7143	EFS-17m		7143	ERS-17	EMD	GP9	23343	Jun 57	to PC	
7144	EFS-17m		7144	ERS-17	EMD	GP9	23344	Jun 57	to PC	
7145	EFS-17m		7145	ERS-17	EMD	GP9	23943	Oct 57	to PC	
7146	EFS-17m		7146	ERS-17	EMD	GP9	23944	Oct 57	to PC	
7147	EFS-17m		7147	ERS-17	EMD	GP9	23945	Oct 57	to PC	
7148	EFS-17m		7148	ERS-17	EMD	GP9	23946	Oct 57	to PC	
7149	EFS-17m		7149	ERS-17	EMD	GP9	23947	Nov 57	to PC	
7150	EFS-17m		7150	ERS-17	EMD	GP9	23948	Oct 57	to PC	
7151	EFS-17m		7151	ERS-17	EMD	GP9	23949	Oct 57	to PC	
7152	EFS-17m		7152	ERS-17	EMD	GP9	23950	Oct 57	to PC	
7153	EFS-17m		7153	ERS-17	EMD	GP9	23951	Oct 57	to PC	
7154	EFS-17m		7154	ERS-17	EMD	GP9	23952	Oct 57	to PC	
7155	EFS-17m		7155	ERS-17	EMD	GP9	23953	Oct 57	to PC	
7156	EFS-17m		7156	ERS-17	EMD	GP9	23954	Oct 57	to PC	
7157	EFS-17m		7157	ERS-17	EMD	GP9	23955	Oct 57	to PC	
7158	EFS-17m		7158	ERS-17	EMD	GP9	23956	Oct 57	to PC	
7159	EFS-17m		7159	ERS-17	EMD	GP9	23957	Oct 57	to PC	
7160	EFS-17m		7160	ERS-17	EMD	GP9	23958	Oct 57	to PC	
7161	EFS-17m		7161	ERS-17	EMD	GP9	23959	Oct 57	to PC	
7162	EFS-17m		7162	ERS-17	EMD	GP9	23960	Oct 57	to PC	
7163	EFS-17m		7163	ERS-17	EMD	GP9	23961	Oct 57	to PC	
7164	EFS-17m		7164	ERS-17	EMD	GP9	23962	Oct 57	to PC	
7165	EFS-17m		7165	ERS-17	EMD	GP9	23963	Oct 57	to PC	
7166	EFS-17m		7166	ERS-17	EMD	GP9	23964	Oct 57	to PC	
7167	EFS-17m		7167	ERS-17	EMD	GP9	23965	Oct 57	to PC	
7168	EFS-17m		7168	ERS-17	EMD	GP9	23966	Oct 57	to PC	
7169	EFS-17m		7169	ERS-17	EMD	GP9	23967	Oct 57	to PC	
7170	EFS-17m		7170	ERS-17	EMD	GP9	23968	Oct 57	to PC	
7171	EFS-17m		7171	ERS-17	EMD	GP9	23969	Oct 57	to PC	
7172	EFS-17m		7172	ERS-17	EMD	GP9	23970	Oct 57	to PC	
7173	EFS-17m		7173	ERS-17	EMD	GP9	23971	Oct 57	to PC	
7174	EFS-17m		7174	ERS-17	EMD	GP9	23972	Oct 57	to PC	
7175	EFS-17m		7175	ERS-17	EMD	GP9	23973	Oct 57	to PC	
7175B	EFS-17m		3800	ERS-17	EMD	GP9B	23997	Nov 57	to PC	
7176	EFS-17m		7176	ERS-17	EMD	GP9	23974	Oct 57	to PC	
7176B	EFS-17m		3801	ERS-17	EMD	GP9B	23998	Nov 57	to PC	
7177	EFS-17m		7177	ERS-17	EMD	GP9	23975	Oct 57	to PC	
7177B	EFS-17m		3802	ERS-17	EMD	GP9B	23999	Nov 57	to PC	
7178	EFS-17m		7178	ERS-17	EMD	GP9	23976	Oct 57	to PC	

Pennsylvania Railroad Diesel Locomotive Roster

ORIG ROAD NUM.	PRR BASE CLASS	PRR REBLT CLASS	1966 ROAD NUM.	PRR CLASS (1966)	BLDR	BLDR MODEL	BLDR SERIAL NUM.	BLDR DATE	RETIRE DATE	NOTE
7178B	EFS-17m		3803	ERS-17	EMD	GP9B	24000	Nov 57	to PC	
7179	EFS-17m		7179	ERS-17	EMD	GP9	23977	Oct 57	to PC	
7179B	EFS-17m		3804	ERS-17	EMD	GP9B	24001	Nov 57	to PC	
7180	EFS-17m		7180	ERS-17	EMD	GP9	23978	Oct 57	to PC	
7180B	EFS-17m		3805	ERS-17	EMD	GP9B	24002	Nov 57	to PC	
7181	EFS-17m		7181	ERS-17	EMD	GP9	23979	Oct 57	to PC	
7181B	EFS-17m		3806	ERS-17	EMD	GP9B	24003	Nov 57	to PC	
7182	EFS-17m		7182	ERS-17	EMD	GP9	23980	Oct 57	to PC	
7182B	EFS-17m		3807	ERS-17	EMD	GP9B	24004	Nov 57	to PC	
7183	EFS-17m		7183	ERS-17	EMD	GP9	23981	Nov 57	to PC	
7183B	EFS-17m		3808	ERS-17	EMD	GP9B	24005	Nov 57	to PC	
7184	EFS-17m		7184	ERS-17	EMD	GP9	23982	Nov 57	to PC	
7184B	EFS-17m		3809	ERS-17	EMD	GP9B	24006	Nov 57	to PC	
7185	EFS-17m		7185	ERS-17	EMD	GP9	24217	Nov 57	to PC	
7185B	EFS-17m		3810	ERS-17	EMD	GP9B	24262	Nov 57	to PC	
7186	EFS-17m		7186	ERS-17	EMD	GP9	24218	Nov 57	to PC	
7186B	EFS-17m		3811	ERS-17	EMD	GP9B	24263	Nov 57	to PC	
7187	EFS-17m		7187	ERS-17	EMD	GP9	24219	Nov 57	to PC	
7187B	EFS-17m		3812	ERS-17	EMD	GP9B	24264	Nov 57	to PC	
7188	EFS-17m		7188	ERS-17	EMD	GP9	24220	Nov 57	to PC	
7188B	EFS-17m		3813	ERS-17	EMD	GP9B	24265	Nov 57	to PC	
7189	EFS-17m		7189	ERS-17	EMD	GP9	24221	Nov 57	to PC	
7189B	EFS-17m		3814	ERS-17	EMD	GP9B	24266	Nov 57	to PC	
7190	EFS-17m		7190	ERS-17	EMD	GP9	24222	Nov 57	to PC	
7190B	EFS-17m		3815	ERS-17	EMD	GP9B	24267	Nov 57	to PC	
7191	EFS-17m		7191	ERS-17	EMD	GP9	24223	Nov 57	to PC	
7191B	EFS-17m		3816	ERS-17	EMD	GP9B	24268	Nov 57	to PC	
7192	EFS-17m		7192	ERS-17	EMD	GP9	24224	Nov 57	to PC	
7192B	EFS-17m		3817	ERS-17	EMD	GP9B	24269	Nov 57	to PC	
7193	EFS-17m		7193	ERS-17	EMD	GP9	24225	Nov 57	to PC	
7193B	EFS-17m		3818	ERS-17	EMD	GP9B	24270	Nov 57	to PC	
7194	EFS-17m		7194	ERS-17	EMD	GP9	24226	Nov 57	to PC	
7194B	EFS-17m		3819	ERS-17	EMD	GP9B	24271	Nov 57	to PC	
7195	EFS-17m		7195	ERS-17	EMD	GP9	24227	Nov 57	to PC	
7195B	EFS-17m		3820	ERS-17	EMD	GP9B	24272	Dec 57	to PC	
7196	EFS-17m		7196	ERS-17	EMD	GP9	24228	Nov 57	to PC	
7196B	EFS-17m		3821	ERS-17	EMD	GP9B	24273	Dec 57	to PC	
7197	EFS-17m		7197	ERS-17	EMD	GP9	24229	Nov 57	to PC	
7197B	EFS-17m		3822	ERS-17	EMD	GP9B	24274	Dec 57	to PC	
7198	EFS-17m		7198	ERS-17	EMD	GP9	24230	Nov 57	to PC	
7198B	EFS-17m		3823	ERS-17	EMD	GP9B	24275	Dec 57	to PC	
7199	EFS-17m		7199	ERS-17	EMD	GP9	24231	Nov 57	to PC	
7199B	EFS-17m		3824	ERS-17	EMD	GP9B	24276	Dec 57	to PC	
7200	EFS-17m		7200	ERS-17	EMD	GP9	24232	Nov 57	to PC	
7200B	EFS-17m		3825	ERS-17	EMD	GP9B	24277	Dec 57	to PC	
7201	EFS-17m		7201	ERS-17	EMD	GP9	24233	Nov 57	to PC	
7201B	EFS-17m		3826	ERS-17	EMD	GP9B	24278	Dec 57	to PC	
7202	EFS-17m		7202	ERS-17	EMD	GP9	24234	Nov 57	to PC	
7202B	EFS-17m		3827	ERS-17	EMD	GP9B	24279	Dec 57	to PC	
7203	EFS-17m		7203	ERS-17	EMD	GP9	24235	Nov 57	to PC	
7203B	EFS-17m		3828	ERS-17	EMD	GP9B	24280	Dec 57	to PC	
7204	EFS-17m		7204	ERS-17	EMD	GP9	24236	Nov 57	to PC	
7204B	EFS-17m		3829	ERS-17	EMD	GP9B	24281	Dec 57	to PC	
7205	EFS-17m		7205	ERS-17	EMD	GP9	24237	Nov 57	to PC	
7206	EFS-17m		7206	ERS-17	EMD	GP9	24238	Nov 57	to PC	
7207	EFS-17m		7207	ERS-17	EMD	GP9	24239	Nov 57	to PC	
7208	EFS-17m		7208	ERS-17	EMD	GP9	24240	Nov 57	to PC	
7209	EFS-17m		7209	ERS-17	EMD	GP9	24241	Nov 57	to PC	
7210	EFS-17m		7210	ERS-17	EMD	GP9	24242	Nov 57	to PC	
7211	EFS-17m		7211	ERS-17	EMD	GP9	24243	Nov 57	to PC	
7212	EFS-17m		7212	ERS-17	EMD	GP9	24244	Nov 57	to PC	
7213	EFS-17m		7213	ERS-17	EMD	GP9	24245	Nov 57	to PC	
7214	EFS-17m		7214	ERS-17	EMD	GP9	24246	Nov 57	to PC	
7215	EFS-17m		7215	ERS-17	EMD	GP9	24247	Nov 57	to PC	
7216	EFS-17m		7216	ERS-17	EMD	GP9	24248	Nov 57	to PC	
7217	EFS-17m		7217	ERS-17	EMD	GP9	24249	Nov 57	to PC	
7218	EFS-17m		7218	ERS-17	EMD	GP9	24250	Nov 57	to PC	
7219	EFS-17m		7219	ERS-17	EMD	GP9	24251	Nov 57	to PC	
7220	EFS-17m		7220	ERS-17	EMD	GP9	24252	Nov 57	to PC	
7221	EFS-17m		7221	ERS-17	EMD	GP9	24253	Nov 57	to PC	
7222	EFS-17m		7222	ERS-17	EMD	GP9	24254	Nov 57	to PC	
7223	EFS-17m		7223	ERS-17	EMD	GP9	24255	Dec 57	to PC	
7224	EFS-17m		7224	ERS-17	EMD	GP9	24256	Dec 57	to PC	

It is a cold February 10, 1962 and the photographer is waiting for hotshot TT-2 at Edgewood, Pennsylvania. The "word" was that GE U25B demonstrators would be on the point. Frozen patience was rewarded later when the red and white GE units appeared. But during the wait, PRR 7186 headed a four-unit GP9 set with an eastbound freight. At the time, these Geeps reigned supreme on through freights. The station platforms are still in reasonable shape for the Pittsburgh commuter service which would last for almost three years more.

222

ORIG ROAD NUM.	PRR BASE CLASS	PRR REBLT CLASS	1966 ROAD NUM.	PRR CLASS (1966)	BLDR	BLDR MODEL	BLDR SERIAL NUM.	BLDR DATE	RETIRE DATE	NOTE
7225	EFS-17m				EMD	GP9	24257	Dec 57	Sep 64	
7226	EFS-17m		7226	ERS-17	EMD	GP9	24258	Dec 57	to PC	
7227	EFS-17m		7227	ERS-17	EMD	GP9	24259	Dec 57	to PC	
7228	EFS-17m		7228	ERS-17	EMD	GP9	24260	Dec 57	to PC	
7229	EFS-17m		7229	ERS-17	EMD	GP9	24261	Dec 57	to PC	
7230	EFS-17m		7230	ERS-17	EMD	GP9	24282	Oct 59	to PC	
7230B	EFS-17m		3830	ERS-17	EMD	GP9B	24322	Oct 59	to PC	
7231	EFS-17m		7231	ERS-17	EMD	GP9	24283	Oct 59	to PC	
7231B	EFS-17m		3831	ERS-17	EMD	GP9B	24323	Oct 59	to PC	
7232	EFS-17m		7232	ERS-17	EMD	GP9	24284	Oct 59	to PC	
7232B	EFS-17m		3832	ERS-17	EMD	GP9B	24324	Oct 59	to PC	
7233	EFS-17m		7233	ERS-17	EMD	GP9	24285	Oct 59	to PC	
7233B	EFS-17m		3833	ERS-17	EMD	GP9B	24325	Oct 59	to PC	
7234	EFS-17m		7234	ERS-17	EMD	GP9	24286	Oct 59	to PC	
7234B	EFS-17m		3834	ERS-17	EMD	GP9B	24326	Oct 59	to PC	
7235	EFS-17m		7235	ERS-17	EMD	GP9	24287	Oct 59	to PC	
7235B	EFS-17m		3835	ERS-17	EMD	GP9B	24327	Oct 59	to PC	
7236	EFS-17m		7236	ERS-17	EMD	GP9	24288	Oct 59	to PC	
7236B	EFS-17m		3836	ERS-17	EMD	GP9B	24328	Nov 59	to PC	
7237	EFS-17m		7237	ERS-17	EMD	GP9	24289	Oct 59	to PC	
7237B	EFS-17m		3837	ERS-17	EMD	GP9B	24329	Nov 59	to PC	
7238	EFS-17m		7238	ERS-17	EMD	GP9	24290	Oct 59	to PC	

ORIG ROAD NUM.	PRR BASE CLASS	PRR REBLT CLASS	1966 ROAD NUM.	PRR CLASS (1966)	BLDR	BLDR MODEL	BLDR SERIAL NUM.	BLDR DATE	RETIRE DATE	NOTE
7238B	EFS-17m		3838	ERS-17	EMD	GP9B	24330	Nov 59	to PC	
7239	EFS-17m		7239	ERS-17	EMD	GP9	24291	Oct 59	to PC	
7239B	EFS-17m		3839	ERS-17	EMD	GP9B	24331	Dec 59	to PC	
7240	EFS-17m		7240	ERS-17	EMD	GP9	24292	Oct 59	to PC	
7241	EFS-17m		7241	ERS-17	EMD	GP9	24293	Oct 59	to PC	
7242	EFS-17m		7242	ERS-17	EMD	GP9	24294	Oct 59	to PC	
7243	EFS-17m		7243	ERS-17	EMD	GP9	24295	Oct 59	to PC	
7244	EFS-17m		7244	ERS-17	EMD	GP9	24296	Oct 59	to PC	
7245	EFS-17m		7245	ERS-17	EMD	GP9	24297	Oct 59	to PC	
7246	EFS-17m		7246	ERS-17	EMD	GP9	24298	Oct 59	to PC	
7247	EFS-17m		7247	ERS-17	EMD	GP9	24299	Oct 59	to PC	
7248	EFS-17m		7248	ERS-17	EMD	GP9	24300	Oct 59	to PC	
7249	EFS-17m		7249	ERS-17	EMD	GP9	24301	Oct 59	to PC	
7250	EFS-17m		7250	ERS-17	EMD	GP9	24302	Oct 59	to PC	
7251	EFS-17m		7251	ERS-17	EMD	GP9	24303	Oct 59	to PC	
7252	EFS-17m		7252	ERS-17	EMD	GP9	24304	Oct 59	to PC	
7253	EFS-17m		7253	ERS-17	EMD	GP9	24305	Oct 59	to PC	
7254	EFS-17m		7254	ERS-17	EMD	GP9	24306	Oct 59	to PC	
7255	EFS-17m		7255	ERS-17	EMD	GP9	24307	Nov 59	to PC	
7256	EFS-17m		7256	ERS-17	EMD	GP9	24308	Nov 59	to PC	
7257	EFS-17m		7257	ERS-17	EMD	GP9	24309	Nov 59	to PC	
7258	EFS-17m		7258	ERS-17	EMD	GP9	24310	Nov 59	to PC	
7259	EFS-17m		7259	ERS-17	EMD	GP9	24311	Nov 59	to PC	
7260	EFS-17m		7260	ERS-17	EMD	GP9	24312	Nov 59	to PC	
7261	EFS-17m		7261	ERS-17	EMD	GP9	24313	Nov 59	to PC	
7262	EFS-17m		7262	ERS-17	EMD	GP9	24314	Nov 59	to PC	
7263	EFS-17m		7263	ERS-17	EMD	GP9	24315	Nov 59	to PC	
7264	EFS-17m		7264	ERS-17	EMD	GP9	24316	Oct 59	to PC	
7265	EFS-17m		7265	ERS-17	EMD	GP9	24317	Nov 59	to PC	
7266	EFS-17m		7266	ERS-17	EMD	GP9	24318	Nov 59	to PC	
7267	EFS-17m		7267	ERS-17	EMD	GP9	24319	Nov 59	to PC	
7268	EFS-17m		7268	ERS-17	EMD	GP9	24320	Nov 59	to PC	
7269	EFS-17m		7269	ERS-17	EMD	GP9	24321	Dec 59	to PC	
7600	ES-17m		6900	ERS-17a	EMD	SD9	24167	Nov 57	to PC	
7601	ES-17m		6901	ERS-17a	EMD	SD9	24168	Dec 57	to PC	
7602	ES-17m		6902	ERS-17a	EMD	SD9	24169	Dec 57	to PC	
7603	ES-17m		6903	ERS-17a	EMD	SD9	24170	Dec 57	to PC	
7604	ES-17m		6904	ERS-17a	EMD	SD9	24171	Dec 57	to PC	
7605	ES-17m		6905	ERS-17a	EMD	SD9	24172	Dec 57	to PC	
7606	ES-17m		6906	ERS-17a	EMD	SD9	24173	Dec 57	to PC	
7607	ES-17m		6907	ERS-17a	EMD	SD9	24174	Dec 57	to PC	
7608	ES-17m		6908	ERS-17a	EMD	SD9	24175	Dec 57	to PC	
7609	ES-17m		6909	ERS-17a	EMD	SD9	24176	Dec 57	to PC	
7610	ES-17m		6910	ERS-17a	EMD	SD9	24177	Dec 57	to PC	
7611	ES-17m		6911	ERS-17a	EMD	SD9	24178	Nov 57	to PC	
7612	ES-17m		6912	ERS-17a	EMD	SD9	24179	Dec 57	to PC	
7613	ES-17m		6913	ERS-17a	EMD	SD9	24180	Dec 57	to PC	
7614	ES-17m		6914	ERS-17a	EMD	SD9	24181	Dec 57	to PC	
7615	ES-17m		6915	ERS-17a	EMD	SD9	24182	Jan 58	to PC	
7616	ES-17m		6916	ERS-17a	EMD	SD9	24183	Jan 58	to PC	
7617	ES-17m		6917	ERS-17a	EMD	SD9	24184	Jan 58	to PC	
7618	ES-17m		6918	ERS-17a	EMD	SD9	24185	Jan 58	to PC	

L.A. MARRE COLLECTION

Builder's photo of PRR 7233B at the EMD plant in October, 1959. This photo shows the end of the unit, which looks quite bare without numberboards. The unit is one of those in the order that the PRR placed early in 1957; they were not delivered until more than two years later. As a result, they had some GP18 equipment. They were the only GP9's on the PRR equipped with magnetic power contactors instead of the older electro-pneumatic type.

Pennsylvania Railroad Diesel Locomotive Roster

ORIG ROAD NUM.	PRR BASE CLASS	PRR REBLT CLASS	1966 ROAD NUM.	PRR CLASS (1966)	BLDR	BLDR MODEL	BLDR SERIAL NUM.	BLDR DATE	RETIRE DATE	NOTE
7619	ES-17m		6919	ERS-17a	EMD	SD9	24186	Jan 58	to PC	
7620	ES-17m		6920	ERS-17a	EMD	SD9	24187	Jan 58	to PC	
7621	ES-17m		6921	ERS-17a	EMD	SD9	24188	Jan 58	to PC	
7622	ES-17m		6922	ERS-17a	EMD	SD9	24189	Jan 58	to PC	
7623	ES-17m		6923	ERS-17a	EMD	SD9	24190	Jan 58	to PC	
7624	ES-17m		6924	ERS-17a	EMD	SD9	24191	Jan 58	to PC	
7900	ES-12		9050	ES-12	EMD	SW1200	24132	Oct 57	to PC	
7901	ES-12		9051	ES-12	EMD	SW1200	24133	Oct 57	to PC	
7902	ES-12		9052	ES-12	EMD	SW1200	24134	Oct 57	to PC	
7903	ES-12		9053	ES-12	EMD	SW1200	24135	Oct 57	to PC	
7904	ES-12		9054	ES-12	EMD	SW1200	24136	Oct 57	to PC	
7905	ES-12		9055	ES-12	EMD	SW1200	24137	Oct 57	to PC	
7906	ES-12		9056	ES-12	EMD	SW1200	24138	Oct 57	to PC	
7907	ES-12		9057	ES-12	EMD	SW1200	24139	Nov 57	to PC	
7908	ES-12		9058	ES-12	EMD	SW1200	24140	Nov 57	to PC	
7909	ES-12		9009	ES-12	EMD	SW1200	24141	Nov 57	to PC	
7910	ES-12		9010	ES-12	EMD	SW1200	24142	Nov 57	to PC	
7911	ES-12		9011	ES-12	EMD	SW1200	24143	Nov 57	to PC	
7912	ES-12		9012	ES-12	EMD	SW1200	24144	Nov 57	to PC	
7913	ES-12		9013	ES-12	EMD	SW1200	24145	Nov 57	to PC	
7914	ES-12		9014	ES-12	EMD	SW1200	24146	Nov 57	to PC	
7915	ES-12		9015	ES-12	EMD	SW1200	24147	Nov 57	to PC	
7916	ES-12		9016	ES-12	EMD	SW1200	24148	Nov 57	to PC	
7917	ES-12		9017	ES-12	EMD	SW1200	24149	Nov 57	to PC	
7918	ES-12		9018	ES-12	EMD	SW1200	24150	Nov 57	to PC	
7919	ES-12		9019	ES-12	EMD	SW1200	24151	Nov 57	to PC	
7920	ES-12		9020	ES-12	EMD	SW1200	24152	Nov 57	to PC	
7921	ES-12		9021	ES-12	EMD	SW1200	24153	Nov 57	to PC	
7922	ES-12		9022	ES-12	EMD	SW1200	24154	Nov 57	to PC	
7923	ES-12		9023	ES-12	EMD	SW1200	24155	Nov 57	to PC	
7924	ES-12		9024	ES-12	EMD	SW1200	24156	Nov 57	to PC	
7925	ES-12		9025	ES-12	EMD	SW1200	24157	Dec 57	to PC	
7926	ES-12		9026	ES-12	EMD	SW1200	24158	Apr 58	to PC	
7927	ES-12		9027	ES-12	EMD	SW1200	24159	Apr 58	to PC	
7928	ES-12		9028	ES-12	EMD	SW1200	24160	Apr 58	to PC	
7929	ES-12		9029	ES-12	EMD	SW1200	24161	Apr 58	to PC	
7930	ES-12		9030	ES-12	EMD	SW1200	24162	Apr 58	to PC	
7931	ES-12		9031	ES-12	EMD	SW1200	24163	Apr 58	to PC	
7932	ES-12		9032	ES-12	EMD	SW1200	24164	Apr 58	to PC	
7933	ES-12		9033	ES-12	EMD	SW1200	24165	Apr 58	to PC	
7934	ES-12		9034	ES-12	EMD	SW1200	24166	Apr 58	to PC	
8100	BS-12		8135	BS-12	BLH	S-12	75945	Feb 54	to PC	
8101	BS-12		8136	BS-12	BLH	S-12	75946	Feb 54	to PC	
8102	BS-12		8165	BS-12	BLH	S-12	75947	Feb 54	to PC	
8103	BS-12		8167	BS-12	BLH	S-12	75948	Feb 54	to PC	
8104	BS-12		8134	BS-12	BLH	S-12	75949	Feb 54	to PC	
8105	BS-12am		8090	BRS-12	BLH	RS-12	75950	Feb 54	to PC	
8106	BS-12am		8091	BRS-12	BLH	RS-12	75951	Feb 54	to PC	
8107	BS-12am		8087	BRS-12	BLH	RS-12	75952	Feb 54	to PC	
8108	BS-12am		8088	BRS-12	BLH	RS-12	75953	Feb 54	to PC	
8109	BS-12am		8089	BRS-12	BLH	RS-12	75954	Feb 54	to PC	
8110	BS-12ams		8085	BRS-12s	BLH	RS-12	75955	Feb 54	to PC	

ORIG ROAD NUM.	PRR BASE CLASS	PRR REBLT CLASS	1966 ROAD NUM.	PRR CLASS (1966)	BLDR	BLDR MODEL	BLDR SERIAL NUM.	BLDR DATE	RETIRE DATE	NOTE
8111	BS-16m		6975	BRS-16	BLH	AS-616	75956	Feb 54	to PC	
8112	BS-16m		6976	BRS-16	BLH	AS-616	75957	Feb 54	to PC	
8113	BS-24m		8966	BRS-24	BLH	RT-624	75958	Feb 54	to PC	
8114	BS-16m		6977	BRS-16	BLH	AS-616	75164	May 51	Sep 67	(19)
8424	AS-10a		9844	AS-10a	Alco	T-6	82857	Mar 58	to PC	
8425	AS-10a		9845	AS-10a	Alco	T-6	82858	Mar 58	to PC	
8426	AS-10a		9846	AS-10a	Alco	T-6	82859	Mar 58	to PC	
8427	AS-10a		9847	AS-10a	Alco	T-6	82860	Mar 58	to PC	
8428	AS-10a		9848	AS-10a	Alco	T-6	82861	Mar 58	to PC	
8429	AS-10a		9849	AS-10a	Alco	T-6	82862	Mar 58	to PC	
8430	AS-10		9830	AS-10	Alco	S-4	80975	Jan 54	to PC	
8431	AS-10		9831	AS-10	Alco	S-4	80976	Jan 54	to PC	
8432	AS-10		9832	AS-10	Alco	S-4	80977	Jan 54	to PC	
8433	AS-10		9833	AS-10	Alco	S-4	80295	Jan 54	to PC	
8434	AS-10		9834	AS-10	Alco	S-4	80296	Feb 54	to PC	
8435	AS-16m		5415	ARS-16	Alco	RS-3	80572	Nov 53	to PC	
8436	AS-16m		5416	ARS-16	Alco	RS-3	80573	Nov 53	to PC	

PRR 7612 pushing the eastbound hump at Enola yard, April 28, 1962. The unit is operating long hood forward and is oriented to shove forward into the cut of cars being humped.

ORIG ROAD NUM.	PRR BASE CLASS	PRR REBLT CLASS	1966 ROAD NUM.	PRR CLASS (1966)	BLDR	BLDR MODEL	BLDR SERIAL NUM.	BLDR DATE	RETIRE DATE	NOTE
8437	AS-16m		5437	ARS-16	Alco	RS-3	80574	Nov 53	to PC	
8438	AS-16m		5438	ARS-16	Alco	RS-3	80575	Nov 53	to PC	
8439	AS-16m		5439	ARS-16	Alco	RS-3	80568	Nov 53	to PC	
8440	AS-16m		5440	ARS-16	Alco	RS-3	80569	Nov 53	to PC	
8441	AS-16m		5441	ARS-16	Alco	RS-3	80570	Nov 53	to PC	
8442	AS-16m		5442	ARS-16	Alco	RS-3	80571	Nov 53	to PC	
8443	AS-16ms		5567	ARS-16s	Alco	RS-3	80576	Nov 53	to PC	
8444	AS-16ms		5568	ARS-16s	Alco	RS-3	80577	Dec 53	to PC	
8445	AS-16ms		5569	ARS-16s	Alco	RS-3	80580	Dec 53	to PC	

Pennsylvania Railroad Diesel Locomotive Roster

ORIG ROAD NUM.	PRR BASE CLASS	PRR REBLT CLASS	1966 ROAD NUM.	PRR CLASS (1966)	BLDR	BLDR MODEL	BLDR SERIAL NUM.	BLDR DATE	RETIRE DATE	NOTE
8446	AS-16a		AS-16am 6800	ARS-16a	Alco	RSD-5	80206	Oct 52	to PC	(13)
8447	AS-16a		AS-16am 6801	ARS-16a	Alco	RSD-5	80207	Oct 52	to PC	(13)
8448	AS-16a		AS-16am 6802	ARS-16a	Alco	RSD-5	80208	Mar 53	to PC	(13)
8449	AS-16a		AS-16am 6803	ARS-16a	Alco	RSD-5	80209	Mar 53	to PC	(13)
8450	AS-16a		AS-16am 6804	ARS-16a	Alco	RSD-5	80210	Mar 53	to PC	(13)
8451	AS-16a		AS-16am 6805	ARS-16a	Alco	RSD-5	80211	Mar 53	to PC	(13)
8452	AS-16m		5452	ARS-16	Alco	RS-3	79927	Jun 52	to PC	
8453	AS-16m		5453	ARS-16	Alco	RS-3	79928	Jun 52	to PC	
8454	AS-16m		5454	ARS-16	Alco	RS-3	79929	Jun 52	to PC	
8455	AS-16m		5455	ARS-16	Alco	RS-3	79930	Jun 52	to PC	
8456	AS-16m		5456	ARS-16	Alco	RS-3	79907	Jun 52	to PC	
8457	AS-16m		5457	ARS-16	Alco	RS-3	79908	Jun 52	to PC	
8458	AS-16m		5458	ARS-16	Alco	RS-3	79909	Jun 52	to PC	
8459	AS-16m		5459	ARS-16	Alco	RS-3	79910	Jun 52	to PC	
8460	AS-16m		5460	ARS-16	Alco	RS-3	79911	Jun 52	to PC	
8461	AS-16m		5461	ARS-16	Alco	RS-3	79912	Jun 52	to PC	
8462	AS-16m		5462	ARS-16	Alco	RS-3	79913	Jun 52	to PC	
8463	AS-16m		5463	ARS-16	Alco	RS-3	79915	Jun 52	to PC	
8464	AS-16m		5464	ARS-16	Alco	RS-3	79916	Jun 52	to PC	
8465	AS-16m		5465	ARS-16	Alco	RS-3	79917	Jun 52	to PC	
8466	AS-16m		5466	ARS-16	Alco	RS-3	79931	Jun 52	to PC	
8467	AS-16m		5467	ARS-16	Alco	RS-3	79932	Jun 52	to PC	
8468	AS-16m		5468	ARS-16	Alco	RS-3	79933	Jun 52	to PC	
8469	AS-16m		5469	ARS-16	Alco	RS-3	79934	Jun 52	to PC	
8470	AS-16m		5470	ARS-16	Alco	RS-3	79935	Jun 52	to PC	
8471	AS-16ms		5571	ARS-16s	Alco	RS-3	79936	Jun 52	to PC	
8472	AS-16ms		5572	ARS-16s	Alco	RS-3	80114	Jul 52	to PC	
8473	AS-16ms		5573	ARS-16s	Alco	RS-3	80115	Jul 52	to PC	
8474	AS-16ms		5574	ARS-16s	Alco	RS-3	79919	Jun 52	to PC	
8475	AS-16ms		5575	ARS-16s	Alco	RS-3	79920	Jun 52	to PC	
8476	AS-16ms		5576	ARS-16s	Alco	RS-3	79921	Jun 52	to PC	
8477	AS-16ms		5577	ARS-16s	Alco	RS-3	79922	Jun 52	to PC	
8478	AS-16ms		5578	ARS-16s	Alco	RS-3	79923	Jun 52	to PC	
8479	AS-16ms		5579	ARS-16s	Alco	RS-3	79924	Jun 52	to PC	
8480	AS-16ms		5580	ARS-16s	Alco	RS-3	79925	Jun 52	to PC	
8481	AS-16ms		5581	ARS-16s	Alco	RS-3	79926	Jun 52	to PC	
8482	AS-16ms		5582	ARS-16s	Alco	RS-3	79937	Jun 52	to PC	
8483	AS-16ms		5583	ARS-16s	Alco	RS-3	79938	Jun 52	to PC	
8484	AS-16ms		5584	ARS-16s	Alco	RS-3	79939	Jun 52	to PC	
8485	AS-10ams		9914	ARS-10s	Alco	RS-1	79940	Jun 52	to PC	
8486	AS-10ams		9915	ARS-10s	Alco	RS-1	79941	Jun 52	to PC	
8487	AS-10		9815	AS-10	Alco	S-4	79582	May 52	to PC	
8488	AS-10		9822	AS-10	Alco	S-4	79583	May 52	to PC	
8489	AS-10		9823	AS-10	Alco	S-4	79792	May 52	to PC	
8490	AS-10m		9770	AS-10m	Alco	S-4	79793	May 52	to PC	
8491	AS-10m		9771	AS-10m	Alco	S-4	79794	May 52	to PC	
8492	AS-10m		9772	AS-10m	Alco	S-4	79795	May 52	to PC	
8493	AS-10m		9773	AS-10m	Alco	S-4	79796	May 52	to PC	
8494	AS-10m		9774	AS-10m	Alco	S-4	79797	Jun 52	to PC	
8495	AS-10m		9775	AS-10m	Alco	S-4	79798	Jun 52	to PC	
8496	AS-10m		9776	AS-10m	Alco	S-4	79799	Jun 52	to PC	
8497	AS-10m		9777	AS-10m	Alco	S-4	79800	Jun 52	to PC	
8498	AS-10m		9768	AS-10m	Alco	S-4	79803	Jun 52	to PC	
8499	AS-10m		9769	AS-10m	Alco	S-4	79804	Jun 52	to PC	
8500	ES-15ms		5950	ERS-15s	EMD	GP7	16756	Aug 52	to PC	
8501	ES-15ms		5951	ERS-15s	EMD	GP7	16757	Aug 52	to PC	
8502	ES-15m		5852	ERS-15	EMD	GP7	16768	Aug 52	to PC	
8503	ES-15m		5853	ERS-15	EMD	GP7	16758	Aug 52	to PC	
8504	ES-15m		5884	ERS-15	EMD	GP7	16759	Aug 52	to PC	
8505	ES-15m		5885	ERS-15	EMD	GP7	16760	Aug 52	to PC	
8506	ES-15m		5886	ERS-15	EMD	GP7	16761	Aug 52	to PC	
8507	ES-15m		5887	ERS-15	EMD	GP7	16762	Aug 52	to PC	
8508	ES-15m		5888	ERS-15	EMD	GP7	16763	Aug 52	to PC	
8509	ES-15m		5889	ERS-15	EMD	GP7	16764	Aug 52	to PC	
8510	ES-15m		5890	ERS-15	EMD	GP7	16765	Aug 52	to PC	
8511	ES-15m		5891	ERS-15	EMD	GP7	16766	Aug 52	to PC	
8512	ES-15m		5892	ERS-15	EMD	GP7	16767	Aug 52	to PC	
8513	ES-12m		9113	ES-12m	EMD	SW9	16724	Dec 52	to PC	
8514	ES-12m		9114	ES-12m	EMD	SW9	16725	Dec 52	to PC	
8515	ES-12m		9115	ES-12m	EMD	SW9	16726	Dec 52	to PC	
8516	ES-12m		9116	ES-12m	EMD	SW9	16727	Dec 52	to PC	
8517	ES-12m		9117	ES-12m	EMD	SW9	16728	Dec 52	to PC	
8518	ES-12m		9118	ES-12m	EMD	SW9	16729	Dec 52	to PC	
8519	ES-12m		9119	ES-12m	EMD	SW9	16730	Dec 52	to PC	
8520	ES-12m		9120	ES-12m	EMD	SW9	16731	Mar 53	to PC	
8521	ES-12m		9121	ES-12m	EMD	SW9	16732	Mar 53	to PC	

L.A. MARRE COLLECTION

PRR 8508 and 8582 in 1955. The 8508 was moved from Trenton, New Jersey to Ohio in 1953. Because 8508 had been purchased without either trainphone or dynamic brakes, both of these pieces of special equipment were added for its Buckeye assignment.

Pennsylvania Railroad Diesel Locomotive Roster

Pennsylvania Railroad Diesel Locomotive Roster

PRR 8592 and 8593 returning from a transfer run to the Canadian National on July 19, 1959. The photo was taken on Canadian soil at Fort Erie, Ontario. This view illustrates the interesting bent bracket for the RS-3 trainphone antenna. The bracket was shaped this way ito allow the hood cover to swing open without interference. In addition, sloganeering signs on cab sides were not commonly seen on the PRR.

ORIG ROAD NUM.	PRR BASE CLASS	PRR REBLT CLASS	1966 ROAD NUM.	PRR CLASS (1966)	BLDR	BLDR MODEL	BLDR SERIAL NUM.	BLDR DATE	RETIRE DATE	NOTE
8522	ES-12m		9122	ES-12m	EMD	SW9	16733	Mar 53	to PC	
8523	ES-12m		9123	ES-12m	EMD	SW9	16742	Dec 52	to PC	
8524	ES-12m		9124	ES-12m	EMD	SW9	16743	Dec 52	to PC	
8525	ES-12m		9125	ES-12m	EMD	SW9	16744	Dec 52	to PC	
8526	ES-12m		9126	ES-12m	EMD	SW9	16745	Dec 52	to PC	
8527	ES-12m		9127	ES-12m	EMD	SW9	16746	Dec 52	to PC	
8528	ES-12m		9128	ES-12m	EMD	SW9	16747	Dec 52	to PC	
8529	ES-12m		9129	ES-12m	EMD	SW9	16734	Mar 53	to PC	
8530	ES-12m		9130	ES-12m	EMD	SW9	16735	Mar 53	to PC	
8531	ES-12m		9131	ES-12m	EMD	SW9	16736	Mar 53	to PC	
8532	ES-12m		9132	ES-12m	EMD	SW9	16737	Mar 53	to PC	
8533	ES-12m		9133	ES-12m	EMD	SW9	16738	Mar 53	to PC	
8534	ES-12m		9134	ES-12m	EMD	SW9	16739	Mar 53	to PC	
8535	ES-12m		9135	ES-12m	EMD	SW9	16740	Mar 53	to PC	
8536	ES-12m		9136	ES-12m	EMD	SW9	16741	Mar 53	to PC	
8537	ES-12m		9137	ES-12m	EMD	SW9	16748	Dec 52	to PC	
8538	ES-12m		9138	ES-12m	EMD	SW9	16749	Dec 52	to PC	
8539	ES-12m		9139	ES-12m	EMD	SW9	16750	Dec 52	to PC	
8540	ES-12m		9140	ES-12m	EMD	SW9	16751	Dec 52	to PC	
8541	ES-12m		9141	ES-12m	EMD	SW9	16752	Dec 52	to PC	
8542	ES-12		9042	ES-12	EMD	SW9	16753	Mar 53	to PC	
8543	ES-12		9043	ES-12	EMD	SW9	16754	Mar 53	to PC	
8544	ES-12		9044	ES-12	EMD	SW9	16755	Mar 53	to PC	
8545	ES-15m		5845	ERS-15	EMD	GP7	18626	Aug 53	to PC	
8546	ES-15m		5846	ERS-15	EMD	GP7	18627	Aug 53	to PC	
8547	ES-15m		5847	ERS-15	EMD	GP7	18662	Sep 53	to PC	
8548	ES-15m		5848	ERS-15	EMD	GP7	18663	Sep 53	to PC	
8549	ES-15m		5849	ERS-15	EMD	GP7	18664	Sep 53	to PC	
8550	ES-15m		5850	ERS-15	EMD	GP7	18665	Sep 53	to PC	
8551	ES-15ms		5952	ERS-15s	EMD	GP7	18666	Sep 53	to PC	
8552	ES-15ms		5953	ERS-15s	EMD	GP7	18667	Sep 53	to PC	
8553	ES-15ms		5954	ERS-15s	EMD	GP7	18668	Sep 53	to PC	
8554	ES-15m		5854	ERS-15	EMD	GP7	18633	Aug 53	to PC	
8555	ES-15m		5855	ERS-15	EMD	GP7	18634	Aug 53	to PC	
8556	ES-15m		5856	ERS-15	EMD	GP7	18635	Aug 53	to PC	
8557	ES-15m		5857	ERS-15	EMD	GP7	18636	Aug 53	to PC	
8558	ES-15m		5858	ERS-15	EMD	GP7	18637	Aug 53	to PC	
8559	ES-15m		5859	ERS-15	EMD	GP7	18638	Sep 53	to PC	
8560	ES-15m		5860	ERS-15	EMD	GP7	18639	Sep 53	to PC	
8561	ES-15m		5861	ERS-15	EMD	GP7	18640	Sep 53	to PC	
8562	ES-15m		5862	ERS-15	EMD	GP7	18641	Sep 53	to PC	
8563	ES-15m		5863	ERS-15	EMD	GP7	18642	Sep 53	to PC	
8564	ES-15m		5864	ERS-15	EMD	GP7	18643	Sep 53	to PC	
8565	ES-15m		5865	ERS-15	EMD	GP7	18644	Sep 53	to PC	
8566	ES-15m		5866	ERS-15	EMD	GP7	18645	Sep 53	to PC	
8567	ES-15m		5867	ERS-15	EMD	GP7	18646	Sep 53	to PC	
8568	ES-15m		5868	ERS-15	EMD	GP7	18647	Sep 53	to PC	
8569	ES-15m		5869	ERS-15	EMD	GP7	18648	Sep 53	to PC	
8570	ES-15m		5870	ERS-15	EMD	GP7	18649	Sep 53	to PC	
8571	ES-15m		5871	ERS-15	EMD	GP7	18650	Sep 53	to PC	
8572	ES-15m		5872	ERS-15	EMD	GP7	18651	Sep 53	to PC	
8573	ES-15m		5873	ERS-15	EMD	GP7	18652	Sep 53	to PC	
8574	ES-15m		5874	ERS-15	EMD	GP7	18653	Sep 53	to PC	
8575	ES-15m		5875	ERS-15	EMD	GP7	18654	Sep 53	to PC	
8576	ES-15m		5876	ERS-15	EMD	GP7	18655	Sep 53	to PC	
8577	ES-15m		5877	ERS-15	EMD	GP7	18656	Sep 53	to PC	
8578	ES-15m		5878	ERS-15	EMD	GP7	18657	Sep 53	to PC	
8579	ES-15m		5879	ERS-15	EMD	GP7	18658	Sep 53	to PC	
8580	ES-15m		5880	ERS-15	EMD	GP7	18659	Sep 53	to PC	
8581	ES-15m		5881	ERS-15	EMD	GP7	18660	Sep 53	to PC	
8582	ES-15m		5882	ERS-15	EMD	GP7	18661	Sep 53	to PC	
8583	ES-15ms		5955	ERS-15s	EMD	GP7	18628	Aug 53	to PC	
8584	ES-15ms		5956	ERS-15s	EMD	GP7	18629	Sep 53	to PC	
8585	ES-15ms		5957	ERS-15s	EMD	GP7	18630	Sep 53	to PC	
8586	ES-15ms		5958	ERS-15s	EMD	GP7	18631	Sep 53	to PC	
8587	ES-15ms		5959	ERS-15s	EMD	GP7	18632	Sep 53	to PC	
8588	ES-15a		6950	ERS-15ax	EMD	SD7	18669	Oct 53	to PC	
8589	ES-15a		6951	ERS-15ax	EMD	SD7	18670	Oct 53	to PC	
8590	AS-16m		5450	ARS-16	Alco	RS-3	81711	Dec 55	to PC	
8591	AS-16m		5451	ARS-16	Alco	RS-3	81712	Dec 55	to PC	
8592	AS-16m		5411	ARS-16	Alco	RS-3	81713	Dec 55	to PC	
8593	AS-16m		5443	ARS-16	Alco	RS-3	81714	Dec 55	to PC	
8594	AS-16m		5444	ARS-16	Alco	RS-3	81795	Dec 55	to PC	
8595	AS-16m		5445	ARS-16	Alco	RS-3	81796	Dec 55	to PC	
8596	AS-16m		5446	ARS-16	Alco	RS-3	81797	Dec 55	to PC	
8597	AS-16m		5447	ARS-16	Alco	RS-3	81798	Dec 55	to PC	
8598	AS-16m		5448	ARS-16	Alco	RS-3	81799	Dec 55	to PC	

Pennsylvania Railroad Diesel Locomotive Roster

ORIG ROAD NUM.	PRR BASE CLASS	PRR REBLT CLASS	1966 ROAD NUM.	PRR CLASS (1966)	BLDR	BLDR MODEL	BLDR SERIAL NUM.	BLDR DATE	RETIRE DATE	NOTE
8620	AS-18m		7620	ARS-18	Alco	RS-11	81923	Aug 56	to PC	
8621	AS-18m		7621	ARS-18	Alco	RS-11	81924	Aug 56	to PC	
8622	AS-18m		7622	ARS-18	Alco	RS-11	81925	Aug 56	to PC	
8623	AS-18m		7623	ARS-18	Alco	RS-11	81926	Aug 56	to PC	
8624	AS-18m		7624	ARS-18	Alco	RS-11	81927	Aug 56	to PC	
8625	AS-18m		7625	ARS-18	Alco	RS-11	81928	Aug 56	to PC	
8626	AS-18m		7626	ARS-18	Alco	RS-11	82330	Feb 57	to PC	
8627	AS-18m		7627	ARS-18	Alco	RS-11	82331	Feb 57	to PC	
8628	AS-18m		7628	ARS-18	Alco	RS-11	82332	Feb 57	to PC	
8629	AS-18m		7629	ARS-18	Alco	RS-11	82333	Feb 57	to PC	
8630	AS-18m		7630	ARS-18	Alco	RS-11	82334	Feb 57	to PC	
8631	AS-18m		7631	ARS-18	Alco	RS-11	82335	Feb 57	to PC	
8632	AS-18m		7632	ARS-18	Alco	RS-11	82336	Feb 57	to PC	
8633	AS-18m		7633	ARS-18	Alco	RS-11	82337	Feb 57	to PC	
8634	AS-18m		7634	ARS-18	Alco	RS-11	82338	May 57	to PC	
8635	AS-18m		7635	ARS-18	Alco	RS-11	82339	May 57	to PC	
8636	AS-18m		7636	ARS-18	Alco	RS-11	82642	Nov 57	to PC	
8637	AS-18m		7637	ARS-18	Alco	RS-11	82643	Nov 57	to PC	
8638	AS-18m		7638	ARS-18	Alco	RS-11	82644	Nov 57	to PC	
8639	AS-18m		7639	ARS-18	Alco	RS-11	82645	Nov 57	to PC	
8640	AS-18m		7640	ARS-18	Alco	RS-11	82646	Nov 57	to PC	
8641	AS-18m		7641	ARS-18	Alco	RS-11	82647	Nov 57	to PC	
8642	AS-18m		7642	ARS-18	Alco	RS-11	82817	Nov 57	to PC	
8643	AS-18m		7643	ARS-18	Alco	RS-11	82818	Nov 57	to PC	
8644	AS-18m		7644	ARS-18	Alco	RS-11	82819	Nov 57	to PC	
8645	AS-18m		7645	ARS-18	Alco	RS-11	82820	Nov 57	to PC	
8646	AS-18m		7646	ARS-18	Alco	RS-11	82821	Nov 57	to PC	
8647	AS-18m		7647	ARS-18	Alco	RS-11	82822	Nov 57	to PC	
8648	AS-18m		7648	ARS-18	Alco	RS-11	82823	Nov 57	to PC	
8649	AS-18m		7649	ARS-18	Alco	RS-11	82824	Nov 57	to PC	
8650	AS-18m		7650	ARS-18	Alco	RS-11	82825	Dec 57	to PC	
8651	AS-18m		7651	ARS-18	Alco	RS-11	82826	Dec 57	to PC	
8652	AS-18m		7652	ARS-18	Alco	RS-11	82827	Dec 57	to PC	
8653	AS-18m		7653	ARS-18	Alco	RS-11	82828	Dec 57	to PC	
8654	AS-18m		7654	ARS-18	Alco	RS-11	82829	Dec 57	to PC	
8655	AS-18am		6855	ARS-18a	Alco	RSD-12	82379	Dec 57	to PC	
8656	AS-18am		6856	ARS-18a	Alco	RSD-12	82380	Dec 57	to PC	
8657	AS-18am		6857	ARS-18a	Alco	RSD-12	82381	Dec 57	to PC	
8658	AS-18am		6858	ARS-18a	Alco	RSD-12	82382	Jan 58	to PC	
8659	AS-18am		6859	ARS-18a	Alco	RSD-12	82383	Jan 58	to PC	
8660	AS-18am		6860	ARS-18a	Alco	RSD-12	82384	Jan 58	to PC	
8661	AS-18am		6861	ARS-18a	Alco	RSD-12	82385	Jan 58	to PC	
8662	AS-18am		6862	ARS-18a	Alco	RSD-12	82386	Jan 58	to PC	
8663	AS-18am		6863	ARS-18a	Alco	RSD-12	82387	Jan 58	to PC	
8664	AS-18am		6864	ARS-18a	Alco	RSD-12	82066	Feb 58	to PC	
8665	AS-18am		6865	ARS-18a	Alco	RSD-12	82067	Feb 58	to PC	
8666	AS-18am		6866	ARS-18a	Alco	RSD-12	82068	Feb 58	to PC	
8667	AS-18am		6867	ARS-18a	Alco	RSD-12	82069	Feb 58	to PC	
8668	AS-18am		6868	ARS-18a	Alco	RSD-12	82070	Feb 58	to PC	
8669	AS-18am		6869	ARS-18a	Alco	RSD-12	82071	Mar 58	to PC	
8670	AS-18am		6870	ARS-18a	Alco	RSD-12	82072	Mar 58	to PC	
8671	AS-18am		6871	ARS-18a	Alco	RSD-12	82073	Mar 58	to PC	

ORIG ROAD NUM.	PRR BASE CLASS	PRR REBLT CLASS	1966 ROAD NUM.	PRR CLASS (1966)	BLDR	BLDR MODEL	BLDR SERIAL NUM.	BLDR DATE	RETIRE DATE	NOTE
8599	AS-16m		5449	ARS-16	Alco	RS-3	81800	Dec 55	to PC	
8600	AS-16m		5400	ARS-16	Alco	RS-3	81801	Dec 55	to PC	
8601	AS-16m		5401	ARS-16	Alco	RS-3	81802	Dec 55	to PC	
8602	AS-16m		5402	ARS-16	Alco	RS-3	81803	Jan 56	to PC	
8603	AS-16m		5403	ARS-16	Alco	RS-3	81804	Dec 55	to PC	
8604	AS-16m		5404	ARS-16	Alco	RS-3	81841	Dec 55	to PC	
8605	AS-16m		5405	ARS-16	Alco	RS-3	81745	Dec 55	to PC	
8606	APS-24ms		6806	ARS-24s	Alco	RSD-7				
8607	APS-24ms		6807	ARS-24s	Alco	RSD-7	81746	Dec 55	to PC	
8608	APS-24ms		6808	ARS-24s	Alco	RSD-7	81747	Dec 55	to PC	
8609	APS-24ms		6809	ARS-24s	Alco	RSD-7	81748	Jan 56	to PC	
8610	APS-24ms		6810	ARS-24s	Alco	RSD-7	81749	Jan 56	to PC	
8611	AS-24m		6811	ARS-24	Alco	RSD-15	81750	Jun 56	to PC	
8612	AS-24m		6812	ARS-24	Alco	RSD-15	81751	Jun 56	to PC	
8613	AS-24m		6813	ARS-24	Alco	RSD-15	81752	Aug 56	to PC	
8614	AS-24m		6814	ARS-24	Alco	RSD-15	81753	Aug 56	to PC	
8615	AS-24m		6815	ARS-24	Alco	RSD-15	81754	Aug 56	to PC	
8616	AS-24m		6816	ARS-24	Alco	RSD-15	81755	Aug 56	to PC	
8617	AS-18m		7617	ARS-18	Alco	RS-11	81920	Aug 56	to PC	
8618	AS-18m		7618	ARS-18	Alco	RS-11	81921	Aug 56	to PC	
8619	AS-18m		7619	ARS-18	Alco	RS-11	81922	Aug 56	to PC	

Westbound ore trains required mid-train helpers on the East Slope grade west of Altoona. Here, PRR 8606, 8608 and 8613 give the big push at Brickyard Crossing on July 24, 1965.

Pennsylvania Railroad Diesel Locomotive Roster

ORIG ROAD NUM.	PRR BASE CLASS	PRR REBLT CLASS	1966 ROAD NUM.	PRR CLASS (1966)	BLDR	BLDR MODEL	BLDR SERIAL NUM.	BLDR DATE	RETIRE DATE	NOTE
8672	AS-18am		6872	ARS-18a	Alco	RSD-12	82074	Mar 58	to PC	
8673	AS-18am		6873	ARS-18a	Alco	RSD-12	82075	Mar 58	to PC	
8674	AS-18am		6874	ARS-18a	Alco	RSD-12	82076	Mar 58	to PC	
8675	AS-18am		6875	ARS-18a	Alco	RSD-12	82077	Mar 58	to PC	
8676	AS-18am		6876	ARS-18a	Alco	RSD-12	82078	Mar 58	to PC	
8677	AS-18am		6877	ARS-18a	Alco	RSD-12	82079	Apr 58	to PC	
8678	AS-18am		6878	ARS-18a	Alco	RSD-12	82080	Apr 58	to PC	
8679	AS-18am		6879	ARS-18a	Alco	RSD-12	82918	Apr 58	to PC	
8699	FS-24m		6708	FRS-24	FM	H24-66	24L897	Aug 56	to PC	
8700	FS-24m		6700	FRS-24	FM	H24-66	24L898	Aug 56	to PC	
8701	FS-24m		6701	FRS-24	FM	H24-66	24L899	Aug 56	to PC	
8702	FS-24m		6702	FRS-24	FM	H24-66	24L900	Aug 56	to PC	
8703	FS-24m		6703	FRS-24	FM	H24-66	24L901	Aug 56	to PC	
8704	FS-24m		6704	FRS-24	FM	H24-66	24L902	Sep 56	to PC	
8705	FS-24m		6705	FRS-24	FM	H24-66	24L903	Sep 56	to PC	
8706	FS-24m		6706	FRS-24	FM	H24-66	24L904	Sep 56	to PC	
8707	FS-24m		6707	FRS-24	FM	H24-66	24L905	Sep 56	to PC	
8708	FS-12		8340	FS-12	FM	H12-44	12L828	Feb 54	to PC	
8709	FS-12		8341	FS-12	FM	H12-44	12L829	Feb 54	to PC	
8710	FS-12		8342	FS-12	FM	H12-44	12L830	Feb 54	to PC	
8711	FS-12m		8327	FS-12m	FM	H12-44	12L637	Nov 52	Oct 67	
8712	FS-12m		8328	FS-12m	FM	H12-44	12L638	Nov 52	Oct 67	
8713	FS-12m		8329	FS-12m	FM	H12-44	12L639	Nov 52	Oct 67	
8714	FS-12m		8330	FS-12m	FM	H12-44	12L640	Nov 52	to PC	
8715	FS-12m		8331	FS-12m	FM	H12-44	12L641	Nov 52	Oct 67	
8716	FS-12m		8332	FS-12m	FM	H12-44	12L642	Nov 52	Oct 67	
8717	FS-12m		8333	FS-12m	FM	H12-44	12L643	Nov 52	Oct 67	
8718	FS-12m		8334	FS-12m	FM	H12-44	12L644	Nov 52	Dec 67	
8719	FS-12m		8335	FS-12m	FM	H12-44	12L645	Nov 52	Oct 67	
8720	FS-12m		8336	FS-12m	FM	H12-44	12L646	Nov 52	to PC	
8721	FS-12m		8337	FS-12m	FM	H12-44	12L647	Nov 52	to PC	
8722	FS-12m		8338	FS-12m	FM	H12-44	12L648	Nov 52	Oct 67	
8723	FS-12m		8339	FS-12m	FM	H12-44	12L649	Nov 52	to PC	
8724	BS-24m				BLH	RT-624	75664	Oct 52	Oct 67	
8725	BS-24m				BLH	RT-624	75665	Sep 52	Oct 67	
8726	BS-24m				BLH	RT-624	75666	Oct 52	Oct 67	
8727	BS-24m				BLH	RT-624	75667	Oct 52	Oct 67	
8728	BS-24m				BLH	RT-624	75668	Nov 52	Oct 67	
8729	BS-24m				BLH	RT-624	75669	Nov 52	Oct 67	
8730	BS-24m				BLH	RT-624	75670	Dec 52	Oct 67	
8731	BS-24m				BLH	RT-624	75671	Dec 52	Oct 67	
8732	BS-12m		8182	BS-12m	BLH	S-12	75631	Sep 52	to PC	
8733	BS-12m		8183	BS-12m	BLH	S-12	75632	Sep 52	to PC	
8734	BS-12m		8184	BS-12m	BLH	S-12	75633	Sep 52	to PC	
8735	BS-12m		8185	BS-12m	BLH	S-12	75634	Sep 52	Oct 67	
8736	BS-12m		8186	BS-12m	BLH	S-12	75635	Sep 52	to PC	
8737	BS-12m		8187	BS-12m	BLH	S-12	75636	Sep 52	to PC	
8738	BS-12m		8188	BS-12m	BLH	S-12	75637	Sep 52	Oct 67	
8739	BS-12m		8189	BS-12m	BLH	S-12	75638	Sep 52	to PC	
8740	BS-12m		8190	BS-12m	BLH	S-12	75639	Oct 52	to PC	
8741	BS-12m		8191	BS-12m	BLH	S-12	75640	Oct 52	Oct 67	
8742	BS-12m		8192	BS-12m	BLH	S-12	75641	Oct 52	to PC	
8743	BS-12m		8193	BS-12m	BLH	S-12	75642	Oct 52	to PC	
8744	BS-12m		8194	BS-12m	BLH	S-12	75643	Oct 52	Oct 67	
8745	BS-12m		8195	BS-12m	BLH	S-12	75644	Oct 52	to PC	
8746	BS-12m		8196	BS-12m	BLH	S-12	75645	Oct 52	Oct 67	
8747	BS-12m		8197	BS-12m	BLH	S-12	75646	Oct 52	to PC	
8748	BS-12m		8198	BS-12m	BLH	S-12	75647	Oct 52	to PC	
8749	BS-12m		8199	BS-12m	BLH	S-12	75648	Oct 52	to PC	
8750	BS-12m		8180	BS-12m	BLH	S-12	75649	Oct 52	to PC	
8751	BS-12m		8181	BS-12m	BLH	S-12	75650	Oct 52	Oct 67	
8752	BS-12m		8178	BS-12m	BLH	S-12	75651	Oct 52	Oct 67	
8753	BS-12		8153	BS-12	BLH	S-12	75619	Aug 52	to PC	
8754	BS-12		8154	BS-12	BLH	S-12	75620	Aug 52	to PC	
8755	BS-12		8155	BS-12	BLH	S-12	75621	Aug 52	Oct 67	
8756	BS-12		8156	BS-12	BLH	S-12	75622	Aug 52	to PC	
8757	BS-12		8157	BS-12	BLH	S-12	75623	Sep 52	to PC	
8758	BS-12		8158	BS-12	BLH	S-12	75624	Aug 52	to PC	
8759	BS-12		8159	BS-12	BLH	S-12	75625	Sep 52	Oct 67	
8760	BS-12		8160	BS-12	BLH	S-12	75626	Sep 52	to PC	
8761	BS-12		8161	BS-12	BLH	S-12	75627	Sep 52	to PC	
8762	BS-12		8162	BS-12	BLH	S-12	75628	Sep 52	to PC	
8763	BS-12		8163	BS-12	BLH	S-12	75629	Sep 52	to PC	
8764	BS-12		8164	BS-12	BLH	S-12	75630	Sep 52	to PC	
8765	BS-12m		8179	BS-12m	BLH	S-12	75652	Oct 52	to PC	
8766	BS-12m		8176	BS-12m	BLH	S-12	75653	Oct 52	to PC	
8767	BS-12m		8177	BS-12m	BLH	S-12	75654	Oct 52	to PC	
8768	BS-12m		8168	BS-12m	BLH	S-12	75655	Oct 52	to PC	
8769	BS-12m		8169	BS-12m	BLH	S-12	75659	Dec 52	to PC	
8770	BS-12m		8170	BS-12m	BLH	S-12	75660	Dec 52	to PC	
8771	BS-12m		8171	BS-12m	BLH	S-12	75661	Dec 52	to PC	
8772	BS-12m		8172	BS-12m	BLH	S-12	75662	Dec 52	Oct 67	
8773	BS-12m		8173	BS-12m	BLH	S-12	75656	Dec 52	to PC	

Full side view of PRR 8751 at Delmar, Delaware, July 23, 1960. Delmar was the operating base for the PRR lines on the Delmarva peninsula. The characteristics of these class BS-12m units as light road switchers is apparent with the multiple unit capability, trainphone and roller bearings visible.

Pennsylvania Railroad Diesel Locomotive Roster

ORIG ROAD NUM.	PRR BASE CLASS	PRR REBLT CLASS	1966 ROAD NUM.	PRR CLASS (1966)	BLDR	BLDR MODEL	BLDR SERIAL NUM.	BLDR DATE	RETIRE DATE	NOTE
8774	BS-12m		8174	BS-12m	BLH	S-12	75657	Dec 52	Oct 67	
8775	BS-12m		8175	BS-12m	BLH	S-12	75658	Dec 52	to PC	
8776	BS-12ams		8086	BRS-12s	BLH	RS-12	75663	Sep 52	Oct 67	
8777	BS-12		8137	BS-12	BLH	S-12	75292	Dec 51	Mar 67	
8778	BS-12		8138	BS-12	BLH	S-12	75293	Dec 51	to PC	
8779	BS-12		8139	BS-12	BLH	S-12	75294	Jan 52	to PC	
8780	BS-12		8140	BS-12	BLH	S-12	75295	Jan 52	to PC	
8781	BS-12		8141	BS-12	BLH	S-12	75296	Jan 52	Jun 67	
8782	BS-12				BLH	S-12	75297	Jan 52	Jan 67	
8783	BS-12		8143	BS-12	BLH	S-12	75298	Jan 52	Mar 67	
8784	BS-12		8144	BS-12	BLH	S-12	75299	Jan 52	to PC	
8785	BS-12		8145	BS-12	BLH	S-12	75300	Jan 52	to PC	
8786	BS-12		8146	BS-12	BLH	S-12	75301	Jan 52	to PC	
8787	BS-12		8147	BS-12	BLH	S-12	75302	Jan 52	to PC	
8788	BS-12				BLH	S-12	75303	Feb 52	Jan 67	
8789	BS-12		8149	BS-12	BLH	S-12	75304	Feb 52	Oct 67	
8790	BS-12		8150	BS-12	BLH	S-12	75305	Feb 52	Sep 67	
8791	BS-12		8151	BS-12	BLH	S-12	75306	Feb 52	to PC	
8792	BS-12		8152	BS-12	BLH	S-12	75307	Feb 52	to PC	
8793	BS-12		8113	BS-12	BLH	S-12	75308	Feb 52	to PC	
8794	BS-12		8114	BS-12	BLH	S-12	75309	Feb 52	Feb 67	
8795	BS-12				BLH	S-12	75310	Feb 52	Dec 67	
8796	BS-12		8116	BS-12	BLH	S-12	75311	Feb 52	to PC	
8797	ES-15m		5897	ERS-15	EMD	GP7	12395	Jan 52	to PC	
8798	ES-15m		5898	ERS-15	EMD	GP7	12396	Jan 52	to PC	
8799	ES-15m		5899	ERS-15	EMD	GP7	12397	Jan 52	to PC	
8800	ES-15m		5840	ERS-15	EMD	GP7	12398	Jan 52	to PC	
8801	ES-15m		5841	ERS-15	EMD	GP7	12399	Jan 52	to PC	
8802	ES-15m		5842	ERS-15	EMD	GP7	12400	Jan 52	to PC	
8803	ES-15m		5843	ERS-15	EMD	GP7	12401	Jan 52	to PC	
8804	ES-15m		5844	ERS-15	EMD	GP7	12402	Jan 52	to PC	
8805	ES-15m		5895	ERS-15	EMD	GP7	12403	Jan 52	to PC	
8806	ES-15m		5896	ERS-15	EMD	GP7	12404	Jan 52	to PC	
8807	FS-16m				FM	H16-44	16L579	Apr 52	Jan 67	
8808	FS-16m		5151	FRS-16	FM	H16-44	16L580	Apr 52	Jun 67	
8809	FS-16m				FM	H16-44	16L581	Apr 52	Jan 67	
8810	FS-16m				FM	H16-44	16L582	Apr 52	Jan 67	
8811	FS-16m		5154	FRS-16	FM	H16-44	16L583	Apr 52	Sep 67	
8812	FS-16m				FM	H16-44	16L584	Apr 52	Jan 67	
8813	FS-16m		5156	FRS-16	FM	H16-44	16L585	Apr 52	Dec 67	
8814	FS-16m				FM	H16-44	16L586	Apr 52	Jan 67	
8815	FS-16m		5158	FRS-16	FM	H16-44	16L587	Apr 52	to PC	
8816	FS-16m				FM	H16-44	16L588	May 52	Jan 67	
8817	AS-16m		5417	ARS-16	Alco	RS-3	79365	Nov 51	Oct 67	
8818	AS-16m		5418	ARS-16	Alco	RS-3	79366	Nov 51	to PC	
8819	AS-16m		5419	ARS-16	Alco	RS-3	79367	Nov 51	to PC	
8820	AS-16m		5420	ARS-16	Alco	RS-3	79368	Nov 51	to PC	
8821	AS-16m		5421	ARS-16	Alco	RS-3	79369	Nov 51	to PC	
8822	AS-16m		5422	ARS-16	Alco	RS-3	79370	Nov 51	to PC	
8823	AS-16m		5423	ARS-16	Alco	RS-3	79371	Nov 51	Oct 67	
8824	AS-16m		5424	ARS-16	Alco	RS-3	79372	Nov 51	to PC	
8825	AS-16m		5425	ARS-16	Alco	RS-3	79373	Nov 51	to PC	
8826	AS-16m		5426	ARS-16	Alco	RS-3	79374	Nov 51	to PC	
8827	AS-16m		5427	ARS-16	Alco	RS-3	79375	Nov 51	to PC	
8828	AS-16m		5428	ARS-16	Alco	RS-3	79376	Nov 51	to PC	
8829	AS-16m				Alco	RS-3	79377	Nov 51	Jan 67	
8830	AS-16m		5430	ARS-16	Alco	RS-3	79378	Nov 51	to PC	
8831	AS-16m		5431	ARS-16	Alco	RS-3	79379	Nov 51	to PC	
8832	AS-16m		5432	ARS-16	Alco	RS-3	79380	Nov 51	to PC	
8833	AS-16m		5433	ARS-16	Alco	RS-3	79381	Nov 51	to PC	
8834	AS-16m		5434	ARS-16	Alco	RS-3	79382	Nov 51	Oct 67	
8835	AS-16m		5435	ARS-16	Alco	RS-3	79383	Nov 51	to PC	
8836	AS-16m				Alco	RS-3	79384	Nov 51	Jan 67	
8837	AS-16ms		5537	ARS-16s	Alco	RS-3	79395	Dec 51	to PC	
8838	AS-16ms		5538	ARS-16s	Alco	RS-3	79396	Dec 51	to PC	
8839	AS-16ms		5539	ARS-16s	Alco	RS-3	79397	Dec 51	to PC	
8840	AS-16ms		5540	ARS-16s	Alco	RS-3	79398	Dec 51	to PC	
8841	AS-16ms		5541	ARS-16s	Alco	RS-3	79399	Dec 51	Oct 67	
8842	AS-16ms		5542	ARS-16s	Alco	RS-3	79400	Dec 51	to PC	
8843	AS-16ms		5543	ARS-16s	Alco	RS-3	79401	Dec 51	to PC	
8844	AS-16ms				Alco	RS-3	79402	Dec 51	Jan 67	
8845	AS-16ms		5545	ARS-16s	Alco	RS-3	79403	Dec 51	Oct 67	
8846	AS-16ms		5546	ARS-16s	Alco	RS-3	79404	Dec 51	to PC	
8847	AS-16ms		5547	ARS-16s	Alco	RS-3	79405	Dec 51	to PC	
8848	AS-16ms		5548	ARS-16s	Alco	RS-3	79406	Dec 51	Oct 67	
8849	AS-16ms		5549	ARS-16s	Alco	RS-3	79407	Dec 51	to PC	
8850	AS-16ms		5550	ARS-16s	Alco	RS-3	79408	Dec 51	to PC	
8851	AS-16ms		5551	ARS-16s	Alco	RS-3	79409	Jan 52	to PC	
8852	AS-16ms		5552	ARS-16s	Alco	RS-3	79410	Jan 52	to PC	
8853	AS-16ms		5553	ARS-16s	Alco	RS-3	79411	Jan 52	to PC	
8854	AS-16ms			ARS-16s	Alco	RS-3	79412	Jan 52	Jan 67	
8855	AS-16ms		5555	ARS-16s	Alco	RS-3	79413	Jan 52	to PC	
8856	AS-16ms		5556	ARS-16s	Alco	RS-3	78914	Jan 52	Oct 67	
8857	AS-10as		9917	ARS-10sx	Alco	RS-1	78377	Mar 51	to PC	
8858	AS-10as		9918	ARS-10sx	Alco	RS-1	79046	Apr 51	to PC	

PRR 5547 at Camden, New Jersey on February 1, 1970, on Penn Central's second birthday. Still in its PRR paint scheme, GG-1-style numbers were used on the cab side when it was renumbered from 8847.

Pennsylvania Railroad Diesel Locomotive Roster

ORIG ROAD NUM.	PRR BASE CLASS	PRR REBLT CLASS	1966 ROAD NUM.	PRR CLASS (1966)	BLDR	BLDR MODEL	BLDR SERIAL NUM.	BLDR DATE	RETIRE DATE	NOTE
8859	ES-12		9059	ES-12	EMD	SW9	13061	Mar 51	to PC	
8860	ES-12		9060	ES-12	EMD	SW9	13062	Mar 51	to PC	
8861	ES-12		9061	ES-12	EMD	SW7	13063	Jan 51	to PC	
8862	ES-12		9062	ES-12	EMD	SW7	13064	Jan 51	to PC	
8863	ES-12		9063	ES-12	EMD	SW7	13065	Jan 51	to PC	
8864	ES-12		9064	ES-12	EMD	SW7	13066	Jan 51	to PC	
8865	ES-12		9065	ES-12	EMD	SW7	13067	Jan 51	to PC	
8866	ES-12		9066	ES-12	EMD	SW7	13068	Jan 51	to PC	
8867	ES-12		9067	ES-12	EMD	SW7	13069	Jan 51	to PC	
8868	ES-12	ES-12m	9094	ES-12m	EMD	SW9	13070	Jan 51	to PC	(14)
8869	ES-12		9095	ES-12	EMD	SW9	13073	Mar 51	to PC	
8870	ES-12		9096	ES-12	EMD	SW9	13074	Mar 51	to PC	
8871	ES-12	ES-12m	9097	ES-12m	EMD	SW7	13071	Jan 51	to PC	(14)
8872	ES-12	ES-12m	9098	ES-12m	EMD	SW7	13072	Jan 51	to PC	(14)
8873	AS-6		9473	AS-6	Alco	S-3	78404	Nov 50	to PC	
8874	AS-6		9474	AS-6	Alco	S-3	78405	Nov 50	to PC	
8875	AS-6		9475	AS-6	Alco	S-3	78506	Nov 50	to PC	
8876	AS-6		9476	AS-6	Alco	S-3	78507	Nov 50	to PC	
8877	AS-6		9477	AS-6	Alco	S-3	78508	Dec 50	to PC	
8878	AS-6		9478	AS-6	Alco	S-3	78509	Dec 50	to PC	
8879	AS-6		9479	AS-6	Alco	S-3	78511	Dec 50	to PC	
8880	AS-6		9480	AS-6	Alco	S-3	78512	Dec 50	to PC	
8881	AS-6		9481	AS-6	Alco	S-3	78513	Dec 50	to PC	
8882	AS-6		9482	AS-6	Alco	S-3	78514	Dec 50	to PC	
8883	AS-6		9483	AS-6	Alco	S-3	78515	Jan 51	to PC	
8884	AS-6		9484	AS-6	Alco	S-3	78516	Mar 51	to PC	
8885	AS-6		9485	AS-6	Alco	S-3	78517	Mar 51	to PC	
8886	AS-10		9803	AS-10	Alco	S-4	78683	Nov 50	to PC	
8887	AS-10		9817	AS-10	Alco	S-4	78684	Nov 50	to PC	
8888	AS-10		9788	AS-10	Alco	S-4	78685	Nov 50	to PC	
8889	AS-10		9789	AS-10	Alco	S-4	78686	Dec 50	to PC	
8890	AS-10		9790	AS-10	Alco	S-4	78687	Dec 50	to PC	
8891	AS-10		9791	AS-10	Alco	S-4	78688	Dec 50	to PC	
8892	AS-10		9792	AS-10	Alco	S-4	78689	Dec 50	to PC	
8893	AS-10		9793	AS-10	Alco	S-4	78690	Dec 50	to PC	
8894	AS-10		9794	AS-10	Alco	S-4	78691	Dec 50	to PC	
8895	AS-10		9795	AS-10	Alco	S-4	78692	Dec 50	to PC	
8896	AS-10		9796	AS-10	Alco	S-4	78693	Dec 50	to PC	
8897	AS-10		9797	AS-10	Alco	S-4	78694	Dec 50	to PC	
8898	AS-10		9798	AS-10	Alco	S-4	78695	Dec 50	to PC	
8899	AS-10		9799	AS-10	Alco	S-4	78696	Dec 50	to PC	
8900	AS-10		9800	AS-10	Alco	S-4	78779	Jun 51	Jul 66	
8901	AS-10		9801	AS-10	Alco	S-4	78780	Jun 51	to PC	
8902	AS-16m		5557	ARS-16s	Alco	RS-3	78585	Apr 51	to PC	
8903	AS-16ms		5414	ARS-16	Alco	RS-3	78586	Apr 51	to PC	
8904	AS-16m		5558	ARS-16s	Alco	RS-3	78579	Apr 51	to PC	
8905	AS-16ms		5406	ARS-16	Alco	RS-3	78587	Apr 51	Oct 67	
8906	AS-16m		5407	ARS-16	Alco	RS-3	78580	Apr 51	Oct 67	
8907	AS-16m		5408	ARS-16	Alco	RS-3	78581	Apr 51	Nov 67	
8908	AS-16m		5409	ARS-16	Alco	RS-3	78582	Apr 51	to PC	
8909	AS-16m				Alco	RS-3	78583	Apr 51	to PC	
8910	AS-16ms		5560	ARS-16s	Alco	RS-3	78588	Apr 51		

ORIG ROAD NUM.	PRR BASE CLASS	PRR REBLT CLASS	1966 ROAD NUM.	PRR CLASS (1966)	BLDR	BLDR MODEL	BLDR SERIAL NUM.	BLDR DATE	RETIRE DATE	NOTE
8911	AS-16ms				Alco	RS-3	78590	Apr 51	Jul 66	
8912	AS-16ms		5562	ARS-16s	Alco	RS-3	78591	Apr 51	to PC	
8913	AS-16ms		5563	ARS-16s	Alco	RS-3	78589	Apr 51	Oct 67	
8914	AS-16				Alco	RS-3	78584	Apr 51	to PC	
8915	AS-16ms		5565	ARS-16s	Alco	RS-3	78592	Apr 51	to PC	
8916	AS-16ms				Alco	RS-3	78593	Apr 51	Jul 66	

PRR 8914 at Morrisville, Pennsylvania on February 22, 1967. This locomotive was the only PRR RS-3 not equipped for multiple unit operation, and classed AS-16. This was perhaps the most extreme example of the PRR ordering locomotives for very specific assignments.

ORIG ROAD NUM.	PRR BASE CLASS	PRR REBLT CLASS	1966 ROAD NUM.	PRR CLASS (1966)	BLDR	BLDR MODEL	BLDR SERIAL NUM.	BLDR DATE	RETIRE DATE
8917	FS-20m		7717	FRS-20	FM	H20-44	21L453	May 51	Dec 66
8918	FS-20m				FM	H20-44	21L454	May 51	Jul 66
8919	FS-20m				FM	H20-44	21L455	May 51	Jul 66
8920	FS-20m		7720	FRS-20	FM	H20-44	21L456	May 51	Mar 67
8921	FS-20m		7721	FRS-20	FM	H20-44	21L457	May 51	Dec 66
8922	FS-20m				FM	H20-44	21L458	May 51	Jul 66
8923	FS-20m		7723	FRS-20	FM	H20-44	21L459	May 51	Feb 67
8924	FS-20m				FM	H20-44	21L460	May 51	Jul 66
8925	FS-20m				FM	H20-44	21L461	May 51	Jul 66
8926	FS-20m				FM	H20-44	21L462	Jun 51	Jul 66
8927	FS-20m				FM	H20-44	21L463	Jun 51	Jul 66
8928	FS-20m				FM	H20-44	21L464	Jun 51	Jul 66
8929	FS-20m		7729	FRS-20	FM	H20-44	21L465	Jun 51	Feb 67
8930	FS-20m		7730	FRS-20	FM	H20-44	21L466	Jun 51	Dec 66
8931	FS-20m		7731	FRS-20	FM	H20-44	21L467	Jun 51	Mar 67
8932	FS-20m				FM	H20-44	21L468	Apr 51	Jul 66
8933	FS-20m				FM	H20-44	21L469	Apr 51	Jul 66
8934	FS-20m		7734	FRS-20	FM	H20-44	21L470	May 51	Sep 67
8935	FS-20m				FM	H20-44	21L471	May 51	Jul 66
8936	FS-20m				FM	H20-44	21L472	May 51	Jul 66
8937	FS-20m				FM	H20-44	21L473	Apr 51	Jul 66
8938	FS-20m				FM	H20-44	21L474	Apr 51	Jul 66
8939	FS-20m		7739	FRS-20	FM	H20-44	21L475	Apr 51	Dec 66
8940	FS-20m		7740	FRS-20	FM	H20-44	21L476	Apr 51	Dec 66

ORIG ROAD NUM.	PRR BASE CLASS	PRR REBLT CLASS	1966 ROAD NUM.	PRR CLASS (1966)	BLDR	BLDR MODEL	BLDR SERIAL NUM.	BLDR DATE	RETIRE DATE	NOTE
8941	FS-20m	FRS-20	7741		FM	H20-44	21L477	Apr 51	Sep 67	
8942	FS-20m				FM	H20-44	21L478	Apr 51	Aug 66	
8943	LS-25m				L-H	2500T	9528	May 51	Jul 66	
8944	LS-25m				L-H	2500T	9529	Jun 51	Jul 66	
8945	LS-25m				L-H	2500T	9530	Jun 51	Jul 66	
8946	LS-25m				L-H	2500T	9531	Jun 51	Jul 66	
8947	LS-25m				L-H	2500T	9532	Jul 51	Jul 66	
8948	LS-25m				L-H	2500T	9535	Aug 51	Jul 66	
8949	LS-25m				L-H	2500T	9536	Aug 51	Jul 66	
8950	LS-25m				L-H	2500T	9533	Jul 51	Jul 66	
8951	LS-25m				L-H	2500T	9534	Aug 51	Jul 66	
8952	BS-24				BLH	RT-624	75123	Jul 51	Jul 66	
8953	BS-24				BLH	RT-624	75124	Jul 51	Jul 66	
8954	BS-24m				BLH	RT-624	75125	Aug 51	Jul 66	
8955	BS-24m				BLH	RT-624	75126	Aug 51	Jul 66	
8956	BS-24m				BLH	RT-624	75127	Sep 51	Jul 66	
8957	BS-24m				BLH	RT-624	75128	Sep 51	Jul 66	
8958	BS-24m				BLH	RT-624	75129	Oct 51	Jul 66	
8959	BS-24m				BLH	RT-624	75130	Oct 51	Jul 66	
8960	BS-24m				BLH	RT-624	75131	Oct 51	Jul 66	
8961	BS-24m				BLH	RT-624	75132	Oct 51	Jul 66	
8962	BS-24m				BLH	RT-624	75133	Nov 51	Jul 66	
8963	BS-24m				BLH	RT-624	75134	Nov 51	Jul 66	
8964	BS-24m				BLH	RT-624	75135	Nov 51	Jul 66	
8965	BS-24m				BLH	RT-624	75136	Nov 51	Jul 66	
8966	BS-16m	BRS-16	6966		BLH	AS-616	75076	May 51	to PC	
8967	BS-16m	BRS-16	6967		BLH	AS-616	75077	Jun 51	to PC	
8968	BS-16m				BLH	AS-616	75078	Jun 51	Jul 66	
8969	BS-16m				BLH	AS-616	75082	Jun 51	Jul 66	
8970	BS-16ms				BLH	AS-616	75083	Jun 51	Jun 67	
8971	BS-16ms				BLH	AS-616	75084	Jun 51	Jul 66	
8972	BS-16m				BLH	AS-616	75079	May 51	Jul 66	
8973	BS-16m	BRS-16	6973		BLH	AS-616	75080	May 51	to PC	
8974	BS-16m	BRS-16	6974		BLH	AS-616	75081	May 51	to PC	
8975	BS-12as	BRS-12sx	8084		BLH	RS-12	75116	Apr 51	to PC	
8976	BS-12				BLH	S-12	74857	Jan 51	to PC	
8977	BS-12		8117		BLH	S-12	74858	Jan 51	to PC	
8978	BS-12		8118		BLH	S-12	74859	Jan 51	Dec 66	
8979	BS-12		8119		BLH	S-12	74860	Jan 51	Jun 67	
8980	BS-12		8120		BLH	S-12	74861	Jan 51	to PC	
8981	BS-12		8121		BLH	S-12	74862	Jan 51	Sep 67	
8982	BS-12		8122		BLH	S-12	74863	Feb 51	to PC	
8983	BS-12		8123		BLH	S-12	74864	Feb 51	to PC	
8984	BS-12		8124		BLH	S-12	74865	Feb 51	Jun 67	
8985	BS-12		8125		BLH	S-12	74866	Feb 51	to PC	
8986	BS-12				BLH	S-12	74867	Feb 51	Jul 66	
8987	BS-12				BLH	S-12	74868	Feb 51	Jul 66	
8988	BS-12		8128		BLH	S-12	74869	Mar 51	to PC	
8989	BS-12		8129		BLH	S-12	74870	Mar 51	to PC	
8990	BS-12		8130		BLH	S-12	74871	Mar 51	to PC	
8991	BS-12		8131		BLH	S-12	74872	Mar 51	to PC	
8992	BS-12		8132		BLH	S-12	74873	Mar 51	to PC	

ORIG ROAD NUM.	PRR BASE CLASS	PRR REBLT CLASS	1966 ROAD NUM.	PRR CLASS (1966)	BLDR	BLDR MODEL	BLDR SERIAL NUM.	BLDR DATE	RETIRE DATE	NOTE
8993	BS-12				BLH	S-12	74874	Mar 51	Jul 66	
8994	BS-7				BLH	S-8	75117	Mar 51	Jul 66	
8995	BS-7				BLH	S-8	75118	Mar 51	Jul 66	
8996	BS-7		7896	BS-7	BLH	S-8	75119	Mar 51	to PC	
8997	BS-7				BLH	S-8	75120	Mar 51	Jul 66	
8998	BS-7		7898	BS-7	BLH	S-8	75121	Apr 51	to PC	
8999	BS-7				BLH	S-8	75122	Apr 51	Jul 66	
9000	BS-6a			BS-6	BLW	DS 4-4-660	73905	Mar 49	May 64	
9001	BS-6a		7801	BS-6	BLW	DS 4-4-660	73906	Mar 49	to PC	
9002	BS-6a		7802	BS-6	BLW	DS 4-4-660	73907	Mar 49	Dec 66	
9003	BS-6a		7803	BS-6	BLW	DS 4-4-660	73908	Mar 49	to PC	
9004	BS-6a		7804	BS-6	BLW	DS 4-4-660	73909	Mar 49	to PC	
9005	BS-6a		7805	BS-6	BLW	DS 4-4-660	73910	Mar 49	to PC	
9006	BS-6a				BLW	DS 4-4-660	73911	Mar 49	Feb 66	
9007	BS-6a		7807	BS-6	BLW	DS 4-4-660	73912	Mar 49	to PC	
9008	BS-6a		7808	BS-6	BLW	DS 4-4-660	73913	Mar 49	to PC	
9009	BS-6a				BLW	DS 4-4-660	74236	Mar 49	May 65	
9010	BS-6a				BLW	DS 4-4-660	74237	Mar 49	May 65	
9011	BS-6a				BLW	DS 4-4-660	74238	Apr 49	Sep 65	
9012	BS-6a				BLW	DS 4-4-660	74239	Apr 49	Nov 65	
9013	BS-6a		7853	BS-6	BLW	DS 4-4-660	74240	Apr 49	to PC	
9014	BS-6a		7854	BS-6	BLW	DS 4-4-660	74241	Apr 49	Jan 68	
9015	BS-6a		7855	BS-6	BLW	DS 4-4-660	74242	Apr 49	Oct 67	
9016	BS-6a		7856	BS-6	BLW	DS 4-4-660	74243	Apr 49	to PC	
9017	BS-6a				BLW	DS 4-4-660	74244	Apr 49	Sep 65	

The charred remains of PRR 9000 after it was consumed by fire a few months previously. It is seen here at Philadelphia's 46th Street engine terminal on May 10, 1964, four days after the unit was retired.

Pennsylvania Railroad Diesel Locomotive Roster

Pennsylvania Railroad Diesel Locomotive Roster

ORIG ROAD NUM.	PRR BASE CLASS	PRR REBLT CLASS	1966 ROAD NUM.	PRR CLASS (1966)	BLDR	BLDR MODEL	BLDR SERIAL NUM.	BLDR DATE	RETIRE DATE	NOTE
9018	BS-6a				BLW	DS 4-4-660	74245	Apr 49	May 66	
9019	BS-6a		7819	BS-6	BLW	DS 4-4-660	74246	Apr 49	to PC	
9020	BS-6a		7850	BS-6	BLW	DS 4-4-660	74247	Apr 49	to PC	
9021	BS-6a		7851	BS-6	BLW	DS 4-4-660	74248	Apr 49	to PC	
9022	BS-6a		7852	BS-6	BLW	DS 4-4-660	74249	Apr 49	to PC	
9023	BS-6a		7842	BS-6	BLW	DS 4-4-660	74250	Apr 49	to PC	
9024	BS-6a		7867	BS-6	BLW	DS 4-4-660	74251	Apr 49	to PC	
9025	BS-6a		7845	BS-6	BLW	DS 4-4-660	74252	Apr 49	to PC	
9026	BS-6a				BLW	DS 4-4-660	74253	Apr 49	May 65	
9027	BS-6a		7827	BS-6	BLW	DS 4-4-660	74254	Apr 49	to PC	
9028	BS-6a				BLW	DS 4-4-660	74255	Apr 49	May 65	
9029	BS-6a		7809	BS-6	BLW	DS 4-4-660	74256	Apr 49	Jan 68	
9030	BS-6a		7880	BS-6	BLW	DS 4-4-660	74410	May 49	to PC	
9031	BS-6a		7881	BS-6	BLW	DS 4-4-660	74411	May 49	to PC	
9032	BS-6a		7882	BS-6	BLW	DS 4-4-660	74412	May 49	Jul 66	
9033	BS-6a				BLW	DS 4-4-660	74413	May 49	Nov 66	
9034	BS-6a				BLW	DS 4-4-660	74414	May 49	Jul 66	
9035	BS-6a				BLW	DS 4-4-660	74415	May 49	to PC	
9036	BS-6a		7847	BS-6	BLW	DS 4-4-660	74416	May 49	to PC	
9037	BS-6a		7837	BS-6	BLW	DS 4-4-660	74417	May 49	to PC	
9038	BS-6a		7838	BS-6	BLW	DS 4-4-660	74418	May 49	to PC	
9039	BS-6a		7839	BS-6	BLW	DS 4-4-660	74419	May 49	to PC	
9040	BS-6a		7840	BS-6	BLW	DS 4-4-660	74420	May 49	to PC	
9041	BS-6a		7841	BS-6	BLW	DS 4-4-660	74421	May 49	to PC	
9042	BS-6a				BLW	DS 4-4-660	74422	May 49	Nov 65	
9043	BS-6a		7843	BS-6	BLW	DS 4-4-660	74423	May 49	to PC	
9044	BS-6a		7844	BS-6	BLW	DS 4-4-660	74424	May 49	Jan 68	
9045	BS-6a				BLW	DS 4-4-660	74425	May 49	May 65	

ORIG ROAD NUM.	PRR BASE CLASS	PRR REBLT CLASS	1966 ROAD NUM.	PRR CLASS (1966)	BLDR	BLDR MODEL	BLDR SERIAL NUM.	BLDR DATE	RETIRE DATE	NOTE
9046	BS-6a		7846	BS-6	BLW	DS 4-4-660	74426	May 49	Mar 67	
9047	BS-6a				BLW	DS 4-4-660	74427	May 49	Sep 65	
9048	BS-6a		7848	BS-6	BLW	DS 4-4-660	74428	May 49	to PC	
9049	BS-6a		7849	BS-6	BLW	DS 4-4-660	74429	May 49	Apr 66	
9050	BS-10a				BLW	DS 4-4-1000	74101	Mar 49	to PC	
9051	BS-10a		8001	BS-10	BLW	DS 4-4-1000	74102	Mar 49	to PC	
9052	BS-10a		8002	BS-10	BLW	DS 4-4-1000	74103	Mar 49	Nov 66	
9053	BS-10a		8003	BS-10	BLW	DS 4-4-1000	74104	Mar 49	to PC	
9054	BS-10a		8004	BS-10	BLW	DS 4-4-1000	74105	Mar 49	to PC	
9055	BS-10a		8005	BS-10	BLW	DS 4-4-1000	74106	Mar 49	Oct 67	
9056	BS-10a		8006	BS-10	BLW	DS 4-4-1000	74107	Mar 49	to PC	
9057	BS-10a		8007	BS-10	BLW	DS 4-4-1000	74108	Mar 49	to PC	
9058	BS-10a		8008	BS-10	BLW	DS 4-4-1000	74109	Mar 49	to PC	
9059	BS-10a		8009	BS-10	BLW	DS 4-4-1000	74110	Mar 49	Dec 67	
9060	BS-10a		8010	BS-10	BLW	DS 4-4-1000	74111	Mar 49	to PC	
9061	BS-10a		8011	BS-10	BLW	DS 4-4-1000	74112	Mar 49	Sep 67	
9062	BS-10a		8012	BS-10	BLW	DS 4-4-1000	74113	Mar 49	to PC	
9063	BS-10a		8013	BS-10	BLW	DS 4-4-1000	74114	Mar 49	to PC	
9064	BS-10a		8014	BS-10	BLW	DS 4-4-1000	74115	Mar 49	to PC	
9065	BS-10a		8015	BS-10	BLW	DS 4-4-1000	74116	Mar 49	to PC	
9066	BS-10a		8016	BS-10	BLW	DS 4-4-1000	74117	Mar 49	Nov 65	
9067	BS-10a				BLW	DS 4-4-1000	74118	Mar 49	to PC	
9068	BS-10a		8018	BS-10	BLW	DS 4-4-1000	74119	Mar 49	to PC	
9069	BS-10a		8019	BS-10	BLW	DS 4-4-1000	74120	Mar 49	to PC	
9070	BS-10a		8020	BS-10	BLW	DS 4-4-1000	74121	Mar 49	to PC	
9071	BS-10a				BLW	DS 4-4-1000	74122	Mar 49	Apr 66	
9072	BS-10a				BLW	DS 4-4-1000	74178	Apr 49	Apr 66	
9073	BS-10a		8023	BS-10	BLW	DS 4-4-1000	74179	Apr 49	to PC	
9074	BS-10a				BLW	DS 4-4-1000	74180	Apr 49	Nov 65	
9075	BS-10a		8025	BS-10	BLW	DS 4-4-1000	74181	Apr 49	to PC	
9076	BS-10a		8026	BS-10	BLW	DS 4-4-1000	74182	Apr 49	to PC	
9077	BS-10a		8027	BS-10	BLW	DS 4-4-1000	74183	Apr 49	to PC	
9078	BS-10a		8028	BS-10	BLW	DS 4-4-1000	74184	Apr 49	Nov 66	
9079	BS-10a		8029	BS-10	BLW	DS 4-4-1000	74185	Apr 49	to PC	
9080	FS-10				FM	H10-44	10L150	Jul 49	Sep 67	
9081	FS-10		8244	FS-10	FM	H10-44	10L151	Aug 49	May 66	
9082	FS-10		8245	FS-10	FM	H10-44	10L152	Aug 49	Oct 67	
9083	FS-10				FM	H10-44	10L153	Aug 49	to PC	
9084	FS-10		8247	FS-10	FM	H10-44	10L154	Aug 49	Jun 67	
9085	FS-10		8248	FS-10	FM	H10-44	10L155	Aug 49	to PC	
9086	FS-10		8249	FS-10	FM	H10-44	10L156	Aug 49	Nov 66	
9087	FS-10		8250	FS-10	FM	H10-44	10L157	Aug 49	Feb 66	
9088	FS-10				FM	H10-44	10L158	Aug 49	Sep 65	
9089	FS-10		8252	FS-10	FM	H10-44	10L159	Sep 49	to PC	
9090	FS-10				FM	H10-44	10L160	Sep 49	Jul 66	
9091	FS-10		8254	FS-10	FM	H10-44	10L161	Sep 49	to PC	
9092	FS-10		8255	FS-10	FM	H10-44	10L162	Sep 49	to PC	
9093	FS-10		8256	FS-10	FM	H10-44	10L163	Oct 49	to PC	
9094	FS-10		8257	FS-10	FM	H10-44	10L164	Oct 49	Oct 67	
9095	FS-10		8258	FS-10	FM	H10-44	10L165	Oct 49	Mar 67	
9096	FS-10		8259	FS-10	FM	H10-44	10L166	Oct 49	to PC	
9097	FS-10		8260	FS-10	FM	H10-44	10L167	Oct 49	to PC	

PRR 9034 looks a lot better than the 9000 did on the page above. It is seen here on November 28, 1965 at Frankford Junction, one of the main bases of switchers in the Philadelphia area during the PRR era. She had been given the full Keystone Only paint image only a short time before, as indicated by the "patch" on the cab side.

Pennsylvania Railroad Diesel Locomotive Roster

ORIG ROAD NUM.	PRR REBLT CLASS	PRR BASE CLASS	1966 ROAD NUM.	PRR CLASS (1966)	BLDR	BLDR MODEL	BLDR SERIAL NUM.	BLDR DATE	RETIRE DATE	NOTE
9098		FS-10			FM	H10-44	10L168	Nov 49	Jan 68	
9099		FS-10	8261	FS-10	FM	H10-44	10L169	Nov 49	Apr 66	
9100		AS-6	9450	AS-6	Alco	S-1	76155	Feb 49	to PC	
9101		AS-6	9451	AS-6	Alco	S-1	76562	Feb 49	to PC	
9102		AS-6	9452	AS-6	Alco	S-1	76563	Feb 49	to PC	
9103		AS-6	9453	AS-6	Alco	S-1	76564	Mar 49	to PC	
9104		ES-6	8504	ES-6	EMD	SW1	6763	Apr 49	to PC	
9105		AS-10	9805	AS-10	Alco	S-2	76597	Feb 49	to PC	
9106		AS-10	9806	AS-10	Alco	S-2	76598	Feb 49	to PC	
9107		AS-10	9807	AS-10	Alco	S-2	76599	Feb 49	to PC	
9108		AS-10	9808	AS-10	Alco	S-2	76600	Feb 49	to PC	
9109		AS-10	9809	AS-10	Alco	S-2	76601	Feb 49	to PC	
9110		BS-6	7810	BS-6	BLW	DS 4-4-660	73632	Jul 48	to PC	
9111		BS-6a	7811	BS-6	BLW	DS 4-4-660	73633	Jul 48	to PC	
9112		BS-6a	7812	BS-6	BLW	DS 4-4-660	73634	Jul 48	Jun 67	
9113		BS-6a		BS-6	BLW	DS 4-4-660	73635	Aug 48	May 66	
9114		BS-6a		BS-6	BLW	DS 4-4-660	73636	Aug 48	Feb 66	
9115		BS-6a	7815	BS-6	BLW	DS 4-4-660	73637	Aug 48	to PC	
9116		BS-6a	7816	BS-6	BLW	DS 4-4-660	73641	Aug 48	to PC	
9117		BS-6a		BS-6	BLW	DS 4-4-660	73638	Aug 48	Feb 66	
9118		BS-6a	7818	BS-6	BLW	DS 4-4-660	73639	Aug 48	May 65	
9119		BS-6a		BS-6	BLW	DS 4-4-660	73640	Aug 48	to PC	
9120		BS-6a	7820	BS-6	BLW	DS 4-4-660	73642	Aug 48	to PC	
9121		BS-6a	7821	BS-6	BLW	DS 4-4-660	73803	Jun 48	Feb 67	
9122		BS-10a	7922	BS-10	BLW	DS 4-4-1000	73616	Jun 48	Sep 67	
9123		BS-10a	7923	BS-10	BLW	DS 4-4-1000	73617	Jun 48	Nov 65	
9124		BS-10a			BLW	DS 4-4-1000	73753	Jun 48	Dec 66	
9125		BS-10a	7925	BS-10	BLW	DS 4-4-1000	73754	Jun 48	Dec 66	
9126		BS-10a	7926	BS-10	BLW	DS 4-4-1000	73755	Jul 48	to PC	
9127		BS-10a	9127	BS-10	BLW	DS 4-4-1000	73756	Jul 48	Apr 66	
9128		BS-10a	9128	BS-10	BLW	DS 4-4-1000	73757	Jul 48	to PC	
9129		BS-10a	9129 7928	BS-10	BLW	DS 4-4-1000	73758	Jul 48	Dec 67	
9130		BS-10a	9130 7929	BS-10	BLW	DS 4-4-1000	73759	Jul 48	to PC	
9131		BS-10a	9131 7930	BS-10	BLW	DS 4-4-1000	73760	Jul 48	Jan 68	
9132		BS-10a	9132 7931	BS-10	BLW	DS 4-4-1000	73761	Jul 48	to PC	
9133		BS-10a	9133 7932	BS-10	BLW	DS 4-4-1000	73762	Jul 48	Jun 67	
9134		BS-10a	9134 7933	BS-10	BLW	DS 4-4-1000	73763	Jul 48	May 66	
9135		BS-10a	9135 7935	BS-10	BLW	DS 4-4-1000	73764	Jul 48	to PC	
9136		BS-10a	9136 7936	BS-10	BLW	DS 4-4-1000	73765	Jul 48	Mar 67	
9137		ES-6	8537	ES-6	EMD	SW1	5371	Jul 48	to PC	
9138		ES-6	8538	ES-6	EMD	SW1	5370	Apr 48	to PC	
9139		ES-6	8539	ES-6	EMD	SW1	5372	Jul 48	to PC	
9140		ES-6	8540	ES-6	EMD	SW1	5373	Jul 48	to PC	
9141		ES-6	8541	ES-6	EMD	SW1	5374	Jul 48	to PC	
9142		ES-6	8542	ES-6	EMD	SW1	5375	Jul 48	to PC	
9143		ES-6	8543	ES-6	EMD	SW1	5376	Jul 48	to PC	
9144		ES-6		ES-6	EMD	SW1	5377	Jul 48	Feb 66	
9145		ES-6	8575	ES-6	EMD	SW1	5378	Jul 48	to PC	
9146		ES-6	8576	ES-6	EMD	SW1	5379	Jul 48	to PC	
9147		ES-6		ES-6	EMD	SW1	5380	Jul 48	Feb 66	
9148		ES-6	8578	ES-6	EMD	SW1	5381	Jul 48	to PC	
9149		ES-6	8579	ES-6	EMD	SW1	5382	Jul 48	to PC	
9150		ES-6	8530	ES-6	EMD	SW1	5383	Jul 48	to PC	
9151		ES-6	8531	ES-6	EMD	SW1	5384	Jul 48	to PC	
9152		ES-6	8532	ES-6	EMD	SW1	5814	Aug 48	to PC	
9153		ES-6	8533	ES-6	EMD	SW1	5815	Aug 48	to PC	
9154		ES-6	8554	ES-6	EMD	SW1	5816	Aug 48	to PC	
9155		ES-10	8655	ES-10	EMD	NW2	5360	Feb 48	to PC	
9156		ES-10	8656	ES-10	EMD	NW2	5361	Feb 48	to PC	
9157		ES-10	8657	ES-10	EMD	NW2	5362	Feb 48	to PC	
9158		ES-10	8658	ES-10	EMD	NW2	5363	Feb 48	to PC	
9159		ES-10	8659	ES-10	EMD	NW2	5364	Feb 48	to PC	
9160		ES-10	8660	ES-10	EMD	NW2	5365	Feb 48	to PC	
9161		ES-10	8661	ES-10	EMD	NW2	5366	Feb 48	to PC	
9162		ES-10	8662	ES-10	EMD	NW2	5367	Feb 48	to PC	
9163		ES-10	8663	ES-10	EMD	NW2	5368	Feb 48	to PC	
9164		ES-10	8664	ES-10	EMD	NW2	5369	Feb 48	to PC	
9165		ES-10	8665	ES-10	EMD	NW2	5802	Oct 48	to PC	
9166		ES-10	8666	ES-10	EMD	NW2	5803	Oct 48	to PC	
9167		ES-10	8667	ES-10	EMD	NW2	5804	Oct 48	to PC	
9168		ES-10	8668	ES-10	EMD	NW2	5805	Oct 48	to PC	
9169		ES-10	8669	ES-10	EMD	NW2	5806	Oct 48	to PC	
9170		ES-10	8670	ES-10	EMD	NW2	5807	Oct 48	to PC	
9171		ES-10	8671	ES-10	EMD	NW2	5808	Oct 48	to PC	
9172		ES-10	8672	ES-10	EMD	NW2	5809	Oct 48	to PC	
9173		ES-10	8673	ES-10	EMD	NW2	5810	Oct 48	to PC	
9174		ES-10	8674	ES-10	EMD	NW2	5811	Nov 48	to PC	
9175		ES-10	8675	ES-10	EMD	NW2	5812	Nov 48	to PC	
9176		ES-10	8676	ES-10	EMD	NW2	5813	Nov 48	to PC	
9177		BS-10a		BS-10	BLW	DS 4-4-1000	73596	Apr 48	May 66	
9178		BS-10a		BS-10	BLW	DS 4-4-1000	73597	Apr 48	Apr 66	

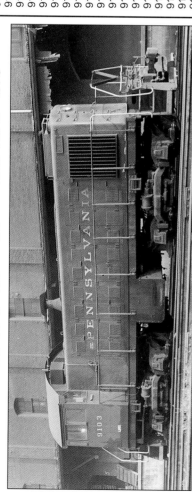

PRR 9103 at Shackamaxon Street, Philadelphia, on June 18, 1966. This was one a large number of switcher storage locations in the area. The large brick warehouse behind the unit is lettered "Shackamaxon Stores," which is believed to be a general warehousing operation.

Pennsylvania Railroad Diesel Locomotive Roster

ORIG ROAD NUM.	PRR BASE CLASS	PRR REBLT CLASS	1966 ROAD NUM.	PRR CLASS (1966)	BLDR	BLDR MODEL	BLDR SERIAL NUM.	BLDR DATE	RETIRE DATE	NOTE
9179	BS-10a		7999	BS-10	BLW	DS 4-4-1000	73598	Apr 48	to PC	
9180	BS-10am		8040	BS-10m	BLW	DS 4-4-1000	73599	Apr 48	Mar 67	
9181	BS-10am		8041	BS-10m	BLW	DS 4-4-1000	73600	Apr 48	to PC	
9182	BS-10am		8042	BS-10m	BLW	DS 4-4-1000	73601	May 48	to PC	
9183	BS-10am		8043	BS-10m	BLW	DS 4-4-1000	73602	May 48	to PC	
9184	FS-10		8218	FS-10	FM	H10-44	10L70	Jun 48	to PC	
9185	FS-10		8219	FS-10	FM	H10-44	10L71	Jun 48	to PC	
9186	FS-10		8220	FS-10	FM	H10-44	10L72	Jun 48	Jun 67	
9187	FS-10				FM	H10-44	10L73	Jul 48	Aug 66	
9188	FS-10		8222	FS-10	FM	H10-44	10L74	Aug 48	Mar 67	
9189	FS-10		8223	FS-10	FM	H10-44	10L75	Aug 48	to PC	
9190	FS-10		8224	FS-10	FM	H10-44	10L76	Aug 48	Sep 67	
9191	FS-10		8225	FS-10	FM	H10-44	10L77	Aug 48	Sep 67	
9192	FS-10		8226	FS-10	FM	H10-44	10L78	Sep 48	Sep 67	
9193	FS-10		8227	FS-10	FM	H10-44	10L79	Sep 48	to PC	
9194	FS-10		8228	FS-10	FM	H10-44	10L80	Sep 48	Sep 67	
9195	FS-10		8229	FS-10	FM	H10-44	10L81	Sep 48	to PC	
9196	FS-10		8230	FS-10	FM	H10-44	10L82	Sep 48	to PC	
9197	FS-10		8231	FS-10	FM	H10-44	10L96	Sep 48	Feb 67	
9198	FS-10		8232	FS-10	FM	H10-44	10L97	Sep 48	Sep 65	
9199	FS-10				FM	H10-44	10L98	Sep 48		
9200	ES-6		8580	ES-6	EMD	SW1	6759	Apr 49	to PC	
9201	ES-6		8501	ES-6	EMD	SW1	6760	Apr 49	to PC	
9202	ES-6		8502	ES-6	EMD	SW1	6761	Apr 49	to PC	
9203	ES-6		8503	ES-6	EMD	SW1	6762	Apr 49	to PC	
9204	AS-10		9804	AS-10	Alco	S-2	75915	Jul 48	to PC	
9205	ES-6		8505	ES-6	EMD	SW1	6764	Apr 49	to PC	
9206	ES-6		8506	ES-6	EMD	SW1	6765	Apr 49	to PC	
9207	ES-6		8507	ES-6	EMD	SW1	6766	Apr 49	to PC	
9208	ES-6		8508	ES-6	EMD	SW1	6767	Apr 49	to PC	
9209	ES-6		8509	ES-6	EMD	SW1	6768	Apr 49	to PC	
9210	BS-6a		7870	BS-6	BLW	DS 4-4-660	73805	Nov 48	to PC	
9211	BS-6a		7871	BS-6	BLW	DS 4-4-660	73806	Nov 48	to PC	
9212	BS-6a		7872	BS-6	BLW	DS 4-4-660	73807	Nov 48	to PC	
9213	BS-6a		7873	BS-6	BLW	DS 4-4-660	73808	Nov 48	to PC	
9214	BS-6a				BLW	DS 4-4-660	73809	Nov 48	May 66	
9215	BS-6a		7875	BS-6	BLW	DS 4-4-660	73810	Nov 48	to PC	
9216	BS-6a		7876	BS-6	BLW	DS 4-4-660	73811	Nov 48	to PC	
9217	BS-6a				BLW	DS 4-4-660	73812	Nov 48	Nov 66	
9218	BS-6a				BLW	DS 4-4-660	73813	Dec 48	May 65	
9219	BS-6a				BLW	DS 4-4-660	73814	Dec 48	May 65	
9220	BS-6a		7800	BS-6	BLW	DS 4-4-660	73815	Dec 48	to PC	
9221	BS-6a		7865	BS-6	BLW	DS 4-4-660	73816	Dec 48	to PC	
9222	BS-6a		7822	BS-6	BLW	DS 4-4-660	73817	Dec 48	Jan 68	
9223	BS-6a		7823	BS-6	BLW	DS 4-4-660	73818	Jan 49	Jul 66	
9224	BS-6a				BLW	DS 4-4-660	73819	Jan 49	Oct 67	
9225	BS-6a		7825	BS-6	BLW	DS 4-4-660	73820	Jan 49	to PC	
9226	BS-6a		7826	BS-6	BLW	DS 4-4-660	73821	Jan 49	to PC	
9227	BS-6a				BLW	DS 4-4-660	73822	Jan 49	May 65	
9228	BS-6a		7828	BS-6	BLW	DS 4-4-660	73823	Jan 49	to PC	
9229	BS-6a		7829	BS-6	BLW	DS 4-4-660	73824	Jan 49	Jun 67	
9230	BS-6a		7830	BS-6	BLW	DS 4-4-660	73825	Jan 49	Dec 67	
9231	BS-6a		7831	BS-6	BLW	DS 4-4-660	73826	Jan 49	Sep 67	
9232	BS-6a		7832	BS-6	BLW	DS 4-4-660	73827	Jan 49	to PC	
9233	BS-6a		7833	BS-6	BLW	DS 4-4-660	73889	Feb 49	to PC	
9234	BS-6a		7834	BS-6	BLW	DS 4-4-660	73890	Feb 49	to PC	
9235	BS-6a		7835	BS-6	BLW	DS 4-4-660	73891	Feb 49	to PC	
9236	BS-6a		7836	BS-6	BLW	DS 4-4-660	73892	Mar 49	to PC	
9237	AS-6		9437	AS-6	Alco	S-1	76565	Mar 49	to PC	
9238	AS-6		9438	AS-6	Alco	S-1	76566	Mar 49	to PC	
9239	AS-6		9439	AS-6	Alco	S-1	76567	Mar 49	to PC	
9240	AS-6		9440	AS-6	Alco	S-1	76571	Apr 49	to PC	
9241	AS-6		9441	AS-6	Alco	S-1	76731	Apr 49	to PC	
9242	AS-6		9442	AS-6	Alco	S-1	76732	Apr 49	to PC	
9243	AS-6		9443	AS-6	Alco	S-1	76733	May 49	to PC	
9244	AS-6		9444	AS-6	Alco	S-1	76734	May 49	to PC	
9245	AS-6		9445	AS-6	Alco	S-1	76735	May 49	to PC	
9246	AS-6		9446	AS-6	Alco	S-1	76736	May 49	to PC	
9247	ES-10		8647	ES-10	EMD	NW2	6755	Dec 48	to PC	
9248	ES-10		8648	ES-10	EMD	NW2	6756	Dec 48	to PC	
9249	ES-10		8649	ES-10	EMD	NW2	6757	Dec 48	to PC	
9250	ES-10		8650	ES-10	EMD	NW2	6758	Dec 48	to PC	
9251	BS-10a		7991	BS-10	BLW	DS 4-4-1000	73864	Dec 48	to PC	
9252	BS-10a				BLW	DS 4-4-1000	73865	Dec 48	Dec 66	
9253	BS-10a		7993	BS-10	BLW	DS 4-4-1000	73866	Dec 48	Mar 67	
9254	BS-10a		7994	BS-10	BLW	DS 4-4-1000	73867	Dec 48	Sep 67	
9255	BS-10a		7995	BS-10	BLW	DS 4-4-1000	73868	Dec 48	to PC	
9256	BS-10a		7996	BS-10	BLW	DS 4-4-1000	73869	Dec 48	to PC	
9257	BS-10a		7997	BS-10	BLW	DS 4-4-1000	73870	Dec 48	to PC	

PRR 9243 at the Reed Street yard in Philadelphia. Locomotives serving the docks along Delaware Avenue worked out of this location. By May 28, 1966, AS-6's had replaced the GE 44-Tonners here.

233

Pennsylvania Railroad Diesel Locomotive Roster

ORIG ROAD NUM.	PRR BASE CLASS	PRR REBLT CLASS	1966 ROAD NUM.	PRR CLASS (1966)	BLDR	BLDR MODEL	BLDR SERIAL NUM.	BLDR DATE	RETIRE DATE	NOTE
9258	BS-10a	BS-10am	8035	BS-10m	BLW	DS 4-4-1000	73871	Dec 48	to PC	(15)
9259	BS-10a	BS-10am	8036	BS-10m	BLW	DS 4-4-1000	73872	Dec 48	to PC	(15)
9260	BS-10a	BS-10am	8037	BS-10m	BLW	DS 4-4-1000	73873	Dec 48	to PC	(15)
9261	BS-10a	BS-10am	8044	BS-10m	BLW	DS 4-4-1000	73874	Dec 48	to PC	(15)
9262	BS-10a		7984	BS-10	BLW	DS 4-4-1000	73875	Dec 48	Sep 67	
9263	BS-10a		7924	BS-10	BLW	DS 4-4-1000	73876	Dec 48	to PC	
9264	BS-10a		7914	BS-10	BLW	DS 4-4-1000	73877	Dec 48	Dec 67	
9265	BS-10a				BLW	DS 4-4-1000	73878	Dec 48	May 66	
9266	BS-10a		7916	BS-10	BLW	DS 4-4-1000	73879	Dec 48	to PC	
9267	BS-10a		7917	BS-10	BLW	DS 4-4-1000	73880	Dec 48	to PC	
9268	BS-10a		7918	BS-10	BLW	DS 4-4-1000	73881	Feb 49	to PC	
9269	BS-10a		7919	BS-10	BLW	DS 4-4-1000	73882	Jan 49	to PC	
9270	BS-10a		7920	BS-10	BLW	DS 4-4-1000	73883	Jan 49	to PC	
9271	BS-10a		7921	BS-10	BLW	DS 4-4-1000	73884	Jan 49	to PC	
9272	BS-10a		8017	BS-10	BLW	DS 4-4-1000	73885	Jan 49	to PC	
9273	BS-10a		7948	BS-10	BLW	DS 4-4-1000	73886	Jan 49	to PC	
9274	BS-10a		8024	BS-10	BLW	DS 4-4-1000	73887	Jan 49	to PC	
9275	BS-10a		7949	BS-10	BLW	DS 4-4-1000	73888	Jan 49	Mar 67	
9276	BS-10as		8050	BRS-10sx	BLW	DRS 4-4-1000	74403	Feb 49	May 66	
9277	BS-10as				BLW	DRS 4-4-1000	74404	Feb 49	to PC	
9278	AS-10		9778	AS-10	Alco	S-2	76602	Feb 49	to PC	
9279	AS-10		9779	AS-10	Alco	S-2	76603	Feb 49	to PC	
9280	AS-10		9780	AS-10	Alco	S-2	76604	Feb 49	to PC	
9281	AS-10		9781	AS-10	Alco	S-2	76605	Feb 49	to PC	
9282	AS-10		9782	AS-10	Alco	S-2	76606	Mar 49	Dec 67	
9283	AS-10		9783	AS-10	Alco	S-2	76607	Mar 49	to PC	
9284	AS-10		9784	AS-10	Alco	S-2	76608	Mar 49	to PC	
9285	AS-10				Alco	S-2	76609	Mar 49	May 65	
9286	AS-10		9786	AS-10	Alco	S-2	76610	Mar 49	to PC	
9287	AS-10		9787	AS-10	Alco	S-2	76611	Mar 49	to PC	
9288	FS-10		8233	FS-10	FM	H10-44	10L120	Mar 49	to PC	
9289	FS-10		8234	FS-10	FM	H10-44	10L121	Mar 49	to PC	
9290	FS-10		8235	FS-10	FM	H10-44	10L122	Mar 49	to PC	
9291	FS-10		8236	FS-10	FM	H10-44	10L123	Mar 49	Dec 67	
9292	FS-10		8237	FS-10	FM	H10-44	10L124	Mar 49	to PC	
9293	FS-10		8238	FS-10	FM	H10-44	10L125	Mar 49	to PC	
9294	FS-10		8239	FS-10	FM	H10-44	10L126	Apr 49	to PC	
9295	FS-10		8240	FS-10	FM	H10-44	10L127	Apr 49	Jun 67	
9296	FS-10		8241	FS-10	FM	H10-44	10L128	Apr 49	Mar 67	
9297	FS-10				FM	H10-44	10L129	Apr 49	Sep 65	
9298	FS-10		8242	FS-10	FM	H10-44	10L130	Apr 49	Jun 67	
9299	FS-10		8243	FS-10	FM	H10-44	10L131	Apr 49	Jun 67	
9300	FS-20		7700	FRS-20x	FM	H20-44	20L42	Jan 49	Jun 67	
9301	FS-20				FM	H20-44	20L43	Jan 49	Sep 65	
9302	FS-20				FM	H20-44	20L44	Feb 49	Nov 66	
9303	FS-20				FM	H20-44	20L45	Feb 49	Sep 65	
9304	FS-20				FM	H20-44	20L46	Feb 49	Nov 65	
9305	FS-20m		7705	FRS-20	FM	H20-44	20L37	Dec 48	Sep 67	
9306	FS-20m				FM	H20-44	20L38	Dec 48	Nov 66	
9307	FS-20				FM	H20-44	20L39	Dec 48	Sep 65	
9308	FS-20				FM	H20-44	20L40	Jan 49	May 66	
9309	FS-20				FM	H20-44	20L41	Jan 49	Sep 65	
9310	FS-20m				FM	H20-44	20L47	Feb 49	May 66	
9311	FS-20m		7711	FRS-20	FM	H20-44	20L48	Mar 49	Nov 66	
9312	GS-4	GS-4m			GE	44-ton	29992	Mar 49	Jun 64	(16)
9313	GS-4				GE	44-ton	29993	Mar 49	Sep 62	
9314	GS-4				GE	44-ton	30132	Mar 49	Jun 64	
9315	GS-4	GS-4m			GE	44-ton	30133	Mar 49	Sep 66	(16)
9316	GS-4				GE	44-ton	30134	Mar 49	Jun 64	
9317	GS-4				GE	44-ton	30135	Mar 49	Jun 64	
9318	GS-4				GE	44-ton	30136	Apr 49	Aug 62	
9319	GS-4				GE	44-ton	30137	Apr 49	Sep 62	
9320	GS-4				GE	44-ton	30138	Apr 49	Jun 64	
9321	GS-4				GE	44-ton	30139	Apr 49	Jun 64	
9322	GS-4	GS-4m			GE	44-ton	30140	Apr 49	Sep 62	(16)
9323	GS-4				GE	44-ton	30141	Apr 49	Jun 64	
9324	GS-4				GE	44-ton	30142	May 49	Sep 66	
9325	GS-4				GE	44-ton	29077	Nov 47	Jun 64	
9326	GS-4				GE	44-ton	29078	Nov 47	Ca. 65	
9327	GS-4				GE	44-ton	29079	Nov 47	Aug 61	
9328	GS-4				GE	44-ton	29961	Jun 48	Ca. 65	
9329	GS-4	GS-4m			GE	44-ton	29962	Jun 48	Feb 65	(16)
9330	GS-4	GS-4m			GE	44-ton	29963	Jun 48	Feb 65	(16)
9331	GS-4				GE	44-ton	29964	Jun 48	Ca. 65	
9332	GS-4	GS-4m			GE	44-ton	29965	Jun 48	Jun 64	(16)
9333	GS-4				GE	44-ton	29966	Jun 48	Jun 64	

While this is not up the desired standard for the photos in this book, PRR 7700 (formerly 9300) was the only non-MU F-M model H20-44 to be renumbered into the 1966 scheme. A long exposure with a block of wood for camera support was used. The location is inside the roundhouse at Columbus, Ohio on March 11, 1967. In June, the 7700 was retired.

Pennsylvania Railroad Diesel Locomotive Roster

ORIG ROAD NUM.	PRR BASE CLASS	PRR REBLT CLASS	1966 ROAD NUM.	PRR CLASS (1966)	BLDR	BLDR MODEL	BLDR SERIAL NUM.	BLDR DATE	RETIRE DATE	NOTE
9334	GS-4	GS-4m			GE	44-ton	29967	Jun 48	Aug 64	(16)
9335	GS-4	GS-4m			GE	44-ton	29968	Jun 48	Dec 64	(16)
9336	GS-4	GS-4m			GE	44-ton	29969	Jul 48	Dec 64	(16)
9337	GS-4				GE	44-ton	29970	Jul 48	Sep 66	
9338	GS-4				GE	44-ton	29971	Jul 48	Apr 65	
9339	GS-4	GS-4m			GE	44-ton	29972	Sep 48	Dec 64	(16)
9340	GS-4				GE	44-ton	29973	Sep 48	Dec 64	
9341	GS-4				GE	44-ton	29975	Sep 48	Dec 64	
9342	GS-4				GE	44-ton	29976	Oct 48	Jun 64	
9343	GS-4				GE	44-ton	29977	Oct 48	Jun 64	
9344	GS-4				GE	44-ton	29978	Oct 48	Mar 62	
9345	GS-4				GE	44-ton	29979	Oct 48	Jun 64	
9346	GS-4				GE	44-ton	29980	Nov 48	Feb 65	
9347	GS-4				GE	44-ton	29981	Nov 48	Dec 64	
9348	GS-4				GE	44-ton	29982	Dec 48	Sep 66	
9349	GS-4				GE	44-ton	29983	Dec 48	Jun 64	
9350	GS-4				GE	44-ton	30144	May 49	Sep 62	
9351	GS-4	GS-4m			GE	44-ton	30143	May 49	Jun 64	(16)
9352	GS-4				GE	44-ton	30145	May 49	Sep 66	
9353	GS-4		9999	GS-4	GE	44-ton	30146	May 49	to PC	
9354	GS-4				GE	44-ton	30243	Aug 49	Sep 66	
9355	GS-4				GE	44-ton	30244	Aug 49	Jun 64	
9356	GS-4				GE	44-ton	30245	Aug 49	Jun 64	
9357	GS-4				GE	44-ton	30254	Feb 50	Ca. 63	
9358	ES-12m		9084	ES-12m	EMD	SW7	10431	Jun 50	to PC	

PRR 9331 in its early days of lease to the Strasburg Rail Road at Leaman Place, Pennsylvania on August 19, 1961. The GE 44-Tonner has just pulled the passenger train from E. Strasburg. Eventually, the unit became Strasburg 33.

ORIG ROAD NUM.	PRR BASE CLASS	PRR REBLT CLASS	1966 ROAD NUM.	PRR CLASS (1966)	BLDR	BLDR MODEL	BLDR SERIAL NUM.	BLDR DATE	RETIRE DATE	NOTE
9359	ES-12m		9085	ES-12m	EMD	SW7	10432	Jun 50	to PC	
9360	ES-12m		9086	ES-12m	EMD	SW7	10433	Jun 50	to PC	
9361	ES-12m		9087	ES-12m	EMD	SW7	10434	Jun 50	to PC	
9362	ES-12m		9088	ES-12m	EMD	SW7	10435	Jun 50	to PC	
9363	ES-12m		9089	ES-12m	EMD	SW7	10436	Jun 50	to PC	
9364	ES-12		9038	ES-12	EMD	SW7	10387	Apr 50	to PC	
9365	ES-12		9035	ES-12	EMD	SW7	10388	May 50	to PC	
9366	ES-12		9036	ES-12	EMD	SW7	10389	May 50	to PC	
9367	ES-12		9037	ES-12	EMD	SW7	10390	May 50	to PC	
9368	ES-12		9068	ES-12	EMD	SW7	10391	May 50	to PC	
9369	ES-12m		9090	ES-12m	EMD	SW7	10437	Jun 50	to PC	
9370	ES-12m		9091	ES-12m	EMD	SW7	10438	Jun 50	to PC	
9371	ES-12m		9092	ES-12m	EMD	SW7	10439	Jul 50	to PC	
9372	ES-12m		9093	ES-12m	EMD	SW7	10440	Jul 50	to PC	
9373	ES-12		9073	ES-12	EMD	SW7	10392	Mar 50	to PC	
9374	ES-12		9074	ES-12	EMD	SW7	10393	Mar 50	to PC	
9375	ES-12		9075	ES-12	EMD	SW7	10394	Mar 50	to PC	
9376	ES-12		9076	ES-12	EMD	SW7	10395	Mar 50	to PC	
9377	ES-12		9077	ES-12	EMD	SW7	10396	Mar 50	to PC	
9378	ES-12		9078	ES-12	EMD	SW7	10397	Mar 50	to PC	
9379	ES-12		9079	ES-12	EMD	SW7	10398	Mar 50	to PC	
9380	ES-12		9080	ES-12	EMD	SW7	10399	Mar 50	to PC	
9381	ES-12		9041	ES-12	EMD	SW7	10400	Mar 50	to PC	
9382	ES-12		9039	ES-12	EMD	SW7	10401	Mar 50	to PC	
9383	ES-12		9040	ES-12	EMD	SW7	10402	Mar 50	to PC	
9384	ES-12		9046	ES-12	EMD	SW7	10403	Mar 50	to PC	
9385	ES-12		9045	ES-12	EMD	SW7	10404	Mar 50	to PC	
9386	ES-12	ES-12m	9081	ES-12m	EMD	SW7	10405	May 50	to PC	(14)
9387	ES-12	ES-12m	9082	ES-12m	EMD	SW7	10406	May 50	to PC	(14)
9388	ES-12	ES-12m	9083	ES-12m	EMD	SW7	10407	Mar 50	to PC	(14)
9389	ES-12		9069	ES-12	EMD	SW7	10408	Mar 50	to PC	
9390	ES-12		9070	ES-12	EMD	SW7	10409	May 50	to PC	
9391	ES-12		9071	ES-12	EMD	SW7	10410	May 50	to PC	
9392	ES-12		9072	ES-12	EMD	SW7	10411	May 50	to PC	
9393	ES-12		9047	ES-12	EMD	SW7	10412	May 50	to PC	
9394	ES-12		9048	ES-12	EMD	SW7	10413	May 50	to PC	
9395	ES-12		9049	ES-12	EMD	SW7	10414	May 50	to PC	
9396	ES-6		8556	ES-6	EMD	SW1	11190	Jul 50	to PC	
9397	ES-6		8557	ES-6	EMD	SW1	11191	Aug 50	to PC	
9398	ES-6		8558	ES-6	EMD	SW1	11192	Aug 50	to PC	
9399	ES-6		8559	ES-6	EMD	SW1	11193	Aug 50	to PC	
9400	ES-6		8560	ES-6	EMD	SW1	11194	Aug 50	to PC	
9401	ES-6		8561	ES-6	EMD	SW1	11195	Aug 50	to PC	
9402	ES-6		8562	ES-6	EMD	SW1	11196	Sep 50	to PC	
9403	ES-6		8563	ES-6	EMD	SW1	11197	Sep 50	to PC	
9404	ES-6		8564	ES-6	EMD	SW1	11198	Sep 50	to PC	
9405	ES-6		8565	ES-6	EMD	SW1	11199	Sep 50	to PC	
9406	ES-6		8566	ES-6	EMD	SW1	11200	Sep 50	to PC	
9407	ES-6		8567	ES-6	EMD	SW1	11201	Sep 50	to PC	
9408	ES-6		8568	ES-6	EMD	SW1	11202	Sep 50	to PC	
9409	ES-6		8569	ES-6	EMD	SW1	11203	Sep 50	to PC	
9410	ES-6		8570	ES-6	EMD	SW1	11204	Oct 50	to PC	

Pennsylvania Railroad Diesel Locomotive Roster

ORIG ROAD NUM.	PRR BASE CLASS	PRR REBLT CLASS	1966 ROAD NUM.	PRR CLASS (1966)	BLDR	BLDR MODEL	BLDR SERIAL NUM.	BLDR DATE	RETIRE DATE	NOTE
9411	ES-6		8571	ES-6	EMD	SW1	11205	Oct 50	to PC	
9412	ES-6		8512	ES-6	EMD	SW1	11206	Oct 50	to PC	
9413	ES-6		8513	ES-6	EMD	SW1	11207	Oct 50	to PC	
9414	ES-6		8514	ES-6	EMD	SW1	11208	Oct 50	to PC	
9415	ES-6		8515	ES-6	EMD	SW1	11209	Oct 50	to PC	
9416	ES-6		8516	ES-6	EMD	SW1	11210	Oct 50	to PC	
9417	ES-6		8517	ES-6	EMD	SW1	11211	Oct 50	to PC	
9418	ES-6		8518	ES-6	EMD	SW1	11212	Oct 50	to PC	
9419	ES-6		8519	ES-6	EMD	SW1	11213	Oct 50	to PC	
9420	ES-6		8520	ES-6	EMD	SW1	11214	Oct 50	to PC	
9421	ES-6				EMD	SW1	11215	Oct 50	Feb 66	
9422	ES-6		8522	ES-6	EMD	SW1	11216	Nov 50	to PC	
9423	ES-6		8523	ES-6	EMD	SW1	11217	Nov 50	to PC	
9424	ES-6		8524	ES-6	EMD	SW1	11218	Nov 50	to PC	
9425	ES-6		8525	ES-6	EMD	SW1	11219	Nov 50	to PC	
9426	ES-6		8526	ES-6	EMD	SW1	11220	Nov 50	to PC	
9427	ES-6		8527	ES-6	EMD	SW1	11221	Nov 50	to PC	
9428	ES-6		8528	ES-6	EMD	SW1	11222	Nov 50	to PC	
9429	BS-10am		8045	BS-10m	BLW	DS 4-4-1000	74708	May 50	Sep 67	
9430	BS-10am		8046	BS-10m	BLW	DS 4-4-1000	74709	May 50	to PC	
9431	BS-10am		8031	BS-10m	BLW	DS 4-4-1000	74710	May 50	to PC	
9432	BS-10am		8032	BS-10m	BLW	DS 4-4-1000	74711	May 50	to PC	
9433	BS-10am		8033	BS-10m	BLW	DS 4-4-1000	74712	May 50	Oct 67	
9434	BS-10am		8034	BS-10m	BLW	DS 4-4-1000	74713	May 50	to PC	
9448A	FF-16				FM	CFA16-4	16L339	Sep 50	Apr 65	
9448B	FF-16				FM	CFB-16-4	16L355	Sep 50	Apr 65	
9449A	FF-16				FM	CFA16-4	16L340	Sep 50	Apr 65	
9450A	FF-16				FM	CFA16-4	16L341	Sep 50	Apr 65	
9450B	FF-16				FM	CFB-16-4	16L356	Sep 50	Apr 65	
9451A	FF-16				FM	CFA16-4	16L342	Sep 50	Apr 65	
9452A	FF-16				FM	CFA16-4	16L343	Sep 50	Apr 65	
9452B	FF-16				FM	CFB-16-4	16L357	Sep 50	Apr 65	
9453A	FF-16				FM	CFA16-4	16L344	Sep 50	Apr 65	
9454A	FF-16				FM	CFA16-4	16L345	Sep 50	Apr 65	
9454B	FF-16				FM	CFB-16-4	16L358	Sep 50	Apr 65	
9455A	FF-16				FM	CFA16-4	16L346	Oct 50	Apr 65	
9456A	FF-20				FM	Erie-A	L1108	Nov 47	Jan 63	
9456B	FF-20				FM	Erie-B	L1103	Nov 47	Mar 63	
9457A	FF-20				FM	Erie-A	L1110	Nov 47	Sep 62	
9458A	FF-20				FM	Erie-A	L1111	Dec 47	Sep 62	
9458B	FF-20				FM	Erie-B	L1106	Dec 47	Sep 62	
9459A	FF-20				FM	Erie-A	L1113	Jan 48	Sep 62	
9460A	FF-20				FM	Erie-A	L1114	Jan 48	Sep 62	
9460B	FF-20				FM	Erie-B	L1109	Nov 47	Feb 63	
9461A	FF-20				FM	Erie-A	L1116	Jan 48	Mar 63	
9462A	FF-20				FM	Erie-A	L1121	Dec 47	Sep 62	
9462B	FF-20				FM	Erie-B	L1112	Nov 47	Mar 63	
9463A	FF-20				FM	Erie-A	L1122	Jan 48	Mar 63	
9464A	FF-20				FM	Erie-A	L1123	Feb 48	Sep 62	
9464B	FF-20				FM	Erie-B	L1115	Dec 47	Sep 62	
9465A	FF-20				FM	Erie-A	L1124	Jan 48	Sep 62	
9466A	FF-20				FM	Erie-A	L1130	Feb 48	Mar 63	
9466B	FF-20				FM	Erie-B	L1125	Dec 47	Mar 63	
9467A	FF-20				FM	Erie-A	L1131	Feb 48	Sep 62	
9468A	FF-20				FM	Erie-A	L1132	Feb 48	Jan 63	
9468B	FF-20				FM	Erie-B	L1126	Dec 47	Dec 62	
9469A	FF-20				FM	Erie-A	L1133	Mar 48	Oct 62	
9470A	FF-20				FM	Erie-A	L1134	Feb 48	Sep 62	
9470B	FF-20				FM	Erie-B	L1129	Dec 47	Sep 62	
9471A	FF-20				FM	Erie-B	L1135	Mar 48	Mar 63	
9472A	FP-20a	FF-20			FM	Erie-A	L1140	Jun 48	Nov 62	(18)
9472B	FP-20a	FF-20			FM	Erie-B	L1146	Jun 48	Sep 62	(18)
9473A	FP-20a	FF-20			FM	Erie-A	L1141	Jun 48	Nov 62	(18)
9474A	FP-20a	FF-20			FM	Erie-A	L1148	Jun 48	Nov 62	(18)
9474B	FP-20a	FF-20			FM	Erie-B	L1147	Jun 48	Mar 63	(18)
9475A	FP-20a	FF-20			FM	Erie-A	L1149	Jun 48	Sep 62	(18)
9476A	FP-20a	FF-20			FM	Erie-A	L1150	Jul 48	Dec 63	(18)
9476B	FP-20a	FF-20			FM	Erie-B	L1144	Jul 48	Dec 63	(18)
9477A	FP-20a	FF-20			FM	Erie-A	L1151	Jul 48	Dec 63	(18)
9478A	FF-20				FM	Erie-A	L1152	Sep 48	Dec 63	(17)
9478B	FF-20				FM	Erie-B	L1158	Sep 48	Dec 63	(17)
9479A	FF-20				FM	Erie-A	L1153	Sep 48	Dec 63	(17)
9480A	FF-20				FM	Erie-A	L1154	Oct 48	Dec 63	
9481A	FF-20				FM	Erie-A	L1155	Oct 48	Dec 63	
9482A	FF-20				FM	Erie-A	L1156	Dec 48	Dec 63	
9483A	FF-20				FM	Erie-A	L1161	Nov 48	Dec 63	
9484A	FF-20				FM	Erie-A	L1162	Oct 48	Dec 63	
9485A	FF-20				FM	Erie-A	L1163	Oct 48	Dec 63	
9486A	FF-20				FM	Erie-A	L1164	Oct 48	Dec 63	
9487A	FF-20				FM	Erie-A	L1165	Oct 48	Dec 63	
9488A	FF-20				FM	Erie-A	L1166	Nov 48	Dec 63	
9489A	FF-20				FM	Erie-A	L1167	Nov 48	Dec 63	
9490A	FF-20				FM	Erie-A	L1168	Nov 48	Dec 63	
9491A	FF-20				FM	Erie-A	L1169	Dec 48	Dec 63	
9492A	FF-16				FM	CFA16-4	16L347	Oct 50	Apr 65	

Full side view of PRR 9461A beside the shop at Conway Yard, Pennsylvania, March 17, 1962. The PRR owned the largest fleet of Erie-builts.

PRR 9501A-9501B-9500B-9500A a few months after delivery. This was the lowest numbered F3 set, but it was not put into service until about three months after the 9506/9508 set. Here at Harrisburg on December 6, 1947.

PRR 9507A was one of the units in the first set of EMD freight units delivered to the PRR in April, 1947. A classic "chicken wire" F3, it was photographed in Toledo, Ohio on May 28, 1961. Retirement was less than two years away, in March, 1963.

Pennsylvania Railroad Diesel Locomotive Roster

ORIG ROAD NUM.	PRR BASE CLASS	PRR REBLT CLASS	1966 ROAD NUM.	PRR CLASS (1966)	BLDR	BLDR MODEL	BLDR SERIAL NUM.	BLDR DATE	RETIRE DATE	NOTE
9492B	FF-16				FM	CFB-16-4	16L359	Oct 50	Apr 65	
9493A	FF-16				FM	CFA16-4	16L348	Oct 50	Apr 65	
9494A	FF-16				FM	CFA16-4	16L349	Oct 50	Apr 65	
9494B	FF-16				FM	CFB-16-4	16L360	Oct 50	Apr 65	
9495A	FF-16				FM	CFA16-4	16L350	Oct 50	Apr 65	
9496A	FF-16				FM	CFA16-4	16L351	Oct 50	Apr 65	
9496B	FF-16				FM	CFB-16-4	16L361	Oct 50	Apr 65	
9497A	FF-16				FM	CFA16-4	16L352	Oct 50	Apr 65	
9498A	FF-16				FM	CFA16-4	16L353	Nov 50	Apr 65	
9498B	FF-16				FM	CFB-16-4	16L362	Nov 50	Apr 65	
9499A	FF-16				FM	CFA16-4	16L354	Nov 50	Apr 65	
9500A	EF-15				EMD	F3A	4914	Jul 47	Sep 62	
9500B	EF-15				EMD	F3B	4918	Jul 47	Feb 63	
9501A	EF-15				EMD	F3A	4915	Jul 47	Nov 62	
9501B	EF-15				EMD	F3B	4919	Jul 47	Mar 63	
9502A	EF-15				EMD	F3A	4916	Jul 47	Dec 62	
9502B	EF-15				EMD	F3B	4920	Jul 47	Dec 62	
9503A	EF-15				EMD	F3A	4917	Jul 47	Jan 63	
9503B	EF-15				EMD	F3B	4921	Jul 47	Feb 63	
9504A	EF-15				EMD	F3A	5389	Sep 47	Mar 63	
9504B	EF-15				EMD	F3B	4922	Sep 47	Nov 62	
9505A	EF-15				EMD	F3A	5390	Sep 47	Oct 62	
9505B	EF-15				EMD	F3B	4923	Sep 47	Dec 62	
9506A	EF-15				EMD	F3A	5043	Apr 48	Mar 63	
9506B	EF-15				EMD	F3B	5055	Apr 48	Mar 63	
9507A	EF-15				EMD	F3A	5044	Apr 48	Mar 63	
9507B	EF-15				EMD	F3B	5056	Apr 48	Oct 62	
9508A	EF-15				EMD	F3A	5045	Apr 48	Sep 62	
9508B	EF-15				EMD	F3B	5057	Apr 48	Sep 62	
9509A	EF-15				EMD	F3A	5046	Apr 48	Mar 62	
9509B	EF-15				EMD	F3B	5058	Apr 48	Sep 62	
9510A	EF-15				EMD	F3A	5047	Apr 48	Nov 62	
9510B	EF-15				EMD	F3B	5059	Apr 48	Nov 62	
9511A	EF-15				EMD	F3A	5048	Apr 48	Sep 62	
9511B	EF-15				EMD	F3B	5060	Apr 48	Sep 62	
9512A	EF-15				EMD	F3A	5049	Apr 48	Jan 63	
9512B	EF-15				EMD	F3B	5061	Apr 48	Feb 63	
9513A	EF-15				EMD	F3A	5050	Apr 48	Sep 62	
9513B	EF-15				EMD	F3B	5062	Apr 48	Sep 62	
9514A	EF-15				EMD	F3A	5051	Apr 48	Oct 62	
9514B	EF-15				EMD	F3B	5063	Apr 48	Feb 63	
9515A	EF-15				EMD	F3A	5052	Apr 48	Mar 63	
9515B	EF-15				EMD	F3B	5064	Apr 48	Mar 63	
9516A	EF-15				EMD	F3A	5053	May 48	Mar 63	
9516B	EF-15				EMD	F3B	5065	May 48	Feb 63	
9517A	EF-15				EMD	F3A	5054	May 48	Sep 62	
9517B	EF-15				EMD	F3B	5066	May 48	Nov 62	
9518A	EH-15	EF-15			EMD	F3A	6496	Jan 48	Dec 62	(20)
9518B	EH-15	EF-15			EMD	F3B	6498	Jan 48	Dec 62	(20)
9519A	EH-15	EF-15a			EMD	F3A	6497	Jan 49	Dec 62	(20)
9519B	EH-15	EF-15a			EMD	F3B	6493	Jan 48	Jan 63	(20)
9520A	EF-15				EMD	F3A	5346	May 48	Oct 62	

Pennsylvania Railroad Diesel Locomotive Roster

ORIG ROAD NUM.	PRR BASE CLASS	PRR REBLT CLASS	1966 ROAD NUM.	PRR CLASS (1966)	BLDR	BLDR MODEL	BLDR SERIAL NUM.	BLDR DATE	RETIRE DATE	NOTE
9520B	EF-15				EMD	F3B	5356	May 48	Oct 62	
9521A	EF-15				EMD	F3A	5347	May 48	Feb 63	
9521B	EF-15				EMD	F3B	5357	May 48	Jan 63	
9522A	EF-15				EMD	F3A	5348	Jul 48	Dec 62	
9522B	EF-15				EMD	F3B	5359	Jul 48	Mar 63	
9523A	EF-15				EMD	F3A	5349	Jul 48	Oct 62	
9523B	EF-15				EMD	F3B	5350	Jul 48	Jan 63	
9524A	EF-15				EMD	F3A	5067	Jul 48	May 66	
9524B	EF-15				EMD	F3B	5068	Jul 48	Apr 66	
9525A	EF-15				EMD	F3A	5351	Jul 48	Aug 66	
9525B	EF-15		3501	EF-15	EMD	F3B	5069	Jul 48	Aug 67	
9526A	EF-15				EMD	F3A	5352	Jul 48	Sep 65	
9526B	EF-15				EMD	F3B	5070	Jul 48	Dec 63	
9527A	EF-15				EMD	F3A	5353	Jul 48	Nov 65	
9527B	EF-15				EMD	F3B	5071	Jul 48	Dec 63	
9528A	EF-15				EMD	F3A	5358	Jul 48	Jul 65	
9528B	EH-15	EF-15a			EMD	F3B	6494	Feb 49	Dec 63	(20)
9529A	EF-15				EMD	F3A	5577	Sep 48	Dec 67	
9530A	EF-15		1402	EF-15	EMD	F3A	5578	Sep 48	to PC	
9530B	EF-15		1403	EF-15	EMD	F3B	5176	Oct 47	Dec 62	(21)
9531A	EF-15				EMD	F3A	5579	Sep 48	Nov 65	
9532A	EF-15				EMD	F3A	5580	Sep 48	Dec 63	

ORIG ROAD NUM.	PRR BASE CLASS	PRR REBLT CLASS	1966 ROAD NUM.	PRR CLASS (1966)	BLDR	BLDR MODEL	BLDR SERIAL NUM.	BLDR DATE	RETIRE DATE	NOTE
9532B	EF-15				EMD	F3B	5177	Oct 47	Sep 62	(21)
9533A	EF-15				EMD	F3A	5581	Sep 48	Sep 65	
9534A	EF-15		1404	EF-15	EMD	F3A	5582	Sep 48	Oct 67	
9534B	EF-15				EMD	F3B	5178	May 48	Sep 62	(21)
9535A	EF-15		1405	EF-15	EMD	F3A	5583	Sep 48	Dec 66	
9536A	EF-15				EMD	F3A	5584	Sep 48	Apr 65	
9536B	EF-15				EMD	F3B	5179	May 48	Oct 62	(21)
9537A	EF-15				EMD	F3A	5585	Sep 48	May 66	
9538A	EF-15				EMD	F3A	5586	Sep 48	Jul 66	
9539A	EF-15				EMD	F3A	5587	Sep 48	Apr 65	
9540A	EH-15				EMD	F3A	5354	Jul 48	Dec 63	(20)
9540B	EH-15		1408	EF-15	EMD	F3B	5072	Jul 48	to PC	
9541B	EH-15	(NOT)			EMD	F3B	7590	Feb 49	Dec 63	(20)
9542B	EH-15	EF-15			EMD	F3B	6467	Oct 48	Sep 65	(20)
9543A	EH-15	EF-15a			EMD	F3A	6481	Oct 48	May 66	(20)
9543B	EH-15	EF-15			EMD	F3B	6468	Oct 48	May 66	(20)
9544A	EH-15	EF-15			EMD	F3A	7591	Feb 49	May 66	(20)
9544B	EH-15	EF-15			EMD	F3B	6469	Oct 48	Apr 66	(20)
9545A	EH-15	EF-15	3504	EF-15	EMD	F3A	6482	Oct 48	Nov 66	(20)
9545B	EH-15	EF-15a	3505	EF-15	EMD	F3B	6470	Oct 48	Dec 63	(20)
9546A	EH-15	EF-15a			EMD	F7B	7592	Feb 49	Dec 63	(20)
9546B	EH-15	EF-15a	3506	EF-15	EMD	F3B	6471	Nov 48	to PC	(20)
9547A	EH-15	EF-15a			EMD	F3A	6483	Nov 48	Dec 63	(20)
9547B	EH-15	EF-15a	3508	EF-15a	EMD	F3B	6472	Nov 48	Dec 66	(20)
9548A	EH-15	EF-15a			EMD	F7B	7593	Apr 49	Oct 67	(20)
9548B	EH-15	EF-15a			EMD	F3A	6473	Nov 48	to PC	(20)
9549A	EH-15	EF-15a			EMD	F3B	6484	Nov 48	Dec 63	(20)
9549B	EH-15	(NOT)			EMD	F3A	6474	Nov 48	Dec 63	(20)
9550A	EF-15	EF-15a			EMD	F7B	7594	Apr 49	Dec 64	(20)
9550B	EF-15	EF-15a	1410	EF-15	EMD	F3B	6475	Dec 48	Dec 63	(20)
9551A	EF-15	EF-15a			EMD	F3A	6485	Dec 48	Sep 65	(20)
9551B	EF-15	EF-15a	1411	EF-15	EMD	F3B	6476	Dec 48	Oct 67	(20)
9552A	EF-15	EF-15a			EMD	F7B	7595	Apr 49	Dec 63	(20)
9552B	EF-15	EF-15a			EMD	F3A	6477	Dec 48	Sep 65	(20)
9553A	EF-15	EF-15a			EMD	F3B	6486	Dec 48	Aug 64	(20)
9553B	EF-15	EF-15a			EMD	F3A	6478	Dec 48	Dec 63	(20)
9554A	EF-15	EF-15a			EMD	F7B	7596	Apr 49	Dec 64	(20)
9554B	EF-15	EF-15a			EMD	F3B	6479	Jan 49	Dec 66	(20)
9555A	EF-15	EF-15a			EMD	F3B	6487	Jan 49	Dec 63	(20)
9555B	EF-15	EF-15a			EMD	F3B	6480	Jan 49	Apr 66	(20)
9556A	EF-15	EF-15a			EMD	F7B	7597	Apr 49	Nov 65	(20)
9556B	EF-15	EF-15a			EMD	F3B	5588	Sep 48	Nov 66	(20)
9557A	EF-15				EMD	F3A	5589	Sep 48	Dec 63	(20)
9558A	EF-15				EMD	F3A	5590	Sep 48	Dec 67	
9559A	EF-15		1414	EF-15	EMD	F3A	5591	Sep 48	Aug 66	
9560A	EF-15				EMD	F3A	5592	Sep 48	to PC	
9561A	EF-15		1416	EF-15	EMD	F3A	5593	Sep 48	May 66	
9563A	EF-15				EMD	F3A	5594	Sep 48	Dec 63	
9564A	EF-15				EMD	F3A	5595	Sep 48	Sep 65	
9565A	EF-15				EMD	F3A	5596	Sep 48	Dec 63	
9566A	EF-15				EMD	F3A	5748	Sep 48		

L.A. MARRE COLLECTION

EMD builder's photo of PRR 9530A and 9529A taken in September, 1948. These units are the first of the PRR's F3 units with what became the F7 carbody. The front coupler cover looks nice but it only lasted for a few years. The cover was another piece of sheet metal that did not hold up to railroad operating conditions.

ORIG ROAD NUM.	PRR BASE CLASS	PRR REBLT CLASS	1966 ROAD NUM.	PRR CLASS (1966)	BLDR	BLDR MODEL	BLDR SERIAL NUM.	BLDR DATE	RETIRE DATE	NOTE
9567A	EF-15	EF-15	1418	EF-15	EMD	F3A	5749	Sep 48	Aug 67	
9568A	BF-15				BLW	DR 4-4-1500	73697	Feb 49	Dec 63	
9568B	BF-15				BLW	DR 4-4-1500	73698	Feb 49	Dec 63	
9569A	BF-15				BLW	DR 4-4-1500	73700	Feb 49	Dec 63	
9569B	BF-15				BLW	DR 4-4-1500	73699	Feb 49	Dec 63	
9570A	BF-15				BLW	DR 4-4-1500	73701	Mar 49	Dec 63	
9570B	BF-15				BLW	DR 4-4-1500	73702	Mar 49	Dec 63	
9571A	BF-15				BLW	DR 4-4-1500	73704	Mar 49	Dec 63	
9571B	BF-15				BLW	DR 4-4-1500	73703	Mar 49	Dec 63	
9572A	BF-15				BLW	DR 4-4-1500	73705	Mar 49	Dec 63	
9572B	BF-15				BLW	DR 4-4-1500	73964	Mar 49	Dec 63	
9573A	BF-15				BLW	DR 4-4-1500	73966	Mar 49	Dec 63	
9573B	BF-15				BLW	DR 4-4-1500	73965	Mar 49	Dec 63	
9574A	BF-15				BLW	DR 4-4-1500	73985	Mar 49	Dec 63	
9574B	BF-15				BLW	DR 4-4-1500	73986	Mar 49	Dec 63	
9575A	BF-15				BLW	DR 4-4-1500	74142	Mar 49	Aug 64	
9575B	BF-15				BLW	DR 4-4-1500	73987	Apr 49	Dec 63	
9576A	BF-15				BLW	DR 4-4-1500	74144	Apr 49	Dec 63	
9576B	BF-15				BLW	DR 4-4-1500	74146	Apr 49	Dec 63	
9577A	BF-15				BLW	DR 4-4-1500	74145	Apr 49	Dec 63	
9577B	BF-15				BLW	DR 4-4-1500	74147	Apr 49	Dec 63	
9578A	BF-15				BLW	DR 4-4-1500	74148	Apr 49	Dec 63	
9578B	BF-15				BLW	DR 4-4-1500	74150	Apr 49	Jun 64	
9579A	BF-15				BLW	DR 4-4-1500	74149	Apr 49	Dec 63	
9579B	BF-15				BLW	DR 4-4-1500	74151	Apr 49	Dec 63	
9580A	BF-15				BLW	DR 4-4-1500	74152	May 49	Dec 63	
9580B	BF-15				BLW	DR 4-4-1500	74154	May 49	Dec 63	
9581A	BF-15				BLW	DR 4-4-1500	74153	May 49	Dec 63	
9581B	BF-15				BLW	DR 4-4-1500	74155	May 49	Dec 63	
9582A	BF-15				BLW	DR 4-4-1500		May 49	Dec 63	
9582B	BF-15				BLW	DR 4-4-1500	74156	May 49	Dec 63	
9583A	BF-15				BLW	DR 4-4-1500	74158	May 49	Dec 63	
9583B	BF-15	ABF-18			BLW	DR 4-4-1500	74157	May 49	May 65	(12)
9584A	BF-15				BLW	DR 4-4-1500	74159	May 49	Dec 63	
9584B	BF-15				BLW	DR 4-4-1500	74160	May 49	Dec 63	
9585A	BF-15				BLW	DR 4-4-1500	74162	May 49	Dec 63	
9585B	BF-15				BLW	DR 4-4-1500	74161	May 49	Dec 63	
9586A	BF-15				BLW	DR 4-4-1500	74163	Jun 49	Dec 63	
9586B	BF-15				BLW	DR 4-4-1500	74164	Jun 49	Dec 63	
9587A	BF-15				BLW	DR 4-4-1500	74166	Jun 49	Jun 64	
9587B	BF-15				BLW	DR 4-4-1500	74165	Jun 49	Dec 63	
9588A	BF-15				BLW	DR 4-4-1500	74167	Jun 49	Jun 64	
9588B	BF-15				BLW	DR 4-4-1500	74168	Jun 49	Jun 64	
9589A	BF-15				BLW	DR 4-4-1500	74170	Jun 49	Jun 64	
9589B	BF-15				BLW	DR 4-4-1500	74169	Jun 49	Jun 64	
9590A	BF-15				BLW	DR 4-4-1500	74171	Jul 49	Aug 64	
9590B	BF-15				BLW	DR 4-4-1500	74172	Jul 49	Jun 64	
9591A	BF-15				BLW	DR 4-4-1500	74174	Jul 49	Jun 64	
9591B	BF-15				BLW	DR 4-4-1500	74173	Jul 49	Jun 64	
9592A	BF-15				BLW	DR 4-4-1500	74175	Jul 49	Jun 64	
9592B	BF-15				BLW	DR 4-4-1500	74176	Jul 49	Jun 64	
9593A	BF-15				BLW	DR 4-4-1500	74177	Jul 49	Jun 64	
9593B	BF-15				BLW	DR 4-4-1500	74178	Jul 49	Jun 64	
9594A	BF-16				BLH	RF-16	74849	Apr 51	Jul 66	
9594B	BF-16				BLH	RF-16	74841	Apr 51	Jul 66	
9595A	BF-16				BLH	RF-16	74850	Apr 51	Jul 66	
9595B	BF-16				BLH	RF-16	74851	Apr 51	Jul 66	
9596A	BF-16				BLH	RF-16	74842	Apr 51	Jul 66	
9596B	BF-16				BLH	RF-16	74852	Apr 51	Jul 66	
9597A	BF-16				BLH	RF-16	74853	Apr 51	Jul 66	
9597B	BF-16				BLH	RF-16	74843	Apr 51	Jul 66	
9598A	BF-16				BLH	RF-16	74854	Apr 51	Jul 66	
9598B	BF-16				BLH	RF-16		Apr 51	Jul 66	
9599A	BF-16				BLH	RF-16		Apr 51	Jul 66	
9599B	BF-16				BLH	RF-16		Apr 51	Jul 66	
9600A	AF-15				Alco	FA-1	75987	Jul 48	Dec 63	
9600B	AF-15				Alco	FB-1	76038	Jul 48	Dec 63	
9601A	AF-15				Alco	FA-1	75988	Jul 48	Dec 63	
9601B	AF-15				Alco	FB-1	76039	Jul 48	Dec 63	
9602A	AF-15				Alco	FA-1	75989	Aug 48	Dec 63	
9602B	AF-15				Alco	FB-1	76040	Aug 48	Dec 63	
9603A	AF-15				Alco	FA-1	75990	Aug 48	Aug 64	
9603B	AF-15				Alco	FB-1	76041	Aug 48	Feb 65	
9604A	AF-15				Alco	FA-1	77010	Mar 50	Feb 65	
9604B	AF-15				Alco	FB-1	76893	Mar 50	Feb 65	
9605A	AF-15				Alco	FA-1	77011	Mar 50	May 65	
9605B	AF-15				Alco	FB-1	76894	Mar 50	Mar 65	
9606A	AF-15				Alco	FA-1	77012	Mar 50	May 65	
9606B	AF-15				Alco	FB-1	76895	Mar 50	Feb 65	
9607A	AF-15				Alco	FA-1	77013	Mar 50	Apr 65	
9607B	AF-15				Alco	FB-1	76896	Mar 50	Mar 65	
9608A	AF-16				Alco	FA-2	78640	May 51	Jul 66	
9608B	AF-16				Alco	FB-2	78664	May 51	Jul 66	
9609A	AF-16				Alco	FA-2	78641	May 51	Jul 66	
9610A	AF-16				Alco	FA-2	78642	May 51	Jul 66	

DOUGLAS COLLECTION

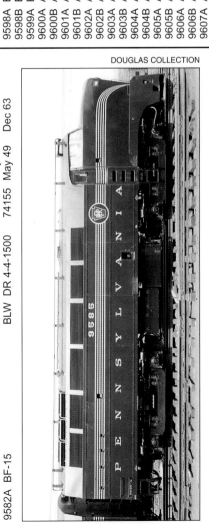

Full side view of PRR 9584A on May 27, 1949. The unit had been placed in service the day before at Enola. This order of units was the first one painted in the five-stripe paint scheme where the stripes extended forward of the PRR monogram in the circle.

Pennsylvania Railroad Diesel Locomotive Roster

Pennsylvania Railroad Diesel Locomotive Roster

ORIG ROAD NUM.	PRR BASE CLASS	PRR REBLT CLASS	1966 ROAD NUM.	PRR CLASS (1966)	BLDR	BLDR MODEL	BLDR SERIAL NUM.	BLDR DATE	RETIRE DATE	NOTE
9610B	AF-16				Alco	FB-2	78665	May 51	Jul 66	
9611A	AF-16				Alco	FA-2	78643	May 51	Jul 66	
9612A	AF-16				Alco	FA-2	78644	May 51	Jul 66	
9612B	AF-16				Alco	FB-2	78666	May 51	Jul 66	
9613A	AF-16				Alco	FA-2	78645	May 51	Jul 66	
9614A	AF-16				Alco	FA-2	78646	May 51	Jul 66	
9614B	AF-16				Alco	FB-2	78667	May 51	Jul 66	
9615A	AF-16				Alco	FA-2	78647	May 51	Jul 66	
9616A	AF-16				Alco	FA-2	78648	May 51	Jul 66	
9616B	AF-16				Alco	FB-2	78668	May 51	Jul 66	
9617A	AF-16				Alco	FA-2	78649	May 51	Jul 66	
9618A	AF-16				Alco	FA-2	78650	May 51	Jul 66	
9618B	AF-16				Alco	FB-2	78669	May 51	Jul 66	
9619A	AF-16				Alco	FA-2	78651	May 51	Jul 66	
9620A	AF-16				Alco	FA-2	79435	Nov 51	Jan 67	
9620B	AF-16				Alco	FB-2	79487	Nov 51	Jan 67	
9621A	AF-16				Alco	FA-2	79436	Nov 51	Jan 67	
9622A	AF-16				Alco	FA-2	79437	Nov 51	Jan 67	

ORIG ROAD NUM.	PRR BASE CLASS	PRR REBLT CLASS	1966 ROAD NUM.	PRR CLASS (1966)	BLDR	BLDR MODEL	BLDR SERIAL NUM.	BLDR DATE	RETIRE DATE	NOTE
9625A	AF-16				Alco	FA-2	79440	Nov 51	Jan 67	
9626A	AF-16				Alco	FA-2	79441	Dec 51	Jan 67	
9626B	AF-16				Alco	FB-2	79490	Dec 51	Jan 67	
9627A	AF-16				Alco	FA-2	79442	Dec 51	Jan 67	
9628A	AF-16				Alco	FB-2	79443	Dec 51	Jan 67	
9628B	AF-16				Alco	FB-2	79491	Dec 51	Jan 67	
9629A	AF-16				Alco	FA-2	79444	Dec 51	Jan 67	
9630A	AF-16				Alco	FB-2	79445	Dec 51	Jan 67	
9630B	AF-16				Alco	FA-2	79747	Dec 51	Jan 67	
9631A	AF-16				Alco	FA-2	79446	Dec 51	Jan 67	
9632A		ABF-18			BLH/A	RF-16/Alco	75198	Jun 51	Jul 66	(12)
9632B		ABF-18			BLW/A	(Note 12)	74157	May 49	May 65	(12)
9633A		ABF-18			BLH/A	RF-16/Alco	75005	Mar 51	Jul 66	(12)
9640A	EF-15a	EF-15a	1440	EF-15a	EMD	F7A	8767	Mar 50	to PC	
9640B	EF-15a	EF-15a			EMD	F7B	8777	Mar 50	May 66	
9641A	EF-15a	EF-15a			EMD	F7B	8768	Mar 50	Jul 65	
9641B	EF-15a	EF-15a	3512	EF-15a	EMD	F7B	8778	Mar 50	to PC	
9642A	EF-15a	EF-15a			EMD	F7A	8769	Mar 50	Aug 66	
9642B	EF-15a	EF-15a	3513	EF-15a	EMD	F7B	8779	Mar 50	Aug 67	
9643A	EF-15a	EF-15a	1442	EF-15a	EMD	F7A	8770	Mar 50	to PC	
9643B	EF-15a	EF-15a	3514	EF-15a	EMD	F7B	8780	Mar 50	Aug 67	
9644A	EF-15a	EF-15a	1443	EF-15a	EMD	F7A	8771	Mar 50	to PC	
9644B	EF-15a	EF-15a	3515	EF-15a	EMD	F7B	8781	Mar 50	Aug 67	
9645A	EF-15a	EF-15a			EMD	F7A	8772	Mar 50	Sep 65	
9645B	EF-15a	EF-15a	3516	EF-15a	EMD	F7B	8782	Mar 50	to PC	
9646A	EF-15a	EF-15a	1444	EF-15a	EMD	F7A	8773	Mar 50	to PC	

PRR 9642A at the Greenwich yard engine terminal on the south side of Philadelphia. This yard served the iron ore docks which the PRR built in the early 1960's to receive ore from new sources. This engine terminal also served electric locomotives as indicated by the overhead wires.

PRR 9625A shows its classic Alco cab unit nose at the engine terminal at Cresson, Pennsylvania on July 15, 1962

ORIG ROAD NUM.	PRR BASE CLASS	PRR REBLT CLASS	1966 ROAD NUM.	PRR CLASS (1966)	BLDR	BLDR MODEL	BLDR SERIAL NUM.	BLDR DATE	RETIRE DATE	NOTE
9622B	AF-16				Alco	FB-2	79488	Nov 51	Jan 67	
9623A	AF-16				Alco	FA-2	79438	Nov 51	Jan 67	
9624A	AF-16				Alco	FA-2	79439	Nov 51	Jan 67	
9624B	AF-16				Alco	FB-2	79489	Nov 51	Jan 67	

ORIG ROAD NUM.	PRR BASE CLASS	PRR REBLT CLASS	1966 ROAD NUM.	PRR CLASS (1966)	BLDR	BLDR MODEL	BLDR SERIAL NUM.	BLDR DATE	RETIRE DATE	NOTE
9646B	EF-15a		3517	EF-15a	EMD	F7B	8783	Mar 50	Aug 67	
9647A	EF-15a				EMD	F7A	8774	Mar 50	Jul 65	
9647B	EF-15a		3518	EF-15a	EMD	F7B	8784	Mar 50	Dec 67	
9648A	EF-15a		1445	EF-15a	EMD	F7A	9826	Feb 50	Aug 67	
9648B	EF-15a		3519	EF-15a	EMD	F7B	9833	Feb 50	Dec 66	
9649A	EF-15a		1446	EF-15a	EMD	F7A	9827	Feb 50	Dec 66	
9650A	EF-15a				EMD	F7A	9828	Feb 50	Sep 65	
9650B	EF-15a		3520	EF-15a	EMD	F7B	9834	Feb 50	Dec 67	
9651A	EF-15a				EMD	F7A	9829	Feb 50	Jul 66	
9652B	EH-15	EF-15a	3521	EF-15a	EMD	F7B	8800	Feb 50	Nov 66	(20)
9653A	EH-15	EF-15a	1449	EF-15a	EMD	F7A	8804	Feb 50	to PC	(20)
9654A	EH-15	EF-15a	1450	EF-15a	EMD	F7A	8801	Feb 50	Nov 66	(20)
9654B	EH-15	EF-15a			EMD	F7B	8802	Feb 50	to PC	(20)
9655A	EH-15	EF-15a			EMD	F7A	8805	Feb 50	Apr 66	(20)
9656A	EF-15a				EMD	F7A	8803	Feb 50	Apr 65	(20)
9661A	EF-15a		1905	EF-15a	EMD	F7A	8791	Mar 50	Nov 66	
9662A	EF-15a		1451	EF-15a	EMD	F7A	8796	Mar 50	to PC	
9663A	EF-15a				EMD	F7B	9830	Feb 50	to PC	
9664A	EF-15a				EMD	F7A	9831	Feb 50	Jul 66	
9665A	EF-15a				EMD	F7B	8775	Feb 50	Aug 66	
9666A	EF-15a		1906	EF-15a	EMD	F7A	9832	Feb 50	Feb 65	
9667A	EF-15a		1454	EF-15a	EMD	F7A	8227	Mar 49	to PC	
9667B	EF-15a				EMD	F7B	8237	Mar 49	Dec 63	
9668A	EF-15a		1455	EF-15a	EMD	F7A	8228	Mar 49	to PC	
9668B	EF-15a		3526	EF-15a	EMD	F7B	8238	Mar 49	to PC	
9669A	EF-15a				EMD	F7A	8229	Apr 49	May 66	
9669B	EF-15a				EMD	F7B	8239	Apr 49	Dec 63	
9670A	EF-15a		1457	EF-15a	EMD	F7A	8230	Apr 49	to PC	
9670B	EF-15a		3527	EF-15a	EMD	F7B	8240	Apr 49	Feb 67	
9671A	EF-15a				EMD	F7A	8231	Jun 49	Dec 63	
9671B	EF-15a				EMD	F7B	8241	Jun 49	Dec 63	
9672A	EF-15a		3528	EF-15a	EMD	F7A	8232	Jun 49	Dec 63	
9672B	EF-15a				EMD	F7B	8242	Jun 49	to PC	
9673A	EF-15a		1458	EF-15a	EMD	F7A	8233	Jun 49	to PC	
9673B	EF-15a				EMD	F7B	8243	Jun 49	Feb 66	
9674A	EF-15a				EMD	F7A	8234	Jun 49	Ca. 63	
9674B	EF-15a				EMD	F7B	8244	Jun 49	Nov 65	
9675A	EF-15a		3530	EF-15a	EMD	F7A	8235	Jun 49	Jul 66	
9675B	EF-15a				EMD	F7B	8245	Jul 49	Aug 67	
9676A	EF-15a				EMD	F7A	8236	Jul 49	Nov 66	
9676B	EF-15a				EMD	F7B	8246	Jul 49	Aug 66	
9677A	EF-15		1419	EF-15	EMD	F3A	8279	Sep 48	to PC	
9678A	EF-15				EMD	F3A	8280	Sep 48	Dec 63	
9679A	EF-15				EMD	F3A	6488	Oct 48	Nov 65	
9680A	EH-15	EF-15			EMD	F3A	6489	Jan 49	Dec 63	(20)
9681A	EH-15	EF-15 (NOT)			EMD	F3A	6490	Jan 49	Dec 63	(20)
9682A	EH-15	EF-15a			EMD	F3A	6491	Feb 49	Nov 65	(20)
9683A	EH-15	EF-15a	1420	EF-15	EMD	F3A	6492	Feb 49	to PC	(62)
9684A	EH-15	EF-15a	1421	EF-15	EMD	F3A	7574	Feb 49	Dec 66	(20)
9685A	EH-15	EF-15a	1422	EF-15	EMD	F3A	7575	Feb 49	to PC	(20)
9686A	EH-15	EF-15a	1423	EF-15	EMD	F3A	7576	Feb 49	Nov 65	(20)
9687A	EH-15	EF-15a	1424	EF-15	EMD	F3A	7577	Feb 49	Oct 64	(20)
9688A	EH-15	EF-15a			EMD	F3A	7578	Feb 49	Nov 64	(20)
9689A	EH-15	EF-15a	1425	EF-15	EMD	F3A	7579	Feb 49	Aug 67	(20)
9690A	EH-15	EF-15a	1461	EF-15a	EMD	F7A	7580	Apr 49	Oct 67	(20)
9691A	EH-15	EF-15a	1462	EF-15a	EMD	F7A	7581	Apr 49	Feb 67	(20)
9692A	EH-15	EF-15a			EMD	F7A	7582	Apr 49	Nov 65	(20)
9693A	EH-15	EF-15a			EMD	F7A	7583	Apr 49	Jul 66	(20)
9694A	EH-15	EF-15a			EMD	F7A	7584	Apr 49	Dec 63	(20)
9695A	EH-15	EF-15a			EMD	F7A	7585	Apr 49	Dec 63	(20)
9696A	EH-15	EF-15a			EMD	F7A	7586	Apr 49	Dec 63	(20)
9697A	EH-15	EF-15a	1464	EF-15a	EMD	F7A	7587	Apr 49	Dec 63	(20)
9698A	EH-15	EF-15a			EMD	F7A	7588	Apr 49	to PC	(20)
9699A	EH-15	EF-15a			EMD	F7A	7589	Apr 49	Dec 63	(20)
9700A	BF-15a				BLW	DR 4-4-1500	74441	Apr 50	Feb 65	
9700B	BF-15a				BLW	DR 4-4-1500	74440	Apr 50	May 65	
9701A	BF-15a				BLW	DR 4-4-1500	74442	Apr 50	Feb 65	
9701B	BF-15a				BLW	DR 4-4-1500	74443	Apr 50	Apr 65	
9702A	BF-15a				BLW	DR 4-4-1500	74444	May 50	Apr 65	
9702B	BF-15a				BLW	DR 4-4-1500	74446	May 50	May 65	
9703A	BF-15a				BLW	DR 4-4-1500	74445	May 50	Feb 65	
9703B	BF-15a				BLW	DR 4-4-1500	74449	May 50	May 65	
9704A	BF-15a				BLW	DR 4-4-1500	74439	May 50	May 65	
9704B	BF-15a				BLW	DR 4-4-1500	74748	May 50	May 65	
9705A	BF-15a				BLW	DR 4-4-1500	74447	May 50	May 65	

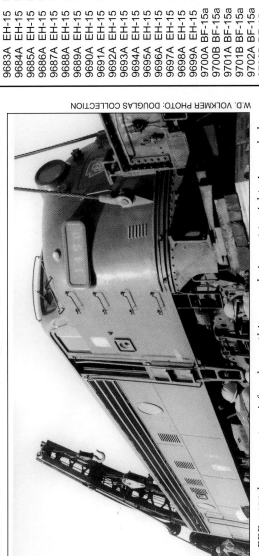

PRR 1450 has come to grief and now things are being set to right. A wreck derrick is lifting each end of the unit. This is why those lifting eyes were installed on the ends of most PRR cab units. The wreck occurred on the Elmira Branch just south of the Pennsylvania-New York border at Snedikerville, Pennsylvania (spelled Snediker by the PRR). The date is September 13, 1967.

Pennsylvania Railroad Diesel Locomotive Roster

ORIG ROAD NUM.	PRR BASE CLASS	PRR REBLT CLASS	1966 ROAD NUM.	PRR CLASS (1966)	BLDR	BLDR MODEL	BLDR SERIAL NUM.	BLDR DATE	RETIRE DATE	NOTE
9705B	BF-15a				BLW	DR 4-4-1500	74749	May 50	May 65	
9706A	BF-15a				BLW	DR 4-4-1500	74448	Jun 50	Feb 65	
9706B	BF-15a				BLW	DR 4-4-1500	74750	Jun 50	Mar 65	
9707A	BF-15a				BLW	DR 4-4-1500	74450	Jun 50	May 65	
9707B	BF-15a				BLW	DR 4-4-1500	74751	Jun 50	Feb 65	
9708A	BF-16				BLH	RF-16	74819	Dec 50	Jul 66	
9708B	BF-16				BLH	RF-16	74831	Dec 50	Jul 66	
9709A	BF-16				BLH	RF-16	74820	Dec 50	Jul 66	
9710A	BF-16				BLH	RF-16	74821	Dec 50	Jul 66	
9710B	BF-16				BLH	RF-16	74832	Dec 50	Jul 66	
9711A	BF-16				BLH	RF-16	74822	Dec 50	Jul 66	
9712A	BF-16				BLH	RF-16	74823	Jan 51	Jul 66	
9712B	BF-16				BLH	RF-16	74833	Jan 51	Jul 66	
9713A	BF-16				BLH	RF-16	74824	Jan 51	Jul 66	
9714A	BF-16				BLH	RF-16	74825	Jan 51	Jul 66	
9714B	BF-16				BLH	RF-16	74834	Jan 51	Jul 66	
9715A	BF-16				BLH	RF-16	74826	Jan 51	Jul 66	
9716A	BF-16				BLH	RF-16	74995	Mar 51	Jul 66	
9717A	BF-16				BLH	RF-16	74996	Mar 51	Jul 66	
9718A	BF-16				BLH	RF-16	74997	Mar 51	Jul 66	
9719A	BF-16				BLH	RF-16	74998	Mar 51	Jul 66	
9720A	BF-16				BLH	RF-16	74999	Mar 51	Jul 66	
9721A	BF-16				BLH	RF-16	75000	Mar 51	Jul 66	
9722A	BF-16				BLH	RF-16	75001	Mar 51	Jul 66	
9723A	BF-16				BLH	RF-16	75002	Mar 51	Jul 66	
9724A	BF-16				BLH	RF-16	75003	Mar 51	Jul 66	
9725A	BF-16				BLH	RF-16	75004	Mar 51	Jul 66	
9726A	BF-16				BLH	RF-16	75005	Mar 51	Jul 66	
9726B	BF-16	ABF-18			BLH	RF-16	75006	Mar 51	Jul 66	(12)
9727A	BF-16				BLH	RF-16	74991	Feb 51	Jul 66	
9728A	BF-16				BLH	RF-16	74838	Feb 51	Jul 66	
9728B	BF-16				BLH	RF-16	74992	Feb 51	Jul 66	
9729A	BF-16				BLH	RF-16	74993	Feb 51	Jul 66	
9730A	BF-16				BLH	RF-16	74839	Feb 51	Jul 66	
9730B	BF-16				BLH	RF-16	74994	Feb 51	Jul 66	
9731A	BF-16				BLH	RF-16	74847	Mar 51	Jul 66	
9732A	BF-16				BLH	RF-16	74840	Mar 51	Jul 66	
9732B	BF-16				BLH	RF-16	74848	Mar 51	Jul 66	
9733A	BF-16				BLH	RF-16	74855	May 51	Jul 66	
9734A	BF-16				BLH	RF-16	74844	May 51	Jul 66	
9734B	BF-16				BLH	RF-16	74856	May 51	Jul 66	
9735A	BF-16				BLH	RF-16	75112	May 51	Jul 66	
9736A	BF-16				BLH	RF-16	74845	Mar 51	Jul 66	
9736B	BF-16				BLH	RF-16	75113	May 51	Jul 66	
9737A	BF-16				BLH	RF-16	75114	May 51	Jul 66	
9738A	BF-16				BLH	RF-16	74846	Mar 51	Jul 66	
9738B	BF-16				BLH	RF-16	75115	May 51	Jul 66	
9739A	BF-16				BLH	RF-16	74827	Jan 51	Jul 66	
9740A	BF-16				BLH	RF-16	74835	Jan 51	Jul 66	
9740B	BF-16				BLH	RF-16	74828	Jan 51	Jul 66	
9741A	BF-16				BLH	RF-16	74829	Feb 51	Jul 66	
9742A	BF-16				BLH	RF-16	74594	Feb 51	Jul 66	
9742B	BF-16				BLH	RF-16	74836	Feb 51	Jul 66	

This what happens when the oil seals on the turbocharger fail. A cloud of oil is propelled out the exhaust and gives the carbody a petroleum shower-bath. The PRR 9734A is parked in the engine terminal at Conway Yard in Conway, Pennsylvania on February 20, 1962.

ORIG ROAD NUM.	PRR BASE CLASS	PRR REBLT CLASS	1966 ROAD NUM.	PRR CLASS (1966)	BLDR	BLDR MODEL	BLDR SERIAL NUM.	BLDR DATE	RETIRE DATE	NOTE
9743A	BF-16				BLH	RF-16	74830	Feb 51	Jul 66	
9744A	BF-16				BLH	RF-16	74989	Feb 51	Jul 66	
9744B	BF-16				BLH	RF-16	74837	Feb 51	Jul 66	
9745A	BF-16				BLH	RF-16	74990	Feb 51	Jul 66	
9764A	EF-15a				EMD	F7A	13578	Jan 51	Aug 66	
9764B	EF-15a		3532	EF-15a	EMD	F7B	13646	Jan 51	Dec 66	
9765A	EF-15a				EMD	F7A	13579	Jan 51	Nov 66	
9766A	EF-15a		1467	EF-15a	EMD	F7A	13580	Jan 51	Aug 67	
9766B	EF-15a				EMD	F7B	13647	Jan 51	Aug 66	
9767A	EF-15a				EMD	F7A	13581	Jan 51	Feb 67	
9768A	EF-15a		1469	EF-15a	EMD	F7A	13582	Jan 51	to PC	
9768B	EF-15a		3534	EF-15a	EMD	F7B	13648	Jan 51	Dec 66	
9769A	EF-15a		1470	EF-15a	EMD	F7A	13583	Jan 51	Aug 67	
9770A	EF-15a				EMD	F7A	13584	Jan 51	Dec 66	
9770B	EF-15a				EMD	F7B	13649	Jan 51	Aug 66	
9771A	EF-15a		1472	EF-15a	EMD	F7A	13585	Jan 51	to PC	
9772A	EF-15a		1473	EF-15a	EMD	F7A	13586	Jan 51	to PC	
9772B	EF-15a		3536	EF-15a	EMD	F7B	13650	Jan 51	Aug 67	
9773A	EF-15a		1474	EF-15a	EMD	F7A	13587	Jan 51	Aug 67	
9774A	EF-15a		1475	EF-15a	EMD	F7A	13588	Jan 51	to PC	
9774B	EF-15a		3537	EF-15a	EMD	F7B	13651	Jan 51	Dec 67	
9775A	EF-15a		1476	EF-15a	EMD	F7A	13589	Jan 51	to PC	
9776A	EF-15a				EMD	F7A	13590	Jan 51	Sep 64	
9776B	EF-15a		3538	EF-15a	EMD	F7B	13652	Jan 51	Aug 67	
9777A	EF-15a		1477	EF-15a	EMD	F7A	13591	Jan 51	to PC	
9778A	EF-15a		1478	EF-15a	EMD	F7A	13592	Feb 51	to PC	
9778B	EF-15a		3539	EF-15a	EMD	F7B	13653	Feb 51	Feb 67	
9779A	EF-15a				EMD	F7A	13593	Feb 51	Nov 66	
9780A	EF-15a				EMD	F7A	13594	Feb 51	Aug 66	
9780B	EF-15a				EMD	F7B	13654	Feb 51	Aug 66	

Pennsylvania Railroad Diesel Locomotive Roster

Pennsylvania Railroad Diesel Locomotive Roster

ORIG ROAD NUM.	PRR BASE CLASS	PRR REBLT CLASS	1966 ROAD NUM.	PRR CLASS (1966)	BLDR	BLDR MODEL	BLDR SERIAL NUM.	BLDR DATE	RETIRE DATE	NOTE
9781A	EF-15a		1481	EF-15a	EMD	F7A	13595	Feb 51	to PC	
9782A	EF-15a		1482	EF-15a	EMD	F7A	13596	Feb 51	to PC	
9782B	EF-15a		3541	EF-15a	EMD	F7B	13655	Feb 51	to PC	
9783A	EF-15a		1483	EF-15a	EMD	F7A	13597	Feb 51	Feb 67	
9784A	EF-15a		1484	EF-15a	EMD	F7A	13598	Feb 51	Oct 67	
9784B	EF-15a		3542	EF-15a	EMD	F7B	13656	Feb 51	Dec 67	
9785A	EF-15a		1485	EF-15a	EMD	F7A	13599	Feb 51	to PC	
9786A	EF-15a		1486	EF-15a	EMD	F7A	13600	Feb 51	Dec 66	
9786B	EF-15a		3543	EF-15a	EMD	F7B	13657	Feb 51	Aug 67	
9787A	EF-15a		1487	EF-15a	EMD	F7A	13601	Feb 51	Dec 66	
9788A	EF-15a		1488	EF-15a	EMD	F7A	13602	Feb 51	to PC	
9788B	EF-15a		3544	EF-15a	EMD	F7B	13658	Feb 51	to PC	
9789A	EF-15a		1489	EF-15a	EMD	F7A	13603	Feb 51	Oct 67	
9790A	EF-15a		1490	EF-15a	EMD	F7A	13604	Feb 51	to PC	
9790B	EF-15a		3545	EF-15a	EMD	F7B	13659	Mar 51	to PC	
9791A	EF-15a		1491	EF-15a	EMD	F7A	13605	Mar 51	Feb 67	
9792A	EF-15a		1492	EF-15a	EMD	F7A	13606	Mar 51	to PC	
9792B	EF-15a		3546	EF-15a	EMD	F7B	13660	Mar 51	Aug 67	
9793A	EF-15a		1493	EF-15a	EMD	F7A	13607	Mar 51	to PC	
9794A	EF-15a		1494	EF-15a	EMD	F7A	13608	Mar 51	to PC	
9794B	EF-15a		3547	EF-15a	EMD	F7B	13661	Mar 51	Dec 67	
9795A	EF-15a		1495	EF-15a	EMD	F7A	13609	Mar 51	to PC	
9796A	EF-15a			EF-15a	EMD	F7A	13610	Mar 51	Aug 66	
9796B	EF-15a		3548	EF-15a	EMD	F7B	13662	Mar 51	to PC	
9797A	EF-15a		1497	EF-15a	EMD	F7A	13611	Mar 51	Nov 66	
9798A	EF-15a		1498	EF-15a	EMD	F7A	13612	Mar 51	Dec 67	
9798B	EF-15a		3549	EF-15a	EMD	F7B	13663	Mar 51	Oct 67	
9799A	EF-15a		1499	EF-15a	EMD	F7A	13613	Mar 51	to PC	

ORIG ROAD NUM.	PRR BASE CLASS	PRR REBLT CLASS	1966 ROAD NUM.	PRR CLASS (1966)	BLDR	BLDR MODEL	BLDR SERIAL NUM.	BLDR DATE	RETIRE DATE	NOTE
9800A	EF-15a		1500	EF-15a	EMD	F7A	13614	Mar 51	to PC	
9800B	EF-15a			EF-15a	EMD	F7B	13664	Mar 51	Jul 66	
9801A	EF-15a		1501	EF-15a	EMD	F7A	13615	Mar 51	to PC	
9802A	EF-15a			EF-15a	EMD	F7A	13616	Mar 51	Nov 66	
9802B	EF-15a		3551	EF-15a	EMD	F7B	13665	Mar 51	Oct 67	
9803A	EF-15a		1503	EF-15a	EMD	F7A	13617	Mar 51	Dec 67	
9804A	EF-15a		1504	EF-15a	EMD	F7A	13618	Mar 51	Oct 67	
9804B	EF-15a		3552	EF-15a	EMD	F7B	13666	Mar 51	Dec 66	
9805A	EF-15a		1505	EF-15a	EMD	F7A	13619	Mar 51	to PC	
9806A	EF-15a			EF-15a	EMD	F7A	13620	Mar 51	Aug 66	
9806B	EF-15a		3553	EF-15a	EMD	F7B	13667	Mar 51	Dec 66	
9807A	EF-15a		1507	EF-15a	EMD	F7A	13621	Apr 51	Oct 67	
9808A	EF-15a		1508	EF-15a	EMD	F7A	13622	Apr 51	Aug 67	
9808B	EF-15a		3554	EF-15a	EMD	F7B	13668	Apr 51	to PC	
9809A	EF-15a		1509	EF-15a	EMD	F7A	13623	Apr 51	to PC	
9810A	EF-15a		1510	EF-15a	EMD	F7A	13624	Apr 51	Oct 67	
9810B	EF-15a		3555	EF-15a	EMD	F7B	13669	Apr 51	to PC	
9811A	EF-15a		1511	EF-15a	EMD	F7A	13625	Apr 51	to PC	
9812A	EF-15a		1512	EF-15a	EMD	F7A	13626	Apr 51	Oct 67	
9812B	EF-15a		3556	EF-15a	EMD	F7B	13670	Apr 51	Oct 67	
9813A	EF-15a		1513	EF-15a	EMD	F7A	13627	Apr 51	to PC	
9814A	EF-15a		1514	EF-15a	EMD	F7A	13628	Apr 51	Dec 67	
9814B	EF-15a		3557	EF-15a	EMD	F7B	13671	Apr 51	to PC	
9815A	EF-15a			EF-15a	EMD	F7A	13629	Apr 51	Nov 66	
9816A	EF-15a		1516	EF-15a	EMD	F7A	13630	May 51	to PC	
9816B	EF-15a		3558	EF-15a	EMD	F7B	13672	May 51	Feb 67	
9817A	EF-15a		1517	EF-15a	EMD	F7A	13631	May 51	Oct 67	
9818A	EF-15a		1518	EF-15a	EMD	F7A	13632	May 51	to PC	
9818B	EF-15a		3559	EF-15a	EMD	F7B	13673	May 51	Oct 67	
9819A	EF-15a			EF-15a	EMD	F7A	13633	May 51	Nov 66	
9820A	EF-15a		1520	EF-15a	EMD	F7A	13634	May 51	to PC	
9821A	EF-15a		1521	EF-15a	EMD	F7A	13635	May 51	to PC	
9822A	EF-15a		1522	EF-15a	EMD	F7A	13636	May 51	Dec 67	
9823A	EF-15a		1523	EF-15a	EMD	F7A	13637	May 51	Oct 67	
9824A	EF-15a		1524	EF-15a	EMD	F7A	13638	May 51	to PC	
9825A	EF-15a			EF-15a	EMD	F7A	13639	May 51	Dec 66	
9826A	EF-15a		1526	EF-15a	EMD	F7A	13640	Jun 51	Aug 67	
9827A	EF-15a		1527	EF-15a	EMD	F7A	13641	Jun 51	to PC	
9828A	EF-15a			EF-15a	EMD	F7A	13642	Jun 51	Dec 66	
9829A	EF-15a		1529	EF-15a	EMD	F7A	13643	Jun 51	Aug 67	
9830A	EF-15a		1530	EF-15a	EMD	F7A	13644	Jun 51	to PC	
9831A	EF-15a		1531	EF-15a	EMD	F7A	13645	Jun 51	to PC	
9832A	EFP-15		4332	EFP-15	EMD	FP7A	12410	Apr 52	to PC	
9832B	EFP-15		4150	EFP-15	EMD	F7B	13075	Apr 52	to PC	
9833A	EFP-15		4333	EFP-15	EMD	FP7A	12411	Apr 52	Oct 67	
9834A	EFP-15		4334	EFP-15	EMD	FP7A	12412	Apr 52	to PC	
9834B	EFP-15		4151	EFP-15	EMD	F7B	13076	Apr 52	to PC	
9835A	EFP-15		4335	EFP-15	EMD	FP7A	12413	Apr 52	to PC	
9836A	EFP-15		4336	EFP-15	EMD	FP7A	12414	Apr 52	to PC	
9836B	EFP-15		4152	EFP-15	EMD	F7B	13077	Apr 52	Dec 67	
9837A	EFP-15		4337	EFP-15	EMD	FP7A	12415	Apr 52	to PC	
9838A	EFP-15		4338	EFP-15	EMD	FP7A	12416	Apr 52	to PC	

PRR 9795A-9790B-7123 are on the head end of a coal train at the Brickyard Crossing just west of Altoona on July 24, 1965. Perhaps the cloud of blue smoke from the brake shoes is not as dense as before the airbrake pressure maintaining feature, but it is still there.

Pennsylvania Railroad Diesel Locomotive Roster

ORIG ROAD NUM.	PRR BASE CLASS	PRR REBLT CLASS	1966 ROAD NUM.	PRR CLASS (1966)	BLDR	BLDR MODEL	BLDR SERIAL NUM.	BLDR DATE	RETIRE DATE	NOTE
9838B	EFP-15		4153	EFP-15	EMD	F7B	13078	Apr 52	to PC	
9839A	EFP-15		4339	EFP-15	EMD	FP7A	12417	Apr 52	to PC	
9840A	EFP-15		4340	EFP-15	EMD	FP7A	12418	May 52	to PC	
9840B	EFP-15		4154	EFP-15	EMD	F7B	13079	May 52	to PC	
9841A	EFP-15		4341	EFP-15	EMD	FP7A	12419	May 52	to PC	
9842A	EFP-15		4342	EFP-15	EMD	FP7A	12420	May 52	to PC	
9842B	EFP-15		4155	EFP-15	EMD	F7B	13080	May 52	to PC	
9843A	EFP-15		4343	EFP-15	EMD	FP7A	12421	May 52	to PC	
9844A	EFP-15		4344	EFP-15	EMD	FP7A	12422	May 52	to PC	
9844B	EFP-15		4156	EFP-15	EMD	F7B	13081	May 52	to PC	
9845A	EFP-15		4345	EFP-15	EMD	FP7A	12423	May 52	to PC	
9846A	EFP-15		4346	EFP-15	EMD	FP7A	12424	May 52	to PC	
9846B	EFP-15		4157	EFP-15	EMD	F7B	13082	May 52	to PC	
9847A	EFP-15		4347	EFP-15	EMD	FP7A	12425	May 52	to PC	
9848A	EFP-15		4348	EFP-15	EMD	FP7A	12426	May 52	to PC	
9848B	EFP-15		4158	EFP-15	EMD	F7B	13083	May 52	to PC	
9849A	EFP-15		4349	EFP-15	EMD	FP7A	12427	May 52	to PC	
9850A	EFP-15		4350	EFP-15	EMD	FP7A	12428	Jun 52	to PC	
9850B	EFP-15		4159	EFP-15	EMD	F7B	13084	Jun 52	to PC	
9851A	EFP-15		4351	EFP-15	EMD	FP7A	12429	Jun 52	to PC	
9852A	EFP-15		4352	EFP-15	EMD	FP7A	12430	Jun 52	to PC	
9852B	EFP-15		4160	EFP-15	EMD	F7B	13085	Jun 52	Oct 67	
9853A	EFP-15		4353	EFP-15	EMD	FP7A	12431	Jun 52	to PC	
9854A	EFP-15		4354	EFP-15	EMD	FP7A	12432	Jun 52	to PC	
9854B	EFP-15		4161	EFP-15	EMD	F7B	13086	Jun 52	Oct 67	
9855B	EFP-15		4355	EFP-15	EMD	FP7A	12433	Jun 52	to PC	
9856A	EFP-15		4356	EFP-15	EMD	FP7A	12434	Jun 52	to PC	
9856B	EFP-15		4162	EFP-15	EMD	F7B	13087	Jun 52	Oct 67	

PRR 4359 at the Pitcairn (PA) engine terminal. Repairs to this FP7 following a head-on crash in 1964 included applying the nose from ex-Great Northern Y-1a electric locomotive No. 5011, which had itself been rebuilt with that EMD nose.

ORIG ROAD NUM.	PRR BASE CLASS	PRR REBLT CLASS	1966 ROAD NUM.	PRR CLASS (1966)	BLDR	BLDR MODEL	BLDR SERIAL NUM.	BLDR DATE	RETIRE DATE	NOTE
9857A	EFP-15		4357	EFP-15	EMD	FP7A	12435	Jun 52	to PC	
9858A	EFP-15		4358	EFP-15	EMD	FP7A	12436	Jul 52	to PC	
9858B	EFP-15		4163	EFP-15	EMD	F7B	13088	Jul 52	Oct 67	
9859A	EFP-15		4359	EFP-15	EMD	FP7A	12437	Jul 52	to PC	
9860A	EFP-15		4360	EFP-15	EMD	FP7A	12438	Jul 52	to PC	
9861A	EFP-15		4361	EFP-15	EMD	FP7A	12439	Jul 52	to PC	
9862A	EFP-15		4362	EFP-15	EMD	FP7A	12440	Jul 52	to PC	
9863A	EFP-15		4363	EFP-15	EMD	FP7A	12441	Jul 52	to PC	
9864A	EFP-15		4364	EFP-15	EMD	FP7A	12442	Aug 52	to PC	
9864B	EFP-15		4365	EFP-15	EMD	FP7A	12443	Aug 52	to PC	
9865A	EFP-15		4366	EFP-15	EMD	FP7A	12444	Aug 52	to PC	
9866A	EFP-15		4367	EFP-15	EMD	FP7A	15643	Aug 52	to PC	
9867A	EFP-15		4368	EFP-15	EMD	FP7A	15644	Aug 52	to PC	
9868A	EFP-15		4369	EFP-15	EMD	FP7A	15645	Aug 52	to PC	
9869A	EFP-15		4370	EFP-15	EMD	FP7A	15646	Aug 52	to PC	
9870A	EFP-15		4371	EFP-15	EMD	FP7A	15647	Aug 52	to PC	
9871A	EFP-15				EMD	FP7A				
9872A	EF-15a		1532	EF-15a	EMD	F7A	16791	Sep 52	Oct 67	
9872B	EF-15a		3560	EF-15a	EMD	F7B	16799	Sep 52	to PC	
9873A	EF-15a				EMD	F7A	16792	Sep 52	Sep 64	
9874A	EF-15a		1533	EF-15a	EMD	F7A	16793	Sep 52	to PC	
9874B	EF-15a		3561	EF-15a	EMD	F7B	16800	Sep 52	to PC	
9875A	EF-15a		1534	EF-15a	EMD	F7A	16794	Sep 52	Oct 67	
9876A	EF-15a		1535	EF-15a	EMD	F7A	16795	Sep 52	Oct 67	
9876B	EF-15a		3562	EF-15a	EMD	F7B	16801	Sep 52	to PC	
9877A	EF-15a		1536	EF-15a	EMD	F7A	16796	Sep 52	Oct 67	
9878A	EF-15a		1537	EF-15a	EMD	F7A	16797	Sep 52	to PC	
9878B	EF-15a		3563	EF-15a	EMD	F7B	16802	Sep 52	to PC	
9879A	EF-15a		1538	EF-15a	EMD	F7A	16798	Sep 52	Apr 71	

PRR 9603A leading a six-unit set of units with an eastbound freight including two Alco B-units, a GP9 unit and two F7A units near Bellwood, Pennsylvania on April 18, 1964. The train has just left Altoona and is on the Middle Division on its way to the Harrisburg area.

Appendix B
Diesel Locomotive Roster Notes

(1) The base class shown is the "1951 Class." This classification system was established in September, 1951.

(2) The class A6 unit 3905 was the first internal combustion locomotive installed in PRR service. The unit was built at Altoona shops by the PRR in 1928. The running gear was similar to the class B1 electric locomotives. The wheel arrangement was 0-4-0 in steam-type nomenclature with all weight on the two driving axles, each of which was driven by a traction motor. The engine finally used was the Winton model 148 gasoline engine rated at 400 horsepower for the 65 ton locomotive. The 3905 was retired in April, 1952.

(3) The other class A6 unit was 3906, built in 1929. It was a duplicate of the 3905. Tho 3905 was retired in August, 1954.

(4) The one A6b built in 1930, was almost identical to the A6 units. Initially this unit was equipped with a Brill-Westinghouse model 860 gasoline engine rated at 535 horsepower. In 1947, the gasoline engine was replaced by a Hamilton model 88SA engine rated at 450 horsepower. The 3907 was retired in late 1962.

(5) The class AS-15m units were Alco RS-3 units originally built for the Delaware and Hudson. The D&H rated these units 1500 horsepower despite the fact that Alco rated the RS-3 model at 1600 horsepower. The units were leased by the PRR by early 1956. The Pennsylvania purchased these units in January, 1958. The PRR also rated these units at 1500 horsepower (reference PRR No.109-M, dated July 1,1960), but this was academic since the continuous tractive effort was the same as the other PRR RS-3 units.

(6) The PRR applied MU controls to three class BS-7 Baldwin model DS 4-4-750 units for operation on Western Maryland trackage near Cumberland, Maryland which had a weight restriction. PRR 5595 and 5597 had MU applied in late 1952 while the 5600 had MU applied in July, 1963. The 5600 had MU applied in order to apply a relief unit for the run to Cumberland.

(7) The fifteen Alco 2000 horsepower passenger units (models PA-1 and PB-1) were converted to dual service freight-passenger units in late 1952 and early 1953. The conversion version involved mostly a regearing from 23:60 (100 mph, max.) to 19:64 (80.5 mph, max.).

(8) Eight of the 27 Baldwin 2000 horsepower passenger units were converted to fright units about between November 1, 1952 and April 1, 1953. The conversion involved regearing from 22:57 (100 mph, max.) to 15:63 (65 mph, max.), and derating the horsepower available for traction from 2000 to 1600.

(9) The PRR Baldwin Centipede units were designed as passenger units with a horsepower for traction of 3000 per unit and a gear ratio of 22:7 (95 mph, max.). Originally numbered 5823A1-5834A1 and 5823A2-5834A2, the first group of units dropped the A1 suffix in 1949 while the second group were renumbered 5813-5822. In 1951, two of the units were converted to helper units by regearing to 17:62 (75 mph, max.), derating each unit to 2500 horsepower for traction and removal of the boiler. The remaining units were subsequently converted by the PRR in a program which lasted until 1954. Before conversion, the units were designated class BP-60a. After rebuilding, the units became class BH-50.

(10) PRR 3908 was the first diesel-electric locomotive purchased by the Pennsylvania. The unit was delivered in June, 1937, owned by EMC and numbered 680. The PRR purchased the unit in September, 1937 and renumbered it 3908 at that time. In 1942, the unit was renumbered 5911. In November, 1956 the unit was re-engined with an EMD, six cylinder model 567 engine but retained the GE electrical equipment. Always an odd unit on the PRR, the unit was actually given class ES-6 (5911) in the 1951 locomotive classification system. The distinction was dropped in the 1966 classification system when the unit was classed ES-6 just like the PRR's model SW-1 units.

(11) The PRR's second diesel-electric locomotive was the 3909 purchased in 1941. It was an EMD model NW2, 1000 horsepower switcher. The original number was short lived since the unit was renumbered 5912 in 1942.

(12) The three class ABF-18 units (An A-B-A set) were the PRR's trial in extending the life of Baldwin freight cab-units by an Alco re-engining. The A-units were originally model RF-16 while the B-unit was a 1500 horsepower freighter. The engine traction generator were replaced in each unit by an Alco 12 cylinder and a GE model GT-581 generator. The horsepower available for traction was raised from 1500 or 1600 horsepower to 1800 horsepower. The conversion was not economical and was not repeated. The units were retired in 1965 (the B-unit) and 1966 (the A-units).

(13) The six Alco model RSD-5 six axle road switchers were built without MU control since they were almost always used as heavy switchers In 1965 the MU control was applied to all units in the class and the classification was changed from AS-16a to AS-16am.

(14) In 1956 and 1957, six class ES-12, model SW7 switcher units received MU control and were reclassed ES-12m. The conversion was made by the PRR. PRR 8871 was converted in early 1956. PRR 8868, 8872, 9386, 9387 and 9388 were converted in mid-1957

(15) Between October 1, 1951 and June 1,1954, four class BS-10a Baldwin switcher units

245

assigned to the Fort Wayne Division of the PRR received MU control.

(16) Between 1955 and 1957, 11 class GS-4, GE 44-ton switchers received MU control and were reclassed GS-4m. On most of these units, the connections were applied to the rear end only, which limited the arrangement to two-unit sets MUed back to back. At least one of the units, the 9332 had MU connections on both ends which enabled the PRR to run three-unit GS-4m sets, which was done in the Altoona area on runs between the various PRR shops in the area.
(16] Between 1955 an~d 1957, 11 class GS-4, GE 44-ton switchers received MU control and were reclassed GS-4m. On most of these units, the connections were applied to the rear end only, which limited the arrangement to two-unit sets MUed back to back. At least one of the units, the 9332 had MU connections on both ends which enabled the PRR to run three-unit GS-4m sets, which was done in the Altoona area on runs between the various PRR shops in the area.

(17) The A-B-A set of Fairbanks-Morse Erie-built units which were classed as FP-20 were built at F-M as passenger units. They were equipped with 23:64 gearing (100 mph, max.) and a 3,000 lb. per hour Vapor DSK-4530 steam generators. In the 1952-53 period, they were rebuilt into freight units by removing the steam generator and regearing to 17:70 (69 mph, max.). In addition, the 1680 gallon boiler water tank was removed from the A-units upon rebuilding. As built, the A-units weighed 331,400 lbs but after rebuilding, they were ballasted to the standard FF-20 A-unit weight of 355,160 lbs.

(18) The three A-B-A sets of Fairbanks-Morse Erie-built units which were classed as FP-20a, were built with freight gearing and steam boilers. In less than a year, the PRR regeared the nine units with passenger gearing and reclassed them as passenger units. The passenger unit characteristics were the same as the FP-20-units except that the A-units weighed 341,180 lbs and the heating water capacity was 1220 gallons on A-units instead of 1680 gallons-on the FP-20 units. The class FP-20a units were rebuilt to FF-20 as described in note (17).

(19) PRR 8114 was formerly Pittsburgh and West Virginia 40. The unit had been leased by the PRR since February, 1954. The PRR purchased the unit in September, 1963.

(20) The class EH-15 consisted of both EMD model F3 and F7 freight cab units which were equipped with a lower than standard gear ratio for helper service. The standard PRR gear ratio on EMD freight and switcher units was 15:62, which resulted in a maximum speed of 65 mph. The EH-15 units were equipped with a 12:65 gear ratio for a maximum speed of 50 mph. Starting in 1959, all but three of the class EH-15 units were converted to either class EF-15 or EF-15a by regearing them to the 15:62 gear ratio. Some of the F3 units were converted to class EF-15a, which indicates some degree of conformity to F7 standards, but it is significant that when the 1966 reclassification was carried out, all the former EH-15 F3 units which were still on the roster were classified EF-15.

(21) PRR 9530B, 9532B, 9534B and 9536B were originally Bangor and Aroostook 600B-603B. The units were purchased by the PRR in 1952.

PRR 9710A leading a three-unit set of Baldwins on an eastbound freight at Federal Street on the North Side of Pittsburgh.

Dispositions

PRR Units Resold After PRR, PC or CR Retirement

This Appendix tabulates former PRR diesels that were sold to other railroads after their retirement by the Pennsylvania Railroad, Penn Central or Conrail. Most sales to dealers are not included.

Almost none of the PRR retired diesel locomotives were sold for further use. A large number were turned into ElectroMotive, Alco or General Electric for credit on new locomotives, and some were scrapped by the PRR itself.

The only significant group of diesels sold by the PRR for further use were the GE 44-Tonners, which the Pennsy classed as GS-4 and GS-4m. In the early 1960s, the PRR came to the conclusion that the small GE units were not very useful and began a sales program to recover as much value from them as possible while they were still in relatively good condition.

The Pennsylvania Railroad was merged with the New York Central to become the Penn Central on February 1, 1968. The Penn Central continued the PRR policy with regard to locomotive disposal. Few locomotives were sold for further use.

Penn Central was merged with several other railroads to form Conrail on April 1, 1976. Conrail adopted a very different policy, becoming quite active in selling locomotives to other railroads and dealers.

The railroad business environment changed significantly after the end of the PRR. This has had a large influence on the locomotive market. New rail operations were formed from sections of the established railroads. The rise of the locomotive rebuilders and dealers and the rising cost of new locomotives have all resulted in a world where used locomotives have considerable value. They are valuable both in the condition in which they were last operated or as "hulks," which can become the basis of major rebuilds. A number of ex-PRR model SD45s were used in this manner after several years of service on the Chicago and Northwestern. A popular rebuild was to replace the 20-cylinder engines with 16-cylinder engine and upgrade control system to current designs.

Southern Pacific 8611 at Bealville, California on July 17, 1999. Originally PRR 6187, rebuilt by Morrison-Knudson with a model 16-645 engine. The locomotive was renumbered UP 2687 in July 2001..

Orig. PRR Road No.	1966 PRR Road No.	Bldr and Model	Last PC Road No.	Last CR Road No.	First Re-sale/ Transfer	Date	Second Re-sale/ Transfer	Date	Third Re-sale/ Transfer	Date	Notes
2200	2200	EMD GP30	2200	2200	Kyle 2200	c1991	AGR 2202	Nov 98			
2202	2202	EMD GP30	2202	2202	Kyle 2202	c1991	(31)				(31)
2204	2204	EMD GP30	2204	2204	Eastern Idaho 2204	Nov 93					
2206	2206	EMD GP30	2206	2206	Ohio Central 3004	Sep 95	ISCX 3004	Sep 95	PCC 3004	c1995	
2210	2210	EMD GP30	2210	2210	Kyle 2210	Sep 94	(31)				
2211	2211	EMD GP30	2211	2211	SK&O 2211	Nov 93	(31)				
2225	2225	EMD GP30	2225	2225	Eastern Idaho 2225	Nov 93	(31)				
2228	2228	EMD GP30	2228	2228	Eastern Idaho 2228	1998					
2230	2230	EMD GP30	2230	2230	LTEX 2230	c1986					In lease fleet
2233	2233	EMD GP30	2233	2233	West Shore 2233	c1992	(34)	c1998			
2234	2234	EMD GP30	2234	2234	LRCX 23	c1991	NKCR 23	c1997			
2238	2238	EMD GP30	2238	2238	Kyle 2238	Nov 93	AGR 2238	1998			
2242	2242	EMD GP30	2242	2242	Eastern Idaho 2242	Sep 95	(31)				
2247	2247	EMD GP30	2247	2247	Ohio Central 2247	Aug 95s					
2249	2249	EMD GP30	2249	2249	West Md Scenic 2249	Aug 92	ISCX 3005		WAMX 3009 (31)	1999	
2250	2198	EMD GP30	2198	2198	"NH&I 2198" (15)	2001					
2254	2254	EMD GP35	2254	2254	Housatonic 3602	Sep 95					
2256	2256	EMD GP35	2256	2256	INCX 2003	Dec 94					
2257	2257	EMD GP35	2257	2257	Ohio Central 2257	Dec 93	MAW 2257	1999			
2262	2262	EMD GP35	2262	2262	Ariz. & Calif. 3501	1993					
2268	2268	EMD GP35	2268	2268	PCC 2268	c1994	(31)	c1997			
2271	2271	EMD GP35	2271	2271	Metro North 102	Aug 92	(31)				
2274	2274	EMD GP35	2274	2274	Metro North 106	1993	(31)				
2290	2290	EMD GP35	2290	2290	SK&O 2290	Aug 92	(31)				
2310	2250	EMD GP35	2250	2250	Housatonic 3601	Aug 92					
2312	2251	EMD GP35	2251	2251	Metro North 103	Aug 92					
2314	2312	EMD GP35	2312	2312	Housatonic 3600	Feb 98					
2336	2314	EMD GP35	2314	2314	Housatonic 3604	c1997					
2339	2336	EMD GP35	2336	2336	Housatonic 3603	1993					
2348	2339	EMD GP35	2339	2339	Ariz & Calif 3502	c1997					
2353	2348	EMD GP35	2348	2348	US Op.	1992					
2350	2353	EMD GP35	2353	2353	PCC 2353						
2357	2350	EMD GP35	2350	2350	Metro North 104						
2363	2357	EMD GP35	2357	2357	PCC 2357						
2369	2363	EMD GP35	2363	7635 (35)	QGRY 7635		QGRY 2006				
	2309	EMD GP35	2309	2309	LRCX 15		NKCR 15				
2415	2415	Alco C-424	2415	2474	GB&W 319		CA&LM 319				
2423	2423	Alco C-425	2423	5062	M-K 6101	c2/84	NY&LE 6101		PCHB 6101		See note (43)
2439	2439	Alco C-425	2439	5073	D&M 381	c80-81	Lake States Ry 381	c5/92			
2442	2442	Alco C-425	2442	5076	D&M 181	c80-81	Lake States Ry 181	c5/92			
2443	2443	Alco C-425	2443	5077	D&M 1280	c80-81	Lake States Ry 1280	c5/92			
2444	2444	Alco C-425	2444	5078	D&M 281	c80-81	Lake States Ry 281	c5/92			
2504	2604	GE U25B	2604	2604	Prairie Cent. 2604	c6/82					
2505	2605	GE U25B	2605	2605	Prairie Cent. 2605	c6/82					
2506	2606	GE U25B	2606	2606	Prairie Cent. 2606	c6/82					
5700A	4300	EMD E8A	4300	--	Amtrak 307	Apr 71	Amtrak 457:2	Jul 77			
5701A	4271	EMD E8A	4271	--	Amtrak 280	Apr 71	Amtrak 448	Nov 77			
5702A	4272	EMD E8A	4272	4272	NJDOT/NJTR 4272:1	Dec 76	NJTR 4305:2 (2)	Dec 79	"DL&W 808" (7)		
5703A	4273	EMD E8A	4273	--	Amtrak 281	Apr 71	Amtrak 453:2	Jul 77			
5704A	4274	EMD E8A	4274	--	Amtrak 282	Apr 71	Amtrak 495	Nov 77			
5705A	4275	EMD E8A	4275	--	Amtrak 283	Apr 71	Amtrak 454:2	Jul 77			
5706A	4276	EMD E8A	4276	--	Amtrak 284	Apr 71	Amtrak 496	Nov 77	BM&R 5706A (5)		Sold for non-railroad use, c1999
5707A	4277	EMD E8A	4277	--	Amtrak 285	Apr 71	Amtrak 499	Nov 77			
5708A	4278	EMD E8A	4278	--	Amtrak 286	Apr 71	Amtrak 454:2	Jul 77			
5709A	4279	EMD E8A	4279	--	Amtrak 287	Apr 71	Amtrak 461:2	Jul 77	"DL&W 807" (6)		
5710A	4280	EMD E8A	4280	--	Amtrak 288	Apr 71	Green Mt. (6)	Oct 87			
5712A	4311	EMD E8A	4311	--	Amtrak 317	Apr 71			CR 4021	Aug 83	See note (41)
5713A	4312	EMD E8A	4312	--	Amtrak 318	Apr 71					
5714A	4313	EMD E8A	4313	--	Amtrak 319	Apr 71					
5715A	4314	EMD E8A	4314	--	Amtrak 320	Apr 71					
5716A	4315	EMD E8A	4315	--	Amtrak 321	Apr 71					
5717A	4316	EMD E8A	4316	--	Amtrak 322	Apr 71					
5761A	4261	EMD E8A	4261	4261	MBTA 4261	Dec 76					

Orig. PRR Road No.	1966 PRR Road No.	Bldr and Model	Last PC Road No.	Last CR Road No.	First Re-sale/ Transfer	Date	Second Re-sale/ Transfer	Date	Third Re-sale/ Transfer	Date	Notes
5762A	4262	EMD E8A	4262	4262	MBTA 4262	Dec 76					
5763A	4263	EMD E8A	4263	4263	MBTA 4263	Dec 76					
5764A	4264	EMD E8A	4264	4264 --	MBTA 4264	Dec 76	BWDX 5764 (24)	c2/91	TCRX 5764	1998	
5765A	4265	EMD E8A	4265	4265	MBTA 4265	Dec 76					
5766A	4266	EMD E8A	4266	4266	MBTA 4266	Dec 76					
5767A	4267	EMD E8A	4267	4267	NJDOT/NJT 4267	Dec 76					To ICG as turn-in, 1981
5768A	4268	EMD E8A	4268	4268	MBTA 4268	Dec 76					
5769A	4269	EMD E8A	4269	--	Amtrak 279	Apr 71					
5788A	4248	EMD E8A	4248	4288	NJDOT/NJTR 4248	Dec 76	"Erie 835" (26)				Lettered and painted ERIE
5790A	4250	EMD E8A	4250	--	Amtrak 277	Apr 71	Amtrak 447	Nov 77			
5791A	4251	EMD E8A	4251	4251	NJDOT/NJTR 4251:1	Dec 76	NJTR 4267:2 (2)	Oct 78			
5792A	4252	EMD E8A	4252	--	Amtrak 278	Apr 71					
5794A	4294	EMD E8A	4294		MBTA 4294	Dec 76	PPCX 5794	c1991	SCRX 5794	c1998	
5793A	4253	EMD E8A	4253	4253	NJDOT/NJTR 4253:1	Dec 76	NJTR 4325:2 (2)	Oct 78			
5797A	4257	EMD E8A	4257	4257	NJDOT/NJTR 4257	Dec 76	WCLC 4257				
5798A	4258	EMD E8A	4258	4258	NJDOT NJTR4258:1	Dec 76	NJTR 4253:2 (2)	Sep 78	URHSNJ 4253	1991	
5801A	4301	EMD E8A	4301	--	Amtrak 308	Apr 71					
5802A	4282	EMD E8A	4282	--	Amtrak 290	Apr 71					
5803A	4283	EMD E8A	4283	--	Amtrak 291	Apr 71	Amtrak 403:2	Nov 77			
5804A	4281	EMD E8A	4281	--	Amtrak 289	Apr 71					
5805A	4270	EMD E8A	4270	4270	NJDOT/NJTR 4270	Dec 76					
5806A	4306	EMD E8A	4306	--	Amtrak 312	Apr 71					
5807A	4307	EMD E8A	4307	--	Amtrak 313	Apr 71					
5808A	4308	EMD E8A	4308	--	Amtrak 314	Apr 71					
5809A	4309	EMD E8A	4309	--	Amtrak 315	Apr 71	Amtrak 498	Nov 77	CR 4020	May 83	See notes (39) and (40)
5810A	4310	EMD E8A	4310	--	Amtrak 316	Apr 71	Amtrak 459:2				
5835A	4317	EMD E8A	4317	--	Amtrak 323	Apr 71					
5836A	4246	EMD E8A	4246	--	NJDOT/NJTR 4246	Dec 76					
5839A	4319	EMD E8A	4319	--	Amtrak 324	Apr 71					
5884A	4284	EMD E8A	4284	--	Amtrak 292	Apr 71	Amtrak 455:2	Jul 77			
5885A	4285	EMD E8A	4285	4285	NJDOT/NJTR 4285:1	Dec 76					
5886A	4286	EMD E8A	4286	--	Amtrak 293	Apr 71					
5887A	4287	EMD E8A	4287	--	Amtrak 294	Apr 71					
5888A	4288	EMD E8A	4288	--	Amtrak 295	Apr 71	Amtrak 456:2	Jul 77			
5889A	4289	EMD E8A	4289	--	Amtrak 296	Apr 71					
5890A	4290	EMD E8A	4290	--	Amtrak 297	Apr 71					
5891A	4291	EMD E8A	4291	--	Amtrak 298	Apr 71					
5892A	4292	EMD E8A	4292	--	Amtrak 299	Apr 71					
5893A	4293	EMD E8A	4293	--	Amtrak 300	Apr 71					
5894A	4294	EMD E8A	4294	--	Amtrak 301	Apr 71					
5895A	4295	EMD E8A	4295	--	Amtrak 302	Apr 71	Amtrak 449	Nov 77			
5896A	4296	EMD E8A	4296	--	Amtrak 303	Apr 71	"Milw 35A" (37)				
5897A	4297	EMD E8A	4297	--	Amtrak 304	Apr 71	Amtrak 431:2				
5898A	4298	EMD E8A	4298		Amtrak 305	Apr 71	Amtrak 497	Nov 77	BM&R 5898A (5)		See note (44)
5899A	4299	EMD E8A	4299	--	Amtrak 306	Apr 71					
5901A	4201	EMD E7A	4201		(36)	c1976					
5902A	4302	EMD E8A	4302	--	Amtrak 309	Apr 71					
5903A	4303	EMD E8A	4303	--	Amtrak 310	Apr 71	Amtrak 458:2	Jul 77			
5904A	4304	EMD E8A	4304	--	Amtrak 311	Apr 71					
5905A	4305	EMD E8A	4305	4305	NJDOT/NJTR 4305:1	Dec 76	NJTR 4324:2 (2)				
5990	8510	EMD SW1	8510	8510	Standard Steel 6732	1986					
5997	8597	EMD SW1	8597	8597	Transco 333						
5999	5999	EMD SW1	5999	5999	BCS	Dec 84					
6040	6040	EMD SD40	6040	6293	CRL 601	1994	HLCX 5016		HLCX 6317		
6041	6041	EMD SD40	6041	6994 (18)	CSX 8883	Jun 99					Was CR 6294 before rebuild
6042	6042	EMD SD40	6042	6295	EMDX 6419		FURX 3028 (18)	Mar 2000			
6043	6043	EMD SD40	6043	6985 (18)	NS (PRR) 3439	Jun 99					Was CR 6296 before rebuild
6044	6044	EMD SD40	6044	6973 (18)	CSX 8874	Jun 99					Was CR 6297 before rebuild
6045	6045	EMD SD40	6045	6971 (18)	CSX 8873	Jun 99					Was CR 6298 before rebuild
6046	6046	EMD SD40	6046	6299	HLCX 5036		DM&E 6067		FURX 3024 (18)	Mar 2000	
6047	6047	EMD SD40	6047	6982 (18)	NS (PRR) 3437	Jun 99					Was CR 6300 before rebuild
6048	6048	EMD SD40	6048	6301	HLCX 5037		HLCX 6068 (30)				
6049	6049	EMD SD40	6049	6995 (18)	CSX 8884	Jun 99					Was CR 6302 before rebuild

Orig. PRR Road No.	1966 PRR Road No.	Bldr and Model	Last PC Road No.	Last CR Road No.	First Re-sale/Transfer	Date	Second Re-sale/Transfer	Date	Third Re-sale/Transfer	Date	Notes
6050	6050	EMD SD40	6050	6303	HLCX 5038		IMRL 201	1997			
6051	6051	EMD SD40	6051	6304	HLCX 5039		HLCX 6074				
6052	6052	EMD SD40	6052	6975 (18)	CSX 8876	Jun 99			FURX 3042 (18)	Apr 2000	Was CR 6305 before rebuild
6053	6053	EMD SD40	6053	6306	HLCX 5040	Oct 94	IMRL 202				
6054	6054	EMD SD40	6054	6307	EMDX 6420	Oct 94	EMDX 420	Oct 94			
6055	6055	EMD SD40	6055	6308	HLCX 5041	Jun 99	HLCX 6066 (30)	Jun 99	TFM 1518		
6056	6056	EMD SD40	6056	6993 (18)	NS (PRR) 3444	1994	HLCX 5020	1994			Was CR 6309 before rebuild
6057	6057	EMD SD40	6057	6310	CRL 605	Jun 99					
6058	6058	EMD SD40	6058	6974 (18)	CSX 8875	Jun 99	HLCX 5025	Jun 99			Was CR 6311 before rebuild
6059	6059	EMD SD40	6059	6312	CRL 611	1994					
6060	6060	EMD SD40	6060	6972 (18)	NS (PRR) 3432	Jun 99	HLCX 6065 (30)	Jun 99			Was CR 6313 before rebuild
6061	6061	EMD SD40	6061	6314	HLCX 5042	Oct 94	EMDX 414	Oct 94	UP 4768 (18)	Oct 99	To UP 2818, Dec 2001
6062	6062	EMD SD40	6062	6315	EMDX 6418	Oct 94	UP 4771 (18)	Nov 99			
6063	6063	EMD SD40	6063	6316	EMDX 6423	Oct 94	FURX 3044 (18)	Apr 00			
6064	6064	EMD SD40	6064	6317	HLCX 6061 (30)						
6065	6065	EMD SD40	6065	6318	EMDX 6401		EMDX 401		FURX 3029 (18)	Mar 00	
6066	6066	EMD SD40	6066	6319	HLCX 6063 (30)						
6067	6067	EMD SD40	6067	6320	CRL 606	1994					
6068	6068	EMD SD40	6068	6321	HLCX 5044	Oct 94	HLCX 6214 (18)				
6069	6069	EMD SD40	6069	6322	EMDX 6415	Jun 99	IMRL 203	1997	UP 4769 (18)	Sep 99	
6070	6070	EMD SD40	6070	6323	EMDX 6069 (30)		EMDX 415	Oct 94			
6071	6071	EMD SD40	6071	6324	CSX 8881				UP 4773 (18)	Nov 99	
6073	6073	EMD SD40	6073	6991 (18)	EMDX 6428	Jun 99	EMDX 428	Jun 99			Was CR 6326 before rebuild
6074	6074	EMD SD40	6074	6327	EMDX 6421	Oct 94	FURX 3033 (18)	Mar 00			
6075	6075	EMD SD40	6075	6328	EMDX 6424	Oct 94	UP 4772 (18)	Oct 99			
6076	6076	EMD SD40	6076	6329	NS (PRR) 3434	Jun 99					
6077	6077	EMD SD40	6077	6977 (18)	EMDX 6402	Oct 94	FURX 3019 (18)	Feb 00			Was CR 6330 before rebuild
6078	6078	EMD SD40	6078	6331	NS (PRR) 3447	Jun 99					
6079	6079	EMD SD40	6079	6998 (18)	NS (PRR) 3441	Jun 99					Was CR 6332 before rebuild
6080	6080	EMD SD40	6080	6987 (18)	HLCX 5045	Jun 99	IMRL 217	1997			Was CR 6333 before rebuild
6081	6081	EMD SD40	6081	6334	NS (PRR) 3431	Jun 99					
6082	6082	EMD SD40	6082	6976 (18)	HLCX 5046	Jun 99	HLCX 6072 (30)	1996			Was CR 6335 before rebuild
6083	6083	EMD SD40	6083	6336	EMDX 6422	Oct 94	NS Mining 651 (30)	c2000			
6085	6085	EMD SD40	6085	6338	EMDX 6416	Oct 94	FURX 3037 (18)	Mar 00			
6086	6086	EMD SD40	6086	6339	HLCX 6064 (30)				HLCX 6086		
6087	6087	EMD SD40	6087	6340	NS (PRR) 3446	Jun 99					
6088	6088	EMD SD40	6088	6997 (18)	EMDX 6403	Oct 94	HLCX 5015	c2000			Was CR 6341 before rebuild
6090	6090	EMD SD40	6090	6343	CRL 600	c1994	NS Mining 652 (30)				
6091	6091	EMD SD40	6091	6344	EMDX 6404	Oct 94					
6092	6092	EMD SD40	6092	6345	CRL 604	Jun 99					
6093	6093	EMD SD40	6093	6983 (18)	HLCX 5047	1994	HLCX 5019	1997	HLCX 5049		Was CR 6346 before rebuild
6094	6094	EMD SD40	6094	6347	HLCX 5048	Jun 99	IMRL 205				
6095	6095	EMD SD40	6095	6348	NS (PRR) 3442	Jun 99	HLCX 6084 (30)				
6097	6097	EMD SD40	6097	6350	CSX 8877	Jun 99					
6098	6098	EMD SD40	6098	6988	NS (PRR) 3435	Jun 99	TFM 1517	Jun 99			Was CR 6351 before rebuild
6099	6099	EMD SD40	6099	6980	HLCX 5049	Jun 99					Was CR 6352 before rebuild
6100	6100	EMD SD40	6100	6978	NS (PRR) 3436	Jun 99					Was CR 6353 before rebuild
6101	6101	EMD SD40	6101	6354	EMDX 6405	Jun 99	EMDX 405	Nov 99	FURX 3035 (18)	Mar 00	To GCFX 3075 (18), Sep 00
6102	6102	EMD SD40	6102	6979	EMDX 6430	Oct 94	UP 4774 (18)	Oct 94	UP 2824	Feb 02	Was CR 6355 before rebuild
6103	6103	EMD SD40	6103	6356	EMDX 6405	Feb 83	EMDX 405				
6104	6104	EMD SD40	6104	6357	EMDX 6430	Feb 83	UP 4774 (18)	Oct 94			
6170	6170	EMD SD45	6170	6170	C&NW 6500	Feb 83	HLCX 6400 (30)	Dec 96			
6172	6172	EMD SD45	6172	6172	C&NW 6501	Feb 83	MKCX 9030 (3)	Sep 93			
6173	6173	EMD SD45	6173	6163	C&NW 6502	Feb 83	CSX 8487 (3)	Oct 90			
6174	6174	EMD SD45	6174	6174	C&NW 6503	Feb 83	HLCX 6506 (3)	Oct 97	MRL 370	Jun 94	To IMRL 370
6175	6175	EMD SD45	6175	6175	C&NW 6504	Feb 83	NRE 6504	Sep 94	MRL 371	Oct 94	
6176	6176	EMD SD45	6176	6176	C&NW 6505	Feb 83	MKCX 9034 (3)	Nov 93			
6177	6177	EMD SD45	6177	6177	(C&NW 6506)	Feb 83	CSX 8478 (3)	Sep 90			Not renum or used on C&NW
6178	6178	EMD SD45	6178	6178	C&NW 6507	Feb 83	NRE 6507	Sep 94			
6180	6180	EMD SD45	6180	6180	C&NW 6508	Feb 83	MPI 9024 (2)	Jul 93			
6181	6181	EMD SD45	6181	6181	(C&NW 6509)	Feb 83	KCS 618:2 (4)	c6/95			Not renum or used on C&NW
6182	6182	EMD SD45	6182	6182	(C&NW 6510)	Feb 83	MKCX 9027 (3)	Aug 93			Not renum or used on C&NW
6183	6183	EMD SD45	6183	6183	(C&NW 6511)	Feb 83	CSX 8486 (3)	Nov 90			Not renum or used on C&NW

250

Orig. PRR Road No.	1966 PRR Road No.	Bldr and Model	Last PC Road No.	Last CR Road No.	First Re-sale/Transfer	Date	Second Re-sale/Transfer	Date	Third Re-sale/Transfer	Date	Notes
6185	6185	EMD SD45	6185	6185	C&NW 6512	Feb 83	Eastern Idaho 6513	c93-94	(31)		
6186	6186	EMD SD45	6186	6186	C&NW 6513	Feb 83	SP 8611 (3)	Oct 94	UP 2687 (21)	Jul 01	
6187	6187	EMD SD45	6187	6187	C&NW 6514	Feb 83	NRE 6515	Jun 94	SP 8608 (3)	Sep 94	See note (45)
6188	6188	EMD SD45	6188	6188	C&NW 6515	Feb 83	MKCX 9032 (3)	Oct 93			
6189	6189	EMD SD45	6189	6189	C&NW 6516	Feb 83	MPI 9029 (3)	Sep 93			
6190	6190	EMD SD45	6190	6190	C&NW 6517	Feb 83					
6191	6191	EMD SD45	6191	6191	C&NW 6518	Feb 83					
6192	6192	EMD SD45	6192	6192	(C&NW 6519)	Feb 83	SP 8655 (3)	Aug 94	(UP 2731) (21)	Jul 01	Not renum or used on C&NW
6193	6193	EMD SD45	6193	6193	C&NW 6520	Feb 83	SP 8695	Jul 94	(UP 2671) (21)	Jul 01	
6194	6194	EMD SD45	6194	6194	(C&NW 6521)	Feb 83	MKCX 9028	Sep 93			Not renum or used on C&NW
6196	6196	EMD SD45	6196	6196	(C&NW 6522)	Feb 83	SP 8595	Jul 95	(UP 2751) (21)	1997	Not renum or used on C&NW
6197	6197	EMD SD45	6197	6197	C&NW 6523	Feb 83	HLCX 6501 (30)	1997			
6198	6198	EMD SD45	6198	6198	C&NW 6524	Feb 83	SP 8615 (3)	Nov 94	(UP 2691) (21)		
6200	6200	EMD SD45	6200	6200	(C&NW 6525)	Feb 83	Eastern Idaho 6525	c93-94	(31)		Not renum or used on C&NW
6201	6201	EMD SD45	6201	6201	C&NW 6526	Mar 83	SP 8614 (3)	Nov 94	UP 2690 (21)	Jul 01	
6202	6202	EMD SD45	6202	6202	C&NW 6527	Feb 83	SP 8610 (3)	Oct 94	UP 2686 (21)	Jul 01	
6203	6203	EMD SD45	6203	6203	C&NW 6528	Feb 83	MRL 372	Oct 94	IMRL 372	1997	
6204	6204	EMD SD45	6204	6204	C&NW 6529	Feb 83					
6205	6205	EMD SD45	6205	6205	C&NW 6530	Oct 83					
6206	6206	EMD SD45	6206	6206	(C&NW 6531)	Feb 83	SP 8654 (3)	Sep 94	(UP 2730) (21)	Jul 01	Not renum or used on C&NW
6208	6208	EMD SD45	6208	6208	C&NW 6532	Feb 83	SP 8616 (3)	Dec 94	(UP 2692) (21)	Dec 97	
6209	6209	EMD SD45	6209	6209	C&NW 6533	Feb 83	MKCX 9504 (3)	Jan 94	HLCX 6513		
6211	6211	EMD SD45	6211	6211	C&NW 6534	Feb 83	SP 8606 (3)	Sep 94	UP 2682 (21)	Apr 02	
6212	6212	EMD SD45	6212	6212	C&NW 6535:2	Feb 83	SP 8607 (3)	Sep 94	(UP 2683) (21)		
6213	6213	EMD SD45	6213	6213	(C&NW 6536)	Feb 83	CSX 8482	Oct 90			Not renum or used on C&NW
6214	6214	EMD SD45	6214	6214	C&NW 6537	Feb 83	HLCX 6504 (3)	1997	SP 8662 (3)	Sep 94	To UP 2738, Jul 01
6215	6215	EMD SD45	6215	6215	C&NW 6538	Feb 83	MKCX 9505	Mar 94			
6216	6216	EMD SD45	6216	6216	C&NW 6539	Feb 83	HLCX 6502 (3)	1997			
6217	6217	EMD SD45	6217	6217	C&NW 6540	Feb 83	MRL 373	Oct 94			
6218	6218	EMD SD45	6218	6218	(C&NW 6541)	Feb 83	CSX 8481 (3)	Oct 90			Not renum or used on C&NW
6219	6219	EMD SD45	6219	6219	C&NW 6542	Feb 83	MRL 368	Aug 94	IMRL 368	Feb 95	
6220	6220	EMD SD45	6220	6220	C&NW 6543	Feb 83	NRE 6543		MRL 374		
6221	6221	EMD SD45	6221	6221	C&NW 6544	Feb 83	HLCX 6500:2 (30)	1997			
6222	6222	EMD SD45	6222	6222	(C&NW 6545)	Feb 83	MKCX 9035 (3)	Nov 93	HLCX 6600 (27)	Jun 97	Not renum or used on C&NW
6223	6223	EMD SD45	6223	6223	C&NW 6546	Feb 83	MKCX 9023 (3)	Jul 93	HLCX 6514 (3)	Nov 97	Renum, not used on C&NW
6224	6224	EMD SD45	6224	6224	C&NW 6547	Feb 83	C&NW 6000 (22)	Feb 86	(UP 2689) (21)		
6225	6225	EMD SD45	6225	6225	C&NW 6548	Feb 83	MKCX 9506	Mar 94			
6226	6226	EMD SD45	6226	6226	C&NW 6549	Feb 83	SP 8613 (3)	Nov 94			
6227	6227	EMD SD45	6227	6227	C&NW 6550	Feb 83	MKCX 9036 (3)	Dec 93			
6228	6228	EMD SD45	6228	6228	(C&NW 6551)	Feb 83					Not renum or used on C&NW
6229	6229	EMD SD45	6229	6229	(C&NW 6552)	Feb 83					Not renum or used on C&NW
6230	6230	EMD SD45	6230	6230	C&NW 6553	Feb 83	SP 8652 (3)	Sep 94	(UP 2728) (21)	Sep 94	
6231	6231	EMD SD45	6231	6231	C&NW 6554	Feb 83					
6232	6232	EMD SD45	6232	6232	(C&NW 6555)	Feb 83	MRL 375	Dec 94	IMRL 375		Renum, not used on C&NW
6233	6233	EMD SD45	6233	6233	C&NW 6556	Feb 83	CSX 8484 (3)	Oct 90			
6234	6234	EMD SD45	6234	6234	C&NW 6557:2	Jan 83					
7000	7000	EMD GP9	7000	7000 (50)	NJT 7000	Jan 83	URHSNJ 7000	1995	CMSL 7000	1998	Leased from URHSNJ
7002	7002	EMD GP9	7002	7568 (50)	LTE	Jul 96					
7003	7003	EMD GP9	7003	7003 (50)	PTRA 9602 (29)	Jan 83					
7005	7005	EMD GP9	7005	7537 (50)	Ohio Central 7537 (37)	Feb 98	Gettysburg 107	Feb 99			
7006	7006	EMD GP9	7006	7006	NJT 7007	Jan 83					
7007	7007	EMD GP9	7007	7007	NJT 7010	Jan 83					
7010	7010	EMD GP9	7010	7010	HP Coop 7516	1986	NHNR 1760	c1989			
7011	7011	EMD GP9	7011	7516 (50)	Mass Cent. 7015	Feb 98					
7015	7015	EMD GP9	7015	7015	NJTR 7016	Jan 83					
7016	7016	EMD GP9	7016	7016	Soo 4102 (20)	Dec 90					
7017	7017	EMD GP9	7017	7017	SEPTA 2-GP9	Dec 82	SEPTA 90		(38)	1999	
7019	7019	EMD GP9	7019	7019	PTRA 9620 (29)	Oct 96					
7020	7020	EMD GP9	7020	7020	SEPTA 1-GP9	Dec 82	SEPTA 91		(38)	1999	
7028	7028	EMD GP9	7028	7520 (50)	OHCR	Dec 90					
7030	7030	EMD GP9	7030	7037	Soo 4101 (20)	Dec 90					
7037	7037	EMD GP9	7037	7558 (50)	FE Co. 7558	Jun 98					
7038	7038	EMD GP9	7038								To State RR Museum of Penna.

Orig. PRR Road No.	1966 PRR Road No.	Bldr and Model	Last PC Road No.	Last CR Road No.	First Re-sale/ Transfer	Date	Second Re-sale/ Transfer	Date	Third Re-sale/ Transfer	Date	Notes
7039	7039	EMD GP9	7039	7039	Soo 4100 (20)	Dec 90					
7041	7041	EMD GP9	7041	7556 (50)	Columbia Grain	Dec 96					
7042	7042	EMD GP9	70402	7042	HB&T 9632 (29)	Aug 96					Horseshoe Curve
7043	7043	EMD GP9	7043	7043	PTRA 9609 (29)	Sep 85					Wellsville, Ohio
7048	7048	EMD GP9	7048	7048	(37)						
7049	7049	EMD GP9	7049	7049	(37)						
7052	7052	EMD GP9	7052	7578 (50)	IT 1	1991					
7056	7056	EMD GP9	7056	7576 (50)	SWP 7576	Nov 95	AVR 1801	c2000			
7057	7057	EMD GP9	7057	7559	AVR 7559	1998					
7058	7058	EMD GP9	7058	7519 (50)	RLGN 1755	Apr 97					
7063	7063	EMD GP9	7063	7570 (50)	Illinois Western 7570	Feb 86					
7065	7065	EMD GP9	7065	7065	NHNR 1756	Jul 96					
7066	7066	EMD GP9	7066	7577 (50)	ADM	Feb 97					
7068	7068	EMD GP9	7066	7557 (50)	LANO 57	c1998					
7079	7079	EMD GP9	7079	7522 (50)	USWX 7522	Jul 86					
7081	7081	EMD GP9	7081	7081	NHNR 1758	Feb 86					
7083	7083	EMD GP9	7083	7083	NHNR 1757						
7089	7089	EMD GP9	7089	7089	Mass Cent. 7089						
7090	7090	EMD GP9	7090	7090	W&W 709	c3/87					
7092	7092	EMD GP9	7092	7523 (50)	RaiLink 1757	Jun 98					
7093	7093	EMD GP9	7093	7093	NHNR 1759:2						
7098	7098	EMD GP9	7098	7562 (50)	Ohio Central	Feb 97	Ga NE				
7111	7111	EMD GP9	7111	7565 (50)	ADM 7565	Dec 96	EIRC 7565				
7118	7118	EMD GP9	7118	7569 (50)	N&BE 1804	Mar 97					
7121	7121	EMD GP9	7121	7579 (50)	SRNJ		CSKR 7579 / NHNR 1759:1	Oct 87	NHNR 1755		
7125	7125	EMD GP9	7125	7125	Mass. Central 7125	Dec 96					
7128	7128	EMD GP9	7128	7580 (50)	CKSR 7580						
7130	7130	EMD GP9	7130	7567 (50)	ADM 7567						
7148	7148	EMD GP9	7148	7517 (50)	Ag Val Coop						
7189	7189	EMD GP9	7189	7189	P&W 1701	May 82	Quaboag Trans. 1701	1984			
7205	7205	EMD GP9	7205	7205	P&W 1702	May 82	Bay Colony 1702				
7210	7210	EMD GP9	7210	7515 (50)	Maywood Coop 7515	1998					
7230	7230	EMD GP9	7230	7583 (50)	Juniata Term. 7250	1996					
7231	7231	EMD GP9	7231	7584 (50)	Kiamichi 1004	1997					
7236	7236	EMD GP9	7236	7587 (50)	Juniata Term. 7251						
7237	7237	EMD GP9	7237	7572 (50)	W&W 572	Dec 96					
7238	7238	EMD GP9	7238	7586 (50)	Ohio Central 7586	1998	ADM 7586	1998			
7239	7239	EMD GP9	7239	7573 (50)	Ohio Central 7573	1998					
7242	7242	EMD GP9	7242	7242	Pocono NE 1751	Oct 83	L&S 1751	Aug 94			
7244	7244	EMD GP9	7244	7585 (50)	Ohio Central 7585	1998					
7248	7248	EMD GP9	7248	7589 (50)	Ohio Central 7589	Feb 84	NY & A 201 (28)	May 97	Lou. & Indiana 201	c1999	
7249	7249	EMD GP9	7249	7249	St. Regis Paper 7249	Aug 96	Champion Paper		Defériet Paper		
7250	7250	EMD GP9	7250	7250	PTRA 9610 (29)	1997					
7253	7253	EMD GP9	7253	7590 (50)	Kiamichi 1005						
7254	7254	EMD GP9	7254	7591 (50)	Ohio Central 7591	Apr 97					
7258	7258	EMD GP9	7258	7594 (50)	Ohio Central 7594	Nov 96					
7259	7259	EMD GP9	7259	7259	HB&T 9626 (29)						
7260	7260	EMD GP9	7260	7596 (50)	Ohio Central 7596	c1977	ADM 7596				
7261	7261	EMD GP9	7261	7595 (50)	Ohio Central 7595	1996	NY & A 202 (28)	May 97	Lou. & Indiana 202	c1999	
7262	7262	EMD GP9	7262	7574 (50)	Ohio Central 7574		W&W 575				
7265	7265	EMD GP9	7265	7575 (50)	Ohio Central	c1992	ADM 35	c1995			
7266	7266	EMD GP9	7266	7266	Ashland Ry 35	c1988					
7267	7267	EMD GP9	7267	7267	Indiana RR 300	1997					
7268	7268	EMD GP9	7268	7597 (50)	Kiamichi 1006	Mar 98					
7900	9050	EMD SW1200	9050	9354	L&C 98	1998					
7901	9051	EMD SW1200	9051	9355	Luria Bros. 151						
7904	9054	EMD SW1200	9054	9358	PHL 35	c1999	Birmingham Steel				To PHL, late 1999
7905	9055	EMD SW1200	9055	9359	Niagara Chem 9359		Geon Canada 9359				
7906	9056	EMD SW1200	9056	9360	Rail Car Ltd 9360						
7907	9057	EMD SW1200	9057	9361	USS-Fairless 11:2	May 89	NJ Steel 11				
7909	9009	EMD SW1200	9009	9328	C&BL 129	1992					
7910	9010	EMD SW1200	9010	9329	USS-Fairless 31	May 89					
7911	9011	EMD SW1200	9011	9330	Cargill	1996					

Orig. PRR Road No.	1966 PRR Road No.	Bldr and Model	Last PC Road No.	Last CR Road No.	First Re-sale/ Transfer	Date	Second Re-sale/ Transfer	Date	Third Re-sale/ Transfer	Date	Notes
7912	9012	EMD SW1200	9012	9331	EC&H 63:2	Feb 98	CCCL 12	c8/87	Shamokin Valley 12		
7913	9013	EMD SW1200	9013	9332	L&C 93	May 83	Cargill 9335				
7914	9014	EMD SW1200	9014	9333	Moxahala. Val 33						
7916	9016	EMD SW1200	9016	9335	Cont. Grain 9335	Mar 98					
7917	9017	EMD SW1200	9017	9336	L&C 97	Sep 97					
7918	9018	EMD SW1200	9018	9337	ADM						
7920	9020	EMD SW1200	9020	9339	USS-Fairless 13:2	c1989	Celenese Corp (17)	c1996			Used as plant switcher
7921	9021	EMD SW1200	9021	9340	Cando Contracting 1003	c1996					
7922	9022	EMD SW1200	9022	9341	EF Coop 9341	1996					
7923	9023	EMD SW1200	9023	9342	Seaport Cent. 9342	1997	Mobile 9335	c1997	DJPX 9335		
7925	9025	EMD SW1200	9025	9344	A. E. Staley	c1997					
7926	9026	EMD SW1200	9026	9345	Ga. NE 9345	1998					
7927	9027	EMD SW1200	9027	9346	L&C 94	Feb 98					
7928	9028	EMD SW1200	9028	9347	NBEC 3703	1996					
7930	9030	EMD SW1200	9030	9349	Cargill 9349	1996					
7931	9031	EMD SW1200	9031	9350	Nucor Steel 610	1998					
7932	9032	EMD SW1200	9032	9351	HLCX 0007	1998					
7933	9033	EMD SW1200	9033	9352	HLCX 0008	1998					
8128	8319	BLH S-12	8319	-	NI&M 8319		NYRR 0008				
8424	9844	Alco T-6	9844	9844	Md & Del 17	c5/84	Eastern Shore 17		Delaware Cst Line 17	May 89	See note (46)
8426	9846	Alco T-6	9846	9846	Md & Del 19		Delaware Cst Line 19		A&M 19		See note (47)
8427	9847	Alco T-6	9847	9847	RR Steel L-3 (8)		Black Riv & Wstn 56	Aug 82	West Jersey RR 56		See note (48)
8428	9848	Alco T-6	9848	9848	Avtex 100						
8429	9849	Alco T-6	9849	9849	North Country 100 (9)	c Apr 80	M&D 15		Avtex Fibre 415 (10)	c10/81	See note (49)
8441	5441	Alco RS-3	5441		Amtrak 117	Apr 76					
8442	5442	Alco RS-3	5442		Amtrak 118	Apr 76					
8445	5569	Alco RS-3	5569		LV 211:2	1971	CR 5487	Apr 76	CR 9920	Aug 79	
8456	5456	Alco RS-3	5456		Amtrak 119	Apr 76					
8458	5458	Alco RS-3	5458		Amtrak 120	Apr 76					
		Alco RS-3			LV 210:2	1971	CR 5486	Apr 76			
8461	5461	Alco RS-3	5461		Amtrak 121	Apr 76					
8465	5465	Alco RS-3	5465		Amtrak 142	Apr 76					
8479	5579	Alco RS-3	5579		PTRA 9614 (29)	Sep 96					
8503	5853	EMD GP7	5853	5853	APD 12						
8522	9122	EMD SW9	9122	9122	NS Steel 1678:2	Sep 98	TDIX 1202	Sep 98			
8523	9123	EMD SW9	9123	9123	CR of I 1202	c1989					
8525	9125	EMD SW9	9125	9125	JRS Milling	1995	QBT 20	1995			
8529	9129	EMD SW9	9129	9129	NDCR						
8530	9130	EMD SW9	9130	9130	APD 13						
8531	9131	EMD SW9	9131	9131	Q & O Paper 9137	Sep 87					
8537	9137	EMD SW9	9137	9137	Rohn & Haas 9043						
8543	9043	EMD SW9	9043	9043	Ohio Central 5407	1994	Ga. NE 5407	Dec 98			
8556	5856	EMD GP7	5856	5407 (13)	Everett 5428						
8574	5874	EMD GP7	5874	5428 (13)	TH&W 6999						
8589	6951	EMD SD7	6951	6999	LV 212:2	1971	CG&B / CR 5488	Apr 76	TRRA 1751	Jan 01	Rebit by TRRA to SD9 rating
8601	5401	Alco RS-3	5401		Amtrak 113	Apr 76					To FGC Museum, 10/85 (12)
8602	5402	Alco RS-3	5402		Amtrak 114	Apr 76					
8604	5404	Alco RS-3	5404								
8640		Alco RS-11	--	7640 (11)							
8641		Alco RS-11	--	7641 (11)							
8642		Alco RS-11	--	7642 (11)							
8643		Alco RS-11	--	7642 (11)							
8644		Alco RS-11	--	7644 (11)							
8648		Alco RS-11	--	7648 (11)							
8797	5897	EMD GP7	5897	5897	LS&BC 4	Jun 82					
8714	8330	F-M H12-44	--	--	USS-Fairless 24	Jun 68					
8721	8337	F-M H12-44	--	--	USS-Fairless 23	Jun 68					
8828	5428	Alco RS-3	5428	--	Amtrak 116	Apr 76					
8860	9060	EMD SW9	9060	9060	GSS Corp 919		Eagle Energy				
8863	9063	EMD SW7	9063	9063	BethEnergy Mines	c1989					
8864	9064	EMD SW7	9064	9064	USS-Fairless 10:2	Aug 79					
8873	9473	Alco S-3	9473	--	Alexander 7	c1989					
8892	9792	Alco S-4	9792	--	Francon 250-60	Feb 68	IVACO 250-60				
8907	5407	Alco RS-3	5407	--	L&N 173:2 (23)	Nov 67					
8908	5408	Alco RS-3	--	--	A&BB 5408						

Orig. PRR Road No.	1966 PRR Road No.	Bldr and Model	Last PC Road No.	Last CR Road No.	First Re-sale/ Transfer	Date	Second Re-sale/ Transfer	Date	Third Re-sale/ Transfer	Date	Notes
8912	5562	Alco RS-3	5562	—	Amtrak 140	Apr 76					
8984	8124	BLH S-12	8124	—	Metro. Stevedores 1						
9051	8001	BLW DS 4-4-1000	8001	—	SCL 3005 (as slug)	1972	SBD 3005 (as slug)	Jan 83			
9069	8019	BLW DS 4-4-1000	8281	—	NH&I 302	Feb 75	SMS 1494	Mar 94	Penn Jersey 302	Aug 97	
9102	9452	Alco S-1	9452	—	Beech Mt. 9452	c1975					
9140	8540	EMD SW1	8540	8540	KCS 203 (16)	Dec 70	KCS 4253	1973			See note (17)
9143	8543	EMD SW1	8543	—	Amtrak 255	Apr 76	Amtrak 742	Jul 77			See note (19)
9145	8575	EMD SW1	8575	—	Amtrak 257	Apr 76	Amtrak 744	Jul 77	CP&F	1973	
9150	8530	EMD SW1	8530	—	Amtrak 254	Apr 76	Amtrak 741	Jul 77	Berlin Mills Ry 741	Feb 86	
9165	8665	EMD NW2	8665	9187	Central Soya		New Eng. Milling 1000	1973			
9167	8667	EMD NW2	9104 (1)	9258	Pocono NE 87	c1982	L&S 87	Aug 94			
9169	8669	EMD NW2	8669	—	CG & C 4		Great Miami 1372	May 92			Lsd by Great Miami from 8/88
9170	8670	EMD NW2	8670	8670	Brandywine Val. 8203	c1982	Chester Valley 8203	Apr 96	Bristol Ind Term 8203		
9172	8672	EMD NW2	8671	8671	Massey Coal 100		SRCT 101	Jul 77			
9200	8580	EMD SW1	8580	—	Amtrak 258	Apr 76	Amtrak 745	Jul 77	Berlin Mills Ry 745	Feb 86	
9206	8506	EMD SW1	8506	8508	Bethlehem Steel 70		BSP 70				
9208	8508	EMD SW1	8508	—	MS&A						
9313	—	GE 44-Tonner	—	—	Cliffside 20	Dec 66	LCH&TD 1	1967			
9315	—	GE 44-Tonner	—	—	Ingalls Shipbuilding						
9317	—	GE 44-Tonner	—	—	Magor Car Co 1663		Fruehuf Corp				
9318	—	GE 44-Tonner	—	—	Seatrain Lines, Inc						
9319	—	GE 44-Tonner	—	—	Seatrain Lines, Inc 231						
9322	—	GE 44-Tonner	—	—	Seatrain Lines, Inc 232	Oct 67	GE, Hornell, NY				For later owners, see (42)
9324	—	GE 44-Tonner	—	—	Bayside Elev.						
9326	—	GE 44-Tonner	—	—	Assoc. Of Amer. RR	1966	Alter Scrap Iron				
9327	—	GE 44-Tonner	—	—	Union Tank Car Co		BS&G 6				
9328	—	GE 44-Tonner	—	—	Berwind-White Coal		Berwind Ry Services 76				
9329	—	GE 44-Tonner	—	—	Lipsett Steel Co						
9331	—	GE 44-Tonner	—	—	Strasburg RR 33 (17)	1961	Strasburg RR 33	1966			
9332	—	GE 44-Tonner	—	—	W&OD 58		Maryland Port Auth 1				
9334	—	GE 44-Tonner	—	—	Vermont 10		L&L 10				
9335	—	GE 44-Tonner	—	—	Pt Richmond Elevator		Bunge Grain Corp.				
9336	—	GE 44-Tonner	—	—	Reynolds Metals						
9337	—	GE 44-Tonner	—	—	Ingalls Shipbuilding						
9338	—	GE 44-Tonner	—	—	Dierks Forest Prod. D-9		Weyerhaeuser D-9	Jan 88	W.A. Smith Const. D-9		To Autex Fibers.200 c1980
9339	—	GE 44-Tonner	—	—	J. B. Goldberg Scrap		SCRR Mus. 33				
9346	—	GE 44-Tonner	—	—	Babcock & Wilcox		Alabama Byproducts				
9348	—	GE 44-Tonner	—	—	Heyden Newport Chem.		Reichold Chemical				
9350	—	GE 44-Tonner	—	—	Berwick Forge 1912		Berwick Forge 1984				
9352	—	GE 44-Tonner	—	—	Ingalls Shipbuilding						
9354	—	GE 44-Tonner	—	—	Vulcan Materials		Celotex 3	1989			
9356	—	GE 44-Tonner	—	—							
9358	9084	EMD SW7	9084	9084	NCP 9084						
9361	9087	EMD SW7	9087	9087	UM&P 9009:2						
9363	9089	EMD SW7	9089	9089	OHRY 50	1997	L&S 50				
9369	9090	EMD SW7	9090	9090	Knox & Kane 9090						
9373	9073	EMD SW7	9073	9073	RELCo RE1251						
9379	9079	EMD SW7	9079	9079	USS-Fairless 9:2						
9385	9045	EMD SW7	9045	9045	BVRY 8206:2						
9387	9082	EMD SW7	9082	9082	RaiLink 137	Sep 96					
9389	9069	EMD SW7	9069	9069	AT&C 9069	Nov 83					
9391	9071	EMD SW7	9071	9071	Atl. City Electric 1200	Oct 92					
9393	9047	EMD SW7	9047	9047	Anthracite Ry 55	Sep 83					
9396	8556	EMD SW1	8556	8556	RaiLink 247						
9399	8559	EMD SW1	8559	8559	Amtrak 256	Apr 76	Amtrak 743	Jul 77			
9404	8564	EMD SW1	8564	8564	A. E. Staley Mfg. 8564		Texas & NW 88				
9408	8568	EMD SW1	8568	8568	Cinci. Ry Exposition 8568		Potlatch For. Prod				
9409	8569	EMD SW1	8569	8569	Great Miami 1371						
9414	8513	EMD SW1	8513	8513	McWCP						
	8514	EMD SW1	8514	8514	North Amer Car 8514	Feb 82	GE Railcar SW1				
9422	8522	EMD SW1	8522	—	Amtrak 251	Apr 76	Amtrak 738	Jul 77			
9423	8523	EMD SW1	8523	—	Amtrak 252	Apr 76	Amtrak 739	Jul 77	NHSR 9423		See note (32)
9425	8525	EMD SW1	8525	8525	West Shore 8525						See note (33)
9428	8528	EMD SW1	8528	—	Amtrak 253	Apr 76	Amtrak 740	Jul 77			

1. Heavy rebuild to 1200 horsepower.
2. Heavy rebuild by Paducah Shops.
3. M-K rebuild to their SD40M-3 standards.
4. VMV rebuild for KCS to SD40-2 standards.
5. Lettered PRR with full five-stripe tuscan red and buff paint scheme
6. Ex-MBTA E8A unit sold to Green Mountain. Traded to the Central New York Chapter, NRHS, who painted and lettered it DL&W 807.
7. Owned by the Central New York Chapter, NRHS, who painted and lettered DL&W 808.
8. Leased from Naporano Iron and Metal, where it was used as road number 1000.
9. Unit purchased by Maryland and Delaware and leased to the North Country.
10. Leased from M&D by FMC. Name changed to Avtex Fiber.
11. PRR rebuilt six class AS-18am units (Alco model RS-11) for the Lehigh Valley Railroad at Juniata in 1964. Part of the rebuild was the upgrading of the units to 2000 horsepower. They were re-classed as AS-20m units at the time, painted and lettered for the LV. All six units were renumbered in the 7600 series in the 1966 number scheme and reclassed as ARS-20. Conrail then acquired the units on April 1, 1976 when CR absorbed the LV without renumbering. The units were never painted or lettered for PC.
12. Unit acquired by Florida Gulf Coast Railroad Museum. By October 1992 it was repainted and lettered as PRR 8604.
13. Heavy Paducah rebuild to IC GP8 standards
14. To Railroaders Memorial Museum, Altoona, Pa.
15. Owned by AF Industries, New Hope, Penna. as number 2198. Painted and lettered New Hope and Ivyland.
16. Rebuilt as yard slug
17. To Cargill 744.
18. Heavy rebuild to SD40-2 standards
19. Berlin Mills Railway sold to St. Lawrence and Atlantic in October, 1997. Berlin Mills Railway 741 became St. Lawrence and Atlantic 741.
20. Heavy rebuild with Caterpillar engine. Identified as GP15C by rebuilder.
21. UP road number not assigned as of December, 1999.
22. Rebuilt by C&NW with a 12-cylinder Caterpillar model 3612 engine. The unit was derated to 3000 horsepower.
23. The L&N rebuilt ex-PRR 5407 with the engine from wrecked L&N 173:1. The unit was renumbered to L&N 173:2.
24. Broadway Dinner Train, operated on (but now owned by) Nashville and Eastern.
25. Unit owned by Tennessee Central Railway Museum. The unit is used in tourist service on the Nashville and Eastern.
26. Owned by United Rail Historical Societies of New Jersey, who have painted and lettered the locomotive as Erie 835.
27. Rebuilt by M-K their SD45-3M rating. The unit was re-engined with an EMD 16-645 engine.
28. The New York and Atlantic, Louisville and Indiana and the Pacific Harbor Lines were operated by Anacosta and Pacific when these units were used.
29. Morrison-Knudson MK1500D locomotives. This unit consists of frames and trucks from the old locomotive. Aside from that virtually its entire remaining locomotive is new. A Caterpillar 12-cylinder model 3512 engine is used, which results in 1380 horsepower for traction.
30. Heavy rebuild designated SD40-3 by rebuilder. Not rebuilt by M-K, but similar to their SD40M-3 standards.
31. During 1999, WATCO, operator of the South Kansas and Oklahoma and the Eastern Idaho (and several other roads), and began applying a company-wide numbering system on their locomotives.
32. To Penn Eastern Lines, Inc. 9423 in 2001. This is former Chester Valley Railway.
33. Leased to Great Miami in August, 1988, then leased to River Services in 1993. Unit owned by West Shore owner.
34. Donated to RR Museum of Pennsylvania by widow of West Shore owner.
35. Rebuilt as a de-turboed EMD GP35 and rated at 2000 HP.
36. Donated to RR Museum of Pennsylvania and repainted in PRR Tuscan Red, five-stripe paint scheme and with the original 5901A road number.
37. On display
38. To Heart of Dixie Railroad Museum.
39. CR 4020 was acquired by the Norfolk Southern when Conrail was split between the NS and CSX. The locomotive was physically renumbered to road number 1000 but the Conrail lettering on the nose was not removed. No Norfolk Southern lettering was applied. See note 40.
40. In July, 2000, the NS 1000 was sold to Mr. Bennett Levin, owner of the Juniata Terminal in Philadelphia. A very extensive renovation was performed to restore the unit to appearance as PRR 5809A, including an accurate single-stripe tuscan red paint job. The unit retained the head-end power sets installed by Amtrak. The unit has subsequently been used on special passenger trains, notably, in MU with ex-PRR 5711A on a trip from Philadelphia to Erie and return starting on August 18, 2001.
41. Conrail 4021, an E8A originally built as PRR 5711A was transferred to CSX when Conrail s were divided between CSX and the Norfolk Southern in June, 1999. The unit was shipped to the CSX shop in Huntington, West Virginia and stored. It was to be numbered CSX 9990 and used on business car specials. By January, 2001, CSX decided to auction the E8A instead and the successful bidder was Bennett Levin, owner of the Juniata Terminal in Philadelphia. The diesel was shipped to Philadelphia from Huntington and arrived in mid-February, 2001. Mr. Levin also purchased a second E8A at the same time as former CR 4022, which was originally Erie 833. The 5711A was also extensively rebuilt as was the former PRR 5809A and run on the trip described as in note 40.
42. After PRR 9324 sold to Bayside Elevator in Reserve, La. in Oct 67. The name of Bayside was changed to Cook Industries. The unit was later sold to Ferruzzi Grain Terminal in Linwood, Iowa (May 75), then sold to Mississippi River Grain Elevator Co in Buffalo, Iowa (1982). The unit was then sold to Harvest States Coop East Elevator in Linwood, Iowa.
43. Transferred back to NY&LE as 6101 in 2001.
44. Sold to St. Louis, Iron Mountain and Southern Feb 98.
45. To UP 4637 in SP to UP merger. Renumbered UP 2684 in March, 2001
46. To Arkansas and Missouri 17.
47. To Queen Anne Railroad 19
48. To Vandalia 56, then PREX 101.
49. To Arkansas and Missouri 15.
50. Heavy rebuild to "GP10" standards by Paducah, Silvis or Morrison-Knudson.

PRR, PC and CR Diesel Resale List Abbreviation List

Abbreviation	Meaning	Abbreviation	Meaning
Ag Val Coop	Ag Valley Coop, Edison, Neb.	MKCX	Morrison-Knudson (now Boise Locomotive Div., MPI)
A&BB	Akron & Barbarton Belt Railroad		
A&M	Arkansas & Missouri Railroad	MRL	Montana Rail Link
ADM	Archer-Daniels-Midland	MPEX	Motive Power Industries
AGR	Alabama & Gulf Coast	MPI	Motive Power Industries
APD	Albany Port District	MS&A	Midwest Steel and Alloy
AT&C	Allied Tube and Conduit, Inc.	N&BE	Nittany and Bald Eagle Railroad
AVR	Allegheny Valley Railroad	NBEC	New Brunswick Southem Railway
AZER	Arizona Eastern Railway	NCP	Nacme Steel Processing
BCS	Buckeye Central Scenic Railroad	NDCR	Northhampton Development Corp,
BSP	Bethlehem Structural Products	NH&I	New Hope and Ivyland Rail Road
BM&R	Blue Mountain and Reading	NHNR	New Hampshire Northcoast Railroad
BS&G	BeckerSand and Gravel	NHRR	New Hope Steam Railroad
BVRY	BrandywineValley Railroad	NI&M	Naporano Iron and Metal
BWDX	Broadway Dinner Train	NJDOT	New Jersey Departmant of Transportation
C&BL	Conemaugh & Black Lick Railroad	NJTR	New Jersey Transit Rail
CA&LM	Caddo, Antoine & Little Missouri Railroad	NKCR	Nebraska, Kansas and Colorado Railroad
CSKR	Carbon and Schuykill Railroad	NRE	National Railway Equipment Company
CCCL	Connecticut Central Railroad	NS Mining	North Shore Mining
CG&B	Consolidated Grain and Barge	NS Steel	North Star Steel
CG & C	Citizens Gas and Coke	NS (PRR)	Norfolk Southern, sublettered PRR, CR units to NS
CMSL	Cape May Seashore Lines	NY&A	New York & Atlantic Railway
CP&F	Charlotte Pipe and Foundry	NYRR	New York Regional Rail
CR of I	Central Railroad of Indianapolis	OHRY	Oswego and Hartford Railway
CRL	Conrail Leasing	PERX	Pioneer Railroad Equipment Co.
D&M	Detroit and Mackinac Railway (Now Lake States RR)	P&W	Providence and Worcester Railroad
		PHL	Pacific Harbor Line
DJPX	Joseph Transportation, Inc.	PPCX	(Private owner in Tennessee)
DL&W	Delaware, Lackawanna and Western Railroad	PCC	Palouse and Coulee City Railroad
DME	Dakota, Minnesota and Eastern Railroad	PTRA	Port Temminal Railroad Association
EC&H	East Camden and Highland Railroad	Q & O Paper	Quebec & Ontario Paper
EF Coop	Eastern Farmers Coop	QBT	Quincy Bay Terminal
EIRC	Eastern Illinois Railroad	QGRY	Quebec-Gastineau Railway
EMDX	Electromotive	RBMN	Reading and Northem Railroad
FE Co	Farmers Elevator Co.	RLGN	Mackenzie Northern Railway
FURX	First Union Rail Corp.	RR Steel	Raritan River Steel
FGC	Museum Florida Gold Coast Museum	SCL	Seaboard Coast Line Railroad
Ga. NE	Georgia Northeastern Railroad	SBD	Seaboard System
GCFX	Alstrom Canada Incorporated Transport	SCRR Mus.	South Carolina Railroad Museum
GSS Corp	Gulf States Steel Corp	SCRX	Santa Clarita Railway
HBT	Houston Belt and Terminal Railway	SEPTA	Southeastern Pennsylvania Transit Authority
HLCX	Helm Financial Corporation	SK&O	South Kansas and Oklahoma Railroad
HP Coop	High Plaines Coop	SMS	SMS Rail Services
ISCX	ISC, Inc	Soo	Soo Line Railroad
IMRL	Iowa-Missouri Rail Link	SRCT	Shipyard River Coal Terminal
INCX	INCO Corporation	SRNJ	Southern Railroad of New Jersey
ITI	IntermodelTechnologies Inc	SWP	Southwest Pennsylvania Railroad
JRS Milling	J. R. Short Milling	TCRX	Tennessee Central Railroad Museum
KCS	Kansas City Southern Railway	TDIX	Trans Dynamic Industries
L&C	Lancasterand Chester Railway	TFM	Grupo Transportacion Ferrovia Mexicana
L&S	Luzerne and Susquehanna Railway	TH&W	Terre Haute & Western
LA&L	Livonia, Avon and Lakeville Railroad	TRRA	Terminal Railroad Association (of St. Louis)
LANO	Lancaster Northem Railroad	UM&P	Upper Merion and Plymouth Railroad
LCH&TD	Lake Charles Harbor & Terminal	URHSNJ	United Railroad Historical Society of New Jersey
LRCX	Livingston Rebuild Center	US Op.	U. S. Operating, Ceder Bay Generating
LS&BC	LaSalle and Bureau County Railroad	USS	United States Steel
LTEX	Larry'sTruck Electric	USWX	USA Waste Services, Inc.
LV	LehighValley Railroad	W&OD	Washington and Old Dominion Railroad
MAW	Maumee and Western Railroad	W&W	Winchester and Western Railroad
MBTA	Metropolitan Boston Transportation Authority	WCLX	Waccamaw Coast Line Railroad
McWCP	McWareCast Iron Pipe		
Milw.	Chicago, Milwaukee, St. Paul & Pacific Railroad (Milw. Road)		